Absolute Destruction

Absolute Destruction

*Military Culture and the Practices of War
in Imperial Germany*

ISABEL V. HULL

Cornell University Press
ITHACA AND LONDON

First published 2005 by Cornell University Press
First printing, Cornell Paperbacks, 2006

Printed in the United States of America

Library of Congress Cataloging-inPublication Data

Hull, Isabel V.
   Absolute destruction : military culture and the practices of war in Imperial Germany / Isabel V. Hull.
     p. cm.
  Includes bibliographical references and index.
  ISBN-13: 978-0-8014-4258-2 (cloth : alk. paper)
  ISBN-10: 0-8014-4258-3 (cloth : alk. paper)
  ISBN-13: 978-0-8014–7293-0 (pbk. : alk. paper)
  ISBN-10: 0-8014–7293-8 (pbk. : alk. paper)
  1. Germany—History, Military—19th century. 2. Germany—History, Military—20th century. 3. Militarism—Germany—History. I. Title.
  DD103.H85 2005
    355.02'13'094309034—dc22

2004013387

Cornell University Press strives to use environmentally responsible suppliers and materials to the fullest extent possible in the publishing of its books. Such materials include vegetable-based, low VOC inks and acid-free papers that are recycled, totally chlorine-free, or partly composed of nonwood fibers. For further information, visit our website at www.cornellpress.cornell.edu.

Clothing printing   10 9 8 7 6 5 4 3 2 1
Paperback printing   10 9 8 7 6 5 4 3 2 1

For George,
whom I loved and admired equally

Contents

Maps

Acknowledgments

I am grateful for the assistance of archivists in the Bundesarchiv Koblenz (Berlin), the Bundesarchiv-Militärarchiv (Freiburg), the Politisches Archiv des Auswärtigen Amts, and the Archiv- und Museumsstiftung Wuppertal (formerly the Archiv der Vereinigten Evangelischen Mission), as well as the cheerful help of the librarians at the Staats- und Universitätsbibliothek Göttingen and the Niedersächsisches Landesbibliothek Hannover.

I am particularly indebted to the von Trotha family for permission to use the papers of Lothar v. Trotha, to Herr Minister Klaus v. Trotha and Herr Gustav-Adolf v. Trotha for their help, and especially to Herr Thilo v. Trotha for his generosity and hospitality. This is also the place to thank the late Mariann Steegman for her interest and intercession.

I thank David Wyatt for his early help with the maps.

For their thoughtful editorial comments, and most of all for their continuing friendship, I thank John Ackerman, Lynn Eden, Laura Engelstein, and Michael Geyer. I could not have written this book without them.

Finally, I am especially grateful to the late Wilhelm Deist for so generously offering me his attention, unsurpassed knowledge of the Imperial German military, and critical insights at a time when he was unwell. I appreciate his support more than I can say.

Abbreviations

AKO	Allerhöchste Kabinetts-Ordre
BA-Berlin	Bundesarchiv (Berlin-Lichterfelde)
BA-Koblenz	Bundesarchiv (Koblenz)
BA-MA Freiburg	Bundesarchiv-Militärarchiv (Freiburg i. Br.)
Col. Dept.	Colonial Department of the Foreign Office (in charge of colonies until May 1907)
Col. Office	Imperial Colonial Office (in charge of colonies after its establishment in May 1907)
KEO	Prussia, War Ministry, *Kriegs-Etappen-Ordnung* (12 March 1914) (D.V.E. Nr. 90) (Berlin, 1914) (regulations for the rear echelon)
Msg. 2	Militärgeschichtliche Sammlung
N	Nachlass
PA-AA	Politisches Archiv des Auswärtigen Amtes (Bonn)
Ober-Ost	Supreme Command on the eastern front
OHL	Supreme Command (Oberste Heeresleitung)
Sten. Ber.	*Stenographische Berichte über die Verhandlungen des Reichstages* (Berlin, 1904–1907) (protocols of Reichstag sessions)
SWA	German Southwest Africa
UA	Germany, Parliament, *Das Werk des Untersuchungsausschusses der Verfassungsgebenden Deutschen Nationalversammlung und des Deutschen Reichstages 1919–1928, Verhandlungen, Gutachten, Urkunden*, ed. Eugen Fischer et al. (Berlin, 1921–1930) (documents of the postwar Reichstag investigating committees)
USW	Unrestricted submarine warfare
VEM	Vereinigte Evangelische Mission (Wuppertal)

Absolute Destruction

Introduction

This is a study of institutional extremism. It examines the German conduct of war from 1870 through 1918. In engagements large and small, in Europe and in the colonies, the Imperial German military repeatedly resorted to terrific violence and destruction in excess of Germany's own security requirements or political goals, in contravention of international norms, and even contrary to ultimate military effectiveness. Routine German military operations developed a dynamic of extremism that could, and did, lead to extermination of civilian populations in the colonies and that characterized German practices in occupied Europe during the First World War.

Military extremism is the repeated and unlimited application of the military's expertise, that is, the use of violence. As Hannah Arendt has written, "Violence, being instrumental in nature, is rational to the extent that it is effective in reaching the end that must justify it."[1] Extremism occurs when the means overwhelms the end, when violence is pursued because the institution keeps on generating violence according to quasi-automatic mechanisms. Following necessary-seeming routines, military extremism gravitates toward final, or total, solutions. In combat, such a solution would mean the utter annihilation of the enemy's armed forces; in occupation, it would mean the establishment of perfect order and complete obedience by the enemy population; in the occupied zones, it would mean the total instrumentalization of all resources for one's own troops, that is, no limits to requisitions and expropriation. Extremism understood as "final solutions" aims at total, unambiguous, permanent results.[2]

1. Hannah Arendt, *On Violence* (New York, 1970), 79.
2. In this book, "final solutions" refers to the practices or policies produced by the military as these develop out of military routines. Final Solution (in capital letters) refers to the National Socialist genocide of the European Jews.

2   We usually think of the extremism of "final solutions," especially when they end in genocide, as the result of ideology. Indeed, in modern times ideology has been responsible for most genocides. But, as we shall see, it has been possible to destroy whole peoples without ideological motives. Genocide can also happen as the by-product of institutional routines and organizational dynamics as they operate during wartime and generate "final solutions" to all sorts of perceived problems.

I have found that the ends, the "final solutions," were in fact expectations and habits that resulted from the means itself, violence, and from the institutional measures taken to wield or control it. This book is the story of how the means overwhelmed the ends, indeed, became the ends. Its focus is therefore not on ideology but on *military practices* and the basic assumptions behind them. These habitual practices, default programs, hidden assumptions, and unreflected cognitive frames I understand in an anthropological and organizational-cultural sense as *military culture.*

This book has three parts. The first reveals the pattern of extreme, even genocidal, conduct of war as it developed in the course of one engagement, in Southwest Africa. The second analyzes that pattern as the result of Germany's military culture. The third shows how the pattern continued to intensify in the First World War.

Let me begin with an overview of part 2, which defines military culture in general and distinguishes the German variant of it in the late nineteenth century. Chapter 5 locates the immediate origins of military culture in the wars of unification (1864–70) and explains how lessons learned then became institutionalized and internalized by its members. Other chapters analyze standard operating procedures and developing doctrine on how best to fight wars; in both, one can identify the tendency toward extreme warfare (*Kriegführung*) produced by military culture. Part 2 is also comparative. Britain's actions in the Boer War (1899–1902) show how similar most late nineteenth-century Western armies were in their tendency to go to extremes. However, other armies' descents into dysfunctional, pure violence were sooner or later halted by intervention from outside the military, either by civilian government and/or by public opinion. Not in Germany—Bismarck's constitution isolated the army sufficiently from external criticism and feedback that its military culture reinforced itself and became ever stronger. Germany's political structure thus profoundly affected the functioning of its military. This process is not nearly so well studied as its reverse, the "militarism" resulting from the penetration of military values into society and government.

Germany's military culture developed a constellation of mutually reinforcing characteristics that enhanced tactical efficacy. Unleashed in war, however, these characteristics propelled the army to ever greater, and in the end, dysfunctional extremes of violence. Part 2 analyzes these interactive and self-generating characteristics, which include risk-taking; the dogmatic conviction that annihilation was the sole goal of war (*Vernichtungskrieg*); resulting prescriptions for correct fighting (the offensive, concentration of force, use of reserves, hectic speed) that all greatly increased casualties; minutely technical planning; focus on the tactical and operative rather than the strategic; disregard of logistics and thus growing unrealism; the conviction (indeed requirement) of one's qualitative superiority over one's enemies; a romantic ruthlessness and actionism (exaggerated drive for action [*Aktionismus*]) on the part of officers in order to bridge the gap between risk and reality; and finally the acceptance of self-destruction (and thus the willingness to destroy everyone else, as well). Some of these qualities were expressed as doctrine, but many more were buried inside organizational routines and the unexamined expectations of the officer corps.

Rather than plunging directly into the analysis of military organizational culture, it seems better to begin with an extended example of military culture in action. The reader can then see for herself the patterns of conduct and spirals of escalation that actually developed in wartime. Part 1, therefore, describes the suppression of the Herero Revolt in Southwest Africa (1904–7) in which two African peoples were almost wiped out. Later, in part 2, I compare these actions to those in two other colonial encounters: the suppression of the Maji-Maji Revolt in German East Africa (1905–7), which resulted in even greater loss of life, and the German intervention in China in 1901.

It might seem surprising that a study of German military culture should begin with colonial wars to establish its habitual pattern of action. After all, contemporaries insisted that "small wars" were of an entirely different character from "real," European conflicts; one could learn nothing about one from looking at the other. Too many historians have accepted this point of view. In fact, for Germany at least, colonial engagements were remarkably European in the operational assumptions about how wars should be fought and won, how enemy populations should be treated, how technology should be used to increase one's power, and how far military necessity reduced limits on total combat. Colonial history is much more central to European history than is often believed. The military history of German imperialism shows clearly and early how the First World War would be fought. The continuities between colonial and European warfare are not due, as I thought at the beginning of this project, to Europeans learning evil lessons in the colonies and then applying them at home (though many an evil lesson was doubtless learned). Rather, Germans approached colonial wars from inside the frames of their military culture as it had developed in Europe. The colonial situation merely provided the opportunity to practice on Africans or Chinese what the military experts took to be the immutable precepts of warfare.

The sociologist Barry Turner has noted that "small-scale failures can be produced very rapidly, but large-scale failures can only be produced if time and resources are devoted to them."[3] We will be examining a series of large-scale failures in the military realm, not just in the colonial sphere but also in Germany's conduct of the First World War, which forms part 3. Some of these engagements deserve the label "failure" because of the enormous imbalance between ostensible goal and means employed; all of them developed a disproportionate, dysfunctional level of death and destruction produced routinely by the military institution; and of course World War I ended in defeat for Germany. One of the great strengths of organizational-cultural analysis is that it can discover the historical and institutional rationality behind seemingly irrational acts of (self-) destruction. We

---

3. Barry A. Turner, "The Organizational and Interorganizational Development of Disasters," *Administrative Science Quarterly* 21:3 (1976): 378–97, here 395.

4   shall see that in Germany's military culture a great deal of time and resources had indeed been devoted to produce institutional failure this large and this repetitive.

Rather than a narrative of the world war, part 3 offers instead an analysis of three of the most defining characteristics of Germany's military culture at war: its immediate propensity for extreme violence, its deadly instrumentalization of civilians, and its tendency when thwarted to repeat its scripts of violence to the point of self-destruction. Chapter 9 therefore examines the conduct of the war in the first two years, before the radicalization that Ludendorff and Hindenburg are supposed to have inaugurated after August 1916. In fact, many of the radical features associated with them were well under way in the first months of the war, some, indeed, in the first week. The treatment of occupied civilians, the subject of chapter 10, is an important measure of institutional extremism. Europeans were instrumentalized for military purposes in ways astonishingly similar to those used against rebellious Africans. Perceived "military necessity" removed one protective limit after another. Ubiquitous forced labor, deportation, and widespread death spread across occupied Europe. In the Ottoman Empire, Germany's Turkish ally claimed "military necessity" as it exterminated its Armenian civilians. Chapter 11 analyzes how putative military necessity paralyzed German policy, silencing objections and rendering Germany impotent to intervene even when genocide actually harmed the Turkish war effort. Finally, chapter 12 analyzes the inability of German military leaders to recognize defeat. Imprisoned in their solipsistic mental world, they launched instead a cycle of unrealistic, costly offensives; they threatened to destroy utterly all occupied lands, and, in the autumn of 1918, even Germany itself, in pursuit of an illusory victory of pure force.

The terrible violence, immense destruction, and mass death caused by the operation of military culture were indeed large-scale disasters, but they had small, literally routine beginnings. Seemingly goal-irrational, the practices of military culture were eminently institutional-rational; they were the product of intelligent professionals working in the finest army of its time. We will now enter their world, a place where, in the words of Norman Maclean, writing about a small forest fire that suddenly turned deadly, "the ordinary can suddenly become monstrous."[4]

4. Norman Maclean, *Young Men and Fire: A True Story of the Mann Gulch Fire* (Chicago, 1992), 217. Maclean is better known as the author of *A River Runs through It*.

PART I

SUPPRESSION BECOMES ANNIHILATION

Southwest Africa, 1904–1907

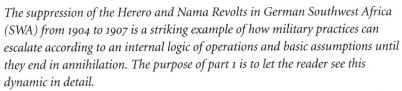

The suppression of the Herero and Nama Revolts in German Southwest Africa (SWA) from 1904 to 1907 is a striking example of how military practices can escalate according to an internal logic of operations and basic assumptions until they end in annihilation. The purpose of part 1 is to let the reader see this dynamic in detail.

There are many puzzling aspects to the SWA story, but the most vexing is the question of intentionality. Was the extermination of the Herero planned, and if so by whom? Was it policy from Berlin, from the Kaiser, or from the General Staff? Was it intended from the beginning by the commander, Lt. Gen. Lothar von Trotha, a natural product of his racism? Was it inherent in colonial dynamics? Or did it, as I think, develop from military-institutional culture as this unfolded in an unsuccessful and difficult war?

Answering these questions requires a detailed reassessment of events based on archival sources. One must pay close attention to the characteristics of fighting: What methods were typically used and which were ordered and which simply "customary"? Were prisoners taken? How were they and noncombatants treated? What were the patterns of executions, of massacres? Establishing the chronological order of these events is critical to uncovering developmental processes. One of the strangest facts about SWA, for example, is that the "order" for extermination came after the genocide had already occurred.

6   *Another important matter is the relation of the internment phase to the actual fighting. Why were prison camps so lethal? And, finally, what tended to hinder the logic of extremes? Who or which institutions resisted the pull toward ever more violence and destruction, and why?*

    The following three chapters present an analytical narrative that offers the raw material to address these questions. The pattern that emerges from these data is analyzed in part 2, using more information about SWA and comparing it with other German and European colonial campaigns.

1

Waterberg

On 14 January 1904 District Judge Richter wired the German Foreign Office: "All farms in the vicinity of Windhuk [Windhoek, the capital of German Southwest Africa] plundered by Herero. Whites living on isolated farms murdered. Situation very grave."[1] Richter's news was shocking. Few in the colony, or in Germany, had foreseen an uprising. Gov. Col. Theodor Leutwein and most of the seven-hundred-man defense force, the Schutztruppe, were in the southern part of the colony suppressing a minor revolt. Their absence left 4,640 German colonists amid an estimated sixty thousand to eighty thousand Herero, who had now apparently determined to throw off German rule.[2]

1. District Judge (*Bezirksrichter*) Richter Windhuk, 14 Jan. 1904, Bundesarchiv Berlin, Reichskolonialamt (R 1001), Nr. 2111, p. 22 (hereafter BA-Berlin, R 1001, Nr.).

2. Germans: Jon M. Bridgman, *The Revolt of the Herero* (Berkeley, 1981), 50. The indigenous population, which consisted of at least six different peoples, has been hard to estimate (Bridgman, 8–29). The lowest contemporary estimate was 30–40,000, by Alfred v. François, "Der Herero-Aufstand," *Militär-Wochenblatt*, vol. 1, Heft 54 (4 May 1905), col. 1284. His estimate was immediately challenged as far too low by an anonymous reporter using military and civilian sources: "Der Verbleib der Herero seit dem Gefecht von Waterberg," *Militär-Wochenblatt*, vol. 2, Heft 96 (8 Aug. 1905), cols. 2211–18. Paul Rohrbach also noted 40,000 as the lowest estimate, without subscribing to it himself: Rohrbach, *Aus Südwestafrikas schweren Tagen* (Berlin, 1909), 160. Gov. Leutwein vacillated: in 1899 he numbered the Herero at 100,000; in 1904 at 60–70,000; and in 1906 he reckoned that at the start of the uprising they had numbered 80,000. Theodor Leutwein, "Die Kämpfe der Kaiserlichen Schutztruppe in Deutsch-Südwestafrika in den Jahren 1894–1896," *Beiheft zum Militär-Wochenblatt* 1 (1899), 2; Leutwein to Colonial Department (hereafter Col. Dept.), Nr. 73, 23 Feb. 1904, Windhuk, BA-Berlin, R 1001, Nr. 2113, pp. 54–55; Leutwein, *Elf Jahre Gouverneur in Deutsch-Südwestafrika* (Berlin, 1906), 11. The missionaries' estimates ranged from 35,000 to 70–85,000 prewar Herero: Nicolai Mossolow, *Waterberg* (Windhuk, [1976]), 41, cited by Gunter Spraul, "Der 'Völkermord' an den Herero," in *Geschichte in Wissenschaft und Unterricht* 39:12 (1988), 725, 739n106; Gerd Sudholt, *Die deutsche Eingeborenenpolitik in Südwestafrika* (Hildesheim, 1975), 40. The highest contemporary estimates were 100,000: General Berthold Deimling, *Südwestafrika* (Berlin, 1906), 14; Gustav Noske, *Kolonialpolitik und Sozialdemokratie* (Stuttgart, 1914), 120. Knowledgeable military participants

8   German rule was only partly established, in any event. Acquired in April 1884 not as a colony but as a protectorate, German Southwest Africa (now known as Namibia) was 580,000 square kilometers of arid, thornbush-studded landscape. Few colonists were attracted to it, and their numbers were dwarfed by two hundred thousand Africans of roughly three main groups: the Ovambo and Herero, who made up about 80 percent of the indigenous population; and the less populous Nama (whom the Germans called "Hottentots" in imitation of their clicking language). The best land was owned by the German Colonial Society of Southwest Africa, which refused to sell to settlers. The colony made no profit. German administration rested on a series of "protective treaties" concluded in the 1890s between Governor Leutwein and the various indigenous peoples. Isolated military stations maintained a German presence in the middle (Hereroland) and the south (Namaland), but not in the north (Ovamboland), where the Germans had barely penetrated. Neither the government nor the private sector was willing to invest much in the unpromising territory.[3] Germans called SWA the "problem child" of its colonies, and now it was in revolt.[4]

The Herero were seminomadic cattle herders recently organized into chieftaincies.[5] The white settlers coveted their cattle, their potential labor, and their grazing land, which the settlers regarded as "property," but the Herero interpreted as common land with usufruct rights. The Herero recognized that their power was slipping. A recent cattle plague had diminished their herds; settlers fenced off land, and they and the colonial police and judicial administration treated the Herero with demeaning brutality. These were the main reasons the Herero united in rebellion, apparently after another incident of provocation by a junior military officer.[6]

In the absence of the governor, and before receiving the fiscal appropriation from the Reichstag, Kaiser Wilhelm II used his extraconstitutional military power of command to order immediate reinforcements. He also directed Captain Gudewill, commander of the *Habicht*, to land in SWA and take over military operations until the governor arrived back in Windhuk.

On 18 January 1904, four days after Richter's telegram arrived in Berlin, Chancellor Bernhard von Bülow asked the Reichstag for a special appropriation to cover sending re-

---

estimated between 60,000 (staff officer Maximilian Bayer, *Mit dem Hauptquartier in Südwestafrika* [Berlin, 1909], 62) and 80,000 (Schutztrüppler Kurd Schwabe, *Der Krieg in Deutsch-Südwestafrika* [Berlin, 1907], 37), and historians have accepted this range as the most probable: Helmut Bley, *South-West Africa under German Rule* (Evanston, Ill., 1971), 150 (60–80,000); Horst Drechsler, *"Let Us Die Fighting,"* trans. Bernd Zollner (London, 1980; orig. 1966), 17, 214 (80,000). Only writers who wish to minimize the demographic catastrophe assume the lowest estimates: Gerd Sudholt cites 40,000 Herero in 1904: *Deutsche Eingeborenenpolitik*, 44; Spraul, "'Völkermord,'" 725, 739n106, and Brigitte Lau, "Uncertain Certainties," *Migabus* 2 (April 1989), 4–5, 8, estimate 35,000.

3. Horst Gründer, *Geschichte der deutschen Kolonien*, 3rd ed. (Paderborn, 1995), 80–81, 118; Bley, *South-West Africa*, 129–32.

4. V. Gädke, "Die militärische Lage in Deutsch-Südwestafrika," *Berliner Zeitung* 63 (4 Feb. 1904), 1; L. Sander, *Zur Lage in Südwest-Afrika* (Berlin, 1904), 1; Conrad Rust, "Der deutsche Reichstag und das südwestafrikanische Schmerzenskind," *Deutsch-Südwestafrikanische Zeitung* 19 (11 May 1904).

5. Jan-Bart Gewald, *Herero Heroes* (Oxford, 1999), chs. 1–3; Gesine Krüger, *Kriegsbewältigung und Geschichtsbewusstsein* (Göttingen, 1999), 30–62; Bridgman, *Revolt of the Herero*, ch. 1.

6. Gewald, *Herero Heroes*, 142–56.

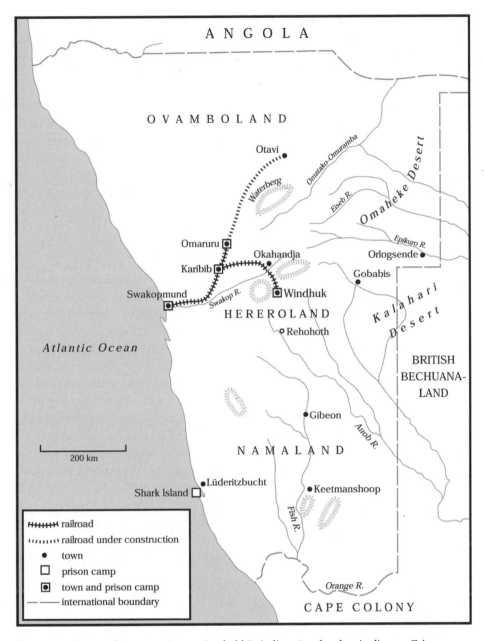

German Southwest Africa, 1904. Source: Berthold Deimling, *Aus der alten in die neue Zeit*, 59.

10   inforcements. The director of the Colonial Section of the Foreign Office, Oscar W. Stübel, read from Richter's dispatch, alluded to the "atrocities" (*Greuel*) Africans committed during such revolts, and set the government's goal: "to end the quasi-independence the natives still enjoyed in politics and in any case to disarm them."[7] The Reichstag reluctantly approved the funds, but representative Müller (Left Liberal Party) was not alone in wondering whether it was worth it, given "the minimal cultural [colonizing] interest in SWA." He concluded that Germany had assumed the duty to protect the colonists and "to reestablish the disturbed order."[8] August Bebel, the Social Democrats' leading spokesman, warned that German troops usually put down colonial revolts "in the most bloody and brutal way conceivable"; he hoped this one would be pursued "with the greatest possible humanity."[9] Christian Storz of the People's Party assumed he spoke for the Reichstag when he concluded: "We urgently insist that the fight be conducted humanely."[10]

The Behavior of the Herero in War and the Initial Military Situation

The prospects for a humane war were not improved by persistent reports of alleged Herero atrocities. Colonial Director Stübel had mentioned these when he first presented the government's case to the Reichstag. Two weeks later, Captain Gudewill, the commander in charge until Governor Leutwein's return, telegraphed the "confirmed losses— murdered and mostly mutilated: 44 settlers, women and children; 26 [soldiers] fallen; 50 others dead."[11] These figures were wrong. The Herero people's paramount chief, Samuel Maherero, had ordered that only German *males* be killed. German women and children were gathered up and gradually released to white outposts. German missionaries and all non-Germans, male and female, were also spared. Conrad Rust, no friend of the Herero people, tallied the dead of the first weeks of the revolt at 158, of whom five were women and none children.[12] However, these facts became available to the German newspaper-reading public only at the end of March 1904.[13] It is typical of the wartime atmosphere that the military memoir (1906) that reprinted Samuel Maherero's order simultaneously reveled in stories of alleged Herero cruelty, so that most readers would have discounted the order's authenticity.[14] Long after everyone knew better, many memoirs—and even the official General Staff account of the campaign—continued to insist that women and children, or simply that "all Germans," had been brutally murdered.[15] So widespread was this

7. Stübel, in Germany, Parliament, *Stenographische Berichte über die Verhandlungen des Reichstages*, XI. legislative period, 1st session, 14th meeting, 19 Jan. 1904, vol. 197, p. 364 (hereafter *Sten. Ber.*).

8. Müller (Sagan), ibid., p. 369.

9. Bebel, ibid., 366, 368.

10. Storz, ibid., 370.

11. Gudewill to Col. Dept., tel. Nr. 26, 3 Feb. 1904, BA-Berlin, R 1001, Nr. 2111, p. 177.

12. Conrad Rust, *Krieg und Frieden im Hererolande* (Leipzig, 1905), 140, 145–47. Gov. Leutwein later reported that only three women had been killed: Leutwein to Col. Dept., tel. Nr. 112, Windhuk, 2 May 1904, BA-Berlin, R 1001, Nr. 2114, p. 114.

13. "Noch ein Wort zum Herero-Aufstand," *Reichsbote*, 22 March 1904.

14. Max Belwe, *Gegen die Herero 1904–05* (Berlin, 1906), 41.

15. Deimling, *Südwestafrika*, 12–13; Bayer, *Mit dem Hauptquartier*, 32; Rust, *Krieg und Frieden*, 142–43; Germany, General Staff, *Die Kämpfe der deutschen Truppen in Südwestafrika*, vol. 1: *Der Feldzug gegen die Herero* (Berlin, 1906), 24, 26, 43 (hereafter General Staff, *Kämpfe der deutschen Truppen*, 1:page).

belief that officers on the spot were "astonished that the Herero had let us go and thereby betrayed their whereabouts," as the wife of one dead settler reported.[16]

Although the Herero were innocent of the charge of wanton killing, their traditional manner of warfare appeared to Germans as cruel and dishonoring. They took no prisoners. They used large knives or clubs (*kirris*) to kill wounded enemy soldiers.[17] When they lacked bullets, they made their own out of bits of scrap metal and glass, which left jagged, often fatal, wounds. They ritually mutilated enemy corpses, which caused the Germans to surmise (probably incorrectly) that they had tortured the wounded. They stripped the dead of their uniforms and wore these themselves. Herero women hid in the thornbushes and encouraged their menfolk with chants, which German soldiers found chilling and which fed the myth that Herero women participated in killing.[18]

The Germans reckoned the Herero, nonetheless, as good fighters. They numbered six to eight thousand warriors and were well armed, with modern rifles.[19] In the first two weeks of the revolt, they dominated all of Hereroland, penning German troops and survivors in the isolated military outposts. But despite their success, the Herero failed to establish strategic superiority.[20] They did not sufficiently appreciate the importance of the feeble railroad as the main supply line for German troops. Their disruption of the telegraph lines was serious but not systematic enough to interrupt communication significantly, and the heliograph (which operated by reflected sunlight) lessened the Germans' reliance on telegraphy. And they did not consider attacking the capital or other strongholds, which, had they fallen, would have dealt a crushing blow to colonial self-esteem and given encouragement to the many voices in the Reichstag who wanted Germany to abandon the colony.

This is not the wisdom of hindsight. Already on 4 February, a week before Leutwein finally made it back to Windhuk, Capt. Viktor Franke achieved the only outstanding German victory of the war. He relieved the central outpost at Omaruru and thereby reestablished a German presence in a strategically important district and, above all, made it possible for the marines from the *Habicht* to secure the railway lines. Captain Gudewill reported that "the war has entered a second phase."[21] These German successes ought to have laid the foundation for a systematic suppression of the revolt in the usual fashion. That is, after the arrival of reinforcements, the governor, who in all German colonies was

16. Else Sonnenberg, *Wie es am Waterberg zuging* (Berlin, 1905), 111.

17. Leutwein to Col. Dept., Nr. 395, Windhuk, 17 May 1904, BA-Berlin, R 1001, Nr. 2115, p. 68.

18. On Herero war practices: missionary August Kuhlmann to inspector of missions, Karibib, 2 June 1904, Archive of the Vereinigte Evangelische Mission, Wuppertal, Kuhlmann papers, B/c II 72, pp. 100–101 (hereafter VEM-Wuppertal). On hostile German interpretation of these: Bayer, *Mit dem Hauptquartier*, 87, 183; Capt. Viktor Franke, diary entries of 8–9 Aug. 1904, Bundesarchiv Koblenz, Nachlass Franke, Nr. 3, p. 90 (hereafter BA-Koblenz, Nl. Franke); Rust, *Krieg und Frieden*, 141; Chief of the General Staff Alfred v. Schlieffen to Bülow, Nr. 13297, Berlin, 16 Dec. 1904, BA-Berlin, R 1001, Nr. 2089, p. 107. Also, Bridgman, *Revolt*, 20.

19. Leutwein, *Elf Jahre*, 436; Deimling, *Südwestafrika*, 11; Berthold Karl Adolf von Deimling, *Aus der alten in die neue Zeit* (Berlin, 1930), 62; Bayer, *Mit dem Hauptquartier*, 62.

20. On Herero military errors: Major Maercker, *Unsere Kriegführung in Deutsch-Südwestafrika* (Berlin, 1907), 30, 45; Bayer, *Mit dem Hauptquartier*, 2, 27, 38, 42, 47, 122, 129–30; Drechsler, *"Let Us Die Fighting,"* 62, 64, 74; Bridgman, *Revolt*, 80, 106–9, 115–17. Cf. Gewald, *Herero Heroes*, 154.

21. Lt. Cdr. (later chief of the admiralty) Magnus v. Levetzow to Col. Dept., Nr. B. 706 IV., Berlin, 4 Feb. 1904, BA-Berlin, R 1001, Nr. 2111, pp. 167–68.

12 also the commander-in-chief of the Schutztruppe, would use his technological advantages to inflict serious casualties and then begin negotiations. Surrender terms were always harsh toward the leaders and those who had laid hands on whites; normally, they would have been court-martialed (that is, tried by a military court) and executed. The rest of the population would have been interned for a while and then released. The size of this revolt and the public consternation it had aroused required harsher negotiation terms: disarmament and the end of the Africans' political organization had already been set as the government's goals, and Leutwein accepted these terms.[22] But he remained true to the maxims he had explained in 1899: After one had destroyed the Africans' military capacity, "one must build the well-known 'golden bridge' necessary for those who want to surrender, as Major [Hermann] v. Wissmann [then governor of German East Africa] stresses in his book on African warfare. In Africa, the diplomat must always stand next to the soldier."[23]

The Herero Revolt was not going to follow this path, however. Three days before Leutwein's return, the first reinforcements arrived. Kaiser Wilhelm placed them and the entire conduct of the war directly under the General Staff and its chief, Gen. Alfred von Schlieffen.[24] The General Staff was the institution charged with operational planning for the next (European) war. After the success of its then chief, Gen. Helmuth von Moltke, against the Austrians in 1866, it had been elevated to a position directly beneath the Kaiser. It was thus independent of the political scrutiny, criticism, or even advice of the chancellor, who, as chief administrator of the colonies and superior of the governor, normally supervised the Schutztruppe. The Kaiser's decision of 8 February meant that the war against the Herero would be conducted like a European war, according to military criteria as interpreted by the General Staff.[25] Military criteria could become paramount because Wilhelminian government was not integrated under civilian leadership but was instead "polycratic." That is, it consisted of separate, vertical units, integrated, if at all, by the Kaiser, who could choose which unit would dominate policy in a given situation. The first stage in the process of military extremism was thus the identification of the revolt in SWA as a national security issue, which encouraged the Kaiser to entrust it to the military experts, the General Staff, rather than to the civilian leadership.

Governor Leutwein arrived back in Windhuk on 11 February. There, he discovered that various forces operating in Berlin had thwarted his freedom of action. Apparently at the Kaiser's urging, the Colonial Department forbade Leutwein from engaging in "negotiations" with Samuel Maherero.[26] The exchange of letters between the governor and his foes was a normal procedure of colonial warfare, which, Leutwein explained, "even if they are only for appearance's sake, make the conduct of war considerably easier and save blood." Only after consulting with the General Staff was the Colonial Department able to

---

22. Leutwein to Col. Dept., Nr. 73, Windhuk, 23 Feb. 1904, BA-Berlin, R 1001, Nr. 2113, pp. 54–55, partly cited in Drechsler, *"Let Us Die Fighting,"* 148.

23. Leutwein, "Kämpfe der Kaiserlichen Schutztruppe," 5.

24. Admiralty to *Habicht*, tel. Nr. 19, Berlin, 8 Feb. 1904, BA-Berlin, R 1001, Nr. 2111, pp. 197–98.

25. For the unsuccessful efforts of the Colonial Department consequently to shift the entire responsibility for the war onto the Prussian War Ministry, see Bley, *South-West Africa*, 155–56.

26. Ibid., 157; Drechsler, *"Let Us Die Fighting,"* 147–48.

assent to "fake negotiations."[27] But Leutwein's leash was very short. In April, when the Colonial Department tried to win more negotiating room for the governor, the General Staff categorically refused.[28] "Negotiations" were a sore point with public opinion, too. When word of Leutwein's letter contact with Samuel Maherero reached the Berlin newspapers, the *Tägliche Rundschau* expressed the widespread indignation at such an idea:

> Humanity belongs in the right place—for the moment, however, the national honor and the future of the colony require punishment and suppression of the rebels via force of weapons and the superiority of the white man, but not via peace negotiations, which would recognize the mutineers as legitimate combatants [*kriegführende Partei*].[29]

Public opinion, the Kaiser, and General Staff were of one mind in demanding a clear victory of weapons.

They also demanded a quick victory. It is understandable that the newspaper-reading public could not appreciate the difficulties that desert, climate, lack of transportation and communication, lack of water and European food, unfamiliarity with the region, and the other myriad hurdles typical of colonial warfare presented to metropolitan troops. In fact, the Herero war showed that most Germans were entirely ignorant of the most basic facts concerning the colony. It is more surprising that the General Staff overlooked all these factors as well. Whereas Leutwein wanted to await further reinforcements and then prepare a careful offensive in which technical superiority would work to his advantage, Schlieffen pressed for immediate operations.[30]

The Conduct of War under Leutwein

An analysis of the movement from regular warfare to extermination must determine exactly how German troops conducted themselves and what orders they received early in the war under Governor Leutwein's command. The destruction of the Army Archives in 1945, before any historians had used them to research the Herero Revolt, does not make our task easier. Let us begin with the contemporary debate launched by August Bebel on 14 March 1904 in the Reichstag.

Before German troops had taken any action at all, Bebel worried that the war would be conducted "in the most bloody and brutal way." Bebel and most Social Democrats reasoned by analogy with the suppression of the Boxer Uprising in China (1900–1901), other colonial "punitive expeditions," and the domestic repression of labor unrest. Going to ex-

---

27. Leutwein to Col. Dept., tel. Nr. 41, Windhuk, 22 Feb. 1904, BA-Berlin, R 1001, Nr. 2112, p. 55. Marginal note: "Die Sache ist mit Gen. Stab besprochen."

28. Bley, *South-West Africa*, 157–58.

29. "Koloniales," *Tägliche Rundschau* 111 (6 Mar. 1904). Similar comments: "Aus den Kolonian," *National-Zeitung*, 9 Mar. 1904. The semiofficial *Norddeutsche Allgemeine Zeitung* thought it necessary to issue a public denial, saying that Leutwein had been instructed on his arrival that real negotiations were out of the question.

30. General Staff, *Kämpfe der deutschen Truppen*, 1:62.

14 tremes was the Wilhelminian way, as Bebel observed: "Acting so that one hinders an outrage at any cost and for all time is simply the method with which such things are done these days."[31] Bebel was therefore not surprised to discover his fears confirmed when in early March letters from Schutztruppler describing German atrocities began showing up in newspapers.[32] On 14 March he read several excerpts aloud to the Reichstag. From a soldier in Karibib: "Here rebels are daily caught and either hanged or shot. The latest order, however, is not to bring in any more prisoners, but simply to shoot everything dead." Another reported: "We're not permitted to take prisoners. Everything alive with black skin is shot down."[33] Bebel therefore asked the government directly if there were such an order and if women and children were indeed being shot.

Colonial Director Stübel denied that orders not to take prisoners or to shoot women and children had been given. "In any event, we have no authentic information in this connection, and in my opinion, our German character does not tend to cruelty and brutality. Even if a temptation to trespass against the laws of humanity might have arisen, the troops in question would not in fact have contravened the laws of humanity."[34] Bebel welcomed this news but wondered if local commanders might not have issued such orders on their own.[35]

Two days later, Bebel weighed in with more evidence from the published letters of a veterinarian, Dr. Baumgart, who had accompanied troops in January 1904: "Bitterness is very great. No one gives quarter; everything is shot down."[36] Bebel now interpellated the government to direct the governor to answer his questions.[37]

Leutwein answered with a quick telegram, followed by a longer report. The report is noteworthy because Leutwein agreed with most of the criticisms Bebel had made before the Reichstag: that the settlers had forgotten that Africans enjoyed political rights guaranteed by the treaties of protection; that many settlers were "wayward sons" sloughed off from the motherland; that the Herero had spared women, children, and missionaries; that the settlers' brutal behavior toward the Herero had helped cause the uprising; that legal injustice was another cause; that many German press reports of Herero atrocities were wildly inaccurate; and so on. But Leutwein rejected Bebel's assertions about the conduct of the war:

> Orders to kill women and children or to take no prisoners at all have nowhere been given. However, after everything that has happened, it is only natural that our soldiers have not proceeded with particular leniency. It is equally natural that no commander has ordered such leniency. If Mr. Bebel apparently believes that one is *obliged* to take prisoners in war, then he doesn't know international law. The his-

31. Bebel, *Sten. Ber.*, XI legis. per., 1st session, 60th meeting, 17 Mar. 1904, vol. 199, p. 1903.
32. It took an average of six weeks for mail to reach Germany from the colony.
33. Bebel, *Sten. Ber.*, XI legis. per., 1st session, 60th meeting, 17 Mar. 1904, vol. 199, p. 1891.
34. Stübel, ibid., p. 1896.
35. Bebel, ibid., p. 1901.
36. Bebel, ibid., 62nd meeting, 19 Mar. 1904, p. 1967.
37. Stübel was therefore constitutionally obligated to do so. Cf. Drechsler, *"Let Us Die Fighting,"* 151.

tory of war tells of enough battles in which pardon was not given or received. International law requires only that one treat the prisoners one has in fact taken, or otherwise unarmed enemies, leniently. And I have always personally acted such that this would happen. However, since in this war the enemy himself expects no leniency, even the wounded defend themselves as long as they are able. I know of an officer, searching a battlefield, whose revolver jammed and who was saved only by the quick action of a subordinate from an attack by a wounded Herero. Under these circumstances it is no wonder that the opportunity to take nonwounded prisoners has not presented itself. To be lenient toward [prisoners] and thus to encourage desertion is necessary [anyway], merely from political motives.[38]

Leutwein then turned to the fate of a different sort of prisoner, those "captured" by settlers, "as cattle thieves or plunderers."

In accordance with the chancellor's regulation of 26 April 1896, these people are brought to trial and regularly condemned to death by the white jurors [*Beisitzern*]. It would have been impossible for the governor to oppose the execution of these judgments, especially at the beginning of the disturbances. . . . Most of these executions took place in my absence, in the south, in Karibib.[39]

Leutwein summed up the war so far:

In battle nonwounded Herero have not been taken at all. I know of only two wounded prisoners, both near Ongangira on 9 April. One died shortly thereafter. The other one, who was lightly wounded, was bandaged and cared for. He was caught later that evening with a hatchet, apparently in an escape attempt. Consequently, he was brought before a court-martial and condemned to death.[40]

By the time Leutwein's report reached the Colonial Department on 25 June, the governor had been relieved of his military duties. For a while the public discussion of the conduct of the war died down. We shall return to consider some of his statements in detail in a later chapter. For now, however, it is necessary to point out that the governor was wrong. His report has misled historians into believing that no prisoners were taken until May, or even until August.[41] But some prisoners, wounded and not, *were* taken. Who were they, and what happened to them?

38. Leutwein to Col. Dept., Nr. 395, Windhuk, 17 May 1904, BA-Berlin, R 1001, Nr. 2115, 64. I have reproduced the entire quotation because Drechsler's partial citation is misleading; Drechsler, *"Let Us Die Fighting,"* 151.

39. The missionary August Kuhlmann gives details of these executions in his letter to Inspector Spiecker, 18 May 1904, VEM-Wuppertal, Kuhlmann papers, B/c II 72, reprinted in Johannes Lucas de Vries, *Namibia* (Neukirchen-Vluyn, 1980), 282.

40. Leutwein to Col. Dept., Nr. 395, Windhuk, 17 May 1904, BA-Berlin, R 1001, Nr. 2115, 68.

41. May: Drechsler, *"Let Us Die Fighting,"* 150–51; Horst Drechsler, *Aufstände in Südwestafrika* (Berlin, 1984), 73. August: Bridgman, *Revolt of the Herero,* 103n9.

16   The gist of the governor's report, that it was extremely difficult for German troops to capture Herero warriors, is certainly true. The Herero used cover so expertly that soldiers rarely glimpsed them, even in battle. Afterward, the Herero melted away into the landscape, taking their dead and wounded with them, so that the Germans rarely knew how many casualties they had inflicted. Of the thirty-five skirmishes that occurred before June 1904, only one, Franke's relief of Omaruru, was an unalloyed German success; none of these engagements was followed by a successful pursuit that might have netted larger numbers of prisoners.[42] The official battle reports, on which Governor Leutwein would have relied, do not mention prisoners being taken.

However, the surviving handwritten war diaries of naval units[43] and the personal diaries and some memoirs of participants sporadically refer to prisoners. Even Baumgart's letter, which Bebel cited, was based on prisoner testimony. In reply to Governor Leutwein's inquiry about the letter, Baumgart denied that he had ever written that no prisoners were taken.

Had Bebel read my entire letter [which might not have been possible, since the published version, in the *Leipziger Neueste Nachrichten*, was an unauthorized, perhaps incomplete, copy], he would have discovered that we had the false information about Mrs. Pilet from "prisoners." Having written this myself, I can hardly have said in the same letter that all Herero, even those incapable of fighting, were being ruthlessly shot down. Furthermore, I know that Nevilecki delivered five Herero women and Kirsten one Herero man to the jail in Windhuk.[44]

The war diary of the 2nd Field Company of the Naval Infantry Battalion for 4 February concurs with Baumgart that "Herero men and women are being held prisoner in the jail [in Okahandja]."[45] More often, one finds in these sources reports that one or two prisoners have given information, or simply that one or several prisoners have been taken, or that wounded prisoners have been taken.[46]

The numbers are small, but the reports are regular enough to indicate that even before Leutwein issued his general order about the conduct of the war (15 Feb. 1904), German troops tried and occasionally succeeded in taking prisoners. Leutwein's order laid

42. List of engagements: Germany, General Staff, *Die Kämpfe der deutschen Truppen in Südwestafrika*, vol. 2: *Der Hottentottenkrieg* (Berlin, 1907), appendix 3 (hereafter General Staff, *Kämpfe der deutschen Truppen*, 2:page).

43. The naval records survived World War II, and because the marines were typically the first troops sent to quell colonial disturbances, these records are invaluable.

44. Copy of Dr. Baumgart to governor, Okahandja, 1 May 1904, BA-Berlin, R 1001, Nr. 2115, p. 71.

45. War diary, 4 Feb. 1904, 2nd Field Company, Naval Infantry Battalion, Bundesarchiv-Militärarchiv, Freiburg im Breisgau, RM 121 I (Landstreitkräfte der Kaiserlichen Marine), Nr. 431, p. 7 (hereafter BA-MA Freiburg, RM 121 I, Nr.).

46. Information: War diary of 2nd Field Comp., 6 Feb. 1904, ibid., p. 10; Lt. v. Winkler to Col. Leutwein, 14 Feb. 1904, ibid., RM 121 I, Nr. 422, p. 168; report of 4 Mar. 1904, ibid., RM 121 I, Nr. 423, p. 6; Leutwein to Oberkommando der Schutztruppe, 2 April 1904, BA-Berlin, R 1001, Nr. 2113, p. 81; war diary of 2nd Field Comp., 14 June 1904, BA-MA Freiburg, RM 121 I, Nr. 431, p. 49; idem., 6 July 1904, ibid., p. 65. Prisoners taken: War diary of 3rd Field Comp., 18 Feb. 1904, BA-MA Freiburg, RM 121 I, Nr. 434; *Deutsch Südwest-Afrikanische Zeitung* 11 (15

down no guidelines for handling prisoners, except to say that "prisoners of any importance are always to be questioned about the causes of the uprising. The protocols of their
answers are to be sent to me."[47] As Leutwein later explained in answer to Bebel's charges,
he assumed that prisoners would be taken and treated in the "usual fashion"
(*naturgemäss*); it was not necessary to order leniency, or indeed to order anything, since
the usual procedures would apply.

Once the debate about war conduct broke out in the Reichstag, Chancellor Bülow ca-
bled Leutwein (28 March 1904): "Press reports of letters from the protectorate cause me to
point out that steps are to be taken to prevent violations against humanity, against enemies incapable of fighting, and against women and children. Orders in this sense are to be
issued."[48] Nevertheless, neither the surviving war diaries nor the personal diaries and
memoirs of participants mention receiving Bülow's order; it was probably never trans-
mitted.[49] The taking and treatment of prisoners in the first phase of the war remained
governed by the unwritten rules of military custom, subject to the interpretation of the
individual commander. From the same sources we may discover what custom dictated.

First, by "prisoner" or "prisoner of war" the Germans understood all Herero, combat-
ant and noncombatant alike, women and children included. This usage is typically colonial, but we shall see that it had firm European precedents as well. When the reports use
the phrase "prisoner testimony" or "prisoner's report" it is thus impossible to tell the sex
or status of the prisoner(s) in question. Some reports do distinguish women and children
from men, but all Herero were subject to being made prisoner. The conflation of combatants with noncombatants had serious repercussions for the later conduct of this war.

Second, adult male Herero prisoners, those who, if they had been Europeans, would
have fallen under the protected status of prisoners of war, were subject to harsh treatment
in several respects. At the very least, they could expect rough questioning. One of the most
humane and fair officers of the Schutztruppe, the "old African" Capt. Viktor Franke, captured a Herero warrior on 10 June 1904. The next day, Franke noted in his diary, "The
Herero is still lying; I'll question him tomorrow, after he's fasted a bit."[50]

The main thing male prisoners had to fear, however, was execution. Governor
Leutwein's general order of 15 February set the usual parameters for handling "enemy"
Africans in colonial uprisings:

Mar. 1904); war diary, 2nd Field Comp. (Estorff), 9 May 1904, BA-MA Freiburg, RM 121 I, Nr. 431, p. 30; idem.,
11 May 1904, ibid., p. 31; idem., 15 May 1904, ibid., p. 35; Viktor Franke, diary entry of 10 June 1904, BA-Koblenz,
Nl. Franke, Nr. 3. For period before Aug. 1904, but without specific dates: Schwabe, *Krieg in Deutsch-Südwestafrika*, 284; Erich von Salzmann, *Im Kampfe gegen die Herero*, 2nd ed. (Berlin, 1905); 119; v. François, "Herero-
Aufstand," col. 2362. Wounded prisoners: Viktor Franke, diary entry, 27 Feb. 1904, BA-Koblenz, Nl. Franke, Nr.
3, p. 20; "March 1904," Belwe, *Gegen die Herero*, 11; "before June," idem., 38; missionary August Kuhlmann to Inspector Spiecker, 18 May 1904 (referring to 1st Lt. Kuhn on 8 May 1904), in de Vries, *Namibia*, 282.

47. Theodor Leutwein, "Truppenbefehl," handwritten draft, Karibib, 15 Feb. 1904, BA-MA Freiburg, RM 121
I, Nr. 422, p. 122.

48. Stübel, *Sten. Ber.*, XI legis. per., 1st session, 87th meeting, 9 May 1904, vol. 200, p. 2790.

49. Gov. Leutwein's son mentions Bülow's order, but it is unclear whether he learned of it in the field or
from the Reichstag debates, where it was announced. Paul Leutwein, *Afrikanerschicksal* (Stuttgart, 1929), 121.

50. Franke diary entry of 11 June 1904, BA-Koblenz, Nl. Franke, Nr. 3, p. 67.

18 Villages [*Werften*] that voluntarily surrender their weapons can be spared. No mercy will be shown to the ringleaders or to those who are proved to have murdered unarmed men, women, or children, or to have robbed or vandalized farms. Insofar as their identities can be ascertained, they are immediately to be tried according to martial law. Trial procedure will be according to the chancellor's decree of 26 April 1896.[51]

The court-martial of rebel leaders and those guilty of major crimes was a standard feature in the suppression of colonial uprisings. However, the addition of robbery and vandalism meant that a very large percentage of Herero men (and possibly women) would now be subject to summary proceedings.

The demand for punishment reflected widespread public opinion in the colony and in Germany. The *Berliner Zeitung* was typical: "We must make a repeat of this uprising impossible under all circumstances by sharp and ruthless punishment."[52] Captain Gudewill used the same language: "The utmost punishment of the enemy is necessary as atonement for the countless brutal murders and as guarantee for a peaceful future."[53] "Exemplary punishment" remained a nonnegotiable, fixed foundation of government policy throughout the war. In his early struggle with the Colonial Department in February over the right to pursue negotiations, Leutwein declared that courts-martial would always follow capitulation.[54] This remained his position. As Leutwein handed over the military reins to his successor, Lt. Gen. Lothar von Trotha, in June 1904, he gave him a proposed proclamation for the surrender of the Herero, which promised that Germany would spare the lives of the innocent, "but those who have killed or robbed whites, or destroyed their property or possessions will receive no mercy; they must appear before a court and be punished for their guilt."[55] Chancellor Bülow also clung to "exemplary punishment" as imperative to the negotiations he tried (unsuccessfully) to persuade Trotha to conduct in late October 1904.[56] In short, punishment was what moderates demanded. As Adolf Stoecker (Christian Social Party) argued before the Reichstag in December 1904, in a speech opposing Trotha's later policy of annihilation: "One accomplishes nothing through mere harshness. I believe severe punishment [*strenge Bestrafung*] is necessary, but when that is accomplished, then the only proper thing is to show the natives, especially the prisoners of war, kindness, so that they will want to become German subjects."[57]

The problem with a policy of exemplary punishment was that it consisted chiefly of the death penalty. As Leutwein had explained to the Colonial Department in February, "Prisoners of war will all be called before courts-martial, and, if they are found guilty of

51. Leutwein, "Truppenbefehl."
52. V. Gädke, "Die militärische Lage in Deutsch-Südwestafrika," *Berliner Zeitung* 63 (4 Feb. 1904), 1.
53. V. Levetzow to Col. Dept., Nr. B. 706 IV, 4 Feb. 1904, BA-Berlin, R 1001, Nr. 2111, pp. 167–68.
54. Leutwein to Col. Dept., Nr. 73, Windhuk, 23 Feb. 1904, BA-Berlin, R 1001, Nr. 2113, pp. 54–55.
55. Leutwein, draft proclamation to the Herero, 30 May 1904, BA-Berlin, R 1001, Nr. 2089, p. 141.
56. Bülow to Trotha, tel., Berlin, 28 Oct. 1904, ibid., Nr. 2116, pp. 92–93.
57. Stoecker, *Sten. Ber.*, XI legis. per., 1st session, 108th meeting, 9 Dec. 1904, vol. 201, p. 3453.

plundering farms, much less of murdering peaceful inhabitants, they will always receive the death penalty."[58] Leutwein's letter was forwarded to the General Staff, and neither it nor the Colonial Department suggested tempering its sweep or vehemence.[59]

Courts-martial were conducted on the spot by field courts consisting of three officers, who were empowered to proceed with executions of African "rebels" without first getting permission from the governor. Regulations thus gave great latitude to individual officers and to their interpretation of military necessity and the customs of war. Some units followed Leutwein's orders and collected eyewitness testimony identifying specific people.[60] That kind of investigation permitted differentiated verdicts, such as one from a field court in June that tried seven Herero and sentenced two to death, three to prison and forced labor, but acquitted two others; or another that occurred sometime before May, in which an Ovambo prisoner was acquitted.[61] But the likelihood that summary proceedings would end in widespread executions was great. The intimate connection between captivity and execution is suggested by the "Excerpt from the Order-Book" of the Naval Expedition Corps (March 1904): "According to higher orders, those persons in charge of leading troops of prisoners or responsible for carrying out executions are to make sure that no photographs are taken."[62] I have discovered in the archives no statistics on how many Herero prisoners were executed by military courts-martial.

In addition to courts-martial conducted by regular troops, there were punitive sweeps carried out by "military patrols," consisting of perhaps one or two Schutztruppler leading deputized male settlers. Paul Rohrbach's published diary gives a good account of their activities. Rohrbach was a political economist charged by the government with surveying the economic potential of SWA. The uprising trapped him along with other whites in the northeast of the colony, in Grootfontein. Although he could barely shoot a gun, Rohrbach felt compelled to volunteer with the other men to ride out on patrol, because "the situation here is such that one can barely get out of it, since, as a man and a government official I'm sort of responsible for the honor of my profession."[63] These patrols operated on their own, out of Leutwein's control. They shot at any Africans they imagined were thieves; if they caught Africans with goods, that was sufficient cause to execute them on the spot. Rohrbach estimated that by the end of March 1904 their patrols had killed twenty men, most of them Bergdamaras and Bushmen, not even Herero.[64]

Spying provided the major justification for regular troops to shoot Africans without trial. This elastic term expanded with anxiety. It covered natives of both sexes, those who did not "belong" in a place, who seemed curious, or who simply tried to run away when

58. Leutwein to Col. Dept., Nr. 73, Windhuk, 23 Feb. 1904, BA-Berlin, R 1001, Nr. 2113, pp. 54–55.

59. Schlieffen to Col. Dept., Nr. 3482, Berlin, 10 Apr. 1904, explicitly agreed with Leutwein's policy. BA-Berlin, R 1001, Nr. 2113, p. 122.

60. Report, signed by Rickmann, 14 Feb. 1904, BA-MA Freiburg, RM 121 I, Nr. 422, p. 131.

61. Belwe, *Gegen die Herero*, 80; Kuhlmann to Inspector, 18 May 1904, in de Vries, *Namibia*, 282. The military used some captured Herero for labor from the beginning: Jan-Bart Gewald, *Towards Redemption* (Leiden, 1996), 221.

62. "Auszug aus dem Parolebuch!" Nr. 729, Windhuk, 7 Mar. 1904, BA-MA Freiburg, RM 121 I, Nr. 423, p. 47.

63. Rohrbach, *Aus Südwestafrikas schweren Tagen*, 79.

64. Ibid., 113, 127, 132.

20   they saw troops. The standard procedure for handling "spies" was to shoot them immediately. Not every officer complied, of course, but Captain Franke's scruples, which he noted in his diary, testify to the expectation that he was supposed to do so. "I am still fighting with myself," he wrote on 26 June 1904, "whether I should have a Herero shot, who was brought in and who is clearly a spy. And then I am freed from my doubts: the prisoner dies [anyway]."[65] Maj. Ludwig von Estorff, another experienced "African," apparently shared Franke's scruples. It is indicative of the cleft between officers with African experience and newcomers from Germany that Paul Leutwein, the governor's son, who came briefly to SWA and fought under Estorff's command, unhesitatingly shot an old Herero woman for spying because he knew Estorff would not.[66]

Thanks to Franke's diary we can confirm another customary military practice: executing the wounded. Franke was an experienced Africa hand. He knew African customs and had good personal relations with a number of Africans. Deeply religious, free-thinking, practical, and hypersensitive, Franke was horrified by gratuitous brutality. He is one of the few whites whom the missionaries singled out as having behaved fairly toward Africans.[67] His diary for 27 February reads:

> A wounded [Herero] is brought in with a horribly mutilated leg. The man does not even brush the flies away from the dreadful ragged flesh. He is questioned and then shot. V[on] Bonin does it well. He had him shot from the back at a moment when the unfortunate man suspected nothing.[68]

Clearly, Franke did not relish this task, nor did he condemn it; it was a regrettable part of colonial warfare. In May the activist Protestant missionary August Kuhlmann sent a blistering report to his superiors about German military conduct, in which he listed nine separate incidents of brutality, three of which, including the one reported by Franke, involved killing wounded prisoners. One of the other executioners he named was First Lieutenant Kuhn, whom Kuhlmann and his fellow missionaries later recalled as fair and just in his treatment of Africans.[69] These executions were therefore not random atrocities but accepted methods of warfare that experienced and decent men employed. Nonetheless, Franke's use of the word "unfortunate" and the protest of a militiaman against the third incident that Kuhlmann cited, indicate that shooting the wounded was right on the boundary of the acceptable. For the present, at least.

65. Franke, diary entry of 26 June 1904, BA-Koblenz, Nl. Franke, Nr. 3, p. 70.

66. Leutwein, *Afrikanerschicksal*, 121–22.

67. Missionaries Bernsmann, Danner, Kuhlmann, Elder, Vedder, Brockmann, Eich, and Diehl to Inspector Spiecker, Karibib, 5 May 1904, VEM-Wuppertal, Diehl papers, B/c II 35, 3, p. 87.

68. Franke, diary entry of 27 Feb. 1904, BA-Koblenz, Nl. Franke, Nr. 3, p. 20. The missionary August Kuhlmann mentions this incident and says Franke's troops bayoneted another Herero at the same time. Franke's diary entry for 26 Feb. mentions finding two wounded Herero, so it is possible that this is what Kuhlmann witnessed. Kuhlmann to Inspector Spiecker, 18 May 1904, reprinted in de Vries, *Namibia*, 282.

69. Kuhlmann to Inspector Spiecker, 18 May 1904; and Bernsmann, Danner, Kuhlmann, Elder, Vedder, Brockmann, Eich, and Diehl to Inspector Spiecker, Karibib, 5 May 1904, VEM-Wuppertal, Diehl papers, B/c II 35, 3, p. 87. For another account of killing the wounded, see the testimony of D. E. Dixon in Union of South Africa, *Report on the Natives of South West Africa and Their Treatment by Germany* (London, 1918), 66.

In the same letter Kuhlmann also reported that around Easter, transport troops had told him that they had received orders to take no prisoners. We have already seen that no such order came from Leutwein. But Bebel's surmise that some local commanders might have been less restrained is possible, above all because Kuhlmann is a highly reliable source. He was punctilious with facts, and where other sources are available, they corroborate his testimonies. Surviving archival documents contain no record of underlings ordering "no quarter," but because records are so spotty and because such an order is likely to have been verbal, no firm conclusion is possible. A number of factors might have encouraged some officers to shed their scruples: the fear and vindictiveness of the settlers, which sanctioned retaliation; the Hereros' own practice of taking no prisoners and of killing wounded enemy soldiers; the difficulty of fighting a canny enemy in an unfamiliar place, especially given the assumption that Europeans were superior to Africans in all things, including warfare.

But above all, the actual, undeniable practices of the early months of warfare contained a dangerous potential to drift further in the direction of more complete destruction. These practices included the identification of the entire people, not just the combatants, as the enemy; the duty to "punish" the enemy, not just for murder but for theft and property destruction; the conviction that such "punishment" merited the death penalty; the swiftness and irrevocability of the court-martial; the custom of shooting "spies"; and the acceptability of executing the wounded. These practices gravitated toward mass death. But they had not reached it. For all of Kuhlmann's justifiable outrage at German military methods in the beginning, when the real campaign of annihilation was later loosed upon the Herero, he recognized that "if [Berlin] had retained Leutwein and given him carte blanche in ending the war, the country today [Feb. 1905] would be in better condition, from the human standpoint."[70]

The Wilhelminian Conception of Defeat and the Appointment of Lothar von Trotha

Although the German strategic situation was sound after Franke's relief of Omaruru and the securing of the railroad in early February, Leutwein's campaign disappointed the public and the General Staff. The Herero fought well; the German reinforcements did not.[71] The naval troops lacked every quality necessary to the colonial soldier. They were indifferent marksmen, unpracticed marchers, and, worst of all, unmounted. These factors and their inexperience combined to produce the greatest disaster of the war, at Owikoko-rero on 13 March 1904, where seven out of eleven officers and nineteen out of thirty-eight

70. Kuhlmann, "Report on the Attempts to Negotiate Peace in Otjimbingue," 16 Feb. 1905, VEM-Wuppertal, Kuhlmann papers, B/c II 72. Many of Leutwein's earlier critics from the other side, those who found his conduct of the war too hesitant, also changed their minds when they experienced his successor's policy of total destruction: Rust, *Krieg und Frieden*, 331; Rohrbach, *Aus Südwestafrikas schweren Tagen*, passim; and the mouthpiece of the settlers, the *Deutsch-Südwestafrikanische Zeitung*, Nr. 50, 14 Dec. 1904.

71. By the end of July, just over 6,000 reinforcements had arrived in SWA; 1,500 Germans fought at Waterberg. For a list of reinforcements: Kommando der Schutztruppen im Reichs-Kolonialamt, *Sanitäts-Bericht über die Kaiserliche Schutztruppe für Südwestafrika* (Berlin, 1909), Beilage 4, pp. 438–40.

22   men died.[72] Compounding the problems the Germans encountered when fighting were the even worse burdens of supply and sanitation. The more reinforcements there were the greater their needs in food, water (which of all things was in shortest supply), ammunition, and medical service. Apart from the frail railroad, SWA lacked infrastructure; the Germans had to provide everything themselves. Here they failed utterly. The survivors of Owikoko-rero and their other mates in the so-called eastern units swiftly fell prey to typhus, which was brought on by undernourishment and contaminated water and aggravated by nonexistent medical care. By mid-April, Leutwein's troops had been reduced by a third.[73]

It is a tribute to Leutwein's military abilities that he was nonetheless able to overcome these disasters and, using his remaining troops, push the Herero back. Leutwein aimed, as always, at inflicting enough damage to force a negotiated surrender. The Herero, and therefore Leutwein, calculated damage on two registers: loss of warriors and loss of cattle, the chief source of tribal wealth. According to these measures, the Germans scored important victories in several difficult battles: at Otjihinamaparero (25 February) the Herero lost two thousand head of cattle; and at Onganjira (9 April) and Oviumbo (13 April) Africans later reported that the Herero had suffered major casualties, causing them to retreat to the Waterberg ["Water Mountain"], the last great water source before the Omaheke Desert to the east-southeast.[74] According to Wilhelminian military reckoning, however, Oviumbo, where Leutwein himself led the troops, was a major defeat.

After a day of very hard fighting, the governor faced the choice of trying a last, desperate charge or assuring his troops' safety by pulling back. Not until later did the Germans learn that the Herero had also retreated. Only one experienced "old African," Major Estorff, urged attack. "[Attack] with what?" Franke asked in his diary. "Without ammunition, without food, with an exhausted train. . . . Thank God the colonel [Leutwein] listened to [Maj. Joachim von] Heydebreck, me, and the others and decided on an orderly retreat."[75] Five thousand miles away the desk soldiers were shocked and ashamed that German troops had retreated before Africans. By 1904 German military doctrine had so thoroughly succumbed to the "cult of the offensive" that military writers had difficulty defending the idea of defensive tactics, including tactical retreat, even in European warfare.[76] The conviction of racial superiority, based not least on technical military prowess, made tactical retreat vis-à-vis blacks simply unacceptable. The General Staff criticized Leutwein's leadership so sharply that the governor offered to resign in favor of "a senior officer who possesses the complete confidence of the General Staff."[77] That officer was Lt. Gen. Lothar von Trotha.

72. General Staff, *Kämpfe der deutschen Truppen*, 1:68.

73. Ibid., 1:118.

74. Cattle: Leutwein, *Elf Jahre*, 500. Casualties: Paul von Lettow-Vorbeck diary entry of 8 Dec. 1904, BA-MA Freiburg, Nl. Lettow-Vorbeck, Nr. 34. Retreat: General Staff, *Kämpfe der deutschen Truppen*, 1:122. Gewald calls Oviumbo a "stand-off"; *Herero Heroes*, 170.

75. Franke, diary entry of 13 Apr. 1904, BA-Koblenz, Nl. Franke, Nr. 3, p. 4.

76. Jehuda Wallach, *Das Dogma der Vernichtungsschlacht* (Frankfurt, 1967), 43–44; Jack Snyder, "Civil-Military Relations and the Cult of the Offensive, 1914 and 1984," *International Security* 9:1 (summer 1984), 108–46, here 122–29; Bley, *South-West Africa*, 158.

77. Leutwein to General Staff, Okahandja, 25 Apr. 1904, cited in Drechsler, *"Let Us Die Fighting,"* 149.

Marine in torn uniform "after four weeks' march in the bush." Kurd Schwabe, *Der Krieg in Deutsch-Südwestafrika, 1904–1906* (Berlin: C. A. Weller, 1907), 184.

Lt. Gen. Lothar von Trotha in colonial uniform. Kurd Schwabe, *Der Krieg in Deutsch-Südwestafrika, 1904–1906* (Berlin: C. A. Weller, 1907), 280.

Trotha's appointment was a stinging defeat for civilian, political authority. Chancellor Bülow and Colonial Director Stübel defended Leutwein and opposed Trotha, whom the experienced colonial expert Heinrich Schnee characterized as "a man capable of thinking only in 'purely military terms.'"[78] That is doubtless what recommended him to Chief of Staff Schlieffen and the chief of the Military Cabinet, Gen. Dietrich von Hülsen-

78. Bley, *South-West Africa*, 159. My discussion follows Bley's analysis of Trotha's appointment, 158–60.

Häseler.[79] Trotha's "friends in high places" arranged for him to be consulted as reinforcements were first being assembled, and newspapers named him as a possible successor to Leutwein as early as March 1904.[80] After the "defeat" at Oviumbo, the Kaiser overrode civilian objections and chose Trotha as military commander. Because the military commander and the governor were normally the same person, Trotha's appointment raised the question, Who would rule in Windhuk? Colonial Director Stübel argued that the governor's political decisions must set policy. Wilhelm overruled him: Trotha received supreme command. On arrival in SWA on 11 June 1904, Trotha declared martial law, thereby transferring supreme authority from civilian government to the military commander, following the model of Germany in wartime.[81] Surprisingly, Leutwein did not resign. He remained governor, overseeing administration but not policy until he was forced out of office in November 1904 because he challenged Trotha's policy of extermination. Thus, from 11 June 1904 to Trotha's recall in November 1905, the war in SWA was conducted entirely according to military calculations, and the administration functioned as a military dictatorship. Although nominally Chief of Staff Schlieffen was in charge, in fact, the commander of the Schutztruppe on the spot determined the conduct of war.[82]

What was it reasonable to expect from a soldier like Trotha? His career had been unusual. As the son of a noble and an officer, Trotha had entered the army in the prestigious 2nd Foot Guards.[83] But he remained there less than a year before being transferred to a mundane infantry regiment, in which he saw action in the Franco-Prussian War. Thereafter he made his name in the colonies. From 1894 to 1897 he served in German East Africa as a lieutenant colonel and, briefly, as deputy governor. Years later, Trotha claimed that he had learned the inevitability of "racial war" in East Africa. Yet, his career there was not unlike that of other commanders of the countless punitive expeditions sent out to quell rebellions. Trotha's troops pursued Sultan Hassan bin Omar (in late 1895) and then engaged in a long expedition into the ill-explored interior of the colony, pro-

79. Schlieffen: ibid., 159. Hülsen: Paul Leutwein, *Afrikanerschicksal*, 172. Hülsen was Trotha's main supporter: Trotha to Hülsen, 7 Dec. 1904, Archive of the von Trotha Family, Nr. 315, Anhang 1, Nr. 14 (hereafter Trotha Papers).

80. "Friends": Ledebour, *Sten. Ber.*, XI legis. per., 2nd session, 5th meeting, 2 Dec. 1905, vol. 214, 92. Successor: "Der Aufstand in SWA," *Berliner Zeitung* 148 (21 Mar. 1904), 1; "Der Aufstand," *Deutsch-Südwestafrikanische Zeitung* 19 (11 May 1904). Eugen Zimmermann, editor of the *Berliner Lokalanzeiger*, asked the Colonial Department only a week after the revolt started whether Trotha would lead the expedition: Zimmermann to Stübel, Berlin, 22 Jan. 1904, BA-Berlin, R 1001, Nr. 2111, p. 87.

81. Allerhöchste Kabinetts-Ordre (AKO) of 19 May 1904; Lothar v. Trotha, "Kriegszustands-Bestimmungen," in Kaiserliche Schutztruppe für Südwestafrika, "Bestimmungen für das Militärgerichts-Verfahren etc.," Swakopmund, 11 June 1904, reprinted in Rust, *Krieg und Frieden*, 344–45. See discussion in Bley, *South-West Africa*, 159.

82. Trotha disagreed with and ignored most of Schlieffen's military recommendations. See Trotha diary, 25 June 1904, 22 July 1904, 20 Jan. 1905, Trotha Papers, Nr. 315, pp. 12, 22, 70. Also, Kirsten Zirkel, "Military Power in German Colonial Policy," in *Guardians of Empire*, ed. David Killingray and David Omissi (New York, 1999), 91–113, here 101.

83. *Deutsches Biographisches Archiv*, Neue Folge, fiche 375.

26 voking various battles along the way, ending in the surrender of the Waha's Sultan Mtau in early 1897.[84]

Trotha described his methods:

> The punishment [of villages that had greeted the expedition with poisoned arrows] consisted of sending small units . . . to the villages, which after a short fight are then taken and burnt down. We cannot determine enemy losses, because most [of the dead and wounded] will have been taken with the people as they retreat, and many will probably have died in the flames. This method of conducting war, through burning, was hardly congenial to me at the beginning. But then and now I cannot help but conclude from later conflicts that any kindness in this regard is interpreted by the natives as weakness.[85]

Trotha understood himself as merely copying the customary war methods of East Africa. He described dealing with one recalcitrant sultan, whom "I punished in the manner customary to the land by burning his residence and taking his cows."[86]

There were other "customary" or at least usual methods of warfare with which Trotha came into contact in East Africa and which he later used in SWA. Governor Wissmann placed bounties (*Kopfgeld*) on the heads of rebel leaders.[87] A local military station master recommended threatening uncooperative populations with starvation by preventing crop cultivation, but Trotha disapproved.[88] However, he did adopt a way of lowering the costs of maintaining prisoners: "I'm going to chase away the rest of those prisoners, who are mostly women and children [anyway], whom we have captured or who have come voluntarily into the camp."[89]

Trotha also relied heavily on execution by court-martial. "Of those we took prisoner," he reported after one episode, "there were two men caught with weapons who were condemned to death the next day by court-martial and hanged, and the fort was consigned to fire."[90] Altogether, Trotha emerged as a confirmed believer in exemplary punishment. After capturing Hassan, he informed Governor Wissmann that "I have not opened court-martial proceedings against him, because I think it more promising if he and the other guilty parties ascend the scaffold in Kilwa before the eyes of his secret followers."[91] Trotha's devotion to exemplary punishment had slid over into "terrorism," as he called it.

---

84. Ernst Nigmann, *Geschichte der Kaiserlichen Schutztruppe für Deutsch-Ostafrika* (Berlin, 1911), 54.

85. Trotha, "Report on the battles in Ururi," Dar es Salaam, 16 Mar. 1897, BA-Berlin, R 1001, Nr. 288, pp. 71–74.

86. Trotha, "Report on the Punishment of the Waha in November 1896," ibid.

87. Wissmann to Chancellor Chlodwig zu Hohenlohe-Schillingsfürst, Nr. 976, Dar es Salaam, 1 Oct. 1895, BA-Berlin, R 1001, Nr. 286, pp. 86–89.

88. Trotha to Wissmann, Lager am Mavuji, 15 Nov. 1895, BA-Berlin, R 1001, Nr. 286, pp. 139–42.

89. Ibid.

90. Trotha, "Report on the Punishment of the Waha in November 1896," BA-Berlin, R 1001, Nr. 288.

91. Trotha to Wissmann, Lager am Mavuji, 15 Nov. 1895, ibid., Nr. 286, pp. 139–42.

When a local population failed to deliver up rebel leaders, Trotha recommended "hanging one prisoner every month" until they complied. "Terrorism can only help."[92]

If Trotha's general profile as a colonial commander was not far out of the ordinary, he nonetheless had begun to distinguish himself as a man prepared to go to extremes, if necessary. He made political minds uneasy. The Colonial Department routinely published excerpts from military leaders' reports as propaganda for the colonies. Trotha's reports were vetted for this purpose. Citing "peculiar circumstances," colonial officials unanimously declared them unfit for publication.[93] Governor Wissmann cancelled sixteen death sentences levied by Trotha's courts-martial during the Hassan bin Omar expedition "because the number of those condemned to death is so great that it would probably lead to unpleasant utterances in our press."[94] When Wissmann learned in 1904 that Trotha was being considered as commander in SWA, he tried to prevent the appointment. He called Trotha "a bad leader, a bad African, and a bad comrade."[95]

After East Africa, Trotha resumed his career in Germany, but as soon as the opportunity arose he volunteered for service in China, as part of the international force to quell the Boxer Uprising. He was present at the public execution of the assassins of German Ambassador Ketteler in Peking, and he led the punitive expedition to the Ming graves to punish Boxers for murdering Chinese Christians in the vicinity.[96] But China offered few opportunities to add luster to his career, so it was probably his reputation in East Africa, plus his dramatic, soldierly bearing that brought him to the attention of Military Cabinet Chief Hülsen and Chief of Staff Schlieffen.[97]

Trotha's Plans at the Waterberg

When Trotha arrived in SWA on 11 June 1904, he inherited a situation and a plan of attack. Virtually the entire Herero people and all their own and the settlers' cattle had retreated to the Waterberg. Leutwein and the "old Africans" had planned a concentric attack at the Waterberg, where they hoped to inflict enough damage to move the Herero to accept a negotiated surrender. Leutwein and most experienced military hands believed a sharp attack with even small forces would be sufficient, but Trotha forbade any engagements in his absence. Leutwein and Estorff contemplated proceeding anyway, as they were sure they could end the war. But Leutwein explained to Estorff that "in Germany

---

92. Ibid.

93. Internal notice to K 8161, BA-Berlin, R 1001, Nr. 288, p. 82.

94. Wissmann to Chancellor Hohenlohe, Nr. 1271, Dar es Salaam, 23 Dec. 1895, BA-Berlin, R 1001, Nr. 287, pp. 14–16.

95. Ludwig v. Estorff, *Wanderungen und Kämpfe in Südwestafrika, Ostafrika und Südafrika* (Wiesbaden, 1968), 117.

96. Execution: Justus Scheibert, *Der Krieg in China* (Berlin, 1909), 381; Ming graves: General Alfred v. Waldersee to General Staff, Nr. 121, Peking, 31 Jan. 1901, and Nr. 134, 13 Feb. 1901, BA-MA Freiburg, RM 121 I, Nr. 399, pp. 71, 72.

97. Estorff, *Wanderungen*, 117. Franke heard of Trotha's reputation as a "Theater-General," diary entry of 5 May 1904, BA-Koblenz, Nl. Franke, Nr. 3, pp. 48–49.

28 [meaning the General Staff] what counts as a success is not a simple victory but only the destruction [*Vernichtung*] of the enemy." Under those conditions, Estorff advised against an attack, and it was left to Trotha to achieve the kind of success "Germany" wanted.[98] The paramountcy of the General Staff thus dictated a particular kind of victory, the pure victory of military force, the *Vernichtungssieg*.

The word "destruction" and the phrase "policy of destruction" (*Vernichtungspolitik*), used to describe Trotha's later annihilation of the Herero people, have raised the question of whether Trotha planned on annihilation from the beginning. Helmut Bley, author of the best political analysis of the colony, has recognized that annihilation developed out of less drastic military policies.[99] Jon Bridgman, however, interprets Trotha's disposition of forces at the Waterberg as proof that Trotha intended mass death. This viewpoint follows Horst Drechsler, whose account was the first based on archival sources and continues to be influential.[100] Drechsler maintains that Trotha pursued a clear "aim of annihilating the Herero [people]," which he accomplished through the "well-thought-out plan" of battle at the Waterberg.[101] To assess Drechsler's claim we must answer three questions: Did Trotha receive orders to annihilate the Herero? Are there other indications that he pursued annihilation from the beginning on his own? Did his battle plan aim to destroy the entire people?

Trotha himself answered the first question in the negative. At two different points the general came under heavy attack for his Vernichtungspolitik: once in late 1904–early 1905 from Chancellor Bülow and Governor Leutwein; and again after the war was over, when tempers had cooled and war costs had been toted up. By then, many public voices excoriated Trotha's policies. Both times the general defended himself vociferously, but he never claimed his superiors had ordered mass destruction. A loyal, self-sacrificing soldier might have hidden such an order from the public, but he would have had no reason to do so in confidential correspondence with the Kaiser's other servants, the chancellor and the governor. To Leutwein, Trotha explained (5 November 1904) that "when I was appointed commander in SWA I received no instructions or directives. His Majesty simply told me that he expected I would defeat the uprising by all means [*mit allen Mitteln*] and explain later why the uprising had begun."[102] Such vagueness was typical of orders commanders received under these circumstances. For example, the "Order for the Leader of the Naval Expedition Corps" at the beginning of the uprising in January 1904 simply told him that,

98. Leutwein to Estorff, heliogram from Owikokorero, 16 June 1904; Estorff to Leutwein, Otjosondu, 16 June 1904, BA-MA Freiburg, RM 121 I, Nr. 431, pp. 50–51.

99. Bley, *South-West Africa*, 162–64. Two other recent studies agree: Zirkel, "Military Power in German Colonial Policy," 100; and Gewald, *Towards Redemption*, 205–9. Gewald, without analyzing the military developments, intimates that Trotha adopted *Vernichtung* at Waterberg: ibid., 209, also *Herero Heroes*, 174–75.

100. The best recent social, not military, history of the Herero follows Drechsler's interpretation: Krüger, *Kriegsbewältigung*, 50, 62. Similarly, John Horne and Alan Kramer, *German Atrocities, 1914* (New Haven, 2001), 169. Jürgen Zimmerer vacillates on this question: *Deutsche Herrschaft über Afrikaner* (Hamburg, 2001), 31, 54–55.

101. Bley, *South-West Africa*, 162–63; Bridgman, *Revolt*, 122; Drechsler, "*Let Us Die Fighting*," 155, repeated in Drechsler, *Aufstände*, 77–78; and reprinted in Drechsler, "The Hereros of South-West Africa (Namibia)," in *The History and Sociology of Genocide*, ed. Frank Chalk and Kurt Jonassohn (New Haven, 1990), 241–42.

102. Trotha to Leutwein, copy, Windhuk, 5 Nov. 1904, BA-Berlin, R 1001, Nr. 2089, pp. 101–3.

unless he received other instructions from the governor, he was "to reestablish order in the protectorate independently by all means at your disposal [*mit allen Ihnen zu Gebote stehenden Mitteln*]."[103] The phrase "by all means" was standard.

In January 1905 Trotha explained to Bülow why he had rejected mediation and instead continued pursuing the Herero people to their deaths: "I asked the General Staff chief several months ago [*vor Monaten*] whether *His Majesty* agreed with my harsh stance. I never received an answer. *Qui tacet, consentire videtur.* I had to assume that my position was approved *at the highest level.*"[104] If Trotha had received direct orders to proceed as he did, he would surely have told Bülow at this time. Four years later, in a letter to a newspaper editor, Trotha specified when he had decided on annihilation and when he had begun asking his superiors for their ex post facto approval: "Already in September 1904 I had made no bones about how I intended to end the uprising, and numerous times I offered my resignation [if this policy was rejected]."[105] The battle of Waterberg occurred on 11 August 1904. Trotha's decision to annihilate occurred a month later. Neither then nor earlier did he receive an order to this effect; otherwise he would hardly have had to inform the General Staff of his new policy, or to ask its blessing.

It is, of course, possible that Trotha received a verbal order from the Kaiser. Bebel speculated along these lines after the annihilation had become fact:

> I don't know whether Mr. v. Trotha acted on his own or according to a similar slogan [*Parole*] to the one made in 1900, "Take no quarter, behave so that no Chinese will dare to look askance at a German for a thousand years." Probably he did take with him from Germany a similar slogan, which one did not want to express publicly a second time.[106]

The "slogan" in question was Wilhelm's speech to troops departing to put down the Boxer Uprising in 1900. If Bebel's point was that a commander could count on Wilhelm's admiration for what he saw as soldierly ruthlessness, then it was a point well taken. But a slogan is not an order.

Nevertheless, Trotha's importunate pleas in the fall of 1904 that the Kaiser approve his Vernichtungspolitik suggest he thought Wilhelm would do so. Wilhelm's tough stand against negotiations announced at the beginning of the uprising made clear that he wanted a decision by force. When Trotha left Germany, the Kaiser's chief of the Militaire

103. "Befehl für den Führer des Marine-Expeditionskorps," signed Wilhelm II, Berlin, 20 Jan. 1904, BA-MA Freiburg, RM 2 (Imperial Naval Cabinet), Nr. 1867, p. 66. Similarly, when Chancellor Leo v. Caprivi sent Kurt v. François to SWA in 1893 to quell disturbances "the only instructions given were to uphold German authority [*Herrschaft*] under all circumstances"; Leutwein, *Elf Jahre*, 15.

104. Trotha to Bülow, Windhuk, 6 Jan. 1905, BA-Berlin, R 1001, Nr. 2089, pp. 138–39, emphasis in original.

105. Lothar v. Trotha, "Die Erwiderung des Staatssekretärs Dernburg am 2. März" (letter dated 9 Mar. 1909) (*Berliner Neueste Nachrichten*), in BA-MA Freiburg, Militärgeschichtliche Sammlung (hereafter MSg. 2), Nr. 3039 (Baron v. Welck). Trotha's first letter to Schlieffen explaining his new policy and threatening resignation if the Kaiser did not approve was 3 Oct. 1904: cf. Trotha diary entries for August and September, and Anhang 1, containing his letters to Schlieffen, Trotha Papers.

106. Bebel, *Sten. Ber.*, XI legis. per., 2nd session, 131st meeting, 1 Dec. 1906, vol. 218, p. 4060.

30   Maison, Gen. Hans von Plessen, told him, "Just don't lose your nerve," which in military parlance meant to hew to the tough military line, regardless of obstacles; and that is how Trotha interpreted it.[107] When Wilhelm finally rescinded Trotha's explicit policy in December 1904 at the chancellor's urging, he responded to practical arguments while rejecting humanitarian and moral ones; universal principles, therefore, would not have hindered the Kaiser from championing harsh action.[108] Finally, pressured by Trotha's military intermediaries to respond to the commander's pleas (and threat of resignation), Wilhelm came close to sanctioning annihilation once it had happened. On 19 January 1905 the Kaiser wrote, "You have entirely fulfilled my expectations when I named you to commander of the Schutztruppe, and it is a pleasure to express to you again my complete recognition for your accomplishments so far."[109] If Trotha had received a verbal order, he would surely have cited it when asking for royal confirmation. Still, the surviving correspondence shows the atmosphere of military hardness at court that Trotha believed backed his extreme policies.

    If Trotha did not receive an actual order to annihilate, he still might have arrived in SWA intent on doing so on his own. Trotha had been an outspoken racist since his time in East Africa. He believed the Herero people were expendable. Indeed, he confided to his diary on 1 July 1904 that all colonies had to be conquered with blood.[110] "The natives must give way [*weichen*]—look at America. Either via the bullet or the mission, with alcohol."[111] The Kaiser had forbidden negotiations without his approval, and Trotha was more than happy to pursue a policy of pure force. On 16 July Trotha quashed negotiation feelers from Salatiel, one of the Herero subchiefs. "In my dying hour I will take responsibility for the black blood that is shed," he wrote in his diary, alluding at the end of the entry to the Herero practice of mutilation.[112] Trotha was therefore personally ready to continue the policy of pure force to the end.

    The main source for the speculation that Trotha planned annihilation from the beginning is the governor's son, Paul Leutwein, who served as a volunteer officer with the Schutztruppe in the opening months of the war, but who had left the colony before Trotha arrived. Years later he described the meeting between Governor Leutwein and the newly arrived general (23 June 1904) in Okahandja: "From the governor's papers I gather

---

107. Trotha to Dietrich v. Hülsen-Häseler, 7 Dec. 1904, Nr. 315, Anhang 1, Nr. 14, Trotha Papers. "I have always held my head high in the most difficult moments."

108. Bernhard von Bülow, *Denkwürdigkeiten*, 4 vols. (Berlin, 1920), 2:21.

109. Wilhelm to Trotha, tel., 19 Jan. 1905, Trotha Papers, Nr. 315, p. 70. Helmut Otto interprets Schlieffen's congratulation as his approval of extermination, but he praised "the extraordinarily energetic and successful pursuit under such difficult circumstances": *Schlieffen und der Generalstab* (Berlin, 1966), 214.

110. The handwritten original of Trotha's diary has been lost. The von Trotha family archive possesses an original typewritten transcript from 1930, made by Trotha's second wife, Lucy, and another, a bound typescript, made later. I have used the 1930 version (Nr. 315). It appears to have been typed from the original by a professional secretary (the keystrokes are quite regular). The retention of small geographical details and numbers and the inclusion of damning statements make it appear that little, if anything, was omitted. The ms. was reread several times, each reading leaving a trace in colored crayon or pencil of passages the reader(s) apparently wished to omit from a possible published version. I thank the von Trotha family for allowing me to use this material.

111. Trotha, diary entry, 1 July 1904, Trotha Papers, Nr. 315, p. 15.

112. Trotha, diary entry, 16 July 1904, Trotha Papers, Nr. 315, p. 20.

that he urged the commander to conduct the war so that the people would survive. General v. Trotha listened to this statement quietly and then replied, 'Your arguments interest me very much, but you must allow me to lead the campaign in my own way.'" Paul Leutwein then maintains that later that evening his father told a public gathering of settlers in Okahandja of Trotha's intentions, and that a report of the governor's exposé, written by military correspondent retired Capt. Otto Dannhauer, appeared in the *Berliner Lokalanzeiger* shortly thereafter. "If those in high office or if public opinion in Germany had wanted to," Paul Leutwein concluded, "one could have stopped Trotha's annihilation strategy in time."[113]

Trotha and Leutwein did meet on 23 June, and Trotha later explained to Chancellor Bülow what they discussed:

> When I took over command, Governor Leutwein gave me a finished proclamation to the Herero, ready for printing, . . . which promised them clemency if they admitted their wrongdoing and came back remorsefully. I immediately declared that I opposed on principle handling the uprising in this way, and that in my opinion, such treatment contradicted the intentions of *His Majesty*. Nothing further happened.[114]

The discussion concerned negotiations, which, as the Colonial Department had reminded Leutwein in February, could be initiated only on the Kaiser's orders. Trotha's tough stand on negotiations increased the probability of more bloodshed, but it does not necessarily indicate that he already intended wholesale annihilation. And it is not at all clear that Leutwein interpreted the discussion that way. On the contrary, he telegraphed Berlin that he had "reached full agreement with Mr. v. Trotha in Okahandja."[115] He continued to serve as governor alongside the general and broke with him only in October, when Trotha openly embraced the policy of annihilation. In his frank memoirs, which lambasted Trotha's Vernichtungspolitik, Leutwein did not mention their June meeting.[116] As for correspondent Dannhauer's account in the *Berliner Lokalanzeiger*, he reported on 23 June 1904: "The result of thorough talks between Excellency Trotha and the governor appear to have reached complete agreement."[117]

Paul Leutwein's memory appears to have amalgamated and elaborated on two separate articles. The most damning of these did not appear "long before the battle of Waterberg,"[118] as he recalled, but on 2 August 1904, just nine days before. It was dated 26 June,

113. Leutwein, *Afrikanerschicksal*, 156–57.

114. Trotha to Bülow, Windhuk, 6 Jan. 1905, BA-Berlin, R 1001, Nr. 2089, pp. 138–39.

115. Leutwein to Col. Dept., tel. Nr. 147, Windhuk, arr. in Berlin 25 June 1904, BA-Berlin, R 1001, Nr. 2115, p. 79. Drechsler cites this telegram but concludes nothing from it: *"Let Us Die Fighting,"* 172n90.

116. Leutwein, *Elf Jahre*.

117. Special correspondent [Dannhauer], "Zum Aufstand in Südwestafrika," *Berliner Lokalanzeiger* 289 (23 June 1904), 1.

118. Leutwein, *Afrikanerschicksal*, 156.

Gov. Col. Theodor Leutwein (middle) and Lt. Gen. Lothar von Trotha (far right) at Command Headquarters, Windhuk, July 1904. Helmut Bley, *South-West Africa under German Rule, 1894–1914* (Evanston: Northwestern University Press, 1971), fig. 22.

however, and describes a ride Dannhauer had taken with Governor Leutwein to Okahandja on the way to meet with Trotha. They discussed, among other things, the Herero
practice of mutilating bodies and killing wounded German soldiers. Dannhauer concluded, in his own voice:

> Forbearance and leniency toward such an enemy is simply a crime committed
> against one's own soldiers. That is also the opinion of the new commander, Lt.
> Gen. v. Trotha, who recently declared while discussing this subject, "Against
> 'nonhumans' [*Unmenschen*] one cannot conduct war 'humanely.'" And he al-
> lowed me to publish his words.[119]

This chilling remark is confirmed by Trotha's diary entry of 16 July, cited above. We shall
see that this attitude probably contributed to atrocities committed in the immediate af-
termath of the battle. But it is not a declaration of annihilation, nor is it an order. Trotha's
opinion, buried on the second page of a rather leisurely reminiscence, was not picked up
by any critics in Berlin, then or later.

The only other article that Paul Leutwein might have had in mind appeared in mid-
July, but was dated 4 July. It did indeed report a "recent" discussion among "a small circle" in Okahandja, in which Leutwein criticized the new military policies. But all he is reported as saying is that a long guerilla war was inevitable unless Germany negotiated with
the Herero. The governor admitted this was unlikely, because "public opinion" rejected
negotiations. He did not mention Trotha.[120] Neither article remotely hinted that Trotha
planned mass annihilation, nor could one expect anyone to have read them that way.[121]

The Battle of Waterberg

It remains, then, to consider the plan of attack at the Waterberg. It was supposed to be
the decisive battle that would end the war, by forcing a negotiated surrender (according to
Leutwein) or by "destroying" the enemy militarily (according to Trotha). German military doctrine was so clear about how to conduct a decisive battle that Governor Leutwein
had already sketched out its contours and moved some troops into place by the time
Trotha arrived on the scene. The concentric battle was to be accomplished by splitting the
troops and loosely surrounding the Waterberg. That assured that the enemy would have
to fight, instead of avoiding the decisive blow by slipping away. At the signal, the units
would attack together. The general simply took over this plan, but instead of striking at

---

119. Otto Dannhauer, "Brief aus Deutsch-Südwestafrika," *Berliner Lokalanzeiger* 358 (2 Aug. 1904), 1–2,
here 2.

120. Dannhauer, "Brief aus Südwest-Afrika," *Berliner Lokalanzeiger* 321 (12 July 1904), 1–2.

121. Paul Leutwein is unreliable on many accounts. For example, he gives the wrong date for the battle of
Waterberg (*Afrikanerschicksal*, 158–59); he confuses the pursuit of August and September with Trotha's extermination proclamation of October 1904 (128); he believes Berlin "immediately" cancelled the proclamation, when
in fact that process was protracted (128); and he believes most of the Herero escaped (128).

34 once, as the "old Africans" desired, he waited for two months in order to bring up as many troops and supplies as possible.[122]

The Waterberg lay over one hundred kilometers from the railroad, and supplies had to be moved by oxcart on indistinct, unmapped paths, as there were no regular roads. The more men Trotha moved in, the more supplies they required; more supplies required more oxen to bring them; and more oxen consumed more scarce water and grass that the men and horses needed to stay alive. That was the vicious cycle that fighting a classic, European-style, decisive, concentric battle brought with it. Throughout June, July, and the first week of August, the inexperienced German reinforcements labored to encircle the Waterberg. By the time they had done so, they were exhausted and ill; their horses were dying of hunger and thirst.[123]

Meanwhile, the united clans of the Herero waited at the Waterberg. That sixty thousand or more people and their cattle could stay there so long was thanks to the unusually heavy rainfall in recent months.[124] But with each passing day, the once plentiful springs diminished, while the herds consumed the last wild grass. Typhus was reported, the first sign of bad water.[125] The Herero were eating the cattle they had taken from the settlers, which reduced the burden on water and grass supplies, but by August their own herds had begun to succumb to thirst. It was these half-dead animals that the Germans reported capturing by the thousands in the first postbattle reports.[126]

No one knows why the Herero did not slip off north into Ovamboland, or northwest into British Bechuanaland, or north again into Portuguese Angola, or simply filter back west and south into the colony. Perhaps they felt confident of victory against the still much smaller, palpably inexperienced German troops; perhaps the Herero people's despair at the prospect of losing land and cattle left them no choice; perhaps they expected an offer of negotiation; perhaps their leadership was divided and uncertain.[127] The one

122. Leutwein to Bülow, tel. Windhuk, 18 May 1904, BA-Berlin, R 1001, Nr. 2114, p. 204; Trotha to General Staff, tel. Okahandja, 25 June 1904, ibid., Nr. 2115, p. 80; Bayer, *Mit dem Hauptquartier*, 121–24; v. François, "Herero-Aufstand," *Mil. Wochenblatt* 98 (16 Aug. 1904), col. 2370. Trotha ultimately assembled 1,500 troops and officers, 30 artillery pieces, and 14 machine guns at Waterberg: General Staff, *Kämpfe der deutschen Truppen*, 1:157.

123. Viktor Franke, "Der Aufstand in Deutsch Südwest Afrika und die nachfolgenden Jahre, 1903–1906," BA-Koblenz, Nl. Franke, Nr. 21, 34.

124. Rohrbach, *Aus Südwest-Afrikas schweren Tagen*, 147.

125. "Der Aufstand," *Deutsch Südwest-Afrikanische Zeitung* 27 (6 July 1904).

126. Rohrbach, *Aus Südwest-Afrikas schweren Tagen*, 159, 170. Sudholt, who wants to deny the genocide (*Völkermord*), argues that limited water could not have sustained 60,000–80,000 people and large animal herds, and therefore, the number of Herero must have been much smaller (he estimates 40,000, but gives no reason for settling on that number). However, both the unusually plentiful water (and grass) in 1904 and the fact that the Herero were close to exhausting their resources argue strongly against Sudholt's surmise. Sudholt, *Deutsche Eingeborenenpolitik*, 41–44, 185–86.

127. V. François, "Herero-Aufstand," *Mil. Wochenblatt* 109, col. 2626; Schwabe, *Krieg in Deutsch-Südwestafrika*, 200, 220; General Staff, *Kämpfe der deutschen Truppen*, 1:89, 136; August Kuhlmann, "Was die Hereros über einen etwaigen Frieden sagten" (6 June 1904), in de Vries, *Namibia*, 287–88; Franke diary entry, 26 June 1904, BA-Koblenz, Nl. Franke, Nr. 3, p. 70; Lettow-Vorbeck, diary entry, 8 Dec. 1904, BA-MA Freiburg, Nl. Lettow-Vorbeck, Nr. 34; Arnold Lequis, diary entry, 23 July 1904, BA-MA Freiburg, Nl. Lequis, Nr. 17, p. 9; Bayer, *Mit dem Hauptquartier*, 129–30; Gewald, *Herero Heroes*, 170; Bridgman, *Revolt*, 109, 113–17; Drechsler, "*Let Us Die Fighting*," 142–44, 150; Jürgen Zimmerer, "Kriegsgefangene im Kolonialkrieg," in *In der Hand des Feindes*, ed. Rüdiger Overmans (Cologne, 1999), 277–94, here 283.

Mountain battery on the march in SWA, 1904. Courtesy of Stadt- und Universitätsbibliothek, Afrikaabteilung, Frankfurt am Main, Nr. 011-0116-06.

thing no one expected them to do, however, was to retreat to the east, into the unmapped and, to white people, unknown Omaheke Desert.[128] "Would [the enemy] want to escape to the east," asked one officer on Trotha's staff, "into the arid, deathly Omaheke? An old soldier's principle says that one should always count on the enemy doing the most intelli-

128. Trotha enumerated all the alternatives once more shortly before the battle. He was satisfied Estorff's troops blocked a breakthrough to the east; he never even mentioned the southeast as a consideration: Trotha to General Staff, tel. arr. Berlin 20 July 1904, BA-Berlin, R 1001, Nr. 2115, p. 124. No contemporary writing before the battle seriously considered this a possibility: Leutwein to Bülow, Windhuk, 25 May 1904, BA-Berlin, R 1001, Nr. 2114; Franke, diary entry, 6 Aug. 1904, BA-Koblenz, Nl. Franke, Nr. 3, pp. 85–87; Capt. Schering to Headquarters, Otjisondusu, 23 June 1904, BA-MA Freiburg, RM 121 I, Nr. 431, p. 55: "[1st. Lt.] Winkler thinks a Herero escape

36

2nd Field Company of the Naval Infantry Battalion in Omaruru, SWA, preparing to go into the field. Courtesy of Stadt- und Universitätsbibliothek, Afrikaabteilung, Frankfurt am Main, Nr. 002-0054-15.

gent thing, always assume he will do what is most unpleasant for us."[129] Most unpleasant would have been an escape west, back into the territory from which the German troops had already expelled them. That is why Trotha overloaded the western unit commanded by Col. Berthold von Deimling. The next strongest unit (Estorff's) faced Deimling's on the east. The units to the north and northwest were smaller, but they could rely on favorable geography (the Waterberg and Klein-Waterberg) to strengthen them. Trotha had placed his own headquarters directly to the south, with moderate strength. By far the weakest unit in troop numbers lay to its right, to the southeast (under Colonel von der Heyde). Heyde and Estorff together could have prevented an eastward escape. To make up for numerical weakness, Trotha had given Heyde eight artillery pieces and more officers, but no machine guns.[130]

in large numbers to the southeast is impossible because of lack of water"; Trotha to General Staff, tel. Okahandja, arr. 21 July 1904, BA-Berlin, R 1001, Nr. 2115, p. 124; Schwabe, *Krieg in Deutsch-Südwestafrika*, 235; General Staff, *Kämpfe der deutschen Truppen*, 1:132–33; Dannhauer's reports in *Berliner Lokalanzeiger* 351 (29 July 1904), 1, and 392 (22 Aug. 1904), 1. None of the "Old Africans" thought it a possibility: Trotha to Schlieffen, Report, repeated in diary entry of 27 Aug. 1904, Trotha Papers, Nr. 315, Anhang 1, Nr. 2, p. 4. Only Salzmann, writing with the benefit of hindsight, claims that "everybody" had suspected the Herero would try to break through to the east. Salzmann, *Im Kampfe*, 151.

129. Bayer, *Mit dem Hauptquartier*, 134.

130. See the information by Bayer, *Mit dem Hauptquartier*, 136.

Paul Leutwein claims that both Estorff and Governor Leutwein warned Trotha that Heyde's unit was too small.[131] Although I have located no archival confirmation and neither man mentions such a warning in his published accounts, it is possible they did so.[132] Certainly, Trotha's adjutant, Capt. Paul von Lettow-Vorbeck, who helped draft the troop dispositions, saw the danger, though late. On 5 August (six days before Trotha launched the battle), Lettow-Vorbeck noted his disagreement with the orders Trotha had just dispatched for the coming battle. The main Herero forces stood south of the Waterberg, by the waterhole Hamakari. "In my draft, I intended the main attack to come at Hamakari and wanted to apply part of Deimling['s troops] here and had therefore ordered a tighter encirclement. I think that the troops that [Trotha's] directive sets against Hamakari are very weak."[133] The day before the battle, Lettow-Vorbeck may have tried to alter Trotha's plans. In the back of one of his diary books is a draft telegram, dated 10 August 1904, with new instructions to the encircling units. These instructions "borrow" some of Deimling's troops for the attack in the south against Hamakari, thus plugging the hole there. The rest of Deimling's troops in the west are ordered not to attack unless the Herero attempt to break out. That would have prevented Deimling's larger numbers from driving the Herero from west to east or southeast, into the desert. But Lettow-Vorbeck's telegram was never sent.[134]

Drechsler interprets Trotha's asymmetrical troop disposition not as "incompetence on the part of the general . . . ; rather it was a well-thought-out plan that the Herero should break through toward the south [*sic*] and perish in the desert there."[135] One of the most tenacious myths of modern military history is that of German military omnicompetence. Even the staunchest critics prefer to believe that military disasters happen by design, rather than to imagine that structural dysfunction, or just plain mistakes, could have riddled the premier institution of the Kaiserreich. But that was precisely what was so embarrassing about the war in SWA: it displayed German military incompetence.

Trotha had indeed set up unbalanced forces, which provided extra insurance in the west, where from his standpoint the greatest danger lay, at the cost of exposing the southeast, where a breakthrough was least harmful, or potentially even helpful, because the desert might force the escaping enemy to turn and fight again. But that was only a second-best outcome. Trotha wanted Waterberg to end the war. His order for the battle stated: "I will attack the enemy simultaneously with all units, in order to destroy [*vernichten*] him."[136] However, the exhaustion of his own troops, the poor condition of their horses, the unavailability of supplies, the lopsided troop arrangement (all things falling under

131. Leutwein, *Afrikanserschicksal*, 157–58.

132. Estorff, *Wanderungen*; Ludwig v. Estorff, "Kriegserlebnisse in Südwestafrika," *Beiheft zum Militär-Wochenblatt* 3 (1911), 79–101; Leutwein, *Elf Jahre*.

133. Lettow-Vorbeck, diary entry, 5 Aug. 1904, Erindi-Ongoahere, BA-MA Freiburg, Nl. Lettow-Vorbeck, Nr. 73.

134. Draft telegram, 10 Aug. 1904, Otjerontjondjo, BA-MA Freiburg, Nl. Lettow-Vorbeck, Nr. 73.

135. Drechsler, *"Let Us Die Fighting,"* 155.

136. Trotha, "Directive for the attack against the Herero," 4 Aug. 1904, cited in General Staff, *Kämpfe der deutschen Truppen*, 1:153.

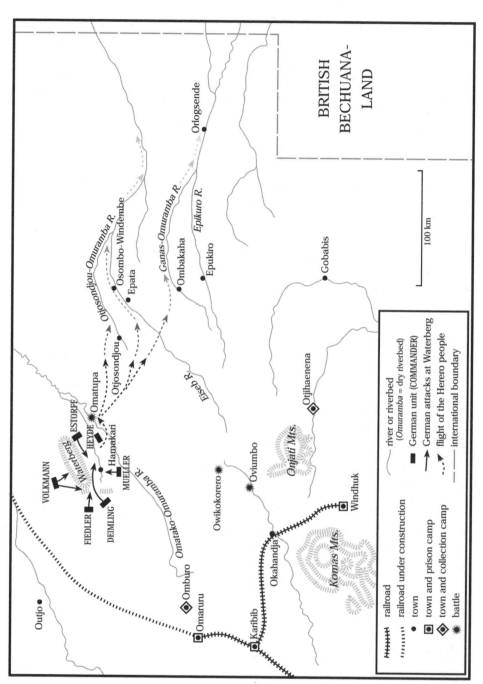

The Battle of Waterberg. Source: Germany, General Staff, *Die Kämpfe der deutschen Truppen in Südwestafrika*, vol. 1, maps 8, 9.

Maj.-Gen. Berthold von Deimling (middle) gives command to Col. Ludwig von Estorff (right), Windhuk, 1907. Courtesy of Stadt- und Universitätsbibliothek, Afrikaabteilung, Frankfurt am Main, Nr. 011-0116-02.

Trotha's and his unit commanders' responsibilities), plus the inevitable friction of battle and the mistakes of two commanders, thwarted the decisive victory.

The battle began on the morning of 11 August. The two units to the north and north-west were supposed to become active only if the Herero tried to break through there; Deimling coming from the west and Estorff from the east were to move toward each other, parallel with the Waterberg, but to hold positions there without forcing the Herero south. Meanwhile, the southern unit (under Lieutenant Colonel Mueller) and Heyde to the southeast were supposed to engage in a concentric attack on Hamakari. Only on the second day were Estorff and Deimling supposed to continue their movement, thus trapping the Herero between themselves and Mueller and Heyde in the south. Unfortunately, Heyde, who had earlier displayed a lack of appreciation for communication and a certain sluggishness, now demonstrated the full range of his incapacity.[137] Hearing gunfire, he rushed his troops off in the wrong direction, later retracing his steps, only to become pinned down by heavy Herero fire. Throughout the day, he failed to contact headquarters, reporting in by radio telephone for the first time at 7 PM, and then again at midnight with the news that not only would he not reach Hamakari that day, but he probably would not

137. Hellmuth Auer von Herrenkirchen, *Meine Erlebnisse während des Feldzuges gegen die Hereros und Witbois nach meinem Tagebuch* (Berlin, 1907), 22, 23, 44; Franke, diary entry, 18 Aug. 1904, BA-Koblenz, Nl. Franke, Nr. 3, p. 97.

Capt. Paul von Lettow-Vorbeck. Courtesy of Stadt- und Universitätsbibliothek, Afrikaabteilung, Frankfurt am Main, Nr. 023-1388-06.

the following morning (the 12th), either.[138] Meanwhile, Deimling had had a relatively easy time of it. He had reached Waterberg Station, and, not pausing as Trotha had planned, he moved swiftly on to Hamakari, driving the Herero before him and through the gap that Heyde's immobility had created.[139] The entire Herero people and those animals not already dying of thirst spilled out into the desert and escaped. Their warriors had suffered relatively light casualties.[140]

Trotha was livid. He wanted to stand Heyde before a court-martial for disobeying battle orders and failing to establish radio contact, but he must have thought better of it.[141] Instead, he dispatched a "lying report," as Franke called it, which began, "The attack started on the morning of 11 August with a complete victory."[142] And newspapers duly reported it as such. But soldiers and observers knew better. In fact, nothing shows more convincingly that Trotha and his troops had aimed not to let the Herero escape but to end the war with one decisive victory than the intense disappointment, indeed the paralysis, that everybody felt afterward. Capt. Heinrich von Welck, whose unit in the north had been part of the plan but had not participated in the fighting, later described the situation to his father:

> Headquarters was not prepared for the eventuality that a people of sixty thousand and perhaps as many cattle, could escape wholesale after so many months of careful preparation. The first order came five days after the breakthrough; until then complete planlessness reigned, and an unbelievable lack of supplies. Medical facilities were not remotely up to the large requirements. Wounded officers lay for weeks on the ground and lacked the barest necessities. Horses died like flies, because the Herero had left not a blade of grass. And then came typhus with its dreadful victims, the result of the concentration of men and animals, of bad water and little food.[143]

Trotha's chief of staff, Lt. Col. Martin Chales de Beaulieu, was crushed. He called the experienced Captain Franke for advice. Franke told him that "only a rapid retreat into pastureland near the railroad could stop catastrophe. The chief of staff said quite openly that the new directives [ordering pursuit of the Herero] were only intended for Berlin, and his only goal was to hinder the complete collapse of the troops. He said convincingly that he was completely surprised by the enemy, whom he had vastly underestimated."[144] German military doctrine called for energetic pursuit of the enemy in cases like this, and

138. Schwabe, *Krieg in Deutsch-Südwestafrika*, 279–80.

139. Ibid., 286; Auer v. Herrenkirchen, *Meine Erlebnisse*, 45.

140. Franke, diary entry, 20 Aug. 1904, BA-Koblenz, Nl. Franke, Nr. 3, pp. 99–100; Lettow-Vorbeck, diary entry, 8 Dec. 1904, BA-MA Freiburg, Nl. Lettow-Vorbeck, Nr. 34; Rust, *Krieg und Frieden*, 381; Drechsler, "*Let Us Die Fighting*," 154.

141. Lequis, diary entry, 30 Aug. 1904, BA-MA Freiburg, Nl. Lequis, Nr. 17, p. 40.

142. Franke, diary entry, 18 Aug. 1904, BA-Koblenz, Nl. Franke, Nr. 3, p. 98; Trotha tel., 12 Aug. 1904, Hamakari, reprinted in Rust, *Krieg und Frieden*, 376–77.

143. Heinrich v. Welck to his father, Waterberg, 16 Dec. 1904, BA-MA Freiburg, MSg. 2, Nr. 3039 (Baron v. Welck).

144. Franke, diary entry, 16 Aug. 1904, BA-Koblenz, Nl. Franke, Nr. 3, pp. 95–96.

42 that is what the "new directives" dictated.[145] Because of the exhaustion of troops and horses, and the hope that the Herero might stop and permit a "real battle," Trotha ordered the pursuit to begin only on the 13th.[146] But the war diary for Deimling's unit for that day reads tersely: "Men are very exhausted"; it noted that there was no water or feed for the horses.[147] And Deimling's had been the most successful unit at Waterberg. Trotha was thunderstruck. "I think I'll collapse," he noted in his diary.

> This 30 km pursuit only makes sense if we can catch the Herero who have a 24 hour head start. . . . I thought they [Deimling, etc.] had 3 days' oats and rations, which I would have stretched to 4. . . . So, we've just frittered away 48 hours just to be able to report back home that we pursued them for 30 km and can't go any further. Ha. . . . Now we can or must start from the beginning, or else it's finished. We must above all stop them from coming back into the territory.[148]

He broke off the pursuit immediately.[149]

The official history of the campaign, written by the historical section of the General Staff, subsequently took pains to deny that Trotha had ever intended "to encircle the Herero and force them to surrender à la Sedan."[150] Deimling and staff officer Schwabe loyally tried to uphold this line, but neither they nor the official history could manage to dissemble consistently.[151] Everyone knew that Waterberg was supposed to be a textbook concentric battle ending in complete victory.[152] Trotha wrote later to Schlieffen, "The operations plan I made originally and held fast to was to surround the majority of Herero at the Waterberg and to destroy them with a simultaneous blow, then to build stations to search out and disarm the ones who escaped, and using bounties on the heads of the cap-

---

145. Trotha tel., 12 Aug. 1904, Hamakari, reprinted in Rust, *Krieg und Frieden*, 376–77.

146. Schwabe, *Krieg in Deutsch-Südwestafrika*, 293.

147. Entry of 13 Aug. 1904, "Nordfeldzug: Kriegstagebuch des Regimentsstabes des 2. Feldregiments für SWA," BA-MA Freiburg, Nl. Deimling, Nr. 7.

148. Trotha diary, 13 Aug. 1904, Trotha Papers, Nr. 315, 29–30.

149. Franke, diary entries, 13–14 Aug. 1904, BA-Koblenz, Nl. Franke, Nr. 3, pp. 93–94; Auer v. Herrenkirchen, *Meine Erlebnisse*, 45; Lequis, diary entry, 30 Aug. 1904, BA-MA Freiburg, Nl. Lequis, Nr. 17, p. 40. Bridgman's claim that "no attempt was made to stop the escaping Hereros nor were they harassed," so that they would escape further into the desert to their doom, is simply incorrect. Bridgman, *Revolt*, 124–25, 122.

150. General Staff, *Kämpfe der deutschen Truppen*, 1:134. Trotha later claimed that, because he could not concentrate the entire 4,000-man force in the colony, Waterberg was not meant to be the classic "decisive battle": Trotha to Schlieffen, 27 Aug. 1904, Trotha Papers, Nr. 315, Anhang 1, Nr. 2.

151. Cf. General Staff, *Kämpfe der deutschen Truppen*, 1:170–71, 185, where it admits the breakthrough was a mistake. Cf. also Deimling, *Südwestafrika*, 30, with Deimling, *Aus der alten in die neue Zeit*, 66; and Schwabe, *Krieg in Deutsch-Südwestafrika*, 235–36, where he begins by denying the intent to provoke a decisive battle by encirclement and ends by admitting it.

152. Apart from Trotha's own clear description of his intentions in the "Directive for the attack against the Herero," 4 Aug. 1904, General Staff, *Kämpfe der deutschen Truppen*, 1:153, see Arnold Lequis: "Waterberg was planned as a great *concentric battle* à la Sedan," BA-MA Freiburg, Nl. Lequis, Nr. 35, p. 343; Franke, diary entry, 5 Aug. 1904, BA-Koblenz, Nl. Franke, Nr. 3, p. 85; Rohrbach, diary entry, 10 Aug. 1904, Rohrbach, *Aus Südwestafrikas schweren Tagen*, 167; Rust, *Krieg und Frieden*, 365; Estorff, *Kriegserlebnisse*, 92; Auer v. Herrenkirchen, *Erlebnisse*, 14; Dannhauer's reports in the *Berliner Lokalanzeiger* 310 (5 July 1904), 1; 319 (10 July 1904), 1; 331 (17 July 1904), 1; and 343 (24 July 1904), 1, among others.

tains to bring them into my control and punish them with death."[153] The shock was all the greater because of Trotha's overconfidence. The commander had telegraphed the General Staff at the end of July that "I believe I will have a complete success."[154] He had ordered a huge detention area erected of thorn branches and barbed wire in Okahandja—large enough to imprison eight thousand men, the highest German estimate of the warrior strength of the Herero at the battle of Waterberg.[155] Franke reported Trotha had even ordered one thousand chains from Berlin, for the Herero prisoners he expected to take.[156] For his part, Governor Leutwein had invited the missionaries to meet with Commissioner Rohrbach on 9 and 10 August to decide how to feed, house, and then distribute the prisoners.[157] Private companies had even begun to place bids for prisoner-workers.[158] Instead, after months of expensive and difficult preparations, the Herero had vanished and the war was not over. The question now was, What to do after Waterberg?

153. Trotha to Schlieffen, 27 Aug. 1904, Trotha Papers, Nr. 315, Anhang 1, Nr. 2, p. 2; also cited in Gewald, *Towards Redemption*, 206, following Gerhardus Pool, *Samuel Maherero* (Windhuk, 1991), 251.

154. Trotha to General Staff, tel. arr. Berlin 20 July 1904, BA-Berlin, R 1001, Nr. 2115, p. 124.

155. Paul Rohrbach, *Deutsche Kolonialwirtschaft*, 2 vols. (Berlin, 1907), 1:342; Rohrbach, *Aus Südwestafrikas schweren Tagen* (diary entry of 10 Aug. 1904), 167, 169.

156. Franke, diary entry, 16 Aug. 1904, BA-Koblenz, Nl. Franke, Nr. 3, p. 96.

157. Dannert, Lang, Hanefeld, Elger, Brockmann, and Wandres to Rohrbach, Karibib, 1 Aug. 1904, VEM-Wuppertal, "Care" (*Fürsorge*), C/o 5; Rohrbach, *Aus Südwestafrikas schweren Tagen*, 167.

158. District Administrator (*Bezirksamtmann*) Burgsdorff to Governor, Nr. 1364, Gibeon, 18 Aug. 1904, BA-Berlin, Kaiserliches Gouvernement Deutsch-Südwest-Afrika, Zentralbureau Windhoek (R 151 F), D.IV.L.3., vol. 1, p. 1 (hereafter BA-Berlin, R 151 F, etc.).

2

Pursuit and Annihilation

T he "failure" of Waterberg was a disaster only because the expectations for victory were so unreasonably high. In fact, the German troops had defeated the Herero, who thereafter offered no systematic resistance. This was the kind of victory that Governor Leutwein had thought the Germans might have achieved in June, and now that it had come in August, he encouraged missionaries to contact General v. Trotha and offer to mediate a negotiated end to the war.[1] Herero clans began indicating from August onward that they were prepared to surrender.[2] Trotha later maintained that he never learned, either from the missionaries or indirectly from the Herero, that a surrender might be possible.[3] Trotha's denial is probably disingenuous, for even in November when he learned definitely that some Herero leaders wished to capitulate, he refused to treat with them.[4] He later (1909) explained why. If Heyde's unit had been in the right place, the Herero would not have broken through.

---

1. Leutwein to Conferenzvorstand, Windhuk, 17 Aug. 1904, copy, VEM-Wuppertal, Diehl papers, B/c II 35, 3, p. 107.

2. Actually, the first attempt to surrender occurred in mid-July, before Waterberg (see ch. 1). The clans offering surrender after Waterberg were those at Waterberg (under Salatiel), at Omaruru (under Mutate), and at Ojimbingue: Rohrbach, *Aus Südwestafrikas schweren Tagen*, 178; Schwabe, *Krieg in Südwestafrika*, 298; testimony of Daniel and Samuel Kariko, in Union of South Africa, *Report on the Natives*, 63; the 1st Field Regt., 8th Comp. (Welck) to the father of their commander, Waterberg, 5 Feb. 1905, BA-MA Freiburg, MSg. 2, Nr. 3039 (Welck).

3. Trotha to Bülow, Windhuk, 6 Jan. 1905, BA-Berlin, R 1001, Nr. 2089, pp. 138–39; Bley, *South-West Africa*, 162.

4. Trotha to Bülow, Windhuk, 6 Jan. 1905, BA-Berlin, R 1001, Nr. 2089, pp. 138–39; and Trotha to Leutwein, Windhuk, 5 Nov. 1904, ibid., pp. 101–3. Trotha also forgot Salatiel's offer to negotiate in July 1904. Cf. Trotha, diary entries, 13 and 17 July 1904, with entries of 10 Dec. 1904 and 17 Nov. 1904, and Estorff to Trotha, Owinana, 12 Dec. 1904, Böttlin to Salatiel, Oruinjoroujombonde, 12 July 1904, Estorff to Trotha, tel. Otjatjingene, 16 July 1904, Trotha to Estorff, Funkentel. Headquarters, 17 July 1904, Leutwein to Foreign Office, copy K. 3862, Auf Erlass vom 28 Feb. 1905, Nr. K 1714/8049, Trotha Papers, Nr. 315, pp. 19, 20, 55, 66, and Anhang 1, Nrs. 23a–e.

If this had been the case, then the possibility of negotiation would have existed, and a regular court would have brought the murderers and ringleaders to the gallows; the weapons and cows would have gone to the government, and the rest of the tribes would have returned to the sunshine of the All-Highest [i.e., His Majesty's] mercy. As the situation was, however, there could be no question of negotiations on the 12th and 13th [of August], if one did not want to testify to one's own weakness and embarrassment [*Ohnmacht und Verlegenheit*]. This would have been immediately clear to the enemy and would have meant a renewal of the war as soon as the band had recovered from the first shock.[5]

To Trotha, then, anything less than a total military victory was evidence of weakness, which, if not rectified, encouraged aggression on the part of one's enemies, and thus endangered security. The logic of this situation required that he continue to try to achieve total military victory. And this is exactly what he did. The first default method for doing so was the decisive, concentric battle; when that failed, the second default method of German military doctrine called for a relentless pursuit of the enemy, forcing them to turn and fight, thus giving the technologically superior force the edge and bringing the war victoriously to a close.

"Pursuit" (*Verfolgung*) was thus what Trotha ordered in his first telegram after Waterberg. The parlous condition of the German troops and their mounts in the end dictated that only two smaller, relatively resilient units chased the Herero people from waterhole to waterhole along the riverbeds Eiseb and Epukiro, harrying them farther and farther into the Omaheke Desert. When pursuit was no longer possible, Trotha ordered the desert "sealed off," so that survivors could not trickle back into the colony. This action killed a majority of the Herero population. The slide from pursuit to outright annihilation is what we must next examine.

Pursuit

"Pursuit" was represented in the military telegrams, and at least partly experienced by the German participants, as a normal military procedure. The official history lists twenty-six further "battles," "patrol engagements," or "pursuit-battles" in its battle calendar from 15 August to 22 December.[6] Only one of these, the first, might have rated that description, however; for here (at Omatupa), the Herero attacked the pursuing Germans. They were quickly thrown back, and "thereafter, their last systematic resistance was broken,"[7] or, as Colonel Deimling later summarized, "There were no real battles during the pursuit—the Herero's resistance was completely broken."[8]

5. Lothar v. Trotha, "Politik und Kriegführung," *Berliner Neueste Nachrichten* 60 (3 Feb. 1909), 1.
6. "Gefecht," "Patrouillengefecht," "Verfolgungsgefecht"; General Staff, *Kämpfe der deutschen Truppen*, 1:338–39.
7. Estorff, "Kriegserlebnisse," 92.
8. Deimling, *Südwestafrika*, 30.

46   Nonetheless, the pursuit continued. Its ostensible aim was "to force the enemy to do battle," as Trotha repeated to his commanders on 26 August.[9] This remained the aim until the end of September, when Trotha made a last effort "to try to surround the enemy."[10] The division chaplain accompanying the exhausted troopers noted on 24 September: "Today at 5 AM begins the march to what will hopefully be the last battle."[11] This was supposed to take place at "the *last* waterholes, so that further escape without fighting will no longer be possible."[12] But the desperation of the surviving Herero made them move quickly; they escaped again, and the "last" battle fizzled out.

While August and September thus brought frustration to the Germans, they brought mass death to the Herero. A great number, especially the old, ill, and women and children, died of starvation and thirst as they ran for their lives through the desert. But a great many were also shot to death, for the conduct of the war changed with Waterberg. The brutal potential of colonial warfare, sporadically evident even under Governor Leutwein, now burgeoned into methodical regularity.

Witnesses, whose testimony we will examine momentarily, describe the wholesale shooting of civilians and captured Herero immediately after the battle of Waterberg. We must again ask whether Trotha ordered this. One witness says he did. During the First World War, Trotha's former African groom in SWA, Manuel Timbu, told British authorities that "when leaving Okahandja [on 9 July 1904], General von Trotha issued orders to his troops that no quarter was to be given to the enemy. No prisoners were to be taken, but all, regardless of age or sex, were to be killed. General v. Trotha said, 'We must exterminate them, so that we won't be bothered with rebellions in the future.' "[13]

Timbu's testimony says two separate things: all Herero, combatants and civilians, were immediately to be shot (not first taken prisoner and then shot); and this action was meant to exterminate the entire people (not just to deliver a message of "terrorism," in Trotha's earlier phrase, or to relieve troops of the burden of taking prisoners). Although the mass shootings he witnessed are undeniable, there is reason to believe that in the intervening years Timbu's memory had elided two separate events: the sharpening of the war to the point of massacre at Waterberg and the intent to exterminate.

Archival records, diaries, and memoirs mention no order of either kind, even when they record the events themselves and/or condemn Trotha's leadership and policies. Moreover, the huge kraal for prisoners that Trotha had built would have been nonsensical had he already ordered extermination. There are many accounts of prisoners taken or giving information, even in the period from August to October.[14] Finally, there is evidence that Trotha was dismayed by the troops' behavior, and acted to limit the massacres.

9. Kommando der Schutztruppe to all commanders, Owikokorero, 26 Aug. 1904, BA-MA Freiburg, Nl. Deimling, Nr. 7; also Anonymous, "Patrouillenritte in Südwestafrika," *Vierteljahrshefte für Truppenführung und Heereskunde* 2, no. 3 (1905): 452.

10. Trotha to Bülow, tel., Okahandja, 25 Sept. 1904, BA-Berlin, R 1001, Nr. 2116, p. 25.

11. Max Schmidt, *Aus unserem Kriegsleben in Südwestafrika* (Berlin, 1907), 50.

12. Bayer, *Mit dem Hauptquartier*, 192, emphasis in original.

13. Testimony of Manuel Timbu, Union of South Africa, *Report on the Natives*, 63.

14. References to prisoners between 11 Aug. and the beginning of Oct. 1904: Lettow-Vorbeck's diary entries for Aug. and Sept. 1904, BA-MA Freiburg, Nl. Lettow-Vorbeck, Nr. 34; war diary of the regimental staff of the 2nd Field Regiment, entries of 6 Sept., 28 Sept., 3 Oct., 4 Oct. 1904, BA-MA Freiburg, Nl. Deimling, Nr. 7;

It seems likely that over ten years after the event, when he gave his testimony, Timbu's memory had elided Trotha's infamous "extermination order" of 2 October 1904, which ordered something close to "no quarter" and which we will analyze presently, with the bloody scenes he had seen during the pursuit.[15] Knowing that the pursuit annihilated the Herero, and knowing that Trotha issued an order to this effect, it was logical to "remember" that the extermination order preceded the events. Other, later accounts make the identical chronological error.[16]

Let us consider the evidence for the conduct of the troops directly after Waterberg. Despite the preparations for great numbers of prisoners, none in fact were taken at the battle.[17] The unexpected escape of the Herero is the main reason, but indiscriminate shooting massacred stragglers who ought to have become prisoners. Capt. Viktor Franke, who fought with Deimling's unit at Waterberg, has left us the most candid account, recorded immediately in his diary. He ridiculed the overwrought atmosphere among the German soldiers. "We come across a strong Herero clan [on 12 August] with several hundred cattle, we deploy against it and—shoot a woman dead." Later that day he noted with disgust: "*In the camp* a Herero woman and child are shot dead; the former requires two shots, the latter one. Vile group."[18] The camp in question was Trotha's, whose diary entry for that date says he ordered an old Herero woman hanged; he does not mention a child.[19] Altogether, Franke excoriated the behavior of officers and men:

> I have contempt for this whole society, because I see only egotistical ends being followed and to those ends only the worst means being used. I continuously observe traits that make me appalled at the lack of discipline of these new, young soldiers. This kind of incompetence on the part of the leadership in combination with such poorly disciplined soldiers must lead to a catastrophe in a war against Germany's enemies at home.[20]

Anonymous, "Patrouillenritte," refers to prisoners on four occasions, 480, 481, 484; war diary of 3rd Field Comp., Naval Infantry Battalion, entries of 26 Sept., 1 Oct., 5 Oct.; Trotha to Bülow, tel., northeast of Epata, 1 Oct. 1904, BA-Berlin, R 1001, Nr. 2116, pp. 35–36; Bayer, *Mit dem Hauptquartier*, 195–96; Estorff, *Wanderungen*, 117; Auer v. Herrenkirchen, *Erlebnisse*, 62.

15. Accompanying Trotha, Timbu could not have seen such things much later, because Trotha left the "front" in mid-October 1904 and thereafter managed the war from the rear. Another African witness who testified to Trotha extolling "extermination" placed his statement after Waterberg, in September. Hendrik Campbell, in Union of South Africa, *Report of the Natives*, 65.

16. Paul Leutwein, *Afrikanerschicksal*, 128; Union of South Africa, *Report on the Natives*, 59–67, which makes it appear that the eyewitness testimonies of Africans refer to events *after* Trotha's proclamation. Cf. Helmut W. Smith, "The Talk of Genocide, the Rhetoric of Miscegenation," in *The Imperialist Imagination*, ed. Sara Friedrichsmeyer, Sara Lennox, and Susanne Zantop (Ann Arbor, 1998), pp. 107–23, here 109–10. Even Drechsler, who knows the chronology very well, bows to the logic by beginning his account of "Von Trotha's Conduct of the War" with the proclamation: Drechsler, *"Let Us Die Fighting,"* 156–62.

17. Leutwein to Burgsdorff, answer to Nr. 1364, Windhuk, 27 Aug. 1904, BA-Berlin, R 151 F, D.IV.L.3., vol. 1, p. 1; Salzmann, *Im Kampfe*, 119.

18. Franke, diary entry, 12 Aug. 1904, BA-Koblenz, Nl. Franke, Nr. 3, pp. 92–93, emphasis in original.

19. Trotha, diary, 12 Aug. 1904, Trotha Papers, Nr. 315, 29. Trotha gave no reason. Manuel Timbu testified to two incidents shortly after Waterberg, the bayoneting of a woman and the shooting of two old Herero women, both allegedly in Trotha's presence. Union of South Africa, *Report of the Natives*, 64, 63.

20. Franke, diary entry, 15 Aug. 1904, BA-Koblenz, Nl. Franke, Nr. 3, p. 95.

48   Franke had a latitudinarian understanding of discipline, which included simple decorum and orderliness; nevertheless, from the context and from the phrase "worst means," it is clear that he was referring to atrocities, like the shooting of captured women. The leadership's "incompetence" in this case must refer to Trotha's gratuitously ruthless hanging order; Franke worried that such incompetence fed wider "indiscipline" among troops whom officers would then be incapable of controlling.

Another of Franke's diary entries (20 August) indicates what had become the expected manner of dealing with Herero of both sexes: "On the way I took a few prisoners, a man and several women. I couldn't bring myself to shoot the miserable creatures."[21] Whether Franke meant he took them prisoner *because* he couldn't bring himself to shoot them, or whether he couldn't bring himself to shoot them *after* he had taken them prisoner, is not clear from his terseness. Either way, it is obvious that the troops were expected to dispatch the Herero, men and women, whom they found. Franke's account does not tell us whether this expectation was official (ordered), quasi-official (by example, as with Trotha's behavior in camp), or had grown out of the practice of the troops in the nine days since the nondecisive "decisive" battle.

African testimony tells us how widespread indiscriminate shooting was directly after Waterberg. We owe these accounts to the British seizure of SWA during the First World War. The occupation government collected testimonies under oath from Africans and some whites who had witnessed German conduct during the uprising. The British were intent on proving the Germans incapable of running a colony humanely and thus bolstering their case for administering SWA themselves. The original affidavits have apparently been lost, but excerpts were published in 1918.[22] The overtly propagandistic motive for collecting the testimonies has led some people to discount them entirely.[23] That is unfortunate, as the motive clearly distorted the accompanying narrative, which is replete with errors, but not necessarily the witnesses' statements, which are reprinted verbatim.

Two different groups of witnesses gave testimony: one on German conduct during the war and another on conditions in the prison camps (three witnesses overlapped). Detailed archival records on the camps make it possible to check those testimonies, and they turn out to be reliable. Eleven men, all nonwhite, gave statements about war conduct. Five were people of high social status (an underchief, a headman, a son of an underchief, an appointed chief, and one war commandant). Only four of the eleven were Herero. The difficulty in assessing their testimony does not come from British propaganda but from the length of time separating them from what they had witnessed. Date and place are sometimes difficult to establish, and one must be wary of the tendency of memory to rearrange events into a more logical-seeming ex post facto order, as we have seen with

21. Franke, diary entry, 20 Aug. 1904, Ojianjondju, BA-Koblenz, Nl. Franke, Nr. 3, p. 99.

22. The national archives of South Africa, Namibia, and Great Britain have been unable to locate the originals: L. Coetzee (head, National Archives Repository) to I. V. Hull, Pretoria, 27 Jan. 1997; J. Kutzner (acting head of Archives) to I. V. Hull, Windhuk, 6 Dec. 1996; and M. K. Banton (Public Record Office) to I. V. Hull, Kew, 29 Nov. 1996. Union of South Africa, *Report on the Natives*.

23. Sudholt, who denies both genocide and atrocity, does not mention them, once he brands their source "war propaganda": Sudholt, *Eingeborenenpolitik*, 40–41, 185–89, 219n2.

Manuel Timbu. But there is no reason to assume that the Africans' memories were any faultier than the Germans'. If the testimonies are used critically, they present rare evidence independent of that of the white Schutztruppler.

Three witnesses described systematic practices (as opposed to isolated atrocities) that occurred directly after the battle of Waterberg. Manuel Timbu, General v. Trotha's groom, "saw the bleeding bodies of hundreds of men, women and children, old and young, lying along the roads as we passed. . . . I know of no instance in which prisoners were spared."[24] Another witness was Jan Cloete, a "Bastard" (which in the parlance of SWA meant a member of a recognized and loyal group of Africans of "mixed blood") from Omaruru who served under Captain Richard in the 4th Field Company (Deimling) at Waterberg. "After the battle, all men, women and children, wounded and unwounded, who fell into the hands of the Germans were killed without mercy. The Germans then pursued the others, and all stragglers on the roadside and in the veld were shot down and bayoneted. The great majority of the Herero men were unarmed and could make no fight."[25] A third witness, Jan Kubas from Grootfontein, also reported that at Waterberg and immediately afterward "the Germans took no prisoners. They killed thousands and thousands of women and children along the roadsides. . . . I saw this every day; I was with them."[26]

These statements confirm that Franke's account was not idiosyncratic; the indiscriminate shooting of civilians had become common practice. To empathetic observers, especially years later, it seemed ubiquitous. They experienced the bloodshed as so massive that they described it as "taking no prisoners," although we know that some prisoners were taken. Nonetheless, their subjective reality tallied with the general scope of the disaster.

Finally, confirmation of the massacres comes from General v. Trotha himself. His chief of staff, Lieutenant Colonel de Beaulieu, reported to the General Staff that directly after Waterberg "the general had forbidden killing women and children, but all armed men who were captured had seen their last hour."[27] Because killing women and children was one of the strongest taboos operating in modern armies, an order explicitly forbidding it would only be necessary if the taboo had already been massively broken. Trotha's order therefore attempted to reestablish control—Franke would have said "discipline"—among the troops.

Trotha's post-Waterberg order extended to troops what he had already ordered for officers in June 1904: that "following the customs of war officers are permitted to shoot without trial black inhabitants who are caught committing treasonous acts against German troops, for example, all rebels who are found armed and with warlike intent." Other Africans suspected of "criminal acts" were to be handed over to field courts-martial.[28]

24. Union of South Africa, *Report on the Natives*, 64.

25. Ibid. The *Report* misspells Richard's name.

26. Ibid., 65.

27. General Staff, *Kämpfe der deutschen Truppen*, 1:186; also Schlieffen to Bülow, Nr. 13297, Berlin, 16 Dec. 1904, BA-Berlin, R 1001, Nr. 2089, p. 107.

28. Trotha order of June 1904, Namibian National Archives, Windhuk, ZBU Geheimakten IX.Z. Bd. 1, B. 1b, cited in Zimmerer, "Kriegsgefangene," 282.

50   From the moment of his arrival, Trotha had thus raised the level of violence by effectively ordering all armed males shot. Under Leutwein, captured warriors were supposed to be court-martialed, and only after the appropriate verdict, executed. We have seen that the pressure to "punish" the rebels had encouraged the tendency to shoot warriors within a day or two of their capture. (Until they rose up against the Germans themselves, Witbooi [Nama] soldiers allied with the Schutztruppe often performed the executions.)[29] Now the legal niceties were openly dispensed with. Trotha's order was ambivalent, for it undermined one taboo (shooting those who surrender) while trying to keep another (not harming women or children, or, presumably, unarmed males). Furthermore, the phrases "treasonous acts" and "warlike intent" easily expanded from armed males to all males, and even beyond, in that the whole people was in revolt. Even without an explicit directive to take no quarter (and none has surfaced in the records), Trotha's order of June 1904 already headed dangerously in that direction. Beaulieu's flip phrase "had seen their last hour" confirmed the atmosphere of casual violence that Trotha had emboldened under his command.

Trotha's directive in June to shoot armed males might explain Manuel Timbu's memory of a sharp order in early July (which he later conflated with the exterminatory practices of October and November). Like most German officers, Trotha often used "Herero" to refer to male warriors, as in the phrase from his diary about a patrol that "shot two Herero, who were standing there with women and cattle."[30] That usage, together with Trotha's vocal racism, could easily have been interpreted to mean he intended harsher measures to apply to the whole society.

Trotha's June order would also explain Paul Rohrbach's repeated emphasis on Trotha's goal, "the absolute destruction of the enemy" (14 July), and his "officially proclaimed program of destruction" (16 August) to characterize methods of warfare that Rohrbach rejected as wasteful.[31] That Rohrbach did not interpret these methods as exterminatory we know from his personal observation of the great prisoner kraal at Okahandja and from his participation in the pre-Waterberg meetings to distribute prisoners. But he was obviously uneasy about Trotha's sharper means. And there are indications that Governor Leutwein interpreted troop behavior at the Waterberg as Trotha's fault. The day after the "victory" of Waterberg was first reported in the *Berliner Lokalanzeiger*, Dannhauer, who enjoyed excellent relations with Leutwein, wrote that the governor was contemplating returning to Germany, allegedly to regain his health.[32] It took a great deal to pry Leutwein loose from his office; the mere breakthrough at the Waterberg would not have accounted for his reaction. Only months later did Leutwein "regain his health" in

---

29. Krüger, *Kriegsbewältigung*, 86–87. Colonial powers often used indigenous collaborators to kill members of other clans, even to the point of near genocide, as in Australia. See Alison Palmer, *Colonial Genocide* (Adelaide, 2000), 48–49.

30. Trotha, diary entry, 19 Aug. 1904, Trotha Papers, Nr. 315, p. 32.

31. Rohrbach, *Aus Südwestafrikas schweren Tagen*, 165, 168. Rohrbach, like most economists, assumed males were superior to female workers.

32. *Berliner Lokalanzeiger*, Nr. 386, 18 Aug. 1904, p. 1.

this way, his departure precipitated precisely by his disagreement with Trotha's by then open and actual policy of extermination.

Finally, Trotha's order to intensify violence against Herero men helps explain why all of a sudden German troops unleashed their potential for massacre. Most of the German troops at the Waterberg were recent reinforcements; they were inexperienced, poorly led, tired, frustrated, hungry, but haughty. Such troops, encouraged to break some taboos, were unlikely to observe others. Trotha's open statements approving inhumane warfare and his gaudy trumpeting of the goal of "destruction of the enemy" created an atmosphere in which soldiers felt that massacre was approved, and even expected. Nonetheless, the massacre at the Waterberg cannot be equated with extermination. Administrative massacre is one of the way stations to that goal, but it is not identical with it, and in most situations does not lead to it.

Whatever Trotha's direct responsibility for troop behavior, his post-Waterberg order tried to direct and therefore limit violence. Did he succeed? How did the Schutztruppe conduct itself from mid-August until Trotha's extermination proclamation of 2 October?

At least one trooper did not wait to find out. On 21 August, Franke quit the pursuing troops, whose goals and means he so abjured. As a hero, ill with malaria and with administrative experience to offer, that route was open to him. The troops Franke left behind in the columns of Estorff and Deimling continued their work of pursuit. The surviving diary accounts mostly note the number of dead Herero at the end of a "battle," but not the manner of their death, or their age, or their sex. Not all of the troops behaved badly, of course. One anonymous reporter in Deimling's unit describes seeing unarmed Herero and not shooting at them, and, at another time, capturing twenty women and making efforts to provide them with water.[33] But the pressure to kill the Herero, rather than to spare them, continued to be very strong. The same reporter describes an incident from around 10 September. Their patrol spotted

> fleeing men and women, who made signs of wanting to surrender. As I was proceeding to take them prisoner, my guide, NCO Kutschke, started shooting against my orders. That caused them to run. Now we all shot at them, but because we did so from our horses, the results were naturally few, only two or three Herero fell. . . . I gathered my people again and forbade further shooting without my order.[34]

This episode reveals two strong tendencies in the practice of the pursuit troops. First, that, even with orders to the contrary, ordinary soldiers thought it right to shoot at non-threatening (i.e., surrendering or unarmed) Herero. Second, once Herero began to run away, they became legitimate targets, even for the officer who had wanted to take them prisoner. Shooting at all fleeing Africans thus appears to have become or, after Waterberg,

33. Anonymous, "Patrouillenritte," 457, 480.
34. Ibid., 462.

52 to have remained customary practice; and fleeing people were the most common targets the soldiers encountered. The 3rd Field Company of the Naval Infantry Battalion, which was still operating around the Waterberg, noted without embarrassment or extenuating circumstance the following incident from 19 September: "Enemy, almost entirely without weapons, flees into the cliffs of the Waterberg, which we then partly climb. Three to four of the hiding Herero are shot in the process. The company has no losses."[35] Obviously, the official company diarist did not expect censure for these actions. These examples indicate that the spiral of violence continued to envelop the entire Herero population as a legitimate target.

Despite the tendency to shoot at Herero, rather than to attempt to capture them, some prisoners were taken. Their fate was not secure, however. Another African witness questioned during World War I, Hendrik Campbell, commanded the "Bastard" unit that accompanied Estorff's troops during the pursuit until October 1904. In the first week of September, his unit captured seventy Herero after a "battle."

> I handed them over to Oberleutnants Volkmann and Zelow [sic, actually Zülow].
> I then went on patrol, and returned two days later, to find the Herero all lying
> dead in a kraal. My men reported to me that they had all been shot and bayoneted
> by the German soldiers. Shortly afterwards, General von Trotha and his staff ac-
> companied by two missionaries, visited the camp.

When Campbell and Zülow argued about what had happened in front of Trotha, Trotha replied, "The entire Herero people must be exterminated."[36] Unfortunately, Campbell does not tell us whether nonmales and noncombatants were among the seventy, so we cannot tell if this mass shooting applied the courts-martial rule to males, or targeted women and children, too. In any event, Campbell's statement does confirm Trotha's recollection that the general had decided sometime in September to extend destruction to the whole people.

Trotha's diary chronicles how he arrived at that decision. On 27 August Trotha ended his report to Schlieffen on the military situation since Waterberg with the words "it can still come to a wearying guerilla war [*Einzelkriegführung*]."[37] Trotha said nothing to indicate plans beyond pursuit. Two days later, Leutwein's recommendation to negotiate jogged him further. For the first time Trotha laid out his radical alternative to negotiation: "For the present I will stick with my idea to pursue and fight them wherever I can, or to drive them [through the desert] into English territory and then leave a strong border oc-

---

35. War diary, 3rd Field Comp., Naval Infantry Battalion, Waterberg, 19 Sept. 1904, BA-MA Freiburg, RM 121 I, Nr. 434.

36. Union of South Africa, *Report on the Natives*, 65. The "battle" can be dated by Campbell's reference to Otjimbende, where he captured the Herero. The Herero quit Otjimbende on 5 Sept., when Estorff's troops moved in: General Staff, *Kämpfe der deutschen Truppen*, 1:194–95; 2:338.

37. Trotha to Schlieffen, 27 Aug. 1904, Trotha Papers, Nr. 315, Anhang 1, Nr. 2, p. 4.

cupation there [so they could not return]."[38] The only two possibilities were therefore military victory or the permanent disappearance of the Herero across the border. Throughout September Trotha pressed to corner the Herero in battle. On 2 September: "They have only the hope for a battle that might go better for them or the hopeless escape into the desert"; 3 September: "So, again pursuit"; 6 September: "After them until either they or we can't go on." On the 23rd Trotha again rejected negotiations (Estorff's plea): "No, my friend, nothing will come of that, so that we have to begin again at the beginning. We will fight as long as it takes."[39]

However, neither water nor provisions were sufficient to carry out Trotha's plan. Noncombatant Africans (women, children, and the so-called Feldherero, the impoverished non-cattleowners who eeked out an existence on the veld) fled the fighting, seeking water and food at the waterholes now occupied by German forces. Sharing provisions meant stopping operations. Rather than give up the chimera of military victory by calling off the pursuit, Trotha ordered these people driven back into the desert. On 13 September Trotha's diary reads: "Feldherero, women, and children come in droves asking for water. I have given renewed orders to drive them all back with force."[40] That Trotha had to repeat the order meant that provisioning had been completely inadequate the entire time and that at least some troops were reluctant to behave so brutally toward civilians.

The pursuit of military victory, the pure victory of superior force, under conditions in which it was impossible to achieve ended in the mass death of noncombatants. That result was compatible with Trotha's racist views, but it actually evolved from standard military doctrine and practices. If these practices were not limited by negotiations (or other brakes), they spiraled into ever widening swaths of destruction. It remained only to declare the resulting extermination as policy, which was easy given Trotha's racist worldview.

In February 1905 the missionary August Kuhlmann received information about the pursuit from a surviving Herero named Victor. Victor described how the hunted Herero disintegrated into smaller and smaller groups as the Germans pursued them, and how they died of agonizing thirst in the desert. "As soon as the troops broke off pursuit for lack of water, the people streamed back, driven by desperation. Many came upon the troops' waterholes and were shot to death there." Victor also was the source for Kuhlmann's observation that "in general, most prisoners were shot to death during the pursuit."[41] Victor describes shooting at noncombatants and killing prisoners (of unspecified sex and age) already taken.

We should expect that there was a spectrum of behavior among soldiers during the pursuit, which took place in small, isolated patrols, where much must have depended on the particular persons involved. But these examples show that the slide from shooting

---

38. Trotha, diary, 29 Aug. 1904, Trotha Papers, Nr. 315, p. 35.

39. Trotha, diary entries, Trotha Papers, Nr. 315, pp. 36, 37, 38, 42; also cited in Gewald, *Towards Redemption*, 208, following Pool, *Samuel Maherero*, 270.

40. Trotha, diary, 13 Sept. 1904, Trotha Papers, Nr. 315, p. 40.

41. August Kuhlmann, "Report on the attempts to negotiate peace in Otjimbingue," 16 Feb. 1905, VEM-Wuppertal, Kuhlmann papers, B/c II 72, 10–15, here 13, 15.

54 warriors to shooting civilians, and from court-martialing to simply shooting all males, continued to characterize the "fighting" as a common, but perhaps not ubiquitous, practice after August.[42] Trotha admitted as much when he told the chancellor on 1 October 1904 that "a part of the people would like to surrender, but fear being shot to death and punished."[43] The targeting of males only, which was Trotha's ostensible aim in the post-Waterberg order, did have an effect, however. That is evident in the very uneven demographic ratio of women to men among the surviving Herero after the war (6 or 7:1), especially when one recalls how few Herero were killed in battle.[44] Military practice thus targeted adult males systematically, even when its violence often engulfed others.

The Herero Victor's statement underscores that the overwhelming majority of deaths came in the desert, as a result of the very conception of the pursuit, not from the manner in which it was carried out. Most Herero died out of sight and earshot of their pursuers. On 29 September the Germans received confirmation of the destruction by an eyewitness, the captured daughter of Herero leader Zacharias, who graphically described the disintegration and mass death of her people in the desert.[45] Yet the officers could not quite believe her. One of the most astonishing aspects of the campaign of destruction is the cleft between deed and recognition. Neither the evidence before their own eyes nor the implacable logic of the situation sufficed to convince the soldiers (or close, well-informed observers) that the Schutztruppe had in fact annihilated the Herero. Trotha himself is the best example of this disbelief. On 1 October, he reported to the chancellor the recent successes against Herero bands, the capture of cows and prisoners, and the information he had received from Zacharias's daughter:

> Abandoned women and children confirm the testimony of prisoners that the enemy's resistance is broken. There is supposed to be dissension among the captains; part of the people would like to surrender but fear being shot to death and punished. The enemy is suffering badly for want of water; many people [*zahlreiche Leute*] including even those of high status are said to have died of thirst.
>
> However, contrary to all previous information, the desert contains no lack of pasturage and many freshly made waterholes. But it is impossible [for us] to operate with strong units there.[46]

Therefore, he was ordering the waterholes along the desert's edge to be occupied, thus sealing the Herero in the desert.

---

42. The testimonies in the *Report of the Natives* relate many examples of individual atrocities. These show a high level of tolerance for violence against the unarmed and against civilians, and suggest an atmosphere of pervasive violence, but by their nature they cannot reveal how representative the episodes they describe were.

43. Trotha to Bülow, tel., northeast of Epata, 1 Oct. 1904, BA-Berlin, R 1001, Nr. 2116, pp. 35–36.

44. Ratio: *Medizinische Berichte über die deutschen Schutzgebiete*, 1904–5 to 1908–9, cited in Karla Poewe, *The Namibian Herero* (Lewiston, N.Y., 1985), 80. Casualties during war: the official history estimates "250?"—indicating their uncertainty. But the figure is still very small: General Staff, *Kämpfe der deutschen Truppen*, 1:108.

45. Bayer, *Mit dem Hauptquartier*, 196.

46. Trotha to Bülow, tel. northeast of Epata, 1 Oct. 1904, BA-Berlin, R 1001, Nr. 2116, pp. 35–36. The waterholes in question were dry: Estorff, *Wanderungen*, 117.

This unwillingness to believe their own success came from several sources. One was the atmosphere of panic, frustration, and anxiety that the "failure" of Waterberg and then especially the pursuit itself engendered. Major Lequis, in charge of provisioning, noted on 30 August that "the pursuit seems to have failed due to the complete exhaustion of the troops, but above all due to the uncertainty of the guides about the landscape, waterholes, and the lack of African informants. Such a guerilla war appears to make even the higher staff [officers] hellishly nervous."[47] Trotha's frustration was palpable in his reports to Berlin.[48] Many officers suspected the pursuit would turn out to be as equivocal as Waterberg had been.[49] Altogether, the ignorance most officers shared about SWA and its people, an ignorance that mightily fed their anxiety, was embodied in the unmapped Omaheke Desert, whose fantastic, hidden sources of water and grass seemed as potentially believable as the equally fantastic idea that German troops had indeed destroyed an entire people.

Surely, a second source of cognitive dissonance lay in the reluctance to take responsibility for wiping out masses of unarmed men, women, and children. The third source, magnified by the all-pervasive anxiety, was the fact that small groups of surviving Herero did manage to slip through the cordon sanitaire back into the colony.[50] Deprived of their cattle, they resorted to theft and, thus, posed a continued threat to the vision of perfect order the Schutztruppe were supposed to realize.

By the beginning of October, then, the post-Waterberg pursuit had reached a geographical limit. German troops, exhausted, lacking water and provisions, could go no further. The pursuit had long since turned into a program of annihilation. But officers vacillated between gloating over the destruction of the enemy and dreading that the Herero still lurked somewhere in the desert, preparing to sneak back. It was under these circumstances that Trotha, on 2 October 1904, issued his extermination proclamation.

The Extermination Proclamation

Five days earlier, on 28 September, Trotha's troops, still pursuing encirclement, had attacked the last known waterhole in SWA, at Osombo-Windimbe along the dry Eiseb riverbed. Trotha recorded the latest disappointment in his diary: "At 11 AM we advanced in a broad front against the waterhole. No enemy to be seen, and also no corpses from the twenty artillery shots [with which they had prepared the attack]. . . . Geographically, the battle was nicely military and it could have been a good one, if the band had not escaped.

---

47. Lequis, diary entry of 30 Aug. 1904, BA-MA Freiburg, Nl. Lequis, Nr. 17, p. 40.

48. A good example: Trotha to General Staff, Oparakan, 14 Sept. 1904, BA-Berlin, R 1001, Nr. 2116, p. 20.

49. For example: Franke, diary entries of 20 Aug. 1904, 27 Oct. 1904, BA-Koblenz, Nl. Franke, Nr. 3, pp. 99–100, 119–20; Lettow-Vorbeck, reporting the views of Lt. Nolte, 4 Dec. 1904, BA-MA Freiburg, Nl. Lettow-Vorbeck, Nr. 34; Salzmann (Nov. 1904), *Im Kampfe*, 170; Maercker, *Unsere Kriegführung in Deutsch-Südwest-afrika*, 47; General Staff, *Kämpfe der deutschen Truppen*, 1:212–13; Hermann v. François, *Der Hottentotten-Aufstand* (Berlin, 1905), 89; Belwe, *Gegen die Herero*, 110; also Rohrbach to parents, 2 Sept., Okahandja, BA-Koblenz, Nl. Rohrbach, Nr. 67; and Rohrbach, 16 Aug. 1904, *Aus Südwestafrikas schweren Tagen*, 168.

50. Trotha to General Staff, tel., arr. Berlin 30 Oct. 1904, BA-Berlin, R 1001, Nr. 2116, p. 98.

56 The two units worked excellently together."[51] The next day they gathered a number of surrendering Herero, some of whom they shot. On the 30th Trotha stopped the pursuit in the Eiseb riverbed, where far ahead they could still glimpse the dust of the retreating Herero. "If they want to stay here [in the desert], they can do so. I am not pursuing them further. Basta." Through the stench of dead cattle they dragged themselves back to the waterhole where they arrived at 5 PM Trotha wrote, "I am so tired [in English]. Our supplies are at an end."[52]

The following day Trotha recorded this diary entry: "In the afternoon worked up proclamation to Herero with help from Kean and Philippus. Otherwise, nothing particular."[53] On 2 October Trotha ordered the prisoners to assemble. The men were hanged. To the women he gave Herero translations of his proclamation, and then they were sent back into the desert. The proclamation read:

> I, the great general of the German soldiers, send this letter to the Herero people. Herero are no longer German subjects. They have murdered, stolen, cut off the ears and noses and other body parts from wounded soldiers, and now out of cowardice refuse to fight. I say to the people: anyone delivering a captain to one of my stations as a prisoner will receive one thousand marks; whoever brings in Samuel Maherero will receive five thousand marks. The Herero people must leave this land. If they do not, I will force them to do so by using the great gun [artillery]. Within the German border every male Herero, armed or unarmed, with or without cattle, will be shot to death. I will no longer receive women or children but will drive them back to their people or have them shot at. These are my words to the Herero people.[54]

To the German troops Trotha added the following explanation:

> This proclamation is to be read to the troops at roll-call, with the addition that the unit that catches a captain will also receive the appropriate reward, and that shooting at women and children is to be understood as shooting above their heads, so as to force them to run [away]. I assume absolutely that this proclamation will result in taking no more male prisoners, but will not degenerate into atrocities against women and children. The latter will run away if one shoots at them a couple of times. The troops will remain conscious of the good reputation of the German soldier.

51. Trotha, diary, 28 Sept. 1904, Trotha Papers, Nr. 315, p. 44.

52. Trotha, diary entries of 29 and 30 Sept. 1904, ibid., pp. 44–45.

53. Trotha, diary, 1 Oct. 1904, ibid., p. 45.

54. Trotha, Proclamation of 2 Oct. 1904, copy, J. Nr. 3737, BA-Berlin, R 1001, Nr. 2089, p. 7; another copy in "Kaiserliche Schutztruppen und sonstige deutsche Landstreitkräfte in Übersee" [RW 51], "Militärgeschichtliches Forschungsamt: Dokumentenzentrale, Schutztruppe Südwestafrika" (vol. 2), BA-MA Freiburg. Reprinted in Rust, *Krieg und Frieden*, 385; *Vorwärts* 294 (16 Dec. 1905); Drechsler, *"Let Us Die Fighting,"* 243; Bridgman, *Revolt*, 128.

Having issued these orders, Trotha left one unit, Estorff's, to continue harrying the Herero, while the remaining, exhausted troops were simply to occupy the waterholes and prevent the Herero from slipping back.

Not surprisingly, Trotha's proclamation was the most controversial document of the war. Before examining the controversies, however, it might be good to summarize what the proclamation says. It begins by making a quasi-legal point, that the Herero are no longer subjects (and thus are *vogelfrei*, that is, beyond the law and may be shot at). It suggests they have lost this status because of dishonorable military behavior (mutilation and cowardice). It then offers rewards for further dishonorable behavior (selling out the leaders), but makes the conditions for fulfillment impossible (all Herero will be shot or shot at, making it hard to see how they could deliver up their captains). The goal of the war is the disappearance of all Herero. This can occur in two ways: by fleeing to British territory, or by dying.[55] All adult men will be killed (this simply ratified ex post facto what was occurring anyway). Women and children will be driven by force back into the desert (where most, having surrendered out of physical desperation anyway, would presumably die of thirst or starvation). In the explanation to German troops, Trotha decreed that his proclamation was indeed an order and that soldiers could collect bounty, but he worried that this manner of warfare could undermine discipline. So he warned that women and children must not be killed directly but simply driven away.

The three most controversial points surrounding the proclamation have been its context and thus Trotha's aim; the extent to which it was put into practice; and the question of who learned of it when. Concerning context, we must clear up one misunderstanding at the outset. Some writers, noting the proximity of Trotha's order to the Witbooi uprising in the colony's south, have taken the logical-seeming path and interpreted the proclamation as Trotha's desperate response to the news that he now had two revolts on his hands.[56] In fact, the Witbooi uprising broke out unexpectedly on the same day that Trotha issued his proclamation, but over 500 km away. Trotha did not learn of the revolt until

---

55. With Trotha's enunciation of intent to make all Herero disappear from SWA, together with his far-reaching accomplishment in fulfilling this goal, he meets the qualifications that many authors have set for "genocide." Intended totality plus a real effort to achieve it, not the complete eradication of a people, are the standards typically used to define a genocide. I believe historical analysis is better done freed of the fetters of this legalistic and rather static definition and the typologies it has spawned, so that we can concentrate instead on how genocide has sometimes developed from smaller causes in the absence of ideological motivation. Trotha's proclamation is interesting precisely because it was ex post facto: the annihilation had been occurring all along. The "policy" followed and retroactively justified the actions that had spiraled from practices and doctrines as they confronted an intractable situation. The following provide a good introduction to scholarly thinking on "genocide": Raphael Lemkin, *Axis Rule in Occupied Europe* (Washington, D.C., 1944); Israel W. Charny, "Toward a Generic Definition of Genocide," in *Genocide*, ed. George J. Andreopoulos (Philadelphia, 1992), 65–94; Israel W. Charny, ed., *Genocide* (London, 1988); Chalk and Jonassohn, ed., *History and Sociology of Genocide*; Helen Fein, "Genocide, Terror, Life Integrity, and War Crimes," in *Genocide*, ed. Andreopoulous, 95–107; Zygmunt Bauman, *Modernity and the Holocaust* (Ithaca, N.Y., 1989); Yehuda Bauer, *Rethinking the Holocaust* (New Haven, 2001); and Norman Naimark, *Fires of Hatred* (Cambridge, Mass., 2001).

56. Tilman Dedering, "The German-Herero War of 1904," *Journal of Southern African Studies* 19:1 (March 1993), 80–88, here 83; Poewe, *Namibian Herero*, 65n14. The official history suggests the same thing: General Staff, *Kämpfe der deutschen Truppen*, 1:207–8.

8 or 9 October, almost a week afterward.[57] The context therefore is the conclusion of the first phase of pursuit.

The timing of the order has suggested to nearly everyone that frustration was its main motive. Trotha, having failed to end the war at Waterberg, had now again failed to do so by a sharp pursuit; his troops, suffering greatly from thirst, hunger, and illness, were physically incapable of achieving the absolute "success" the homeland demanded. But what did such an order achieve? Those who wish to minimize the order's seriousness represent it as merely psychological warfare with two aims. By driving the Herero away, it was supposed to save troopers from more casualties inflicted by Herero sharpshooters. And it was designed for domestic propaganda: if one could not actually defeat the Herero, one could at least appear properly fierce.[58] The first suggestion is simply not credible. The suffering of the German troops had long been primarily due to lack of provisioning, exhaustion, and resultant illness; Trotha and his officers repeatedly stated that the military capacity of the Herero was ended. The suggestion that Trotha wished to impress the Kaiser or the General Staff chief with tough words is possible, but it seems unlikely as a complete explanation for such an extraordinary document. Helmut Bley, who takes the proclamation seriously (as did the governor, chancellor, director of the Colonial Department, and the Reichstag), believes that its aim was to prevent the Herero from infiltrating back into the colony.[59] That is surely true and had long been Trotha's goal. But the violence and finality of the order seem out of proportion to such an aim.

If we ask what the order achieved from the military perspective, the answer is, not much. It essentially sanctioned practices (the shooting of all men) that were already customary.[60] It tried, as Trotha had done in August, to reassert disciplinary control relating to the shooting of women and children, which had become widespread, while granting explicitly the very objective that justified shooting: the "disappearance" of all Herero.

The order accomplished only one thing: it made negotiations practically impossible. It did so by scaring the Herero away, and even more so by attempting to lock the military leadership into the most drastic possible policy. That kept the war out of civilian hands and entirely within the military's bailiwick, which was the order's major purpose. For a negotiated settlement was the logical next step, now that the resistance of the Herero people had been broken but while German troops were incapable of ending the war militarily. This is precisely what Trotha wanted to avoid, as he explained to the General Staff chief in the cover letter (4 October) to the proclamation:

> For me, it is merely a question of how to end the war with the Herero. My opinion is completely opposite to that of the governor and some "old Africans." They have wanted to negotiate for a long time and describe the Herero nation as a necessary labor force for the future use of the colony. I am of an entirely different

57. 8th: Auer v. Herrenkirchen, *Erlebnisse*, 62. 9th: v. François, "Hottentotten-Aufstand," 44.

58. Sudholt, *Deutsche Eingeborenenpolitik*, 188–89; Poewe, *Namibian Herero*, 65–66.

59. Bley, *South-West Africa*, 163–64. Drechsler, who also takes the order seriously, never explains why Trotha issued it. Drechsler, *"Let Us Die Fighting,"* 156–57.

60. Gewald also reaches this conclusion: *Towards Redemption*, 216.

opinion. I believe that the nation must be destroyed as such, or since this was not possible using tactical blows, it must be expelled from the land operatively and by means of detailed actions.

Trotha continued that he believed it would be possible to dispose of small bands trying to reenter the colony, though provisioning problems prevented him from capturing the captains. If Estorff did not succeed in forcing the Herero into British Bechuanaland, then it only remained to be seen if they would go voluntarily,

> or if they will try to regain possession of their old pastureland by force or by complete submission. Because I neither can treat with these people, nor do I want to, without the express direction of His Majesty, a certain rigorous treatment of all parts of the nation is absolutely necessary, a treatment that I have for the present taken and executed on my own responsibility, and from which, as long as I have command, I shall not detour without a direct order. My detailed knowledge of many Central African tribes, Bantu and others, has taught me the convincing certainty that Negroes never submit to a contract but only to raw force. Yesterday before my departure, I had the warriors who were captured in the last several days, [and who were] condemned by court-martial, hanged, and I have chased all the women and children who had gathered here back into the desert, taking with them the proclamation to the Herero people. This proclamation (enclosed), which will unavoidably become known, will be attacked. I only ask that it be explained to His Majesty that these means are absolutely necessary, and that my order to the troops (who are [still] excellently disciplined and with three characters like Deimling, Estorff, and Mühlenfels will surely remain so) gives the necessary instruction and guarantee for the execution of the order. On the other hand [*sic*] accepting women and children, who are mostly ill, is an eminent danger to the troops, and taking care of them is impossible. Therefore, I think it better that the nation perish rather than infect our troops and affect our water and food. In addition, the Herero would interpret any kindness on my side as weakness. They must now die in the desert or try to cross the Bechuanaland border. This uprising is and remains the beginning of a race war, which I already predicted in 1897 in my reports to the chancellor on East Africa. . . . Whether this uprising was caused by poor treatment [of the Africans] remains irrelevant to its suppression.[61]

I have quoted this letter at length because it clears up many questions. In it, Trotha explains that he has elevated the *tactic* of destruction to an operative level and adopted this (the destruction of the nation, rather than of its military force) as the goal of the war.

---

61. Trotha to Schlieffen, Okatarobaka, 4 Oct. 1904, BA-Berlin, R 1001, Nr. 2089, pp. 5–6. Partly reprinted in Drechsler, *"Let Us Die Fighting,"* 160–61; Drechsler, *Aufstände,* 86–87; Drechsler, "Hereros," 244–45; and Bley, *South-West Africa,* 164.

60 Therefore, negotiations are out of the question. Instead, the solution to the war must be military, violent, physical, and total. Even the "complete submission" of the Herero is no longer acceptable to him. They must disappear. Believing that the deaths of women and children needed more justifying, and because the principle of their "disappearance" actually developed out of the severe provisioning problems the troops faced, Trotha adds that they, too, pose a physical danger to the German soldiers. Therefore, they too must die. Finally, Trotha makes clear that he has received no orders to exterminate. He has arrived at this conclusion on his own, through the force of events, and now seeks All-Highest recognition of the logical necessity of his actions.

One of the "old Africans" Trotha must have meant was Major Estorff, whose unit now was ordered to carry on the pursuit alone. Although he loyally carried out his order, Estorff believed "crushing the people like this was in equal measure cruel and insane [töricht]. One could have saved many of them and their herds, if one had spared them and given them refuge; they were punished enough. I suggested this to General von Trotha, but he wanted their complete destruction [gänzliche Vernichtung]."[62]

So Estorff soldiered on against his better judgment, while the other units occupied the waterholes and shot at Herero trying to break through the cordon, or conducted sweeps nearby. Because Trotha's order basically ratified existing practice, it will come as no surprise to learn that in the two months between the proclamation and its cancellation by Berlin (8 December 1904), the method of "fighting" continued much as before. The war diary of the 3rd Field Company of the Naval Infantry Battalion gives a good idea of how occupation units operated:

3 Nov. (Klein-Waterberg). They see thirty Herero searching for food. "After a difficult descent we attack the latter in their camp and take 14 men and women prisoner. We didn't see animals or guns. 4 Herero are shot to death, we have no losses."

4 Nov. They return to their own camp. "The 10 captured women and children are taken along and in the afternoon transported by wagon to work in the typhus hospital at Waterberg."[63]

23 Nov. (near Klein-Waterberg). "We surprised Herero in the flats, south of the hill; 2 men are shot to death, 1 boy captured. Pontoks [huts, where Herero lived] are burnt down."

27 Nov. (near Okateitei). "1 Klipp-Kaffern [i.e., not Herero, but members of another tribe] pontok is attacked."

6 Dec. (near Klein-Waterberg). They surprise a party of thirty Herero, of whom fifteen to twenty are shot to death, "including several well-armed warriors; 6 guns with ammunition are bagged [erbeutet]."[64]

These entries tell us that the accepted practice was to attack all groups of Herero and even non-Herero blacks, armed and unarmed, warrior and civilian. All men were shot dead.

---

62. Estorff, *Wanderungen*, 117.
63. War diary of 3rd Field Comp., Naval Inf. Batt., BA-MA Freiburg, RM 121 I, Nr. 434.
64. Diary entry, 3rd Field Comp., Naval Inf. Batt., ibid., Nr. 435.

Women and children (contrary to Trotha's order) were taken prisoner and put in work
details. The huts were burnt down.

Trotha's own reports to Berlin tell us how the more active units along the desert's edge operated:

3 Nov. "[Captain] Klitzing [of Mühlenfels's unit] conducts a successful battle east of Okunjahi with a large Herero troop of 250 with 20 guns. Enemy leaves 6 dead behind; on our side cavalryman Urschech is lightly wounded on the knee."

4 Nov. "Klitzing follows tracks leading north. Breaks up 2 small Herero bands. 4 Herero shot dead. 1 gun bagged."[65]

11. Nov. (Eiseb riverbed). "Several hundred Herero flee as he [Estorff] approaches"; in his pursuit, he kills nineteen.

12–13. Nov. Captain Wilhelmi at Otjosondjou-Okunjahi. "He met only women, children, and old people and found a few discarded guns."[66]

2 Dec. "Herero *Werften* [groups of huts] attacked near Onandowa north of Namutoni; 58 animals and 7 guns with ammunition bagged, several Herero shot to death."[67]

6 Dec. Reports that First Lieutenant Brockdorff at Okasaberg meets thirty Herero and kills twenty.[68]

11 Dec. "15 Herero dead, 1 gun bagged."[69]

Here the noteworthy numbers relate to the discrepancy between the number of Herero killed and the number of guns captured. This discrepancy makes clear that, at the very least, unarmed men were routinely being shot down. The reports mention no prisoners, so we do not know, for example, what Captain Wilhelmi did with the women, children, and old men whom he encountered. Chief of Staff Schlieffen later claimed that in this period Estorff treated prisoners kindly and released them.[70] (This is possible, because Estorff disagreed with Trotha's policies and, as we shall see, was quite capable of acting independently on Africans' behalf.) Missionaries reported that Capt. Joachim von Heydebreck was also taking "quite a number of prisoners" in this period.[71]

Trotha's reports never describe the dead Herero by sex or age, but it would be surprising if no women and children were killed in these attacks on whole groups of Herero, fleeing or in Werften. The diary of the 3rd Field Company, above, suggests that the main targets of shooting were probably men, however. The widespread slaughter of women and children by shooting may have been more characteristic of the period immediately after Waterberg; it is hard to tell for certain.

One other event during the period after Trotha's order deserves mention. Trotha reported to Berlin that "on 3 November, First Lieutenant v. Beesten lured Herero into a trap

65. Trotha to Bülow, copy, tel. arr. 7 Nov. 1904, BA-Berlin, R 1001, Nr. 2133, p. 124.

66. Trotha to General Staff, tel., Windhuk, 16 Nov. 1904, BA-Berlin, R 1001, Nr. 2116, p. 175.

67. Trotha to General Staff, tel. Nr. 21, Windhuk, 19 Dec. 1904, BA-Berlin, R 1001, Nr. 2117, p. 51.

68. Trotha to General Staff, tel. Nr. 247, Windhuk, 2 Dec. 1904, ibid., p. 37.

69. Trotha to General Staff, tel. Nr. 28, Windhuk, 27 Dec. 1904, ibid., p. 55.

70. Schlieffen to Bülow, Berlin, 23 Nov. 1904, BA-Berlin, R 1001, Nr. 2089, pp. 3–4.

71. Eich to Inspector, 16 Nov. 1904, cited in de Vries, *Namibia*, p. 305.

62 at Ombakaha. 4 clan leaders [*Grossleute*] fell."[72] This action was entirely consonant with Trotha's policy to destroy the possibility of negotiations, for the Herero had come to Beesten in order to negotiate a surrender, under the repeated assurance that they would not be killed. When he demanded they surrender their guns, they began to run. Beesten's troops had meanwhile surrounded the Herero; they opened fire and killed them.[73] Ombakaha left a lasting impression on the Herero. As a colonial official noted over a year later, "In light of this kind of behavior, it is no wonder that the Herero have no trust in our assurances and therefore don't turn themselves in."[74] Obviously, Trotha saw nothing wrong with these methods, though he had not "engineered them," as Drechsler claims.[75] He described them matter-of-factly in his report to his superiors. The General Staff ordered an inquiry, but no disciplinary proceedings seem to have resulted.[76] "Ombakaha" continued to be listed as a genuine "battle."[77] The military's satisfaction with these means was also shared by the settlers.[78]

The last point of controversy surrounding Trotha's proclamation concerns how widely it was known. The instruction to the order said it was to be read at roll-call to the German troops. The two surviving war diaries from this period do not mention the proclamation.[79] But it is hard to know how to interpret their silence, since, for example, Captain v. Lettow-Vorbeck, who was with Trotha during those days and who notes the hanging of the male Herero that accompanied the distribution of the proclamation, does not mention the proclamation itself in his diary.[80] Other military diarists, stationed elsewhere, say nothing about it. The proclamation also does not appear in the standard military reports sent to Berlin and now in the archives. As we have seen, Trotha did not intend it to affect the method of fighting, except possibly to limit the shooting of women and children. It merely put a seal of approval on the methods already in use. The kind of fighting and the goal of fighting remained the same before and after the proclamation, regardless of its circulation.

Nonetheless, word of the proclamation began to spread, as Trotha predicted it would. The extraordinarily well-informed Paul Rohrbach learned of it in Omaruru, five days after it was drafted.[81] He may have been the first civilian to do so, since, with one possible exception, Trotha informed only military leaders, because he intended the proclamation to solidify a *military* policy before civilian policy makers could inaugurate a counterpol-

---

72. Trotha to Bülow, copy, tel. arr. 7 Nov. 1904, BA-Berlin, R 1001, Nr. 2133, p. 124.

73. Drechsler, *"Let Us Die Fighting,"* 159–60.

74. Marginalium, dated 25 Jan. 1906, to "Report on the events of 29.10—2.11 and on the battle near Ombakaha on 2 Nov.," arr. Col. Dept., 25 Feb. 1905, BA-Berlin, R 1001, Nr. 2117, pp. 113–17, here 113. Also, missionary August Kuhlmann, "Report on the attempts to negotiate peace in Othimbingue," 16 Feb. 1905, VEM-Wuppertal, Kuhlmann papers, B/c II 72; and Rohrbach, *Aus Südwestafrikas schweren Tagen,* 265.

75. Drechsler, *"Let Us Die Fighting,"* 161.

76. Oberkommando of Schutztruppe to Col. Dept., Berlin, 22 May 1905, BA-Berlin, R 1001, Nr. 2118, p. 112.

77. General Staff, *Kämpfe der deutschen Truppen,* 1:339.

78. "Der Aufstand," *Deutsch-Südwestafrikanische Zeitung* 45 (9 Nov. 1904).

79. War diary, 3rd Field Comp., Naval Inf. Batt., BA-MA Freiburg, RM 121 I, Nr. 434; war diary, Regimental Staff of the 2nd Field Regt. (Deimling), ibid., Nl. Deimling, Nr. 7.

80. Lettow-Vorbeck, diary, BA-MA Freiburg, Nl. Lettow-Vorbeck, Nr. 34.

81. Rohrbach, *Aus Südwestafrikas schweren Tagen,* 177–78.

icy of their own. The struggle between military and civilian policy makers was perhaps the
most important outcome of Trotha's proclamation.

Canceling the Proclamation: Civilian versus Military Leadership

Trotha later claimed that he had sent a copy of his proclamation to Governor Leutwein "immediately," presumably meaning 4 October, when he also sent a copy to the General Staff chief.[82] However, Trotha never notified the Colonial Department or the chancellor—and Leutwein always maintained that he had never received a copy "officially."[83] Indeed, it was not until 23 October that Leutwein, galvanized into action by the proclamation (as he later explained),[84] telegraphed the Colonial Department asking for authority to begin negotiations. If Leutwein had known earlier, it is hard to see why he would have waited so long. Only on the 28th did Leutwein send a copy of the proclamation (by ship) to the Colonial Department, which later told the General Staff historians that the department first learned of the proclamation in "late November."[85]

The military worked faster. No sooner had Leutwein telegraphed the Colonial Department than Trotha sprang to his own defense, pretending to take umbrage at the suggestion that he had known of Herero peace-feelers and quashed them. Trotha next ordered Leutwein to cease any political activity, and finally, on 28 October, Trotha threatened to resign if his complete authority over politics and military matters, including negotiations, were not upheld.[86] Two days later it was Leutwein who had to resign, despite the fact that both the director of the Colonial Department and the chancellor supported him and his policies.[87] As long as Trotha was covered by the chief of the General Staff, with his direct connections to the Kaiser, military rule would continue. Trotha had accepted command under the express condition that, as Wilhelm had told him, "you will have nothing to do with the chancellor," that is, Trotha would be completely inside the military command chain (Kaiser–chief of the General Staff–commander), and that he, not the governor, would determine politics in the colony.[88] That is why Trotha insisted on proclaiming a state of emergency even before he arrived in SWA.

Having lost the power struggle, Leutwein recommended that the Colonial Department and the chancellor let the "military dictatorship of Lt. Gen. v. Trotha" run its course, which is almost what they did.[89] For, once Leutwein resigned, the chancellor re-

---

82. Trotha to Leutwein, copy, Windhuk, 5 Nov. 1904, BA-Berlin, R 1001, Nr. 2089, pp. 101–3.

83. Leutwein to Col. Dept., Nr. 437, 28 Oct. 1904, ibid., pp. 21–22.

84. Ibid.

85. Leutwein to Col. Dept., Nr. 437, Rehoboth, 28 Oct. 1904, BA-Berlin, R 1001, Nr. 2089, pp. 21–22; Kellwig notice of 3 Aug. 1905, ibid., Nr. 2118, p. 153. Surface mail normally required six weeks to arrive in Germany.

86. Leutwein to Trotha, tel., Rehoboth, 24 Oct. 1904; Trotha to Leutwein, tel., Windhuk, 27 Oct. 1904, ibid., Nr. 2089, pp. 24–25, 36; Trotha to General Staff, 28 Oct., Windhuk, ibid., Nr. 2116, p. 91.

87. Stübel report to Bülow, 26 Oct. 1904, and draft of telegram from Bülow to Trotha, 26 Oct. 1904, which was approved by Bülow but stopped by Foreign Minister Baron Oswald v. Richthofen, after Trotha's resignation threat arrived: Richthofen note of 29 Oct. 1904, ibid., Nr. 2116, pp. 85–86, 92–93, 94.

88. Trotha to Hülsen-Häseler, 7 Dec. 1904, Trotha Papers, Nr. 315, Anhang 1, Nr. 14.

89. Leutwein to Bülow, Rehoboth, 28 Oct. 1904, BA-Berlin, R 1001, Nr. 2089, pp. 21–22.

64 fused to appoint another governor until Trotha had left and the new governor was guaranteed supreme political authority over the commander of the Schutztruppe.

In the meantime, three more weeks elapsed before the civilian leadership learned of the proclamation. It did so through Chief of Staff Schlieffen, who, though he wanted to keep Trotha in command and thus uphold military control, nonetheless judged Trotha's proclamation unworkable. Schlieffen sent the Colonial Department a copy of the proclamation, along with a cover letter in which he admitted that "the campaign against the Herero has come to a standstill."[90] He agreed with Trotha's assessment of the uprising as a "race war [that] can be concluded only by the destruction or complete servitude of one of the parties. . . . The intentions of General v. Trotha can only be commended. Only he does not have the power to carry them out." Therefore, only a "rapid concluding of peace" would save Germany from a protracted guerilla war, "with all the horrors of typhus, malaria, and heart disease."[91] Schlieffen recommended setting a higher bounty for Herero leaders and issuing a new proclamation promising life to innocent Herero who chose to surrender.

Bülow and the colonial officials saw things differently. They were appalled by both the methods and the goals outlined in the proclamation. Colonial officials drafted, and Bülow approved, a report for the chancellor to present to the Kaiser personally.[92] The report immediately assumed a moral stance, describing its contents as "a matter of conscience." The shooting of all men and the driving away of women and children were "contrary to the principles of Christianity and humanity." Although the Herero deserved to be punished, "a complete and systematic annihilation [Ausrottung] of the Herero would exceed all the demands of justice and of the reestablishment of authority." Only as a third point did the report use Schlieffen's argument (citing him) that the plan was infeasible and tremendously expensive. Fourth, the loss of the Herero to death or flight would seriously harm the colony's economy. And finally, Bülow argued that the proclamation "will demolish Germany's reputation among the civilized nations and feed foreign agitation against us." These were unusually powerful words, the kind one rarely sees in such official documents. But Bülow obviously feared they were not powerful enough, for he ended the report by saying, "For these reasons, I ask Your Majesty, in agreement with the chief of the General Staff," to order Trotha to issue a new proclamation offering life to those who surrender. The report made it seem that the military leadership made common cause with the civilians. Because raising the bounty on the heads of African leaders contradicted the purpose of encouraging surrender, Bülow left it out.

When the Kaiser made his decision, however, he was no longer in Berlin, but hunting at Slawentzitz, surrounded by his mostly military entourage. Wilhelm chose Schlieffen's path: a new proclamation, but also increased bounty.[93] Bülow was now obliged to meet with Schlieffen. In protracted and difficult discussions he managed to get Schlieffen to drop the bounty idea; it was even harder to get him to accept the missions as mediators.

90. Schlieffen to Col. Dept., Nr. 12383, Berlin, 23 Nov. 1904, ibid., pp. 3–4.

91. The high altitude and strenuous conditions led to dangerous enlargement of the heart in many soldiers.

92. Bülow report to the Kaiser, draft, Berlin, 24 Nov. 1904, BA-Berlin, R 1001, Nr. 2089, pp. 8–11.

93. Friedrich v. Schoen to Foreign Office, tel. Nr. 204, Slawentzitz, 29 Nov. 1904, ibid., p. 13.

For it had finally dawned on Bülow that only the missionaries could overcome the Herero people's distrust of the soldiers, and only they could provide the care that sick and hungry refugees required to survive. Like Trotha, Schlieffen found the idea repellent, and said the Kaiser would never accept it. Eventually he relented, as did Trotha's protector, Military Cabinet Chief Hülsen, whom Schlieffen had called in to the meeting.[94] Therefore, it was only after Bülow had convinced the military leaders that he eventually received Wilhelm's approval of his policies. The telegram canceling Trotha's proclamation went out through the General Staff on 8 December. It said the German kaiser wanted "to treat mercifully those Herero who voluntarily surrender and to spare their lives, except for those directly guilty and their leaders." It also put the missions in charge of the Herero people's "immediate accommodation."[95] Bounty was not mentioned.

Just how precarious Bülow's victory was became clear during the next month. Not surprisingly, Trotha obstructed the order at every turn.[96] He demanded (unsuccessfully) that the Kaiser's order be published, presumably to relieve himself of the odium of having "negotiated."[97] And he insisted (again unsuccessfully) that a new civilian governor be appointed immediately to deal with the surrendering Herero, a problem for which he steadfastly refused responsibility.[98]

But it was Schlieffen, not Trotha, who determined how Wilhelm's order would be carried out. Schlieffen set the narrowest possible parameters: Trotha was merely to accept surrendering Herero; "negotiations are out of the question."[99] The bounty could be raised later.[100] Above all, military operations were to continue unchanged. Trotha wired his (correct) understanding of Schlieffen's orders: "Continuing the offensive against the mass of Herero is not supposed to be hindered by the All-Highest order. Negotiations are not to be begun, but voluntarily surrendering Herero are not to be shot down but accepted."[101] This is the wording the troops in the field received.[102]

One of the most interesting aspects of the colloquy between civilian and military leadership was the exchange on shooting at women and children. Shooting women and children (not just shooting at them) had already erupted in March as a serious issue, after Bebel raised his questions in the Reichstag. The government had explicitly denied that German troops shot women and children, a practice that public opinion condemned as utterly unthinkable. Apparently Schlieffen had neglected to send Bülow Trotha's "instruction" directing troops to shoot above, not actually at, women and children. Trotha's and Schlieffen's obstruction now moved Bülow to pursue this point. He wanted a precisely

94. Bülow notice, 3 Dec. 1904, ibid., pp. 17–18.

95. General Staff to Trotha, tel. in code, 8 Dec. 1904, ibid., p. 48.

96. Stübel to Bülow, memorandum of 12 Dec. 1904, ibid., pp. 64–65.

97. Trotha to Bülow, tel. Nr. 2, Windhuk, 9 Dec. 1904, ibid., p. 52; Trotha to General Staff, 11 Dec. 1904, ibid., p. 62.

98. Trotha to Bülow, tel. Nr. 2, Windhuk, 9 Dec. 1904, ibid, p 52.

99. Schlieffen to Trotha, Berlin, 10 Dec. 1904, ibid., p. 83; Bley, *South-West Africa*, 167–68.

100. Schlieffen to Trotha, tel., 8 Dec. 1904, BA-Berlin, R 1001, Nr. 2089, p. 49.

101. Trotha to Schlieffen, copy, Nr. 16, Windhuk, 13 Dec. 1904; acknowledging Schlieffen to Trotha, tel., Berlin, 12 Dec. 1904, ibid., pp. 85, 87.

102. Trotha to Schlieffen, copy, Nr. 16, Windhuk, 13 Dec. 1904, ibid., p. 87.

66 worded instruction to tie Trotha's hands. He therefore asked Schlieffen to direct Trotha "that in any event under no circumstances were women and children to be shot at any longer," and Trotha was to make actual efforts to get Herero to surrender, not just wait for them to do so on their own.[103] Schlieffen took umbrage at the words "any longer."[104] He denied that German troops had ever done so. Before the proclamation, Trotha had forbidden shooting at women and children, Schlieffen assured Bülow, and afterward, the proclamation was just for purposes of "intimidation." But he continued:

> If, in one or another exceptional case, women have been shot, then one must re-member that women have not only participated in the fighting, they have also been the main originators of the cruel and horrible martyrdom that our wounded have often been subjected to, and that the sight of these victims, who were dis-played with bestial intention, provoked the comrades to forgivable fury.

Schlieffen was thus careful to represent the practice as an individual, regrettable, but un-derstandable exception. Bülow, unmollified, returned to the matter two weeks later and repeated that it was the civilian leadership's assumption "that, apart from an actual mili-tary action, women and children will not be shot at."[105] The civilians were thus prepared to grant "actual military action" as an exception but wanted the practice itself expressly forbidden. Schlieffen replied that Trotha had assured him "his prohibition to shoot at women and children has been repeated once more to the troops."[106]

Trotha Continues the War

In accordance with Schlieffen's instructions, "offensive" operations continued. Tak-ing advantage of the rainy season in January and February 1905, German troops chased two Herero leaders, Wilhelm Maherero and Traugott, and their followers across the bor-der into Bechuanaland.[107] A typical battle report during this pursuit claimed six Herero had fallen, but no prisoners had been taken.[108] On 23 February Trotha decreed "the oper-ations in Hereroland ended."[109] Nevertheless, "cleansing actions" (*Säuberungs-Aktionen*) continued in the occupied areas.[110] These consisted of approaching Herero Werften and,

103. Bülow to Schlieffen, draft tel., 14 Dec. 1904, ibid., p. 89.

104. Schlieffen to Bülow, Nr. 13297, Berlin, 16 Dec. 1904, ibid., p. 107.

105. Bülow to Schlieffen, Berlin, 30 Dec. 1904, ibid., pp. 108–9.

106. Schlieffen to Bülow, Nr. 13752, Berlin, 5 Jan. 1905, ibid., p. 114. Cf. the account in Bridgman, *Revolt*, 126–27, and Drechsler, *"Let Us Die Fighting,"* 158.

107. See Gewald's account of the flight of the Herero after Waterberg: *Towards Redemption*, 210–24.

108. Trotha to General Staff, tel. Nr. 86, Windhuk, 22 Feb. 1905, BA-Berlin, R 1001, Nr. 2117, p. 111.

109. Lettow-Vorbeck, diary entry, 23 Feb. 1905, BA-MA Freiburg, Nl. Lettow-Vorbeck, Nr. 34; and Trotha to General Staff, tel. Nr. 90, Windhuk, 7 Mar. 1905, BA-Berlin, R 1001, Nr. 2117, pp. 134–35.

110. Trotha to General Staff, tel. Nr. 95, Windhuk, arr. Col. Dept. 15 Mar. 1905, BA-Berlin, R 1001, Nr. 2117, pp. 144–46.

if the people failed to surrender, attacking and burning them down.[111] The official history lists these episodes in the "battle calendar," the last one for 23 August 1905.[112]

Meanwhile, the brunt of the war had shifted to the south, where the various clans of the Nama, or Hottentots, as whites called them, had been in united rebellion since October 1904.[113] The fighting in the Nama war never escalated to annihilation, however. For one thing, Namaland was even less accessible than Hereroland, and in the absence of any railroad at all, and with a fatal epidemic among the oxen, the Germans could not sustain the cumbersome reinforcements that had permitted the encirclement attempt at the Waterberg. But more than this, the Nama never gave them such a target. Instead of provoking a European-style battle by collecting themselves and waiting in a single spot, the Nama stuck to the style of warfare at which they excelled: hit-and-run guerilla warfare with fast-moving, small, mounted units of excellent marksmen. Furthermore, women and children did not accompany the warriors, so the opportunities even for individual atrocities were very limited.[114] Finally, the Germans felt considerably less threatened by the Nama than by the Herero: they were a much smaller group (perhaps twenty thousand people with a maximum of eighteen hundred warriors), located on the very underpopulated southern fringe of the colony; they possessed much less wealth (cows) than the Herero; and they did not demonstrate their victories over German troops by marking the bodies of the dead.[115]

Nevertheless, Trotha approached the Nama exactly as he had the Herero. His object was to bring as much technological force as possible to bear, as that was the source of European superiority. Because no railroad existed to move supplies, Trotha wanted to postpone all operations until one was built. When that outrageous suggestion was rejected,[116] Trotha ordered Colonel Deimling, in charge of operations in the south, to move very cautiously, in hopes the Nama would collect their forces and permit a decisive battle. Deimling, however, attacked head on, and confirmed the inevitability of a lengthy guerilla war. Despite the advisability under these circumstances of dividing and conquering, among other means, by negotiation, Trotha rigidly refused his commanders permission to do so. And just to make sure, he destroyed the first tentative negotiations with one African leader by issuing another proclamation, this one to the Nama people. It began by following the Kaiser's order of 8 December 1904, promising life to those who freely surrendered

---

111. Trotha to General Staff, 28 Apr. 1905, ibid., Nr. 2118, pp. 75–76; Lettow-Vorbeck, diary entry, 3 May 1905, BA-MA Freiburg, Nl. Lettow-Vorbeck, Nr. 34.

112. General Staff, *Kämpfe der deutschen Truppen*, 2:339–40.

113. For accounts of the fighting: General Staff, *Kämpfe der deutschen Truppen*, vol. 2: *Der Hottentottenkrieg*; Drechsler, "*Let Us Die Fighting*," 176–230; Bridgman, *Revolt*, 132–63.

114. General Staff, *Kämpfe der deutschen Truppen* 2:118, 175–76.

115. Less threat: General Staff, *Kämpfe der deutschen Truppen*, 2:16. Numbers: Leutwein, *Elf Jahre*, 436.

116. Trotha to General Staff, copy, 29 Dec. 1904, and Trotha to General Staff, tel. Nr. 33, Windhuk, 30 Dec. 1904, BA-Berlin, R 1001, Nr. 2134, pp. 93, 100. Although the General Staff agreed with Col. Dir. Stübel that this was a virtual "declaration of bankruptcy" by Trotha, Schlieffen covered for Trotha by not presenting this request to the Kaiser, which would have given the civilian leadership another opportunity to try to remove Trotha: Stübel draft report, Berlin, 4 Jan. 1905 (with Bülow's mark on it), ibid., pp. 102–3.

68 and were not guilty of murder or of leading the revolt. But then it promptly slipped into the old language:

> Further, those few who refuse to surrender will have happen to them what happened to the Herero people, who in their blindness also believed they could successfully make war on the mighty German kaiser and the great German people. . . . The whole Herero people have had this happen, part of them have died of hunger and thirst in the desert, part were killed by German troops, part were killed by the Ovambo. The same will happen to the Hottentot people, if they do not freely surrender themselves and their weapons. . . . Those who believe that [because they have murdered or are leaders] they will receive no mercy, should leave the land, because if they are seen on German territory, they will be shot at, until all are destroyed.[117]

The proclamation ended by placing bounties on the heads of three Nama leaders.

Despite Trotha's thunder, the war in the south went its slow, difficult, but different, course. The almost accidental death in late October 1905 of Hendrik Witbooi, one of the chief leaders of the revolt, provided the opportunity to declare a premature victory and to remove Trotha, whose methods had not brought success. Sentiment in the colony had turned against Trotha, after he had in late November 1904 publicly announced his intention to exterminate the Herero. In response to questions posed by the Windhuk council (*Beirat*), Trotha told the colonists that "at the moment the destruction [*Vernichtung*] of all rebellious tribes is the goal of military measures. Supporting the settlers' prosperity naturally ranks behind this goal."[118] The editors of the *Deutsch-Südwestafrikanische Zeitung* spoke for the settlers when they countered this view: "The economic interest of the country argues against the rigid maintenance of this viewpoint, because the natives represent a colonial possession of high economic value. . . . Not their destruction but their actual submission must therefore be the goal of the current war."[119]

General Schlieffen, too, had been disappointed by Trotha's inability to end the war, or to pursue it more successfully with the means at his disposal.[120] But for almost a year he covered for Trotha. Schlieffen's impending retirement, planned for the end of 1905, probably eased Trotha's ouster. Certainly, the general did not leave willingly: one of his young staffers reported how hard he found it to be removed before the job was done.[121] In mid-November 1905 Trotha began the journey back to Germany, where he received Prusso-

---

117. Trotha, proclamation of 22 Apr. 1905, reprinted in General Staff, *Kämpfe der deutschen Truppen*, 2:186; Bridgman, *Revolt*, 145.

118. Trotha, "Bescheid," of 24 Nov. 1904, printed in *Deutsch-Südwestafrikanische Zeitung* 49 (7 Dec. 1904), 2, "Aus dem Schutzgebiet."

119. *Deutsch-Südwestafrikanische Zeitung* 50 (14 Dec. 1904), 2.

120. Stübel, draft, 4 Jan. 1905, BA-Berlin, R 1001, Nr. 2134, pp. 102–3.

121. 1st Lt. Eberhard v. d. Hagen to Heinrich v. d. Hagen, Keetmanshoop, 12 Nov. 1905, BA-MA Freiburg, Militärbiographische Sammlung (MSg. 1), Nr. 2038 (Eberhard v. d. Hagen).

Germany's highest military decoration, the Pour-le-mérite, four other prestigious medals from other German states, and a full pension.[122]

The war against first one Nama band and then another continued into 1907. Trotha's command was taken over on an interim basis by Colonel v. Dame and then permanently by Major-General v. Deimling, who eventually ended the war by negotiation. With Trotha's departure and the appointment of a new civilian governor (Friedrich von Linde-quist), SWA returned to the usual arrangement whereby a civilian government set general political policy, and military commands were given inside those parameters. The military dictatorship was over.

122. Bley writes that Trotha's pension was too low for his rank, but the cabinet order of 21 May 1906 spelled out that Trotha would receive the "legal pension." Bley, *South-West Africa*, 165n46; AKO of 21 May 1906, Trotha Papers, Nr. 315, Anhang 2, Nr. 30b. Medals: ibid., 30a.

3

Death by Imprisonment

We must return to January 1905, when Chancellor Bülow's difficult, partial victory over the military leadership ushered in a new aspect of the war: imprisonment.[1] Imprisonment had two phases: one under Trotha, which coincided with ongoing military sweeps, and another under Governor Lindequist (after December 1905), which until September 1906 operated under almost a truce. But in both phases the mortality rate among prisoners (men, women, and children) was extraordinarily high, raising the question whether annihilation had not merely reappeared under a different mask. And death by imprisonment hit Herero and Nama equally, despite the radical differences in the methods of warfare against each.

Trotha's Principles of Imprisonment

The transition from shooting to imprisonment was difficult. It appears that instructions to local officers about how to handle the situation arrived late, if at all. It was left to the missionaries to improvise and to cajole cooperation from the district officers. Depending on the personality, experience, and political convictions of the officer in question, this could go well or badly. But there was also some system in this, for Trotha's leadership style tended to replicate itself among many of his underlings. Trotha's own recalcitrance was crystal clear. Forced against his will to accept prisoners, Trotha informed Berlin he was placing them all in chains. Once again, Bülow had to intervene and order Trotha to desist from this practice, except in extraordinary cases, since knowledge

---

1. Recent articles: Zimmerer, "Kriegsgefangene"; Joachim Zeller, "'Wie Vieh wurden hunderte zu Tode getrieben und wie Vieh begraben,'" *Zeitschrift für Geschichtswissenschaft* 49:3 (2001): 226–43.

of the procedure prevented Herero from surrendering.[2] Forced to lift the chain order, Trotha reported, "I have ordered the people to be told that, if they don't reveal where they have buried guns and ammunition, which they have clearly done, I will have one warrior shot every eight days, until they tell the truth."[3] Bülow replied that "it is beyond my competence to judge whether such rigorous measures as shooting warriors is necessary. Your Excellency must decide on your own responsibility."[4]

With their commander setting such an example, it is not surprising that subalterns mimicked Trotha's forceful extremism. So, for example, in Otjimbingue, where First Lieutenant Friedrichs grew impatient at the reluctance of the Herero to surrender. He told missionary Kuhlmann that if they did not hurry up, he would "saddle up and shoot down the Werften." Kuhlmann hastened to Friedrichs' superior, District Chief First Lieutenant Kuhn, who replaced Friedrichs with two more understanding officers.[5] Or in Omaruru, where First Lieutenant Cramer's first response to the news that Herero were nearby was to lead a patrol against them. The best the missionary could wrest from him was the promise not to shoot those who wanted to surrender. Cramer's superior, First Lieutenant Count v. Brockdorff, short-circuited Cramer's dash by ordering that African messengers be sent out in place of soldiers.[6] This became the main method of luring Herero to give themselves up. The pattern here is that lieutenants with less experience in SWA tended to cleave to Trotha's example, whose adamantine attitude, as missionary Eduard Dannert noted, was "that one would rather let the Herero die and rot, than save them for the colony."[7] Inspector of Missions Gottlob Haussleiter summed up the problem of the first few months: "It was especially difficult for victorious soldiers in the field to set aside their weapons and reach out to the beaten and dispersed enemy. Later, however, the idea of peace gained ground."[8] Nevertheless, relatively sensible and experienced officers had trouble reconciling their profession with treating with the enemy, even with noncombatants and prisoners. District Chief First Lieutenant Kuhn defended himself against the possible charge that his policies showed he was "soft" on the Herero by declaiming in public that "I have not made this suggestion from considerations of humanity—I am completely free of dizzy humanitarianism [*Humanitätsduselei*]."[9]

Administering prisoners at all, much less in a way that might guarantee their survival, was so alien to the proper task of a "real" soldier that prisoner management was the

2. Trotha to General Staff, copy, tel., 29 Dec. 1904, BA-Berlin, R 1001, Nr. 2134, p. 93; Tecklenburg to Col. Dept., tel. Nr. 7, Windhuk, 6 Jan. 1905, ibid., Nr. 2089, pp. 118–19; Trotha to Bülow, tel. Nr. 6, Windhuk, 7 Jan. 1905, ibid., p. 115; Bülow to Trotha, tel., Berlin, 13 Jan. 1905, ibid., p. 116.

3. Trotha to Bülow, tel. Nr. 13, Windhuk, 14 Jan. 1905, BA-Berlin, R 1001, Nr. 2089, p. 120; Drechsler, *"Let Us Die Fighting,"* 165–66.

4. Bülow to Trotha, tel., Berlin, 21 Jan. 1905, BA-Berlin, R 1001, Nr. 2089, pp. 124–26.

5. Kuhlmann, "Report on the attempts to negotiate peace in Otjimbingue," 16 Feb. 1905, VEM-Wuppertal, Kuhlmann papers, B/c II 72, pp. 10–15. The quotation gives Kuhlmann's words.

6. Dannert to Spiecker, Omaruru, 11 Mar. 1905, VEM-Wuppertal, Dannert papers, B/c II 43, p. 116. Brockdorff had earlier been stationed at Omaruru and knew how the station worked.

7. Ibid. Another example was Lt. Reuss: Vedder to inspector, Swakopmund, 7 Nov. 1906, VEM-Wuppertal, Vedder papers, B/c II 87, p. 97.

8. Haussleiter to Bülow, Barmen, 22 Apr. 1905, BA-Berlin, R 1001, Nr. 2118, pp. 70–72.

9. Dannert to Spiecker, Karibib, 8 Oct. 1905, VEM-Wuppertal, Dannert papers, B/c II 43, pp. 107–8.

72 stepchild of military administration. Prisoners of war (and civilians interned for military reasons) fell under the purview of the commander of the rear (*Etappe*), or occupied zones, who also managed provisioning. In SWA this was Major von Redern (later Colonel v. Dame, then Major Maercker), whose chief of staff was Maj. Arnold Lequis. Prisoners were such a low priority, however, that Lequis's table of administration on arrival in SWA (June 1904) lists no position for them.[10] Trotha abjured all responsibility for accepting or maintaining them the instant he received the order to take prisoners in December 1904, and tried to shift the burden to the civilian administration.[11] The colonial government turned back this attempt, although Bülow asked it to report to Berlin on the situation, apparently trusting that its interest in maintaining an African workforce would spur it to effective supervision over the military.[12] Bülow's move recognized that civilian administration might, in fact, be better able to provide for prisoners, but it did not change the fact that under military law and practice, prisoners were the military's responsibility.[13]

In mid-January 1905, in an order to all troops, Trotha laid down the principles by which prisoners were to be treated:

> The chancellor has canceled my order that all male Herero are to be put in chains. Troops and stations, instead, are to send back surrendering or otherwise captured Herero as they see fit. The offensive capacity for further operations in the east [Omaheke] and the provisioning of troops must under no circumstance suffer. Depending on geographical location, the bands are to be sent to Windhuk, Oka-handja, or Karibib. . . . The rear areas that receive Herero prisoners are to contact the local missions for accommodating the prisoners and should also seek the co-operation of the district chief [who was invariably an officer]. I await telegraphic reports concerning the provisioning of prisoners already in Swakopmund, Karibib, Omaruru, and Okahandja. Guarding them without chains is impossible. Guarding is to be limited to a daily check in the presence of the missionary, to ascertain escapes. If possible, a doctor should examine and watch over prisoners. If a contagious disease breaks out, the camp is immediately to be moved several kilometers into the bush and the old camp burned down. I intend to affix to prisoners of both sexes a nonremovable tin badge with the letters "G.H." (*gefangener Herero* [Herero prisoner]).[14]

Treatment of prisoners under the Trotha regime was therefore to follow these principles: first priority always went to battle-readiness and provisioning of German troops; "prison-

10. "Wirklich Iststärke der einzelnen Formation des Etappenkommandos," Doc. 25, BA-MA Freiburg, Nl. Lequis, Nr. 35.

11. Tecklenburg to Col. Dept., tel. Nr. 249, Windhuk, 10 Dec. 1904, BA-Berlin, R 1001, Nr. 2089, p. 60.

12. Bülow to Schlieffen, Berlin, 30 Dec. 1904, ibid., pp. 108–9.

13. Cf. Bridgman, *Revolt*, 155, where he blames the prisoners' deaths on the civilian government. The commander of the Schutztruppe had supreme authority over prisoners, as Trotha insisted to the end: Trotha to Bülow, coded tel., 22 Aug. 1905, Trotha Papers, Anhang 1, Nr. 37.

14. Trotha, "To all troops and stations in Damaraland," copy sent to Bülow, tel. Nr. 14, Windhuk, 16 Jan. 1905, BA-Berlin, R 1001, Nr. 2089, pp. 122–23.

ers" were all Herero, regardless of age and sex, and no distinction was made between those captured and those who surrendered following the Kaiser's invitation; the local officer was given remarkable latitude in determining how to transport and provision prisoners; guarding was to be kept to an absolute minimum, with the result that draconian security requirements like chains became necessary; missionaries were to run accommodations at the collection camps, thus relieving the military of this responsibility; aside from escapes, the chief anxiety concerned contagious disease; finally, the Herero were to be visibly and permanently identified. Bülow approved these principles, or at least did not fight to have them rescinded. He agreed to the last item provided it did not "involve cruelty," and he reiterated that chains were to be used sparingly.[15] Apparently, Governor Leutwein had already in May 1904 successfully tested a system of tin "passes" for Africans in Swakopmund.[16]

Prison Camp Conditions under Trotha

By the beginning of April, 4,033 prisoners were alive in German hands, only 25 percent of them adult males; by the beginning of December 1905, when Lindequist's new system replaced Trotha's, there were 13,216 prisoners.[17] But many more than this must have surrendered or been captured, for the death rates among prisoners were very high. What happened to Herero and Nama prisoners? They arrived, many of them starved and ill from their desert experience, at the collection camps listed in Trotha's order.[18] Occasionally, contemporaries, including the chancellor, referred to these as "concentration camps."[19] At the turn of the century that term meant internment camp, primarily for large numbers of civilians. Such camps, and also the name "[re]concentration camp," had first appeared in Cuba in 1896, when the Spanish military governor Valeriano Weyler y Nicolau had attempted to suppress the revolt there by imprisoning the civilian population and thus separating it from the guerillas who hid in its midst. Four years later, British military leaders Generals Frederick Sleigh Lord Roberts and Hubert Horatio Kitchener did the same thing in the Transvaal, during the Boer War. In short, concentration camps were a colonial, military phenomenon. Because "concentration camp" has since come to have a rather different meaning, I will use the term "collection camp" to refer to the first holding areas for African prisoners in SWA.

15. Bülow to Trotha, tel., Berlin, 21 Jan. 1905, ibid., pp. 124–26.

16. Zeller, " 'Wie Vieh,' " here 238n37. On the origin of the idea of tin IDs in 1900: Zimmerer, *Deutsche Herrschaft*, 73n56.

17. Trotha to General Staff, tel. Nr. 104, Khub, 10 Apr. 1905, BA-Berlin, R 1001, Nr. 2118, pp. 61–64; Maj. Maercker, appendix to report Nr. 26176, Windhuk, 8 Dec. 1905, BA-Berlin, R 151 F/D.IV.L.3., vol. 1, pp. 187–88.

18. The Nama also retreated into the desert, the Kalahari, in which one could survive, but at a high physical cost. For a description of the poor condition of surrendering Nama, see Hermann Alverdes, *Mein Tagebuch aus Südwest; Erinnerungen aus dem Feldzuge gegen die Hottentotten* (Oldenburg, 1906), 172.

19. Bülow to Trotha, tel., Berlin, 11 Dec. 1904, BA-Berlin, R 1001, Nr. 2089, p. 54; Bülow to Trotha, tel., Berlin, 21 Jan. 1905, ibid., Nr. 2089, pp. 124–26; Lindequist to Col. Dept., tel. Nr. 4, Windhuk, 4 Jan. 1906, ibid., Nr. 2118, p. 201.

Starving Herero returning from the desert where they had been driven by the Germans. Two women are unable to stand. Union of South Africa, *Report on the Natives of South West Africa and Their Treatment by Germany* (London: HMSO, 1918), plate 3.

From the collection camps, prisoners were very quickly shipped by train or wagon to other camps: to labor camps along the Otavi railroad, to prison camps in Windhuk, Swakopmund, and Lüderitzbucht, and sometimes from there still further to private companies or farms, which often ran camps of their own.[20] The ostensible reason was the labor shortage that had held SWA in its grip since even before the uprisings.[21] Imprisoned Herero, working without pay, were supposed to fill this gap. The military had first call on prisoner labor. By the end of March 1905, it had filled its needs and had begun to redirect prisoner labor into the private sector. In the absence of preexisting rules regulating such an enterprise, the occupation command and the government reached an agreement stipulating the following: families with young children should not be split apart, if possible; prisoners should remain locked up at night; the private "employer" was responsible for food, clothing, and shelter, but was admonished "to observe the right proportion: the people must receive adequate food and be protected from the cold with blankets, but one should never forget that these people are prisoners and are to be maintained as such"; prisoners were not to be paid for their work; and, finally, "employers" were to pay a tax of

20. Zeller, " 'Wie Vieh,' " 227; Gewald, *Towards Redemption*, 221–22; Zimmerer, *Deutsche Herrschaft*, 45.
21. Zimmerer, *Deutsche Herrschaft*, ch. 5.

10 marks per month per prisoner to the district office (*Bezirksamt*).[22] The military occupation command and the civil government split these proceeds, using them to finance the maintenance of their prisoners.[23] These rules would not have been necessary had the civil and military authorities intended for the prisoners to die.[24] The authorities nevertheless insisted that prisoner status required rigid limits to good treatment. Punishment required harshness; if death resulted, that was acceptable. Hard-liners such as Trotha and Deputy Governor Tecklenburg, who set the parameters of policy, though they did not closely supervise actual administration, thought death appropriate punishment.[25] The invention of a "tax" to help pay for prisoners indicates the reluctance to divert money or matériel from the Schutztruppe to its prisoners, whose cost should have been entirely covered by government subsidy. The low priority that prisoners received in an institution focused on combat, the definition of the enemy as the entire population, together with the stubborn requirement to punish Africans who had dared resist German authority, created standards of treatment below the subsistence level.

After only two months, the impact of the imprisonment policy was already obvious. The missionary Heinrich Vedder visited the Swakopmund prison camp in late February–early March 1905, only a month after it had received its first large shipment of prisoners.[26] He reported its catastrophic conditions to his superiors.[27] Most of the surrendering Herero, he wrote, were being sent to Swakopmund, and after far too short a recovery time in the collection camps. They arrived "completely impoverished, naked, starved, weakened, and mostly ill." Their treatment in Swakopmund then did the rest, because unlike Hereroland, Swakopmund (and Lüderitzbucht, the other main prison camp) lay on the coast. From April to October (winter in the south of Africa) it was exposed to a cold, damp, ocean wind. Most of the Herero lived in huts "that consist only of stakes over which canvas cloth is thrown as a wall and roof, which provides no real protection during the night. On the ground are nailed boards taken from boxes. Thirty to forty Herero sleep in these huts each night." They received no warm clothes. The government provided eighty blankets for twelve hundred to fifteen hundred prisoners. Food was "in no sense adequate. The only thing the people receive is rice, which even the commandant [Major Bauer] admits is in insufficient quantity." Because they lacked pots, the prisoners could not cook the rice enough to make it digestible. "[The commandant] would like some flour and sent in a request." "If an ox or horse dies, the people get some meat. A couple of days ago they received as an extra ration some ham that had been meant for the troops. As Major Bauer exclaimed, 'This [ham] really stinks!' The results were inevitable. Along with

22. Maj. Dame, memorandum attached to Nr. 7957, Windhuk, 29 Mar. 1905, BA-Berlin, R 151 F/D.IV.L.3., vol. 1, p. 45.

23. Maercker to Lindequist, Nr. 9070, Windhuk, 10 May 1906, BA-Berlin, R 151 F/D.IV.L.3., vol. 2, pp. 190–92.

24. Zeller vacillates between attributing to the authorities intention or mere acceptance: "'Wie Vieh,'" 242.

25. See below for their reaction to the deaths of the Witbois in captivity.

26. Dr. Fuchs, report Nr. 1035, Swakopmund, 29 May 1905, BA-Berlin, R 151 F/D.IV.L.3., vol. 1, pp. 58–59.

27. Vedder to mission inspector, Swakopmund, 3 Mar. 1905, VEM-Wuppertal, Vedder papers, B/c II 87, pp. 50–57.

76 the weak and those with lung diseases, now many suffer from dysentery." Under these circumstances it is hard to imagine how the prisoners could work, but each day they were taken out of the camp, leaving the sick behind with no medical or nursing care, and in the evening they returned. Their treatment by the guards was uniformly "harsh." "I have never seen an overseer without a *sambok* [a club], whip, or truncheon."

Vedder described Major Bauer as "a serious and God-fearing man," whose efforts to improve the situation were blocked by the governor (Trotha).[28] Bauer's request for warm clothing had gone unanswered. Vedder expected the same regarding the flour, since Bauer had told him "that the administration [*Behörde*] have told the rear to 'send the weak and sick back into the bush,'" or, less drastically, "'to accept the help of the missionaries in medical-sanitary matters.'" In fact, the military tried to unload all prisoners unable to work onto the missionaries, but Trotha, suspicious to the end, insisted that a doctor make sure there were no malingerers. And while Trotha accepted the possible substitution of flour for rice, he adamantly refused to allocate more money "for the *better* provisioning of prisoners."[29]

Under these circumstances, the mission, whose own resources were scant, saw itself blocked by the same intransigence that faced Major Bauer. Vedder's superior, Haussleiter, therefore turned to Berlin. After meeting with Haussleiter at the beginning of May, Colonial Director Stübel ordered Deputy Governor Tecklenburg to look into the matter.[30] Tecklenburg warned District Administrator Dr. Fuchs of Swakopmund to do so "discreetly and without saying why."[31] A week later Tecklenburg received the devastating results. Dr. Fuchs minced no words: "In agreement with the government doctor, I regard the cause [of the high mortality rate among native prisoners in Swakopmund] as inadequate accommodation, clothing, and food, in combination with the raw, unaccustomed climate and the weakened condition of the prisoners brought here." The major causes of death were pneumonia and scurvy. Stopping these deaths was relatively simple. Dr. Fuchs recommended "accommodation in dry, ventilated but wind-fast rooms, warm clothing (flannel shirts, pants, blankets, shoes) and some variation in the diet (rice, flour, if possible frequently meat, onions, or oil), and medical care." He also asked that the collection camps keep debilitated or sick Herero, sending only strong and healthy people to Swakopmund. The most damning aspect of the report was the figures. Whereas the annual death rate among Africans incarcerated in the city jail for 1903 and 1904 was 1.7 percent, the prisoner camp had in just the last two weeks of May compiled a death rate of 10 percent. Annually, that was enough to wipe out the entire camp population two and a half times over. Because mortality among Herero working and living for private persons was

28. Vedder to inspector, Swakopmund, 1 Mar. 1905, ibid., pp. 48–49. After Leutwein's departure, Trotha exercised power as interim governor: Bley, *South-West Africa*, 159; Lettow-Vorbeck, diary entry of 13 Nov. 1904, BA-MA Freiburg, Nl. Lettow-Vorbeck, Nr. 34.

29. Trotha marginalium to First Lieutenant Adjutant Starck to commando of the Schutztruppe, Okahandja, 11 Mar. 1905, BA-Berlin, R 151 F/D.IV.L.3., vol. 1, pp. 39–40, emphasis in original.

30. Stübel to Tecklenburg, tel. Nr. 52, Berlin, 18 May 1905, ibid., p. 56.

31. Tecklenburg to dist. admin. Swakopmund, Windhuk, 21 May 1905, ibid., p. 57.

lower, Dr. Fuchs recommended that more prisoners be shifted from the military to the private sector.[32]

Despite these figures, both Deputy Governor Tecklenburg and Rear Commander Colonel v. Dame rejected the missionaries' advice, which Stübel had forwarded, to remove sickly Herero prisoners to the interior to regain their health "and avoid decimation."[33] Tecklenburg hoped the prisoners would acclimate themselves to Swakopmund with the help of warmer rooms.[34] Dame was more candid. So many workers were needed to unload ships at Swakopmund and Lüderitzbucht that "no substitute could be found for them," he wrote.[35] Both men agreed that "especially weak" prisoners should be sent to neither place, but they placed solving the labor shortage above the prisoners' lives. This seemingly straightforward, materialist motive foundered in illogic, however, for dying Africans provided at best only brief, poor-quality labor. At worst, they provided none at all. Just before the debate about Swakopmund erupted, the district administrator in Windhuk, where conditions were better, reported to Tecklenburg that he was unable to provide any workers at all for the construction office, "because the majority of prisoners of war are ill."[36] We see here one of the abiding patterns of militarily organized forced labor, not just in the colonies but also later in World War I: force constantly overwhelmed the ostensible economic goal.

Although better treatment would have served the economic interests of the occupation and civil authorities, improvements were made only stingily and haphazardly. Vedder's interventions in March, for example, brought the following results: "While the occupation command [Dame] distributed old uniforms to them, an instruction from the high command [Trotha] took them away again and replaced them with rough sacks that, without underwear, worn right next to the skin, give no warmth." Trotha had okayed alternating flour with rice, and "for a short time flour was actually available but then unfortunately for some unknown reason was quickly removed again."[37] In the month after Stübel's intervention, it appears that some efforts were made to make the dwellings more wind-resistant, and the occupation command built a hospital of corrugated tin, but still at the end of June, Dame could report only that "the question of better nutrition for the prisoners is being considered."[38] The wheels of bureaucracy ground slowly, but that is not

32. Dr. Fuchs, report Nr. 1035, Swakopmund, 29 May 1905, BA-Berlin, R 151 F/D.IV.L.3., vol. 1, pp. 78–79. Figures are unreliable for prisoners in private hands, but Dist. Admin. Fuchs estimated that about three hundred Herero were with private people. In the same two-week period where the military camp had a 10% death rate, the private figure was 4.6%, which still would have more than wiped out the prisoner laborers over the year. Ibid. and Dist. Admin. Fuchs to Tecklenburg, Nr. 686, Swakopmund, 27 Apr. 1905, BA-Berlin, R 151 F/D.IV.L.3., vol. 1, p. 73.

33. Stübel to Tecklenburg, tel. Nr. 52, Berlin, 18 May 1905, BA-Berlin, R 151 F/D.IV.L.3., vol. 1, p. 56.

34. Tecklenburg memorandum, Nr. 7689/05, 7 June 1905, ibid., p. 57.

35. Dame to Tecklenburg, Nr. 13131, Windhuk, 27 June 1905, ibid., pp. 60–61.

36. Dist. Admin. Capt. Puder to Tecklenburg, Windhuk, 20 Apr. 1905, ibid., p. 52.

37. Vedder to district administration in Swakopmund, 27 May 1905, VEM-Wuppertal, Vedder papers, B/c II 87, pp. 60–63.

38. Dwellings: two doctors reporting to the occupation command described the housing in June as acceptable: Dr. Lowade to occupation command, Nr. 1029, Swakopmund, 15 June 1905, BA-Berlin, R 151 F/D.IV.L.3.,

78 the whole explanation—it took the district office just two days to act on the mission's suggestion that alcohol be forbidden to African prisoners.[39]

Although conditions in the Swakopmund prison camp were worse than in camps in Windhuk, Karibib, and Okahandja, they were better than those in Lüderitzbucht. There, prisoners were shut up on a rocky island (Shark Island) in the middle of the bay, even more exposed to damp, cold winds. "The native [prisoners in Swakopmund] are so afraid of Lüderitzbucht," Vedder reported, "that when recently 150 men were due to be transferred there, 60 of them escaped despite guards and fences. . . . Another time [when such a transfer was to occur] a man slit his own throat with a pocket knife."[40] Missionary Kuhlmann's superiors sent him to check on Shark Island at the end of July 1905. He discovered the same mixture of neglect, malice, and uneven attempts at amelioration that reigned in Swakopmund.[41] "Housing" consisted of pieces of wood leaned up against the rocks, covered by sacks. Or it consisted of nothing at all; some prisoners slept completely in the open, others, between clefts in the rocks. "The result was a terrible dying-off; in the beginning, as the commandant's manager, First Lieutenant Wagenführer told me, each week twenty-five, twenty, or fifteen prisoners died." Kuhlmann hastened to add, however, "that people here are not being starved; they receive more meat than in other camps, and rice is also plentiful." He complained, however, of lack of flour. Worse, warm clothing was unavailable. Death rates had fallen, but still, in the week of Kuhlmann's visit, eleven inmates died. Sanitation was disastrous. Many prisoners suffered from diarrhea, and without medical or nursing care as their strength left them, they lay in their own excrement.

Shark Island also suffered from inadequate leadership and vicious caprice. The commandant led an absentee administration. Apparently Wagenführer never set foot on the island himself but delegated complete authority to a brutal overseer named Benkesser. One day during Kuhlmann's visit, Benkesser, a former police sergeant, called the prisoners to work detail. "A women so weak from illness that she could not stand, crawled to some prisoners to beg for water. The overseer fired five shots at her; two shots hit her, one in the thigh, the other smashing her forearm. This inhuman creature left her there. In the night she died. Benkesser told another soldier of his deed." Yet word apparently never reached the camp manager, Wagenführer. When Kuhlmann reported the incident to him, he was surprised and incensed, and told Kuhlmann he would investigate. Unlike at other camps, charitable donations (for example, ten blankets that Kuhlmann wished to distribute to the prisoners) were not permitted at Shark Island; instead, all "requests" had to go through the overseer. Benkesser's may have been an isolated atrocity, but it was lax

vol. 1, p. 64; Dr. Plappe (Plagge?), Nr. 14376/I, Windhuk, 26 June 1905, ibid., p. 65; Chefarzt Dr. Berger, "Report," Swakopmund, 8 June 1905, ibid., p. 65. Hospital: Vedder to district administration in Swakopmund, 27 May 1905, VEM-Wuppertal, Vedder papers, B/c II 87, pp. 60–63. Dame: Dame to Tecklenburg, Nr. 13131, Windhuk, 27 June 1905, BA-Berlin, R 151 F/D.IV.L.3., vol. 1, p. 61.

39. Note of 29 May 1905 appended to Vedder to district administration in Swakopmund, 27 May 1905, VEM-Wuppertal, Vedder papers, B/c II 87, p. 63.

40. Vedder to inspector, Swakopmund, 26 May 1905, ibid., p. 67.

41. August Kuhlmann, "Report on a trip to Lüderitzbucht," 10 Aug. 1905, VEM-Wuppertal, Kuhlmann papers, B/c II 72.

administration that permitted the ever-present potential for brutality to become real. Laxity (or administrative incompetence) was the systemic result of making prisoners a low priority.

Deportation was another method of handling prisoners of war. It had many advantages: no guards needed to be detached from the fighting forces, escape was impossible, and "problem natives" disappeared from the colony entirely. Deportation was a "final solution." But it was also the first solution to the prisoner problem that occurred to Governor Leutwein. Already in January 1904, Herero living in Swakopmund or who had been captured along the railroad lines were interned in the first prisoner-of-war "camp," the ship *Eduard Bohlen* belonging to the Woermann Line. It sailed for Cape Town on 20 January, just six days after the revolt began, carrying 282 Herero, who thereafter worked as miners in South Africa.[42] Colonial administrators, who thought in terms of populations and their instrumentalization, easily arrived at deportation as a solution to security problems.

Deportation was the fate of a unit of ninety or so Witbooi soldiers who had fought with the Schutztruppe but were disarmed and interned when news of the Witbooi uprising reached the troops in early October 1904. It appears to have been Governor Leutwein, not Trotha, who suggested deportation: "The natives would understand it better if we shot the 80 [sic] Witboois, than if we fed them at state's expense. Using them as workers is out of the question because of danger of escape."[43] There was widespread agreement that deportation was the best way to maintain security.[44] Thereupon, the Witboois, whose numbers had swelled to 118,[45] were sent to another German colony, Togo.

For the first month, the Witboois were healthy. But as soon as a group was sent to work in the interior, they acquired malaria, and then, weakened, dysentery and lung diseases.[46] By 15 May, sixteen had died, and then in just a week, a contagious illness claimed another thirty-six.[47] By mid-July the dead had reached sixty-three; only eleven prisoners were healthy.[48] The climate, unaccustomed pathogens, and strange food made Togo deadly. Missionaries checking on the Witboois since December did not report ill-treatment.[49] But the mission concluded that the Witboois had to be repatriated if they were to survive.[50] Meanwhile, the Togo administration improved rations further (the Witboois had already been receiving more meat than was usually allotted to Africans), providing meat and fish soup on alternate days, "rice, Zwieback, tea, coffee, sugar, tobacco (and oc-

42. Zeller, " 'Wie Vieh,' " 227.

43. Leutwein, tel. Nr. 210, Windhuk, 21 Oct. 1904, BA-Berlin, R 1001, Nr. 2090, p. 5.

44. Rohrbach, *Aus Südwestafrikas schweren Tagen*, 178; Viktor Franke, diary entry, 25 Oct. 1904, BA-Koblenz, Nl. Franke, Nr. 3, p. 118; *Deutsch-Südwestafrikanische Zeitung* 43 (26 Oct. 1904), 2. See also Zimmerer's account, *Deutsche Herrschaft*, 49–55.

45. Not all of the deportees were necessarily soldiers or Witboois but Nama of other clans: Rohrbach, *Aus Südwestafrikas schweren Tagen*, 178–79.

46. Dr. Krueger, Report, Lome, 24 June 1905, BA-Berlin, R 1001, Nr. 2090, pp. 37–38.

47. Dep. Gov. Schlettwein to Col. Dept., Lome, 26 June 1905, ibid., p. 36.

48. Station administrator Pfeil to Col. Dept., tel., Lome, 15 July 1905, ibid., p. 28.

49. August Schreiber to Spiecker, Bremen, 20 Dec. 1904, VEM-Wuppertal, papers relating to Witboois, C/i 17; excerpt from a letter from missionary Osswald, Lome, 30 Mar. 1905, ibid.

50. Schreiber to Haussleiter, Bremen, 22 Apr. 1905, VEM-Wuppertal, papers relating to care (*Fürsorge*), C/o 5, p. 86.

Lt. Gen. Lothar von Trotha and Witbooi troops at Okahandja, SWA, June or July 1904. Courtesy of Stadt- und Universitätsbibliothek, Afrikaabteilung, Frankfurt am Main, Nr. 010-2112-04.

casionally corned beef)."[51] It gave quinine prophylaxis against malaria, but either in insufficient quantities or too late to help. But it despaired of providing guards sufficient to force the Witboois to achieve German standards of cleanliness.[52]

As none of these measures seemed to work, the governor of Togo, supported by the doctors, at the end of June 1905 demanded that the surviving Witboois be sent back to their homeland.[53] The Colonial Department relayed this request to Deputy Governor Tecklenburg and General Trotha, who, acting independently, but with a united vehemence, rejected it. Tecklenburg remarked that the "high mortality was not surprising; it must be regarded as retaliation for the uprising."[54] A Colonial Department official underlined "retaliation" in pencil and put a question mark beside it. Meanwhile, Trotha played the patriotic-security card. He claimed it was impossible to guard the Witboois without chains. "Every German shot to death by one of these Witboois shall be the responsibility of the person who orders them repatriated. I suggest you send them to Kilimanjaro in East [Africa]."[55]

51. Dr. Krueger, Report, Lome, 24 June 1905, BA-Berlin, R 1001, Nr. 2090, pp. 37–38.
52. Ibid.
53. Dep. Gov. Schlettwein to Col. Dept., Lome, 26 June 1905, BA-Berlin, R 1001, Nr. 2090, p. 36.
54. Tecklenburg to Col. Dept., tel. Nr. 65, Windhuk, 4 July 1905, ibid., p. 22.
55. Trotha to Col. Dept., tel., Keetmannshoop, 24 July 1905, ibid., p. 34.

The Colonial Department bowed to this stiff resistance and transferred the surviving Witboois to the German Cameroons, instead, whose governor was under the impression they could work as cattle herds. When he laid eyes on them, he was quickly disabused. "Their current condition makes a pitiable impression," he wrote.[56] Following the instructions of government doctor Krueger for a plentiful and varied diet, and vigorous quinine administration, the Witboois' further slide into extinction was halted.[57] But the Witboois were never physically capable of more than light work, and Governor Jesco von Puttkamer pressed from the beginning and continuously thereafter for the return of these "useless eaters" to SWA.[58] As long as the Colonial Department deferred to Trotha and Tecklenburg, however, the Witboois stayed where they were.

The only other possibility for African prisoners was to fall under the control of private persons or companies. How many prisoners ended up on farms or in individual households is unknown.[59] Contemporaries all assumed these prisoners received comparatively the best treatment, though an individual's fate depended entirely on the personality of the "employer."[60] The largest group of prisoners working for private persons were those building the railroad for the Otavi Company. They numbered over a thousand at any one time. This mass project operated out of Karibib, and perhaps because of its size, the heavy labor, and the national-security interest involved, conditions for Africans resembled those in the regular prison camps. There was little provision for housing, though the better climate in the interior made this omission less fatal than it was elsewhere. The diet was similarly inadequate, which led to noticeable scurvy by mid-August 1905.[61] By October, scurvy was rampant; three hundred persons were ill.[62] However, the Otavi Company, unlike the military, was more interested in work than in punishment. It employed a good doctor; it made at least partially successful efforts to remedy the diet; missionaries reported less brutality in handling prisoners; and the company requested permission to pay a token wage to the prisoners in order to encourage better work.[63] The annual death rate for 1905 was high, 11.6 percent, but nevertheless a third less than what the next "healthiest" military prisoner camp managed to achieve.[64]

56. Puttkamer to Col. Dept., Nr. 14133, Buea, 23 Sept. 1905, ibid., pp. 45–46.

57. Apparently, Dr. Krueger's prescription was forwarded from Togo. Public health doctor Waldow to Puttkamer, Victoria, 16 Nov. 1905, ibid., p. 55.

58. Puttkamer to Tecklenburg, Nr. 15020, Buea, 7 Oct. 1905, BA-Berlin, R 151 F/D.IV.M.2., vol. 7, p. 48.

59. A document from 8 Feb. 1906 lists 3,251 prisoners as having been distributed to private persons or firms by that date, 1,556 of them to either the Otavi railroad or the Lüderitzbucht railroad. Then 1,695 must have gone to individuals or much smaller operations. "Nachweisung über an Private abgegebene Kriegsgefangene nach dem Stande vom 1 February 06," signed Maj. Maercker, Nr. I J. 3191, Windhuk, 8 Feb. 1906, BA-Berlin, R 151 F/D.IV.L.3., vol. 2, p. 1.

60. Krüger, *Kriegsbewältigung*, 133–34.

61. August Kuhlmann, "First report on my work in Karibib with the prisoners of war on the Otavi railroad," Karibib, 14 Aug. 1905, VEM-Wuppertal, Kuhlmann papers, B/c II 72, pp. 42–43.

62. Dannert to Spiecker, Karibib, 8 Oct. 1905, VEM-Wuppertal, Dannert papers, B/c II 43, pp. 106–9.

63. Doctor: ibid. Diet: August Kuhlmann, "Second report on the work on the Otavi railroad," Omburo, 2 Jan. 1906, VEM-Wuppertal, Kuhlmann papers, B/c II 72. Less brutality: Kuhlmann, "First report," ibid., pp. 42–43. Wages: Tecklenburg to Occupation Command, Windhuk, 5 Sept. 1905, BA-Berlin, R 151 F/D.IV.L.3., vol. 1, p. 105.

64. "Sterblichkeit in den Kriegsgefangenenlagern," Nr. KA II. 1181, copy of undated report compiled by the Schutztruppe Command, read in Col. Dept. 24 Mar. 1908, BA-Berlin, R 1001, Nr. 2040, pp. 161–62. The other an-

82   As long as Trotha was commander and acting governor, there was no hope for real improvement in the military prison camps. In mid-October 1905, just a month before he was relieved of command, the suggestion was made to give the prisoner workers on the Otavi railroad a token payment to encourage productivity. Trotha's response expressed his unalterable philosophy: "The Herero are still to be regarded as prisoners, and [therefore] no privileges may be granted for the time being."[65]

Imprisonment under the New Administration

When Friedrich v. Lindequist assumed office as governor in late November 1905, he immediately set about canceling the policies of Trotha's military dictatorship. On 25 November he met with the missionaries to arrange their mediation in bringing the rest of the Herero in from the field. He explained that "the prisoner-of-war status in the earlier sense will end" and would be replaced by a system of low-wage labor. The new collection camps run by the missionaries would play a larger role than before: "There the surrendering Herero will remain for a time to regain their strength and [only] later will be sent to workplaces."[66] On 1 December 1905 Lindequist issued a proclamation that African messengers distributed among the Herero. It assured them that Lieutenant General Trotha had returned to Germany: "His departure means that the war should now end." Lindequist urged all remaining Herero to turn themselves in to the two collection camps at Omburo and Ojtihaenena. He assured them that no soldiers were present there. All military patrols and sweeps were ended for the time being. He promised the Herero adequate food. "I have taken every precaution that you will be justly treated," he told them.[67] To the German troops he ordered "military operations in Hereroland and the destruction of Herero-*Werften* by patrols to be suspended until further notice."[68] At home, Chancellor Bülow told the Reichstag (5 December 1905) that the Schutztruppe had succeeded "in completely breaking the resistance of the Herero," and that that part of the war was virtually over.[69]

Given Lindequist's acceptance of negotiations (and thus of a nonmilitary conclusion to the war), and his strong interest in reviving the colony's economy (and thus in preserving the Herero as a workforce), one would have expected the high death rates in the prison camps to fall. But they did not. In Windhuk and on Shark Island, they reached

---

nual average death rates (for the period Oct. 1904 to Mar. 1907) were as follows: Okahandja, 37.2%; Windhuk, 50.4%; Swakopmund, 74%; Shark Island in Lüderitzbucht, 121.2% for Nama, 30% for Herero. Traugott Tjienda, headman of the Herero at Tsumeb and foreman of a large group of prisoners at the Otavi lines for two years, testified years later to a death rate of 28% (148 dead of 528 laborers) in his unit. Union of South Africa, *Report on the Natives*, 101.

65. Citing Trotha, Dame to Tecklenburg, No. 19929, Windhuk, 12 Oct. 1905, BA-Berlin, R 151 F/D.IV.L.3., vol. 1, p. 106.

66. August Kuhlmann, memorandum of 3 Jan. 1906, Omburo, VEM-Wuppertal, Kuhlmann papers, B/c II 72, p. 6.

67. Lindequist Proclamation of 1 Dec. 1905, BA-Berlin, R 1001, Nr. 2119, p. 14; reprinted in Union of South Africa, *Report on the Natives*, 102–3.

68. Lindequist to Col. Dept., tel. Nr. 142, Windhuk, 30 Nov. 1905, BA-Berlin, R 1001, Nr. 2118, p. 185.

69. Bülow, *Sten. Ber.*, 6th legis. per., 2nd session, 8th meeting, 9 Dec. 1905, vol. 214, p. 191.

their pinnacle under Lindequist's administration.[70] Yet, Lindequist's relatively enlightened attitude was genuine. He approved the Otavi Company's request to pay prisoner laborers a small wage, for example.[71] And when missionaries complained that work requirements made church attendance impossible for prisoners, Lindequist intervened on their behalf.[72] Lindequist's attitude encouraged or permitted ameliorative policies by the occupation command that Trotha had blocked. The order calling for more Herero prisoners to be sent to Swakopmund in December 1905, for example, stipulated that families were not to be broken up, that only healthy prisoners be sent, and that prisoners "be carefully provided with clothing and blankets suitable to the raw climate; further, they are to take with them two days' rations (generously measured)."[73] This was a different atmosphere from the Trotha era. Why did it not bring greater benefit?

Part of the reason lies in the extreme debility of the surrendering Herero, six thousand more of whom had surrendered between December 1905 and the end of April 1906.[74] Although some of the first to arrive were in fair shape, the rest "were so skinny and weak that they could not immediately be used for work. They generally stay several weeks in the [collection] camp, before being sent on."[75] Even those who appeared to be well were highly susceptible to illness. Kuhlmann, the most understanding and empathetic of the missionaries, who ran the camp at Omburo, reported that "as soon as they [the healthy ones] are put on strange food, they become sick."[76] And strange food was all the military and missionaries had to offer. The condition of the Herero, therefore, required generous, long-term, patient, and attentive treatment. This they did not receive.

But the Herero people's poor health, which was of course a result of German military policy, is an inadequate explanation of the tremendous mortality rates. For the Nama prisoners, who were usually in better shape on their arrival in the prison camps, died in even greater proportion than the Herero. And their deaths occurred primarily under the Lindequist administration.

Several factors worked against the positive effects one might have expected from Lindequist's interest in preserving African prisoners as a workforce. One was the very interest in work itself; the labor shortage (a result of military policy) and the purely instrumental view of Africans moved Lindequist to comb the collection camps for every potentially able "worker," even though he knew that only the disabled remained in the camps.[77] Lindequist came under very strong pressure from the military authorities to provide labor

70. "Sterblichkeit in den Kriegsgefangenenlagern in SWA," Nr. KA II. 1181, BA-Berlin, R 1001, Nr. 2140, pp. 161–62.

71. Lindequist to Dame, Windhuk, 5 Dec. 1905, BA-Berlin, R 151 F/D.IV.L.3., vol. 1, p. 116.

72. Vedder to inspector, Swakopmund, 29 Nov. 1906, VEM-Wuppertal, Vedder papers, B/c II 87, 97.

73. Maercker to Occupation Command, Windhuk, 14 Dec. 1905, BA-Berlin, R 151 F/D.IV.L.3., vol. 1, p. 121.

74. Lindequist to Col. Dept., Nr. 458, Windhuk, 17 Apr. 1906, BA-Berlin, R 1001, Nr. 2119, pp. 42–43.

75. Ibid.; cf. Lindequist to Col. Dept., Nr. 137, Windhuk, 8 Feb. 1906, BA-Berlin, R 1001, Nr. 2119, pp. 12–13.

76. August Kuhlmann, "Reports on the mediation work," Omburo, 23 Apr. 1906, VEM-Wuppertal, Kuhlmann papers, B/c II 72, pp. 18–20.

77. Lindequist to Kuhlmann, Windhuk, 13 Mar. 1906, VEM-Wuppertal, Kuhlmann papers, B/c II 72; Kuhlmann to Lindequist, Omburo, 19 Mar. 1906, ibid., and in BA-Berlin, R 151 F/D.IV.L.3., vol. 1, p. 202; and, again, Lindequist to Kuhlmann, Nr. 2174, draft, Windhuk, 17 Apr. 1906, ibid., p. 215.

84 for railroad building. Unless the missionaries complained and Lindequist intervened against the military (which on at least one occasion he did), Herero continued to be shipped out of the collection camps too soon, and with inadequate clothing or blankets.[78] As governor, Lindequist was also beholden to the settlers, who had so completely undermined Leutwein's policies before him. It was to calm their nervousness at the number of Herero and the relative "freedom" they enjoyed at the collection camp in Omburo that Lindequist in August 1906 closed first that camp, and then the camp at Otjinaenena, and in September resumed armed military sweeps.[79] Typically, Governor Lindequist's orders to close the Omburo camp were interpreted by the local lieutenant, Hellmich, to mean close it by force, which he did in a surprise morning raid, much to the governor's disgust.[80]

If Lindequist was ground down by the combined pressure of the military and the settlers, the civilian government's commitment to "punishment" was another factor making it hard for Lindequist to break cleanly from the military and settler viewpoints. Lindequist's proclamation, he assured the chancellor, contained the obligatory phrase, "the strictest punishment of criminals and ringleaders will not be touched by [this order]."[81] This was not merely a formal sine qua non for "negotiations," slipped in to satisfy the chief of the General Staff, the Kaiser, or public opinion. Lindequist truly believed that punishment and penitence were the cornerstones of wise policy. When he first arrived back in SWA as governor, Lindequist wanted to meet with some imprisoned Herero, whom the missionaries duly cleaned up and brought before him. The governor told them that they would go free once the war was over and the murderers had been punished. He ended their meeting with a question and answer ceremony: "Do you admit that you began the war without cause and are yourselves responsible for your own suffering?" the governor asked them. "Yes, we know it," they answered.[82] This extraordinary colloquy was meant to demonstrate the total sway of German authority; it was a civilian version of complete military victory. The governor's conception of guilt, punishment, and responsibility undermined his policy of preservation for work.

The main cause of prisoner deaths, however, was the continued operation of military administration and its principles. The management of the military prison camps was characterized by a fatal combination of neglect, red tape, ignorance of the needs of civilians (mothers, children, the aged, and the severely ill), and ignorance and contempt for Africans' accustomed lifestyles. More than anything else the rigid maintenance of military priorities determined prison policy. The two most imperative commandments were "the needs of the Schutztruppe come before those of prisoners" and "the prisoners' status as

78. Wilhelm Eich to Lindequist, Okahandja, 9 Mar. 1906, BA-Berlin, R 151 F/D.IV.L.3., vol. 1, p. 199; Lindequist to Eich, Nr. 4253, Windhuk, 16 Mar. 1906, ibid., p. 200.

79. Lindequist to Eich, Windhuk, 22 July 1906, BA-Berlin, R 151 F/D.IV.L.3., vol. 2, p. 160; Eich to Spiecker, Okahandja, 22 July 1906, VEM-Wuppertal, Eich papers, B/c II 36, p. 76; Lindequist to Col. Dept., Nr. 1087, Windhuk, 23 Aug. 1906, BA-Berlin, R 1001, Nr. 2119, pp. 73–74.

80. Lindequist to Col. Dept., Nr. 1087, Windhuk, 23 Aug. 1906, BA-Berlin, R 1001, Nr. 2119, pp. 73–74. See Drechsler, "Let Us Die Fighting," 208–9.

81. Lindequist to Col. Dept., tel. Nr. 142, Windhuk, 30 Aug. 1905, BA-Berlin, R 1001, Nr. 2118, p. 185.

82. Vedder to Inspector Spiecker, Swakopmund, 27 Nov. 1905, VEM-Wuppertal, Vedder papers, B/c II 87, pp. 30–32.

prisoners must always be visible and palpable." Time and again well-meant efforts to improve the prisoners' health ran up against these limits.

Once Trotha was gone, the occupation command was much more willing to agree to improvements. On 24 January 1906, Major Mühlenfels, commander of the rear, issued new regulations "to stem the continuing illnesses of native prisoners of war."[83] All prisoners were to receive an additional portion of dried vegetables and more fat. The twice-weekly portion of meat was to be augmented by tinned beef. "Where supplies exist, *as long as the threat of scurvy persists,* 200 g of legumes can be substituted for the rice, corn, or flour portion." Those with scurvy could receive in addition preserved fruit and chocolate. "The garrison doctor will decide how much of these semiluxury foods [*Genussmittel*] are to be provided, but the limit is 30 g per day." These regulations "are only to be fulfilled if the provisioning of the troops depending on the same warehouse is absolutely secure. Therefore, allotment is left to the dutiful judgment of the warehouse manager." This order betrays the persistent anxiety that prisoners could take food from the mouths of the Schutztruppler, and that prisoners might be too well treated.

The Death of the Nama

The greatest scandal of military occupation administration was the annihilation of the Nama in the prison camps. The death of the Nama began as deportation. Governor Lindequist had intended to deport the Nama clans to the German colonies of Samoa and Adamaua after the war was over.[84] Colonial wisdom held the Nama to be useless as workers, while the military judged them to be far more dangerous fighters than the Herero.[85] Although Lindequist had permitted the surviving Witbooi soldiers (who were Nama) to return from the Cameroons, his ultimate solution was to remove all Nama permanently.[86] This project was sped up by the return to SWA of Colonel v. Deimling, who replaced Colonel v. Dame as the permanent commander of the Schutztruppe. The recent escape from prison of some Witboois encouraged Lindequist to assent to Deimling's demand that all Nama prisoners immediately be deported as security risks.[87] This solution, which Lindequist explicitly said applied to the entire Nama peoples, was seriously considered at a Colonial Department conference in mid-July but ultimately rejected by the director, Prince Ernst zu Hohenlohe-Langenburg.[88] He did approve deporting clan leaders; but

83. Mühlenfels to governor, Nr. IVa. 17486, Windhuk, 24 Jan. 1906, BA-Berlin, R 151 F/D.IV.L.3., vol. 1, p. 189.

84. Lindequist to Col. Dept., tel., Windhuk, 10 July 1906, BA-Berlin, R 1001, Nr. 2090, p. 62.

85. *Deutsch-Südwestafrikanische Zeitung* 50 (14 Dec. 1904), 2; Rohrbach, *Deutsche Kolonialwirtschaft,* 349; Deimling, *Südwestafrika,* 14–16, 35, 46; Estorff, "Kriegserlebnisse," 96; General Staff, *Kämpfe der deutschen Truppen,* 2:16–17.

86. Dame to Lindequist, tel., Keetmanshoop, 6 Feb. 1906, BA-Berlin, R 151 F/D.IV.M.2, vol. 8, p. 55; Lindequist to Col. Dept., Nr. 61, Windhuk, 11 Feb. 1906, BA-Berlin, R 1001, Nr. 2090, p. 58.

87. Lindequist to Col. Dept., tel., Windhuk, 10 July 1906, BA-Berlin, R 1001, Nr. 2090, p. 62; Deimling, *Aus der alten in die neue Zeit,* 113. Settler hysteria contributed to the urgent-seeming atmosphere: Referent v. Jacob (Col. Dept.), "Essay for the Reichstag on the native prisoners on Shark Island," Nr. KA II. 1167, 23 Mar. 1908, BA-Berlin, R 1001, Nr. 2140, pp. 157–60.

88. Memorandum of meeting of 13 July 1906, BA-Berlin, R 1001, Nr. 2090, p. 64; Hohenlohe to Lindequist, Berlin, 28 July 1906, ibid., p. 72.

86 high transportation costs (130,000 marks) doubtless killed even this reduced version of the plan.[89] Meanwhile, the district administrator in Windhuk, to whom Lindequist had "given" the returning Witboois from the Cameroons as non-prisoner-of-war labor, insisted on locking them up with extra guards, because he so feared them as soldiers.[90]

Prevented from the complete solution of deportation, Deimling and the civilian government agreed to a kind of internal deportation: all Nama were sent to Shark Island. The appalling conditions on Shark Island did not improve with the influx of Nama. Although food and warm clothing seem to have been more plentiful than earlier, they were still inadequate to stop rampant scurvy and, finally, death.[91] Conditions worsened in late 1906, hitting the nadir in December, when 276 of 1,464 Nama died (18.9 percent).[92] Under the circumstances, the local missionary, Fenchel, requested a meeting with Colonel v. Deimling, at Deimling's southern headquarters. "Then I told him," Fenchel reported, "about the conditions on Shark Island and asked if he couldn't put the hundreds of women and children, who were unnecessarily dying there, someplace else. He said: 'It hadn't occurred to me that there are actually more women than men there. Certainly, I'll take steps immediately.'"[93] Colonel v. Deimling had not been paying attention.[94] The association of the rubric "prisoner" with men was so strong as to blot out the obvious facts. When Deimling learned from Fenchel that the leaders were, not surprisingly, embittered at their treatment, he replied, "I'll have to be all the more careful in letting the people go." But he ordered the immediate transfer of the women and children to the missionaries' care inland, and searched for another camp for the men.[95]

But the Nama were not saved. When the remaining men complained at the removal of their families, the women and children were returned to the island.[96] Most of them never left it alive.

When the head of the mission, Haussleiter, received Fenchel's report of his meeting with Deimling, Haussleiter forwarded it to the new director of the Colonial Department, Bernhard von Dernburg, who in turn directed the civil government of SWA to intercede to remedy matters.[97] Whether it would have done so is questionable. As it was, Deimling's successor, Major Estorff, preempted it. Estorff had received a report that Deimling had

---

89. Norddeutscher Lloyd to Col. Dept., Bremen, 29 Aug. 1906, ibid., pp. 89–90; Aktennotiz of 12 Dec. 1906, ibid., p. 100.

90. District Administration Windhuk to Dep. Gov. Oskar Hintrager, Nr. 10818, Windhuk, 31 Oct. 1906, BA-Berlin, R 151 F/D.IV.M.2., vol. 8, p. 217.

91. Missionary Laaf to Director (*Präses*) Fenchel, Lüderitzbucht, 5 Oct. 1906, copy, Col. Dept., BA-Berlin, R 1001, Nr. 2140, p. 18; testimony of Edward Fredericks, Union of South Africa, *Report on the Natives*, p. 99 (Samuel Kariko's testimony to the contrary refers to conditions in 1905, 101).

92. "Sterblichkeit in den Kriegsgefangenenlagern."

93. Fenchel report, Keetmanshoop, 26 Dec. 1906, copy, BA-Berlin, R 1001, Nr. 2140, p. 18.

94. Capt. Zülow told another missionary, Laaf, that when he had asked Deimling to transfer the Nama inland, Deimling had replied, "As long as I command, no Hottentot is permitted to leave Shark Island alive." It is unclear when this exchange occurred, but it indicates that Deimling's inattention was overdetermined. Zimmerer, *Kriegsgefangene*, 292.

95. Fenchel report, Keetmanshoop, 26 Dec. 1906, copy, BA-Berlin, R 1001, Nr. 2140, p. 18.

96. Jacob, "Essay."

97. Dernburg to Dep. Gov. Hintrager, draft, 21 Feb. 1907, BA-Berlin, R 1001, Nr. 2140, p. 19.

solicited from camp commandant Captain von Zülow. It said "that of 245 men only 25 were periodically capable of work (all of whom, moreover, can only walk with canes), so that staying on Shark Island would lead to a slow but certain death, [and that] since September 1906 of 1,795 natives on Shark Island 1,032 had died." Estorff was horrified. He ordered everybody to be removed to an inland camp immediately, which Zülow accomplished in under two days.[98] Estorff informed his superiors in Berlin that "for such hangmen's services I can neither detail my officers, nor can I accept responsibility, because holding the Hottentots in this way breaks the promise I made to the people and [their leader] Samuel Izaak, with the permission of the commander [Dame]."[99] Estorff had negotiated the surrender of Samuel Izaak and his clanspeople and had promised they would not be interned. But Deimling soon replaced Dame and reneged on Estorff's promise.[100] Estorff now intended to recoup his good name. But he was a week late. On 31 March 1907 Germany had declared victory and an end to martial law. On 1 April authority over the prison camps shifted to the civilian administration, which was no longer led by Governor Lindequist, who had left the colony in mid-October 1906, but by his deputy, Oscar Hintrager. Hintrager had thoroughly absorbed the military-security perspective. He immediately wired Berlin that, in his view, "Prisoners should remain on the island until the complete pacification of the land, because except on the island their escape cannot be hindered and the escape of each one of the very embittered prisoners can cause renewed unrest and hostilities."[101]

In the interests of humanity, Dernburg overlooked the letter of the law: he recognized in principle the governor's authority over the prison camps but upheld Estorff's decision.[102] In just two weeks after the transfer, the death rate among the Nama had shrunk by 80 percent.[103] Meanwhile, Dernburg wanted to know why his February order to improve conditions had never been carried out; and, above all, he wanted to know how long the civil government had known about the fatal conditions.[104] Hintrager claimed he learned of them only in February 1907, from Estorff, but he went on to say that he opposed removing even women and children at that time for security reasons.

> But even if [the government had learned earlier], I would not have been able to intercede [to improve conditions], and I have avoided giving the district administration in Lüderitzbucht any instructions whatsoever regarding the Shark Island captives, because the All-Highest Cabinet Order of 19 May 1904 gives the deputy governor no authority in this regard.[105]

98. Estorff to Schutztruppe Command in Berlin, tel. Nr. 461, Windhuk, 10 Apr. 1907, ibid., p. 88.

99. Ibid.

100. Estorff, *Wanderungen*, 123.

101. Hintrager to Col. Dept., tel. Nr. 89, Windhuk, 10 Apr. 1907, BA-Berlin, R 1001, Nr. 2140, p. 87.

102. Dernburg to Hintrager, copy, tel., Berlin, 11 Apr. 1907, ibid., p. 89; Dernburg to Hintrager, tel., Berlin, 18 Apr. 1907, ibid., p. 95.

103. Böhmer's enclosure to Hintrager to Lindequist, Nr. 10834, Windhuk, 26 Apr. 1907, ibid., p. 111.

104. Dernburg to Hintrager, tel., Berlin, 11 Apr. 1907, and Dernburg to Schutztruppe Command in Windhuk, copy, tel., Berlin, 11 Apr. 1907, ibid., p. 89.

105. Hintrager to Lindequist, Nr. 10834, Windhuk, 26 Apr. 1907, ibid., pp. 109–10.

88   Hintrager was referring to the Kaiser's decree giving the military full control over policy, which was a convenient alibi for civilian administrators, like himself, to whom mass death was an acceptable price for security.

The Dead

On 31 March 1907, then, the war was over, the inflated Schutztruppe was gradually withdrawn, and government returned, if not to normal,[106] at least to civilian administration. At home, taxpayers had paid 600-million marks to put down the revolts. This was an extraordinary cost, given that the normal yearly subsidy for the colony was only 14.5-million marks.[107] Three times the government had spent money illegally, before the Reichstag had appropriated it.[108] Almost 19,000 German troops had gone to SWA, but only 3,000 of them had fought there; the rest were absorbed in the tasks of upkeep and administration.[109] Of the troops, 676 had been killed in fighting (752, if one counts the 76 missing), while 689 had died of disease—a typical colonial proportion.[110]

Against these figures, the loss of African lives is staggering. The census of 1911 listed 19,962 Herero and 13,858 Nama still alive in SWA.[111] Reports indicate 1,275 Herero had escaped safely to British Bechuanaland; at a very generous estimate several thousands may have survived in Ovamboland or as "field Herero" in Hereroland itself.[112] That still leaves approximately 20,000 survivors (allowing for some demographic recovery after 1907). Even if one were to accept the artificially low estimate of an original population of 40,000, offered by those who wish to minimize the catastrophe, this still amounts to a death rate of 50 percent.[113] The more likely and more generally accepted figure of 60–80,000 yields a death rate for the Herero of 66–75 percent. The Nama death rate remains accepted at 50 percent.[114] Because we lack perfect statistics, the exact death rates will never be known. But their magnitude can also be gauged by the observations of knowledgeable contempo-

106. See Bley's excellent account of the paranoid violence loosed by the settlers in the postwar, "peacetime" colony: *South-West Africa*, pt. 3, and Zimmerer, *Deutsche Herrschaft*, chs. 2–6.

107. Klaus Epstein, "Erzberger and the German Colonial Scandals," *English Historical Review* 74 (1959), 637–63, here 645; Bley, *South-West Africa*, 150–52.

108. Epstein, "Erzberger," 650.

109. Kommando der Schutztruppen, *Sanitäts-Bericht*, 2:438–40; Maercker, *Unsere Kriegführung*, 5.

110. General Staff, *Kämpfe der deutschen Truppen*, 2, Anlage 2, p.335. A later official report slightly revised these figures: 648 dead from wounds, 699 from illness: Kommando der Schutztruppen, *Sanitäts-Bericht*, 2:table 310, p.405.

111. Diedrich Baedeker, "Kolonialstatistik und Bemerkungen," *Jahrbuch über die deutschen Kolonien* 4 (1911), 218–37, here 230. Drechsler cites the 1911 census as showing only 15,130 Herero and 9,781 Nama survivors. Drechsler, *"Let Us Die Fighting,"* 246.

112. General Staff, *Kämpfe der deutschen Truppen*, 1:212; Drechsler, *"Let Us Die Fighting,"* 166–67, 213–14; Sudholt, *Deutsche Eingeborenenpolitik*, 186.

113. Sudholt, *Deutsche Eingeborenenpolitik*, 40–44, 185–86; Poewe, *Namibian Herero*, 59–62.

114. This rate is not accepted by Sudholt, who claims Bley has misread the 1911 census as 9,800 Nama instead of 13,858: Sudholt, *Deutsche Eingeborenenpolitik*, p.43. Bley was simply following Drechsler, *"Let Us Die Fighting,"* 214. Cf. Drechsler, 229n189, who says that he could not find the 1911 census in "official annual reports or in other sources," so he relied on the citation in the Union of South Africa, *Report*, p.35, whose figures Germany never challenged.

raries. Paul Rohrbach had estimated in March 1905 that "probably half the Herero" had died in the desert (with the war only one-third over).[115] Estorff, who was nearer to the dead than any other German officer, since he led the "pursuit" to the bitter end, thought "the greatest part" of the Herero people had died there.[116] Governor Leutwein reckoned that two-thirds of the Herero had died altogether.[117] And Major Maercker, who commanded the rear in late 1905 and 1906 and thus was in charge of prisoners of war, wrote in 1907 that of the seven Nama clans, four "have been so decimated that only pitiful remnants are left over."[118]

The question of how many of these people died in captivity is also hard to answer with certainty. The only official summary report I have been able to find is the 1908 compilation by the Schutztruppe Command, which estimated 15,000 Herero and 2,000 Nama captured, of whom 7,682 died.[119] The Schutztruppe thus admitted a death rate of 45.2 percent. But their figures are incomplete. They lack any numbers for Karibib for 1906 and 1907. And internal evidence, interpreted in the most conservative possible way, shows a minimum of 20,702 prisoners taken, not 17,000.[120] The official history says that at the war's end, 16,000 prisoners were alive in German hands; if this were true, then, together with the 7,682 dead listed by the 1908 Schutztruppe report, that would mean a total of 23,682 prisoners had been taken.[121] In November 1907, in front of the German Colonial Society, Major Maercker claimed that 20,000 prisoners had surrendered in just the period after Governor Lindequist's proclamation of 1 December 1905.[122] If that is true, then the Schutztruppe took over 33,000 Africans prisoner, since Maercker had listed 13,216 prisoners alive and in German hands on 8 December 1905.[123] If 16,000 of these survived, as the

---

115. Rohrbach, *Aus Südwestafrikas schweren Tagen*, 195.

116. Estorff, *Kriegserlebnisse*, 92.

117. Leutwein, *Elf Jahre*, 542.

118. Maercker, *Unsere Kriegführung*, 57–58.

119. "Sterblichkeit in den Kriegsgefangenenlagern in SWA," Nr. KA II. 1181, minuted in Col. Dept. on 24 Mar. 1908, BA-Berlin, R 1001, Nr. 2140, pp. 161–62.

120. The figure 20,702 comes from adding the 13,216 prisoners listed as alive and in German hands on 8 Dec. 1905 (Maercker, Anlage to Report Nr. 26176, Windhuk, 8 Dec. 1905, BA-Berlin, R 151 F/D.IV.L.3., vol. 1, pp. 187–88) to the 1,400 who surrendered from the beginning of Dec. 1905 to 1 Jan. 1906 (Dame to General Staff, Nr. 203, Windhuk, 3 Jan. 1906, BA-Berlin, R 1001, Nr. 2118, p. 202) to the 4,497 total who surrendered at Omburo from 1 Jan. 1906 to its closing in Aug. 1906 (August Kuhlmann, "Abschluss der Sammelarbeit," Omburo, 31 July 1906, VEM-Wuppertal, Kuhlmann papers, B/c II 72, pp. 49–52) to the 1,503 who had to have surrendered at Otjihaenena (since Gov. Lindequist reported to Berlin that 6,000 prisoners had surrendered at Omburo and Otjihaenena from 1 Jan. to 17 Apr. 1906: Lindequist to Col. Dept., Nr. 458, Windhuk, 17 Apr. 1906, BA-Berlin, R 1001, Nr. 2119, pp. 42–43), plus 86 members of the "Red Nation" Nama, who surrendered on 13 Jan. 1906 (Mühlenfels to Lindequist, Nr. 949, Windhuk, 13 Jan. 1906, BA-Berlin, R 151 F/D.IV.M.2., vol. 8, p. 105). It is certain that many more surrendering Herero were gathered in at Otjihaenena, which remained open over three months longer, and at new collection camps that operated until Feb. 1907 farther east, but whose statistics are unavailable (missionary Olpp, copy of report, Otjosongombe, 14 Aug. 1906, BA-Berlin, R 1001, Nr. 2119, pp. 77–79; Hintrager to Col. Dept., Nr. 245, Windhuk, 24 Feb. 1907, BA-Berlin, R 1001, Nr. 2140, pp. 81–83).

121. General Staff, *Kämpfe der deutschen Truppen*, 2:298. Zimmerer estimates between 21,000 and 24,000; Zimmerer, "Kriegsgefangene," 289, and Zimmerer, *Deutsche Herrschaft*, 44.

122. Maercker, *Unsere Kriegführung*, 48.

123. Maercker, Anlage to Report Nr. 26176, Windhuk, 8 Dec. 1905, BA-Berlin, R 151 F/D.IV.L.3., vol. 1, pp. 187–88.

90   official history says, then around 17,000 had died, a death rate of 51 percent, not far from that officially admitted by the Schutztruppe Command.

It is therefore probable that the number of prisoners taken and the number dead were much larger than the 1908 report tally. In any event, it is striking that in the periodic reports sent to Berlin, the number of prisoners alive barely changes, despite the influx of thousands surrendering. From 8 December 1905 to 21 January 1906, for example, more than 2,137 new prisoners were taken, yet the number of prisoners in German hands dropped by 1,026.[124] Major Quade reported 12,549 prisoners alive on 1 May 1906, a drop of 667 from December, when by official count a minimum of 7,400 new prisoners had been taken from December 1905 to mid-April 1906.[125] Some of these people must have been transferred into private hands and thus disappeared from the military statistics.[126] But surely most of them had perished. The death rates calculated in the 1908 Schutztruppe report are consistent with this massive disappearance, which appears to have consumed numerically almost all the prisoners taken in 1906.[127] Two of the prison camps, Windhuk and Shark Island, reached their highest death rates in 1906. Annualized, these rates would have been 61 percent for Windhuk, and at Shark Island, 86 percent for the Herero, and 227 percent for the Nama. The latter figure means that death would have consumed the entire original Nama prison population plus over twice that number in incoming captives.[128] But even the yearly rate of death averaged out for the period October 1904 to March 1907 yields staggering figures: death rates of 37 percent (Okahandja), 50 percent (Windhuk), 74 percent (Swakopmund), 30 percent (Herero at Shark Island). The average annualized death rate for the Nama at Shark Island (121 percent) means that the original camp population plus twenty percent more newcomers would all have died in the course of a year.

Despite their incompleteness, these figures show that captivity was as deadly as war. Far from being a haven from the fighting and pursuit, imprisonment was a continuation of annihilation by other means.

And so, as Paul Rohrbach observed, the "peace of the graveyard" settled over SWA.[129]

124. Ibid.; Dame to General Staff, Nr. 1648, Windhuk, 21 Jan. 1906, BA-Berlin, R 151 F/D.IV.L.3., vol. 2, p. 83; 2,137: Dame to General Staff, Nr. 203, Windhuk, 3 Jan. 1906, BA-Berlin, R 1001, Nr. 2118, p. 202.

125. Quade to General Staff, copy, 5 June 1906, BA-Berlin, R 1001, Nr. 2119, p. 46. 7,400: Dame to General Staff, Nr. 203, Windhuk, 3 Jan. 1906, ibid., Nr. 2118, p. 202; Lindequist to Col. Dept., Nr. 458, Windhuk, 17 Apr. 1906, ibid., Nr. 2119, pp. 42–43.

126. In 1908 Maercker estimated that 15,000 Herero "might" (*mag sein*) be in private hands, in addition to the 15,000 in military or mission camps. This estimate is hard to square with the 1911 census figure of just under 20,000 Herero. Maercker, "Die militärische Lage in Süd-Westafrika," *Jahrbuch über die deutschen Kolonien* 1 (1908): 39–41, here 39–40.

127. 20,000: Maercker, *Unsere Kriegführung*, 48; 12,000: Bley, *South-West Africa*, 169.

128. "Sterblichkeit in den Kriegsgefangenenlagern in SWA," Nr. KA II. 1181, minuted in Col. Dept. on 24 Mar. 1908, BA-Berlin, R 1001, Nr. 2140, pp. 161–62.

129. Rohrbach, *Aus Südwestafrikas schweren Tagen*, 182. Prein incorrectly attributes this expression to historian Horst Drechsler; Philipp Prein, "Guns and Top Hats," *Journal of Southern African Studies* 20:1 (1994): 99–121, here 100. Cf. Zimmerer's objections to the phrase, *Deutsche Herrschaft* 5, 13–14. For a similar contemporary metaphor, see Südekum, *Sten. Ber.*, vol. 202, 30 Jan. 1905, col. 4123.

PART II

MILITARY CULTURE

Events in SWA followed a pattern that we should summarize before analyzing it in part 2. First, military practices developed on the spot. The General Staff did not run events in SWA; instead, it set the expectations (for victory, forceful leadership, and proper priorities) that suffused operations. Scripts and routines then unfolded, if not automatically, then almost thoughtlessly: the single concentric battle of annihilation, the fierce pursuit, and the punitive internment of the rebel population. Courts-martial with frequent executions led to immediate executions, then to the wholesale targeting of all fleeing Africans, and, finally, to massacre. Unrealism permeated planning and execution. As Germans began to suffer from scarcity and poor logistics, their standard for treatment of Africans sank to a below-subsistence level. Failure to achieve the Siegfrieden, the victory of military force, resulted in repeated, widening spirals of violence and finally suggested an equally total analogue, the disappearance of the native problem, either by deportation, expulsion, or death. Only after annihilation had occurred did Trotha raise it to the level of policy.

The slide to extremes in SWA thus had several characteristics: it was developmental, not ordered; it was dysfunctional (it destroyed the African workforce and the colony's cattle and it prolonged the war, thus raising German casualties and expenses); and it was irrational from the perspective of goals or real limits to action. We must therefore seek its rationality elsewhere, in the unexamined assumptions and institutional habits of the military, that is, in military culture.

92

Military culture is a particular variant of organizational culture. The organizational-cultural perspective of social science is valuable for its focus on patterns of cognition and practice that organizations, including militaries, build from the past and embed in methods of operation, routines, expectations, and basic assumptions. Organizational culture is liable to produce irrationality and dysfunction because the lessons of the past may be a poor guide to problems of the present, and because its most influential tenets are often unconscious, hidden, or taken for granted, and therefore difficult to correct. Nevertheless, organizational culture is more likely to determine action than is explicit policy or ideology.

Germany's particular military culture was strongly the consequence of the military's peculiar status in the constitution and politics. In SWA we saw how the government's decision to treat the revolt as a national security issue immediately shifted power to the military. But the Kaiser's legal ability to cancel civil government (by handing affairs to the General Staff, impeding negotiations, choosing Trotha, and approving martial law) was decisive in permitting the untrammeled sway of military authority. Freedom from civil-political oversight had dramatic repercussions on Germany's military culture.

We will begin the analysis of Germany's military culture by looking at its historical development in the wars of unification and how the "lessons" learned became institutionalized and codified. The distance between Germany's rules and contemporary international law is striking.

The next step is to look at operational practices: Were Germany's other wars before 1914 prosecuted in the same way as in SWA? Do we find typical expectations for warfare, planning shortfalls, and treatment of enemy fighters and civilians? Are these characteristic only of colonial warfare, or also of European conflicts?

From practices and operations we move up a notch of abstraction to doctrines, where one would expect to find strategic reflection, or at least explicit statements about how to wage war. The Schlieffen Plan provides a convenient distillation of military culture at the doctrinal level.

Two questions are especially important to pose at each stage of analysis: How different was Germany's military culture from that of other Western armies? and, How did explicit norms (embodied in doctrine or regulations) contain hidden assumptions with powerful consequences for action? In other words, how did norms create circumstances with systematic but unintentional results? The relation between the explicit and the unconsciously implicit is extremely important.

I also examine how the juggernaut of military extremism could be interrupted or stopped, comparing Germany in SWA with Britain during the Boer War. My conclusion, that military extremism was more likely to be prevented by intervention from outside the military than from within, returns to the beginning of part 2: the relation of politics to the military.

Once the template of military culture is clear, we can then turn to how it played out during World War I, the subject of part 3.

4

National Politics and Military Culture

ontemporary critics, and many subsequent scholarly studies, have identified the baleful effects that the German military had on national politics and public opinion. They labeled this phenomenon "militarism."[1] Few observers have focused on the reverse process. Yet, the peculiar functioning of the German military was strongly a product of Germany's constitution and the political culture it engendered.

Military Culture

"Military culture" is a way of understanding why an army acts as it does in war. Unlike military sociology, which mostly has focused on military organizations in peacetime, a military-cultural perspective concentrates on practices during war.[2] By "practice" I

1. Michael Geyer, "Militarismus," in *Geschichtliche Grundbegriffe*, vol. 4, ed. Otto Brunner, Werner Conze, and Reinhart Koselleck (Stuttgart, 1978), 1–48; Volker R. Berghahn, *Militarism* (Leamington Spa, U.K., 1981); Volker R. Berghahn, ed., *Militarismus* (Cologne, 1975); Alfred Vagts, *A History of Militarism, Civilian and Military*, rev. ed. (London, 1959); Gerhard Ritter, *The Sword and the Scepter*, 3 vols., trans. Heinz Norden (Coral Gables, Fla., 1969–73; orig. 1960–68); Laurence J. Radway, "Militarism," in *International Encyclopedia of the Social Sciences*, vol. 10 (New York, 1968); Nicholas Stargardt, *The German Idea of Militarism* (Cambridge, 1994). On the relation of the military to society: Ute Frevert, *Die kasernierte Nation* (Munich, 2001); Ute Frevert, ed., *Militär und Gesellschaft im 19. und 20. Jahrhundert* (Stuttgart, 1997).

2. Klaus Roghmann and Rolf Ziegler, "Militärsoziologie," in *Handbuch der empirischen Sozialforschung*, ed. René König (Stuttgart, 1967), 2:514–66; Karl Demeter, *Das deutsche Offizierskorps* (Berlin, 1930); Franz Carl Endres, "Militarismus als Geistesverfassung des Nichtmilitärs," in *Militarismus*, ed. Berghahn, 99–101; Vagts, *History of Militarism*; Samuel P. Huntington, *The Soldier and the State* (Cambridge, 1957); Morris Janowitz, *Military Conflict* (Beverly Hills, Calif., 1975); Karl Rohe, "Militarismus, soldatische Haltung, und Führerideologie," in *Militarismus*, ed. Berghahn, 267–82; Hans Paul Bahrdt, *Die Gesellschaft und ihre Soldaten* (Munich, 1987); Emilio Willems, *Der preussisch-deutsche Militarismus* (Cologne, 1984); Wilfried von Bredow, "Erkundungsziel Militärwelt," in *Militär als Lebenswelt*, ed. Wolfgang R. Vogt (Opladen, Germany, 1988); Wolfgang R. Vogt, ed., *Militär*

94 mean two things: the actions that result consciously from applied doctrine and training, and the habitual actions that seem obvious by virtue of unquestioned assumptions or necessary by virtue of the unintended consequences of regular military procedure. Two fields analyze practices in this sense: anthropology and the sociological subfield of organizational culture. Using both one can develop a conception of military culture that will help explain how and why a particular military behaved as it did in wartime.

Cultural anthropologist Clyde Kluckhohn provides especially useful observations on what "culture"[3] is:

> By "culture" we mean all those historically created designs for living, explicit and implicit, rational, irrational, and nonrational, that exist at any given time as potential guides for the behavior of men.

> "Design" denotes both "theory" and "practice." "Design" is meant to designate both "behavioral patterns" and "ideal patterns."

> Some of the most critical premises of any culture are often unstated, even by the intellectuals of the group. Likewise, some basic categories of "thinking" are implicit.

> [These implicit parts of culture operate unconsciously, in the sense of being] "not verbalized" or "not habitually verbalized"—the unstated premises, for example. . . . In every culture there are certain pervasive principles of "orderings" . . . certain clusters that persistently turn up.[4]

Kluckhohn's definition of culture contains several important elements. First, culture consists of an interrelation between norms and actual behavior (practices) tested through time, both affecting each other. It is not simply an idea template that stamps out approved behavior. Second, much of culture operates implicitly; it is unexamined and unverbalized. That means, third, that it does not necessarily operate in relation to "rational" goals.

---

als Gegenkultur (Opladen, Germany, 1986), 171–79; Paul Klein and Ekkehard Lippert, eds., *Militär und Gesellschaft* (Munich, 1979).

3. On different anthropological interpretations of "culture" see Marietta L. Baba, "Organizational Culture," in *Encyclopedia of Cultural Anthropology*, ed. David Levinson and Melvin Ember, vol. 3 (New York, 1996), 891–95, here 894. A convenient history: Ino Rossi, "The Development of Theories of Culture," in *People in Culture*, ed. Ino Rossi (New York, 1980), 31–78; Ward H. Goodenough, "Culture," in *Encyclopedia of Cultural Anthropology*, vol. 1, ed. David Levinson and Melvin Ember (New York, 1996), 291–99.

4. Clyde Kluckhohn, "The Concept of Culture," in *Culture and Behavior*, ed. Richard Kluckhohn (New York, 1962), 19–73, here 54, 54, 59, 62–63, respectively. I partially quote Kluckhohn and Edgar Schein in an abbreviated discussion of "military culture" in "Military Culture, Wilhelm II, and the End of Monarchy in the First World War," in *The Kaiser*, ed. Wilhelm Deist and Annika Mombauer (Cambridge, 2003), 235–58, here 239–41.

Therefore, functional analyses according to goal orientation (à la Weberian sociology) will be inadequate for a complete understanding of cultural processes.

Militaries are, of course, organizations, and organizations develop cultures in somewhat more specific ways than do cultures at large. The failure of functional analyses to explain dysfunction and seeming irrationality in organizations led to the development of the subfield of organizational culture. One of the most useful and influential definitions of organization culture comes from one of the first social scientists to study it, Edgar Schein. He writes:

> [Culture is] the total of the collective or shared learning of that unit as it develops its capacity to survive in its external environment and to manage its own internal affairs. Culture is the solution to external and internal problems that has worked consistently for a group and that is therefore taught to new members as the correct way to perceive, think about, and feel in relation to those problems. Such solutions eventually come to be assumptions about the nature of reality, truth, time, space, human nature, human activity, and human relationships—they come to be taken for granted and, finally, drop out of awareness. The power of culture is derived from the fact that it operates as a set of assumptions that are unconscious and taken for granted.[5]

The operation of culture, Schein continues, occurs on three levels (and is therefore accessible to analysis on three levels): (1) artifacts, "the visible behavior manifestations of underlying concepts"; (2) overt beliefs or professed values, the level of justification for actions; and (3) learned basic assumptions, which motivate action.[6] Surprisingly, levels two and three are often discrepant.[7] Not only is it common for individual and organizational behavior to contradict stated beliefs, it is common for individuals and organizations to deny the discrepancy. Summing up the social science literature on this subject, Steven Ott writes that "many organizations actually reward behaviors that are inconsistent with their stated cultural beliefs and values."[8] The common disjunction between practice and norms means that analyses of military action and decision making derived solely from

---

5. Edgar H. Schein, "How Culture Forms, Develops, and Changes," in *Gaining Control of Corporate Culture*, ed. Ralph H. Kilmann, Mary J. Saxton, and Roy Serpa (San Francisco, 1985), 17–43, here 19–20.

6. Ibid., 21–23.

7. Argyris and Schön call this discrepancy the disjuncture between "theory-in-use" (i.e., practice) and "espoused theory"; Chris Argyris and Donald A. Schön, *Organizational Learning II* (New York, 1996), 13–15. Vaughan refers to the "frame of reference" or "predispositions, scripts, conventions, and classification schemes" that operate in a "pre-rational, preconscious manner" in decision making; Diane Vaughan, *The Challenger Launch Decision* (Chicago, 1996), 404–5. See also Scott A. Snook, *Friendly Fire* (Princeton, 2000), 209–10.

8. J. Steven Ott, *The Organizational Culture Perspective* (Chicago, 1989), 95, also 44; Alexander George, "The Causal Nexus between Cognitive Beliefs and Decision-making Behavior," in *Psychological Models in International Politics*, ed. Laurence S. Falkowski (Boulder, Colo., 1979), 95–124, here 97; Alice M. Sapienza, "Believing Is Seeing," in *Gaining Control of the Corporate Culture*, 66–83, here 69.

96 doctrine will miss much of the actual motivation and most of the tension, dysfunction, and irrationality that frequently occur in military organizations and that are a major focus of this book.

The basic assumptions that remain hidden from the actors, and consequently are not easily accessible to outside observers, are the results of past learning. Some lessons sink in deeper than others: those that occur at the founding moments of an institution, for example, or that are associated with an especially influential leader. One of the most indelible learning processes is what Schein calls "trauma-learning." Organizations that have overcome extreme threats or challenges tend to reify whatever procedures they think saved them. The resulting lessons are doubly memorable: as solutions to the problem and as prescriptions against the anxiety the trauma caused. Trauma-learning is therefore especially resistant to change and testing. "Cultural assumptions learned by this means can thus be thought of as defense mechanisms that the group has learned to cope with anxiety and potential trauma."[9] One might say that militaries are in the trauma business; a great deal of their learning occurs in times of existential threat. Trauma-learning is thus a common characteristic of militaries, and is, as we shall see, a major foundational factor in Imperial German military culture.

The basic assumptions that organizations acquire, by whatever means, structure their perceptions of their own essence and purpose, of the problems they must solve, and of the ways they should solve them. Culture defines, and therefore narrows, perceptions and, by reducing the alternatives, makes it easier for individuals and organizations to define tasks and make decisions. This strength can also be a weakness, however. It can lead to rigid thinking, to "collective blindness to important issues," to a reluctance to seek further information, and to unrealistic assessments.[10] The quality of perception strongly affects decision making, to the extent that some perceptions (of the dangerousness of an enemy, for example) are in themselves already decisions; that is, they short-circuit the process of collecting and evaluating information, weighing alternatives, and making decisions.[11]

For many reasons, basic assumptions tend to coalesce into a pattern.[12] The resulting constellation of mutually supporting assumptions lends stability and consistency to the whole. Similar or analogous beliefs developed by other organizations or subcultures will also be more readily accepted as obvious, "natural," or true.[13] But the internal consistency of basic assumptions does not necessarily mean that they are logical or rational in an external sense; that is, they would not necessarily pass the test of evidence or argument independent of their own perceptual base. The interlocking, self-generating quality of the

---

9. Schein, "How Culture Forms," 25, whole discussion 24–27.

10. Blindness: Turner, "Organizational and Interorganizational Development of Disasters," 378–97, here 388; information: George, "Causal Nexus," 101–3.

11. George, "Causal Nexus," 103; Nils Brunsson, "The Irrationality of Action and Action Rationality," *Journal of Management Studies* 19:1 (1982), 29–44, here 38.

12. Schein, "How Culture Forms," 23; George, "Causal Nexus," 100–101.

13. Martha Finnemore, "Constructing Norms of Humanitarian Intervention," in *The Culture of National Security*, ed. Peter J. Katzenstein (New York, 1996), 153–85, here 173–74.

German army's basic assumptions about conflict and violence is striking, for example. Their coincidence with widespread social Darwinist views, which arose independently, seemed to confirm for officers their correctness.

Basic assumptions are the products of historical experience. They therefore fall into the category of "irrational beliefs," as Alasdair MacIntyre would term them, meaning they are functions of social processes rather than of rigorous procedures of thinking.[14] Their rationality lies in their social history; from other perspectives, they will appear "irrational."

There are other sources of seeming irrationality in organizational culture, too.[15] Nils Brunsson considers irrationality "a basic feature of organizational behavior." "Some irrationalities are necessary requirements for organizational action," he writes. "Choices are facilitated by narrow and clear organizational ideologies, and actions are facilitated by irrational decision-making procedures which maximize motivation and commitment." This latter he terms "action rationality."[16] Few organizations are more dedicated to action than the military, and few actions require more motivation and commitment than exposing oneself to deadly fire in battle. We should therefore expect action rationality to be particularly well developed in militaries.

Finally, the type of organization influences its culture. Militaries are "strong" organizations. They are led by long-serving professionals (officers); they aspire to be total institutions that control their charges around the clock, even off duty. They devote tremendous resources to training and indoctrination. They consciously inculcate values (of strict obedience, indifference to danger, use of violence, for example) at odds with those of the surrounding society. They attempt extreme regulation via printed rules, and so forth.[17] In short, they produce a strong organizational culture. And strong organizations are often more disaster-prone than weak ones; they are less flexible and less innovative.[18] Furthermore, the disasters militaries produce are likely to be extensive because their task is wielding concerted violence.

The motor of organizational behavior is its basic assumptions. Because these remain hidden from the actors and often contradict their stated beliefs, discovering the constellation of basic assumptions is not always straightforward. One must begin by examining the patterns in their practices. But basic assumptions are also revealed in the group's language (which indicates categories of perception), myths, explanations of events, standard oper-

---

14. Alasdair MacIntyre, "Rationality and the Explanation of Action," in *Against the Self-Images of the Age* (New York, 1971), 244–59, here 246.

15. James G. March, "Decision Making Perspectives," in *Perspective on Organization Design and Behavior*, ed. Andrew H. Van de Ven and William F. Joyce (New York, 1981), 205–44.

16. Brunsson, "Irrationality of Action," 29, 36.

17. Elizabeth L. Kier, *Imagining War* (Princeton, 1997), 28–30; Schein, "How Culture Forms," 26; Anonymous, "Informal Society in the Army," *American Journal of Sociology* 51:5 (March 1946), 365–70; Maury Feld, "A Typology of Military Organization," in *The Structure of Violence* (Beverly Hills, Calif., 1977), 31–69, here 33.

18. Kier, *Imagining War*, 32; Barry R. Posen, *The Source of Military Doctrine* (Ithaca, N.Y., 1984), 32–33, 54–57.

98 ating procedures, and doctrines.[19] All of these will be objects of examination in the next chapters.

The Military Culture of Late-Nineteenth-Century European Armies

When one asks what produces military culture, rather than simply what it is, one moves onto somewhat different ground. Here, the breadth of the phenomenon is important. Elizabeth Kier insists, for example, that military culture is not synonymous with the "military mind," meaning the assumptions or habits that all militaries share.[20] She would like to reserve the term "military culture" to refer to a specific military at a given historical time.[21] But if one is trying to determine what distinguished one army from another (why one moved from administrative massacre to attempted extermination, when others did not, for instance), then it makes sense to define military culture broadly as the culture of comparable militaries in the same era, and to include as wide a spectrum of determinants of military culture as possible. Only in that way can one see which factors made a difference in a given situation.

It is possible to identify seven main factors determining how general military culture fashioned itself over time: (1) its place in state and society (constitutional limits to its power, its social prestige, its openness to fashionable ideas or ideologies); (2) its task (in general the legitimate wielding of deadly force, but it may have acquired other tasks as well); (3) its hierarchical and (relative to other formal organizations) rigidly imperative organization; (4) the resources at its disposal (especially technology, funding, and education); (5) its social base (both for the officer corps and the common soldiers); (6) its gender constituent (which in the late nineteenth-century was, of course, purely masculine); and (7) its past history (especially the last major war or engagement it fought).

Late-nineteenth- and early-twentieth-century western and central European armies differed in important ways. The most important of these was the position of the armed forces in state and society. They also had somewhat different social bases and different past histories, and some had acquired other main tasks (for example, the protection of an overseas empire, or internal police functions, or integration of subject minorities). But they all existed in the post-Napoleonic world of stronger, activist states with more resources of money, manpower, technology, and industrial strength that made armed force much stronger than it had ever been. These modern armies shared the general task of wielding legitimate violence in the name of and (presumably) in the interest of national security; they shared imperative organization, extensive resource base (especially regarding colonial warfare), and gender homogeneity. Their similarities far outweighed their

19. Andrew M. Pettigrew, "On Studying Organizational Cultures," *Administrative Science Quarterly* 24:4 (1979), 570–81, here 575–76; Sonja A. Sackmann, "Culture and Subcultures," *Administrative Science Quarterly* 37:1 (1991), 140–61, here 141–42; Sonja A. Sackmann, "Uncovering Culture in Organizations," *Journal of Applied Behavioral Science* 27:3 (1991), 295–317, here 297–98.

20. Elizabeth Kier, "Culture and French Military Doctrine before World War II," in *The Culture of National Security*, 186–215, here 203.

21. See discussion in Deborah D. Avant, *Political Institutions and Military Change* (Ithaca, N.Y., 1994), 14.

differences. Furthermore, they learned from one another: they sent observers to report on foreign wars and annual maneuvers; they read one another's journals and treatises. Most European militaries shared significant aspects of military culture, whose features we must discuss to establish a base line before considering their differences.[22]

The most formative aspect of military culture is clearly the general task of exercising violence on a mass, systematic scale for national ends.[23] From this task flow most of its other distinguishing peculiarities. Exercising violence in this way requires the military to reconcile or accommodate two major paradoxes. First, violence destroys social stability. Wielded by any other agent except the military, violence is the epitome of social harm, and therefore its suppression is the first and founding duty of the state. Max Weber's famous dictum that the state is the monopolist of legitimate violence (*Gewalt*) is only half the story, for in wielding violence the state at once demonstrates its sovereignty and threatens to undermine it fundamentally. If violence lasts too long or destroys too much, it delegitimizes the state that is responsible for it. The military, as the designated agent of violence, therefore represents this foundational aspect of the modern state (and is thus symbolically synonymous with the state and its order) and at the same time officiates over the greatest instrument of disorder and existential threat. Because the military operates in the realm of the most powerful social taboo, it enjoys exceptional status among state organs. The second paradox arises from the fact that violence is the province of emotion: the terror of being killed and the anxiety of killing (the breaking of a fundamental taboo) release powerful emotions. Yet, the military is supposed to channel violence in a systematic fashion toward specific ends. It is supposed to calculate and operate coolly under circumstances of white-hot passion.

Modern European armies tried to reconcile these paradoxes through bureaucratic organization. The hierarchical command structure, the imperative of near-absolute obedience (*Kadavergehorsam*: corpse-like obedience), obsessive drill, constant practice, detailed planning, and by-the-book management were supposed to overcome the difficulties inherent in the military's assigned task. Discipline had to outweigh terror, exhaustion, and uncertainty; doctrine had to produce decisions in the absence of adequate information or time for reflection; planning had to counterbalance the inevitable chaos of battle; and routine had to tame the explosively extraordinary.

In order to fulfill these, in many ways, impossible tasks, military bureaucracy became more bureaucratic and overly organized than civilian organizations. All the typical failings of bureaucracy—sluggishness, pedantry, cleaving to the formal process at the expense of the goal, expense, redundancy, inflexibility—were likely to reach luxuriant heights in the military. Most late-nineteenth-century European militaries were rigid and resisted criticism and innovation.[24] They were loath to reexamine the standard operating procedures and doctrines they had worked out to deal with crisis. Where they had professionalized war planning in general staffs dedicated to this purpose, militaries risked bu-

---

22. On tactical, technical, and learning similarities: Dieter Storz, *Kriegsbild und Rüstung vor 1914* (Herford, Germany, 1992).

23. Feld, *Structure of Violence*.

24. Posen, *Sources of Military Doctrine*, 32–33, 46–47, 54–57; Avant, *Political Institutions*, 15.

100 reaucratically induced unrealism. Future planning was by definition both secret and visionary; neither outside critics nor real circumstances normally intruded into the illusions that flourished there. Uncorrected by outside influences, war planning tended to become self-referential. Planners proceeded from what they could control, namely, their own military-political necessities, and these, rather than the enemy, often determined their war plans.[25]

The balancing act of using violence to create order, and using order to control violence, encouraged two seemingly opposite characteristics, which in fact were closely related and mutually reinforcing. One was control mania.[26] Necessary discipline and the understandable wish to exert as much control as possible in chaotic, dangerous conditions encouraged both higher standards of order and a stronger devotion to upholding them. The symbols of order were omnipresent: the uniform, exact drill, spic-and-span appearance of the barracks, the day divided precisely into its constituent parts, the myriad regulations. The more pervasive the demand for order, the more opportunity for disorder was created, and thus, the greater the danger to order and the more watchfulness it required. All militaries were vulnerable to this vicious cycle.

The second characteristic exaggerated the violence end of the spectrum from order to violence. Not surprisingly, organizations specializing in the use of force will tend to value force as the best solution to military-political problems. Such a conviction, however, reduces the panoply of possible military options, which is actually quite broad: threat, feint, defensive positioning, blockade, negotiation, divide and conquer, *Sitzkrieg*, and so on. In the late nineteenth century the exaltation of the violent solution was especially prevalent and took many forms: for example, the "cult of the offensive"; the fixation on superior armament or numbers; or the demand for unconditional surrender. Another variant conceived of peace in terms of an "order" so perfect that it required the disappearance of any potential enemy. This type of thinking led to the wish to exterminate.

A further effort to master the problems posed by the military's task of order via violence was the institution of the rigid command structure and the requirement of stringent discipline. This imperative quality brought further dangers with it. It hindered criticism coming from inside the institution, making external feedback all the more important to it. Yet the military task, risking and perpetrating death, produced a sense of specialness and bonding that set its members apart from others and made it harder to hear or accept criticism coming from outsiders, from mere civilians.

Military discipline required that soldiers and officers give up certain basic freedoms for the period of their service. Foremost among these was the realm of personal choice, which included the right to question orders. In fact, German military regulations were more accommodating in this regard than were those of other Western armies (including the United States), but still, the premium on obedience to orders left little room for critical thinking, especially among common soldiers. Military discipline, which was partly

25. Maury D. Feld, "Information and Authority, the Structure of Military Organization," in *Structure of Violence*, 71–84, here 74, 80.

26. Bahrdt, *Die Gesellschaft und ihre Soldaten*, 31.

designed to stop individual atrocities, also meant, however, that massacres ordered or even suggested from above would likely be carried out. Under these circumstances, resisting orders for mass destruction, not conforming to them, is the behavior that requires explanation.

Even fully democratic regimes energetically tried to guarantee that their soldiers would carry out orders regardless of personal conviction. A range of restrictions aimed to isolate soldiers from critical influences emanating from civil society. Thus, they typically needed to receive permission to marry; they were forbidden from joining political parties; and their rights to free assembly and speech were curbed.[27] Soldiers were, therefore, everywhere intentionally stunted; wherever the military existed, civil society stopped. That is why liberals (and social democrats) were antimilitarist. It is also why conservatives and others who rejected what they viewed as the baleful tendencies of modern society championed the military as the upholder of (social) deference, order, and simpler virtues. The marriage of convenience between the military and the conservative or right-wing spectrum of politics was a general European phenomenon.

The premium on obedience, order, and discipline not surprisingly produced (or continued) a system of repressive, physical punishment presided over by a military legal system that lacked the safeguards of regular courts. Military justice was short and sharp. Military punishment was physical and often brutal, among other reasons because the treatment of ordinary recruits was already harsh and often demeaning.[28] Military organizations were characterized by a readiness to be punitive and to conceive of punishment in terms of physical suffering. The anxiety and carnage of war only reinforced this readiness. The "punitive expeditions" of imperial campaigns exemplified the propensity of militaries to regard themselves as agents of brutal punishment.

The fact that the military was an all-male institution did little to put a brake on the organizational predisposition toward greater use of force. The (not only) late-nineteenth-century identification of males with strength, violence, decisiveness, success, relative lack of emotion, and so forth, gave individual soldiers a powerful, personal incentive to conform to military ideals and do their duty to the point of massacre and gratuitous destruction. Masculine identity made the military's task easier, but it was also another factor pulling in the direction of potentially greater violence.[29]

These tendencies of military culture, which came partly from its sociology but primarily from the military task and the rigid organization designed to meet it, were common to all Western armies. So were the resources at their disposal in the colonial theater.

---

27. Vagts, *Militarism*, 160.

28. Anthony Clayton, *France, Soldiers, and Africa* (London, 1988), 13–18; István Deák, *Beyond Nationalism* (Oxford, 1990), 104–7.

29. Herbert C. Kelman, "Violence without Moral Restraint," *Journal of Social Issues* 29:4 (1973), 25–61, here 54, 58; Morris Janowitz, "The Ineffective Soldier," *Administrative Science Quarterly* 5:2 (Sept. 1960), 296–303, here 302; Neil J. Smelser, "Some Determinants of Destructive Behavior," in *Sanctions for Evil*, ed. Nevitt Sanford and Craig Comstock (San Francisco, 1971), 15–24, here 22–23. Generally: Ruth Seifert, "Militär und Ordnung der Geschlechter," in *Ordnung zwischen Gewaltproduktion und Friedensstiftung*, ed. Klaus Dieter Wolf (Baden-Baden, 1993), 213–29; Ruth Seifert, *Individualisierungsprozesse, Gechlechterverhältnisse, und die soziale Konstruktion des Soldaten* (Munich, 1993), 64–65, 74, 138, 141–45.

102   The whirring and grinding of the late-nineteenth-century arms race was of course predi-
cated on the possibility that one state or another would achieve technical or resource
paramountcy.[30] But this possibility, which did not in fact materialize, was irrelevant to
imperial conditions, where all colonial powers enjoyed overwhelming technical superiority over the native populations.[31] That was the very precondition of imperialism, and consequently technical (military) superiority became the symbol of European ("racial") superiority.[32] As a result, Western militaries fought very similar imperial campaigns guided
by almost identical doctrines calling for the best exploitation of their superior firepower
and the most impressive display of their material power generally (for purposes of moral
intimidation). In planning for the First World War and fighting it, resource differentials
were more significant, however.

In sum, nineteenth-century European military culture tended toward rigidity, encapsulation, control mania, and overvaluation of force. Its professional expertise and discipline tended to make it all too successful in realizing goals of mass destruction. Nonetheless, this potential for mass destruction did not always become actual. It was, instead, a
possible outcome that—if a campaign ran into difficulty, if a war lasted too long, if no
forces intervened to hinder it—was more likely to occur than other possibilities.

In regard to these possibilities that were inherent in general military culture, Germany was not much different from other European nations. But several of the determinants of its military culture were unique. Its immediate past military history, the Franco-
Prussian War of 1870–71, was formative for its military doctrine and much of its actual
tactical practice, as we shall see.

The social base of its officer corps was also somewhat different from that of other European armies, but less so than some histories make it appear.[33] Nobles were overrepre-
sented in all late-nineteenth-century officer corps. It is true that the Prussian Junkers had
a special political significance, but this was more important for domestic politics than for
military practice. By 1900 the status of officer and the ethos of the corps had become
largely independent of the social caste with which they were originally identified. The officer corps had become a *Stand*: it socialized and assimilated its members according to its
own professional and cultural values.[34] It might even be argued that the Junkers had become a function of the officer corps, rather than vice versa. At any rate, it is difficult to
identify Junker characteristics that affected practice in warfare.[35]

30. David G. Herrmann, *The Arming of Europe and the Making of the First World War* (Princeton, 1996).

31. With rare exceptions, such as Menelek of Eritrea.

32. Michael Adas, *Machines as the Measure of Men* (Ithaca, N.Y., 1989); Joseph Conrad, *Heart of Darkness* (London, 1902).

33. Hanns Hubert Hofmann, ed., *Das deutsche Offizierkorps, 1860–1960* (Boppard am Rhein, 1980); Martin Kitchen, *The German Officer Corps, 1890–1914* (Oxford, 1973); Manfred Messerschmidt, "The Military Elites in Germany since 1870," in *The Military, Politics, and Society in France and Germany in the Twentieth Century*, ed. Klaus-Jürgen Müller (Oxford, 1995), 43–72.

34. Michael Geyer, "The Past as Future," in *German Professions, 1800–1950*, ed. Geoffrey Cocks and Konrad Jarausch (New York, 1990), 183–212, here 192.

35. For an attempt to do so: Bernd F. Schulte, "Die Armee des Kaiserreichs im Spannungsfeld zwischen struktureller Begrenzung und Kriegsrealität, 1871–1914," in Schulte, *Europäische Krise und Erster Weltkrieg* (Frankfurt am Main, 1983), 45–124.

More than anything else, it was the differing constitutional and political parameters that distinguished German military culture from that of its neighbors. These gave the army additional tasks and created a vacuum in which military culture developed its peculiarities relatively unchecked.

Military and National Political Culture in Germany

The army's unique place in Germany's constitution was the most important factor shaping its military culture. That place derived from the oddity that the (Prussian) army's most important task after 1815 was not national defense but defense of the monarchy against its internal political enemies, and later national consolidation and definition.[36] This is probably the best-studied subject in German history, and we need only summarize it here.

The greatest victory the Prussian army achieved in the nineteenth century came in 1849 against the proponents of national revolution and reform.[37] However, this negative victory of repression could not indefinitely retard the ever-growing, differentiated movement for unity and liberal and/or social reform. After a decade of reaction, the economic, political, and social forces pressing for reform coalesced in the Prussian parliament and squared off against the monarch.[38] The issue was, broadly, civilian versus monarchical control over the army, whose monopoly over violence had determined Prussia's (and the other German states') political course in 1849 and would do so again.[39] In this constitutional crisis, Prussian War Minister Albrecht von Roon pushed the monarch to accept the military's candidate—Otto von Bismarck—as chancellor. Bismarck's political acumen transformed a negative politics of obstruction into a far cleverer politics of preemption. Instead of merely blocking reform, Bismarck used the army to unify Germany by war, which gave the military a positive halo of national heroism while enabling Bismarck to draft an incomplete national constitution designed to keep the army firmly in the monarch's hands. This bifurcated heritage, in which the army was both the instrument of reactionary repression *and* the quintessence of national integration, helped produced the Kaiserreich's characteristic political culture, in which the military as symbol and real institution played a central role.

Bismarck wrote the intentional, negative, or repressive aspects of this heritage into the German constitution of 1871. Together with the Kaiser's control over foreign policy, his command of the military (*Kommandogewalt*) constituted his major power. Every effort was made to protect this power from criticism by the civilian government and the public.

---

36. Michael Geyer, "Die Geschichte des deutschen Militärs von 1860 bis 1945," in *Die moderne deutsche Geschichte in der internationalen Forschung 1945–1975*, ed. Hans-Ulrich Wehler (Göttingen, 1978), 256–86; Manfred Messerschmidt, *Militär und Politik in der Bismarckzeit und im wilhelminischen Deutschland* (Darmstadt, 1975); Wilhelm Deist, "Armee in Staat und Gesellschaft, 1890–1914" in Deist, *Militär, Staat, und Gesellschaft* (Munich, 1991), 19–42; Bernd F. Schulte, *Die deutsche Armee, 1900–1914* (Düsseldorf, 1977).

37. Dieter Langewiesche, "Die Rolle des Militärs in den europäischen Revolutionen von 1848/49," in *Ungarn-Deutschland*, ed. W. Bachofer and H. Fischer (Munich, 1983), 273–88.

38. Wolfram Siemann, *Gesellschaft im Aufbruch* (Frankfurt, 1990).

39. Eugene Newton Anderson, *The Social and Political Conflict in Prussia, 1858–1864* (Lincoln, Neb., 1954).

104   The Reichstag's budgetary power over the military was curtailed by setting army strength in perpetuity and fixing military budgets for seven-year (later five-year) periods. That gave the Reichstag only intermittent opportunity to debate military policy. There was no secretary of war; at most the Prussian war minister might answer questions posed by Reichstag representatives. But after the mid-1880s, he was intentionally kept ignorant of planning, personnel, and even many financial matters, so his answers were not especially instructive.[40] Where ministerial links between the army and Reichstag were lacking, those between the military and the monarch continued as in absolutist times through the Military Cabinet (and with the founding of the navy, the Naval Cabinet), which after 1883 ran personnel matters.[41] To protect the Kaiser's power of command from civilian oversight within the government, the chief of the General Staff (in charge of war planning), the military and naval cabinet chiefs, and numerous other higher-level commanders gradually acquired the right of meeting with the monarch in the chancellor's absence, which vastly increased the probability that policy would be formed according to military rather than civilian-political considerations. Finally, in the event of war or domestic uprising, Article 68 decreed that all civilian government ceased; its functions automatically went over to the district military commanders. We shall examine the consequences of the military's isolation below.

Not surprisingly, such formal, constitutional measures also encouraged informal accommodation, since political power flowed through military channels. The monarchy successfully manipulated and thus nationalized its military image. Both Kaiser Wilhelm I and his grandson, Wilhelm II, conceived of themselves as military men, appearing in public exclusively in uniform. They cultivated strong personal relations with the members of the officer corps, and Wilhelm II (ruled 1888–1918) surrounded himself with military advisors.[42] Prussian court ceremonies, which after 1871 took on national importance, were saturated with uniforms and military custom. Because both real and symbolic power were so heavily militarized, ambitious social groups, particularly from bourgeois strata, acquired military trappings to aid their upward mobility. Bourgeois sons coveted reserve officer status for this reason, despite its many fetters to their political and social freedom.[43] Military service became synonymous with manhood and with citizenship, providing another reason for the exclusion of women from politics. And military mannerisms—the "hard look" (*forscher Blick*), the command tone, stiff bearing, and so forth—penetrated deep into civilian life.[44]

---

40. Gordon Craig, *The Politics of the Prussian Army, 1640–1945* (Oxford, 1955), 217–51.

41. Rudolf Schmidt-Bückeburg, *Das Militärkabinett der preussischen Könige und deutschen Kaiser* (Berlin, 1933).

42. Isabel V. Hull, *The Entourage of Kaiser Wilhelm II, 1888–1918* (Cambridge, 1982), 175–235.

43. Manfred Messerschmidt, "Die Armee in Staat und Gesellschaft—die Bismarckzeit," in *Das kaiserliche Deutschland*, ed. Michael Stürmer (Düsseldorf, 1970), 107; Deist, "Armee in Staat und Gesellschaft," 30–31; Eckart Kehr, "Zur Genesis des Königlich Preussischen Reserveoffiziers," in Kehr, *Primat der Innenpolitik*, ed. Hans-Ulrich Wehler (Berlin, 1965), 53–55.

44. The classic contemporary fictional account is Heinrich Mann, *Man of Straw*, trans. Ernest Boyd (London, 1947).

The military self-presentation of the monarchy and the enthusiastic identification of bourgeois circles with military symbols for a long time made it seem that the monarchy and its noble supporters successfully controlled nationalist politics by manipulating "militarism." Recent research has shown, however, that the monarchy lost control of nationalist politics, despite (or rather because of) the ubiquity of national-military priorities.[45] The repressive-reactionary side of the military could not integrate disparate social strata into a national whole nor could it define the goals of the nation any better in 1900 than it had in 1860. It was the other side, the army as heroic instrument of unification and exemplar of patriotic self-sacrifice, that alone could fulfill these functions. And this was precisely the aspect of the military that was "captured" by bourgeois and lower-middle-class groups organized into agitation societies.[46] As government foreign policy seemed increasingly unsuccessful to these groups, they wielded the national-military bludgeon against the monarchy in vicious criticism of governmental weakness and ineptitude. These groups had come to define what successful national policy was; they had given it content. This is the process that Stig Förster has labeled "double militarism."[47] Because it produced a hothouse effect on Germany's military culture, we need to examine it more closely.

Significantly, double militarism began in the 1880s and 1890s in colonial politics. The Pan-German League, the most extreme and vociferous agitation group, developed out of the colonial organizations, while the Navy League, the largest and best-funded group, was founded surreptitiously by the government to whip up popular support for the new instrument of *Weltpolitik*, the navy. These agitation groups and others, such as the Army League, wholeheartedly endorsed the main outlines of government policy: identification of Germany with its military strength and, in lieu of immediate domestic reform, an activist, expansionist, and bellicose-sounding foreign policy fit for a world power. The difference between the agitation groups and the government was that, not having to pay for these policies or realize them in fact, they were free to demand immediate, grandiose successes. When these were not forthcoming, they held the government responsible. For, unlike the relatively conservative national leadership, which at most hoped to use foreign political changes to shore up the status quo at home, the agitation groups recklessly embraced the revolutionary potential of German foreign policy abroad and at home. They embraced the transformation of mere nationalism into dynamic, high-stakes, imperialist, and populist ultranationalism. Above all, as other nations reacted to German imperial, military, and foreign political actionism by increased armament and protective alliances, the agitation groups defined the new situation according to their own extreme social Darwinism. The world was a place of ubiquitous, inevitable, existential conflict, and only that nation that was prepared to give itself up entirely to military preparedness would sur-

---

45. Geoff Eley, *Reshaping the German Right* (New Haven, 1983).

46. Ibid.; Roger Chickering, *We Men Who Feel Most German* (Boston, 1984); Thomas Rohkrämer, *Der Militarismus der "kleinen Leute"* (Munich, 1990); Stig Förster, *Der doppelte Militarismus* (Stuttgart, 1985).

47. Förster, *Der doppelte Militarismus*.

106 vive.[48] That required a mobilization of popular masses and a diversion of resources for military purposes far beyond anything most government leaders dreamed of or wanted.

In short, the agitation groups took the military, foreign political, national premises of Wilhelminian government literally, and they took them to their extremes. They came to dominate public opinion on national politics. They were able to do so because they were more adept at wielding commercial propaganda than the government was, because their organizations gave a political voice and satisfying activism to hundreds of thousands of Germans dissatisfied with the narrowness and ineffectuality of the political parties, because they seemed like "experts" on colonial and military matters, and because the government had nothing better to offer. Furthermore, the "logic" of nationalism and national security made it impossible for the government to counter the agitation groups: after all, they were the most pro-German, patriotic, promilitary people in the country. Increasingly, the government lost control over the national arena; it faced enormous pressure from the agitation groups for colonial expansion, arms increases, and war. This was especially true after 1911, but the process began the moment Germany first embarked on colonialism in the early 1880s.

As for the Reichstag, it, too, succumbed to the intertwined logic of national security and national imperialism. It did so in 1904–5 because of the revolts in Southwest Africa. The first debates in January 1904 show how reluctant most members were to throw more resources into Germany's exotic and unsuccessful colonies. The most powerful argument causing them to overcome their colonial tepidness was duty: "Because we have established a German protectorate in the area, we owe SWA every protection."[49] The government played the national security card by claiming the "dignity" of the nation was at stake.[50] Once troops were committed and had sacrificed themselves, then the regular mechanisms of fortress patriotism came into play and even Left Liberals announced that "the current moment, when our troops are risking life and blood in the battle against the Herero, is inappropriate [for questioning]."[51] By the end of 1904, despite all the wrangling over railroad building, it was clear that two main blocs of former colonial opponents had swung around to supporting colonialism: parts of the Center Party and the Left Liberals. In short, military engagement made the colony into an issue of national pride and security, which dampened criticism and converted opponents to proponents. This was a profound political transformation, for it brought a much larger spectrum of liberal, bourgeois opinion into the government camp than had ever before been possible. Chancellor Bülow merely cashed in on these changes during the famous "Hottentot" elections of 1907.[52] Even though the 1912 elections produced a Social Democratic Party (SPD) victory, the reconfiguration of liberal-bourgeois politics remained steadfast.

48. Chickering, We Men, 96, 122–23, 129.

49. Spahn, Sten. Ber., 11th legis. per., 14th meeting, 19 Jan. 1904, vol. 197, p. 365, and entire debate, pp. 361–70.

50. Stübel, ibid., 14 Mar. 1904, vol. 199, p. 1772. Also Patzig, p. 1895.

51. Richter, ibid., 17 Mar. 1904, 1896–97. Also, Schrader, p. 1897, and Patzig, p. 1895.

52. George Dunlap Crothers, The German Elections of 1907 (New York, 1941); Jonathan Sperber, The Kaiser's Voters (Cambridge, 1997), 241–47

The story of Germany's forced unification and of the "double militarism" that followed from it has been often told, but almost always it has been from the standpoint of the invidious effects "militarism" had on policy, politics, and/or society.[53] But this process also worked in reverse; the peculiar constitution, the unintegrated ("polycratic")[54] governance structure, and the symbolic importance of the military to German populist nationalism all affected the military and its functioning. They strongly shaped Germany's military culture by defining the framework in which it operated and the force field to which it responded.

The Effects of Political Parameters on German Military Culture

The constitution, drafted to ensure maximum power to the military, had two major unintended consequences for military culture. First, it created a vacuum in which military-institutional dynamics could freely develop without being crosscut or interrupted by extramilitary considerations. Although militaries tend toward encapsulation, the German case was unusual. This did not necessarily shape the *content* of German military culture but it increased the probability that whatever content arose would tend to develop to an extreme. Furthermore, civilian leaders accepted the military's insularity and preeminence in times of crisis and intentionally absented themselves from decision making or curtailed their own critical influence, as we have seen Bülow do in SWA, and as Chancellor Theobald von Bethmann Hollweg did in July 1914 and throughout World War I.

Second, the constitution thwarted policy coordination in two different ways. The political, legal, economic, diplomatic, and social considerations a civilian chancellor and cabinet ought to have brought to military thinking were missing. That is, strategy, which is the combination of these, was blocked institutionally. Bismarck's constitution vested the Kaiser with sole responsibility for coordinating these realms, and either he or his chancellor had to be extraordinarily gifted to accomplish this task without having an institutional venue regularly providing the occasion to coordinate policy. After Bismarck's dismissal in 1890, no such personality filled the gap. The polycratic potential of Wilhelminian government, with its many uncoordinated founts of policy, could not exercise oversight, much less domination, over the military. Military policy tended to be solipsistic, even in matters of national security. Incredible as it may seem, Germany's military planning after 1871 occurred largely without reference to its foreign policy.

If there was no integration of politics and the military, there was no coordination among the various military organs, either. The General Staff, in charge of planning for war, the Prussian War Ministry, in charge of matériel and troop strength, and the Military Cabinet, in charge of personnel, proceeded along their separate tracks without regard for one another. The General Staff consequently developed a war plan (the Schlieffen Plan) that required eight army corps (about sixteen divisions) more than the War Ministry had

53. For example, concerning responsibility for the war: Ritter, *Sword and the Sceptre*; Egmont Zechlin, *Krieg und Kriegsrisiko* (Düsseldorf, 1979).

54. "Polycratic" was Hans-Ulrich Wehler's term for the Kaiserreich. It has since more widely been used to characterize Nazi Germany. Hans-Ulrich Wehler, *The German Empire, 1870–1918* (Leamington Spa, U.K., 1985).

108 provided by 1914.[55] German army organization was radically segmented. The segments were inadvertently encouraged to act solipsistically, that is, in reference to their own requirements or judgments without the feedback or restraint that comes from inconvenient reality. Scholars have used the term "autism" to describe the resulting organizational behavior, which tended to wishful thinking instead of realism, to projection, and to vicious circles.[56]

The organizational weaknesses bequeathed to the military by the constitution meant that the military was unable to fulfill the enormous national roles and tasks expected of it by "double militarism." Hungry to legitimate itself and strongly identified with the military, the monarchy was powerless to counter the populist military enthusiasm generated by the agitation groups and apparently adopted by much wider circles. Double militarism enormously inflated the military's symbolic importance to national identity. This went far beyond the usual equation of the military with national security, which would have made it important enough. Instead, the military was also the foremost instrument of national integration ("the school of the nation"); the main guarantee of Germany's world power status; the exemplar of its national virtues of technological prowess, discipline, rational planning, and practicality; and the instrument of its future in a cut-throat, competitive world. The military was, thus, an overfreighted symbol. And it was impossible for most people to separate the symbol from the real institution and its actions.

Symbolic overload had at least two important consequences for German military culture. One was stereotyping. Popular enthusiasm for the military and projection onto it expressed itself in all sorts of commercial venues, cheap books, daily newspapers, magazine supplements, picture postcards, and the like. All of this encouraged a larger-than-life picture of military characteristics and virtues that was not without effect on the officers and men. The colonial-military memoir literature, for example, describes the expectations and then the experiences of the writers in repetitive little stories and snapshots that constitute abiding tropes: the experienced, fatherly senior officer; the dashing, reckless lieutenant; the nervousness before the "baptism by fire"; the pride, patriotism, and satisfaction afterward; the comradeship of physical suffering; the tenderness toward one's own wounded; the cunning and ruthlessness of the solitary hero; the perfidy and cowardice of the enemy; the nobility of and attachment to one's horse; and so forth. This stereotype, while useful for building identity and identification, was also a straitjacket reinforcing insularity and inflexibility.

The most important result of symbolic overload, however, was the imperative to succeed. The widespread public identification of the military with Germany's essence, with its world power and future prosperity, or simply with Germany itself, meant that the public expected it always and under every circumstance to acquit itself successfully. We have already seen in the case of SWA what "success" meant: quick, smooth, unquestionable victory. In that the military's métier was force, the victory was expected to be in the same

55. Stig Förster, "Dreams and Nightmares," in *Anticipating Total War*, ed. Manfred F. Boemeke, Roger Chickering, and Stig Förster (Cambridge, 1999), 358.

56. Dieter Senghaas, *Rüstung und Militarismus* (Frankfurt, 1972), 50–62; Schulte, *Die deutsche Armee*, 72.

coin, that is, the physical defeat of the enemy. And because the military operated so strongly in a symbolic mode, the enemy's defeat had to be similarly expressed in clear symbols of deference and humiliation. These sorts of expectations placed an enormous burden on the military. It was simply unthinkable that Germany's premier institution should fail. The most astonishing sign of the ubiquity of this conviction is the ease with which right-wing officers convinced most Germans, in the face of every physical and political indication to the contrary, that Germany had not in fact lost World War I but had instead been "stabbed in the back" at home.[57]

An enormous cleft thus opened up between the huge national tasks it faced and the army's ability to fulfill them. For conservative social reasons, the constitution inadequately tapped Germany's burgeoning wealth (for example by omitting a national income tax), so the army remained underfunded. For reasons of domestic control, the War Ministry restricted army growth to socially "reliable" groups, so Germany never took full advantage of universal military service.[58] The desire to escape Reichstag scrutiny was so strong that the army put a premium on handling crises with the available resources, rather than asking the Reichstag for supplementary funding. And the national tasks may have been too large to fulfill even if all possible material resources had been exploited. In the event, the army was left to overcome the cleft between reach and grasp by cultivating its peculiar qualitative virtues and its officers' zealotry.

The elements of Germany's political culture that we have just examined—its constitution and "double militarism"—set the parameters within which German military culture developed and flourished. They affected the shaping of military doctrine, self-understanding, training, decision making, and practice. It is to these subjects that we now turn in detail, beginning with the founding event of the German army, the Franco-Prussian War of 1870–71.

---

57. Wilhelm Deist, "Der militärische Zusammenbruch des Kaiserreichs," in Deist, *Militär, Staat, und Gesellschaft* (Munich, 1991), 211–33; Friedrich Frhr. Hiller von Gaertringen, " 'Dolchstoss-Diskussion' und 'Dolchstoss-Legende' im Wandel von vier Jahrzehnten," in *Geschichte und Gegenwartsbewusstsein* (Göttingen, 1963), 122–60.

58. In 1914 only 36.5% of potential draftees served in the German army, as opposed to 60% in the French army: Holger Afflerbach, " 'Bis zum letzten Mann und letzten Groschen?' " in *Die Wehrpflicht*, Beiträge zur Militärgeschichte, vol. 43, ed. Roland F. Foerster (Munich, 1994), 71–90, here 76; Stig Förster, "Militär und staatsbürgerliche Partizipation," in *Die Wehrpflicht*, 55–70.

5

Lessons of 1870–71

Institutions and Law

Prussia entered the mid-nineteenth century with a formidable military tradition. It was the product of self-contradictory parentage: the pragmatic "absolutism" of Frederick the Great, the liberal reforms of the Napoleonic period (epitomized in the writings of Carl von Clausewitz), the hostile revisions of those reforms that accreted after the post-Napoleonic restoration, and the antiliberal but technically modernizing "reform" of King Wilhelm I in the early 1860s.[1] These doctrinal, institutional, and cultural inheritances were galvanized and transformed during the three wars of German unification in 1864 (against Denmark), in 1866 (against Austria and the other German states), but especially in 1870–71 (against France). The Franco-Prussian War of 1870–71 set the model for the subsequent standard practices of the German army. This is hardly surprising since the Franco-Prussian War was the first German "national" war and was thus formative in a number of respects. The armies of the several, independent German states, which had fought against Prussia just four years earlier, now fought victoriously under the leadership of the Prussian General Staff. The war created the German state, revolutionized the state system of Europe, and seemed to inaugurate a new kind of warfare.[2]

For the military, the wars of unification were foundational doctrinally and institutionally. Chief of the General Staff Helmuth v. Moltke's modernization of the older Prussian military view that the proper way to fight was to concentrate nearly all one's forces at a single point with the Clausewitzian aim of totally destroying the foe's military force was established as canonical in 1866 and 1870. Doctrine will be the subject of chapter 7.

---

1. Geyer, "Past As Future."
2. Watershed in warfare: Daniel Pick, *War Machine*, 88–114; Bucholz, *Moltke, Schlieffen, and Prussian War Planning*, 85; Martin van Crefeld, *Command in War* (Cambridge, Mass., 1985), 144; Mark Stoneman, "The Bavarian Army and French Civilians in the War of 1870–1871," *War in History* 8:3 (July 2001), 271–93, here 290–91, 293.

Here we concentrate on the institutional revolution that 1870 created. This occurred on four fronts: the elevation of the General Staff to paramountcy, the establishment of "mission tactics," the laying down of principles governing treatment of civilians, and the consequent development of the theory of war and "military necessity." As we shall see, Germany's military regulations and its interpretation of military necessity diverged ever more widely from the principles that were being codified in international law.

The General Staff

After 1871 the General Staff became the main arbiter of Germany's modern military culture. It selectively interpreted the lessons of the past and institutionalized them (in explicit doctrine, regulation, and bureaucratic routine, as well as in implicit basic assumptions and unexamined thought patterns). The General Staff educated several generations of military leaders in these precepts and through them and their professional habits helped disseminate these patterns throughout the army.

The Prussian reformers of the Napoleonic period had created the General Staff to ensure systematic, professional planning. It stayed a small and overlooked subunit of the War Ministry until its chief, Helmuth v. Moltke, demonstrated in 1864 how effectively it could coordinate operations.[3] Moltke's General Staff received credit for defeating the Austrians at Königgrätz in 1866, thanks to its meticulous prewar planning, audacious use of the new technology the railroad, and effective staff work.[4] Consequently, in 1866 the chief of the General Staff received the right to oversee troops in war, not simply to plan. The operative effectiveness of the General Staff was demonstrated yet again in 1870–71, and its prestige thereafter was unapproached by any other unit in the military.

After 1871 the power of the General Staff increased until its purview encompassed operational planning, oversight in wartime, mobilization, communication and railroad coordination, and training of the officer corps.[5] In the absence of an overall coordinating institution, the General Staff filled that vacuum.[6] The consistency it lent (through war planning, the staff system, bureaucratic procedure, and example) was the main avenue through which its version of military culture became hegemonic inside the army.

Its officers incorporated the virtues of the officer corps and became models. Serving in the General Staff was the goal of every ambitious officer, so it attracted the very best candidates. A competitive examination selected 150 men per year for the war college, of whom only a third graduated. These select few then served two years with the General Staff, and of these, only three or four officers were chosen to become permanent members of the General Staff. The rest commonly rotated between service in the General Staff and

3. Arden Bucholz, *Moltke and the German Wars, 1864–1871* (New York, 2001).

4. Gunther Rothenberg, "Moltke, Schlieffen, and the Doctrine of Strategic Envelopment," in *Makers of Modern Strategy*, ed. Peter Paret (Princeton, 1986), 296–325, here 304; Wilhelm Deist, "Remarks on the Precondition to Waging War in Prussia-Germany, 1866–1871," in *On the Road to Total War*, ed. Stig Förster and Jörg Nagler (New York, 1997), 311–25, here 321–22.

5. Colonel Trevor Nevitt Dupuy, *A Genius for War* (Englewood Cliffs, N.J., 1977), 46–47, 112–13.

6. Bucholz, *Moltke, Schlieffen*, 99–102, 226. Hew Strachan appears to disagree, at least for the later army: *The First World War*, vol. 1 (Oxford, 2001), 172.

Division staff between Mława and Sierpc in Poland, First World War. *Der Weltkrieg, illustrierte Kriegs-Chronik des Daheim* (Bielefeld: Velhagen & Klasing, 1915–), vol. 2, 109.

"line" commands, which created a cadre of like-trained officers throughout the army, who were in charge of operative planning and coordination at army, division, and regimental levels.[7] The General Staff operated according to merit, not social background (noble predicate). It cultivated a colossal work ethic and an ethos of selfless, goal-oriented duty.[8] The relatively small number of officers who had enjoyed General Staff training made up a disproportionately large number of troop commanders and inspectors, and most military attachés. They also represented the German military internationally, for example, during the negotiations to codify the rules of war at the Hague Conferences.[9]

The German General Staff was a modern bureaucracy, organized according to the principle of the specialization of knowledge. It was divided into sections (operations, mobilization, railroad, topography, maneuvers, etc.) that functioned separately and without much knowledge of the other sections.[10] Technical efficacy was heightened through rotation to line commands, which kept tactical problems in the focus of planning, and through regular staff rides, war games, and "homework," all of which encouraged periodic, critical self-appraisals.[11]

The advantages the general staff system produced were so obvious to contemporaries that states without it swiftly introduced the system after 1871.[12] As it was meant to

7. Theodor Ropp, *War in the Modern World* (Durham, N.C., 1959), 137, cited in Dupuy, *Genius*, 48.

8. Hugo Frhr. von Freytag-Loringhoven, *Menschen und Dinge, wie ich sie in meinem Leben sah* (Berlin, 1923), 135, 268; Wilhelm Groener, *Lebenserinnerungen*, ed. Friedrich Frhr. Hiller von Gaertringen (Göttingen, 1957), 69.

9. Otto, *Schlieffen*, 53.

10. Groener, *Lebenserinnerungen*, 84; Germany, Reichsarchiv, *Der Weltkrieg 1914 bis 1918*, 14 vols. (Berlin, 1925–44), vol. 12:3; Wiegand Schmidt-Richberg, *Die Generalstäbe in Deutschland, 1871–1945*, vol. 3, ed. Militärgeschichtliches Forschungsamt (Stuttgart, 1962), 11–120, here 33–36, 49–51; Otto, *Schlieffen*, 35–52.

11. See Bucholz's excellent descriptions in *Moltke, Schlieffen*, 85–93, and passim.

12. Dupuy, *Genius*, 113–14.

Staff officers observe a battle from a hill, First World War. *Der Weltkrieg, illustrierte Kriegs-Chronik des Daheim* (Bielefeld: Velhagen & Klasing, 1915–), vol. 2, 301.

do, the General Staff guaranteed focused, professional, systematic, operative planning. It selected the cream of military talent and trained it to high standards, producing a uniform set of motivated, hard-working professionals who could perform almost interchangeably.[13] Through this system Germany created the finest army in Europe, meaning that it could win battles against superior numbers and it could inflict more casualties per soldier than could its opponents.[14] The German army was extremely effective at the level of fighting.

The palpable successes of the general staff system were so great that they eclipsed the main danger inherent in its organization: that it could become ever more narrowly focused on perfecting the technical management of violence, until the means became the end. The triumph of technical narrowness and its counterproductive effects are clearest in doctrine and in the conduct of World War I, where we will examine them more closely. For now, it is enough to indicate the direction of developments and the relation of these to the founding events of 1870–71.

Hyperspecialization is a common dynamic in modern organizations. Its foundations were laid in the functional structure of the General Staff (its division into sections). Arden Bucholz has shown, for example, how the railroad section gradually assumed preemi-

---

13. Rothenberg, "Moltke," 301–2; Schulte, *Die deutsche Armee*, 106–8, 156, 160; Gerhard Granier, "Einleitung," in Adolf Wild von Hohenborn, *Briefe und Tagebuchaufzeichnungen des preussischen Generals als Kriegsminister und Truppenführer im Ersten Weltkrieg*, ed. Helmut Reichold and Gerhard Granier (Boppard am Rhein, 1986), 2; see also the uniform leadership standards for all levels of officers in Prussia, War Ministry, *Exerzir-Reglement für die Infanterie*, 2nd ed. (Berlin, 1889) (often spelled "Exerzier").

14. Dupuy, *Genius*, 177–78; Bucholz, *Moltke and the German Wars*; Dennis E. Showalter, "German Grand Strategy," *Militärgeschichtliche Mitteilungen* 42 (1990), 65–102; superior numbers: Deist, "Remarks," 315, 317.

Regimental scribe in the field, First World War. *Der Weltkrieg, illustrierte Kriegs-Chronik des Daheim* (Bielefeld: Velhagen & Klasing, 1915–), vol. 2, 64.

nence inside the General Staff because of its task to plan for the next war[15] and, above all, because it construed that task technically, as the solution to discrete organizational problems (for example, mobilization and deployment). This view is already visible in the experts' interpretation of Moltke's victories in 1866 and 1870 as the result of superior organization and technical manipulation. The institutional and the cognitive mutually supported and mutually determined each other. The resulting narrow view of war then replicated itself, producing further "lessons" upholding its validity. Schlieffen's excursions into military history are famous examples.[16]

Professional narrowness tended to spiral downward toward the ever more specific use of violence. Instead of the strategic, the General Staff focused on operations, or even tactics.[17] This institutional bias (in planning, for example) also had cognitive aspects apparent in the model character of Moltke's victories. Moltke had won battles; the wars were actually concluded by diplomacy. The professionals' interpretation of the wars of unification placed the battles at the center. Thereafter, the battle became the focus of

15. Bucholz, *Moltke, Schlieffen*, 145–50.

16. Ibid., 314.

17. Showalter, "German Grand Strategy," 76–78; Dennis E. Showalter, "From Deterrence to Doomsday Machine," *Journal of Military History* 64 (July 2000), 679–710, here 697; Walter Goerlitz, *Kleine Geschichte des deutschen Generalstabes* (Berlin, 1967), 131; Messerschmidt, "Military Elites," 60–65; Förster, *Doppelte Militarismus*, 20; Deist, "Remarks," 322–23; Detlef Bald, *Der deutsche Generalstab, 1859–1939* (Munich, 1977), 44–48.

planning, as if it could end war by itself; the military-technical displaced the political-diplomatic.

The organizational-cultural dynamic pressed the spiral ever downward. Decision making and problem solving tended to revolve inside the narrow frame of the battle, predisposing General Staff officers to seek solutions to military problems at the same level, or lower (i.e., tactics). As we saw in SWA, when officers faced problems, they were likely to launch another battle or try new tactics rather than to rethink the problem strategically, structurally, or extramilitarily.

Planning, the original task of the General Staff, displayed these same tendencies. Organizations frequently have difficulty avoiding self-referential, and therefore unrealistic, planning.[18] In the German case, the narrow focus on battle relegated everything else, even including provisioning one's own troops, to the background. Again, the template was set in 1870: Moltke's brilliant use of the railroads to deploy huge armies used every single train, leaving none for logistics.[19] The organizational split between the General Staff and the War Ministry, which was in charge of resources, did not help the General Staff overcome its propensities. We will examine planning in detail in chapter 7.

The General Staff's flaws derived from its strengths. Its excellence in solving complex management problems, its superior, "strong" organization made it supremely successful at fighting on the operative level. As World War I showed, these very operative strengths blinded Germany to its strategic weaknesses. Success, in the 1860s and 1870s and later, measured in terms of fighting capacity, helped block the General Staff from reexamining itself as an institution.

Similarly, its fabled success in producing a cadre of like-minded professional officers insulated its military culture from critical scrutiny inside the military. The uniformly trained staff officers shared so many of the basic assumptions about the nature of war, the paramountcy of battle, the irrelevancy of other considerations, and the exploitation of operative and tactical mastery, that they were *betriebsblind* (organization blind), that is, unlikely to see the problems plaguing their own institution. The more successful their training, the blinder they were likely to be.

Mission Tactics

As the General Staff incorporated the lessons of 1870 in institutional form, "mission tactics" (*Auftragstaktik*) did so in command and leadership on the battlefield. In 1866 and again in 1870 Moltke had gotten the drop on his opponents by deploying his forces separately and having them converge at the time of battle. This solution to the problem of swiftly maneuvering mass armies, together with the expectation that commanders would attack aggressively, required that officers think and act independently without waiting for

18. Feld, "Information and Authority," 74; Jack Snyder, *The Ideology of the Offensive* (Ithaca, N.Y., 1984); Posen, *Sources of Military Doctrine*, 47–50; Stephen van Evera, "The Cult of the Offensive and the Origins of the First World War," *International Security* 9:1 (summer 1984), 58–107.

19. Martin van Crefeld, *Supplying War* (Cambridge, 1977), 105–7; Deist, "Remarks," 322–23; Goerlitz, *Kleine Geschichte*, 131.

116   orders that inevitably would arrive too late. It took until 1888 for this principle to be enshrined in training regulations, and probably longer before it saturated actual training, but over time Auftragstaktik became the unique hallmark of the German army.[20] It contributed substantially to the German army's singular effectiveness, but, like its institutional counterpart, the General Staff, it also encouraged dangerous dynamics; it made excessive zeal and actionism on the part of officers more likely.

Under mission tactics, commanders issued general orders outlining the task at hand and left the details of accomplishment to their subordinates. This system operated from the senior-most general to the junior-most lieutenant and held good for the fighting as well as the occupation forces. Mission tactics demanded thinking and initiative. The combat manual (*Felddienst-Ordnung*) for 1900 made the principle clear: "In every situation, even the most extraordinary, each officer should apply his entire personality, without shrinking from responsibility, to fulfill his mission, even without waiting for orders concerning all the details. Superiors must encourage this application of personality."[21] A popular, unofficial handbook for officers glossed this rule: "The officer's obedience must be self-activating, voluntary and not slavish." It continued, "The officer must early on fashion his own viewpoint and may express this tactfully and modestly to his superior."[22]

Two things prevented anarchy in this system. First, uniform training in operative and tactical principles ensured that officers would judge military situations and "solve" problems similarly.[23] Second, initiative was to be exercised only in fulfillment of the mission. As the exercise manual (1888) put it, "The decisions to be taken independently must always be guided by the coherence [of the plan]."[24] Mission tactics did encourage critical thinking and therefore was one potential source of resistance to standard operating procedures and their consequences. But the critical thinking that mission tactics encouraged was sharply bounded by tactical and operative parameters; it was self-delimiting, making it more likely to increase the army's effectiveness at ground level and even to produce policy drift toward greater violence, than to challenge it.

In order to allow their subordinates latitude, commanders were warned to avoid "intervening immediately in [the operation of] lower units."[25] The directives German officers received were usually less detailed than those characteristic of other armies. Nonetheless, while the mission tactics system produced broad orders, it still contained explicit expectations of its officers. Moltke himself had inserted the following sentence in the 1888

20. Daniel J. Hughes, "Schlichting, Schlieffen, and the Prussian Theory of War in 1914," *Journal of Military History* 59 (April 1995), 257–78, here 265, 270; Rothenberg, "Moltke," 296; Dupuy, *Genius*, 116; Schulte, *Die deutsche Armee*, 477–78; Storz, *Kriegsbild*, 31–32, 167–70.

21. Prussia, War Ministry, *Felddienst-Ordnung* (Berlin, 1900), 9–10. The revised manual of 1908 was less emphatic but made the same point: *Felddienst-Ordnung* (Berlin, 1908), 9.

22. *Eiswaldt's Handbuch für Einjährig-Freiwillige, Reserve-Offizieraspiranten, und Offiziere des Beurlaubtenstandes des Trains*, 10th ed. (Berlin, 1915), 45, 46. This handbook, finished in the summer of 1914, reflected military thinking just as war began.

23. Rothenberg, "Moltke," 301–2.

24. Prussia, War Ministry, *Exerzir-Reglement*, 2nd ed., 126–27. This and other sections on the general duties of officers are unchanged from the 1888 edition.

25. Ibid., 129.

manual: "The highest commander and the youngest soldier must always be conscious of the fact that omission and inactivity are worse than resorting to the wrong expedient."[26] In short, mission tactics pressured officers into actionism. The expectation that the good officer would go beyond the book in the interests of the greater mission became a fundamental principle of German military culture.[27] It encouraged risk taking and excess, and it promised to forgive mistakes ("wrong expedients") taken in that spirit.

The Treatment of Civilians

The Franco-Prussian War had the same foundational effect on military practices and their justifications as it had on institutions. The practices that developed in 1870–71 were codified in army regulations that remained substantially the same down to 1914, because no European war occurred to challenge them and because the colonial punitive expeditions, which were Germany's main military experience from 1871 to 1914, seemed to confirm their aptness. Furthermore, the basic interpreter of the lessons of 1870 was the General Staff, and its subsequent hegemony over doctrine, planning, and preparation ensured that its interpretation became canonical.[28] The controversial "lessons" of 1870 concerning treatment of civilians, consistently challenged afterward by other nations in international conferences on the laws of war, were nevertheless written into German military regulations and almost univocally defended by German jurists. Unofficial guidebooks to proper military conduct intended for use in combat defended the practices of 1870 and took them as their foundation.[29]

The knowledge and habits that developed from 1870 proved especially resistant to questioning or change because they were both institutionally formative and the result of "trauma-learning."[30] The year 1870 deserves the epithet "traumatic" because it was literally "existential"—the (future) existence of Germany hung in the balance—and also because its course was unexpected and supremely frustrating to the self-understanding of the army. On 2 September 1870 the Prusso-German army won the spectacular victory at Sedan that "annihilated" the enemy in the Clausewitzian sense, that is, the French Emporer's army surrendered. Yet the war did not end. Instead, an armed popular uprising raised by republicans and radical French nationalists confounded the Prussian General Staff, which found itself facing unconventional troops and occupying a surly and uncooperative populace. French popular forces in the end were limited and largely ineffective; the

26. *Exerzir-Reglement*, cited in Dupuy, *Genius*, 116.

27. Max von Gallwitz, *Meine Führertätigkeit im Weltkriege, 1914–1916* (Berlin, 1929), 185.

28. Manfred Messerschmidt, "Völkerrecht und 'Kriegsnotwendigkeit' in der deutschen militärischen Tradition," in Messerschmidt, *Was damals Recht war . . . NS-Militär- und Strafjustiz im Vernichtungskrieg* (Essen, 1996), 191–230, here 196; Geyer, "Past as Future," 189–90, 193–94.

29. For example, Felix Dahn, "Der deutsch-französische Krieg und das Völkerrecht," in Dahn, *Bausteine*, vol. 5, no. 1 (Berlin, 1884), 122–224, written "especially for the German officer and every educated soldier," 122; and Germany, General Staff (Maj. Rudolf v. Friedrich, author), *Kriegsbrauch im Landkriege* (Berlin, 1902) (hereafter General Staff, *Kriegsbrauch*). Cf. Dahn's 1884 work with that written at the start of the 1870 war, before its "lessons" had been learned: Dahn, *Das Kriegsrecht* (Würzburg, 1870).

30. Schein, "How Culture Forms," 25.

118 Franco-Prussian War never became a full-scale guerrilla war. But guerrilla fighters (whom the Germans dubbed "francs-tireurs") threatened railways and communications enough that one hundred thousand German troops had to be diverted from fighting to occupation duties.[31] Worse, it was no longer clear how to end the war, now that straightforward military victory was insufficient.

Chief of the General Staff Moltke, who originally had envisioned a conventional war to be ended by diplomacy, now in the fall and winter of 1870–71 went beyond these limits to embrace a more total form of war. Moltke "no longer reckoned with an equal partner with whom he could negotiate but instead an enemy [who must be forced] to surrender unconditionally [*auf Gnade und Ungnade*—literally, at the mercy of the victor]."[32] This enemy now included civilians.

The precedents for harsh treatment of civilians developed in a complex dialectic among troop expectations, innovative ad hoc practices, officers' retrospective approval, and official orders. We saw this pattern in SWA and it reappeared in 1914 in Belgium and northern France. Expectations were apparently set by a Prussian decree of 21 July 1866 that ordered the death penalty for civilian snipers.[33] In the heat of action, some soldiers omitted the obligatory courts-martial and resorted to summary execution; others torched houses where they thought francs-tireurs might be hiding. Their actions were at first tacitly approved by officers, encouraged further by broad, mission-tactic orders, and soon incorporated in orders at first from junior, and then from senior, commanders. Moltke then legalized a panoply of harsh responses, though not summary execution.

Moltke recognized the regular army and the national guard as legitimate soldiers who, when captured or wounded, enjoyed the status of protected prisoners of war. However, he noted, "Francs-tireurs are not soldiers and thus are subject to . . . the laws of war and to death."[34] Mayors of occupied towns were ordered to report francs-tireurs operating in their districts on penalty of having their houses burnt down.[35] The "order concerning the punishment of enemy inhabitants in case of actions against the German army" set collective, villagewide fines reckoned at between ten and twenty francs per head and added: "Furthermore, experience has shown that the more effective means [to deter francs-tireurs] is destroying the relevant farm or, in the case of more widespread participation, the entire locality."[36] To secure the railway lines, Moltke ordered "harsh reprisals against those localities in whose vicinity any disruption of the railroad has occurred. It would be recommended that, in those places where rail disturbances have often occurred, hostages consisting of local mayors or otherwise prominent persons should be taken on the trains

31. Albrecht von Boguslawski, *Der kleine Krieg und seine Bedeutung für die Gegenwart* (Berlin, 1881), 57–72, esp. 67–69; Michael Howard, *The Franco-Prussian War* (New York, 1961), 249–56, 371–81, 407–12; Walter Laqueur, *Guerrilla* (London, 1977), 85–87.

32. Rudolf Stadelmann, *Moltke und der Staat* (Krefeld, 1950), 246.

33. This account follows Stoneman, "Bavarian Army," and Howard, *Franco-Prussian War*, 250–51, 252, 379.

34. Moltke to Lt. Gen. von Werder, Nr. 193, 22 August 1870, in Germany, General Staff, ed., *Moltke's militärische Korrespondenz* (Berlin, 1896), 241–42; Howard, *Franco-Prussian War*, 378.

35. Christian Meurer, *Die Haager Friedenskonferenz*, vol. 2: *Das Kriegsrecht der Haager Konferenzen* (Munich, 1907), 109.

36. Order Nr. 380, 7 Nov. 1870, in Germany, General Staff, ed., *Moltke's Militärische Korrespondenz*, 368.

as hostages, preferably in the locomotives."[37] Civilians forced to act as guides for the oc- 119
cupiers were liable to execution if the information they gave was false. In addition to these
reprisals, the German army, after initially living off its own supplies, shifted the burden of
its own maintenance to the occupied country and resorted to heavy requisitions to feed itself and pay for military administration.[38]

Later apologists interpreted harsh reprisal orders as mere threats. But in fact civilian
hostages were placed on trains; localities were dunned stiff fines; guides, "spies," and suspected francs-tireurs were executed (with and without trial); and houses and villages were
destroyed in reprisals. As in SWA, men were targeted far more than women. And, as in
SWA, soldiers continued to profess allegiance to moral values, even when they trans-
gressed them, by blaming the victims or citing the necessities of warfare.[39] Some, like
Trotha and Schlieffen in 1904, even claimed the conflict was a "racial war."[40] Nonetheless,
one should not exaggerate the harshness; the foremost modern historian of the war,
Michael Howard, concludes that in general the German armies exercised disciplined restraint in the face of sometimes irresponsible provocation by French ultranationalists.[41]

The Methods of 1870 and the Laws of War

The significance of the 1870 war lies instead in the precedents it set. Chancellor Otto v.
Bismarck recognized the harshness of military conduct as something new in Germany's
history.[42] The new methods deemed acceptable after 1870 related mostly to the treatment
of enemy civilians, who were pulled into the vortex of war and who were less protected
from severe treatment than were prisoners of war.

The practical lessons of 1870 became part of Germany's military culture in several
different ways, ranging from official regulation to not-quite-official regulation, to memoirs and myths (for example, about the francs-tireurs).[43] The manual for the rear echelons, the *Kriegs-Etappen-Ordnung* (KEO), is an instance of official regulation. It made
enemy civilians liable to collective punishment in case of sabotage and to service as
hostages on threatened railways. It also suggested that requisitions could be raised regardless of the welfare of the occupied population.[44] All three points violated international law
at the time the KEO was written.

The fact that not one official German law book codified the proper treatment of civilians and prisoners of war testifies to the skepticism with which military leaders viewed laws
regulating combat. Their views were translated into troop training and behavior. Recruits

---

37. Order Nr. 309, 1 Oct. 1870, in ibid., 318; also Order Nr. 321 and Nr. 350, pp. 328, 351.

38. Stoneman, "Bavarian Army," 283–85, 287–88.

39. Ibid., 276–81, 278n43, 285–86, 291–92.

40. Ibid., 288.

41. Howard, *Franco-Prussian War*, 379–80. Stoneman agrees; "Bavarian Army," 290, 293.

42. Cited in Felix Dahn, "Zur neueren Praxis und Literatur des Völkerrechts," in Dahn, *Bausteine*, vol. 5,
no. 1, 45–121, here 63.

43. Myths and memoirs: Horne and Kramer, *German Atrocities*, 143–44.

44. Prussia, War Ministry, *Kriegs-Etappen-Ordnung* (KEO) (12 Mar. 1914) (D.V.E. Nr. 90) (Berlin, 1914),
p. 68 (para. 137), p. 69 (para. 141), and p. 52 (para. 103). See discussion in ch. 10.

120   had few opportunities to learn the international laws of war. They were probably most conversant with the Geneva Convention concerning recognized prisoners of war, because the convention had been printed in the back of the *Felddienst-Ordnung* since at least 1900, and because most officers and military writers approved of the Geneva Convention. The broader laws of war as codified at the Hague Conventions (1899, slightly modified 1907) were not included in the *Felddienst-Ordnung* until December 1911. Recruits apparently received no instruction in the general laws of war; of the twenty books customarily used for their training, only one (published first in 1917) briefly mentioned the Hague rules.[45]

The resulting ignorance of recruits reflected the convictions and priorities of their officers. Until 1907, when the instructor was fired, future General Staff officers at the War Academy received each week a thirty-minute lecture on international law.[46] So little did the laws of war apparently rank in the opinion of the academy that the post was left vacant for four years, and thereafter the legal lectures focused on domestic law.[47] The army did not even bother to draft regulations for executing the laws relating to prisoners of war.[48] The officers' lack of interest in law is also reflected in the complete absence of articles on the subject in the *Militär-Wochenblatt* (the main professional journal) after 1906.

The most obvious bellwether of officer opinion was the 1902 manual on the laws of war, *Kriegsbrauch im Landkrieg*. Allied propaganda pilloried this book during the First World War, because it denied the binding nature of any agreements save the Geneva Convention, virtually ignored the Hague rules, and defended by reference to "military necessity" the methods of 1870–71, many of which the Hague and other agreements had since outlawed.[49] Commissioned by the historical section of the General Staff and written in six weeks by Maj. Rudolf von Friederich, the book appeared under the imprint of the General Staff and thus assumed "quasi-official" character, as a Reichstag investigatory committee later admitted, even though strictly speaking only the War Ministry had the authority to issue official volumes. Asked by the committee to explain the absence of the Hague rules, which had previously been published in the *Reichsgesetzblatt* as officially binding for Germany, Friederich replied that he was not a lawyer. His intention had been "to describe and explain the reigning opinions in Germany," "the general opinion of the most influential persons in the contemporary war literature."[50] Friederich based his compilation on a preexisting card catalog and the libraries of the War Academy and the General Staff. There is

---

45. Germany, Parliament, *Das Werk des Untersuchungsausschusses der Verfassungsgebenden Deutschen Nationalversammlung und des Deutschen Reichstages, 1919–1928, Verhandlungen, Gutachten, Urkunden*, Reihe 3: vol. 1, *Das Völkerrecht im Weltkrieg*, ed. Eugen Fischer, Berthold Widmann, and Johannes Bell (Berlin, 1927), 26–27 (hereafter *UA* 3:1, page). Also Ernst Stenzel, *Die Kriegführung des deutschen Imperialismus und das Völkerrecht* (Berlin, 1973), 36–37.

46. The War Academy was careful to discuss Germany's reservations about the applicability of certain of the Hague Conventions: Horne and Kramer, *German Atrocities*, 149–50.

47. *UA* 3:1, 26.

48. The report of Christian Meurer, "Verletzungen des Kriegsgefangenenrechts," in ibid., 3.1: 29–909, here 181.

49. General Staff, *Kriegsbrauch*, 2–3, 9, 12, 16, 18, 19, 25, 30–31, 47–48, 49, 51–52, 59, 61–63. The book is heavily indebted to Lueder, *Krieg und Kriegsrecht* and *Landkriegsrecht*, whose language it often borrows.

50. *UA* 3:1, 48, 47, 27–28.

every reason to believe that his account is an accurate snapshot of what officers believed about the laws of war, since the pattern of undervaluation, rejection, and misconstrual is consistent with most German writings on the subject and, above all, with the training and omissions in actual practice mentioned above.

Recruits trained according to the opinions compiled by Friederich would have been under the impression that the following acts were legal and proper. Regarding civilians: killing civilians guilty of taking up arms against an occupier loosely defined (*Kriegsrebellion*); killing civilians guilty of harming the German war effort (*Kriegsverrat*); forcing civilians to act as guides, to give information harmful to their own country, to act as hostages, to work on public works with potentially military value; killing civilians for giving false information; subjecting them to collective fines for sabotage; killing them as "spies" without a trial, though a trial was "desirable"; destroying their property if military necessity, defined as mere success, required it. Regarding recognized prisoners of war: subjecting them to collective penalties; killing them in reprisal, as security risks, or if it was impossible to feed them. Regarding native populations in colonies: starving them en masse to win a guerrilla war.[51]

The recruits' training provided few safeguards against the drift to such harsh methods. Above all, ambivalence and lack of interest blighted the tentative beginnings to promote international law. The *Felddienst-Ordnung* (1900) is a typical example. It began well, but shrank back after the first sentence: "Mild treatment of enemy civilians is usually the most useful method. However, harshness appropriate to the earnestness of the situation should not be omitted regarding hostile inhabitants. Mildness and leniency in the wrong place can become harshness toward one's own troops."[52] This kind of skepticism came from the adamantine priority given to narrowly construed military operations, and it pushed all other considerations, including the treatment of civilians, the wounded, prisoners of war, and so forth, far into the background.[53]

The behavior of German officers and troops from the very beginning of World War I indicates that the panoply of harsh methods developed in 1870 were widely considered to be perhaps unfortunate, but in any case necessary, expedients in wartime.[54] The excep-

---

51. General Staff, *Kriegsbrauch*, civilians: 12, 13, 31, 48, 49, 50, 51, 53, 54, 62, 63; prisoners of war: 14, 15, 16; "savages": 53.

52. Prussia, War Ministry, *Felddienst-Ordnung* (1900), §433, p. 127. This precept had a long pedigree. Hartmann may have penned it first: "Leniency and mildness become cruelty, if they let the goal of war slip away and thus hinder the conclusion of peace"; Julius v. Hartmann, "Militärische Nothwendigkeit und Humanität," *Deutsche Rundschau* 13 (1877), 123–24. Thereafter, it was virtually a cliché. Col. Deimling, for example, informed the Reichstag in 1904 that "mildness toward natives is cruelty toward one's own troops"; in Gustav Noske, *Kolonialpolitik und Sozialdemokratie* (Stuttgart, 1914), 114. Or, Dep. Gov. Tecklenburg: "It would be a crime against our own sick soldiers in hospital, against the settlers and their children, if we used even one cow they needed to provide milk to save the lives of a few Herero prisoners." Tecklenburg to Col. Dept., Nr. 600, 3 July 1905, Windhuk, BA-Berlin, R 1001 Nr. 2118, p. 154.

53. This principle is nicely explained in the *Kriegs-Etappenordnung*: "The field army requires for the maintenance of its effectiveness . . . the removal of every burden that can hinder it (the sick, wounded, useless war matériel, prisoners or war, booty, etc.). These tasks fall to the rear." Prussia, War Ministry, *Felddienst-Ordnung* (1908), Anhang 1, 21.

54. See ch. 9.

122 tions of 1870 had become the rule. The hegemony of the exceptional inside the military institution was doubtless aided by its exceptional task of wielding violence. It was easy to argue that violence had laws of its own that ran counter to the laws of society, indeed, that cancelled them out. But behind such justifications one can discern basic assumptions of which contemporaries were only dimly, if at all, aware.

Justifications: "Military Necessity" and the Law of War

German government and military officials and law professors had many occasions to justify the practices of 1870–71, not only because France, England, and many smaller European states objected to them but because the creation of Germany coincided with an upsurge in the codification and extension of the international laws of war. The Geneva Convention of 1864 (on prisoners of war, revised 1906), the Brussels Conference on Land Warfare of 1874, and the Hague Conventions of 1899 and 1907 were opportunities for military and civilian representatives of many states to debate and reach agreement on international norms governing war.[55] These debates made explicit reasoning that might otherwise have remained submerged and inarticulate.

The various codifications of international law from 1864 to 1914 aimed to eliminate violence and destruction unnecessary to the accomplishment of military aims. The Geneva Convention defined wounded soldiers as no longer combatants; they and medical aides (military and private) were not legitimate targets. Similarly, prisoners of war were guaranteed humane treatment at the same standards as one's own troops. Nonofficers might work, for pay, but not on war-related projects. The Hague Convention on Land Warfare (1899) was the first international summary of the laws of war. Its signatories, including Germany, were bound to refrain from a list of techniques that spread suffering beyond the fighting troops: bombarding undefended cities; using new, cruel weapons (like dumdum bullets, aerial bombardment, or poison gas); or using occupied civilians for military purposes (as guides, hostages, war workers). Collective punishment and fines and unlimited requisitions were also forbidden in occupied areas.[56] In addition to the specific acts the nations had agreed on, the Martens Declaration declared that other inhumane or unnecessary practices were equally forbidden, even though they were not contained in positive law: "In cases not included in the present arrangement, populations and belligerents remain under the protection and empire of the principles of international law, as they result from the usages established between civilized nations, from the laws of humanity, and the re-

---

55. Geoffrey Best, *Humanity in Warfare* (London, 1980); Jost Dülffer, *Regeln gegen den Krieg?* (Berlin, 1981); Stenzel, *Kriegführung*; Messerschmidt, "Völkerrecht und 'Kriegsnotwendigkeit'"; Philipp Zorn, *Die beiden Haager Friedenskonferenzen von 1899 und 1907*, vol. 5, pt. 1 of *Handbuch des Völkerrechts*, ed. Fritz Stier-Somlo (Stuttgart, 1915); C. Lueder, "Krieg und Kriegsrecht im Allgemeinen" and "Das Landkriegsrecht im Besonderen," in *Handbuch des Völkerrechts*, ed. Franz von Holtzendorff (Hamburg, 1889), 169–367, 369–544; John Westlake, *International Law*, part 2: *War* (Cambridge, 1907); Meurer, *Haager Friedenskonferenz*; James Brown Scott, ed., *The Proceedings of the Hague Peace Conferences* (New York, 1920).

56. The discussion below considers several other controversial issues.

quirements of the public conscience."[57] The direction of international legal development, then, was to prohibit the practices Germany had used in 1870–71.

The most thorough German justification for the methods of 1870–71 appeared in the popular journal *Deutsche Rundschau* in 1877–78.[58] The arguments that Gen. Julius von Hartmann, a retired cavalry officer, gave there summarized the official German position thereafter, and not only among military men. Hartmann was arguing against the conclusions of the Brussels Conference, which had rejected using civilians as guides or as hostages, collective fines and destruction of localities as reprisals against civilians who could not be proven saboteurs, broad bombardment of undefended areas, unlimited requisitions, and the narrow definition of legitimate soldiers as only regular, uniformed troops. As a cavalry officer, Hartmann had helped crush the revolution of 1848–49 and had earned promotion to general while fighting against France in 1870–71. In defense of the practices condemned at Brussels he argued "military necessity," which thereafter was the main justification used by German representatives at subsequent international conferences and by German legal experts on international law.[59]

Military necessity, Hartmann wrote, was dictated by "the great, final purpose of war: *the defeat of the enemy's power, the overcoming of the enemy's energy, the overwhelming of the enemy's will.* This *one* goal commands absolutely, it dictates law and regulation. The concrete form of this law appears as *military necessity.*"[60] War was the great exception in human affairs:

War, as compared to peace, is something entirely *abnormal*; it produces exceptional/emergency situations [*Ausnahmezustände*—"declarations of emergency"] in the most decisive sense of that word. Indeed, it is itself an exceptional situation because it contradicts in its innermost nature the foundation on which civilization and culture rest, the laws according to which they have developed. In their stead it returns to conditions that permit the unlimited justification of individual power and might [*Kraft und Macht*].[61]

The exceptionality of war raises it above law.

War interrupts the legal condition of peace explosively, so to speak, and during its activity completely suspends the entire legal norms characteristic of peace.[62] . . .

57. Named after Fedor Fedorovitch Martens, the Russian representative. Cited in Best, *Humanity in Warfare*, 166; original in Scott, *Proceedings*, 547–48.

58. Hartmann, "Militärische Nothwendigkeit und Humanität," *Deutsche Rundschau* 13 (1877), 111–28, 450–71; 14 (1878), 71–91.

59. The best discussion of this concept and the relation of the German military to international law is in Messerschmidt, "Völkerrecht und 'Kriegsnotwendigkeit.'" Also, Best, *Humanity in Warfare*, 172–79. Subsequent German works on the law of war began from Hartmann's positions; for example: Lueder, "Krieg und Kriegsrecht," 186–87, 254–57, 262–63, 275–76; General Staff, *Kriegsbrauch*; Meurer, *Haager Friedenskonferenz*, 8–15, 213.

60. Hartmann, "Militärische Nothwendigkeit," 453–54. Emphasis in original.

61. Ibid., 123. Emphasis in original.

62. Ibid., 124.

124 War means the temporary suspension of [the international legal] order, which it replaces with battle.[63]

In these passages Hartmann has done two things. He has reified the existential, exceptional quality of the 1870–71 war as characteristic of all wars: all are unlimited, existential emergencies. From this follows the second principle, that anything that will win them must be permitted ("The warlike action is defined by its postulated goal, to lead the battle to victory").[64] As the contemporary British critic John Westlake pointed out, this view was an argument from "a necessity, not of war but of success."[65]

The first set of basic assumptions, then, concerned the always existential, unlimited nature of war. The second set concerned enemy civilians. As the experience in 1870 had shown, civilians were a legitimate target of war. "Modern war targets the entirety of the enemy's war power," which meant that "war goals emerge that leave behind a specifically military character and include general damage to the enemy."[66] Unlimited requisitions followed this principle; "Misery and torment should not be spared the enemy—they actually serve to break his energy and conquer his will."[67] Most of the measures wielded against civilians, however, came under another category: keeping order in the occupied zone. Here, too, the 1870–71 example was decisive, for Hartmann imagined that the worst case scenario, popular uprising, set the rules. In cases of popular uprising (guerrilla war), the people's "excesses can only be reined in when their paroxysm is met with drastic means. If individuals are hit hard, as warning examples to others, that is certainly deeply regrettable, but this harshness is a healthy and preserving good deed for the whole. Where there is popular uprising, *terrorism* becomes a necessary military principle."[68] It should be underscored that Hartmann's approval of "terrorism" was meant for European populations. No wonder that colonials would expect the same.

The international debate over popular uprisings revolved around two issues. The narrower one was solved at the Second Hague Convention (1907), which recognized uprisings occurring before effective occupation as legitimate and their irregular troops as soldiers protected by the Geneva Convention. The larger question, however, concerned the character of occupation itself and the rights of civilians under it. The German (and Russian) position was that occupation began immediately behind the front lines, regardless of whether the "occupier" actually controlled the area. The counterposition required effective administration. In addition, the Hague Convention (1899) ratified the view that occupation was temporary, pending the conclusion of peace; thus occupiers were to up-

---

63. Ibid., 128.

64. Ibid., 116.

65. Westlake, *International Law*, 117; Best, *Humanity in Warfare*, 175–76. Westlake was arguing against Lueder's restatement of Hartmann's maxim and pointed out that international law already amply acknowledged true necessity as a consideration in the legal limits to warfare, Westlake, *International Law*, 57, 115–17. Lueder, "Krieg und Kriegsrecht," 186–87, 254–55.

66. Hartmann, "Militärische Nothwendigkeit," 455, also 126–27, 461.

67. Ibid., 459.

68. Ibid., 462. Emphasis in original.

hold local laws and to limit requisitions to the ability of the area to raise them, and they   125
were forbidden to force civilians to swear allegiance to them, to treat them as spies, to use
them as guides, or to make them help the war effort against their own nation.[69]

From the very beginning of the 1870 war, the German–Prussian position was different; the instructions for the occupying authorities announced (25 July 1870) that local,
French law would henceforth be superseded by German military law.[70] That is, Germany
treated occupied areas (even before it could establish effective control) as if they were annexed.[71] Section 161 of the Military Penal Code (1872) made "all foreigners or Germans in
foreign territory occupied by German troops" subject to German domestic law, "just as if
their act had been committed in Germany." Among those laws was Section 89 of the Imperial Penal Code, which forbade "intentionally aiding a foreign power or harming the
war power of the German Empire during a war."[72] Doing so was treason for a German
(*Landesverrat*) or *Kriegsverrat* (literally, treason against war) for others.

The timing of the occupation instructions shows that this view of occupation and its
correlate, Kriegsverrat, was not a product of 1870 but belonged to an older conception of
order, legality, and state authority. It was confirmed by 1870, however. As Hartmann
noted, "No contagion is more dangerous than anarchy."[73] The vision of order contained
in German expectations of (enemy) civilian docility was extreme and unrealistic. It is perhaps most clearly expressed by the specialist in international law C. Lueder, who was at
pains to underscore that civilians were not the enemy: "They are and remain *subjects of
law*" whose "life and limb, honor and freedom, family circumstance and religious obser-
vance are not to be diminished or harmed."[74] But, he continued:

> The condition and correlate of their protected and free position is that they for
> their part will truly behave completely peacefully, will refrain from every partici-
> pation in battle and support of their countrymen's war campaign, that they will
> not deny obedience to the occupying power and will refrain from all attacks on or
> damage to the troops and occupying power. If these conditions are not met, there
> can be no talk of a protected position of the inhabitants. Instead, they will be sub-
> ject to the full violence and harsh punishment of the laws of war.[75]

"Obedience" meant the following:

> The inhabitants must submit to the limitations, burdens, and forceful measures
> made necessary by the state of emergency or war, and they are obliged to give

69. See Best's excellent discussion in *Humanity in Warfare*, 180–89.

70. Hartmann, "Militärische Nothwendigkeit," 76–77.

71. Best, *Humanity in Warfare*, 184.

72. Militär-Strafgesetzbuch of 20 June 1872, in Kurt Elsner von Gronow and Georg Sohls, ed., *Militärstrafrecht für Herr und Marine des Deutschen Reichs* (Berlin, 1906).

73. Hartmann, "Militärische Nothwendigkeit," 464.

74. Lueder, "Landkriegsrecht in Besonderen," 469–70. Emphasis in original.

75. Ibid., 470.

126 their temporary obedience to the occupying power as the actual and legal legitimate power, which when necessary may force the fulfillment of every duty.[76]

These duties were practically boundless: "The inhabitants must put up with all the extraordinary limits to their personal independence, even the most far-reaching and burdensome, which pursuing the goal of war requires, and can furthermore equally be forced to positive personal service and work," which included aiding the occupying army as hostages, guides, or workers.[77] Lueder's interpretation was the dominant one inside Germany, including in the Foreign Office and the Chancellor's Office, as the First World War proved. It foresaw intensive instrumentalization of enemy civilians for military purposes, yet barely recognized protections to save them from extremes.

Basic Assumptions

Among the premises contained in the German position as it developed after 1870 are several fundamental assumptions that had major implications for military practice.

First, as we have seen, war, all war, was existential, which meant that it contained no limits and tended to develop its capacity for violence and destruction to the extreme.

Second, the counterpart to this unsettling picture was a conception of equally extreme order, which the military was instantly to establish in the occupied areas. Order in this conception was practically lifeless, for it required an extreme of self-abnegation (of emotional loyalty to one's land or people, of self-preservation) that could hardly exist in real life. Holding enemy civilians to the same standards as one's own citizens fostered the expectation that not even passive friction would slow the wheels of administration or the success of the war effort. It is difficult not to conclude that this exaggerated, sterile sense of order was somehow required by the equally exaggerated vision of war as essential violence (Lueder: "violence [*Gewalt*], which must achieve victory at any cost"; Hartmann: "violence and passion . . . suffuse the entire essence [of war]"; Zorn: "war is in its essence violence [*Gewalt*], [and] the violent force [*Gewalt*] of the conqueror in the conquered land is completely unlimited").[78] That is, the only commensurate justification for risking limitless destruction would be to create limitless order (security). The expectation of complete docility also had its analogue in the vision of domestic harmony cherished by monarchists and nationalists for Germany itself, a vision marred by noisy democrats and socialists.

Third, the unrealistic expectation of perfect order artificially produced occasions for disorder, which turned enemy civilians into criminals subject to harsh military law. In short, "order" encouraged reprisals when it inevitably failed. Punishment thus became a major military duty, and civilians became as dangerous as enemy soldiers. The instru-

76. Ibid., 469.
77. Ibid., 475, also 476–77.
78. Lueder, "Krieg und Kriegsrecht," 186; Hartmann, "Militärische Nothwendigkeit," 122; Zorn, *Die beiden Haager Friedenkonferenzen*, 25.

mentalization of civilians for victory and the high, but unrecognized, likelihood that the failure to instrumentalize them smoothly would result in their criminalization, are the third basic set of assumptions that developed from 1870.

A fourth basic assumption concerned international law, the only limit to the violence of war. Some writers, heady with the success of German arms in 1870–71, opined immediately thereafter that international law simply did not exist: there could be no limits to the sovereignty of the nation-state.[79] Subsequent writers, beginning with Hartmann, rejected this position. Hartmann believed that most actual limits to war's violence came from the ethical and legal convictions of the warriors, which over time became customary and were later codified in international agreements. Hence, he accepted the Geneva Convention (as did all other German writers and military men) but was skeptical about the Brussels Convention or any conference designed to extend limits to war *before* these had developed from actual practices in battle.[80] Hartmann's requirement that the laws limiting war develop out of war itself was the hegemonic position thereafter, both among Germany's military and civilian representatives to international conferences and among its international lawyers. Unlike the enthusiasts immediately after the 1870 war, however, later writers seem to have indulged the military point of view because they appreciated its strength in setting actual state policy. Even Lueder, the most promilitary of the scholars, explained why he feared "hyperhumane demands that do not fit real circumstances": "These only feed the preexisting mistrustful rejection of all codification and humanization altogether among those in positions that determine practice . . . and thereby endanger the creation of humane codes."[81] In fact, Lueder favored international law and its extension but dared not challenge the pervasive military standpoint, which cloaked itself as "realism."[82]

Another limit to international law universally recognized in Germany was reciprocity. After enumerating the limits that everyone recognized as customary (wearing a recognizable uniform; carrying arms openly; eschewing dishonorable weapons, poison, and bounties; rejecting spies as dishonorable; treating prisoners of war and the wounded humanely; sparing hospitals; respecting the white flag; etc.), Hartmann concluded: "Everywhere there exists *reciprocity*."[83] Some, but not all, German writers interpreted this principle to mean that "if one side does not fulfill [its recognized obligations], then . . . the other side cannot be required to do so."[84] This facile suspension of international law

79. This was the position of Adolf Lasson and Max Seydel: Messerschmidt, "Völkerrecht und 'Kriegsnotwendigkeit,'" 191–92.

80. Hartmann, "Militärische Nothwendigkeit," 123–25, 79–84, 86–88.

81. Lueder, "Krieg und Kriegsrecht," 275, also 257, 262–63, 276. Same position: Meurer, *Haager Friedenskonferenz*, 213; Albert Zorn, cited in Stenzel, *Kriegführung*, 29.

82. "No process in the life of a people carries so decisively the quality of immediate reality as does war": Hartmann, "Militärische Nothwendigkeit," 111.

83. Ibid., 86. Emphasis in original.

84. Lueder, "Krieg und Kriegsrecht," 255; also General Staff, *Kriegsbrauch*, 2–3, 5, 40. Meurer, who accepted that "international law stands under the sign of reciprocity" (50), nonetheless stressed the prior obligation to obey the law and to refrain from reprisals, much less wholesale abandonment of the law when the other side broke it: *Haager Friedenskonferenz*, 11, 103, 123, 135, 152n6.

128   seems to have been the more widespread interpretation in Germany, but not internationally, where it met sharp rejection.[85]

Aside from weakening the general validity of international law, "reciprocity" smug-
gled in two other assumptions with potentially far-reaching effects on the conduct of war.
Reciprocity suggested equality between combatants, since only like-minded foes could be
trusted to restrain themselves. This is one reason why those who were not western Europeans were so easily bracketed a priori from the rules of "civilized" warfare and subjected
to practices Europeans at least overtly shunned regarding themselves. And just as "occupation" rested on the spreading of domestic German law, "reciprocity" postulated a German model of right warfare. So, for example, because German industry produced ample
regulation ammunition, that was the norm, whereas the homemade bullets (of scrap
metal or glass) to which Africans had to resort were violations. Or, closer to home, because Germany had a well-trained, well-equipped standing army based on universal military service, when it confronted smaller states, such as Belgium, with its regular troops
plus a rag-tag militia of undertrained, non-uniformly uniformed troops, this by definition violated German standards of proper conduct.[86]

These four assumptions (the existential, unlimited nature of war; the vision of perfect
order in the occupied zones; the resulting instrumentalization and probable criminalization of civilians and the transformation of German soldiers into agents of punishment;
and the nature of international law as derivative of force and in any case reciprocal) were
all discussed openly in various forums. But many of their implications and necessary consequences in practice were not reflected upon or consciously understood. These aspects
deserve the label "basic assumptions" in the sense of lessons that had become submerged
and that operated almost automatically.[87]

Although these basic assumptions operated like a riptide undercutting international
law, the German army was not completely indifferent to the agreements the government
had signed. The inclusion in the *Felddienst-Ordnung* of the Geneva Convention and, after
1911, the Hague rules, the sometime instruction of General Staff officers, and the revision
of the Military Penal Code (in 1916) to conform with the Hague Conventions concerning
foreigners and prisoners of war, all show some concern.[88] Still, other major powers gave
these matters higher priority. Both Britain and France relatively quickly reprinted the
Hague rules in their own manuals and provided convenient excerpts and explanations of
them in instruction manuals.[89] While other governments pressed to extend international
law, Imperial Germany uniformly worked to limit it.

85. Best, *Humanity in Warfare*, 174–76; Messerschmidt, "Völkerrecht und 'Kriegsnotwendigkeit,' " 193;
Westlake, *International Law*, 114.

86. The clashing expectations of big versus small European states were a standard feature of late-nineteenth-century international conferences.

87. March, "Decision Making Perspectives," 222–24.

88. Art. 47, Pt. 2 of the Military Penal Code (1872) permitted a soldier to disobey an order he knew to be a
violation of military or civilian penal codes, but this provision was spelled out only in the commentary to the
provision and was not well known. Elsner von Gronow, *Militärstrafgesetzbuch*, §47, p. 52, and note 7, pp. 54–55.

89. *UA* 3:1, 26; Stenzel, *Kriegführung*, 37. In general: Geoffrey Best, "How Right Is Might?" in *War Economy
and the Military Mind*, ed. Geoffrey Best and Andrew Wheatcroft (London, 1976).

The Boer War (1900–1902) helps put the German military in perspective. Three months into the war, War Secretary Lord Lansdowne asked his aides whether Britain should conduct the war according to the Hague rules. The chief of military intelligence, Maj.-Gen. Sir John Ardagh, who had represented Britain at the Hague Conference, replied that the acts were merely the codified "customs and usages" of war and thus applied even to nonsignatories, such as the Boer Republics. Field Marshal Lord Garnet Wolseley disagreed, arguing that the Boers would not abide by the laws. Subsequently, the government told Parliament that Britain accepted the Hague rules and was conducting the war accordingly; the military intelligence division told the cabinet the same thing. After the war, in a report designed for future planning, Colonial Secretary Joseph Chamberlain asked directly whether certain actions committed in the war were consonant with international law.[90] The point is not that Britain's methods in the Boer War were always legal, or that the government felt obliged to uphold international law in public before Parliament (Bülow had done the same before the Reichstag in 1904), but that *inside* the military there were influential voices upholding international law as binding for military practice—even in a colonial war where that law would not seem to apply. Further, these military voices found support in the major institutions of government: Parliament, the cabinet, and within the bureaucracy, which independently asked for reassurance that British troops were abiding by international norms. Such support would have encouraged the Ardaghs in the military against the Wolseleys. Even Britain's future war planning took international law at least into consideration. Such institutionalized and energetic concern for the international law of war was missing in Imperial Germany, and therefore it was missing from the training and from the expectations of its troops.

We turn now to one final basic assumption, a collective self-understanding that repeatedly emerged in Germany's argumentation at the international conferences. Geoffrey Best has referred to it as the "arch-occupier" position, which Germany shared with Russia.[91] Both countries argued as though they would always be the occupying power. For the Russian Empire, whose very existence consisted of occupation, this made sense. But for Germany, it had a different meaning. It meant that the German government thought of itself as always *victorious*, and of victory as always territorial (and probably aggressive), that is, as involving the movement of German troops into other lands. It was apparently unthinkable that Germans might ever lose, suffer occupation, and therefore require the protections international law afforded to the occupied. It was not coincidental that the one area in which German representatives ever tried to extend international law concerned the transportation of wounded soldiers through neutral countries.[92] Otherwise, international law represented an annoying series of impediments to military practice.

The official German point of view was thus military, not civilian; bellicose, not peaceful; and utterly devoted to victory. This self-understanding made Imperial Germany unique among the other states at the international conventions; no other country, includ-

---

90. S. Burridge Spies, *Methods of Barbarism?* (Cape Town, 1977), 12–14, 270.
91. Best, *Humanity in Warfare*, 180–81.
92. Scott, *Proceedings*, 501.

130 ing Russia, the other great continental military power, was so distant from the emerging international norms.[93] For our purposes, the most important point is the premium on victory, which was so powerful that defeat was inconceivable, and thus could never be factored into decision making or planning as a (regrettable) possibility.[94] The self-generated pressure to succeed at all cost was one of the chief parameters influencing officers' decisions in actual wars.

93. Ibid., 483, 487–88, 509–12, 520, 529–30, 552–53; Geoffrey Best, "How Right Is Might?" 120–35; Dülffer, *Regeln gegen den Krieg*, 122–23, 345; Stenzel, *Kriegführung*, 32–33, 42; Zorn, *Die beiden Haager Friedenskonferenzen*, 30, 35–37, 53, 82, 94.

94. Lueder, for example, can only imagine a spiral of war that increases the cost, stakes, and effort; he never entertains the possibility that statesmen might end a war whose cost had escalated beyond the original goal. Lueder, "Krieg und Kriegsrecht," 366–67.

6

Standard Practices

After 1871, how did the German army fight wars? How closely did it follow the 1870 precedents? We have examined one example in detail, Southwest Africa, but was it representative of German combat practices? Is colonial warfare properly comparable with European warfare? These are some of the questions we must now address as we examine standard practices in Germany's wars down to 1914.

Colonial Warfare

Contemporary military men claimed that colonial warfare was entirely different from European warfare; it operated according to different rules, and therefore little could be learned from it.[1] However, even the brief discussion of the Franco-Prussian War will have shown many similarities in the drift to extreme treatment of civilians, the slide from courts-martial to summary executions, even the ex post facto justification of atrocities by reference to "racial war," when war failed to end with a tidy, decisive victory of military force, and when the population seemed untrustworthy. Although World War I will offer the best evidence that modern colonial and European warfare are closely related, there are other reasons to conclude that, in the period before 1914, at least the military behavior of Germans in the colonies was mostly the consequence of Germany's own military culture.[2]

1. See Bernd F. Schulte, *Europäische Krise und Erster Weltkrieg* (Frankfurt, 1983), 70–71. The *Vierteljahrshefte für Truppenführung und Heereskunde* devoted under 10% of its pre-1914 column space to colonial wars.

2. Porch found the same to be true for France: "Bugeaud, Galliéni, Lyautey," in *Makers of Modern Strategy*, ed. Paret, 376–407, here 399–400. On Britain, see Michael Howard, "Colonial Wars and European Wars," in *Imperialism and War*, ed. J. A. de Moor and H. L. Wesseling (Leiden, 1989), 218–223, here 223.

132   For one thing, Imperial Germany's combat history from 1871 to 1914 was purely colonial. All its military engagements were extra-European. There were countless "punitive expeditions" in Germany's colonies—between 1891 and 1894 German East Africa recorded fifty-four of these, for example.[3] They were handled by the local Schutztruppe, which consisted of white officers and troops, supplemented by black NCOs and troops under white command. Three military engagements were large and expensive enough, however, to qualify as real wars: the Boxer Uprising in China (1900–1901), and the revolts in Southwest Africa (1904–7) and in German East Africa (1905–7). Only in East Africa, where Gov. Count Gustav Adolf von Götzen had learned from the mistakes in SWA, were white troops carefully limited, leaving the fighting to African mercenaries and recruits. In both China and SWA most combat fell to marines and volunteers drawn from the various contingents of the German army.

Unlike Britain and France, Germany lacked a specialized colonial army. The common denominator for all white soldiers in Germany's colonial campaigns was the standard military training they received in Germany. Regular Schutztruppler, who served long years in the colonies, supplemented that training with valuable on-the-spot experience. Not surprisingly, they were the most effective fighters. However, the volunteers (twenty thousand in China, fifteen thousand in SWA, almost none in East Africa)[4] received no special training for colonial warfare, and, surprisingly, neither did the marines (naval troops), though they were expected to hold the fort until further reinforcements arrived. Thus, the men who fought in Germany's two largest colonial engagements (China and SWA) did so with the formation, habits, and expectations characteristic of the regular army.

The number of volunteers, both for the various Schutztruppen and, especially, for the China and SWA campaigns, so exceeded the demand that only the most suitable-seeming men were chosen; whatever misdeeds later occurred, they cannot be attributed to recruitment problems.[5] However, the volunteers may not have been representative of the German army. Although the desire for battle experience and consequent career advancement presumably had a general appeal, especially to officers in the peacetime army, there are some indications that colonial "small wars" attracted a peculiar set of volunteers. Captain v. Lettow-Vorbeck noted "many names of former officers, which had appeared in the

3. Karl-Martin Seeberg, *Der Maji-Maji-Krieg gegen die deutsche Kolonialherrschaft* (Berlin, 1989), 73. Trutz v. Trotha counts thirteen colonial wars and hundreds of punitive expeditions: " 'The Fellows Can Just Starve,' " in *Anticipating Total War*, ed. Boemeke et al., 415–35, here 420.

4. There were 100–200 white Schutztruppler in East Africa at the beginning of the uprising. They were reinforced by 228 marines, who were mainly used to man military stations and thus release the Schutztruppler for fighting. Governor Götzen then requested (20 Aug. 1905) 20 white officers to command 500 additional black troops. Ernst Nigmann, *Geschichte der Kaiserlichen Schutztruppe für Deutsch-Ostafrika* (Berlin, 1911), 93; Walter Nuhn, *Flammen über Deutschost* (Wilhelmshaven, 1991), 25, 105, 115; Gustav Adolf Graf von Götzen, *Deutsch-Ostakfrika im Aufstand 1905/06* (Berlin, 1909), 74; cf. figure of 150 marine reinforcements: Bülow to Foreign Office, Nr. 84, Wilhelmshöhe, 19 Aug. 1905, BA-Berlin, R 1001, Nr. 721, p. 74.

5. Götzen, *Deutsch-Ostafrika*, 39–41; Nuhn, *Flammen*, 26; Justus Scheibert, *Der Krieg in China 1900–1901* (Berlin, 1909), 397; Bley, *South-West Africa*, 160–61. Generals volunteering for China: Annika Mombauer, "Wilhelm, Waldersee, and the Boxer Rebellion," in *The Kaiser*, ed. Annika Mombauer and Wilhelm Deist (Cambridge, 2003), 91–118, here 106.

press [in scandals], who now wanted to rehabilitate themselves" (as common soldiers).[6] 133
Deimling, who supervised the collection of the first volunteers for SWA, observed the disproportionate number of "rough fighters" among them and wondered "if perhaps not all company commanders permitted only those men to volunteer, about [whose departure] they shed honest tears."[7] But Deimling dismissed the worst offenders of this sort. In any event, colonial wars (or perhaps actual combat, anywhere) were particularly attractive to certain officers; many veterans of the China campaign reenlisted for SWA.[8] Only further research might permit more detailed conclusions as to the sociological difference between the regular army and the colonial contingents.

One further, organizational factor distinguished the colonial military experience from that of the regular army. Except for the marines, the men fought in new, temporary units formed especially for the purpose. These units lacked the cohesiveness and specific group culture that regimental history and long service together encouraged. Their general training and the military culture that they had absorbed was thus unusually important in determining their collective behavior.

As with training, the command principles (mission tactics) remained identical in the colonies and in Europe. In fact, the colonial situation epitomized the expectations embedded in the mission-tactical system and even exaggerated them, because difficult terrain and poor communications typically isolated officers from their commander and forced them to act on their own. As we saw in SWA, colonial orders usually ceded broad interpretive room to the unit officer. So, for example, a typical order from Governor Götzen during the Maji-Maji Revolt in East Africa in 1905 said that "the mission of the expedition corps is the relief of the country around Ssongea, which appears strongly threatened, and the defeat [*Unterwerfung*] of the Wangoni [the rebellious local tribe]. Further tasks will develop from the situation there."[9] How to achieve these goals was left to the officer's judgment. In East Africa even commanders of small units had the right to levy collective fines and to execute those whom they thought to be rebel leaders—and they did so.[10]

The German army in the colonies was, in terms of its operating principles, sociology, and experience, a European army. It brought with it from Europe certain operational *expectations* and habits of *logistical planning*. The cleft that opened up between these was supposed to be bridged by the *officers' military virtues* or character traits. When the army

6. Paul von Lettow-Vorbeck, *Mein Leben* (Biberach an der Riss, 1957), 76–77.

7. Deimling, *Aus der alten in die neue Zeit*, 52.

8. Salzmann, *Im Kampfe*, 1–2; Leutwein, *Elf Jahre*, 441.

9. "Order for the expedition corps bound for Ssongea," copy, 15 Oct. 1905, Dar es Salaam, MA-Freiburg, RM 121 I, Nr. 441, Doc. 98. Similar orders: "Befehl für Oberleutnant von Grawert," copy, 15 Oct. 1905, Dar es Salaam, ibid., Nr. 441, Doc. 99; "Befehl für das Detachement Merker," copy, 26 Sept. 1905, ibid., Nr. 441, Doc. 7. Cf. Leutwein's "Truppenbefehl," copy, 15 Feb. 1904, Karibib, ibid., Nr. 422, Bl. 122–23, or Leutwein, "Operationsbefehl," 11 Mar. 1904, ibid., Nr. 423, Bl. 41; and Leutwein, "Operationsbefehl Nr. 4," Windhuk, 1 Apr. 1904, ibid., Nr. 423, Bl. 169.

10. Götzen, Runderlass Nr. 8040, Dar es Salaam, 13 Nov. 1905, BA-Berlin, R 1001, Nr. 724, p. 118; Götzen to Foreign Office, Nr. 249, secret, Dar es Salaam, 12 Dec. 1905, ibid., Nr. 723, p. 191. For China: Mombauer, "Wilhelm," 109.

134 met the enemy it used *standard practices*, most of which were either already familiar or developed logically from deeply held basic assumptions about the nature of war. The same is true for its *treatment of civilians*. We will now examine in turn these aspects of German war conduct before 1914.

Expectations

Inexperienced European soldiers—and it is well to remember that most German soldiers and their officers were inexperienced in both colonial warfare and warfare generally—shared broad expectations about colonial warfare. The volunteer soldiers who embarked for combat in China and SWA looked forward to achieving an easy victory over an inferior, but cruel, opponent.[11] This double expectation (the easy victory and the nature of the foe) helped determine much of the conduct during the wars.

In retrospect, it seems possible to identify at least two main sources for the belief in a quick, easy victory. The first is the assumption of European superiority, manifested in material, technological, managerial, and disciplinary preeminence over non-Europeans (including those with ancient, high civilizations, such as the Chinese). This pan-European belief was expressed both racially and culturally, and it saturated public opinion, government, and the military. The postulate of superiority tended to encourage escalation in all Europe's colonial wars. The clamor of public opinion, the desire of government to placate it, and, in Germany, the myth of military perfection and its identification with the nation, all fed the pressure on troops to succeed. The more intense this pressure, the greater the tendency to believe in one's own superiority, since that guaranteed victory. The dynamics of motivating soldiers to fight also encouraged this spiral, as officers, who believed in European superiority and who *needed* to believe in it, built up their men's self-confidence by belittling the opponent.[12]

The second source is the "short war illusion": the belief prevalent throughout Europe after 1870 that industrialism and the nature of the modern state made war so destructive of economies and societies that long wars were impossible. All European military planning began from the premise that future European wars would be short. If that were true among the nearly equally equipped and trained Great Powers, then surely no colonial war between unequals could last longer. As Alfred Vagts has pointed out, the short war illusion was a way of "getting something for nothing." It ran on the principle of "limited liability," permitting great dreams of conquest at limited cost.[13] That, of course, was the entire principle behind imperialism, so it should not be surprising to find the analogue of the short war illusion operating in the colonial sphere.

The second feature of soldiers' expectation—the inferior, but cruel, enemy—was the standard colonial foe. This trope was generated almost automatically as the opposite of

11. For example: Bayer, *Mit dem Hauptquartier*, 2, 11; Auer v. Herrenkirchen, *Meine Erlebnisse*, 5; and Max Schwabe, "Einige Lehren aus dem Kriege in Südwestafrika," *Vierteljahrshefte für Truppenführung und Heereskunde* 1:3 (1904), 461–79, here 480.

12. This is a feature of the rationality of action: Brunsson, "Irrationality of Action," 32–33.

13. Vagts, *History of Militarism*, 349–50.

the superior, law-abiding and moral European, following cultural principles of "we" and "other" that have been well researched.[14] The stereotype of native cruelty justified in advance "reciprocal" cruelty by Europeans. In Germany this pattern of stereotyping seemed to receive the imprimatur of national military policy by Kaiser Wilhelm II himself, in his famous "Hun speech," delivered in July 1900 to the first reinforcements embarking to quell the Boxer Uprising in China.[15] The Chinese government had attempted to use the spontaneous uprising of patriotic-xenophobic young men in several of China's northern provinces to eradicate Western penetration of the Middle Kingdom. Germany joined seven other powers in intervening against the Chinese after its envoy, Baron Wilhelm Emmanuel von Ketteler, had been assassinated and the foreign embassies in Peking put under siege (a violation of international law). Because this was Germany's first major military engagement since 1870 and its first outside Europe as a Great Power, the Kaiser's speech occurred at a critical symbolic moment when the public and the soldiers might assume that basic principles of conduct would be laid down. The Kaiser presented their mission to the troops. "You are to avenge grave injustice," he told them, accusing the Chinese of "discarding thousand-year-old international law" and claiming that these acts proved that Chinese culture was inferior to Christian culture. And then he said the following, part of which he extemporized:

> So, I send you out so that you will demonstrate, first, your traditional German efficiency, second, the sacrifice, braveness, and joyful bearing of all discomfort, and, third, the honor and fame of our weapons and flags. You should give an example of discipline [*Manneszucht und Disziplin*], but also of overcoming and self-control. You will fight against a well-armed power, but you should also avenge, not only the death of the envoy, but of many Germans and Europeans, too. When you meet the enemy, you will beat him; you will give no pardon and take no prisoners. Those whom you capture are at your mercy. As the Huns a thousand years ago under King Etzel made a name for themselves that has lasted mightily in memory, so may the name "Germany" be known in China, such that no Chinese will ever again even dare to look askance at a German.[16]

The virtues the Kaiser praised will be discussed shortly. At the time, hardly anyone noticed them, so riveted were they by the Hun image and the injunction to take no prisoners. In some quarters, including outside Germany, the speech was immensely popular; it struck a deep chord of anger and vengefulness. To the civilian leadership, however, the speech was a dreadful embarrassment because it contravened Chancellor Bülow's express policy of moderation. Bülow tried to contain the damage by removing from the official,

14. John W. Dower, *War without Mercy* (New York, 1986), 10, 147–80, 320n8, 342n3.

15. Bernd Sösemann, "Die sogenannte 'Hunnenrede' Wilhelms II," *Historische Zeitschrift* 222:2 (1976), 342–58. My account follows his. See also Mombauer, "Wilhelm," 95, 97, 112.

16. Sösemann, "Die sogenannte 'Hunnenrede,'" 349–50. Sösemann gives the actual words that Wilhelm delivered, as reconstructed from the notes of newspapermen.

136 printed version the references to Huns and taking no prisoners. But Wilhelm's utterances were so striking, they soon leaked out.

The instant notoriety of the Hun speech showed that, along with civilian government leaders, probably most of the German public rejected the harsh military methods the Kaiser had praised.[17] But conservatives and ultranationalists welcomed them and scorned the "whole sentimentality [*Zimperlichkeit*]" typical of the critics.[18] More telling is the response of the troops. Whereas in previous days they had written slogans such as "Express Train to China" on their troop trains, they now wrote "Revenge Is Sweet" and "No Pardon."[19] The Kaiser's carte-blanche fitted the comforting self-stereotype of the hard, uncompromising military man and provided immediately popular expressions for men about to subject themselves to peril. The slogans pithily expressed the extreme possibilities latent in their training and in the situation of avengers in a foreign land.

The hullabaloo surrounding the Hun speech caused Bülow to muzzle the Kaiser successfully when the revolt in SWA in 1904 provided the next opportunity for such an oration.[20] Nevertheless, Colonial Director Stübel opened the government's request for emergency funding by characterizing the Herero as "cruel [*grausam*]," and that word became epithetic for the Herero thereafter in government publications, newspapers, speeches, and later memoirs. The Herero practice of mutilating dead German soldiers, stripping their bodies, using homemade "dirty" ammunition, and fighting while wounded provided a foundation for the accounts. The Boxers in China and the Maji-Maji rebels in East Africa also engaged in outlandish and expressive killing (mostly of Chinese Christians and African villagers, respectively), vengeful destruction, and other acts that Europeans found sickening and in violation of the norms of European warfare. Such actions made reprisals and escalation of combat more likely. But that is not the point here, for we are looking at a process of political labeling that took place outside the military, away from the theater of war, often before extensive fighting had occurred, and in which exaggeration and extrapolation overwhelmed observation. Again, stereotyping the enemy was not peculiar to Germany; it was a general Western political phenomenon common at times of (complete or incomplete) national mobilization. The late- nineteenth–early-twentieth-century variant was heavily racialist, and it tapped into domestic discourses of danger, disorder, and threat. In times of war (even "small" ones), it placed the enemy outside the moral universe of Europeans and thus beyond the protection of legal limits to war. In short, stereotyping created the most important precondition for "authorized" massacres: it dehumanized the enemy and legitimized extreme measures to punish them and protect the European soldier (as fighter, or as representative of national power and honor).[21]

17. The Catholic Center Party, the socialists, and the Left Liberal Party denounced the speech in a lengthy Reichstag debate: ibid., 355–56.

18. Friedrich Naumann's phrase, in ibid., 355.

19. Ibid., 345.

20. The Kaiser's brother delivered the speech to the embarking troops in Kiel, while the Kaiser confined himself to calling for the reimposition of "law and order" (*Ruhe und Ordnung*) in a short speech in Berlin a few days later. *Reichsbote*, Nr. 16, 20 Jan. 1904, and Nr. 18, 22 Jan. 1904; Spraul, *Der "Völkermord,"* 718.

21. On the mechanisms by which mass destruction of life is authorized see the articles in Nevitt Sanford and Craig Comstock, ed., *Sanctions for Evil* (San Francisco, 1971), esp. Sanford and Comstock, "Sanctions for Evil," 1–11; Neil J. Smelser, "Some Determinants of Destructive Behavior," 15–24; Troy Duster, "Conditions for Guilt-

The basic assumptions behind German troop expectations were more political than military and more European than German. However, there was added pressure for German troops to succeed. As SWA demonstrated, the organizational and cultural values of the German officer corps defined victory more absolutely than did other European armies—as the annihilation of the enemy. And the national importance of the military as symbol of the German nation seemed to require unequivocal demonstrations of German power and authority. Together, these factors created a potential for disappointment and frustration when the easy victory did not materialize, and it encouraged a readiness to resort to exemplary harshness, even when it did.

Logistical Planning

Perhaps the most astonishing aspect of Imperial German military organization is the cleft between the ambitious, often bombastic, goals and the real preparations taken to achieve them. This gap is so great that failure seems, in retrospect, to have been preprogrammed. Deficient preparation was the dual result of the administrative chaos typical of Wilhelminian government and willful neglect inside the military.

A certain degree of administrative chaos was typical of all European armies fighting outside the Continent. The troops in SWA, for example, were (mis)managed by five separate agencies: the Colonial Department of the Foreign Office, the Navy, the War Ministry, the high command of the Schutztruppe (under the chancellor), and the General Staff.[22] In China only three had jostled with each other.[23] But the situation elsewhere was hardly better. The British official investigation into the management of the Boer War took 143 pages to outline the administrative deficiencies it had uncovered, and even before its assessment, the government had already reorganized the War Office and created the Defence Committee and a clearer command structure at the top to address the mistakes revealed during the war.[24] In France, various aspects of the administration and command of colonial troops were shared by or transferred among the Colonial Office (which itself was shifted to the Commerce Department in 1889 and became independent in 1894) and the Naval and War Ministries.[25]

But German planning suffered under structural deficits all its own. The first was political: the desire of both the civilian and military leadership to avoid asking the Reichstag for money. Appropriations opened the door to scrutiny and criticism. Besides, before the revolts of 1904–5, the Reichstag had had little stomach for colonies and was loath to pay much for them. Miserliness had ensured small Schutztruppe forces and thin, underdevel-

Free Massacre," 25–36; and Viola W. Bernard, Perry Ottenberg, and Fritz Redl, "Dehumanization," 102–24; also the excellent article by Kelman, "Violence without Moral Restraint." On exclusion from the moral universe of the perpetrator: Helen Fein, *Imperial Crime and Punishment* (Honolulu, 1977), 19.

22. General Staff, *Kämpfe der deutschen Truppen*, 1:129–30.

23. Germany, Admiralty, *Die Kaiserliche Marine während der Wirren in China 1900–1901* (Berlin, 1903), 171.

24. Great Britain, Parliament, *Report of His Majesty's Commissioners Appointed to Inquire into the Military Preparation and Other Matters Connected with the War in South Africa* (London, 1903), Cd. 1789, 132–35.

25. A. S. Kanya-Forster, "The French Marines and the Conquest of the Western Sudan, 1880–1899," in *Imperialism and War*, ed. J. A. de Moor and H. L. Wesseling (Leiden, 1989), 121–45, here 123; C. Fourniau, "Colonial Wars before 1914," in ibid., 72–86, here 76.

138 oped colonial infrastructures the military could make use of in case of revolt.[26] The length
to which the leadership would go to keep the military independent of the Reichstag is best
illustrated by the Maji-Maji Revolt of 1905–7.[27]

German East Africa was not a settler colony like SWA. Vast (almost two hundred
thousand square kilometers) and economically productive, in 1905 East Africa contained
between four and seven million African inhabitants but only two thousand Germans.[28]
German authority in the interior was nominally upheld in a symbolic way by military stations. In summer 1905 the southern provinces rose in revolt against the newly imposed tax
system, the plantation economy, and the use of forced labor for public works.[29] Inspired
by religious wise men, who claimed to make them invulnerable to bullets by dousing
them with sacred water (*maji*), the members of many different tribes united against the
Germans; the revolt spread throughout the whole southern half of the colony.

At Governor Götzen's request, the Kaiser sent two cruisers and 150 marines as rein-
forcement. Chancellor Bülow was disappointed to hear from the undersecretary of the
treasury that the cruisers and men exceeded the peacetime budget, "not to speak of the
question whether a peacetime budget can be stretched in the same way a war budget
can."[30] Undeterred, Bülow called a meeting of naval, treasury, and Colonial Department
officials to see how to circumvent the Reichstag. Admiral Alfred von Tirpitz, chief of the
Naval Office, rescued them by agreeing to cover the cost, as Bülow explained, "through
savings in other areas, so that [we] can avoid calling the Reichstag, which in my opinion
would create an uncomfortable precedent."[31] The price of this arrangement was divided
command: the Schutztruppe remained under the governor, and the marines were under
naval command, which insisted that the marines be used only to hold military stations,
releasing the Schutztruppe for fighting. The governor was forced to agree. Only through
good personal relations with the naval commanders did he create an acceptable administrative modus vivendi.[32]

The second structural deficit in German planning was the result of the narrow interpretation of operational priorities. Only actual fighting was deemed important. Adminis-

26. Captain von Haeften, "Eine Deutsche Kolonialarmee," *Vierteljahrshefte für Truppenführung und Heereskunde* 2:4 (1905), 609–31, here 614–16; Nuhn, *Flammen über Deutschost*, 15, 25.

27. Kaiser Wilhelm kept the Reichstag out of the China expedition, as well: Mombauer, "Wilhelm," 97.

28. Iliffe estimates four million; Götzen, seven million: John Iliffe, *Tanganyika under German Rule, 1905–1912* (Cambridge, 1969), 9; Götzen, *Deutsch-Ostafrika*, 20. Detailed contemporary description: Hans Meyer, ed., *Das Deutsche Kolonialreich*, vol. 1: *Ostafrika and Kamerun* (Leipzig, 1909), 3–416.

29. The best account of the uprising is Detlef Bald, "Afrikanischer Kampf gegen koloniale Herrschaft," *Militärgeschichtliche Mitteilungen* 19 (1976), 23–50. Other useful works are Seeberg, *Der Maji-Maji-Krieg*; John Iliffe, *A Modern History of Tanganyika* (Cambridge, 1979), 168–202; Nigmann, *Geschichte der Kaiserlichen Schutztruppe*; and Nuhn, *Flammen über Deutschost*. Less useful: Kurt Büttner and Heinrich Loth, ed., *Philosophie der Eroberer und koloniale Wirklichkeit* (Berlin, 1981).

30. Bülow to Foreign Office, Nr. 84, Wilhelmshöhe, 19 Aug. 1905, BA-Berlin, R 1001, Nr. 721, p. 74; Undersecretary Twele to Bülow, Nr. I. 6114, 19 Aug. 1905, ibid., p. 82.

31. Bülow to Richthofen, Nr. 102, Norderney, 23 Aug. 1905, ibid., p. 149.

32. Götzen to Col. Dept., Nr. 61, Dar es Salaam, 26 Aug. 1905, BA-Berlin, R 1001, Nr. 722, p. 13; Naval Office (signed v. Ahlefeld) to Col. Dept., Nr. A I e 8171, Berlin, 5 Sept. 1905, ibid., p. 80; Götzen to the "eldest officer" of the *Bussard*, Dar es Salaam, 10 Sept. 1905, MA-Freiburg, RM 121 I, Nr. 443; Glatzel, "Bericht über die mit den Marinetruppen in Ostafrika gewonnenen Erfahrungen," Dar es Salaam, 28 Mar. 1906, MA-Freiburg, RM 5/Nr. 6036, pp. 344–52.

Rifle practice in Morogoro, German East Africa. Courtesy of Stadt- und Universitätsbibliothek, Afrikaabteilung, Frankfurt am Main, Nr. 042-1388-06.

tering occupied land, providing for the wounded and for prisoners of war, even provisioning troops, were all ancillary activities; no ambitious officer could make a successful career specializing in them. As a result, they simply withered from lack of attention.

The lack of training that troops received regarding enemy civilians and prisoners of war had its analogue at the highest levels. In 1894 the Administrative Department suggested to Chief of Staff Schlieffen that the old rules for the treatment and provisioning of prisoners of war, which dated from the beginning of the campaign against France in 1870, be updated. Schlieffen found this unnecessary. In 1870, he replied:

> One hundred fifty to one hundred sixty thousand prisoners were provided for without our having made any peacetime preparations. It is unlikely that we would take more prisoners in a future war. I therefore suggest that in peacetime we restrict ourselves to very general regulations, as we have done for clothing, pay, and provisioning, and refrain from special preparations.

The result was, as a later Reichstag committee investigating the subject put it, "Germany entered [the First World War] completely unprepared" regarding prisoners of war (a situation common to other European armies, too).[33] The handling of enemy civilians was equally neglected.

33. Fischer et al., *Völkerrecht*, 3.1: 179; Alon Rachamimov, *POWs and the Great War* (Oxford, 2002), chs. 1–2.

140   Ignoring the defeated enemy might be understandable, given the institutional fixation on pure fighting, but neglecting the basic maintenance of one's own troops is much harder to explain. This is especially true given the universal agreement in the late nineteenth century that military superiority rested on numbers of men plus their technical-material support. The worship of matériel is visible in the arms race, which grew to fetishistic proportions, and in the fatal insistence of all European colonial armies on burdening their troops with "kitchen ranges, pianos, and harmoniums," as Lord Kitchener put it.[34] Indeed, the huge amount of stuff and the thicket of regulations, tables, and lists at first glance makes it hard to see the basic inadequacy of German preparations; it seems instead that overpreparation might have been the fault. But, in fact, underplanning (lack of investment of time and reflection) was the problem, visible in all aspects of provisioning from choice and amount of goods to packing and transport to distribution and administration. Fabled German efficiency is one of the myths one must drop to understand how the military (and for that matter the civilian) bureaucracy actually worked.[35]

It is true that some bad planning resulted from lack of experience. Packing freighters "backward," that is, putting the immediately necessary items in first, which meant they were inaccessible on arrival, was a mistake one could expect from a land power in its first overseas campaign (in China).[36] The gleaming silver buttons on the Schutztruppe uniforms, which made such splendid targets, and the inappropriate riding boots were both youthful errors of a new colonial power.[37] However, the absence of anything in the rations to counteract scurvy (a problem solved by a well-known British reform in 1870),[38] the wholly inadequate medical provisions (especially in SWA), "the complete chaos at the beginning, concerning mobilization, substitution, and replacement," as Maj. Arnold Lequis characterized it (in SWA),[39] the blithe trust of the Schlieffen Plan that men and horses could subsist off what they found in Belgium and France in 1914[40]—all these examples point to much deeper problems. They were a result of inveterate disdain for practical, economic management.

To some extent all militaries are un-, or even anti-, economical. They produce nothing except destruction; they remove people from productive labor; they live from subsidies (at home) or requisitions (abroad); their soldiers do not "work," they serve; the military has no competitors inside the nation, and so forth.[41] Military principles are thus in many ways antithetical to economic ones. Nevertheless, the Prussian military's rejection

---

34. Eversley Belfield, *The Boer War* (London, 1975), 137.

35. From the inside, German organization appeared as "overorganization" according to Quartermaster General v. Eisenhart-Rothe during World War I: Eisenhart-Rothe, *Im Banne der Persönlichkeit* (Berlin, 1931), 129. On the European myth of German efficiency, see Pick, *War Machine*, 100–110, 138.

36. Germany, Admiralty, *Kaiserliche Marine*, 171–84.

37. Lettow-Vorbeck diary entry, 3 June 1904, MA-Freiburg, Nl. Lettow-Vorbeck, Nr. 73.

38. Brian Bond, "Editor's Introduction," in *Victorian Military Campaigns*, ed. Brian Bond (London, 1967), 23.

39. Arnold Lequis, "Meine Erfahrungen in Südwest Afrika" (written in Aug. 1905), MA-Freiburg, Nl. Lequis, Nr. 35, 361.

40. Van Crefeld, *Supplying War*, 115–40.

41. Bahrdt, *Die Gesellschaft und ihre Soldaten*, 31, 70–74.

of economic management was overwhelming and overdetermined. Economic proficiency was associated not just with civilians in general but with the bourgeoisie and with political liberalism in particular—both directly at odds with the convictions and identification of the officer corps. The Wilhelminian epithet that summed up everything civilian, unheroic, militarily inept, and consequently anti-Prussian was "British commercialism," characteristic of that "nation of shopkeepers," those "military amateurs and dilettantes" from whom nothing worthwhile militarily could be expected.[42] Major Lequis, the General Staff officer assisting the commander of the rear and thus in charge of provisioning during the war in SWA, fulminated against the incompetence he diagnosed as willful. Lequis was a Rhinelander who referred to himself as an "involuntary Prussian [*Musspreussen*]." The Prussian convictions he identified as responsible for the conduct of the war and the failure of provisioning were cheapness, short-sightedness, devotion to destruction (*Vernichtung*) instead of to the economic future of the colony, impatience at the kind of long-range planning a well-fought war required, and haughty disregard for "experts." In his eyes, all of this compared very unfavorably with the way any well-run business (for example, in his Rhenish homeland) would have administered things.[43]

The rejection of economically realistic planning saturated practices sufficiently to become an enduring part of Prusso-Germany's military culture.[44] That made this habit especially resistant to change. Even before the wars of unification, Prussian maneuvers were held as if provisioning would take care of itself, so that, in the words of one student, "the officer corps barely worried about provisioning and busied itself almost exclusively with exercise and combat training."[45] In the 1866 campaign against Austria, the resulting food shortfalls caused a near military disaster and provoked hungry troops to unusually violent behavior.[46] Consequently, more attention was spent on provisioning, and the beginning of the 1870 war saw much improved handling of the problem. But as the war lengthened, the army reverted to living from requisitions, rather than from its own supplies, and so the brief lesson of 1866 was forgotten again.[47] Afterward, maneuvers reverted to type, and living off the enemy, supplemented by some of one's own provisions, became again the (non)planning norm. In 1913, the Reichstag raised the issue of inadequate provision-

42. Hence, the ubiquitous belief in German military circles that England could not possibly win the Boer War: Belfield, *Boer War*, 67. "Dilettantes" was Gustav Stresemann's phrase applied to the entire Entente, 22 Oct. 1918: Gustav Böhm, *Adjutant im preussischen Kriegsministerium Juni 1918 bis Oktober 1919*, ed. Heinz Hürten and Georg Meyer (Stuttgart, 1977), 44–45.

43. Lequis, "Meine Erfahrungen in Südwest Afrika," MA-Freiburg, Nl. Lequis, Nr. 35, 337–45, 353.

44. Van Crefeld, *Supplying War*, 231–37, who remarks that Germany was not unique in this regard; Schulte, *Die deutsche Armee*, 306n3; Deist, "Remarks," 321–23; Goerlitz, *Geschichte*, 83, 131; Lothar Burchardt, *Friedenswirtschaft und Kriegsvorsorge* (Boppard am Rhein, 1968), who shows civilian-political restraints on logistical planning, as well.

45. Major Renner, "Wechselwirkung zwischen Herreszucht und Verpflegung im Kriege," *Vierteljahrshefte für Truppenführung und Heereskunde* 6:3 (1909), 413–420, here 417.

46. Ibid., 418.

47. Despite a logistical war game held in 1906, Renner mentions no institutional or training changes since 1870 and concludes that modern mass armies would be forced to live partly off the land, even though he believed self-sufficiency and one's own administration were far preferable. Ibid., 419. 1906: Bucholz, *Moltke, Schlieffen*, 250–54.

142 ing and recommended reforms, which the army rejected, clinging instead to the 1870 model.[48] The degree to which provisioning was left to circumstances is suggested in the *Felddienst-Ordnung*, which instructed that all officers had the duty "unfailingly to see to the most adequate possible provisioning of their troops and to secure this, if necessary, through their own, independent measures."[49] Lequis thought it hopeless to try to change the entrenched view. He had been in China, too, and noted later in his SWA diary that "it's funny, how many experiences we had in China and how little we learned from them." He concluded, "There is really no reason for me to fashion a sharply logical, well-styled report [on deficiencies in provisioning]," since it would not make any difference; so he kept his notes to himself.[50] Lequis's despairing silence is a nice example of the power of military culture (unintentionally) to stifle internal criticism.

The result of lack of realistic planning was that adequate provisioning and medical services for German troops depended largely on luck. In China, the richness of the countryside masked the organizational deficiencies.[51] In East Africa, the governor, wiser because of the SWA example, saved the situation by radically restricting the number of white troops, drilling the few newcomers in stringent hygiene measures, and successfully pushing to raise the monetary allotment for food.[52] But in SWA the full measure of inadequacy had been bared for all to see. Both medical and food provisioning were catastrophic. Two-thirds rations were the rule in the field, with the result, as the military committee later charged with investigating the failures laconically put it, that "malnourishment and resulting illnesses, especially scurvy, were not unusual among field troops."[53] They were not unusual among troops in the rear, either. The ratio of losses (casualties, not deaths) by disease to losses by wounds or death in battle was 25:1.[54] Twenty percent of the ill had to be returned to Germany.[55] The ill and wounded received little, late, or poor medical attention: even in late 1904, after almost a year of war, the sick in Windhuk, where vegetables were available, were receiving none to counteract their scurvy.[56] The gigantic size and

48. Anonymous, "Der Train in den Verhandlungen der Kommission für den Reichshaushaltsetat," *Militär-Wochenblatt* 98:72 (1913), cols. 1643–45. For inadequate planning to feed German civilians in wartime see Burchardt, *Friedenswirtschaft*, 193–231.

49. Prussia, War Ministry, *Felddienst-Ordnung* (1900), 126; Prussia, War Ministry, *Kriegs-Etappen-Ordnung* (KEO), para. 23 and 26, pp. 17, 19; typical, also Eiswaldt, *Handbuch*, 256; Germany, General Staff, *Heeresverpflegung* (Berlin, 1913), 285–86, 288, 297.

50. Lequis, diary (in SWA), no date, MA-Freiburg, Nl. Lequis, Nr. 16, 73, 74.

51. Lequis, "Allgemeine Erfahrungen," ibid., Nr. 30, 94; Scheibert, *Krieg in China*, 469.

52. Götzen, "Befehl für das Detachement Merker," Dar es Salaam, 26 Sept. 1905, MA-Freiburg, RM 121 I, Nr. 441, Doc. 7, point 8; "Sanitäre Vorschriften für die an Land befindl. Marinemannschaften," Dar es Salaam, 16 Sept. 1905, ibid., Nr. 443; Ahlefeld to Col. Dept., Nr. M. 4440, Berlin, 19 Sept. 1905, BA-Berlin, R 1001, Nr. 722, 137.

53. "Ergebnis der Arbeiten der durch AKO vom 14.11.1908 berufenen Kommission zur Beratung aufgrund der bei der Entsendung von Verstärkungen für die Schutztruppen in SWA gesammelten Erfahrungen," 1908, MA-Freiburg RW 51, vol. 19, 69.

54. Kommando der Schutztruppen, *Sanitäts-Bericht*, 2:404.

55. Ibid., table 13, p. 30. Of the 73% who returned to the troops, few of them (even officers) were sent to their original unit, which increased the administrative chaos that already reigned: Lettow-Vorbeck diary entry, 27 Nov. 1904, MA-Freiburg, Nl. Lettow-Vorbeck, Nr. 34.

56. Lettow-Vorbeck diary entry, 17 Nov. 1904, ibid.; also, Heinrich v. Welck to his father, copy, Okomiparum near Waterberg, 16 Dec. 1904, MA-Freiburg, MSg. 2, Nr. 3039.

staggering pedantry of the later official report on the medical situation (*Sanitäts-Bericht*) is a perverse measure of the lack of resources expended at the time.

Unrealistic planning had real consequences in unnecessary suffering and death for German troops and in preprogramming their failure to fulfill their original military goals. The combination of frustration at one's own failure and physical suffering commonly leads to greater violence among soldiers.[57] As Captain Bayer remembered about his experiences in SWA, "Pain and anger are related, because they come from the same source of sensation."[58] Faulty planning had the unintended consequence of at least preparing troops to accept gratuitous violence, even if they did not initiate it themselves.

If the consequences of unrealistic planning were often unintended, it is still important to recall that defective preparation had a systematic character and was produced on several different levels. It reflected the valuation of fighting over every other consideration. It was supported by the inherent cleft between the unrealistic, racialist-inspired expectations of colonial warfare and that warfare's intractable reality. Both of these situations were common to other European militaries. But in the German case, systematic underplanning was strengthened by two further forces: the political convictions and traditional values of the officer corps, and what one scholar of provisioning calls "the conflict between strategic and logistic considerations."[59] That is, the (politically inspired) requirements of grand victory exceeded the ability to fulfill them. Realistic planning would have revealed the impossibility of the grand goals; rather than give these up, planning itself was truncated.[60]

The resulting gap between goal and grasp was to be bridged by virtues: "discipline," "will," "self-sacrifice." Because the gap was not the product of happenstance (or mere incompetence or bad luck) but of system, the saving virtues were systematically encouraged through training, mythmaking, models, and rewards. Once again, the German army was not alone in its predicament; one can recognize analogues in the French army's devotion to élan and the British army's promotion of pure stubbornness. But the national importance of the army and, above all, the grandiosity of the Wilhelminian goal of becoming a World Power produced a qualitative difference in degree, while the virtues had a different valence in the German system.

Extremism and the Virtues of the Officer

If we return to Kaiser Wilhelm's Hun speech, we can see the virtues German soldiers were expected to embody in the order in which the Kaiser enumerated them: "first, your traditional German efficiency, second, the sacrifice, braveness, and joyful bearing of all discomfort, and, third, the honor and fame of our weapons and flags. You should give an example of discipline [*Manneszucht und Disziplin*], but also of overcoming and self-control [*Ueberwindung und Selbstbeherrschung*]."[61] What I have translated as "efficiency"

---

57. On this phenomenon in the Boer War: Spies, *Methods of Barbarism?* 115; in French Indochina: Fourniau, "Colonial Wars before 1914," 83–84; generally, Ervin Staub, *The Roots of Evil* (Cambridge, 1989), 35–50.

58. Bayer, *Mit dem Hauptquartier*, 21.

59. Van Crefeld, *Supplying War*, 115.

60. Vagts, *History of Militarism*, 354; Wallach, *Das Dogma der Vernichtungsschlacht*, 55–56, 71–72, 81, 84.

61. Sösemann, "Die sogenannte 'Hunnenrede,'" 349–50.

144   (*Tüchtigkeit*) is more accurately rendered as experienced, energetic activity. Neither braveness nor upholding honor and fame are surprising in a list of military virtues. But the repeated call for sacrifice, joyful bearing of discomfort, overcoming (in the sense of surmounting obstacles), and self-control (in the sense of self-denial) is remarkable for its glorification of suffering. The immediate movement in the speech from this list to avenging and taking no prisoners follows an emotional logic in which one's own suffering justifies the greater suffering and punishment of one's enemies (the twinning of "pain and anger" that Captain Bayer noted).

The Kaiser's speech occurred at a symbolically significant moment: the first sending out of German troops overseas. That his list of virtues was canonical is confirmed by the myth of Captain Klein. Myths are cultural lessons repeated and believed because they exemplify truths for groups to live (or die) by. They may be inconsistent, illogical, or even untrue, but that does not matter: "Myths are too important for people to be embarrassed about factual inaccuracy."[62] The event that ought to have epitomized soldierly virtue in SWA was Franke's relief of Omaruru. Accomplished with few resources, much bravery, and only seven deaths, this battle saved the strategically important railroad for German use.[63] But Franke was an old Schutztruppler, not a regular officer; and, besides, he survived. And so it was the exploit of Captain Klein that became the most repeated "story" of the war.

Captain Klein's patrol (26–31 October 1904) occurred under the aegis of Trotha's October proclamation, before Berlin had rescinded it. Exercising his own initiative, Klein decided to attack a band of Herero reported to be at the last waterhole before the Omaheke Desert, a place dubbed by the soldiers "Orlogsende"—war's end. Arriving at Orlogsende on the 27th, Klein and his thirty horsemen, artillery, and twenty-five foot soldiers had a brief firefight with Herero at the well. The survivors, as usual, scattered into the desert. Lacking water, Klein was forced to divide his unit, sending some south and leaving others at Orlogsende. Klein led a small band in pursuit of the Herero eastward into the desert. As they were setting out, a captive Herero woman told them that Chief Tetjo and his clan (whom they were now pursuing) had already died of thirst. But Klein pressed on. After fifty kilometers with no water anywhere, Klein was forced to send more men and horses back. Klein forged ahead, first with four and then with two riders, farther and farther into the waterless desert, until "only a few footsteps and no [dead] animals" could be found.[64] And still Klein continued another thirty kilometers, to a rise that afforded him an unobstructed view toward the east and south. He saw nothing. Only then did he break off the pursuit and struggle back. The units he had left behind were in such desperate straits that they had to abandon their munitions and artillery. Their horses and donkeys died of thirst. The men sickened. But, as the official history says, they were "saved" by the heroic efforts of other troopers, who brought them in from the desert. Klein and his two companions also made it back alive. But, like the rest of their men, they

---

62. Ott, *Organizational Culture*, 31.
63. Casualties: General Staff, *Kämpfe der deutschen Truppen*, 2:228.
64. Ibid., 1:204.

had contracted typhus at waterholes contaminated by dead animals. Klein died of the disease a few weeks later, in a miserable desert hut, without adequate medical attention.[65] "The same sad fate struck a great number of his soldiers."[66]

Despite this admission, the official history placed its imprimatur on the myth of Captain Klein: "The daring pursuit [*Verfolgungszug*] of Captain Klein, which went to the *outermost* limit of human capacity, put the crown on everything that German soldiers had suffered and accomplished in the war against the Herero."[67] It is hard to avoid concluding that it was the very extravagant uselessness of Klein's action that merited such praise. For Klein had accomplished nothing, except his own suffering and death and that of many of his men. He was told at the beginning that his quarry had died, a message confirmed again and again by the bodies of people and animals he discovered along the way. And how effective would he and two men have been against the Tetjo clan, had it still existed? But Klein nonetheless exemplified the virtues necessary to hopeless endeavors: "restless energy,"[68] boundless initiative, inordinate capacity for suffering, and blind self-sacrifice, matched only by the willingness to sacrifice others. He had gone literally and figuratively beyond "war's end" and had died of his exemplary attention to pure duty for its own sake.

Standard Practices in the Treatment of Enemy Soldiers

German Southwest Africa was exceptional in that practically every systemic deficiency inherent in training, planning, and basic assumptions became visible; everything that could go wrong did go wrong. When one examines the other military campaigns the Kaiserreich conducted, however, one discovers very similar treatment of enemy soldiers and civilians and the same general conduct of war.

Actual operations differed in each instance, depending on the particular situation. German Southwest Africa was the only place where conventional operations (the single battle of annihilation) seemed possible. In China, most of the fighting was already over when the bulk of German troops arrived; in East Africa, guerilla war raged almost from the beginning of the revolt. Both China and East Africa offered opportunities for energetic pursuit and punitive sweeps, however. These typically involved much exemplary violence that was seldom limited to enemy fighters. But even the treatment of armed men showed the tendency we saw in SWA to become steadily more violent.

One of the most striking features of the surviving accounts, archival and published, of the German campaigns in China and East Africa is the widespread practice of shooting captured enemy soldiers or warriors. In Africa, exemplary executions could be justified by the warriors' status as "rebels."[69] Their status of being outside the law was further con-

65. Lettow-Vorbeck diary, 1 Dec. 1904, MA-Freiburg, Nl. Lettow-Vorbeck, Nr. 34.

66. General Staff, *Kämpfe der deutschen Truppen*, 1:206. Naturally, the official report is silent on medical care.

67. Ibid. Emphasis in original. For similarly approving contemporary accounts: Bayer, *Mit dem Hauptquartier*, 204–5; Schwabe, *Krieg in Südwest-Afrika*, 298–300; Deimling, *Aus der alten in die neue Zeit*, 68–69; Deimling, "Südwest-Afrika," 30–31.

68. General Staff, *Kämpfe der deutschen Truppen*, 1:204.

69. Bald, "Afrikanischer Kampf," 40.

146 firmed by the general assumption among Europeans that international law, as a compact among the "civilized" organized into states, did not apply to colonial conflicts.[70] But this principle was weakening, even in Germany. In response to a query of December 1904, the Colonial Department, for example, explicitly recognized the enemy warriors in SWA as prisoners of war, though it seems not to have understood the full implications of such status.[71] Reichstag members argued on both sides of the question.[72] In China, shooting prisoners could not be justified by the same arguments. Nevertheless, the practice was commonplace.

In East Africa, shooting those suspected of being rebel leaders began immediately as legally sanctioned policy. Already on 4 August 1905 the official war diary of Navy Lieutenant von Paasche recorded that "at the suggestion of [the local administrator] Keudel, Captain Merker arrived [at a village near Mohorro] and proclaimed a state of war so that he could immediately hold a court-martial and hang three main magicians [rebel leaders], whom Keudel feared might be freed. The execution is said to have made a good impression on the populace."[73] Executions could be ordered by the local administrator (*Bezirksamtmann*), the commander of the naval troops, or the unit military commanders.[74] Executions were routinely reported in the war diaries and reports sent in to the governor and naval commander, who then sent digests on to the Foreign Office and the naval administration, respectively. All of these offices approved the practice implicitly—I have found no archival record of a higher authority criticizing it, and in an early message, Governor Götzen explicitly expressed his "thanks and recognition to [Paasche] and [his] men" for their work in August 1905.[75]

As in SWA, legally sanctioned exemplary executions of rebel leaders opened the floodgates to executions for all sorts of reasons. It is difficult to believe, for example, that the "almost one hundred" men executed in Jakobi on 6 October 1905 were all rebel leaders, or the forty-seven whom Bezirksamtmann Richter had put to death on 27 February 1906 in Ungoni.[76] Captain Kleist shot over fifty men at a single time for being unsatisfactory guides, and the war diary of Ensign Schröder simply notes, "8 September 1905: execution of twenty rebels by shooting," and then, one week later, another thirty-seven.[77]

70. Meurer, *Die Haager Friedenskonferenzen*, 2:250; Lueder, "Landkriegsrecht," 395–96; Germany, General Staff, *Kriegsbrauch im Landkriege* (Berlin, 1902), 53; Stenzel, *Kriegführung*, 25; Büttner and Loth, *Philosophie*, 54–55.

71. Col. Dept. to governor of the Kamerun, Berlin, 7 Jan. 1905, BA-Berlin, R 1001, Nr. 2090, p. 12.

72. Ledebour (SPD), 25 May 1905, *Sten. Ber.*, vol. 204, pp. 6159–60, versus Erzberger (Catholic Center), 2 Dec. 1905, ibid., vol. 214, p. 111.

73. War diary of Lt. Paasche, 6 Aug. 1905, MA-Freiburg, RM 121 I, Nr. 452, p. 7; Nuhn, *Flammen über Deutschost*, 30.

74. War diary of v. Jastrzembski, Kilwa, pt. 2, entries of 8 and 9 Aug. 1905, ibid., Nr. 448, pp. 2–3; Götzen to Foreign Office, Nr. 249, secret, Dar es Salaam, 12 Dec. 1905, BA-Berlin, R 1001, Nr. 723, p. 191.

75. Paasche to Cdr. Back (cdr. of the *Bussard*), Mayenge, 3 Sept. 1905, MA-Freiburg, RM 121 I, Nr. 448.

76. Mission Superintendent Schumann, "Die Schreckenstage auf der Missionsstation Jakobi," *Missionsberichte der Gesellschaft zur Beförderung der evangelischen Missionen unter den Heiden zu Berlin für das Jahr 1906* (Feb.), 62–76, here 75; Nuhn, *Flammen über Deutschost*, 141.

77. Nuhn, *Flammen über Deutschost*, 148; war diary of Ensign Schröder, 8 and 15 Sept. 1905, near Lindi, MA-Freiburg, RM 121 I, Nr. 441, Doc. 55.

War diaries note that prisoners were executed "for participation in the uprising," for giving false information, for having killed a German soldier in battle, and for spying; sometimes they say simply "people shot," which makes it impossible to know whether these were prisoners or battle casualties.[78] The colonial administration estimated in 1913 that twenty-six thousand Africans had been shot during the rebellion.[79]

There are nonetheless many accounts of prisoners taken but not later shot, so the goal of troop practice did not become, as it did in SWA, the complete annihilation of the male population.[80] Other aspects of war conduct against an armed enemy were identical to those used in SWA, however, such as bounties and using prisoners as guides or as workers.

In China the picture was much the same. Sometimes executions of Boxer prisoners were preceded by courts-martial that gathered Chinese testimony via interpreter and targeted only leaders or Boxers guilty of massacring Chinese Christians.[81] At other times, when those executed numbered twenty-five or even one hundred seventy, it appears that all suspected Boxers were summarily executed.[82] These executions were not spontaneous "excesses"; they were policy, ordered by the commanders of the different divisions. The General Staff's official reporter on the China expedition, Baron Binder-Krieglstein, faithfully recorded executions of large numbers of Boxer prisoners, including those guilty of nothing more than sniping at German troops during a battle. He ends his account by noting that "discipline, thank heavens, was so excellent that no excesses on marches occurred."[83] Paul von Lettow-Vorbeck, who, like Lothar von Trotha, also served in China, noted the final act of a punitive expedition west of Peking, which shows that many officers and troops regarded executions as an unfortunate part of their duty.

The next morning a court-martial was held. The three principal accused were condemned to death, the other guilty ones received whippings. "Jenowitsch, will you be so good as to have these people shot?" was Zajetz's unintentionally grotesque order. A group of sailors pulled the condemned men out of the crowd and forced them to kneel. A fat man screamed horribly for his "Ma" (mother). Four men aimed at each head. When the salvo came, those who were shot flew into the air. Two were dead at once, another received another shot. It was the man who

78. War diary of v. Jastrzembski, 6 Sept. 1905, Kilwa, pt. 8, MA-Freiburg, RM 121 I, Nr. 448; Report of Ensign Dollmann to cdr. of the *Thetis*, ca. 15 Nov. 1905, ibid., Nr. 439, Doc. 204; war diary of Paasche, 18 Aug. 1905, Hirnsee, ibid., Nr. 448; war diary of Paasche, 12 Jan. 1906, Kitanga, ibid., Nr. 452, p. 39; report of Lt. Baron v. Stengel, 4 Oct. 1905, Kilwa, ibid., Nr. 450, p. 14; war diary of Paasche, 19 Aug. 1905, Utete-Mayenge, ibid., Nr. 452, p. 13.

79. Noske, *Kolonialpolitik*, 123.

80. For example, the one hundred male prisoners mentioned in "Report on the condition and events of the detachment Lindi-Massassi," signed Lt. Stieler v. Heydekampf, 26 Nov. 1905, Massassi, MA-Freiburg, RM 121 I, Nr. 439, Doc. 275.

81. Scheibert, *Krieg in China*, 481–82; Lettow-Vorbeck personal diary, 5 Nov. 1900, MA-Freiburg, Nl. Lettow-Vorbeck, Nr. 44; E. Baron Binder-Krieglstein, *Die Kämpfe des Deutschen Expeditionskorps in China und ihre militärischen Lehren* (Berlin, 1902), 64, 67.

82. Binder-Krieglstein, *Kämpfe des Deutschen Expeditionskorps*, 11, 57, also 190.

83. Ibid., 233.

148   had screamed. This executioner's work must be done, but it is repulsive. I thought
I saw on most faces as they marched by afterward an expression of repulsion.[84]

In addition to mass executions of prisoners, the Boxer campaign saw much indiscriminate shooting. It recalled the 1870 war because of the difficulty Europeans had in distinguishing innocent farmers from Boxers who had thrown off their identifying armbands and fled to the fields. Many, many civilian males were shot as Boxers, because, as Lettow-Vorbeck put it, "in such a franc-tireur's war, who can tell?"[85] It is impossible to determine how much the Kaiser's Hun speech encouraged troops to shoot at everything before them.

Germany was by no means alone in wreaking massive destruction on Boxers and civilian Chinese alike. The other nations (Britain, France, Russia, the United States, Japan, Austria, and Italy) engaged in killing of innocents, limitless plunder, repeated rape, and widespread, vindictive property destruction—the uprising brought out the worst in all the armies present.[86] German troops played a very limited role in the first two phases of the war—British Admiral Seymour's unsuccessful attempt to relieve Peking in June 1900 and the successful race among the allied contingents in August to do so. It was only in the last phase of the war, when the East-Asian Expeditionary Corps arrived under the command of Field Marshal Alfred von Waldersee, that German troops began to distinguish themselves from their allies. By the time Waldersee and his troops arrived in Peking in mid-October 1900, the war was virtually over; Peking had been taken and thoroughly plundered. Only the humiliating demands of the allies and the diplomatic maneuvering of the Chinese government prevented a quick conclusion of peace.

It was in this period from October 1900 through spring 1901 that the Germans launched seventy-five punitive expeditions, designed to end all Boxer resistance in the countryside and force the Chinese government to sign a peace treaty.[87] The Germans' zeal, exemplary violence, and policy of widespread execution were recognized, and condemned, by contemporary observers as unique.[88] The official reporter for the German army expressed the difference: "Whereas the German grasps the casus belli with joy, the Briton [elsewhere, he adds Frenchman] postpones the decision as long as possible and tries to move the opponent to retreat by negotiation."[89] The casus belli had largely disappeared, of course; German action was designed instead to demonstrate allied armed might and to take revenge in areas where Chinese Christians had died at Boxer hands. German violence was therefore exemplary, in two senses, and that largely accounts for its ferocity.

---

84. Lettow-Vorbeck, "Diary-like entries," MA-Freiburg, Nl. Lettow-Vorbeck, Nr. 43.

85. Ibid.

86. See the excellent brief account of Paul A. Cohen, *History in Three Keys* (New York, 1997), 15–56.

87. Mombauer, "Wilhelm," 109.

88. Ibid., 184–85; Sabine Dabringhaus, "An Army on Vacation?" in *Anticipating Total War*, 459–76, here 475; Binder-Krieglstein, *Kämpfe des Deutschen Expeditionskorps*, 204.

89. Binder-Krieglstein, *Kämpfe des Deutschen Expeditionskorps*, 265; same thing concerning France, 144, 202–4.

Trying to separate analytically the treatment of enemy soldiers from that of enemy civilians, as I have done, is somewhat artificial and hence inaccurate. The fate of civilians and fighters was bound together; in all these engagements, German troops could not, or would not, distinguish them. All males were suspected of being actual or potential soldiers. During skirmishes, German soldiers tended to fire at whatever targets revealed themselves, and often enough these were noncombatant women, children, and unarmed men trying to flee.[90] In engagements where prisoners were interned, as in SWA and East Africa, civilians were equally reckoned as "prisoners."[91]

Noncombatants in all these wars suffered the same treatment as had the French in 1870–71: recruitment as guides (and punishment if they misled); execution as spies; punitive fines and "contributions"; and the routine destruction of their houses, villages, and places of worship.[92] These practices were not isolated atrocities; they were systematic policy, openly reported in official war diaries and published accounts. Obviously, the exceptional methods of 1870 had become simply routine.

In addition to these systematic practices endured by civilians, however, there were indeed atrocities, or "excesses" as they were called at the time. "Excesses" were examples of

90. Some typical examples: War diary, Saamanga [*sic*], signed Lt. Cdr. Konis, 9 Aug. 1905, MA-Freiburg, RM 121 I, Nr. 448; Lettow-Vorbeck, report on his second punitive expedition in China, Dec. 1900–Jan. 1901, MA-Freiburg, Nl. Lettow-Vorbeck, Nr. 43.

91. Paasche to Glatzel, Utanza, 4 Oct. 1905, MA-Freiburg, RM 121 I, Nr. 439, Doc. 135; Report of Ensign Dollmann to cdr. of *Thetis*, 15 Nov. 1905, Mtumba, ibid., Doc. 204; "Report on the condition . . . ," Lt. Stieler v. Heydekampf, 26 Nov. 1905, Massassi, ibid., Doc. 275.

92. Guides: China: Scheibert, *Krieg in China*, 475, 511; Rudolf Giehrl, *China-Fahrt* (Munich, 1903), 39–40, 70; Binder-Krieglstein, *Kämpfe des Deutschen Expeditionskorps*, 37–38, 93, 97, 122–23.

Collective fines and "contributions": East Africa: Bald, "Afrikanischer Kampf," 41; Paasche war diary, 7 Sept. 1905, Mayenge, MA-Freiburg, RM 121 I, Nr. 452, p. 18; Götzen, Runderlass Nr. 8040, Dar es Salaam, 13 Nov. 1905, BA-Berlin, R 1001, Nr. 724, p. 118; Götzen to Foreign Office, copy, 7 Dec. 1905, Dar es Salaam, ibid., Nr. 723, p. 188; in China: Giehrl, *China-Fahrt*, 143; Binder-Krieglstein, *Kämpfe des Deutschen Expeditionskorps*, 31, 53.

Destruction of individual houses, East Africa: war diary of detachment of Lt. Cdr. Konis, 30 Aug. 1905, MA-Freiburg, RM 121 I, Nr. 448; war diary of Paasche, 3 and 27 Oct. 1905, ibid., Nr. 452, pp. 23–24, 27; war diary of detachment of SMS *Seeadler*, signed Sommerfeld, 25 Nov. 1905, Mtingi, ibid., Nr. 439, Doc. 271; in China: Binder-Krieglstein, *Kämpfe des Deutschen Expeditionskorps*, 64–65, 67.

Destruction of villages, China: Scheibert, *Krieg in China*, 290, 299; Giehrl, *China-Fahrt*, 41; Binder-Krieglstein, *Kämpfe des Deutschen Expeditionskorps*, 50–51, 56, 80; Germany, Admiralty, *Kaiserliche Marine*, 41, 190; Westermayer diary, 22 Nov. 1900, MA-Freiburg, MSg. 2, Nr. 5196, p. 28; Lettow-Vorbeck, diary, 4 Dec. 1900, MA-Freiburg, Nl. Lettow-Vorbeck, Nr. 44; in East Africa: Nuhn, *Flammen über Deutschost*, 121; Jastrzembski diary, 28 and 29 Aug. 1905, MA-Freiburg, RM 121 I, Nr. 448; Schumann, "Die Schreckenstage," 1 Oct. 1905, p. 74; war diary of Lt. Stieler v. Heydekampf, 5 Oct. 1905, MA-Freiburg, RM 121 I, Nr. 459; war diary of Lt. Paasche, 3 and 27 Oct. 1905, ibid., Nr. 452, pp. 23–24; "Military-political report on the activity of the cruiser and marines stationed in East Africa (20 Oct. to 30 Nov. 1905)," 7 Dec. 1905, MA-Freiburg, RM 5/Nr. 6036, 20R-21; Götzen to Foreign Office, Nr. 118, Dar es Salaam, 11 Nov. 1905, MA-Freiburg, RM 121 I/Nr. 438, p. 32; war diary of sailor detachment Wachtel, 10 Nov.–25 Dec. 1905, Lindi-Kiswere, ibid., Nr. 455; Report of Lt. Baron v. Stengel, 10 and 13 Nov. 1905, Kilwa, ibid., Nr. 450, pp. 4–6; Report of Ensign Dollmann to cdr. of *Thetis*, ca. 15 Nov. 1905, ibid., Nr. 439, Doc. 204; war diary of Paasche, 30 Nov. 1905, ibid., Nr. 452, p. 35; "Official Report of the Government on the Rebellious Districts," 26 Nov. 1905, ibid., Nr. 439, Doc. 236.

Destruction of temples, China: Giehrl, *China-Fahrt*, 59; Binder-Krieglstein, *Kämpfe des Deutschen Expeditionskorps*, 31, 64.

150 indiscipline, dreaded by officers who feared being unable to reestablish control over their troops. The line separating "excesses" from purposive policy is not always easy to draw. For one thing, contemporaries often used "excess" or "atrocity" to refer to acts we can in retrospect identify as widespread and accepted behavior, or even the result of orders. For another, armies tolerated some kinds of "excesses" but punished others. Toleration made certain "excesses" systemic; they became latent policy but were never officially acknowledged.

The German army was especially sensitive to the issue of plunder. Judging from the attention devoted to property offenses, the Military Penal Code mimicked the Criminal Code in placing a higher value on protecting property than life and limb—a characteristic of nineteenth-century law generally. The *Felddienst-Ordnung* was equally emphatic about reducing the occasions for plunder, especially in requisitioning: "Contact between individual soldiers and inhabitants is to be avoided as much as possible," and it, too, devoted more space to the protection of civilians' belongings than to the protection of the civilians themselves.[93] (Exempt from the rubric "plunder" were enemy state property and items deemed necessary to maintain the army.) The orgy of looting that characterized allied behavior in China was therefore very disturbing to Field Marshal v. Waldersee, the titular head of the allied troops in China after mid-October 1900. On 27 November 1900 he admonished German officers to "be strict regarding crimes against property and cruelty against defenseless and peaceful Chinese," as Lettow-Vorbeck noted in his diary that day.[94] Waldersee later admitted his lack of success: the type of warfare in China, he wrote, "made people coarse and insensible and confused their conceptions about property."[95] Waldersee's intervention may not have privileged life over property, but it was at least a clear statement that not everything was permitted.[96]

Unlike plunder, the rape and sexual coercion of women appears to have been widely tolerated in non-European theaters of war.[97] It was a standard feature of the war in China among all the allied troops.[98] It appears to have been ubiquitous among German soldiers in SWA, too. The memoirists always denied it, but there is contemporary testimony from missionaries and later evidence given to British investigators by Africans that nightly rape was common in the internment camps and that soldiers routinely forced women captives to act as concubines.[99] The best corroborating evidence comes from the *Sanitäts-Bericht*,

---

93. Prussia, War Ministry, *Felddienst-Ordnung* (1908), 137–38; *Felddienst-Ordnung* (1900), 134–36; also, Germany, General Staff, *Heeresverpflegung*, 297.

94. Lettow-Vorbeck diary, 27 Nov. 1900, MA-Freiburg, Nl. Lettow-Vorbeck, Nr. 44.

95. Cited in Spraul, " 'Völkermord,' " 718.

96. The German diarists and memoirists are univocal in their condemnation of plunder (as opposed to massive destruction and loss of life), and the other armies may indeed have plundered more extensively than the Germans. Scheibert, *Krieg in China*, 317; Binder-Krieglstein, *Kämpfe des Deutschen Expeditionskorps*, 35.

97. In general: Ruth Seifert, "Krieg und Vergewaltigung," in *Massenvergewaltigung*, ed. Alexandra Stiglmayer (Freiburg, 1993).

98. Cohen, *History in Three Keys*, 182–83; Esherick, *Origins*, 189.

99. Denials: Rohrbach, 27 Feb. 1904, *Aus Südwestafrikas schweren Tagen*, 122; Bayer, *Mit dem Hauptquartier*, 99; Hermann Alverdes, *Mein Tagebuch aus Südwest* (Oldenburg, 1906), 21. Missionaries: August Kuhlmann to Gov. Lindequist, 28 Feb. 1906, Omburo, VEM-Wuppertal, B/c II 72, 28–29; Kuhlmann, "Mitteilung für die Gesellschaft," 15 May 1906, Omburo, ibid., 36–37; Fritz Meier, "Bericht," 1 Feb. 1906, Windhuk, BA-Berlin, R 151 F/D.IV.L.3., vol. 2, p. 35. African testimony: Union of South Africa, *Report on the Natives*, 9, 65, 67, 99–102.

which detailed the troops' medical condition. It lamented the astonishing venereal disease rate among soldiers. The contemporary Bavarian army at home had a VD rate of 19.4 percent; during the 1870–71 war, the percentage of infected soldiers had risen to 42.6 percent, approximately the same as for British soldiers during the Boer War (1900). In SWA, the figure was 93.3 percent; in China, 140 percent (including those infected more than once).[100] Normally, troops in the rear areas were much more at risk for venereal disease than fighting units. In SWA, however, this ratio was reversed: field troops had infection rates over twice as high as those in the rear guard.[101] The monthly medical report for April 1906 located the cause when it noted "the remarkable rise in venereal diseases in the last five months in the northern lines. It obviously stands in a certain relation with the rise in prisoners."[102] The *Sanitäts-Bericht* admitted the source was "free and captive native women," but it would only describe the circumstances as "the generally great ease with which sexual relations could be undertaken with the female native population, even when they were not prostitutes."[103]

The unwillingness of the military to acknowledge endemic sexual "excesses" is an example of the typical discrepancy between stated beliefs or values and actual behavior.[104] As opposed to the oft-repeated claims of male chivalry, the basic assumptions that motivated actual behavior and encouraged the army to tolerate sexual excesses included the following: male dominance and female inferiority, with its corollary, the right of soldiers to display domination over defeated peoples in a sexual manner; the myth of the "easy" sexuality of the "uncivilized"; the hydraulic model of male sexual functioning, in which male sexual activity was an unquestioned imperative; the desirability of male bonding and camaraderie via sexual display; and so forth.[105] These convictions, which one rarely finds articulated, were not confined to common soldiers but shared throughout the military system. One sees this in the *Sanitäts-Bericht*'s assumption, for example, that "long periods of forced sexual abstinence" would invariably result in the field troops engaging in "indiscriminate" sex, or in the army's solicitude for presumptive sexual necessity by erecting official bordellos with "mostly white inmates," whose venereal health was regularly checked.[106] In the rare instance when someone protested sexual "excess," as missionary Fritz Meier did in February 1906, the army bureaucracy quickly closed ranks to protect its comrades.[107]

"Excesses," or atrocities, could be so pervasive as to qualify as unarticulated policy. But for analytical purposes, it is important to distinguish them from official policy, whose

100. Kommando der Schutztruppen, *Sanitäts-Bericht*, 2:339.
101. Ibid., 2:341.
102. Ibid., 2:343. Also, staff doctor Kuhn, "Die Gesundheitsverhältnisse in unseren Kolonien," *Jahrbuch über die deutschen Kolonien* 1 (1908), 42–61, here 54.
103. Kommando der Schutztruppen, *Sanitäts-Bericht*, 2:340.
104. Schein, "How Culture Forms," 19–20, 22–23; Ott, *Organizational Culture*, 39–44; Sapienza, "Believing Is Seeing," 60.
105. Cf. Stoneman's discussion for 1870: "Bavarian Army," 276–81.
106. Kommando der Schutztruppen, *Sanitäts-Bericht*, 2:341, 343.
107. Meier, "Bericht," 1 Feb. 1906, Windhuk, BA-Berlin, R 151 F/D.IV.L.3., vol. 2, p. 35; Capt. Baumgärtner, "Bericht über Missionar Meyer [*sic*]," 6 Feb. 1906, ibid., pp. 36–37; Etappenkommando to governor, 4 Mar. 1906, Windhuk, ibid., p. 39.

152 sources were somewhat different. The official policies regarding civilians we have examined so far—firing on civilian populations, forced services, collective fines, punitive destruction of houses and whole villages—could have a tremendous impact on civilian survival. Dabringhaus estimates German punitive expeditions made "hundreds of thousands" of Chinese homeless; the number of Chinese dead from allied actions is thought to be many tens of thousands.[108] The percentage of dead is even more staggering in the two African wars. This resulted from the last two standard practices we shall consider: internment and "hunger war."

The internment of large numbers of civilians is a hallmark of colonial fighting. Because internment became so widespread during the First World War, it is important to put German colonial practices in their European context. Military motives were mixed: on the one hand, internment removed noncombatants from the perils of warfare against guerrillas and made it easier to feed them; on the other, it permitted control of them as potential enemies. Despite the more and more frequent recourse to civilian internment camps after 1898, no European army appears to have examined the logistic and hygiene problems connected with this new institution, nor were administrators trained to deal with it. They took no account of the differing food requirements of nursing mothers, small children, or the sick as against healthy young men; they forgot that internment camps tended to become permanent and erected them instead like temporary bivouacs; they allotted no more space to civilians who lived all day in the tents than they did to soldiers who merely slept there at night; they ignored elementary hygiene rules of every sort; and they chose camp administrators with no regard to the extraordinary practical skills (in engineering, plumbing, medicine, nutrition, hygiene, and so forth) that the position required.[109] Consequently, civilian internment camps compiled high death rates. Nonetheless, before the First World War, they remained unmentioned and unregulated by international law.

Before World War I the most infamous internment camps were those run by the British army from July 1900 to summer 1902 in South Africa to house Boer noncombatants (with separate camps for black Africans). These camps featured the same lethal combination of maladministration, lack of attention, and "lovelessness" that characterized the German camps in SWA.[110] Poor sanitation, inadequate rations, and inferior medical care produced epidemics of pneumonia, measles, and dysentery. At their highest, monthly death rates in the winter of 1900–1901 compare to those in the German camps. In the end, almost twenty-eight thousand Boer women and children died in these camps: a death rate of between 17 and 24 percent, probably nearer the latter.[111] In addition, fourteen thousand

---

108. Sabine Dabringhaus, "Anticipating Total War?" paper presented at the conference "Anticipating Total War? The United States and Germany, 1871–1914," Augsburg, 27–29 July 1994, 6; Cohen, *History in Three Keys*, 51, 174–75. German losses were 188 dead in battle, 409 wounded, 8,070 ill: Roland Felber and Horst Rostek, *Der "Hunnenkrieg" Kaiser Wilhelms II* (Berlin, 1987), 36; *Sanitäts-Bericht* 2: Beilage 1, 426–27.

109. These deficiencies are pithily summarized in Great Britain, Parliament, *Report on the Concentration Camps in South Africa, by the Committee of Ladies Appointed by the Secretary of State for War*, Cd. 893 (London, 1902), 1–24.

110. Estorff, *Wanderungen*, 118.

111. Spies, *Methods of Barbarism?* 265 (numbers dead); S. Burridge Spies, "Women and the War," in *The South African War*, ed. Peter Warwick and S. B. Spies (London, 1980), 161–85, 169 for total number of inmates

blacks died—a death rate of 12 percent.[112] Obviously, general European military culture tended to produce catastrophes when armies attempted to "concentrate" large numbers of civilians, which, in colonies, they were tempted to do.

If the British army is quite comparable in its fatal ineptitude, there is still one striking difference between it and the German military administration in SWA.[113] This difference is visible in table 1, which sets out various contemporary model rations for adults. The most punitive meat ration the British military doled out to enemy civilians was still five times greater than the official ration for African prisoners in SWA.[114] The official prisoner ration was set in September 1905 under Lieutenant General v. Trotha's regime. When he departed, the ration was minimally raised by the addition of under an ounce of dried vegetables and under an ounce of extra fat per day. The total meat portion remained unchanged.[115] When one recalls that the Nama were a primarily meat-eating people (and the Herero a dairy-dependent people—and there was no set milk allotment), that most prisoners were ill or severely debilitated, that they were expected to work, and that in some cases food was allotted to the male head of the family only (who then had to share it with his dependents), then one must conclude that the original rations as set under Trotha were intentionally designed to produce extreme suffering and that starvation, disease, and death were acceptable outcomes. Even an inattentive military administrator would have had to have noticed that the rations were deadly. Field troops already experienced undernourishment and scurvy as a result of the two-thirds rations they received, and these contained (at least theoretically) six times more meat than what African prisoners received, twice as many carbohydrates, plus fruit jam that contained vitamin C, which was not present in the official prisoner ration. The amelioration ordered by Lieutenant Colonel Mühlenfels after Trotha's departure shows that not all officers regarded death as an acceptable result, but the minimal changes equally show how reluctant officers were to break with the whole system and introduce new principles of rationing.

In short, general European military culture can account for some of the horrendous conditions in the SWA internment camps, but German policy must be held responsible

---

(over 116,000). Spies's figures make a death rate of 24%. The figure of 160,000 internees, which seems high (Smuts estimated a total Boer population of 200,000, of whom 87,000 fought in the war), would give 17%: Andrzej J. Kaminski, *Konzenstrationslager 1896 bis Heute* (Munich, 1990), 35. Smuts: Spies, "Women and War," 170; number of Boer fighters: Thomas Pakenham, *The Boer War* (London, 1979), 572.

112. Peter Warwick, "Black People and the War," in *The South African War*, 204.

113. The military erected an internment camp for surrendering women and children in East Africa in September 1905, near Kibata. Gov. Götzen claimed that this camp made it easier to provide the inmates with food. I have discovered no further information on the camp. Götzen, *Deutsch-Ostafrika*, 133; Nigmann, *Geschichte der Kaiserlichen Schutztruppe*, 98; Seeberg, *Maji-Maji-Krieg*, 83; Büttner and Loth, *Philosophie*, 282.

114. Furthermore, the meager meat ration was supposed to consist of "fresh meat or inferior but still edible meat, ham, or sausage conserves." The rice was also to be second, not first, class. Stellvertr. Kommando, 5 Apr. 1906, Windhuk, BA-Berlin, R 151 F/D.IV.L.3., vol. 2, p. 149.

115. The original ration was set on 2 Sept. 1905 through regulation IVa 8821. In Jan. 1906, to combat scurvy, Lt. Col. Mühlenfels ordered substituting legumes for rice if possible and adding fruit jam, conserved fruit, or chocolate. But these were sharply limited to 30 grams per day and cancelled if provisioning for German troops was not "completely secured." Mühlenfels to governor, Nr. IVa 17486, 24 Jan. 1906, Windhuk, BA-Berlin, R 151 F/D.IV.L.3., vol. 1, p. 189. Mühlenfels's order to permit sick prisoners to have corned beef or boiled beef was silently dropped and the original language of "inferior but still edible" meat conserves reinstituted in Apr. 1906: Stellvertr. Kommando, 5 Apr. 1905, Windhuk, ibid., vol. 2, p. 149.

Table 1. Rations for One Adult per Day

Food Item	Germany — German 1870 Official	Germany — Feld-Ord 1900 Official	Britain, S. Africa — 1901 Official	Britain, S. Africa — 1901 Actual Avg.	Britain, S. Africa — 1901 Ladies' Recomm.	Germany, SWA — 1904–7 Official Whites	Germany, SWA — 1904–7 Official Blacks	Germany, SWA — 1904–7 Actual Field	Germany, SWA — 1905 Official POWs	Germany, SWA — Jan. 1906 Official POWs
Meat	500 g.[a]	375 g.	224 g.	224 g.	320 g.	428 g.	266 g.	287 g.	43 g.	43g.
Rice or	—	125 g.	—	—	—	33 g.	333 g.	22 f.	400 g.	400 g.
Potatoes or	—	1500 g.	—	—	—	400 g.	—	268 g.	—	—
Flour or	—	250 g.	—	—	—	80 g.	533 g	54 g.	—	—
Meal	—	—	336 g.	224 g.	448 g.	—	.	—	—	—
Bread	750 g.	750 g.	—	—	—	—	—	—	—	—
Vegetables	—	150 g.	—	—	224 g.	64 g.	—	44 g.	—	20 g.
Sugar	—	17 g.	56 g.	56 g.	56 g.	80 g.	50 g.	53 g.	40 g.	40 g.
Fat	250 g.	—	—	—	—	80 g.	50 g.	53 g.	30 g.	50 g.
Fruit jam or	—	—	—	—	—	46 g.	—	31 g.	—	30 g.[b]
Lime juice	—	—	—	—	limes	—	—	—	—	—
Milk[c]	—	—	1/12 tin	1/12 tin	1/7 tin	—	—	—	—	—
Salt	—	25 g.	28 g.	28 g.	28 g.	26 g.	30 g.	17 g.	30 g.	30 g.
Coffee	30 g.	25 g.	28 g.	28 g.	28 g.	31 g.	40 g.	21 g.	30 g.	30 g.

Sources: Meurer, *Die Haager Friedenskonferenz*, 2:273 (German 1870 Official); *Felddienst-Ordnung*(1900), 126–7 (Feld-Ord 1900 Official); Spies, *Methods of Barbarism?* 357n210, 186 (South Africa 1901 Official; South Africa Actual Average); *Report on the Concentration Camps*, 2, 23 (South Africa 1901, Ladies' Recommendations); *Ergebnis der Arbeiten*, Anlage 8, pp. 121–22, BA-MA Freiburg, RW 51, vol. 19 (SWA 1904–7 Official Whites; SWA 1904–7 Official Blacks); ibid., p. 69 (SWA 1904–7 Actual Field); Stellvertr. Kommando, 5 April 1906, Windhuk, BA-Berlin, R 151 F/D.IV.L.3, vol. 2, p. 149, and Mühlenfels to Governor, Nr. IVa 17486, 24 January 1906, Windhuk, ibid., D.IV.L.3, vol. 1, p. 189 (SWA 1905 Official POWs; SWA Jan. 1906 Official POWs).
[a]28 g. = 1 oz. [b]Ill prisoners only [c]Children only

for the rest. As we have seen, this policy developed out of a number of premises that in all 155
probability were never explicitly examined, and certainly never examined together. The
ration system for troops assumed that even allied African soldiers ought to receive less
food than white troops, reflecting the basic assumptions that white superiority must be
reflected in better treatment and that blacks required less food to survive than did whites.
Rations for prisoners were then depressed even further by two additional principles: that
prisoners must never be treated better than one's own (in this case, African) troops,[116] and
that rebels deserved punishment. Withholding food, or sharply reducing its variety, were
classic methods (and signs) of punishment in Germany, widely used in prisons and even
in families. The military's punitive role applied these usages to warfare. Starvation was the
logical extreme of punishment by hunger. Most higher officers and civilian administrators, when their attention could be momentarily redirected from what they regarded as
more important matters than prisoners' conditions, rejected starvation as official policy.
But they did not reject the minipolicies and working assumptions that produced this end
effect. And some few accepted explicitly the logic of the ration system, of punishment, and
of racially inspired indifference, and were led to the position pithily expressed by Deputy
Governor Tecklenburg when he learned that the Witbooi prisoners were dying in great
numbers in Togo: "[Their] rapid mortality is not considered surprising here; it must be
seen as a retaliation for the uprising."[117]

The greatest mortality in numbers occurred not in SWA but in German East Africa. It
was the result of a type of total war Europeans regarded as peculiarly colonial: the destruction of all dwellings, food stores, domestic animals, and planted fields. *Kriegsbrauch*
(the semi-official manual of war conduct) specifically permitted such a war only against
"wild people and barbarians"; the British expert on "small wars" thought these tactics
"unfortunate," but sometimes necessary.[118] A "hunger war" of this type appears to have
been conducted by Germans for the first time in East Africa in 1897 against holdouts in the
Wahehe rebellion.[119] The Maji-Maji rebels used this tactic themselves, and it was obviously widely enough appreciated that just two weeks into the German response, detachment leader Lieutenant Paasche already regarded it as the key to stopping the uprising.[120]
As the rebels abandoned large-scale attacks for guerrilla warfare, unit commanders immediately adopted the tactic. As Lieutenant von der Marwitz reported on 23 September
1905, "The systematic search of the bush is time-consuming, but next to the destruction of

116. Germany, General Staff, *Kriegsbrauch*, 15; Lueder, "Landkriegsrecht," 435; Meurer, *Die Haager Friedenskonferenz*, 122.

117. Tecklenburg to Col. Dept., Nr. 65, tel., 4 July 1905, Windhuk, BA-Berlin, R 1001, Nr. 2090, p. 22. Tecklenburg's view was not held by everyone: one Col. Dept. official underlined the word "retaliation" and put a
question mark in the margin.

118. Germany, General Staff, *Kriegsbrauch*, 53; Charles Callwell, *Small Wars*, 3rd ed. (London, 1976 [orig.
1906]), 41; the *Felddienst-Ordnung* (1900), 136, placed destruction of food stores solely in the hands of higher
commanders.

119. "Even the last adherents will leave [the Wahehe dynast], when the new manner of conducting the war,
which consists only in the systematically repeated destruction of planted fields, works in the long run." Gov.
Liebert to Col. Dept., Nr. 1005, 15 Oct. 1897, Dar es Salaam, BA-Berlin, R 1001, Nr. 6467, p. 383.

120. Paasche notes, sent to Cdr. Back on 19 Aug. 1905, Mohorro, MA-Freiburg, RM 121 I, Nr. 448,
pp. 25–26.

156 food supplies, it is the only way to become master of the fanatical rebels."[121] Thereafter, total war against dwellings, fields, and food stores became the norm.[122] Only several months later, however, after the uprising had been broken in a number of districts, was this tactic recognized as the normal method of warfare and elevated to the level of operation. The "military-political report" (7 December 1905) of the commander of the naval forces in East Africa described the new operative task in the relieved districts as "forcing the rebels to a lasting capitulation through permanent harassment, destruction of their villages (which they rebuild again and again), and removal of livestock and food stores."[123] By the summer of 1906 there were only a few isolated regions where the revolt still smoldered, but German units, seeking a kind of total victory, pursued every single remaining leader until the last was killed in 1908.[124]

As in SWA, so in East Africa a tactic came to determine operations. Unlike in SWA, however, the result of this tactic, mass death, never became proclaimed as policy. The policy remained "lasting capitulation," a total solution of a different sort. It consisted in the elimination of all leaders, which in practice meant the destruction of the indigenous political infrastructure of the rebellious areas.[125] It meant also the ritual humiliation of the population, which was thus made to demonstrate its subservience to the German government.[126] And it meant the transformation of the population from traditional pastoralists into an available wage-labor workforce.

Where "lasting capitulation" occurred, military units and local civilian administrators distributed grain and encouraged rebuilding.[127] Governor Götzen's successor, Baron Albrecht von Rechenberg, was probably not assiduous enough in doing so, and some local military leaders and administrators were more worried about food production for themselves than for the local population.[128] Nevertheless, partly because East Africa was not a settler colony, and thus had no cause to flirt with visions of a colonial tabula rasa,

121. Cited in war diary of detachment leader Jastrzembski, 23 Sept. 1905, Kilwa, ibid., Nr. 441, Doc. 56.

122. War diary of Paasche, 30 Sept. 1905, Mtanza, ibid., Nr. 452, p. 22; war diary of Jastrzembski, 30 Sept. 1905, Kilwa, ibid., Nr. 448; Report of Lt. Baron v. Stengel, 5 Oct. 1905, Kilwa, ibid., Nr. 450, pp. 14–15; Götzen, *Deutsch-Ostafrika*, 132, 139–40, 135; Bald, "Afrikanischer Kampf," 40.

123. Military-political report on the activity of the cruisers and marines stationed in East Africa (20 Oct. to 30 Nov. 1905), signed Glatzel, cdr. of the *Thetis*, sent to Kaiser Wilhelm II, 7 Dec. 1905, Dar es Salaam, MA-Freiburg, RM 121 I, RM 5, Nr. 6036, pp. 20–36, here 20–21; also cited in Bald, "Afrikanischer Kampf," 40.

124. Bald, "Afrikanischer Kampf," 36–37.

125. Seeberg, *Der Maji-Maji-Krieg*, 89–90.

126. Kommando der Schutztruppe, "Order to the troop leaders in the rebellious areas," 11 Nov. 1905, Dar es Salaam, which gives the conditions for capitulation and the demand for penal labor, in BA-Berlin, R 1001, Nr. 724, p. 119; Götzen to Col. Dept., 7 Dec. 1905, Dar es Salaam, where he refers to fines as "signs of capitulation": ibid., Nr. 723, p. 188; Dep. Gov. Haber to Col. Dept., Nr. 860, Dar es Salaam, ibid., Nr. 724, pp. 115–17, where he insists on methods "to keep their capitulation permanently awake in the minds of the natives."

127. Military-political report Nr. 4 (1 Jan. to 6 Feb. 1906), 6 Feb. 1906, MA-Freiburg, RM 121 I, Nr. 438, p. 112; Gov. Rechenberg to Col. Office, Nr. 606, 24 May 1907, Dar es Salaam, BA-Berlin, R 1001, Nr. 725, pp. 176–77. Götzen was interested in economic recovery from the beginning: Götzen to Foreign Office, Nr. 120, Dar es Salaam, 16 Nov. 1905, MA-Freiburg, RM 121 I, Nr. 438, Bl. 33.

128. Rechenberg to Col. Office, Nr. 382, 25 Mar. 1907, Dar es Salaam, BA-Berlin, R 1001, Nr. 771, p. 166; idem, Nr. 606, 24 May 1907, Dar es Salaam, ibid., pp. 176–77; Nuhn, *Flammen über Deutschost*, 157.

and partly because Governor Götzen had learned from the SWA debacle, mass death never became the intentional goal of warfare.

But mass death is what the hunger tactic achieved. A German trader described the catastrophe in a letter from March 1907:

> People are dying like flies in the area around Ssongea; in Ssongea itself dead bodies are often discovered in the deserted, collapsing structures only because of the pestilential odor. . . . The population has gone down from probably 30,000 . . . to 3,000, which proves that Ssongea exists in name only—and it was such a rich district![129]

The government at first estimated the African dead at seventy-five thousand, but the last governor of the colony, Heinrich Schnee, later believed "it seems more accurate to assume much higher estimates of the victims of the Maji-Maji uprising and to compare it in cause and effect with the Hottentot and Herero uprising in SWA."[130] One contemporary scholar estimated a death toll of one hundred and fifty thousand; a modern estimate is two hundred and fifty to three hundred thousand, or one-third of the population of the rebellious areas.[131] Whole districts were so thoroughly depopulated and the human ecology so transformed that they were later turned into reserves for big game.[132]

Given the extensive human devastation, it is perhaps surprising that East Africa never became a cause célèbre like SWA. In fact, East Africa barely made it into the headlines. Here Governor Götzen's strategy of circumventing Reichstag appropriations paid off; without Reichstag scrutiny, the military was much freer to pursue its tactics to the bitter end. Götzen and the Colonial Department also became clever manipulators of the news, and that, too, had a soporific effect.[133] But the main factor was probably that the public focused on a different death statistic: during the entire revolt, rebels killed just fifteen Europeans, only five of whom were soldiers.[134]

Standard Practices and Going to Extremes

We have been examining operations in the three wars Germany fought between its establishment and the outbreak of World War I. All of these took place in colonies, and only

---

129. Richard Peter to retired Bezirksamtmann Richter, 5 Mar. 1907, BA-Berlin, R 1001, Nr. 771, pp. 169–70.

130. *Sten. Ber.*, 1907–9 session, vol. 239, Anlage Nr. 622, p. 3693; Schnee cited in Bald, "Afrikanischer Kampf," 45.

131. Noske, *Kolonialpolitik*, 123; Iliffe, *Modern History of Tanganyika*, 200.

132. Iliffe, *Modern History of Tanganyika*, 199–202.

133. Götzen to Col. Dept., Nr. 173, "secret," 26 Aug. 1905, Dar es Salaam, BA-Berlin, R 1001, Nr. 722, pp. 109–10: this early news summary was carefully edited for public reaction by a colonial official. Other examples of controlling the news: Stübel to Götzen, tel. Nr. 84, Berlin, 12 Oct. 1905, ibid., Nr. 723, p. 24; Col. Dept. to Götzen, tel., 17 May 1906, ibid., Nr. 724, p. 77.

134. Iliffe, *Modern History of Tanganyika*, 200; Nigmann, *Geschichte der Kaiserlichen Schutztruppe*, 136. Seventy-three black soldiers fighting for the Germans died, and seventy more were missing (Nigmann, p. 144).

158 one, in SWA, permitted a large, European-style battle. The rest of the operations in SWA, and those in China and German East Africa, were all disjointed pursuits. Their course was strongly influenced by unexamined basic assumptions that were a mixture of the typically European and the specifically German. These assumptions concerned expectations (of easy, unequivocal victory and of perfect postvictory order and docility), wishful thinking (which ignored the systematic shortfalls in planning and provisioning), and characterological expedients (the virtues of extreme self-sacrifice to overcome all real obstacles). The course of the pursuits was also determined by tactics: widespread shooting of males and extensive instrumentalization and punishment of civilians. To those tactics of European origin were added hunger war and internment, which until 1914 were confined to the colonies.

Both the SWA and East African cases make clear that standard practices can have devastating consequences that de facto amount to extinguishing human life in entire areas. In neither case, however, was the original military intention to destroy the entire rebel population but, instead, to end the uprisings. The "finality" of the solution developed from the smaller logics of the organizational apparatus, its tactics, and its (hidden) basic assumptions. Once mass death had occurred, however, the perpetrators faced a choice: they could reject these consequences and change the habits of organization and mind that had created them; they could accept the consequences tacitly, while publicly regretting them (as in East Africa); or they could accept the consequences openly, as the logical result of priorities and techniques so important that they should remain above criticism, and make annihilation the stated goal of policy (as Trotha did in SWA, using the ideological template of "race war").

Berlin ultimately rejected Trotha's path. But, as operations in World War I made clear, no basic organizational rethinking occurred. That omission raises the question of doctrine and its relation to the unthinking scripts, tactics, and automatisms of practice. For standard practices to tend toward extremes of destruction and mass death, and in one case to reach acknowledged extermination, they must have found support on the level of military doctrine. Otherwise, their deadly development would have been cut short from above, from inside the military itself. We therefore must now turn to doctrine, where we might expect some of the basic assumptions of military culture to be made explicit and thus the objects of reflection.

7

Doctrines of Fear and Force

Doctrines and Military Culture

With doctrine, we move from operations and tactics to the level of strategy. Wilhelminian Germany's strategic military doctrine is most clearly visible in the Schlieffen Plan. It is tempting to suppose that standard practices, as technical-administrative means to an end, would result from doctrine, but in Imperial Germany, the reverse seems truer. At least, military doctrine after 1890 was both astonishingly technical and formally remarkably similar to the principles behind standard practices at the tactical and operational levels.[1] Explicit doctrine, on the one hand, and the (often unconscious) basic assumptions of military culture and unexamined standard practices, on the other, seem to have been in a dialectical relation. They affected and changed each other constantly, but unevenly, over time.

Against this messier view is one that might be termed "doctrinalism," which sees doctrine as the prime mover of militaries and understands it as a more or less rational product of the real situation of the military ("realism"), its function ("functionalism"), or its

---

1. Distinguishing the tactical, operational, and strategic levels of military planning and action is difficult. Barry Posen defines tactics as "the study of how fights are fought," operations as how battles are conducted and coordinated, and strategy as the overarching political-military security goal that a war or subsequent peace is supposed to ensure. He vacillates as to whether military doctrine belongs to operations or strategy. Posen, *Sources of Military Doctrine*, 13–14, 245n3. Clausewitz defined tactics as "the theory of the use of military forces in combat. Strategy is the theory of the use of combats for the object of the war." Carl von Clausewitz, *On War*, ed. Anatol Rapaport (London, 1982), bk. 1, p. 173, cited and discussed in Wallach, *Vernichtungsschlacht*, 15. Wilhelm Deist uses Andreas Hillgruber's sensible definition of strategy as "the integration of domestic and foreign policy, of military and psychological planning, and the administration of the economy and armaments by the top-level leadership of a state, in order to carry out a comprehensive ideological and political design." Deist, "Strategy and Unlimited Warfare in Germany," in *Great War, Total War*, ed. Roger Chickering and Stig Förster (Cambridge, 2000), 265–79, here 266. From my perspective, doctrine is codified organizational knowledge that might apply to any level of functioning.

160 organizational structure ("structuralism").[2] Following this logic, Barry Posen has adduced excellent bureaucratic reasons why militaries might favor offensive doctrines such as the Schlieffen Plan. Because the aggressor initiates action to which the opponent must respond, the offensive is easier to plan; because it is expensive, the offensive permits one to claim more resources; and because it is difficult to execute, it enhances the status of the military's expertise.[3] Jack Snyder, writing more historically, examined the different security reasons impelling Germany, France, and Russia to adopt the offensive before 1914.[4] But as Elizabeth Kier has pointed out, all the advantages the offensive offers can also accrue to the defensive, and in fact, militaries do not always choose the offensive. She advocates a more organizational-cultural perspective, because it is freer to account for diversity among militaries, multiple determinants of policy, and policy irrationality.[5] The cultural perspective is especially useful because it raises questions about doctrine; that is exactly what Imperial Germany's offensive doctrine, the Schlieffen Plan, requires, for it poses enormous problems of interpretation. It was grander, riskier, more extreme, and above all more unrealistic than anything comparable in Europe at the time. It had a long history of development, which reveals it to have been a codification and intensification of Germany's military culture, not a cause of it, and certainly not a "rational" policy decision.

The Schlieffen Plan

Prussia had a long history of favoring the offensive or, in Dennis Showalter's phrase, "total force applied in limited wars for limited objectives." Concentrating the entire military potential aggressively at a single point for a brief time was the policy most suited to a middle-sized power with limited means.[6] Chief of the General Staff Helmuth v. Moltke built on this tradition, but transformed it. The modern history of Prusso-Germany's military doctrine began with him and the wars of unification. Moltke, like his predecessors, sought a solution to Prussia's limited financial and manpower resources; he, too, found it in the offensive. But Moltke's solution became with time a prescriptive template. It contained virtually all of the particular characteristics that later defined Schlieffen's plan, and that the reader has already seen at Waterberg, a kind of sedentary version of Moltke's conception.

Moltke began from the premise that the goal of battle was the annihilation of the enemy's military forces, that is, a complete, purely military victory. This conception was

---

2. Kier, *Imagining War*, 10.

3. Posen, *Sources*, 46–50.

4. Jack Snyder, "Civil-Military Relations and the Cult of the Offensive, 1914 and 1984," *International Security* 9:1 (summer 1984): 108–46. See also Stephen van Evera, "The Cult of the Offensive and the Origins of the First World War," *International Security* 9:1 (summer 1984), 58–107; and Herrmann, *Arming of Europe*.

5. Kier, *Imagining War*, chs. 1 and 2.

6. Showalter, "German Grand Strategy," 66, 68–69. Showalter may exaggerate offensive tendencies before 1870; see, for example, a typical handbook from 1840 that only slightly prefers the offensive: Ferdinand von Bentheim, *Leitfaden zum Unterricht in den Kriegswissenschaften: Für Lehrer und zum Selbstunterricht* (Berlin, 1840), 143–44.

originally Clausewitz's, but Moltke revived it and then seemed to demonstrate its validity at Königgrätz (1866) and Sedan (1870). He counterbalanced Prussia's resource deficiencies by meticulous, detailed prewar planning relying on Prussia's technical advantages (the railroads and superior infantry firepower). He foresaw a single battle of annihilation in which the enemy was enveloped and attacked at its flanks "in one continuous strategic-operational sequence combining mobilization, concentration, movement, and fighting."[7] Such a battle risked everything in a single event. It blurred the distinction between strategy and operations; in fact, it cultivated operations in a kind of flight from strategy.[8] In 1866 Moltke ignored logistics. He learned from his mistake, however, and prepared for the war against France in 1870; but as that war lengthened, he reverted again to living off the enemy's land. Finally, Moltke's way of war depended for success on aggressive, independent commanders (the beginning of mission tactics). In the unexpectedly longer war of 1870–71 two further characteristics developed. One was Moltke's insistence that in wartime the military should have sole power to conduct the war, which he conceived of in a purely military way.[9] The other was the chief of staff's (reluctant) conclusion that republican France must be defeated totally. That is, in extreme circumstances, where annihilation of the army had not defeated the state, society became a legitimate target for terror in pursuit of unconditional and permanent defeat of the enemy.[10] It is these last tendencies that moved one military historian to conclude that "a Moltke without a Bismarck would very possibly have been a prototype Ludendorff."[11]

After the war was safely won, Moltke stayed on as chief of staff until 1890. Several times between 1871 and 1890 Moltke yielded to the military logic of extremes. He twice advocated preventive war to offset Germany's numerical weakness against its potential foes. And he continued to distrust political solutions to security problems, for example, by not letting Germany's alliance with Russia deter him from imagining, and even proposing, a preventive war against it.[12] In 1879 Moltke even planned for a war against Germany's firm ally, Austria![13]

In the last two years of his tenure, however, Moltke abandoned the purely military-aggressive way of thinking. His basic realism caused him to conclude that Germany's manpower and resource limits, plus its position in central Europe potentially facing a two-front war, made it impossible for Germany to win such a war against France and Russia,

---

7. Rothenberg, "Moltke," 296; Stig Förster, "The Prussian Triangle of Leadership in the Face of the People's War," in *On the Road,* 115–40, here 124.

8. Förster, "Prussian Triangle," 127; Hugo Frhr. von Freytag-Loringhoven, *Heerführung im Weltkriege* (Berlin, 1920), 45–46.

9. Deist, "Remarks," 325; Stadelmann, *Moltke,* 208, 392.

10. Stadelmann, *Moltke,* 238–60. Moltke was not as bloodthirsty as Bismarck, however (260–61). See also Stig Förster, "Optionen der Kriegführung im Zeitalter des 'Volkskrieges,'" in *Militärische Verantwortung in Staat und Gesellschaft,* ed. Detlev Bald (Koblenz, 1986), 83–108, here 92–94, and Förster, "Prussian Triangle," 137–38.

11. Dupuy, *Genius,* 109.

12. Förster, "Optionen der Kriegführung," 96; Michael Schmid, *Der "Eiserne Kanzler" und die Generäle* (Paderborn, 2003), 371–78, 403–18.

13. Rothenberg, "Moltke," 306.

162   no matter how audacious, well-planned, or well-executed an offensive it tried. The best he foresaw was a stalemate in which a defensive Germany protected its territory while ending the war diplomatically.

Why did Moltke's realistic insight not become doctrine? After all, Moltke was by far the most prestigious figure in modern German military history. Stig Förster points out that Moltke did little to secure his viewpoint by, for example, lobbying for a successor who agreed with him.[14] But Moltke would have had trouble finding one. Even sober-sided senior officers, like Wilhelm von Blume, Prince Kraft zu Hohenlohe-Ingelfingen, or Colmar von der Goltz believed that an initially successful defense needed to shift to the offensive, because only that promised a true victory.[15] Moltke's successor, his longtime assistant Alfred v. Waldersee, was an energetic proponent of offensive preventive war. Younger officers were even less ready to embrace dour military self-abnegation; instead, they considered the existential situation of 1870–71 to be rule setting and, therefore, the norm; the solutions Moltke had earlier discovered then remained valid for them.[16] Moltke was, therefore, practically alone, because his late views ran counter to twenty years of institutionalized military culture that he had helped to create. Indeed, the very lateness of Moltke's realization, his vacillation in expressing it, and his continued underestimation of diplomacy (in the form of alliances) as against military solutions to security issues—all show how much he was still in the grip of Germany's military culture, even at the end of his career.

Waldersee's adventurism cut short his tenure as chief of the General Staff in 1891. Nonetheless, his response to growing French and Russian military strength anticipated the drift of German strategic thinking under his successors Alfred von Schlieffen and Moltke's nephew Helmuth von Moltke the younger, chief of staff from 1906 to 1914. Expanding on the elder Moltke's model, Waldersee emphasized greater concentration of forces, more detailed premobilization planning, and heavier emphasis on operations. But Waldersee also moved down the road of wishful thinking. His reckoning on quick, seriatim defeats of France and Russia relied on two assumptions: German technical superiority and strategic errors by his opponents (namely, that they too would abandon the stronger defensive for the riskier offensive).[17]

Schlieffen followed Waldersee as chief of staff and remained in that office through 1905, time enough to train an entire generation of officers. Schlieffen himself had been carefully prepared by both Moltke and Waldersee for the post,[18] so Schlieffen, too, was a refined product of post-1870 German military culture as interpreted by the General Staff.

Recent scholarship has revised our view of Schlieffen, emphasizing his flexibility and raising questions about the relation of his plan to Germany's war plan of 1914.[19] Schlieffen

---

14. Förster, "Optionen," 103.

15. Rothenberg, "Moltke," 310.

16. Stadelmann, *Moltke*, 238–39.

17. Bucholz, *Moltke, Schlieffen*, 102–3, 124; Schmid, *Der "Eiserne Kanzler,"* 704, 716.

18. Dupuy, *Genius*, 129.

19. Terence Zuber, "The Schlieffen Plan Reconsidered," *War in History* 6:3 (1999), 262–305; idem, "Terence Holmes Reinvents the Schlieffen Plan," ibid. 8:4 (2001), 468–76; idem, "Terence Holmes Reinvents the Schlieffen

(like all the chiefs of staff) revised Germany's war plans yearly in response to the changing military situation, and he routinely honed two alternatives, an eastern and a western offensive, to suit different political circumstances.[20] Like all chiefs of staff, he tested the plans in war games and staff rides. Schlieffen's rigidity thus lay not in cleaving to a single, fixed blueprint but rather in how he defined and went about "solving" Germany's strategic dilemma.

What has gone down in history as the Schlieffen Plan is more accurately a memorandum probably written in 1906 at the very beginning of Schlieffen's retirement. This memorandum proposed to defeat France and then Russia, beginning with a single, swift encircling movement involving almost all of Germany's troops, which were to sweep through neutral Belgium, go around Paris, and defeat the entire French army in six weeks, before turning against the slower-moving Russian armies in the east.[21] Moltke the younger's subsequent plans naturally took account of growing French and Russian strength, just as did Schlieffen's later revisions written up until his death in 1912.[22] Schlieffen's 1906 memorandum was, therefore, not identical with the plans with which Germany entered the war in 1914.

Much of the disagreement, both in the latest and in earlier scholarship, revolves around how to define the essence of the Schlieffen Plan. There are two narrow constructions: one that defines it as the sweep around Paris and another that understands it as grand encirclement.[23] In my view both are too narrow to apprehend the enormous continuities stretching from Moltke the elder through Waldersee, Schlieffen, and even Moltke the younger. Except for Moltke the elder's brief apostasy in 1888 (when he embraced the strategic defensive), all planners attempted to solve Germany's strategic problems in the same way: they advocated an offensive (to occur on one front, be it east or west) that demanded concentration of force flanking around fortified or strong fronts—an offensive that aimed for a decisive battle of annihilation requiring speed, risk, and minute prewar planning and that focused on operations rather than actual strategy. This is the sense in which the following analysis understands Schlieffen's thinking, but it is equally true of both Moltkes and of Waldersee. "Schlieffen" is therefore shorthand for a remarkably consistent institutional view of how to wage war.

Schlieffen elaborated on and developed the principles that Moltke the elder had worked out, going farther in the same direction, as Waldersee had done. Schlieffen gradu-

---

Plan—again," ibid. 10:1 (2003), 92–101; Terence M. Holmes, "The Reluctant March on Paris," ibid. 8:2 (2001), 208–32; idem, "The Real Thing," ibid. 9:1 (2002), 111–20; Robert T. Foley, "The Origins of the Schlieffen Plan," ibid. 10:2 (2003), 222–32. Zuber's argument has now appeared in book form, which I have not seen: *Inventing the Schlieffen Plan: German War Planning, 1871–1914* (Oxford, 2002).

20. Zuber, "Schlieffen Plan Reconsidered," 284–85.

21. Gerhard Ritter, *Der Schlieffenplan* (Munich, 1956); Ritter, *Sword and Scepter*, 2:193–206; Wallach, *Dogma*; Rothenberg, "Moltke"; Martin Kutz, "Schlieffen contra Clausewitz," in Kutz, *Realitätsflucht und Aggression im deutschen Militär* (Baden-Baden, 1990), 12–48; Förster, "Optionen"; Förster, "Dreams and Nightmares," 343–76.

22. On Moltke's tactical/technical changes: Storz, *Kriegsbild*, 167–206; Mombauer, *Moltke*, 94–100.

23. Paris: Zuber, "Schlieffen Plan Reconsidered," 299; encirclement: Otto, *Schlieffen*, 120. On Zuber's narrowness: Holmes, "Reluctant March"; Strachan, *First World War*, 170.

164 ally shifted the first offensive from east to west (Russia to France) in response to the development of Russian railroads; in order to avoid French fortifications, he grasped at an ever larger envelopment to the north, which brought him eventually to advocate violating Belgian (and even Dutch) neutrality.[24] The flanking maneuver developed as an idea inside the General Staff and was honed and strengthened in response to war games and staff rides.[25] All of these modifications were technical responses to what planners perceived as changing technical situations. They did not engage in fundamental rethinking. Schlieffen's memorandum of 1906, despite its audacity in concentrating 87 percent of Germany's forces in the west, "was merely the logical continuation of a plan of operation that had been in effect since 1899," as one historian remarks.[26] Chief of Staff Moltke studied Schlieffen's memorandum closely in 1911.[27] After the Marne debacle in September 1914, disappointed generals pilloried Moltke for his famous emendations to the basic plan (strengthening the center and thus diminishing the ratio of troops engaged in the encirclement)—changes that were the result of usual staff work and of which Quartermaster General Erich Ludendorff approved.[28] From the historian's perspective, the continuities in strategic thinking are overwhelming; both Schlieffen's plan and Moltke's were modifications of the same basic strategic thought. Furthermore, even with Moltke's changes, the Schlieffen Plan remained the conceptual war plan on which Germany gambled in 1914.[29]

Schlieffen's plan was so audacious that one is tempted to think it the product of hubris or expansionism.[30] But it was the reverse. For, despite all the differences in Germany's actual political and strategic situation between the 1870s and 1914, the General Staff built its plans to overcome the same dilemma, namely, the German military's numerical weakness vis-à-vis France plus Russia and its inability to sustain a war of attrition.[31] Much of this dilemma was self-made. The army's internal task to defend the monarchy against revolution, plus the desire not to plead for more money from the democratically elected Reichstag, caused the Prussian War Ministry to oppose army expansion, lest unreliable socialists flood the ranks and undesirable bourgeois, the officer corps. The same sort of thinking shied away from long wars that, in the absence of popular legit-

24. Railroads: Schmid, "*Eiserne Kanzler*," 660–61; fortifications: ibid., 666, and Foley, "Origins," 223.

25. Zuber, "Schlieffen Plan Reconsidered," 280; Holmes, "Reluctant March," 217–20.

26. Foley, "Origins," 223. Zuber disagrees ("Schlieffen Plan Reconsidered"), but the only researcher (Dieckmann) who saw the original documents before their destruction in 1945 also concluded that the memorandum ran seamlessly from previous planning (Zuber, "Schlieffen Plan Reconsidered," 271). Strachan also rejects Zuber's view; *First World War*, 167.

27. Zuber, "Schlieffen Plan Reconsidered," 298–99.

28. On Moltke's decisions regarding Paris, see Holmes, "Reluctant March," 222–24. On Moltke as an outsider, who never grasped Schlieffen's ideas: Bucholz, *Moltke, Schlieffen*, 223, 242–43; Strachan, *First World War*, 176–78.

29. Hence the frequent criticism among officers of Moltke and his staff after the Marne, that they "were only capable of reeling off the 'Schlieffen film,' and were perplexed and distraught when the roll got hung up." Diary entry of Lt. Gen. Karl Ritter von Wenninger, 6 Sept. 1914, cited in Holger Afflerbach, *Falkenhayn* (Munich, 1984), 185n178.

30. Ritter, *Sword and Scepter*, 2:199; Kutz, "Schlieffen," 30; Holger Herwig, *The First World War* (London, 1997), 47.

31. Wallach, *Dogma*, 59; Förster, *Doppelte Militarismus*, 158–65.

imation, would encourage civil unrest or even revolution. Finally, the General Staff regarded alliances as being of negligible strategic help; it reckoned danger by adding up the troop strengths of its neighbors, regardless of whether they were allied or not (after 1894, of course, the Russo-French alliance confirmed this bleak view).[32] In short, the "weakness" that promoted aggressive planning, and that seemed to the General Staff to be a natural given, was in fact both political and self-generated.

Fear of weakness (a trope we shall consider shortly) was thus a powerful source of Germany's obsession with the offensive. As Gen. Friedrich von Bernhardi explained in 1911, "The offensive offers greater chances for success, especially for the weaker [power]." This is why "only the offense [was] suitable to a state like Germany, which is ringed with enemies and which must perish [*zugrunde gehen*] if it were to regard the defensive as the stronger form of pursuing war."[33] For the same reason, the offensive had to be huge and definitive. In Schlieffen's words, "Complete annihilation [of the enemy's military capacity] is necessary in order to stop once and for all the possibility that the opponent will recover and his allies rush to his aid."[34] The Schlieffen Plan allowed Germany to concentrate its strength against one enemy at a time; the offensive allowed it to determine the timing and place of attack and to offset its deficits by meticulous planning; the single battle of annihilation promised a short war.

There seems little doubt that in the years after 1890 the elder Moltke's knowledge of how to think about problems was lost in the search for what Schlieffen called the "prescription for victory."[35] Moltke's solutions became fixed laws rather than contingent answers. According to Schlieffen, "The basic laws of warfare remain the same."[36] Not all of that hardening occurred under Schlieffen; it was a continuous process to which the younger Moltke also contributed, for example, by stressing the ineluctable timetable and the technical integration of the various parts in war games.[37] Therefore, only part of what the elder Moltke "knew" survived as a permanent part of Germany's military culture.

The Schlieffen Plan as Organizational Knowledge

The Schlieffen Plan, as the retiring chief of staff set it down in 1906, gives us the clearest distillation in a single source of the army's organizational knowledge and thus represents a summary at the doctrinal level of Wilhelminian military culture. It clearly shows how the dynamic toward extremes was (unintentionally) built into the system, and it reflects and accounts for the actual conduct of Germany's wars in the colonies and during

32. Schmid, *"Eiserne Kanzler,"* 371–73.

33. Friedrich von Bernhardi, "Clausewitz über Angriff und Verteidigung," Beiheft of *Militär-Wochenblatt* 12 (1911), 399–412, here 407, 411, 412.

34. Cited in Wallach, *Dogma,* 73, also 89–90.

35. Schlieffen's phrase, cited in Wallach, *Dogma,* 129; see also 69, 73.

36. Cited in Otto, *Schlieffen,* 114.

37. Timetable: Holmes, "Reluctant March," 228n71; timetable and war games: Bucholz, *Moltke, Schlieffen,* 242. On Schlieffen's rigidity: Wallach, *Dogma,* 53, and passim; Otto, *Schlieffen,* 111–37; Strachan, *First World War,* 172.

166 the First World War. Furthermore, it illustrates how explicit doctrine can also be riddled with implicit, but unacknowledged, basic assumptions.

The essence of Schlieffen's plan consisted of these points:

1. The plan was *purely military*. It accepted and built on the constitutional split of civil from military policy. Foreign policy, economics, and domestic politics played no role in it. It would unroll regardless of the cause or goal of the particular war that broke out. So encapsulated was military planning that Chancellor Theobald v. Bethmann Hollweg (who came to office in 1909) first learned of its vague outlines in December 1912. The plan's most famous aspect from the standpoint of diplomacy was its violation of Belgian neutrality, which virtually assured Britain's entry into the war. Both Chancellors Bülow and Bethmann silently accepted this enormous subordination of the political to military convenience. Political considerations, therefore, did not interrupt the self-replicating solipsism of military thinking.

2. *Risk* was the heart of the plan, at once its most astonishing feature and its most consequential. The most daring military plan of its age, the Schlieffen Plan required feats of marching, provisioning, resupply, and coordinated communication that were unparalleled at the time and that the German army was in fact unable to accomplish in 1914. More than this, the plan proposed not merely to defeat the two major powers that surrounded and outnumbered Germany but to defeat one of them in merely six weeks (it had taken the elder Moltke, with numerical superiority, seven months to do so). And it proposed to do so without the necessary material base or logistical planning.[38] Finally, it risked Germany's entire future on the outcome of a single battle. In the words of one scholar, the Schlieffen Plan "made no sense."[39] That is true in the larger sense of strategy and politics. But it made perfect sense in the smaller world of organizational knowledge and practical techniques. The plan was a coherent extension and application on a large scale of what every officer knew to be true at the level of combat. The extreme risk produced the other defining features of the plan, which may be understood as basic assumptions about the nature of warfare and compensatory techniques to overcome (relative) weakness.

3. The plan assumed the elder Moltke's definition of victory: the *complete military annihilation* of the enemy's force. This *Vernichtungsgedanke* (idea of annihilation) had been hegemonic in German military circles since the early 1870s.[40] It was limited to destruction of enemy troops, but as we have seen, when that goal was frustrated, it slipped easily to encompass civilians and society, as in 1870–71 and in 1904–5.[41] Annihilation was victory; everything short of it was unacceptable. That included "ordinary victories," such as even

38. The German army never had the troops necessary to execute the Schlieffen Plan: Förster, "Militär und staatsbürgerliche Partizipation," 62–63, 68; Herwig, *First World War*, 49.

39. Förster, "Dreams and Nightmares," 361. On the impossibility of the plan see Rothenberg, "Moltke," 318–20.

40. Messerschmidt, "Völkerrecht und 'Kriegsnotwendigkeit,'" 196–97; Rothenberg, "Moltke," 296.

41. Otto believes that "criminal acts" were inherent in its very conception of "Blitzkrieg"; *Schlieffen*, 138–41. See also his list of essential features, 113.

Königgrätz (1866), in Schlieffen's view.[42] And it certainly included negotiated settlements, which were tantamount to military failure. The struggle to achieve annihilation tended to lengthen combat, as in SWA, and therefore it perpetuated the cycle of violence.

4. The plan was *purely offensive*. The "cult of the offensive" was a European phenomenon that gripped all the Continental armies before 1914.[43] But it was nowhere more assiduously cultivated or more thoroughly adopted as the single foundation for all military training and planning than in Germany.[44] It was so ubiquitous that writers unabashedly identified it with the very essence of Germandom: "We love the offensive and want to hold tight to it because it has its origin and justification as much in the character of the German people as in purely tactical considerations."[45] Germany consequently spent less on defensive measures (such as fortifications) than any other European major power; knowledge of how to wage defensive war atrophied among officers and in Germany's military handbooks, and troops were not trained in defensive techniques (such as trench building).[46] As we saw, Governor Leutwein in SWA was removed from command for engaging in a strategic retreat; in World War I at least one officer was sacked in 1915 simply for mentioning retreat as a possibility.[47] But the offensive is both riskier and bloodier than the defensive, as Clausewitz had long ago noted. The conviction that the offensive was the only way to fight war, and that mastery of it was Germany's chief military advantage, predisposed officers to choose bloody actionism over other alternatives.

5. The plan was designed to end the war *quickly, at a single blow*, before it developed into a war of attrition that Germany would surely lose (in the sense of being unable to annihilate the enemy). All contemporary European armies indulged in the "short war illusion," which predicted that wartime disruption of sensitive commercial-industrial economies would simply prevent a long war.[48] However, short wars had been the Prusso-

---

42. Hughes, "Schlichting," 271; Rothenberg, "Moltke," 313.

43. Storz, *Kriegsbild*, 143–53, 226–31, 254–57, 371–72, and passim; van Evera, "Cult of the Offensive"; Snyder, *Ideology of the Offensive*; Posen, *Sources of Military Doctrine*, 46–50, 69–71; Herrmann, *Arming of Europe*.

44. Wallach, *Dogma*, 43–44, 85–88; Schulte, *Europäische Krise*, 61–64; Immanuel, "Der offensive Geist in unserer neuen Felddienst-Ordnung," *Militär-Wochenblatt* 93:71 (1908), cols. 1664–67; Friedrich von Bernhardi, *Deutschland und der nächste Krieg* (Stuttgart, 1912).

45. Major v. François, *Lehren aus dem Südafrikanischen Kriege für das Deutsche Heer* (Berlin, 1900), 54, also 57.

46. Hew Strachan, "From Cabinet War to Total War," in *Great War, Total War*, ed. Chickering and Förster, 19–31, here 20; compare sections on attack with those on defense in Prussia, War Ministry, *Exerzir-Reglement*, 2nd ed., 117–23; Groener, *Lebenserinnerungen*, 150; Rupprecht Kronprinz von Bayern, *Mein Kriegstagebuch*, 3 vols., ed. Eugen von Frauenholz (Munich, 1929), diary entry of 10 Dec. 1914, 1:274; Wild, *Briefe*, 23; Burchardt, *Friedenswirtschaft*, 39–41.

47. Karl von Einem, *Ein Armeeführer erlebt den Weltkrieg*, ed. Junius Alter (Leipzig, 1938), 184.

48. Lancelot L. Farrar, *The Short-War Illusion: German Policy, Strategy, and Domestic Affairs, August–December 1914* (Santa Barbara, 1973). Stig Förster points out how many German officers expressed anxiety that the war might not in fact be short, but their fears did not materially change Germany's lack of preparation for a long war. Fear of failure was in any case an ever-present emotion in the officer corps. Förster, "Der deutsche Generalstab und die Illusion des kurzen Krieges, 1871–1914," in *Lange und kurze Wege in den Ersten Weltkrieg*, ed. Johannes Burkhardt et al. (Munich, 1996), 115–58; see also Lancelot L. Farrar, *Arrogance and Anxiety* (Iowa City, 1981).

168   German ideal for decades before the "illusion" became current. In Germany's case, the short war was probably more the result of military wishful thinking than a cause of it. The important aspect is the tight timetable that placed terrific pressure on officers and troops to accomplish unrealistic goals swiftly.[49] Unrealistic expectations of rapid, smooth success replayed the colonial dilemma on the European continent and helped precipitate the massacre of French and Belgian civilians in 1914. When the race ran late and the war lengthened, desperate searches for shortcuts and quick solutions became a hallmark of war conduct and encouraged the use of experimental wonder weapons (such as poison gas or the submarine), whose lethality could not be controlled.

  6. Having eschewed strategic planning, the Schlieffen Plan codified the tendency, already partly visible under the elder Moltke, to *overvalue operations*. It focused organizational strength away from strategy and the level of war, downward to the level of the individual battle, operations, or even tactics.[50] The lack of political-military coordination made this drift likely, but not inevitable. The victories of 1864, 1866, and 1870–71 seemed to confirm the success of narrow operational planning.[51] And, after all, planning was the General Staff's main task, so it is hardly surprising that it imagined it could solve fundamental strategic problems at that level.[52] Framing problems in this way encouraged solutions discovered at the level of practice to rise upward and be applied to larger issues. Practices, standard and newly minted, might then become significant and even policy-setting in the absence of overarching policy or principle. World War I was replete with examples of this process.

  7. The hegemony of the operative encouraged reliance on technique to bridge over deficits of various kinds. So, for example, the Schlieffen Plan codified two of Moltke's *operative maxims*: envelopment with flanking attacks, and ruthless pursuit should that fail. These techniques hardened into unquestioned truths. Even in colonial warfare, where the single concentric battle of annihilation and ruthless pursuit were almost impossible to accomplish, German officers attempted them again and again.[53] Abandoning these methods required detailed justification, not just to military authorities but before the public, too, which shared these expectations of correct military action.[54] World War I saw German of-

49. Even Moltke the younger, who feared war might be long, polished and tightened the timetable to keep it short. Förster, "Dreams and Nightmares," 364–67; on Moltke's other preparations, all of which increased pressure to succeed, see Annika Mombauer, *Helmuth von Moltke and the Origins of the First World War* (Cambridge, 2001), 106–81.

50. Kutz, *Realitätsflucht*, 27–30; Showalter, "From Deterrence to Doomsday Machine," 708; Showalter, "German Grand Strategy," 76–77; Bruno Thoss, "Militärische Entscheidung und politisch-gesellschaftlicher Umbruch," in *Kriegsende 1918*, ed. Jörg Duppler and Gerhard P. Gross (Munich, 1999), 30; Groener, *Lebenserinnerungen*, 173; Rupprecht Kronprinz v. Bayern, *Mein Kriegstagebuch* 2: 58, 270, 372, 429, 436.

51. Dupuy, *Genius*, 110.

52. Michael Geyer, "German Strategy in the Age of Machine Warfare, 1914–1945," in *Makers of Modern Strategy*, ed. Paret, 527–97. Geyer emphasizes the central role in German strategic thought played by the General Staff's desire to retain its position as the sole expert manager of war.

53. In SWA, Trotha never gave up trying. These had been Leutwein's tactics, too: operation order of 11 Mar. 1904, MA-Freiburg, RM 121 I, Nr. 423, p. 41; Bayer, *Mit dem Hauptquartier*, 33. In China: Binder-Krieglstein, *Kämpfe des Deutschen Expeditionskorps*, 231–31. In East Africa, Nigmann, *Kaiserliche Schutztruppe*, 115, 117–18.

54. Amtliche Nachrichten des Gouvernements aus den unruhigen Gebieten vom 11 October 1905, MA-Freiburg, RM 121 I, Nr. 441, Doc. 78; Militärpolitischer Bericht . . . (26 Sept.–20 Oct. 1905), Dar es Salaam, ibid.,

ficers attempt concentric attacks repeatedly, in the west, the east, and the Balkans.[55] The hegemony of the operative meant that repeated failure did not lead to rethinking, which would have required rising to the level of strategy, but to more repetition. Germany's very tactical and operative strengths disinclined the military to question or abandon them.

8. The flight into technique is also visible in the Schlieffen Plan's *detailed planning.* Overcontrol was the pendant to extraordinary risk; control through planning was meant to lessen risk by preempting problems—a method common to organizations.[56] But in the Schlieffen Plan this technique reached astonishing heights.[57] It was clearest in the fantastically detailed railroad planning for mobilization, which inspired such confidence that its chief, Gen. Wilhelm Groener, was "not even particularly excited" when war was declared.[58] And it continued in the timetable for the sweep through Belgium and northern France. But how could one expect to eliminate the accidental, the very "friction" that Clausewitz had identified as one of the defining characteristics of war?[59] Furthermore, on the battlefield the taut central planning necessary to keep to the timetable clashed with the principle of mission tactics. And it ignored the enemy's response, not to mention the long lines and consequent difficult communication that a sweeping battle of movement would surely produce. In short, planning had moved into unrealism while keeping the semblance of rationality. In addition to everything else, the husk of planning without its content promoted self-delusion. Having organizational talent was a national stereotype that Wilhelminians commonly held of themselves, and that also encouraged faith in detailed planning. We shall see that during the world war, as things went wrong, supreme commanders grasped at this straw and lost themselves in minutiae. Planning drifted farther down to the level of mere tactics, which were supposed to function in the place of operations and strategy (as in the German offensives of 1918).

9. Among the detailed plans that were never made were those concerning *logistics and provisioning.* As in 1866 and in the colonial campaigns, these central elements of preparation were left largely to luck.[60] Logistics had frequently been eclipsed by the narrow focus of resources and creative energy on pure combat. The General Staff found it easy to continue this focus because material resources were not in its province but be-

---

Nr. 438, p. 12. Also, Götzen, *Deutsch-Ostafrika,* 75; Leutwein, *Elf Jahre,* 532–37. Public expectations: v. Gädke, "Die militärische Lage in Deutsch-Südwestafrika," *Berliner Zeitung* 63 (4 Feb. 1904), 1. The public was subjected to a flood of publications by military men extolling these methods; e.g., Curt v. François, *Kriegführung in Süd-Afrika* (Berlin, 1900), 44–45; Capt. Frhr. v. Maltzahn, "Der Abschluss des Burenkrieges," *Vierteljahrshefte für Truppenführung und Heereskunde* 6:3 (1909), 435–67; Major General v. François, "Der Herero-Aufstand," *Militärisches Wochenblatt* 89:1 (1904), Heft 33, col. 837, 840; Heft 34, col. 863; Heft 40, col. 987, 989.

55. Max von Gallwitz brings many examples: *Meine Führertätigkeit im Weltkriege 1914–1916,* 266, 377–78, 462–63; see also Rupprecht Kronprinz v. Bayern, *Mein Kriegstagebuch* 1: 208, 236–37.

56. Turner, "Organizational and Interorganizational Development of Disasters," 378; Snook, *Friendly Fire,* 230.

57. Van Crefeld, *Command in War,* 142.

58. Groener, *Lebenserinnerungen,* 143. On the impact of railroads on General Staff functioning: Bucholz, *Moltke, Schlieffen,* 149–50, 173–75, 287–300, 318–20.

59. Clausewitz, *On War,* bk. 1, ch. 7, 164–67.

60. Van Crefeld, *Supplying War,* ch. 4; Burckhardt, *Friedenswirtschaft;* Wallach, *Dogma,* 81, 84, 89; Schulte, *Europäische Krise,* 275.

170   longed to the War Ministry.[61] The Schlieffen Plan, therefore, proposed to live off the occupied territory, leading to extreme exploitation of civilians in the First World War. Lack of genuine preparation is another mark of the wishful thinking that permeated the Schlieffen Plan.

    10. In place of realistic planning the Schlieffen Plan relied not only on clever techniques but on the *qualitative superiority* of the army's officers and men, which it took to be axiomatic.[62] The effectiveness of the German army when compared with other European forces lent substance to this view. But the assumption of superiority was impervious to revision, for example, in colonial warfare, where new arrivals were decidedly not superior to native fighters, or in the world war after November 1914, when the original army had been destroyed, wiping out the training, planning, and preparation advantages that officers always cited. And the assumption of superiority operated the same way that racialism did in the colonies: it built in expectations of easy success, and it encouraged foolhardy underestimation of the enemy. The first set in motion vicious spirals of violence, the second discouraged learning from mistakes.

    11. Finally, the Schlieffen Plan depended for success on specific *moral and emotional qualities* in its officers. It risked so much—the gap between its reach and its grasp was so great—that daring to carry it out required ignoring its huge improbabilities. This was no job for the cautious or contemplative. The plan demanded of its practitioners optimism bordering on the foolhardy, will, daring, and ruthless determination. General Groener, a south German and political moderate, was nonetheless utterly typical in his conclusion, expressed in a letter during World War I, that "one cannot be hard enough in war to be successful. . . . One must always go to the end; one cannot be satisfied with halfway measures: there is no golden mean in war."[63] Crown Prince Rupprecht, Bavarian and a politically astute critic of pure Prussianism, is for that very reason an excellent witness. In August 1914 he opined that "pessimists and excitable people don't belong in the General Staff." After four years of reaping the consequences of military optimism, he recognized his own and his organization's error: "It was a false mental orientation, especially visible in Prussian military circles, that one did not want to hear doubts. Anyone who expressed doubts or an opinion different from what was desirable was all too easily taken to be a pessimist, weakling, or faint-hearted, and if possible was removed."[64] Will, extreme daring (*Kühnheit*), optimistic recklessness, and one-sided actionism were not simply self-selected among officers (who could not serve unless approved by their fellows in the regiment) but were systematically inculcated by Schlieffen into a generation of General Staff officers.[65] At the time of Schlieffen's retirement in 1905, his successor, the younger Moltke,

---

61. Förster, "Dreams and Nightmares," 360–61.

62. Kutz, *Realitätsflucht*, 37.

63. Groener, *Lebenserinnerungen*, 157–58.

64. Rupprecht Kronprinz v. Bayern, *Mein Kriegstagebuch*, diary entry of 25 Aug. 1914, 1:48, and of 21 Sept. 1918, 2:448.

65. On Schlieffen as *Erzieher*: Ritter, *Sword and Scepter*, 2:200; Goerlitz, *Kleine Geschichte*, 129–30; Dupuy, *Genius*, 132–34; Rothenberg, "Moltke," 313–14; Groener, *Lebenserinnerungen*, 69, 93; Freytag-Loringhoven, *Menschen und Dinge*, 135; Freytag-Loringhoven, *Heerführung im Weltkriege*, 47, 152; Eisenhart-Rothe, *Im Banne der Persönlichkeit*, 28–45. Will as characteristic: Dieter Storz, "'Aber was hätte anders geschehen sollen?'" in *Kriegsende 1918*, 51–95, here 82–83. Ernst von Wrisberg held this characterological schooling responsible for the

recognized this achievement as Schlieffen's finest. Schlieffen, he told his audience, had directed everyone's eyes toward the single goal. "All energy should be directed to this highest goal, and the will that leads to it was the will to victory. This unrelenting, emotional will to victory is the legacy that Your Excellency has left to the General Staff. It is up to us now to hold it sacred."[66] The emotional or nonrational was thus fundamental to the Schlieffen Plan. It also helped cement the romantic picture of the military commander as intuitive genius, nowhere more clearly expressed than by General Ludendorff, who remarked in his memoirs that "during the entire war I did not think as much as I have in writing these memoirs. Waging war is an art, not a science."[67] The image of the ideal officer incorporated these emotional and characterological traits that determined the professional officer's expectations of himself and his fellows. And finally, joy in risk taking, relentless willpower, and obligatory optimism had far-reaching cognitive effects for those who had internalized them.

This list of characteristics might seem to suggest that German military culture and its expression in the Schlieffen Plan were static. They were not, though the principal assumptions operating in them were quite constant. As Schlieffen refined his war plan from 1892 to his retirement in 1905, it became steadily grander and riskier. The assumptions behind it produced a dynamism that tended toward expansion, a movement if anything encouraged by the political situation after 1905.[68] His successor, the younger Moltke, tried to dampen this internal dynamism by lessening the risky, one-sided deployment and by paying more attention to logistics. But the essential features of the Schlieffen Plan still remained Germany's main war plan (and after April 1913 its only war plan);[69] its tenets guided Germany's war conduct in World War I, as they had in the colonies. What accounts for their dominance over twenty-five years?

The Durability of the Schlieffen Principles

There were strong internal military-organizational reasons to enshrine Schlieffen's principles. His plan elaborated on, and made into explicit doctrine, the wisdom about fighting that had developed as Germany's military culture since the wars of unification. The Schlieffen Plan, therefore, rested on firm foundations. Its principles, which the historian Gunther Rothenberg has summed up as "the offensive, maneuver, mass, and economy of force," made sense to the junior-most officer, because these were operative, or

---

high death rate of War Ministry officers, most of whom had passed through the General Staff, when they reached the front in World War I: "Most of the comrades in the War Ministry soon died heroes' deaths on the battlefield. Actionism [*Tatendrang*] and inexperience . . . will have been mostly responsible." *Heer und Heimat, 1914–1918* (Leipzig, 1921), 140.

66. Groener, *Lebenserinnerungen*, 91.

67. Cited in Hans Meier-Welcker, "Die deutsche Führung an der Westfront im Frühsommer 1918," *Die Welt als Geschichte* 21 (1961), 164–84, here 176. See also Kutz, "Schlieffen," 42–44.

68. Förster says that in 1905 Schlieffen succumbed to popular expansionary fervor and no longer viewed his plan as purely security oriented but as providing the basis for Germany's world-power status. "Dreams and Nightmares," 362.

69. Mombauer, *Moltke*, 100–105.

172 even tactical, principles that were now said to apply at the strategic level.[70] The experience of battle, maneuvers, and war games—the palpable reality of actual combat—made the plan seem real, even as it developed more and more into the realm of wishful thinking and unreality. On top of this came Schlieffen's assiduous training in the General Staff of the most meritorious young officers in the army. Only a few future military leaders escaped this thorough schooling. Schlieffen's own reputation and personal charisma added to the effect of his lessons. The German military was obviously susceptible to the myth of the romantic military genius; it idolized first Moltke, then Schlieffen, and then the duo Ludendorff and Hindenburg. The more daring, even foolhardy, the plan the more it fitted the trope of intuitive genius. On the more prosaic level, the very effort the General Staff poured into the meticulous plan increased its incentive to hang on to it. And then there were the other standard military-bureaucratic reasons that Posen has enumerated for preferring an offensive war plan.

The mutually supporting logic of its parts also protected the Schlieffen Plan from criticism from within the military. One can begin with almost any of the eleven points above and derive the others from it. For example, if one assumed the necessity for a quick victory, then one recognized the utility of a risky offensive aiming at achieving it unequivocally. Or, one could begin by believing that only military victory "counted," which also required the offensive to destroy the enemy. Or, if one believed in the qualitative superiority of German troops and organization, then the risk of the all-out offensive seemed lower and the expectation of quick, purely military victory was heightened, predisposing you to choose these, and so on. Historians have entered these circular thoughts at different points and adduced different causal explanations for the Schlieffen Plan. But the Schlieffen Plan was not "caused" in a logical-functional way. Its logic is historical; it is the logic of development out of a series of interlocking practices and organizational experience, which ended up intensifying and then freezing organizational knowledge in a solipsistic doctrine.[71]

The details of the Schlieffen Plan were, of course, secret. But its basic principles (the single, offensive, swift concentration of force to produce a [probably] flanking battle of annihilation) were well known; they were discussed publicly in military journals and books, and they were embodied in the actions of German officers in the colonies and during maneuvers and war games. In a remarkable example of organizational mimicry, the German navy also adopted these principles. The navy was new; in its modern form it was the creation of Kaiser Wilhelm II in 1897–98. It is not surprising that, in its efforts to find legitimacy, it should have patterned itself after the model of the established, successful, and prestigious army. The navy also shared the fundamental dilemma that Schlieffen addressed: it was much weaker than its chosen opponent, the British navy. Admiral v. Tirpitz, head of the Naval Office and father of the new battleship fleet, foresaw a single battle of annihilation in the North Sea. He called this battle "the unmovable goal of our tactics,

---

70. Rothenberg, "Moltke," 314; Kutz, "Schlieffen," 32.

71. Travers points out that, while Britain and France also developed offensive plans, only in Germany was the offensive actually doctrine: Tim Travers, *The Killing Ground* (London, 1993), 254, 257.

always to be kept in mind in our training and organization."[72] Tirpitz was as good as his word; the navy, like the General Staff, trained its officers and sculpted its organization in the same tradition of reckless offensive as found in the Schlieffen Plan, to which it held firm to the very end of World War I.

There was thus little incentive inside the armed forces to criticize the principles embedded in the Schlieffen Plan (and its naval equivalent). Of course, not every officer was a Schlieffen acolyte. We have seen the opposition of the "old Africans" in SWA, and we will meet more examples in World War I. More important, we shall see that it was possible to subscribe to the basic operational tenets of the Schlieffen Plan and still resist its dynamic toward extremes and unrealism. A firm grip on practical goals, political interest, regard for world opinion, or humanitarian values (whether encouraged by religion or otherwise) are some of the reasons for such resistance. But the example of the silence of Major Lequis reminds us how hard it was to buck the organizational tide; and the interlocking dynamism of the plan's parts made it difficult to accept some of its tenets while rejecting others.

Organizational cultures may sometimes be corrected by negative experiences, in this case by war. Before 1914 that meant colonial war. Yet Germany's colonial experience also seemed to bear out the assumptions embedded in the Schlieffen Plan. The colonial situation replicated perfectly in real life the imagined world of danger and its triumphant, daring overcoming through technical superiority and élan. In all the European colonies, the offensive leading to total victory was an unquestioned maxim. In 1909, for example, German First Lieutenant Prager reviewed and summed up the message of the official French guidebook to colonial warfare:

> The main goal of operations is to force the foe to a decisive battle in which one can utilize one's superior weapons and the better military training of one's troops. Each operation should be crowned at the end with the complete submission of the opponent.[73]

Colonial warfare thus put the same premium on speed, the decisive, demonstrative victory of force, the exploitation of technical and organizational advantages, the assumption of one's own superiority, and the vision of perfect victory followed by perfect order ("complete submission") that animated the Schlieffen Plan. The correspondence between colonial methods and those embedded in the Schlieffen Plan removed this source of potentially salutary feedback. And the dogma that "small wars" were irrelevant to European warfare, anyway, was a further shield to learning from the unpleasant reality of unsuccessful campaigns.

---

72. Tirpitz, "Denkschrift über die Neuorganisation unserer Panzerflotte" (1892), cited in Gerhard P. Gross, "Eine Frage der Ehre?" in *Kriegsende 1918*, 349–65, here 358; and Volker R. Berghahn, "War Preparations and National Identity in Imperial Germany," in *Anticipating Total War*, 307–26, here 317.

73. Oberlt. Prager, "Ein französisches Reglement für die Kriegführung in Afrika," *Vierteljahrshefte für Truppenführung und Heereskunde* 6:3 (1909), 475–92, here 477–78 and 491. See also the standard British handbook, Callwell, *Small Wars*.

174   If all these reasons meant that the military was unlikely to produce much healthy self-criticism, it received little from outside, either. Although the Schlieffen Plan had developed without coordination with the Reich political leadership, it nonetheless seemed to fit two different, almost antithetical, contemporary interpretations of German foreign policy. The first was *Weltpolitik* (world policy), the not very clearly worked out pursuit of elevating Germany from a merely European Great Power to a world power. World policy is particularly associated with Bernhard v. Bülow (foreign minister from 1897 to 1901 and then chancellor until 1909). Germany was not large, rich, or powerful enough to revolutionize the world order as the propaganda for Weltpolitik suggested, so Bülow tried to finesse it through a combination of bluff and opportunism.[74] The Schlieffen Plan resonated with both the dilemma and the goals. It was similarly a prescription for producing the absolute maximum power effect from a (relatively) weak position. Had it succeeded, it would indeed have revolutionized the world order by establishing a single continental hegemonic nation for the first time since Napoleon. Bülow and Bethmann could not publicly give up Weltpolitik, even when it had palpably failed after 1905, because the legitimacy of the monarchy was too strongly identified with it. General Staff officers were in a similar position. If they had accepted the elder Moltke's conclusion that only diplomatic-political means, not military victory, could save Germany, then they would have delegitimized the supreme place of the army in the constitutional order.[75]

Once France, Russia, and Britain responded to the threat that Weltpolitik seemed to pose by establishing the Entente, a second interpretation of German foreign policy began to displace that cheery one. It was the paranoid vision of the Pan-Germans who saw Germany encircled by its envious enemies, bent on destroying the newcomer. Beginning in 1905 and accelerating after 1911, wider circles of the German public adopted this anxious view. Its negativity dovetailed better with the Schlieffen Plan, whose purpose was defensive, even if its means were offensive. But the Schlieffen Plan's combination of ostensible security-mindedness and aggressive means suited the vague possibilities inherent in Wilhelminian foreign policy, as it did the various competing versions of social Darwinism, which ranged from conservative-protectionist to a racialist Hobbesian war of all against all.[76] It is worth remembering that the Schlieffen Plan antedated the advent of Weltpolitik and the heyday of social Darwinism. But their existence helped confirm its precepts.

The Hidden Dynamism of Violence

The Schlieffen Plan was not a lifeless, preprogrammed script. Its unusual mix of daring and desperation contained an explosive dynamic that the plan's unrealism and imperviousness to reexamination made worse. Only when one understands the link between

74. Peter Winzen, *Bülows Weltmachtkonzept* (Boppard am Rhein, 1977).

75. Förster, "Dreams and Nightmares," 360.

76. Bernard Semmel, *Imperialism and Social Reform* (Cambridge, Mass., 1960); Hans-Günter Zmarzlik, "Social Darwinism in Germany," in *The Human Creature*, ed. Günther Altner (Garden City, N.Y., 1974), 346–77; Daniel Gasman, *The Scientific Origins of National Socialism* (London, 1971); Storz, *Kriegsbild*, 79–81, 373, and passim.

aggression and fear, and between fear and the panacea of order, does the systematic drift implicit in doctrine toward extremes in practice make sense.

Planning is normally a way organizations handle and defend against anxiety.[77] Plans give the comforting illusion of control; they reduce the number of irritating options and the necessity to think or to choose. The Schlieffen Plan, however, had anxiety built into its very premise. On the one hand, Schlieffen promised that his plan was a "prescription for victory"; on the other, the plan forced its practitioners to overcome Germany's perceived weakness by risking everything. The technique of overcoming weakness by the daring use of force did not diminish anxiety, it fed it, unleashing in practice a spiral of aggression, anxiety, and more aggression that officers experienced as compulsive.

Organizational technique is one way to account for pervasive anxiety and the wish for perfect order visible in the Schlieffen Plan. But like most durable characteristics, these idées fixes were overdetermined. A military's task of wielding violence and the hyperbolic conception of discipline and order that it develops to manage its task predispose it to these preoccupations. In the German case, the political framework added to these propensities. The army's privileged position seemed under attack by growing hordes of socialists; the monarchical order seemed the only bastion against them; but Germany's increasing foreign-political "encirclement" imperiled the monarchy and threatened fatal weakness at the national level. Thus, implicit, unconscious features of the Schlieffen Plan seemed confirmed by structures beyond the plan.

We turn now from Schlieffen's doctrine to the practices of fear and force that developed logically from it. The fear of weakness and the panaceas of victory and order were as hidden from most officers as they were ubiquitous and deadly in their dynamism. The resulting spiral of violence before 1914 was clearly visible in the colonial engagements, which then became a kind of dress rehearsal for the world war.

The Fear of Weakness

The fear of being thought weak by the enemy surfaces again and again as a determinant of military policy in the field. To some extent, fear of weakness is a general military predisposition, in that the military's métier is the successful use of force. Furthermore, giving the appearance of strength was entrenched colonial policy. The British expert on small wars, Charles Callwell, warned officers against delaying a march, because "every pause is interpreted as weakness," and he spoke for most Europeans when he supported harsh treatment of native rebels, because "uncivilized races attribute leniency to timidity."[78] The conviction that the colonial opponent "always takes leniency and forbearance for weakness and *cowardice*" was simply universal among German officers and policy-

---

77. Posen, *Sources*, 44–45.

78. Callwell, *Small Wars*, 72–73, 148. The same point: the French guidebook "Guerre d'Afrique, guide-annex des réglements sur le service en campagne et de manoeuvres," cited in Prager, "Ein franzöisches Reglement," 476; Hartmann, "Militärische Nothwendigkeit," 466.

176 makers.[79] It accounted for a great number of decisions at the micro and macro levels. For example, fear of appearing weak moved officers to chance risky marches, premature attacks, or especially difficult operations in order to impress the opponent with German strength.[80] More important, however, far-reaching decisions to prolong or escalate combat were taken from this same motive.

The reluctance of German commanders to end conflict by negotiation is one of the most noteworthy characteristics of prewar German military culture. In SWA, the Kaiser had forbidden negotiations without his approval, and public opinion supported his forceful stance. Still, no contemporary ever expressed doubt that Lieutenant General v. Trotha would have been permitted to open negotiations after the battle of Waterberg. But Trotha refused to do so, later explaining that "there could be no question of negotiations if one did not wish to testify to one's own weakness and embarrassment."[81] Fear of showing weakness was not just an idiosyncrasy of Trotha's. His decision not to negotiate was entirely consistent with basic assumptions permeating the military, which one of Trotha's staff officers clearly expressed in his defense of Trotha's decision:

> Was the pursuit really necessary? Some voices have declared it an unnecessary cruelty. Surely, *every* pursuit is a harsh measure, but often, as here, it was the lesser of two evils, because it ended the war more quickly and with less bloodshed than a long, drawn-out war would have.
>
> Imagine that, out of false humanity, we had not pursued [the enemy]. Then the fleeing foe, instead of giving up resistance, would have gathered and organized. He would have interpreted our lack of pressure as weakness, and strengthened [by this thought], he would have recovered and armed for a new, energetic battle. . . . Then the war would have gone on indefinitely, and for each Herero whom we spared, a German soldier would have fallen, and in the end, we would *still* have had to force the enemy down with weapons. Instead of dying of thirst and hunger, the enemy would have died of lead. An energetic pursuit was therefore more humane than a long struggle in which *both* warring parties would have slowly bled to death.[82]

Here we see the familiar chain of assumptions: pursuit is an unquestioned dogma; war is existential, it cannot be interrupted (by "false humanity") in its development toward the extreme; the foe will interpret humane policy as weakness and continue fighting for total victory; and, therefore, only total victory or total defeat (death) is possible.

79. Schwabe, *Krieg in Südwestafrika*, 70, emphasis in original. Other examples of virtually the same sentence: Bayer, *Mit dem Hauptquartier*, 33, 279; Lettow-Vorbeck, *Mein Leben*, 81; Rohrbach, *Aus Südwestafrikas schweren Tagen*, 113–14.

80. Nuhn, *Flammen über Deutschost*, 64, 109; Leutwein to General Staff, tel., 10 June 1904, Okahandja, BA-Berlin, R 1001, Nr. 2115, p. 13; Lettow-Vorbeck diary, 4 Dec. 1900 (China), MA-Freiburg, Nl. Lettow-Vorbeck, Nr. 44.

81. Trotha, "Politik und Kriegführung," *Berliner Neueste Nachrichten* 60 (3 Feb. 1909), 1.

82. Bayer, *Mit dem Hauptquartier*, 159–60, emphasis in original.

There was another version of total defeat held open by German officers; however, it 177 was not more conducive to negotiated settlements in that it demanded unconditional surrender. This kind of total defeat required the enemy to publicly demonstrate that it did not interpret settlement as German weakness; that is, it required ritual humiliation acknowledging the Germans' superior position and authority. In China, where the allies joined Germany in demanding a humiliating settlement, the terms included the following measures symbolic of allied strength: the execution or suicides of several high-ranking court figures, official apologies to Germany and Japan (for assassinations of their representatives), a monument to Germany's murdered ambassador, and the stationing of more allied troops in China.[83] These demands delayed peace for almost a year, during which time Germany carried out forty-eight punitive expeditions of exemplary destructiveness.[84]

The surrender terms offered in East Africa similarly show that ritual humiliation of the enemy was necessary to overcome the fear of having shown weakness by settling a conflict by any means short of ultimate force.[85] In addition to complete disarmament and the handing over of rebel leaders (who were, of course, the political leaders of the districts), Governor Götzen also insisted on a "punishment fine" for each warrior and the deliverance of large groups of laborers "for punishment and forced labor on the coast."[86] Eight months later (in July 1906), the deputy governor had to inform Berlin that "the surrender conditions demanded by the government could not be fulfilled to the degree one expects of an unconditional surrender." In fact, leaders and rebels had to be captured, and almost no fines or work gangs materialized. "This way will not serve to rebuild the authority of German power vis-à-vis the natives," he wrote. Instead, he suggested "a punishment that will keep their subjection permanently awake in the natives' memory"— namely, expropriating their usufruct rights to the products of the land. This measure happily combined administrative feasibility with profitability, but, above all, it demonstrated the Africans' dependency and subjection with nearly every economic transaction.[87] In the end, however, the war did not end by negotiated settlement or voluntary surrender but by force. The pursuit of rebel leaders in East Africa continued for another two years, until the very last one was dead, along with probably hundreds of thousands of other Africans. The *Felddienst* manual for East Africa (1911) summed up the lessons of power and weakness the military had found confirmed in the revolt: "The Negro does not love us but only fears our power. Any sign of weakness that he thinks he sees in us will be a temptation to him to take up arms and to drive us from his country."[88]

---

83. Cohen, *History in Three Keys*, 55–56.

84. Felber and Rostek, *Der "Hunnenkrieg" Kaiser*, 31.

85. Demonstrating "the required military display of power": Militärpolitischer Bericht über die Tätigkeit der in Ostafrika befindlichen Kreuzer und Marinetruppen, 7 Jan. 1905, Dar es Salaam, cited in Bald, "Afrikanischer Kampf," 40.

86. Götzen, "Befehl an die Truppenführer im Aufstandsgebiet," 11 Nov. 1905, Dar es Salaam, MA-Freiburg, RM 121 I, Nr. 438, p. 60.

87. Dep. Gov. Haber to Foreign Office, 16 July 1906, Nr. 860, Dar es Salaam, BA-Berlin, R 1001, Nr. 724, pp. 115–17.

88. Introduction to *Felddienst in Deutsch-Ostafrika* (Dar es Salaam, 1911), 2, cited in Iliffe, *Tanganyika under German Rule*, 28–29.

178   Real negotiations were thus basically out of the question for the military.[89] This stance prolonged war, while the methods of pursuit, punishment, and demonstration of authority meant that prolongation equaled escalation. Fear of appearing weak undermined every opportunity to stop the process of spiraling escalation, as SWA showed. Even after Chief of Staff Schlieffen had agreed with Chancellor Bülow that Trotha's October proclamation had to be rescinded, he still refused to support any further efforts to encourage the Herero people's voluntary submission:

> To go further in our invitation seems to me not undangerous. At the moment we are completely unable to harm the Herero. . . . If we choose the course of appealing, after our threats [Trotha's proclamation] have been in vain, then the Herero will recognize in our shift an admission of weakness. Every sign of weakness will ignite in one place or another a new uprising.[90]

Efforts to ameliorate the appalling conditions in the internment camps met with the same reluctance, born of fear that the inmates would extract revenge; thus the fear of appearing weak became the fear of being weak.[91] Even in 1908, nine months after Germany had officially declared victory in the war, one still finds a county administrator arguing that the Herero must not be freed from camps lest "too much conciliation awaken the appearance of weakness and bring out the dominating nature of the Herero."[92]

      In terms of military policy there was not much to distinguish fear of appearing weak and fear of actually being weak; they both resulted in deadly conduct. The atmosphere of pervasive fear fosters decision making that runs toward extremes; fear is, therefore, one of the inciters of the genocidal process.[93] The extreme toward which fear impelled German military policy was not at first intended as mass death, however, but as complete victory and total order.

The Imperative of Absolute Victory and Order

      For modern military organizations victory means the successful establishment of order through force. This is true of all militaries, not just the German. As the sociologist Maury Feld has observed, "The emergence of armed forces into their modern professionalized, disciplined form has had the effect of transforming violence into a mode of order and making its victims appear to be destructive threats."[94] Because militaries are state bu-

---

89. As Estorff discovered in SWA, the negotiated settlements individual commanders reached with the various Nama clans were often abrogated by superior officers who preferred the more complete solution of mass imprisonment to whatever minimal compromises the commanders had worked out.

90. Schlieffen to Bülow, Nr. 13297, 16 Dec. 1904, Berlin, BA-Berlin, R 1001, Nr. 2089, p. 107.

91. Report of Director Fenchel, 26 Dec. 1906, Keetmanshoop, copy, BA-Berlin, R 1001, Nr. 2140, p. 18.

92. Bezirksamtmann (Seitz?) to governor, Nr. 1164, 30 Jan. 1908, Windhuk, BA-Berlin, R 151 F/D.IV.L.3., vol. 6, p. 99.

93. Peter du Preez, *Genocide* (London, 1994), 29–30; Smelser, "Some Determinants of Destructive Behavior," 19; Chalk and Jonassohn, "Conceptual Framework," 40.

94. Feld, *Structure of Violence*, 16–17.

reaucracies, the order they tend to envision is a bureaucratic one: a hierarchy consisting of authorities, who administer, and passive objects of administration, who accept as legitimate their subordination to those in command. Colonialism provided the perfect threat to such a vision of order, with the rebel who rejects state authority and disrupts bureaucratic functioning. Rebels are, therefore, in Governor Götzen's words, "representatives of anarchy."[95]

In 1870, before war against France had become a desperate, guerrilla war, the international lawyer Felix Dahn defined the goal of war as "peace, the establishment of a relation between the warring parties that approximates, better than did the prewar situation, reason and political requirements and, therefore, that holds the prospect of longevity."[96] Dahn, like Clausewitz before him, placed political considerations at the center of military victory. General v. Hartmann, summing up the lessons of 1870–71, typically divided the political from the military. The political goal concerned the conflict that had led to war. "The *military goal* rests in what the act of violence of war immediately creates—overcoming the enemy's will by smashing the personnel and material means by which the enemy seeks to carry out or uphold his will."[97] After 1870, the narrow military understanding of victory as the destruction of the enemy, not the establishment of viable peace, became dominant. Just as German jurists had accepted military necessity as the realistic and binding limit to international law, they and civilian leaders accepted the military definition of victory that focused on eliminating the threat. In doing so, they weakened the autonomy of the political sphere and helped reinforce the military's fatal autism.

When the uprising in SWA broke out, leading government spokesmen, such as Colonial Director Stübel, defined the terms of war and of victory by making the rebellion a matter of the "reputation of the Reich," by characterizing the Herero as "opponents of the state and social order," and by calling for a "quick and complete vanquishment of the uprising," which would eliminate the "political quasi-independence" of the Herero people.[98] These phrases found a wide echo in National Liberal, Conservative, and procolonial circles, and in nonsocialist newspapers generally. The threat to German sovereign authority, and thus to "national honor," was taken seriously: "Our sovereignty," averred the National Liberal Deputy Patzig, "has been severely damaged and must be restored to full authority."[99] Calls for "punishment" were ubiquitous. Stübel's words "complete vanquishment" or "complete subjection" became epithetic, and the drift toward the extreme is also clear in the call for sending the natives a message "that they won't forget for generations."[100] As one might expect, settler opinion was even more rabid. Where it did not ex-

95. Götzen, *Deutsch-Ostafrika*, 224.

96. Dahn, *Das Kriegsrecht*, 32.

97. Hartmann, "Militärische Nothwendigkeit," 121. Emphasis in original.

98. Col. Dir. Stübel before the Bundesrat, 12 Mar. 1904, BA-Berlin, R 1001, Nr. 2113, p. 36; Stübel before the Reichstag, 19 Jan. 1904, *Sten. Ber.*, 6th legisl. per., 1st session, vol. 197, col. 363.

99. Patzig, 17 Mar. 1904, *Sten. Ber.*, vol. 199, col. 1895. "National honor": "Koloniales," *Tägliche Rundschau*, Nr. 111, 6 Mar. 1904, BA-Berlin, R 1001, Nr. 2112, p. 172.

100. "Die künftige Rechtsstellung der Hereros," *National-Zeitung*, Nr. 209, 29 Mar. 1904, BA-Berlin, R 1001, Nr. 2113, p. 98; "Koloniales," *Tägliche Rundschau*, Nr. 111, 6 Mar. 1904, ibid., Nr. 2112, p. 172; General Staff, *Kämpfe der deutschen Truppen*, 1:4.

180 press itself in racist terms, such as calling for the "unlimited maintenance of the supremacy of the [white] race," or in a mood of "terrible revenge" and "bloodthirstiness," as one missionary described it, it demanded "the establishment of a new order of things, such that the rebels will lose once and for all the desire and possibility" of rebelling.[101]

Government policy became the prisoner of the sentiments it had, in part, helped to unleash. It was not possible later, when the war was going badly, to demote the uprising from an issue of national security and sovereignty. Chancellor Bülow's dilemma is clear in his speech before the Reichstag on 5 December 1904. He had just finished days of arguing with Chief of the General Staff Schlieffen and Chief of the Military Cabinet Hülsen to get Trotha's October proclamation rescinded. An extreme policy of Vernichtung was the last thing he wanted. He set out the government's modest war aims in SWA as "the reestablishment of law and order [*Ruhe und Ordnung*] and security for life and property." He denied that the surviving Herero would be shot down. "There can be no question of that," he told the Reichstag. But he felt impelled in the very next sentence to say, "Certainly, gentlemen, I consider it our holy duty to make a repeat of such an uprising impossible for all time."[102] The phrase "for all time," like "once and for all" or "for generations," is the language of final solutions. Despite his clear opposition to such policies, Bülow, one of the most gifted orators of his day, could not escape the compulsion to pander to extremity.

If civilians in ever wider circles had adopted the vision of unlimited victory and perfect order, it is not surprising that the military continued to live by this creed. "The final pacification of the former Herero area," the "complete securing and domination of the occupied area" (in China), "the final pacification of the Matumbi Mountains" (in East Africa) were the repeated goals of military policy.[103] The requirements of "final pacification" were high; they were equivalent to the expectations military guidebooks held for enemy civilians in occupied zones, and they were not far from the Kaiser's injunction that no Chinese should dare look askance at a German. In SWA, even cattle rustling was enough to make officers regard an area as "unsecured" or even, as one put it, "to place everything we have accomplished into question."[104]

The world of total victories and perfect order in the end rested completely on force, on the demonstration of it in punitive expeditions and exemplary destructions and executions, and on the philosophy of it. Although not many Wilhelminians were simpleminded, brutally logical, or desperate enough, before World War I, openly to embrace the endpoint, genocide, the developmental logic was nonetheless clear. One of the desperate was Deputy Governor Tecklenburg in SWA, who, in a masterpiece of projection onto the Herero, expressed the logic running from fear to force:

101. "Zu den Unruhen in Deutsch-Südwestafrika," *Flugblätter des Deutschen Kolonial-Bundes*, Nr. 9, Jan. 1904, BA-Berlin, R 1001, Nr. 2111, p. 27; Missionary Elger, 10 Feb. 1904, cited in Drechsler, *Aufstände*, 66; *Deutsch-Südwestafrikanische Zeitung* 6, Nr. 3, 19 Jan. 1904, p. 1.

102. Bülow, 5 Dec. 1904, *Sten. Ber.*, vol. 201, col. 3376.

103. Schwabe, *Krieg in Südwestafrika*, 303; Waldersee to General Staff, Nr. A 8886 I, 28 Oct. 1900, Peking, MA-Freiburg, RM 121 I, Nr. 399, p. 17; Götzen to eldest officer of the *Bussard*, 22 Sept. 1905, Dar es Salaam, ibid., Nr. 443.

104. General Staff, *Kämpfe der deutschen Truppen*, 2:282; Estorff, "Kriegserlebnisse," 96.

Even when the uprising will have been put down, security of life and property as they existed before the uprising will not have returned. We cannot hide one thing. Our prestige among the natives, the prestige of the white man, is completely gone. Our enemies have too often had the opportunity of testing their strength . . . against our troops. Our black helpers have too often been able to laugh at the clumsiness of the white newcomers. . . . Yes, a "personality" would still be able to arouse respect and submission from the natives. But these feelings will simply not be forthcoming to every white man. What [the natives] respect is only our power, our "machines," our guns.[105]

Where Tecklenburg set all his stock and store on power (*Macht*), his addition of machines and guns makes clear he actually meant violence (*Gewalt*). As Hannah Arendt has observed, "Power and violence are opposites; where the one rules absolutely, the other is absent." Power in this sense means political, legitimate government that is expressed when people "act in concert." "Rule by sheer violence comes into play where power is being lost,"[106] as was the case in SWA. The military's métier is violence, not power, and where military doctrine and practices unfold without limit, violence crowds out government.

105. Letter of Tecklenburg, 15 Oct. 1904, cited in "Auszüge aus jüngst eingegangenen Berichten über die Lage der Dinge in Südwest-Afrika," BA-Berlin, R 1001, Nr. 2089, pp. 105–6.
106. Arendt, *On Violence*, 56, 44, 53.

8

Stopping the Process

The Imperial German patterns of military practice and doctrine differed only in degree from those operating in the armies of other major European powers. The German army placed itself under greater pressure to succeed, held a more extreme conception of order and of victory, and was less mindful of the limits set by international law. But other armies facing the frustrations of colonial conflict showed the same tendency to drift toward final solutions. The French army in Sudan shook off metropolitan shackles and erected a virtual slave empire with itself as master.[1] French Indochina suffered systematic, gratuitous devastation at the hands of the army.[2] But the best example of the temptation to wage war to extremes is the British conflict with the Boers from 1899 to 1902. The Boer War shows how extreme war practices developed, but also how they could be stopped.

Militaries generally had a hard time exercising effective self-criticism or braking their tendencies toward extremes. It fell, then, to extramilitary sources (civil government, public opinion, political parties, private groups, etc.) to counter military extremism. This was Germany's greatest disadvantage and the factor that most distinguished it and fed the cycle of military destructiveness. Germany's constitution (governmental lack of coordination, the chancellor's dependence on imperial favor, the Kaiser's untrammeled Kommandogewalt, the weakened Reichstag) and the political culture that developed from it (weak political parties, "double militarism") crippled effective extramilitary intervention. Nothing illustrates this better than comparing two colonial disasters, the Herero Revolt and the Boer War.

---

1. Kanya-Forster, "French Marines," 121–45. On French colonial methods generally, see Porch, "Bugeaud, Galliéni, Lyautey," 376–407.
2. Fourniau, "Colonial Wars before 1914."

The Boer War

The Boer War pitted the world's largest empire against two hundred thousand descendants of Dutch settlers in the Boer republics in southern Africa. After two and a half years of war, Britain annexed the Boer republics, but it cost over two hundred million pounds, over four hundred thousand troops (against sixty to eighty thousand for the Boers), and twenty-two thousand British dead to do so.[3] After a poor beginning, new leadership under Frederick Sleigh Roberts managed to control the main towns by early 1900, and most people believed the war was over. In June 1900, however, the Boers shifted to a highly successful guerrilla war, which elicited greater and greater severity from British commanders. Horatio Herbert Kitchener, who had recently subdued the Sudan, succeeded Roberts in November 1900 and determined to end the war no matter what it took. What it took, he thought, were three extreme tactics that he resolutely applied: the removal of the entire civilian population to internment camps; the systematic sweeping of the republics with flying columns, whose job was maximum destruction of property and food; and the erection of a grid of cement blockhouses linked by barbed wire, which was to expand to cover the entire area of the republics.[4] Together, these tactics were supposed to confine guerrilla warfare to an ever smaller space, until the last guerrillas were killed, gone, or had surrendered. Kitchener's methods were indeed total.[5]

There are many similarities between the Boer War and the Herero Revolt. The British effort was poorly organized and badly provisioned, and many of the technical problems were identical: naval troops were especially ill-prepared and suffered high losses; the infantry never learned to ride or handle horses; the loss by death of horses and pack mules was tremendous; intelligence was poor; the Boers were frustratingly brilliant at using and reading the landscape; death by disease was three times greater than death in battle; and so forth.[6] These failures were made worse by high expectations at home for a quick and glorious victory. The Boer War elicited the first sustained criticism of modern imperialism. Two of these lasting monuments were John Hobson's famous polemic, *Imperialism*, and Joseph Conrad's *Heart of Darkness*, both published in 1902.

The tactics British commanders used to counter guerrilla warfare were also very similar to those the Germans had used in 1870 and later.[7] Under Roberts, selective burning of farms began in March 1900 as reprisal and then swiftly expanded into the wholesale destruction of Boer farms and villages. To protect railroads from sabotage, British officers

---

3. Between six and seven thousand British soldiers died in battle, the rest of disease. Pakenham, *Boer War*, 572; Belfield, *Boer War*, xxiv, 10, 148; Howard Bailes, "Military Aspects of the War," in *South African War*, 67; also J. F. Maurice and M. H. Grant, ed., *History of the War in South Africa, 1899–1902*, 8 vols. (London, 1906–10), and L. S. Amery, ed., *The Times History of the War in South Africa*, 7 vols. (London, 1900–1909).

4. An early form of blockhouses and sweeps was used by French General Joseph Simon Galliéni in Tonkin in the 1890s: Porch, "Bugeaud, Galliéni, Lyautey," 388.

5. Du Preez, *Genocide*, 18.

6. Belfield, *Boer War*, 29–30, 36–38, 108, 115–18.

7. My discussion of British war conduct follows S. B. Spies's thoughtful and thoroughly researched account, *Methods of Barbarism?*

184 took civilians hostage, citing precedents from the Franco-Prussian war.[8] Prisoners of war were deported to camps abroad.[9] Collective fines were levied against communities near sabotaged facilities. At first as reprisal and later to prevent guerrillas from getting food, the British pursued a policy of "laying waste." Asked what that meant, one commander replied, "Gather all food, wagons, Cape carts, sheep, oxen, goats, cows, calves, horses, mares, foals, forage, poultry. Destroy what you cannot eat or remove . . . burn all houses and explain reason is that they have harboured enemy and not reported to British authorities as required. Give no receipts."[10] Civilians made destitute by this policy began to be gathered up in internment camps (July 1900), where the British thought they could be more easily fed and, in any case, better controlled.

These tactics were all in use by the time Kitchener replaced Roberts in November 1900. Along with introducing the blockhouse and the sweeps, or "drives," Kitchener transformed the civilian internment camps. Not just refugees created by the drives, but all Boer and even black African civilians were now to disappear from the landscape. A whole network of camps administered by the military sprang up. When these tactics of totality still did not end the war, Kitchener could think of no other solution than to introduce more extremes. In the summer of 1901 he demanded the deportation of recalcitrant Boer women and the punitive confiscation of the property of all Boers who refused to surrender. By that time, however, civilian leaders and public opinion had grown skeptical of severe methods, and Kitchener's push to go further down the road of extremism was halted.

Nonetheless, the costs of severity were high. Along with the tens of thousands of deaths in the internment camps came the widespread destruction of farms. After the war, Boers submitted sixty-three thousand claims for restitution of property.[11]

Occasionally, opposition to severe methods arose from within the military itself. One of Roberts's motives for curtailing indiscriminate farm burning in November 1900 was the protest of an officer about its effects.[12] Roberts also struggled to keep reprisals from developing into exemplary cruelty. One of his field commanders, Lt.-Gen. Sir Archibald Hunter, wished to hang those caught destroying railroads, kill ten prisoners of war for every British soldier hurt in sabotage attack, deport the wives and children of Boer guerrillas, and put them and prisoners of war on half rations as reprisal for sabotage. Roberts flatly rejected the suggestion.[13] Nevertheless, even under Roberts the military tended toward greater harshness against civilians and totality of method.

If in the last six months of the war no further extreme measures were adopted and the conditions in the internment camps were remedied, the reason was intervention from outside the military. Britain's political culture broke the development toward final solutions fostered by its military culture. The elements of political culture most active in stopping the process were strong civilian oversight of the military, effective parliamentary in-

---

8. Ibid., 104.
9. Bailes, "Military Aspects," 98.
10. Lt. Gen. Sir Archibald Hunter, cited in Spies, *Methods of Barbarism?* 122.
11. Pakenham, *Boer War*, 572.
12. Spies, *MetBarbarism?* 126.
13. Ibid., 115.

tervention, and robust public criticism. One aspect of British military culture contributed to this outcome: greater willingness to permit civilian scrutiny of military conduct.

Civilian oversight came primarily from Secretary of State for Colonies Joseph Chamberlain, the high commissioner in South Africa, Sir Alfred Milner, and War Secretary Lord Lansdowne (until November 1900) and his successor, St. John Brodrick. Prime Minister Lord Salisbury left matters to these men, while the cabinet remained ill-informed—and complained about it.[14] The civilian leadership gave the military substantial leeway for a long time. Milner, who was nearest the fighting and best informed, complained neither about hostage taking nor farm burning when Roberts announced these as policies in June 1900. The cabinet, the Colonial Office, and Milner all acquiesced to the establishment of internment camps for civilians, but apparently none of them knew or approved of Kitchener's intent to expand the camps to swallow up all civilians.[15] Two things seem to have moved the civilians to intervene more energetically in military policy: public criticism and their own observation that severity was ineffective, or even counterproductive.

By September 1900, High Commissioner Milner urged Roberts to stop farm burning, population clearance, and laying waste, and concentrate on the fighters instead. Two months later, Milner repeated his views to Chamberlain:

> There has been a great deal too much burning of farms. As a *punishment* I feel that the destruction of a homestead is fully justified. . . . But such *discriminating* destruction which really has a deterrent effect is one thing. The indiscriminate burning of all houses in a particular district simply to make it untenable by the enemy is quite another. To that I object thinking it 1) barbarous and 2) ineffectual. By making a large number of people homeless, you increase the army of desperadoes roaming the country which it is our object to reduce. For my part, I am going as soon as I take over the civil administration, to set my face against wholesale destruction.[16]

Partly as a result of Chamberlain's and Milner's interventions, Roberts formally rescinded the policy of indiscriminate farm burning in November 1900. However, Chamberlain (and Milner) specifically recognized that military necessity "must of course be dealt with according to circumstances," meaning that "discriminating destruction" was still permissible.[17] Some farm burning therefore continued under Kitchener, though most of it was already over by November 1900.[18] Milner continued to protest the practice when it occurred.[19]

Once the civilian leaders had become skeptical of military promises, they were energetic in stopping policies before they began. Kitchener's repeated request for banishment of oppositionist Boer civilians and prisoners of war, and confiscation of their property, was rejected out of hand by War Secretary Brodrick. "Hitherto the effects of severity have

14. Ibid., 300–301.
15. Ibid., 152, 190.
16. Cited in ibid., 126, emphasis in original.
17. Ibid.
18. Ibid., 118.
19. Ibid., 177.

186 not been all we could have hoped," he noted. "Those who knew South Africa best expected the same results from farm burning as are now claimed for confiscation—but we were led quite wrong in this."[20] Chamberlain agreed. Confiscation "is contrary to the laws of the Cape Colony and Natal and also contrary to international usage," he noted. Permanently banishing all prisoners of war he termed "absurd." "What are we to do with the twenty thousand more or less who are not in the colonies? Are we to keep them there [in camps abroad] for life or where are we to dump them?" Chamberlain continued:

> I do not blame [Kitchener] for these absurd proposals, but they show that he was too much occupied with military matters to be able to give his mind to other things, and we poor civilians have therefore to think for him. . . . We have shown ourselves ready to adopt every reasonable suggestion, but we cannot authorize proclamations which would make us ridiculous in the eyes of the Home and Foreign nations.[21]

The (civilian) secretary of war arrived at his position a month before Chamberlain added his views. Both men judged extreme military policies as both ineffective and illegal. It is possible that British civilian leaders would have permitted continued severity had it been effective—the acute spasm of cruelty that German writers repeatedly equated with true humanitarianism.[22] As it was, civilian leaders showed themselves ready and willing to subject military policies to criticism and, if they found them wanting, to stop them. And they were concerned about domestic and foreign public opinion, which they identified as supporting the limits of international law.[23] The cabinet, too, swung away from permitting extremism in the name of military necessity. In July 1901, it officially disapproved of Kitchener's military policies; it blocked the commander's deportation scheme for women and children; it rejected his suggestion to pay for the internment camps by expropriating Boer property; and it protested the execution of Cape rebels.[24]

Public opinion played an important role in abandoning military harshness. It was the crucial element in reforming the horrible conditions inside the internment camps. These were exposed by a Liberal reformer, Emily Hobhouse, who gained access to the camps through party political connections to High Commissioner Milner.[25] Kitchener and the

20. Brodrick, 20 July 1901, cited in ibid., 237.

21. Chamberlain to Brodrick, 20 Aug. 1901, cited in ibid., 237.

22. "True humanity requires a quick end and therefore energetic conduct of the war"; Lueder, "Krieg und Kriegsrecht," 193; also 277. "Apparent harshness and severity become the opposite, if they hasten the foe's decision to sue for peace; mercy and leniency become cruelty if . . . they prolong the conclusion of war"; Hartmann, "Militärische Nothwendigkeit," 123–24; also 465–66. "Even the most complete, most dangerous, and most massively deadly means are permitted in war, indeed, because they achieve the goal of war quickest, they are indispensable and, strictly speaking, they are the most humane"; Germany, General Staff, *Kriegsbrauch,* 9. The same sentiment: Bayer, *Mit dem Hauptquartier,* 159–60; Deimling, "Südwest-Afrika," 13.

23. Brodrick worried that "Europe would be needlessly scandalized" by Kitchener's policies; Spies, *Methods of Barbarism?* 237. Best has found that there was widespread European public opinion favoring the extension of international law to curb cruelty in warfare: Best, *Humanity in Warfare,* 132–34, 139–40.

24. Pakenham, *Boer War,* 512–14.

25. Ibid., 503–4.

military commanders of the camps cooperated with Hobhouse, who visited several of them early in 1901. On her return to England in May, she informed War Secretary Brodrick of her findings. Even before receiving Hobhouse, Brodrick had been uneasy about reports of poor conditions in the camps and had intervened to improve rations. But his suggestions for further reforms had met resistance from both Kitchener and Milner, who cited technical problems.[26] Meanwhile, Hobhouse had alerted Liberal MP Henry Campbell-Bannerman to the misery in the camps. In a famous public address, Campbell-Bannerman pilloried the military's "methods of barbarism."[27] A few days later Parliament received statistics on civilian deaths in the internment camps. If these had remained steady, they would have reached 12 percent per annum, which was high enough for a leader of the Liberal Party, David Lloyd George, to accuse the government of pursuing a "policy of extermination" against women and children.[28]

Because the radical Hobhouse was dismissed in some quarters as prejudiced, War Secretary Brodrick appointed an official commission of "ladies" to inspect the camps and recommend reforms. These women were mostly upper-class Conservatives, headed by Millicent Fawcett, though two of them were doctors. The Fawcett, or Ladies' Commission, as it was popularly called, inspected only the white camps from August to December 1901, but their report to Brodrick was thorough, candid, and unsparing. Referring to the Aliwal North Camp in the Orange River Colony, for example, the report's pithy recommendation was: "Remove the Superintendent, and thoroughly re-organise the camp."[29] The "ladies" did not shrink from practical details; the Mafeking camp hospital required the following, they wrote: "disinfectants, mosquito netting, drugs, already indented for, urine-testing apparatus, waterproof sheets."[30] In general, the Ladies' Commission recommended higher and better rations (including milk and vegetables), better sanitation and hygiene, and more attentive and professional camp administration.

Even before the commission's report arrived, Chamberlain (November 1901) removed the camps from the military's administration and ordered Milner to spare no expense in reforming them and reducing the death rate.[31] Milner followed the commission's recommendations; the death rate promptly fell to 6.9 percent in February 1902 and soon thereafter to 2 percent.[32]

Comparing Disasters

The comparison between the Boer War and the Herero Revolt illuminates important structural differences in how the political cultures of Britain and Germany handled disas-

26. Spies, *Methods of Barbarism?* 198–200, 216.

27. Pakenham, *Boer War*, 508.

28. Ibid. Spies's careful study concludes that the high death rate (of about 24%, twice as high as what shocked Lloyd George) was due to maladministration and militaristic inattention, not an intention by military or civilian leaders to exterminate the Boers. Spies, *Methods of Barbarism?* 268.

29. Great Britain, Parliament, *Report on the Concentration Camps*, 56.

30. Ibid., 183.

31. Spies, *Methods of Barbarism?* 256.

32. Pakenham, *Boer War*, 518.

188 ters caused by military extremism. Beginning at the top, the British cabinet may have been ill-informed, slow to counteract pernicious military policies, and not always effective against military obstructionism, but Germany did not even possess a cabinet. This was a double deficiency. There was no institution where elected officials accountable to a parliament oversaw military policy. Worse, there was no institution where civilian government officials met to coordinate military with national, economic, or foreign policy. The thinness of civilian institutions was compounded by the Kaiser's decision, spurred by his military advisors, to suspend civilian administration in SWA, first by restricting it to nonmilitary matters (beginning with Trotha's arrival in June 1904), and then by making Trotha acting governor. Thus there was also no SWA equivalent of a high commissioner, who might have provided the viewpoint that Milner expressed when he said, "In the upper ranks of the army there is nothing like sufficient ability to manage their own business properly, much less to do other people's."[33]

Robbed of institutional allies within government, a chancellor seeking to rein in the military would have been forced to rely even more heavily on the Reichstag or public opinion. Here, too, he was blocked, but not for institutional reasons (for example, because the Reichstag lacked the budgetary power to throttle military policies). The Reichstag was as powerful as the British Parliament in that regard. Rather, a chancellor who openly used the Reichstag against the military would have been instantly dismissed for encouraging the growth of democracy against the monarchical principle. In 1908, Chancellor Bülow's seeming attempt to strengthen the Reichstag as an ally against the Kaiser's quixotic political interventions led to his dismissal barely eight months later.[34] Criticism by the Reichstag was equally powerless on its own. In Britain, even hyperbolic and unfair criticism, like Lloyd George's claim of "extermination," would be likely to have a more sympathetic hearing than would, in Germany, the reasoned criticism of Socialists such as August Bebel or Georg Ledebour, or even of Center Party leaders such as Matthias Erzberger. Decades of systematic official calumny of Socialists and—even after the end of the Kulturkampf—of Catholics as traitors made it impossible for government officials to agree with their viewpoints publicly (even if they did so privately) and predisposed other parties, and presumably wide circles of voters, to reject whatever they said out of hand. This strategy of divide and rule had the corollary of identifying the government (and especially the military) with the nation *tout court*. That, too, made it hard for Reichstag critics to present themselves successfully as patriots, whereas in Britain opposition was not a priori denigrated as unpatriotic.

Public critics in Germany faced similar obstacles. Germany did not lack its own Emily Hobhouses. Socialist, Left Liberal, Roman Catholic, and some Protestant circles produced very similar denunciations of harsh, gratuitous military policy. In SWA the best informed and most outspoken critics were Protestant missionaries. Their early reports that settlers' misdeeds had caused the uprising and that the Herero had not been indiscriminate killers raised a furor in the right-wing and nationalist press. Typically, Bülow felt compelled to

---

33. Spies, *Methods of Barbarism?* 73.
34. Katherine Lerman, *The Chancellor as Courtier* (Cambridge, 1990).

attack the missionaries in the same way he dismissed Socialist and Roman Catholic critics—as traitors. He told the Reichstag, "In a war, the place of missionaries is on the side of their fellow countrymen. I can grant them neither the right of neutrality between Germans and Herero nor the office of complainant or judge."[35] When the Rhenish Missionary Society complained, Bülow repeated these views and placed himself on the side of "the justified national sentiment of indignation and fury over the [Herero] atrocities."[36] In doing so, Bülow contributed to the climate of revenge he would later try to stem, and he weakened the only organized force in SWA capable of pursuing an alternate course to Trotha's Vernichtungspolitik.

The missionaries were forced to spend a great deal of energy combating their new national reputation as traitors.[37] The largest source of their weakness as critics of military policy, however, was their dependence on government goodwill. Unlike Emily Hobhouse, who traveled to South Africa as a private person, the missionaries worked at the government's sufferance. The Rhenish Missionary Society had received the privilege of missionizing in SWA without competition from Roman Catholics, a privilege it fought to retain.[38] Nothing illustrates the missionaries' resulting paralysis better than the last example of gratuitous death that security mania dealt to the surviving Nama.

Oskar Hintrager had distinguished himself as deputy governor during the uprising by appropriating Trotha's extreme views on the colony's security. In March 1910, three years after the uprising had ended, three Nama prisoners serving criminal sentences in Karibib escaped. Deputy Governor Hintrager claimed that such escapes were "a constant, unpredictable danger for the security of the colony." The only solution was a final one—deportation. "I am urgently renewing my request for the deportation of all the Hottentots interned in Grootfontein to another colony. That is 120 in all, 42 of them men."[39] At least ninety-six Witbooi Nama were thereupon deported to the Cameroons, where the identical scenario of incarceration, poor treatment, and widespread death repeated itself.[40] By June, the Witboois had started to die. Although they received twice the meat and fish ration of native prisoners during the uprising (87 g per week), it was not enough for survival, especially since it was not supplemented with oil or fat. The lack of variety alone would have resulted in malnutrition. And, once again, no clothing or blankets seem to have been provided.[41] At the urging of military doctors and missionaries, Cameroon authorities improved conditions, but in the end, only thirty-seven Witboois survived their captivity.[42]

35. Bülow, 9 May 1904, *Sten. Ber.*, vol. 200, col. 2788.

36. Bülow letter to Rheinische Missionsgesellschaft, cited in "Aus Inland und Ausland," *Berliner Lokalanzeiger* 308 (4 July 1904), 1.

37. See VEM-Wuppertal, C/i 22, for their many documents of defense.

38. See correspondence in BA-Berlin, R 1001, Nr. 2140, pp. 20–39.

39. Hintrager to Col. Dept., Nr. 4669, "secret," 1 Mar. 1910, Windhuk, BA-Berlin, R 1001, Nr. 2090, p. 119.

40. J. Spiecker to Gov. Lindequist, Auszug, 26 June 1910, VEM-Wuppertal, C/i 17, says ninety-six Witboois were deported. Later government correspondence refers to ninety-three; director of Col. Office to Governor Seitz (SWA), 18 Mar. 1913, Berlin, BA-Berlin, R 1001, Nr. 2090, p. 178.

41. Chief staff doctor Ziemann, report of 21 June 1910, Duala, and chief doctor Friese, report of 30 June 1910, Duala, ibid., pp. 130–31.

42. That is a total death rate of 60%, or 24% per year. Colonial Office to Seitz, 18 Mar. 1913, Berlin, BA-Berlin, R 1001, Nr. 2090, p. 178.

190   The missionaries began an immediate campaign to free their parishioners. The director of the mission intervened with Colonial Secretary Lindequist in June 1910. "It surely cannot be the intention of the government and the Colonial Office to send these people to their certain deaths," he wrote, especially since no legal proceedings or charges seemed to have preceded the deportation.[43] But neither his intervention nor the request of the Cameroon government for repatriation persuaded SWA to relent. For Hintrager it was unthinkable "that humanitarian considerations relating to these few should make us forget the same considerations toward thousands of whites in the colony."[44] As long as SWA remained adamant, the Colonial Office bowed to its "political" reasons, though it expressed sympathy for the counterargument based on "pity and Christian charity."[45] Finally, at the end of 1912, the mission's director lost his patience and threatened to make a public scandal. This brought a sharp reply and counterthreat from the otherwise sympathetic colonial official Karl Heinrich Berner. The mission, he wrote, "must leave the decisive judgment to the government alone, in that it alone bears responsibility for the security of the colony." The mission would merely be accused "of intervening in a dangerous way in matters of state. That this would disturb the good understanding between the government and the mission not only in SWA but in Cameroon is obvious."[46]

Faced with this threat, the mission went behind closed doors to several Reichstag members, who raised the issue in session and petitioned the chancellor for repatriation in March 1913. This form of public pressure did indeed move the Colonial Office to overcome its timidity and override the opposition from SWA.[47] The thirty-seven survivors were finally returned. But the entire process had taken almost three years. Despite their fury, the missionaries dared not act swiftly or publicly, for fear of losing their colonial concession. And the security argument again and again trumped the humanitarian better judgment of the Colonial Office. Finally, anything that could be construed as a "matter of state" was, in principle, beyond the criticism of the public.

That the government responded to Reichstag pressure shows it was not deaf to public opinion. But public opinion was not necessarily a panacea against military extremism in any country. There were, for example, many voices in Britain favoring harsh and vengeful

43. J. Spiecker to Lindequist, excerpt, 26 June 1910, VEM-Wuppertal, C/i 17, p. 9. When Spiecker specifically asked the government to confirm that a court judgment lay behind the deportation, Berner replied that it had been a "judgment of the government." Berner's evasive reply suggests that the deportation was strictly an administrative, not a legal, measure. Berner to Spiecker, 13 Oct. 1912, Berlin, ibid., p. 42. An internal government document notes that only seven of the deportees were criminals: four were serving terms for cow theft, one for attempted rape, one for incitement, and one for disobedience and lying to his master. All the rest of the deportees were simply members of various Nama clans: Witbooi, Stürmann, and Jefta-Ortmann, "Nachweisung der nach Kamerun abtransportierten Eingeborenen," undated, but from 1910, BA-Berlin, R 1001, Nr. 2090, pp. 134–35.

44. Hintrager to Colonial Office, Nr. 211, 1 Feb. 1912, Windhuk, ibid., p. 141.

45. Berner to Spiecker, Berlin, 13 Oct. 1912, VEM-Wuppertal, C/i 17, p. 42.

46. Berner to Spiecker, 13 Nov. 1912, Berlin, ibid., pp. 43–44.

47. Secretary of Colonial Office to Gov. Seitz, 18 Mar. 1913, BA-Berlin, R 1001, Nr. 2090, pp. 178–79; MP Mumm to Spiecker, Berlin, 20 Nov. 1913, VEM-Wuppertal, C/i 17, p. 56, and Spiecker to Vielhauer, 24 June 1913, Barmen, ibid., p. 59.

military practices during the Boer War.[48] In Germany, as elsewhere, historians are forced to gauge public opinion before 1914 through newspapers, which method at least makes plain that a unified public opinion did not exist. Regarding the uprising in SWA, the shock of the revolt created a sense of national crisis that encouraged strong promilitary sentiment.[49] In Conservative, but especially in procolonial and National Liberal papers, calls for a politics of mass expropriation of Africans and punishment were common, but there were no calls for the outright extermination of the people.[50] Nonetheless, vituperative language and the loose use of "Vernichtung" (meaning destruction of military capacity, but not explicitly excluding mass civilian death) are characteristic of the early months of the uprising in these papers. Socialist, Left Liberal, and Roman Catholic publications represented a moderate or even critical point of view. Once Trotha's policy was clearly revealed, both in its extent and its expense to the colony and the taxpayer, public extremism virtually disappeared.[51]

Apart from the peculiar case of SWA, however, two general factors especially tended to pull public opinion in Germany after 1900 toward, rather than away from, extremism. The novelty of Germany's colonies and the tepid support for them before 1907 meant that the discourse of colonial security and warfare was monopolized by procolonial "experts" and agitation groups. They were the only ones who cared or knew anything about the new territories, and consequently their vocal activism filled the silence created by ignorance or antipathy. The colonists themselves, radicalized by the colonial experience and by fantasies of revenge and seemingly legitimized by practical knowledge and by suffering, pulled in the same direction. Therefore, colonial issues had an unusual potential to activate extremism.

More important, the government's constant search for popular legitimacy in lieu of more democratic processes condemned it to a kind of Caesarism in which it posed as the guarantor of the national enthusiasms of the "loyal" classes (especially of the various middling strata). The narrowly military monarchical state then struggled to keep up with nationalism as it was reinterpreted outside government in imperial, economically expansionist, and social Darwinist ways. The result was Weltpolitik, whose aggressive dynamic welded into a mutually reinforcing constellation the valorization of the nation, empire, military strength, social Darwinist struggle, and war. The process by which nationalism meant all these things simultaneously was a long one, stretching the length of the Wilhelminian period. The process was driven on the one hand by government and on the other by mostly bourgeois, postliberal agitators organized into cultural, colonial, anti-Se-

48. Spies, *Methods of Barbarism?* 171, 240, 272–73.

49. Bley, *Southwest Africa,* 156–57; Theodor Leutwein, *Elf Jahre,* 522; Paul Leutwein, *Afrikanerschicksal,* 150–51.

50. Bebel, 17 Mar. and 19 Mar. 1904, *Sten. Ber.,* vol. 199, cols. 1892, 1967; Stoecker, 17 Mar. 1904, ibid., col. 1904; Jahresbericht 1904 of Deutsche Kolonialgesellschaft Abteilung Berlin.

51. For example, "Die Hereros nach dem Kriege, Falsche Politik," *Berliner Tageblatt,* Nr. 75, 11 Feb. 1908, BA-Berlin, R 1001, Nr. 2119, p. 86; M. J. Bonn, "Die wissenschaftliche Begründung der Trotha'schen Eingeborenenpolitik," *Frankfurter Zeitung,* Nr. 45, 14 Feb. 1909, ibid., Nr. 2141, p. 6; Spraul, "'Völkermord,'" 724.

192 mitic, and promilitary groups. The government ultimately failed in its attempt to lead or master the new nationalism, though it left its unmistakable imprint in the almost paranoid military-security preoccupation and the glorification of war that became synonymous with prewar German nationalism. The foreign policy setbacks of 1905–1911 robbed the government of its leadership claim, which passed to the most extreme, vociferous, and therefore authentic-seeming proponents of the new nationalism, the Pan-Germans.[52] The failure of the government's foreign policy sowed among its growing public critics the same fear of weakness and concomitant worship of force that permeated military culture.[53] In the years just before World War I, extreme nationalists and the military drew palpably closer together, not just organizationally but, above all, ideologically.[54] The historian of the symbiotic relation between government and public opinion, Klaus Wernecke, concludes that the government was not the prisoner of public opinion so much as of the ideology of world prestige (*Weltgeltung*), which it had created in tandem with the agitation groups.[55] In any case, the new nationalism meant that public opinion was less and less a reliable brake on military extremism and more and more the opposite, a force pushing toward total, violent military solutions.[56]

The government's encouragement of imperial expansion, chauvinistic nationalism, and bellicose posturing was not a merely cynical tactic of mass manipulation. It reflected basic assumptions of the Reich leadership, which furthered the drift toward final solutions, even if that was not the conscious intention. Once again, the starting point was Germany's three-fold weakness: its putative internal disunity (the Socialist and Roman Catholic threats to the monarchy and the military); its exposed position between France and Russia; and above all, the gap between its power potential and that of Russia and Britain. In a perceptive study of the assumptions behind Imperial German foreign policy, Jost Dülffer has analyzed how the Kaiser, his chancellors, and high Foreign Office officials managed their fear of Germany's weakness. Their pervasive sense of national insecurity caused them to imagine a bellicose, lawless world of state jackals bent on destroying one another. Thus, the Kaiser interpreted the Russian invitation to the First Hague Conference on disarmament as being "directed more or less against our military development, which Russia wants to stop in order to freeze us in the subordinate, inferior position relative to itself."[57] The suspicion that international agreements were always aimed at keeping Germany weak determined Germany's frequent obstructionism and, in Dülffer's words, "led to the tendency to seal itself against the outside world and to blindness about the realities of the international system."[58] Subjectively defensive, but in effect aggressive, isolation was justified in Hegelian terms as absolute state sovereignty. As the chief advisor in

---

52. Förster, *Der doppelte Militarismus*, 208–16; Chickering, *We Men*, 197.

53. Chickering, *We Men*, 96, 122–23.

54. Marilyn Shevin Coetzee, *The German Army League* (Oxford, 1990); Förster, *Der doppelte Militarismus*, 227; Rohrkrämer, *Der Militarismus der "kleinen Leute,"* 201, 245, 254–60; Chickering, *We Men*, 268–90; Klaus Wernecke, *Der Wille zur Weltgeltung* (Düsseldorf, 1970), 302–8.

55. Wernecke, *Der Wille zur Weltgeltung*, 312–13.

56. Smith, "Talk of Genocide."

57. Cited in Dülffer, *Regeln gegen den Krieg*, 109.

58. Ibid., 114.

the Foreign Office, Friedrich von Holstein, wrote in his draft instructions to German delegates to the first Hague Conference, "The state has no higher purpose than preserving *its* own interests. Among great powers the latter will not necessarily be identical with upholding peace, but more likely with the rape [*Vergewaltigung*] of the enemy and competitors."[59] One of those delegates, Philipp Zorn, later (1915) protested this point of view:

> Certainly every state, and especially every Great Power, must think in the first instance of its own interests. But if one first gets used to the idea of not suspecting in every suggestion made by another state a priori a trap or intrigue against oneself, if one with earnest and goodwill regards an understanding about differences of opinion as the primary goal . . . then one . . . will recognize more and more that the unity of [international state] interests is much greater than one usually supposes.[60]

Zorn's views were in the decided minority. Instead, the conviction of universal danger and threat logically moved the Reich leadership to greater and greater reliance on military force rather than on international or even bilateral agreement, or on normal diplomacy. The fear–force dynamic encouraged the view that war was inevitable, and from there it was a short step to risking war at a seemingly opportune moment. The Reich leadership's basic assumptions about power and politics favored military force and were therefore inappropriate instruments to limit or confine the potential of military culture to develop extreme solutions.

Learning from Mistakes

Both the Boer War and the war in SWA were recognized at the time to have been disastrously conducted. Perhaps the greatest difference between how Britain and Germany handled their respective disasters lies in who was permitted to criticize. The British army and government permitted outsiders, civilians, to gather evidence, judge, and recommend reform of military practices and institutions. The most remarkable example is the Ladies' Commission, which was created by the secretary of war and which inspected and reported while the war was still going on. Such a commission was simply inconceivable in Germany. Civilian oversight contravened the monarchical principle that regarded the hermetically sealed military as its guarantor and bulwark. Every constitutional and institutional safeguard had been taken to thwart civilian prying into military affairs. Furthermore, the conduct of a war in progress was held to be the business of military experts alone—chancellors had difficulty enough insinuating themselves into the process, much less civilians outside government. If civilians were already impossible, then women inspectors were preposterous. Whatever expertise they might have brought to a situation was closed to the German military from the start.

---

59. Holstein cited in Dülffer, ibid., 124, emphasis in original.
60. Zorn, *Die beiden Haager Friedenskonferenzen*, 78.

194   Once the war was over, the British government continued to believe that military reform was too important to be left to the military. Following recommendations contained
in the report (1903) of Reginald Baliol, Viscount Esher, the government reorganized the
War Office, created the Defence Committee, and streamlined command at the highest
levels of administration. In addition, a commission headed by Victor Alexander, Earl of
Elgin and Kincardine, and Viscount Esher heard 144 witnesses over fifty-five days detail
deficiencies in army administration. The resulting Elgin Report (1904) criticized conditions from top to bottom: it began with the niggardly military outlays by the cabinet,
moved on to note systematic deficiencies in actual fighting and incompetence among senior and inexperienced staff officers, and moved in detail to consider ineffective armaments and inadequate clothing, medical care, handling of horses, and transport.[61] Neither
report considered the conduct of war in the largest sense, that is, the blockhouses, laying
waste, or the internment camps. The last two issues, of course, had already been the objects of official investigation, internment camps by the Ladies' Commission, and laying
waste and other controversial tactics by the Colonial Office during the war. Chamberlain
had ordered harsh tactics to be examined from two perspectives: "What can be done
without violating international law and usage?" and "Will any action proposed help to
end the war?" The results were designed to guide Britain in future wars.[62] The Boer War
disaster thus produced officially sanctioned criticism, much of it from civilians, which re-
formed the military-governmental structure and vastly improved Britain's capacity to
wage land warfare.[63]

    The contrast with Germany is striking. In November 1908 the Kaiser called a commis-
sion to examine the SWA experience. It consisted of officers only, headed by Major General and Chief Quartermaster Erich von Gündell. The commission met thirty-five times;
it collected information by circulating a questionnaire and then an interim report for criticism. It produced two final reports, one for internal consumption and a shorter one for
the Kaiser.[64] Both reports were much narrower in scope than what Britain produced. Proceeding from the assumption that colonial warfare was fundamentally different from European warfare, the investigation was limited to problems arising from colonial revolts.
No lessons were applied to the regular army. The reports contained only one suggestion
for administrative reorganization: the creation of a permanent unit to respond to colonial
rebellions. Because the navy would not permit the marine infantry to do this, the Prussian
war minister agreed to train a brigade for this purpose. The reports also made two quasi-
political recommendations. One was to "strengthen the military element in the adminis-

    61. Great Britain, Parliament, *Report of His Majesty's Commissioners.*
    62. Spies, *Methods of Barbarism?* 270–72.
    63. Jay Stone and Erwin Schmidl, *The Boer War and Military Reforms* (Lanham, Md., 1988).
    64. "Überblick über die bei der Entsendung von Verstärkungen für die Schutztruppe in Südwest-Afrika
gesammelten Erfahrungen und die in den Kommissionsberatungen zu erörternden Fragen," 1 Nov. 1908, MA-
Freiburg, RW 51, vol. 18; "Ergebnis der Arbeiten der durch AKO vom 14.11.1908 berufenen Kommission zur Beratung aufgrund der bei der Entsendung von Verstärkungen für die Schutztruppen in SWA gesammelten Erfahrungen," 1908, ibid., vol. 19; and Kommission zur Bewertung der bei der Entsendung von Verstärkungen für
die Schutztruppen in Südwest-Afrika gesammelten Erfahrungen, Bericht des Gen.-Majors und Quartiermeisters
v. Gündell an Seine Majestät Kaiser Wilhelm II, copy, 28 Mar. 1909, MA-Freiburg, Nl. Lequis, Nr. 59.

tration of the Schutztruppe" by removing disciplinary authority over soldiers from the chancellor and/or governor and investing it in the military commander.[65] The purpose was to ease the integration of reinforcements from the regular army into the Schutztruppe command structure by eliminating the unacceptable possibility that a civilian official could punish soldiers. The second political recommendation was to allow commanders to negotiate with rebels. This would have removed Trotha's excuse for not doing so (namely, having to wait for authorization from Berlin), but it would not have checked the pursuit of extreme goals, nor was it designed to do so. The rest of the recommendations addressed specific problems. The reports advised expanding the administration of the rear and improving medical care. To combat scurvy and malnutrition, they suggested raising the amount of sugar and fruit preserves, including flour in the vegetable ration, and eliminating tobacco and alcohol altogether.

The most interesting aspect of the official investigation into SWA is what disappeared from the final report. The interim report contained a thirteen-page section on "conduct of the war" (*Kriegführung*). Significantly, Vernichtungspolitik was absent; apparently that subject was too sensitive to discuss. Indeed, the report disclaimed responsibility for the "great success" of the pursuit, saying that occurred "because the foe voluntarily retreated to the waterless territory, which destroyed both him and his cattle."[66] Colonel Estorff corrected this prevarication in the margin: "The intentional flight of the Herero down the riverbed from Waterberg," he noted, "would have permitted a retreat without very great losses. That retreat was redirected on orders from headquarters by a strenuous march of the Estorff unit and by its battle on 15 August. Thereafter, they [the Herero] wandered into the desert."[67] This colloquy is yet another indication that Trotha's logical extremism was not consciously accepted by the military institution whose practices led to it.

If Vernichtungspolitik remained off limits for investigative criticism, the failure of the concentric battle of Waterberg did not. The interim report rejected concentric battles of annihilation as almost impossible to achieve in the colonial theater, and it acknowledged the almost equal difficulty of mounting a successful pursuit. Failing both, a "more defensive" tactic was required, such as holding all waterholes, removing all cattle from the land, and/or sealing the borders so that the rebels could not import ammunition or food.[68] These suggestions are noteworthy for two reasons. The admission that a defensive tactic was preferable to the offensive was daring in an atmosphere where praise of the offensive was so hegemonic. François's assessment of the Boer War was about as far as even knowledgeable German colonial fighters would usually go: "We must resort to the defensive only as a makeshift, always bearing in mind that the defense is only half, if it renounces attack."[69] Challenging this doctrine exhausted the report writers' boldness, however, for in fact their suggestions to hold *all* waterholes, remove *all* cattle, or seal the *entire* border were still versions of a total vision of control. Again, Estorff's marginalium jerked them

65. "Ergebnis der Arbeiten," 5.
66. "Überblick," 127.
67. Ibid.
68. Ibid.
69. François, *Lehren aus dem Südafrikanischen Krieg*, 57.

196   back to reality. "This will never lead to the goal," he wrote. "If you cannot force the foe energetically and pursue him, then you must end the war politically like the English frequently have done."[70] In a way, the final report indirectly acknowledged Estorff's point by asking that commanders receive the right to negotiate with rebels. Still, the commission was unable to enunciate directly the principle that political solutions might be preferable to military ones. Instead, it was constantly tempted to dream up total, technical solutions to the problems it faced.

The final report omitted the section on conduct of war altogether. The only remaining residue was the recommendation concerning negotiation. Passing over actual conduct of fighting in silence, and thus tacitly leaving doctrine and practices intact, the report presented the key to victory as extensive prewar preparation. The interim report had already reached the same conclusion: "Everything . . . can be organized in peacetime, from mobilization, provisioning, weapons, munitions, medical, etc. depots distributed according to the peculiarities of the colony, down to the mobilization designation of the last oxcart." To this end, the commission called for "complete, understanding cooperation between military and civil authorities."[71] More than this, the military wanted the infrastructure of the colonies, especially the railroads, laid out for military purposes, and even offered to build them itself.[72] These suggestions subordinated the civil and economic development of the colonies to military considerations. They turned on its head the principle that the military serves and protects society. Mobilization mania was, of course, partly a reflection of the technical-mechanical obsession worked out to such perfection in the Schlieffen Plan. But these suggestions for the colonies went further, since they proposed to shape at least partly the very development of civil institutions.

Apart from technical adjustments, the military assimilated the debacle in SWA with no changes to its doctrines or customary practices. Without the necessity of explaining shortcomings to outsiders, without a fresh critical perspective, the military's basic assumptions remained insulated from empirical testing. Germany's military culture remained unchallenged. The army therefore entered World War I with its patterns of doctrine and practice intact.

70. "Überblick," 127.
71. "Überblick," 134; "Ergebnis der Arbeiten," 86.
72. "Überblick," 135; "Ergebnis der Arbeiten," 87, called for the building of railroads, but omitted the offer to have the military do so.

PART III

THE FIRST WORLD WAR

World War I presented the German army and its military culture with their greatest opportunity and greatest crisis. The civil-military split that had allowed military culture to reinforce itself now also set the parameters of war conduct. In the near absence of political oversight and coordination, and locked into endless combat by reciprocal Allied intransigence that matched its own, the German army waged a hopeless war in pursuit of a pure, military victory of annihilation, unleashing instead the destructive micro-logics implicit in its military culture. Gratuitous violence multiplied, consuming soldiers and civilians alike, to the very brink of Germany's own self-destruction.

In part 3 we shall analyze that process. I do not offer (yet another) narrative of the war. Instead, I identify those events, decisions, or actions in which the workings of military culture seem to have been especially determining. The purpose is to demonstrate, as briefly as possible, patterns that the reader will already recognize, even as they are taken to extremes.

As in part 2, we begin with the political-strategic vacuum that military-cultural practices filled. In this section we ask whether the Kaiserreich was coherent enough to have war aims that actually guided war conduct, or whether its very incoherence opened the door for the spiraling habits of pure force. We must also grapple with the widespread view that the war became radicalized because of its length, a process that would happen in any war and to any belligerent(s). There is some truth to this observation, especially on the home front. The German variant of this view claims that radicalization occurred first under Hindenburg and Ludendorff, after August 1916. That is why chapter 9 examines the pattern of extremes in war operations before then: in the "Belgian atrocities" of 1914 and in operations under the leadership of Chief of Staff Erich von Falkenhayn from September 1914 to August 1916. We shall see that even Falkenhayn, who tried to escape the compulsions of military culture, nonetheless fell victim to them.

The occupied territories give us the opportunity to test whether European warfare offered significantly greater protections to enemy civilians than colonial warfare did to Africans or Chinese. As we explore the kinds of instrumentalization civilians suffered and the limits to them, we must also ask whether eastern Europeans were treated worse than western Europeans. Did the occupation in the east run along more ideological lines (which prepared the ground for the policies of the Third Reich, as one recent work has suggested)? The occupation of northern France will be of special interest for this reason. Finally, in chapter 11 the German response to the Armenian genocide provides the most stunning example of how unlimited the use of "military necessity" regarding noncombatants had become as early as 1915.

The final chapter returns to operations and to the period of generally acknowledged radicalization under Ludendorff and Hindenburg. The virtual collapse of civilian government in this period permitted them to override limits (political, legal, and economic) to which Falkenhayn had reluctantly submitted. The logic of limitless violence now proliferated in the Belgian deportations, the Hindenburg program, unrestricted submarine warfare, and the destruction of northern France in 1917. The apogee of pure, violent means was reached in the decision to seek a military victory (Siegfrieden) by a last, all-or-nothing offensive in March 1918. When this final reprise of military-cultural precepts failed, the Supreme Command, unable to learn from defeat or to relinquish the chimera of military victory, repeated the tactic over and over until Germany was so weakened that the Allies could begin the final attacks of the war in the summer and fall of 1918. Now, in the ultimate display of violent solipsism, the military leaders, denying defeat, called for Germany to lay waste to occupied western Europe and risk destroying itself in a hopeless Endkampf *(final battle) inside Germany.*

9

Waging War, 1914–1916

Risk, Extremes, and Limits

Strategic Vacuum

Germany's conduct in the First World War is often explained as the result of policy. Its goal of continental hegemony and world (not just European) power status unleashed a bitter war of unfettered imperialism, which took on the characteristics of wars of "pacification" in the occupied zones.[1] This interpretation has the merit of simplicity. It explains Germany's expansionist war aims—the frankly imperialist peace treaties Germany forced on Russia (Brest-Litovsk) and Romania (Bucharest), and its tenacious grip on Belgium and Longwy-Briey in Lorraine, which made a negotiated settlement impossible. It explains the remarkable agreement among civilian government leaders, important interest groups (owners of heavy industries, Prussian agrarians), bourgeois ideologues (Pan-Germans, patriotic professors, and pundits), the third Supreme Command (OHL) under Ludendorff and Hindenburg, and the navy on winning a pure victory of force regardless of sacrifices. It is logical to assume that war conduct this repetitively destructive to self and others should have followed from policy, as it is logical to assume that Lothar v. Trotha's order for genocide should have preceded its realization in practice. But Germany's prosecution of World War I was much more like its bungled efforts in SWA than conventional logic recognizes. For the same radical split between the military and the political spheres that produced Germany's peculiar military culture made policy in the sense of coordinated strategy impossible. The absence of policy created a vacuum that the standard

---

1. Fritz Fischer, *Germany's Aims in the First World War* (New York, 1967); Fritz Fischer, *World Power or Decline* (New York, 1974); Fritz Klein, ed., *Deutschland im Ersten Weltkrieg*, 3 vols. (Berlin, 1968–69). On "pacification": Trutz von Trotha, " 'The Fellows Can Just Starve' "; and Trutz von Trotha, *Koloniale Herrschaft* (Tübingen, 1994), 37–44.

operating procedures and assumptions of the military filled; they then developed further according to their own narrow logic inside the vortex of a long war that nobody had foreseen.

Chancellor Theobald v. Bethmann Hollweg had risked war in July 1914 hoping that either Russia would back down and lose credibility as a Great Power, or that Britain and/or France would decline to support their partner during the latest Balkan crisis.[2] Either way, the Entente would dissolve, freeing Germany from its "encirclement" and greatly increasing its relative power, since it could henceforth weigh in against each of the former partners separately, instead of facing their combined strength. This was world power on the cheap. It opened pleasing vistas of continental economic expansion that would lead—who knew exactly how?—to that Wilhelminian place in the sun. But neither Bethmann's risk in 1914 nor Germany's Weltpolitik of the preceding two decades had been framed in accord with military planning or with Germany's actual strength. Germany, a continental power lacking Britain's enormous financial resources, had prematurely challenged the world's greatest naval power while possessing neither a finished (nor experienced) navy of its own, nor the economic basis to win a naval race without allies. Bethmann saw these limits to the naval gamble and shifted German priorities to the Continent.[3] Despite increased military spending just before the war, however, the armies of Germany and its ally, Austria-Hungary, were smaller than those of France and Russia, and inadequate even for the demands of Germany's only war plan, the Schlieffen Plan.[4] Although Bethmann, like Bülow before him, was aware of the Schlieffen Plan, he conducted foreign policy in 1914 without regard to it and without consulting military or naval leaders, just as the General Staff and the navy had developed their war plans without consulting the chancellors or even each other.

When the Entente powers refused to behave as Bethmann had hoped, genuine military danger developed and the chancellor in late July lost control of policy to the military experts in the General Staff. Their calculations were not political but military, and their decisions and requirements precipitated the world war.[5] Thus it happened that Germany entered war without war aims. The military's goal was complete military victory. Until 1916, the General Staff had few or no territorial aims.[6] Thereafter, the second OHL, under Erich v. Falkenhayn (modestly), and the third OHL (grandiosely) championed annexations. Falkenhayn advocated keeping control over Belgium "for military reasons," that is, to prevent Belgium from becoming an enemy staging point in a future war. Ludendorff and Hindenburg began their annexationism with similar military worries, arguing that a border strip detached from Russian Poland would prevent Russian armies from penetrating East Prussia as they had in 1914. But they soon developed fantastically broad territorial ambitions stretching from Antwerp and northern France to the Ukraine. These aims were

2. Among the huge literature on war origins, see especially Imanuel Geiss, ed., *July 1914: The Outbreak of the First World War* (New York, 1968); John W. Langdon, *July 1914: The Long Debate, 1918–1990* (New York, 1991); Luigi Albertini, *The Origins of the War of 1914*, ed. and trans. Isabella Massey, 3 vols. (Oxford, 1952–57); R.J.W. Evans and Hartmut Pogge von Strandmann, ed., *The Coming of the First World War* (Oxford, 1988); and H.W. Koch, *The Origins of the First World War* (London, 1984).

3. Volker R. Berghahn, *Germany and the Approach of War in 1914*, 2nd ed. (New York, 1993).

4. Holger Afflerbach, "'Bis zum letzten Mann und letzten Groschen?'" 90.

5. Geiss, *July 1914*.

6. Hans W. Gatzke, *Germany's Drive to the West* (Baltimore, 1966), 10–11.

largely derivative, however; Ludendorff and Hindenburg had taken them from Pan-Germans, leaders of heavy industry, and Prussian agrarians who had developed them after the war had already begun, after Germany's early, heady victories in the west in 1914 and in the east the following year. In his memoirs Ludendorff insisted that the Supreme Command had not fought to achieve specific territorial goals.[7] Ludendorff lied about many things, but careful scrutiny of his and Hindenburg's actions in 1917 and 1918 bears out his disclaimer.[8] Ludendorff used annexationism as a *means* to achieve military victory, not the reverse. After years of war, heavy losses, and hunger and dissatisfaction at home, Ludendorff believed (wrongly) that only the prospect of huge gains would keep the troops fighting and the home front loyal. Ludendorff clung to annexation as the material and military-strategic foundation for the inevitable next war. More than anything else, Ludendorff, together with most officers and many civilians, saw territorial expansion as a *sign* of military victory. Renouncing annexations meant admitting defeat, admitting that Germany could not force its enemies to its will. This is the reason Ludendorff and Hindenburg clung to absurd territorial gains even as they were negotiating the armistice. And it is why the call for annexations expanded with Germany's military successes—no specific content defined the achievement of victory.

For his part, Bethmann never committed himself to specific war aims. He drew up the (objectively immoderate) September 1914 program in order to limit the even more fantastic aims the Pan-Germans and some Reichstag members were publicizing.[9] But he kept it secret. Bethmann's sibylline public statements on war aims continued his prewar "policy of the diagonals," an attempt to patch over domestic differences by shifting compromises that robbed his government of coherence. Bethmann would have been pleased to preside over annexations, but what they would be depended entirely on Germany's military situation. "Never during the entire war did I present to the Supreme Command a general war aims program whose achievement would have determined how long we had to fight," Bethmann told his successor, Georg von Hertling, in 1917. Instead, he proposed waiting for peace negotiations, during which Germany "would get what the military-political situation would permit and which Germany felt was useful."[10] The meaning of Bethmann's (in)action for the military becomes clearer in an off-the-cuff remark he made in 1917 to

7. Erich Ludendorff, *Kriegführung und Politik* (Berlin, 1922), 250, paraphrased in Gen. Hermann Kuhl's report, in Germany, Parliament, *Das Werk des Untersuchungsausschusses der Verfassunggebenden Deutschen Nationalversammlung und des Deutschen Reichstages 1919–1928, Verhandlungen, Gutachten, Urkunden*, Reihe 4: vol. 3, *Die Ursachen des deutschen Zusammenbruchs im Jahre 1918*, Erste Abteilung: *Der militärische und aussenpolitische Zusammenbruch.* ed. Eugen Fischer, Walther Block, and Albrecht Philipp (Berlin, 1928), 226 (hereafter *UA* Reihe: volume, page).

8. Peter Graf Kielmansegg, *Deutschland und der Erste Weltkrieg* (Frankfurt am Main, 1968), 305–6; Schwertfeger Gutachten, in *UA* 4:2, 102–6; Germany, Reichsarchiv, *Der Weltkrieg 1914 bis 1918*, 14 vols. (Berlin, 1943), 14:3–4 (hereafter Reichsarchiv, *Weltkrieg*).

9. Fischer, *Germany's Aims*, 103–5.

10. Bethmann to Hertling, 26 Jan. 1918, Hohenfinow, cited in *UA* 4:2, 143; also Bethmann's testimony before the Reichstag, 31 Oct. 1919, in Germany, National Constituent Assembly, *Official German Documents Relating to the World War*, trans. Division of International Law, Carnegie Endowment for International Peace, vol. 1 (New York, 1923), 339; and Theobald von Bethmann Hollweg, *Betrachtungen zum Weltkriege*, vol. 2: *Während des Krieges* (Berlin, 1922), 153.

202   Gen. Hans von Boehn, who asked the chancellor what his war aims were: "I'll wait and see how big the Supreme Command wins; when they're out of ideas, then *I* must intervene and make peace!"[11] The chancellor thus explicitly left the military in charge of both conducting the war and determining when it was won or lost.

War aims ought to have been overall policy, uniting political, economic, and military considerations into strategy, but instead of guiding military practices, policy was contingent on them. Germany had no strategic plan. The constitutional split between politics and the military, Germany's political "curse" as Bethmann called it, prevented strategic planning.[12] The constitution vested sole responsibility for coordinating policy in the Kaiser; no institution, such as a cabinet, aided him. Unequal to this huge task, the Kaiser withdrew into passivity, except on the rare occasions when the chief of staff or chancellor specifically sought his intervention.[13] Contemporaries commonly blamed Wilhelm and the wartime chancellors for personal failure, but only the rare genius could fairly have been expected to overcome the constitutional hurdles to effective policy making.[14]

Germany's bifurcated institutions had had serious effects on the country's political culture. The split encouraged chancellors to stick to their own bailiwick; through the years the military sphere, as part of the Kaiser's power of command (*Kommandogewalt*), became taboo.[15] The war further inflated the prestige of the soldier-experts. The Austrian representative to supreme headquarters noted that civilian leaders "seemed to feel ill at ease and constrained" in the military atmosphere.[16] Civilian leaders took to disguising themselves as soldiers: most wore their (reserve) uniforms when they visited supreme headquarters, and Bethmann gave all of his wartime speeches to the Reichstag in uniform.[17] But none felt competent to judge military matters. "It was simply impossible for a military layman to presume to judge military possibilities, much less military necessities," Bethmann explained later. "But military necessities were precisely what seemed to me to have guided military conduct. Even the most brilliant initiatives that the General Staff undertook were done from military necessity. How to respond to that necessity was some-

11. Recounted in Albrecht von Thaer, *Generalstabsdienst an der Front und in der OHL*, Abhandlungen der Akademie der Wissenschaften in Göttingen, philologisch-historische Klasse, Dritte Folge, Nr. 40, ed. Siegfried Kaehler (Göttingen, 1958), diary entry of 30 June 1918, 212, and in slightly different words, 241.

12. Bethmann: Germany, National Constituent Assembly, *Official German Documents*, 1:348. The best modern analysis of Germany's strategic planlessness is Deist, "Strategy and Unlimited Warfare," 265–79; and his superb analyses in Deist, *Militär, Staat und Gesellschaft*, in his article in *Anticipating Total War,* ed. Boemeke et al., and in his edited volume, *Militär und Innenpolitik im Weltkrieg, 1914–1918* (Düsseldorf, 1970). See also Gerhard Ritter's classic account in *Sword and the Scepter,* vol. 3, and Karl-Dietrich Erdmann, *Der Erste Weltkrieg,* 5th ed. (Munich, 1985), 65.

13. The Kaiser's decisions tended toward the moderate alternative, especially from 1914 to 1917, which angered extremists. See Hull, "Military Culture," 237.

14. Typical for the contemporary view: Schwertfeger's report, 88, 169–76; Alfred Niemann, *Kaiser und Heer* (Berlin, 1929), 60–62; and Eisenhart-Rothe, *Im Banne der Persönlichkeit,* 175–93.

15. Deist, "Voraussetzungen innenpolitischen Handelns des Militärs im Ersten Weltkrieg," in *Militär, Staat und Gesellschaft,* 115–17; Karl-Heinz Janssen believes that Bethmann was slightly more assertive: *Der Kanzler und der General* (Göttingen, 1967), 207.

16. Josef Stürgkh, *Im deutschen grossen Hauptquartier* (Leipzig, 1921), 26.

17. Friedrich v. Payer, *Von Bethmann Hollweg bis Ebert* (Frankfurt, 1923), 67, 121.

thing only the military could decide, including in areas where military and political demands went hand in hand."[18]

The self-abnegation of the civilians and the imperious self-assurance of the military experts caused the information flow between them to wither, despite the existence of regular briefings and competent mutual representatives in both camps.[19] Falkenhayn kept Bethmann as ignorant of operations as Bethmann kept Falkenhayn of diplomatic initiatives.[20] They never worked together, which is why Falkenhayn's at least incipient strategic views were never transformed into actual policy. Bethmann never took advantage of the only chief of staff who had a realistic view of Germany's limited options.[21] Ludendorff and Hindenburg replaced Falkenhayn in August 1916, and together (with the help of the Reichstag) they pushed out Bethmann in July 1917; with each step, the information flow between civilians and the military became worse. In September 1918 Chancellor Hertling was unable to tell the Bundesrat (which a Reichstag vote in August 1914 had charged with overseeing the prosecution of the war on the homefront) how long Germany could continue to fight, because, in the interests of secrecy, he "conscientiously avoided becoming informed about military details."[22] The nadir of civil-military relations came in 1918, as military leaders hid the coming defeat from others and, above all, from themselves. But— except for a brief moment in November 1914, which we will examine—at no time during the war was the civilian leadership well informed about the military situation. The Reichstag, dependent mostly on official press reports, was even more in the dark.

Civilian leaders were thus in no position to force the military to engage in strategic thinking, nor to engage in it themselves. Instead, one finds among civilian ministries widespread mimicry of military attitudes and ways of defining and handling problems. Like Deputy Governor Tecklenburg in SWA, many officials were apparently convinced that the exceptional situation of war required the suspension of civilian procedures and the adoption of the professional habitus of the military experts. Once again they were encouraged in this supposition by German law. The state of siege law, in effect since 31 July 1914, subordinated the entire civilian administration to the oversight of the military— specifically, to the commanding general of each military district. Only the Kaiser had the authority to reverse their decisions.

Yet wartime Germany was not a military dictatorship in the conventional sense, even under Ludendorff and Hindenburg.[23] None of the chiefs of staff aspired to total power, and dozens of mediate sources of power (or at least friction) continued to exist throughout the war. Military leaders remained narrowly focused on what they took to be their duty: fighting the war to military victory.

Furthermore, the military establishment was no better coordinated than the govern-

18. Bethmann, *Betrachtungen*, 9.

19. Schwertfeger's report, *UA* 4:2, 330.

20. Afflerbach, *Falkenhayn*, 244–45, 253.

21. Ibid., 453.

22. Prince Max von Baden, *Erinnerungen und Dokumente* (Stuttgart, 1927), 303.

23. Kitchen disagrees, but see his definition and concluding discussion: Martin Kitchen, *The Silent Dictatorship* (London, 1976), 22, 274–77.

204   ment as a whole. The Kaiser held sole responsibility here, too, and was if anything even less active in exercising it. Inside Germany, at least sixty-two deputy army commanders (of army districts or fortresses), each reporting directly to the Kaiser, exercised authority in his own district. These *Militärbefehlhaber* operated independently, often beyond the knowledge and always beyond the control of either the chief of the General Staff or the chancellor.[24] The deputy army commanders became lawmakers in their separate districts, thus preventing Germany from developing a uniform and effective food policy, for example.[25] "Instead of order, [they create] a whir of orders, resulting in disorder!" Crown Prince Rupprecht complained.[26] After May 1916 the Prussian war minister gained some control over the deputy military commanders, but balkanization remained the guiding principle.[27]

Partly to protect the Kaiser's command power from civilian oversight, and partly through sheer bureaucratic proliferation, Germany's military disorganization had grown worse between 1870 and 1914.[28] The war encouraged even further fissiparousness. It brought new areas of control, the occupied zones, which were, variously, under a military governor-general or, when they were close to the front lines, under the commander of the local army, or, in the east, under "Ober-Ost," the Supreme Command in the east under Ludendorff and Hindenburg. Occupation policy remained typically uncoordinated. War-caused scarcity made matters worse by encouraging competition for scarce resources, rather than cooperation among the various military fiefdoms.

The war automatically elevated the chief of the General Staff from a mere planner to de facto supreme commander who issued orders in the Kaiser's name. His focus on operations was quite different from that of the war minister, whose purview was resources, manpower, and, increasingly, the entire economic and financial basis of the war effort. Under Falkenhayn (September 1914 through August 1916) relations between the General Staff and the war ministry were smooth, but the potential for conflict always existed. Beneath the chief of the General Staff were General Staff officers posted to all major units of the field army from army groups on down. They were junior in rank to the commanders, yet they were charged with planning operations and making sure that General Staff thinking permeated practice. Not surprisingly, there was recurrent friction between them and the titular commanders, who bore final responsibility for orders.

If army subdivisions were not well coordinated, the army and navy were positively remote. The 1914 army and navy war plans had taken absolutely no notice of each other. Britain and France entered the war with better coordination among themselves than Germany had achieved within its own services. "Ministerial particularism" (*Ressortpartiku-*

24. Wilhelm Deist, "Zur Institution des Militärbefehlshabers und Obermilitärbefehlshabers im Ersten Weltkrieg," *Jahrbuch der Geschichte Mittel- und Osteuropas* 13–14 (1965): 228.

25. Lothar Dessauer, *Der Militärbefehlshaber und seine Verordnungsgewalt in der Praxis der Weltkrieges* (Berlin, 1918), 27–34; Deist, "Voraussetzungen," 127–37; Roger Chickering, *Imperial Germany and the Great War, 1914–1918* (Cambridge, 1998), 44–45.

26. Rupprecht Kronprinz v. Bayern, *Mein Kriegstagebuch*, diary entry of 5 May 1916, 1:457.

27. Deist, "Voraussetzungen," 133; Groener, *Lebenserinnerungen*, 353.

28. Deist, "Voraussetzungen," 112–13.

larismus), that hallmark of Wilhelminian government, did not weaken after 1914, and it affected the military as well as the civilian administration. Each service remained profoundly ignorant of the other. The following exchange occurred between Chief of the General Staff Falkenhayn and Navy Captain Widenmann in February 1916, during a proposed reorganization of the navy:

> Falkenhayn: "Then it appears the chief of the Admiralty is actually superfluous? Doesn't he have the power of military decision?"
> Widenmann: "No, he just reports to His Majesty about the division of resources among the various theaters of war."
> Falkenhayn: "So, it's not the same as my job?"
> Widenmann: "Not as far as I can judge."[29]

Mutual ignorance meant that naval and army officers deferred uncritically to each other's expertise. Even quite fantastic assertions (about how quickly a handful of submarines could defeat Britain, or how long the army in the west could hold out) tended to be gullibly accepted by the other service, especially when they confirmed what it wanted to hear. There was no critical feedback here.

Lack of coordination between military and political leaders and within the military itself meant that Germany never achieved the "total war" that Ludendorff later claimed as the ideal type of modern warfare and that many historians use to judge the Great War. "Total war" in this usage means the complete mobilization of civilians, of civil society, and especially of the economy for the war effort. A recent, three-volume comparative study of total war and its antecedents concluded that World War I was a major stage in the process of totalization but that it stopped short of its complete development. Roger Chickering, one of the editors and main contributors to the project, identified the dynamics leading toward totality primarily in nonmilitary sectors: "demographic growth, technological innovation, industrial integration, social conflict, the redefinition of political society, the expansion of public power, and the heightening of diplomatic tension, to say nothing of technological and organizational changes within the narrower realm suggested by the term 'military history.' "[30] In this widespread view, these dynamics were loosed by the war itself. They "emerged suddenly, by improvisation, and without a shred of foresight,"[31] gathering momentum especially after 1916.[32] Therefore, in the words of the

29. Alfred von Tirpitz, *Politische Dokumente* (Hamburg, 1926), 476.

30. Roger Chickering, "Total War: The Use and Abuse of a Concept," in *Anticipating Total War*, ed. Boemeke et al., 13–28, here 27. The other two volumes in the series are Stig Förster and Jörg Nagler, ed., *On the Road to Total War* (New York, 1997), and Roger Chickering and Stig Förster, ed., *Great War, Total War* (Cambridge, 2000).

31. Roger Chickering, "World War I and the Theory of Total War," in *Great War, Total War*, ed. Chickering and Förster, 37.

32. John Horne, "Introduction: Mobilizing for 'Total War' 1914–1918," in *State, Society, and Mobilization in Europe during the First World War*, ed. Horne (Cambridge, 1997), 1–18.

206   historian Stig Förster, "No direct line led from the combat of the 1860s and 1870s to total war."[33]

Yet, in the German case, the continuities in military practices, doctrines, and micrologics, and their steadfast tendency to go to extremes, are astonishing. Perhaps the vantage point of total war obscures our view of this phenomenon by its focus on the nonmilitary. Wilhelm Deist has suggested "total combat" as more descriptive of the extremes that military conduct of the war produced.[34] But this phrase does not do justice to the enormous effects that military priorities had on civilians, especially in the occupied zones.

The continuities in German military practices resulted from the policy void and from Germany's strategic situation. The structural and institutional barriers to strategic planning meant that military viewpoints were not coordinated with or subordinated to political-economic-legal calculations but were free to develop according to their own unexamined internal logic. The new challenges posed by the war (the unprecedented expenditure of munitions, huge loss of life, and then the war's duration and extent) meant that no expert in any field had an obvious policy remedy. In wartime, military expertise seemed most apposite. But no degree of military expertise could have overcome Germany's strategic deficits. It and its weak ally Austria-Hungary faced a coalition vastly superior demographically and economically (even before the United States entered the war in April 1917) and which could effectively cut off food and raw materials on which the landlocked Central Powers depended. The longer the war continued the more the power discrepancy tipped to Germany's disadvantage. Genuine strategic planning would have been forced to acknowledge that Germany was too small to become a world power, or to win a world war. For those who wanted to avoid this conclusion, purely military thinking was attractive. For the German military had developed its culture on the very premise of overachievement, of using quality, daring, and tactical proficiency to overcome strategic disadvantage. By acquiescing to German military culture, civilians could conveniently deny the discouraging truth of Germany's situation. This motive operated powerfully to silence criticism of the military's actions during the war.

In many ways World War I recapitulated for Germany the colonial situation. The Schlieffen Plan in 1914 and its principles of rapid envelopment and pursuit in 1915 were just successful enough to ensure that Germany fought the war on foreign soil. As in the colonies, there were insufficient troops to control the hostile population according to military standards. The twin temptations of imperial exploitation and violent pacification were ever present. At home, as in earlier colonial conflicts, the war raised enormous popular and governmental expectations of success (a quick military victory by the army everyone assumed to be the best, an end to internal discord, the achievement of world power, the acquisition of the fundamentals of future prosperity, and permanent military security). The national stakes were inflated from the very beginning, not just after the war had taken such a heavy toll of life. Yet there was a high likelihood that these expectations

---

33. Stig Förster, introduction, *Great War, Total War*, 3.

34. Wilhelm Deist, "The German Army, the Authoritarian Nation-State, and Total War," in *State, Society, and Mobilization*, ed. Horne, 160–72, here 160n2.

would be disappointed. In the colonies, lack of resources hampered imperial wars because of long transportation lines, stingy parliaments, and the absence of colonial infrastructure; in the world war Germany simply lacked manpower, food, and raw materials, both comparatively, and even absolutely. The cleft between expectation and reality was too large to permit a graceful or honest exit, however. Instead, the policies of bluff and saving face recommended themselves. But unlike "small" colonial wars, which boosters only claimed were matters of life and death, the world war truly did involve national security interests—the security mania of the professional officer corps and its more ideologized Pan-German version was suddenly justified. War really was existential, just as General v. Hartmann had written in 1876.

To address this situation, the military experts filled the policy void with their default plans, doctrinal frameworks, practical habits, and unconscious assumptions. It was these that drove German military conduct (*Kriegführung*) into its spiral of extremity and that ended in catastrophe. German military conduct distinguished itself by adamantine consistency; neither failure in battle, nor widespread foreign criticism (of "atrocities," forbidden weapons, or treatment of occupied civilians), nor even the impending loss of the war itself, shook the normal procedures by which military leaders understood, defined, and handled the problems of war. They learned little that they had not "known" when the conflict started. Military learning was confined almost solely to the tactical level. Impervious to experience on any other plane, uncorrected by other institutions, and facing an impossible self-imposed task, military leaders drifted into self-delusion and unreality. Military culture, whose operations they did not see or understand, worked together with other factors to turn the very strengths of the German military into fatal weaknesses.

The rest of this chapter and the next three focus on the workings of Germany's military culture during the war, and especially on five aspects: patterns of repetition; uncoordinated instances of the movement toward extremes, which nonetheless strongly resembled one another; the replacement of larger strategic goals with mere means (tactics) or, put another way, the adoption of short-term expedients over long-term thinking; the movement to irrational and dysfunctional action; and the inability to recognize or admit defeat.

Autumn 1914

During the war and afterward Germany's military and civilian leaders commonly claimed that objective circumstances had propelled Germany down the path to extremes.[35] The sheer duration and extent of the war, they said, the stalemate in the west, and above all the blockade created extreme necessities, which only extreme measures could address. Historians often accept this logic, which would seem to explain the excesses of Ludendorff and Hindenburg in 1917 and 1918. But if this were true, then we should expect to see the process unfold only after the war was well underway. In fact, the spiral toward the extreme began immediately. The opening weeks of war showed how

---

35. *UA* 3:4; English version: Germany, National Constituent Assembly, *Official German Documents*; *UA* 3:1, Volkmann's report, 168; Meurer's testimony, 88–89; Prussia, War Ministry and Supreme Command, *Die deutsche Kriegführung und das Völkerrecht* (Berlin, 1919), iv, and passim.

208 much German war conduct was determined by the patterns of military culture already familiar to us.

From the war's outbreak at the beginning of August 1914, the General Staff took charge of running it. The Schlieffen Plan's "secret of victory"[36] was now to unfold. Lt. Col. Hans von Seeckt, who became chief of the army in the Weimar Republic, was hardly alone in feeling that "it is like a dream that these operations, so long thought through, are running in reality exactly as they were planned on paper."[37] But not simply the advantages of the plan now emerged—rapid mobilization and deployment, crushing strength on the right wing, initial victories, and occupation of foreign territory—but also the potential problems—the enormous goal of *Siegfrieden* (victory of pure military force), the exhausting timetable (four hundred miles of marching in forty days), the assumption of qualitative troop superiority (though relying on reserve officers and men years removed from military training), the pressure on officers to blind themselves to adversity and to "will" victory, the logistics left to chance.[38]

In fact, the Schlieffen Plan went wrong immediately. Belgium contradicted the expectation that such a small state would surely permit German troops free passage on their way to France. On 3 August Belgium refused and took up arms. The Belgian government's statement was never published in Germany, which meant that soldiers had no reason to revise their expectations of an easy march. To their surprise German troops encountered real resistance from small units, sometimes from individual snipers who used houses and trees for cover, a form of warfare unlike the sweeping mass movement of troops for which they had been trained. On 4 August, the day Germany invaded Belgium, Gen. Otto von Emmich ordered the Belgian population to give Germany "free passage"; destruction of bridges or railroads (a normal military measure that the retreating Belgian army could be expected to take) would result in reprisals.[39] The next day Chief of Staff Moltke admitted to his Austrian counterpart, "Our method in Belgium [referring to the siege at Liège] is certainly brutal, but for us it is a matter of life or death, and anybody who gets in our way has to take the consequences."[40] To Foreign Secretary Gottlieb von Jagow, Moltke explained on the same day that Britain's entry into the war forced Germany "to exhaust every means that could contribute to victory. . . . The grave situation in which the fatherland finds itself makes the use of every means that can harm the enemy a duty."[41] The logic of Germany's predicament was clear to those at the top: it demanded force limited only by the achievement of victory.

36. Groener, *Lebenserinnerungen*, 87, also 91, 420.

37. Hans von Seeckt, *Aus meinem Leben 1866–1917*, ed. Friedrich von Rabenau (Leipzig, 1938), diary entry of 29 Aug. 1914, 69.

38. Crown Prince Rupprecht of Bavaria, commander of the German 6th Army, reported that "we were told that, if necessary, we would have to rely on the abundant stores we would capture"; he discovered that such staples as wheat and flour, for example, were far from abundant. Rupprecht Kronprinz v. Bayern, *Mein Kriegstagebuch*, 1:127. As for ammunition, it "somehow" arrived in time: Crefeld, *Supplying War*, 140.

39. Lothar Wieland, *Belgien 1914* (Frankfurt, 1984), 4n16.

40. Ibid., 7.

41. Ibid., 7n35.

At the bottom, the situation was messier. German troops began shooting Belgian and French civilians for a variety of reasons: frustration at resistance, suspicion of the foreign population, surprise at sniper fire, shock at the first sight of disfiguring wounds and at the heavy casualties caused by inexperienced officers hastening to achieve victory, incredulity that friendly fire could be so costly, the stress of meeting the goals of the Schlieffen Plan, exhaustion from unaccustomed marching, drunkenness, lack of discipline, and poor leadership.[42] The pattern of troop behavior was remarkably similar to that in 1870 and in the colonies. It had three significant qualities. First, crimes of excess began immediately; the use of human shields in combat, the punitive destruction of buildings, and the mass execution of noncombatants began on 5 August 1914, the first day of the real shooting war.[43] Second, they were widespread; half of all the German regiments in the western theater of operations committed such acts. In the first two months of the war there were 129 major incidents of execution (involving ten or more civilians). The historians of these events, John Horne and Alan Kramer, conclude that "violence against enemy civilians was endemic throughout the German army."[44] Third, as in 1870, these acts were first committed by common soldiers or low-ranking officers, but they were swiftly approved by higher-ranking officers and systematized in orders at the army level and above. On 14 August, Moltke, for example, ordered that civilians engaging in combat would be summarily executed, an order repeated on the 26th.[45]

The speed, extent, and systematic nature of the atrocities show that they had been long prepared, not in the sense of ordered outright but in Barry Turner's sense that large-scale failures require "time and resources [to be] devoted to them."[46] Unintentional preparation for excesses had occurred at the level of myth- and expectation-building, training for combat, and the unrealistic Schlieffen Plan. The army and officer corps had assiduously cultivated the myth of the francs-tireurs of 1870 until it had become part of the folklore of German military culture. Officers and men expected French and Belgian civilians to engage in illegal acts of resistance; it was easy to blame them for the discrepancy between the easy victory they expected and the difficult and sometimes horrible reality of war they encountered. Their credulity was then confirmed and reinforced by superior orders and newspaper accounts.[47] Even the apparently new practice of using human shields must have seemed merely an extension of the already permissible. After

---

42. Ibid., 3–10; Alan Kramer, " 'Greueltaten,' " in *"Keiner fühlt sich hier mehr als Mensch . . . ,"* ed. Gerhard Hirschfeld and Gerd Krumeich (Essen, 1993), 87–92.

43. Horne and Kramer, *German Atrocities,* 13, appendix 1:435. Human shields: John Horne and Alan Kramer, "War between Soldiers and Enemy Civilians, 1914–1915," in *Great War, Total War,* ed. Chickering and Förster, 153–68, here 157–58; Carl Ernst, *Der grosse Krieg in Belgien* (Gembloux, Belgium, 1930), 30, 56; Georges Gromaire, *L'occupation allemande en France, 1914–1918* (Paris, 1925), 73; Dana C. Munro, George C. Sellery, and August C. Krey, eds., *German War Practices,* Part 1: *Treatment of Civilians* (Washington, D.C., 1917), 40.

44. Horne and Kramer, *German Atrocities,* 76 (one half of all regiments), 74 (129 incidents).

45. John Horne and Alan Kramer, "German 'Atrocities' and Franco-German Opinion, 1914," *Journal of Modern History* 66:1 (March 1994): 17, 22; Horne and Kramer, *German Atrocities,* 162, 164.

46. Turner, "Organizational and Interorganizational Development of Disasters," 395.

47. Wieland, *Belgien 1914,* 4, 20; Horne and Kramer, *German Atrocities,* 132.

all, the *Kriegs-Etappen-Ordnung* (12 March 1914) had recommended using civilian hostages to protect trains from sabotage and to protect villages unexpectedly attacked by enemy troops.[48] It had therefore already breached the principle of civilian inviolability from direct combat, as had the General Staff publication *Kriegsbrauch*. The massacres of August and September must have seemed to the perpetrators to have been "sanctioned."[49]

The pattern of acts is quite similar to what was done in SWA and elsewhere in the colonies. One finds, for example, an order by the commander of the 33rd Reserve Division "to shoot all male inhabitants [of the village of Nomény] and expel the women in the direction of France."[50] Burning of homes, and even whole villages, was common. The transgression of the gender taboo appears in Falkenhayn's order of 26 August 1914 making any civilian caught engaging in resistance, "regardless of age and sex," liable to summary execution. As in SWA, the niceties of courts-martial swiftly gave way to common summary executions.[51] Harsh orders tended to lead to harsher behavior. One soldier from the 108th Infantry Regiment described to a French investigator after his capture how that happened: "We were given the order to kill all civilians shooting at us, but in reality the men of my regiment and I, myself, fired at all civilians we found in the houses from which we suspected there had been shots fired; in that way we killed women and even children. We did not do it light-heartedly."[52] Bad provisioning increased contact with civilians and also the chances for lethal misunderstandings. Finally, as in the colonies, the francs-tireurs myth placed the blame for extreme troop behavior on civilians, whose alleged armed resistance placed them outside the protection of international law, indeed made them savages, as one of Germany's newspapers of record claimed on 9 August, when it spread the already widespread tale that civilians (often women, in the stories) had mutilated or tortured German troops in a fashion rivaled only by the Herero.[53]

This wave of systematic violence in August and September 1914 killed six thousand civilians, possibly more, and destroyed fifteen to twenty thousand buildings, including some entire villages.[54] The allies dubbed these actions the "Belgian atrocities," which became the first staple of propaganda labeling the Germans brutal breakers of international law. When the haze of appeasement settled over Europe in the 1920s, the "Belgian atrocities" were interred as propaganda lies until historians in the 1980s and 1990s unearthed them and found they were true. Neither the wartime German government nor the Weimar parliament denied them.[55] Instead, they defended them as regrettably necessary reprisals against illegal francs-tireurs (whom subsequent historical scholarship has shown did not

48. Prussia, War Ministry, *Kriegs-Etappen-Ordnung* (KEO), p. 68 (para. 137), p. 69 (para. 141).
49. Sanford and Comstock, "Sanctions for Evil."
50. Horne and Kramer, *German Atrocities*, 64; more examples: 33, 49.
51. Ibid., 164–65.
52. Ibid., 163–64.
53. Ibid., 135.
54. Horne and Kramer, "War between Soldiers," 157–58; Kramer, "Greueltaten," 86; Horne and Kramer, *German Atrocities*, 74–75.
55. Germany, Foreign Office, *Die völkerrechtswidrige Führung des belgischen Volkskriegs* (Berlin, 1915); UA 3:2, 129–260; Prussia, War Ministry and Supreme Command, *Die deutsche Kriegführung*, 46–51.

exist).[56] The diaries of the time strongly suggest that Germans high and low believed the francs-tireurs myth. But this belief did not cause the atrocities, any more than anti-Catholicism or social Darwinism did, though all three made it easier for them to happen.[57] The atrocities occurred because two forces converged: the unintended consequences to ordinary soldiers of a far too ambitious war plan, and the conscious and customary acceptance among officers that making the risky plan work might require using terror against civilians. These same officers did not understand how the Schlieffen Plan and their own professional expectations had generated atrocity; they experienced the situation as compulsive, beyond their control. Like Moltke, they felt forced to respond to friction according to the logic of ever greater violence.

The object of the atrocities was to force civilian obedience and to re-create in the occupied zones the reliable order of home (the *Kölnischer Zeitung* asked, "Is there a person in the world who would imagine that the Belgian capital, Brussels, would have permitted us to live there doing as we please, as if in our own country, if the inhabitants did not tremble at our [possible] revenge?").[58] The projection of military hierarchy and perfect orderliness onto civilians is also clear in the frequency with which German officers assumed that mayors actually controlled their citizens' actions.[59]

There was a more perfect way to do achieve order, however—deportation. Not three weeks into the war, German authorities were already using this extreme measure. The first deportees were civilian hostages from Belgium and northern France, from places such as Dinant or Louvain, where major atrocities had occurred. After being marched about aimlessly for hours, the civilians were crowded onto cattle cars and shipped off to internment camps in Germany; most were repatriated after several months, but some remained prisoners for the entire war.[60] The deportation of hostages was apparently a hastily improvised measure, because few of the necessary provisions for food, water, clothing, or shelter were provided.[61] On 23 August General Moltke proposed that deportation should be a permanent feature of occupation policy. He suggested to the chancellor that "part of the numerous working class [of Belgium] . . . be pushed across the border to Antwerp," where, instead of Germany, the Belgian government-in-exile would have to feed them. Bethmann did not reject this suggestion out of hand; instead, he blocked it temporarily. The guidelines issued on 27 August to the military governor of Belgium read that deportation of the working class would depend on "special consideration."[62] Deportation was obviously a widespread temptation. A month after Moltke's suggestion, the chief of the

56. Horne and Kramer, *German Atrocities*, 123–29; Kramer, "Greueltaten," 96–99; Wieland, *Belgien 1914*, 11–16.

57. Horne and Kramer stress ideological stereotyping: "War between Soldiers," 162–65.

58. Walter Bloehm, "Greuelhetze," *Kölnische Zeitung* 146 (10 Feb. 1915), morning edition, p. 1: paraphrased in Ernst, *Der grosse Krieg*, 83.

59. Horne and Kramer, *German Atrocities*, 103.

60. Annette Becker, *Oubliés de la Grande Guerre* (Paris, 1998), 55.

61. Great Britain, *Report of the Committee on Alleged German Outrages*, Cd. 7894 (London, 1915), 19, 22, 28, 30–37; Ernst, *Der grosse Krieg*, 62–66; Horne and Kramer, *German Atrocities*, 77, 166, 436–38.

62. Frank Wende, *Die belgische Frage in der deutschen Politik des Ersten Weltkrieges* (Hamburg, 1969), 21–22; Horne and Kramer, *German Atrocities*, 158.

212 rear (*Etappeninspekteur*) of the 1st Army ordered all males of military age (eighteen to forty-eight) in St. Quentin, France, to be transported to Germany, where they would be less likely to escape to unoccupied France and where, above all, the 1st Army would not have to feed them. His commander, Crown Prince Rupprecht, whittled down the number of deportees to those capable of bearing arms, so that the rest could be used for labor behind the German lines.[63] Altogether, some twenty-three thousand French and Belgian civilian deportees disappeared into German camps in the first weeks of the war.[64]

Despite extreme measures against civilians, the ruthless sacrifice of thousands of German troops in hopeless attacks against strong positions,[65] and tremendous daily exertions in executing the Schlieffen Plan, the risk failed. It proved impossible to orchestrate the independently acting armies within Schlieffen's sweeping scheme.[66] But more fundamentally, Germany's strength in manpower, transportation, and matériel (especially munitions) was simply not enough to beat Britain and France together, much less with the addition of Russia. On 9 September 1914 the German armies were checked at the Marne and had to retreat and dig in. The grand offensive was through, the enemy undefeated. Chief of Staff Moltke had always appreciated more than most the tremendous risks involved and, for example, had tried to improve the logistical basis of Schlieffen's plan and to reduce Germany's vulnerability to enemy breakthrough while the bulk of German troops were attempting their difficult one-sided sweep.[67] Moltke therefore recognized that failure at the Marne meant the failure of the Schlieffen Plan and with it Germany's only hope to win the war. That had been the calculation: all or nothing. Moltke, who days earlier had seemed to think that Germany had already won,[68] now recognized the true extent of defeat. He lapsed into apathy, and his health collapsed.

Moltke's response was entirely appropriate for a man who took the Schlieffen Plan seriously as a *strategic* concept. Germany had not simply lost a battle, it had lost the war. The widespread "resignation," "pessimism," or "irritability" among high-ranking officers in the weeks after 9 September suggests that, at least subliminally, Moltke was not alone in his insight.[69] But it proved almost impossible to sustain this logical, but dour, view. The broken Moltke was replaced in mid-September as chief of the General Staff by Erich v. Falkenhayn, who briefed the chancellor on the new military situation on the 19th. Neither Falkenhayn nor Bethmann concluded at that time that the war was lost.[70] Bethmann successfully pressed Falkenhayn to misrepresent the Marne to the German people as a volun-

---

63. Rupprecht Kronprinz v. Bayern, *Mein Kriegstagebuch*, 1:144–45.

64. Horne and Kramer, *German Atrocities*, 166.

65. Bernd F. Schulte, *Europäische Krise und Erster Weltkrieg* (Frankfurt am Main, 1983), 245–46; Groener, *Lebenserinnerungen*, 150.

66. German officers and too many historians have blamed the Marne on Moltke's poor leadership. For a recent summary of the extensive literature see Strachan, *First World War*, 242–62, and Holmes's interesting interpretation, "Reluctant March," 228–32.

67. Gunther Rothenberg, "Moltke, Schlieffen, and the Doctrine of Strategic Envelopment," in *Makers of Modern Strategy*, ed. Paret, 296–325, here 321–22; Förster, "Dreams and Nightmares," 343–76; Burchardt, *Friedenswirtschaft*, 26, 27, 48, 175, 193.

68. Fritz von Lossberg, *Meine Tätigkeit im Weltkriege 1914–1918* (Berlin, 1939), 128.

69. Seeckt, *Aus meinem Leben*, 72–74; Janssen, *Der Kanzler und der General*, 20; Stürgkh, *Im deutschen Grossen Hauptquartier*, 41–42.

70. Afflerbach, *Falkenhayn*, 191.

tary strategic correction. The thinking at general headquarters was so fuzzy that the Austrian military representative there could not judge the situation clearly: "It was not easy to understand the significance of the battle of the Marne at the time."[71] Already by 18 September, Moltke seemed to have backtracked.[72] Later he ascribed his behavior to having been "nervous" and "pessimistic," the recurring epithets military men used to discredit advocates of unpleasant realism.[73]

It is therefore not surprising that Falkenhayn handled the problem by denying it. But Falkenhayn was not alone; he was typical. No one among Germany's higher military leaders accepted the defeat at the Marne, and therefore none was in a position to rethink Schlieffen's precepts.[74] On the one hand, the press of circumstances surely hindered fundamental criticism. On the other, in the absence of rethinking, the automatisms of military culture determined action. Except for Gen. Karl von Einem, who advocated a strategic retreat in order to lure the French into a trap where they could be destroyed, everybody favored a continuation of the offensive.[75] Everyone without exception agreed that military annihilation was still the goal and the way to achieve it was through concentration of forces and the relentless forcing of a single-battle victory.[76]

Falkenhayn therefore attempted the Schlieffen solution again, in the Moltke guise. That is, he aimed to envelop the British by using as much strength as possible on the right wing, while pinning the Allies down by attacks from the center, which the army commanders there believed might on their own succeed in achieving a total military victory.[77] Repetition produced the same failure and ignited yet another technical debate among officers about whether enough troops had been concentrated on the right wing.[78]

Denial of defeat and inability or unwillingness to rethink left the spiraling dynamic of military culture in effect. The compulsion to escalate the use of violence was extremely strong. When fighting bogged down at Ypres, the last chance for encirclement, Falkenhayn committed wave after wave of German troops, leading to the death of eighty thousand of them and using up the precious new army of post–August 1914 volunteers. German losses were finally so staggering that many high-ranking officers criticized Falkenhayn for not stopping the battle sooner—he did so on 13 November 1914 when Germany came within six days of having *no* artillery shells.[79] But Falkenhayn's repetitive actionism and loyalty to the Schlieffen Plan was the default position. Newly appointed Min-

71. Stürgkh, *Im deutschen Grossen Hauptquartier*, 81.

72. Rupprecht Kronprinz v. Bayern, *Mein Kriegstagebuch*, 1:126.

73. Moltke to Gen. Hans v. Plessen, 2 May 1915, cited in Herwig, *First World War*, 106.

74. Strachan, *First World War*, 262; Janssen, *Der Kanzler*, 26–27; Groener, *Lebenserinnerungen*, 328; Kronprinz Wilhelm v. Preussen, *Meine Erinnerungen aus Deutschlands Heldenkampf* (Berlin, 1923), 91; Hermann von Kuhl, *Der Weltkrieg 1914–1918* (Berlin, 1929), 2:45.

75. Einem, *Armeeführer*, 61, 62; Groener, *Lebenserinnerungen*, 180.

76. For example, Groener, *Lebenserinnerungen*, diary entry of 13 Sept. 1914, 176; Rupprecht Kronprinz v. Bayern, *Mein Kriegstagebuch*, diary entry of 15 Sept. 1914, 1:124; ex post facto criticism of this position by Freytag-Loringhoven (8 June 1915), in Wild, *Briefe*, 68–69.

77. Afflerbach, *Falkenhayn*, 191–95; Strachan, *First World War*, 264–65.

78. Groener, *Lebenserinnerungen*, 180–81; Lossberg, *Meine Tätigkeit*, 99.

79. Afflerbach, *Falkenhayn*, 198. Plessen, 16 Nov. 1914: "Falkenhayn does not want to stop the violent attack on Ypres until the last attack (again made by new troops) and the last heavy shell is fired." Reichsarchiv, *Weltkrieg*, 6:93.

214   ister of War Adolf Wild von Hohenborn summed it up, "What a soldier sets his mind to, he must execute ruthlessly. If Ypres had been a victory, everybody would have been satisfied."[80] But at Ypres, the Schlieffen principles had failed again.

At the end of September, as Falkenhayn ordered the armies to attack, he was already experimenting with the first of a series of technical wonder weapons to extract victory from defeat—gas.[81] Fritz Haber, the scientist in charge of the program, remembered, "It was thought up in great haste, created, and tried out at Neuve Chapelle in the same month."[82] These early gas grenades contained an irritant to make enemy troops abandon their positions; only in the next year did the Germans first develop a lethal gas. The gas war ultimately developed on both sides until, for example, five hundred thousand Russian soldiers became gas casualties, while Germany devoted 25 percent of its shell-making capacity to gas shells.[83] No one could have foreseen such effects from this small beginning, especially given the widespread early opposition to the new weapon from officers who found it morally repugnant.[84] They all overcame their objections as the weapon became more widely used. For our purposes, however, the decision to try gas grenades is a good indicator of the grooves in which military problem-solving ran. First, the decision occurred very early, before the trench stalemate was complete. Desperation came quickly to the Supreme Command, because its task was desperate by definition. Second, the method tried was experimental and technical; it attempted to achieve a tactical advantage over the enemy. Third, it tried to do so hastily, without much investment or forethought, and it was based on short-term calculations. For example, the decision ignored the fact that the prevailing winds in Europe are almost always westerly (which would blow gas back at the German troops).[85] If the weapon had worked, the war would have been over before anyone had to worry about this. Fourth, the decision rested on underestimating the capacity of the enemy to retaliate in kind: Haber told Falkenhayn that Britain could not possibly develop poison gas, because it lacked Germany's scientific advantages.[86] Gas warfare obviously violated international law, but no discussion of that fact or its potential effects preceded the adoption of the experiment. After the war, the legal expert who investigated gas warfare for the Reichstag justified it legally as a "compulsory necessity of war."[87] Finally, gas was designed for purely conventional purposes to achieve a tactical advantage; the escalation it represented was unintentional and was surely experienced as the "compulsory necessity of war" by which it was later defended.[88]

80. Wild, *Briefe*, diary entry of 23 Dec. 1914, Mézières, 47.

81. The scientist in charge of the program, Fritz Haber, thought Falkenhayn had contacted him in early October, but the legal expert who examined the case for the postwar Reichstag investigation noted that the gas program began in late September: *UA* 3:4, 20–21; Rolf-Dieter Müller, "Total War as the Result of New Weapons?" in *Great War, Total War*, ed. Chickering and Förster, 95–111, here 96.

82. *UA* 3:4, 19–20.

83. Müller, "Total War," 103; *UA* 3:4, 14.

84. Müller, "Total War," 107.

85. Crown Prince Rupprecht argued against the new weapon for this reason. Diary entry 1 Mar. 1915, *Mein Kriegstagebuch*, 1:304–5.

86. Afflerbach, *Falkenhayn*, 261.

87. Dr. Kriege's report, *UA* 3:4, 34.

88. Dennis E. Showalter, "Mass Warfare and the Impact of Technology," in *Great War, Total War*, ed. Chickering and Förster, 90–91, citing Rolf-Dieter Müller and Tim Travers.

In the weeks before the stalemate on the western front had solidified, Germany's war conduct already showed the outlines it would pursue to the end. From the very beginning it used ruthless methods and outright terror against civilians to fulfill the unrealistic schedule of the Schlieffen Plan and to create a docile order that one could hardly expect of civilians, much less of enemy civilians. Commanders rapidly arrived at the most final-seeming solution to civilian order—deportation—which they suggested and partly used to solve logistical and governmental problems. When the Schlieffen Plan was frustrated, one of the first responses was to grasp at a cheap, experimental, technical weapon that operated at the tactical level. And, rather than admitting that the Schlieffen gamble had failed, officers supported repeating its basic idea of sweeping attack over and over again, at greater and greater human cost. With one exception, this template defined how Germany fought the war right to the end. We turn now to that exception.

Falkenhayn and the Abandonment of Military Victory

With the defeat at Ypres, Falkenhayn became the second chief of staff to admit defeat, or almost. He informed Bethmann on 18 November, "As long as Russia, France, and England hold together, it will be impossible for us to beat our enemies such that we will get an acceptable peace. We would instead run the danger of slowly exhausting ourselves."[89] In short, Germany could not win a purely military victory—the Siegfrieden that constituted real victory for the Imperial German military. Like the elder Moltke in the 1880s, Falkenhayn thought that only diplomacy could end the war. The military's job now became twofold, to avoid an Allied breakthrough in the west, which would end in Germany's outright military defeat, and to provide the conditions in the east whereby Russia could be driven to a separate peace. "If Russia made peace, France would surely succumb, too. Then if England did not completely bow to our will, we could beat it [*niederzwingen*] by starving it with a naval blockade using our base in Belgium, even if this would take months."[90] Unlike the younger Moltke, Falkenhayn did not, consequently, think they had lost the war: "If we do not lose the war [via an Allied breakthrough], we will have won it," he used to tell his staff.[91] In fact, Falkenhayn proposed a subtler version of the Schlieffen Plan: victory against one foe (through a combination of military action and diplomacy), followed by military victory against the others.

Historians generally do not credit Falkenhayn's conclusion with being truly strategic, that is, with having an overarching political and economic framework to contain and guide military operations.[92] And it is certainly true that Falkenhayn had no realistic idea of how England could be "forced," or even why France should sue for peace, as long as England remained stalwart. Still, Falkenhayn's admission that Germany could not win a purely military victory was extraordinary. It caused him to adopt unusually moderate war aims and limited military goals. Throughout 1915 Falkenhayn directed the eastern cam-

89. Bethmann reported Falkenhayn's letter in Bethmann to Arthur Zimmermann, 19 Nov. 1914, cited in Afflerbach, *Falkenhayn*, 204.
90. Ibid.
91. Ibid., 198.
92. Deist, "Strategy and Unlimited Warfare," 274; Janssen, *Der Kanzler*, 85; Kielmansegg, *Germany*, 72–73.

216 paign explicitly *not* to annihilate the Russian forces through a grand encirclement, as the commanders in the east, Hindenburg and Ludendorff, strove to do but instead to achieve a defeat just large enough to encourage Russia to negotiate a separate peace.[93] And he gave up the principle of risking all, which had been the heart of German military practice and doctrine for decades. In preparing for the battle of Verdun, Falkenhayn told all the army commanders and their chiefs of staff that Germany could not afford to risk everything in a single attack for fear of so weakening the rest of the (western) front that Britain and France could break through and defeat Germany. "For this reason," he told them, "we must *consciously* abandon the principle of concentrating *everything* for the great attack."[94]

But Falkenhayn remained almost alone in his logical conclusions from the failure of the Schlieffen Plan. His student, Crown Prince Wilhelm, who commanded the 5th Army and afterward the Army Group Crown Prince Wilhelm opposite Verdun, supported Falkenhayn's strategic insight, though he arrived at it slightly later and shrank from publicizing his views.[95] Gen. Max Hoffmann, chief of staff at Ober-Ost, was another.[96] But Germany's other senior commanders rejected Falkenhayn for his apostasy regarding a Siegfrieden and a single victory of annihilation.[97] Crown Prince Rupprecht, one of the most moderate and politically well-informed generals, was nonetheless typical. He learned on 12 November 1914 about Falkenhayn's assessment of the Marne, yet that did not move Rupprecht to draw any larger conclusions about Germany's ability to win the war. A year and a half later, Rupprecht summed up his dissatisfaction: "What bothers me the most," he confided to his diary, "is that General Falkenhayn apparently thinks a decisive victory is no longer possible. How is the war supposed to end for us under these circumstances?"[98] Col. Fritz von Lossberg, Germany's genius for defensive battles, said essentially the same thing: "A two-front war requires daring, drastic decisions with the broad goal of destroying the enemies one after another through strong offensives. But General von Falkenhayn could never bring himself to adopt this will to destroy, either in the east or in the west."[99]

The memoirs and diaries suggest that the other military leaders shifted blame to the bearer of bad tidings. They saw personal failure instead of a reasonable response to Germany's objective position of inferiority. Falkenhayn did not fit the ideal of Prusso-German command. "He is a man of small means, without large goals; he is inclined to make his measures dependent on those of the enemy, instead of dictating the law."[100] But Ger-

93. Afflerbach, *Falkenhayn*, 295, 298, 305, 307–8.

94. Lossberg, *Meine Tätigkeit*, 206. Emphasis in original.

95. Kronprinz Wilhelm v. Preussen, *Meine Erinnerungen*, 116, 152–57. Falkenhayn had been the crown prince's first military governor.

96. Max Hoffmann was another: Max Hoffmann, *Die Aufzeichnungen des Generalmajors Max Hoffmann*, 2 vols., ed. Karl-Friedrich Nowak (Berlin, 1929), 1:232. Hugo v. Freytag-Loringhoven, whose deafness kept him from command positions, praised Falkenhayn for having recognized "the natural limits of the Schlieffen doctrine"; *Menschen und Dinge, wie ich sie in meinem Leben sah* (Berlin, 1923), 285.

97. On the legions of Falkenhayn's enemies: Afflerbach, *Falkenhayn*, 211–17; Herwig, *First World War*, 131–34.

98. Rupprecht Kronprinz v. Bayern, *Mein Kriegstagebuch*, diary entries of 12 Nov. 1914 and 20 Mar. 1916, 1:250–52 and 430.

99. Lossberg, *Meine Tätigkeit*, 141–42.

100. Rupprecht Kronprinz v. Bayern, *Mein Kriegstagebuch*, diary entry of 2 Mar. 1915, 1:306.

many had only (relatively) small means at its disposal. Germany was forced onto the defensive, whose nature is responding to the enemy's initiatives. Karl von Einem, commander of the 3rd Army, felt relieved when Falkenhayn was dismissed in August 1916: "He was simply not a field marshal, because he never anticipated events—he lacked intuitive ability."[101]

The Marne and, at the latest, Ypres were powerful reality checks to the professional assumptions of the German military. Except for Moltke, Falkenhayn, and Hoffmann, however, the upper military leadership ducked the unhappy strategic conclusions and drew instead more comfortable operative or merely tactical conclusions. That is, they stayed within the framework of the Schlieffen Plan, which itself was operative, not strategic. They concluded that the plan would have worked except for the personal leadership failures of Moltke, who watered it down and lost control of his armies, and of the commanders in the field, who did not follow the plan in their lust for victory. As Groener said at the time, "The 'plan' of the late [or blessed: *seligen*] Schlieffen has been temporarily lost; perhaps we'll find it again."[102] The remedy was therefore more of the Schlieffen Plan and its premises, not less.[103] More risk taking, grander goals, more daring intuitive leadership, more concentration of strength, more uncompromising execution of force—in short, a higher round in the spiral of violence and destruction. Schlieffen's principles, which epitomized modern military thinking, were wonderfully effective operatively; even Falkenhayn and Hoffmann clung to them for conduct in battle.[104] It was difficult for most other commanders to imagine that these same tenets might spell strategic doom. For the vast majority of believers, the Marne and Ypres were occasions for positive, not negative, feedback.

Falkenhayn and the Logic of Extremes

Historians usually use the third Supreme Command under Chief of Staff Hindenburg and Quartermaster General Ludendorff (29 August 1916–26 October 1918) to illustrate the "military dictatorship" and the extreme, counterproductive measures that now developed.[105] But these were all prefigured by Falkenhayn in 1916. Falkenhayn's odyssey proves the patterned nature of the developments. Ludendorff's willfulness, vehemence, and,

---

101. Einem, *Armeeführer*, diary entry of 29 Aug. 1916, 253.

102. Groener, *Lebenserinnerungen*, diary entry of 13 Sept. 1914, 176.

103. Hindenburg, *Aus meinem Leben*, 118–19; Lossberg, *Meine Tätigkeit*, 79 and passim. Even after the war this was the common lesson military men drew from the Marne: Bernhard von Schwertfeger's report, *UA* 4:2 (1928), 177; Freytag-Loringhoven, *Heerführung im Weltkriege*, 126–27; Reichsarchiv, *Weltkrieg*, 6:444–45; Kuhl, *Weltkrieg*, 1:510–11.

104. See Falkenhayn's orders to keep the offensive spirit alive, despite going on the defensive: Reichsarchiv, *Weltkrieg*, 6:480, or his conduct of the offensive at Gorlice in 1915, despite its limited goals: Afflerbach, *Falkenhayn*, 297–308; Max Hoffmann, "Gedanken über 1914," in *Aufzeichnungen*, 2:228–34, here 233–34.

105. "Dictatorship" is meant figuratively, in that neither Hindenburg nor Ludendorff ever aspired to one-man rule; in fact, both explicitly rejected the suggestion when it was broached. Heinz Hagenlücke, *Deutsche Vaterlandspartei* (Düsseldorf, 1997), 278–81; Werner Jochmann, "Die Ausbreitung des Antisemitismus," in *Deutsches Judentum in Krieg und Revolution 1916–1923*, ed. Werner E. Mosse (Tübingen, 1971), 430–31; Kuno von Westarp, *Konservative Politik im letzten Jahrzehnt des Kaiserreiches*, 2 vols. (Berlin, 1935), 2:469.

218   toward the end, frank irrationality can make it seem that his personality shaped events more than was true. But Falkenhayn was nothing like Ludendorff. Falkenhayn served only two short stints in the General Staff, thus missing the typical Schlieffen saturation.[106] Instead, he combined a colonial career, as military inspector in Qing-Dao (including fighting during the Boxer Uprising), with regular commands. He rose to brigade commander and chief of the General Staff of the 4th Army before becoming Prussian war minister in 1913. He spoke several languages, thrived in the international atmosphere of Peking, and was interested in foreign affairs. Falkenhayn's relative cosmopolitanism may have helped him recognize the significance of Germany's defeats in autumn 1914, but it did not free him from military culture. No professional can forge such a successful career independent of organizational knowledge. Falkenhayn was clearly very good at playing the game; he did not need Schlieffen—who only systematized certain aspects of Germany's military culture but did not create it—to tell him how to think like a professional.

Since November 1914, when he had recognized that Germany could not win a purely military victory, Falkenhayn had pursued a strategy of dogged defense in the west and limited offense in the east, designed to bring Russia to a separate peace. However, Germany's civil-military split meant that the chief of staff and the chancellor did not coordinate their policies. Indeed, Bethmann arrived at Falkenhayn's realistically dour conclusion only in late 1916. Until then Bethmann undermined peace feelers in hopes that Germany would win greater battlefield victories.[107] In any case, Russia refused Germany's (weak) signals for negotiation in August 1915 and brought Falkenhayn up short. Throughout the war, the Allies' uncompromising stance confirmed the all-or-nothing assumptions of German military culture. For months Falkenhayn had fought the lonely fight of moderation against the outright opposition of every army commander, of the twin heroes of Ober-Ost, and the foot-dragging of the chancellor. But it became too difficult to sustain a differentiated view. Falkenhayn now lost grip on his strategic insight and slipped back into the all-or-nothing school of thought. On 29 November 1915 he informed the chancellor that Germany did not have the choice between a compromise peace and a purely military victory:

> The view is false that Germany can choose between concluding peace soon by documenting its acceptance of conditions acceptable to the enemy or, instead, pursuing the war until the enemy's will to win and therefore to stand fast is broken, at the risk that Germany must fight to the last man and the last penny. In reality we only have the latter choice; we are forced to go down that path to a good or bitter conclusion, whether we want to or not. . . . This is no longer a war of the sort we knew earlier; this war has become for all participants literally a battle for existence.[108]

106. My account follows Afflerbach, *Falkenhayn*.
107. Afflerbach, *Falkenhayn*, 265; Deist, "Strategy and Unlimited Warfare," 273.
108. Falkenhayn to Bethmann Hollweg, 29 Nov. 1915, in Afflerbach, *Falkenhayn*, 352.

Falkenhayn's conversion was probably eased by the large battlefield victories against the Russians in the summer of 1915. These may have slightly buoyed him,[109] but it was Russia's intransigence that forced him to confront again the situation of July 1914: envelopment, material inferiority, and only the military way out. If we take his words seriously, then Falkenhayn accepted the possibility of Germany's self-destruction, the "bitter conclusion" that meant ruin to "the last man and the last penny." (In fact, the middle way, a status quo ante peace, was never attempted—Bethmann had not offered it to the Russians in 1915, nor did he or his successors do so later.) So Falkenhayn faced the classical Wilhelminian all-or-nothing dilemma ("world power or defeat" [*Weltmacht oder Niedergang*], "the necessity of the impossible" [*die Erforderlichkeit des Unmöglichen*]), only this time without a Schlieffen Plan.[110]

Beginning in mid-1915, and until his dismissal on 28 August 1916, Falkenhayn attempted to solve the dilemma in four ways. The first addressed Germany's most pressing problem: the shortage of manpower in the army and in industry. He began (June 1915) in Germany by trying to squeeze every able-bodied man into the army—by extending the draft to fifty year olds and reexamining the physically unfit—and by militarizing industry. That is, workers would be drafted but would continue factory work under military discipline and with the state controlling wages, hours, and benefits. The leader of heavy industry Gustav Krupp von Bohlen und Halbach had helped the economic neophyte draft this proposal, which the chancellor, the Prussian war minister, and the interior secretary all rejected as impossibly anti-union, anti-economic, and politically suicidal.[111] Falkenhayn dropped the idea for Germany, but shifted his attention to the occupied zones. In August 1915, he proposed drafting a Polish army to fight in the west. Bethmann pointed out that using force for this purpose contravened international law and that an appeal for volunteers was unlikely to be fruitful. So Falkenhayn let this idea drop, too.[112] But there were other ways to gain soldiers. In order to release German workers for the front, the war minister in March 1916 proposed forcibly deporting four hundred thousand Belgian workers to German factories. This time it was the governor-general of Belgium, Gen. Moritz von Bissing, supported by the chancellor and interior secretary, who quashed the idea, citing foreign opinion, international law, and the economic fact that forced labor was never as efficient as volunteer labor.[113]

Falkenhayn's second proposal to overcome comparative material weakness was to radically revise the state sovereignty and economic borders of the Central Powers (Germany, Austria, Bulgaria, and Turkey), lumping them into an allegedly more efficient,

---

109. Ibid., 357.

110. These contemporary phrases (from Gen. v. Bernhardi and Kurt Riezler, Bethmann's private secretary) have become emblematic for the Kaiserreich's self-imposed predicament. Riezler, *Die Erforderlichkeit des Unmöglichen* (Munich, 1913); Fritz Fischer, *Weltmacht oder Niedergang* (Frankfurt, 1965), 38.

111. Afflerbach, *Falkenhayn*, 317–320.

112. Ibid., 315.

113. Bissing to Bethmann Hollweg, Nr. CC. IV. A. 2804 Chef. Nr., Brussels, 12 Apr. 1916, *UA* 3:1, 333–34; Herbert Hoover, *An American Epic*, vol. 1: *Introduction: The Relief of Belgium and Northern France, 1914–1930* (Chicago, 1959), 41.

220 semipermanent middle European union. This fantasy, which quickly died, would not merit mention except as further proof of the enthusiasm for provoking foreign revolution evident in German military and political thinking. It was of a piece with the Ottoman call for jihad against the West under German auspices, and with Germany's attempts to underwrite revolution in the British and Russian empires.[114]

Falkenhayn's third solution was, by contrast, quite real, if not realistic, for it was a military plan that civilian opposition could not stop. It was the attack on Verdun.

Verdun brilliantly shows how pragmatic calculation undertaken in an impossible situation can spiral into unreality and, in this case, great loss of life. For Falkenhayn did not believe that Germany was suddenly capable of a classic battle of annihilation, nor was he entirely optimistic about victory—he promised the Kaiser only a "high probability" of success, a quite subdued claim, given the hyperpositive language characteristic of senior commanders.[115] Verdun was supposed to achieve a favorable peace by the fall of 1916, since Falkenhayn did not believe Germany, and especially its ally, Austria, could hold out much longer. He factored in Germany's relative weakness and focused the attack at the demographically weaker foe, France, hoping that France's resolve would falter if it lost more soldiers than Germany. The stalemated war of attrition would thus be speeded up and concentrated on the weakest Allied link. Falkenhayn was also careful not to commit all troops to the attack but to save reserves in case Britain rushed to France's aid. The Verdun plan combined activism with a grisly numerical calculation aiming at tremendous numbers of dead. Although France was supposed to "bleed" more, Falkenhayn clearly accepted an immense German death rate. This cold, self-wasting calculation is all the more remarkable for resting ultimately on a psychological gamble, that French morale would crumble (before Germany's).

But one could not calculate away Germany's inferiority in even a shorter war of attrition. Prudently saving reserves forced Falkenhayn to limit the attack to the eastern hills around Verdun, leaving the western positions to France, from which it rained down murderous artillery fire on the attacking German troops below. France and Germany lost almost equal numbers of men, negating the original idea. This self-contradiction was visible in the planning; it caused Crown Prince Rupprecht to surmise "that General von Falkenhayn is not clear about what he really wants, and that he is waiting for luck to bring a positive result."[116]

The conceptual fragility of the Verdun campaign is also clear in the confusion among many high-ranking officers about whether Falkenhayn intended a "victory," that is, to take the fort (he did not), or simply to use the attack to lure as many French defenders to their deaths as possible.[117] Either Falkenhayn did not dare disappoint the conventional expectations of his officers, or he tightly restricted information. But even Falkenhayn wa-

---

114. Egmont Zechlin, "Friedensbestrebungen und Revolutionierungsversuche im Ersten Weltkrieg," *Aus Politik und Zeitgeschichte*, Beilage to *Das Parlament*, B20/1961, B24/1961, B25/1951, B20/1963, B22/1963.

115. Janssen, *Der Kanzler*, 184.

116. Rupprecht Kronprinz v. Bayern, *Mein Kriegstagebuch*, diary entry of 12 Feb. 1916, 1:427.

117. For different interpretations: Groener, *Lebenserinnerungen*, 320; Hoffmann, *Aufzeichnungen*, 136–37; Thaer, *Generalstabsdienst*, 91, 96; Janssen, *Der Kanzler*, 182.

vered when the fall of Fort Douaumont raised hopes that Germany might after all be able to take the entire Verdun complex. He seemed then to press ahead. And even after it was clear that the casualty calculation was entirely wrong, he refused to break off the battle.

There are three recurrent patterns here: a lack of clarity in the original goal (which resulted from the large cleft between reach and grasp); the tendency to follow "victory," even if it ran counter to the original plan or ran in an anti-strategic direction (in this case, used up more precious manpower without the probability of ending the war); and the inability to acknowledge defeat.

Far from acknowledging defeat, Falkenhayn began swerving in the opposite direction. He started by self-delusion. He convinced himself that the ratio of French to German dead was far, far higher than it was—he estimated 9:1 and then trimmed it to 3:1 or 5:2 (when it was in fact close to 1:1).[118] If this error originated in "wishful thinking and lack of information," it ended in lies.[119] To keep up the fiction of success, Falkenhayn shaved thirty to forty thousand off the number of German dead in a report to the chancellor in May 1916.[120] In May and June 1916, despite the fact that Verdun had not succeeded, Falkenhayn suddenly began proclaiming a Siegfrieden by fall. He expanded what had been rather moderate war aims to include demands for parts of the Verdun fort complex and the important ore basin, Longwy-Briey, in the Côte Lorraine. His illusions went so far that he (and Ober-Ost) interpreted the major Russian troop buildup of spring 1916 as a positive sign of a last-gasp Russian offensive that would give Germany victory in the east, too. In fact, the Brussilov offensive (4 June) almost knocked Austria out of the war, and it was timed to coincide with the enormous British attack on the Somme (1 July), which shook the German army like no other single event. Five days later, Falkenhayn admitted to the Kaiser that his optimism was unfounded.[121] On 19 July Falkenhayn summed up the military situation as "bad, critical, mushy as a plum."[122]

Falkenhayn was not an irrational man. After he left the post of General Staff chief, he became a highly successful battlefield commander. It is therefore all the more striking how quickly and how far wishful thinking led him to self-delusion, to lying, and to the inability to recognize or respond to reality. The misinterpretation of the Brussilov offensive is particularly striking because it is another instance where a stark occasion for critical learning became transformed into the opposite, a tendentious confirmation of wishful thinking. But to Falkenhayn's credit, when the cataclysm of the Somme broke, he recognized and admitted it. Ludendorff did not do the same two years later.

Falkenhayn responded to the pressures of summer 1916 in another characteristic way—he immersed himself in detail. He fiddled with battalion-sized units in the east and west, as if details could save the larger catastrophe.[123] And when he finally did agree that Verdun could not be pursued further, instead of breaking off the battle cleanly and shift-

118. The ratio was 1.1:1. Afflerbach, *Falkenhayn*, 371, 506.
119. Ibid., 371.
120. Ibid., 407–8.
121. Ibid., 408–20; Janssen, *Der Kanzler*, 201–4.
122. Janssen, *Der Kanzler*, 297.
123. Afflerbach, *Falkenhayn*, 437.

ing as many troops as possible to the defense of the Somme, he wound down the attack gradually and even renewed the attack in August to try to fool the Allies into thinking Germany was strong enough to continue.[124] Falkenhayn thus continued in the military sphere the politics of bluff that had characterized prewar Wilhelminian foreign policy.

Finally, the fourth way in which Falkenhayn tackled the insoluble dilemma of providing military victory against a coalition of much stronger foes was through wonder weapons. The battleship fleet had been the wonder weapon of prewar Wilhelminian policy, insofar as it had promised using technical innovation and daring virtuosity to overcome Britain's naval numbers and traditional expertise and gain for Germany world power status. It is therefore not surprising that wonder-thinking during the war should have largely focused on the navy, particularly on the submarine. Admiral v. Tirpitz had from the beginning pressed for submarine warfare, unrestricted by the international-legal requirements of dealing with merchant ships—prize-warfare. These rules dated from the presubmarine era and demanded that warships check the freighters' bills of lading and then disembark all persons aboard before sinking the vessel. Prize rules were unrealistic for submarines because they had to surface to fulfill them. The slower submarines risked being rammed, or shot at and sunk by armed freighters. Therefore, naval officers argued for unrestricted warfare, which could more safely and efficiently sink neutral freighters bearing food to Britain, but which risked angering neutrals and especially causing the United States to enter the war on the Allied side.

In 1915 Falkenhayn had joined Bethmann in rejecting the navy's calls for unrestricted submarine warfare (USW), because he feared driving neutral states in the Balkans into the enemy camp. That fear subsided when Bulgaria declared war on Serbia in October 1915. By September 1915 the navy argued frankly for USW as the last hope and projected that it would take only six months to "force England to its knees."[125] The treasury secretary, on the contrary, believed that the British blockade would eventually cause Germany to lose the war, and Falkenhayn doubted that submarines were capable of beating England. Captain Michaelis's response (30 September 1915) to their skepticism shows that USW was a compulsive attempt to stave off recognition of Germany's limits:

> If this [skeptical] view were true, then it would mean we will never be able to force England to a peace according to our wishes and that sooner or later we must submit to its conditions. Can we even contemplate such an idea so long as there is a single war weapon left with which we can harm the enemy? In my view: no.[126]

Once Falkenhayn felt trapped by the logic of total military victory, he now (December 1915) also grasped at the USW panacea, but he did so cautiously. In place of the military defeat that he knew Germany could not achieve he again postulated a psychological vic-

124. Janssen, *Der Kanzler*, 242; Lossberg, *Meine Tätigkeit*, 215, 247; Kronprinz Wilhelm v. Preussen, *Deutschlands Heldenkampf* (Berlin, 1923), 219–20, 223.

125. Tirpitz, *Politische Dokumente*, 525–26.

126. Captain Michaelis, "The Meaning of Submarine Warfare—A Memo from the Commander of the High Seas Fleet," Wilhelmshaven, 30 Sept. 1915, in Tirpitz, *Politische Dokumente*, 444.

tory—Britain would behave like a shopkeeper and calculate that the harm Germany was capable of inflicting by USW was more than Britain was willing to tolerate.[127] This was Verdun logic, and a reprise of Tirpitz's original idea behind building the battle fleet.

Falkenhayn now initiated a decision-making process that is unique in appearing to provide the strategic coordination that Germany otherwise lacked. On 30 December 1915 the General Staff chief and the Prussian war minister met with the head of the Naval Office (Tirpitz), the chief of the Admiralty (Grand Admiral Henning von Holtzendorff), and the deputy chief of the Admiralty (Admiral Reinhard Koch). Falkenhayn posed three questions: Would USW be so effective that it would outweigh a possible U.S. entry into the war? Would England sue for peace by the end of 1916? and When could USW realistically and effectively be launched? Holtzendorff answered "yes" to the first two questions and April 1916 to the third. A week later the naval and military leadership agreed to go ahead as much as possible without civilian involvement, but Falkenhayn, recognizing the political implications, informed Bethmann. Falkenhayn's argument was identical to Captain Michaelis's and to the position he had sketched out earlier to Bethmann about the necessity of pursuing military victory: "We can no longer choose *whether* or not we want to use it [USW]. We are simply compelled to do so."[128]

Strategic coordination now widened beyond just the military to include Bethmann and Treasury Secretary Karl Helfferich. The navy, with its flood of statistics, set the terms of the debate.[129] The civilians argued that the navy's data were in fact uncertain; that even if Germany could damage England to the extent the navy claimed, it did not guarantee England would sue for peace; and that U.S. entry was a far more serious problem and would tip the scales against Germany, whatever happened with Great Britain.[130] In the spring of 1916, as the debate raged and the Kaiser was pulled first in one direction and then another, the decision was ultimately made on the basis of the data. Bethmann discovered that Tirpitz had inflated the number of submarines at Germany's disposal by counting those under construction. Tirpitz resigned, and the Kaiser decided for the restricted version of submarine warfare demanded by the United States.

The decision against USW was not a rejection of the logic of military necessity but a recognition that the risk was greater than the probability of success. Falkenhayn had originally been skeptical of the navy's numbers; when he added them up in February, he arrived at less tonnage sunk than did the navy.[131] But, driven by the logic of his situation, he overcame his own doubts and let himself by convinced by the "experts."[132] When the decision went against him, he thought the Kaiser and chancellor had shown weakness in backing down from a calculated risk.[133] When one of the opponents of USW at the Foreign Office asked Falkenhayn how he could still support USW, Falkenhayn replied that

127. Afflerbach, *Falkenhayn*, 380, 384.
128. Bethmann memo of 7 Jan. 1916, in Janssen, *Der Kanzler*, 289, emphasis in original.
129. Deist, "Strategy and Unlimited Warfare," 275–76.
130. Bethmann, memo of 29 Feb. 1916, in Bethmann, *Betrachtungen*, 2:261–69.
131. Tirpitz, *Politische Dokumente*, 475–77.
132. Janssen, *Der Kanzler*, 186, 203–4.·
133. Afflerbach, *Falkenhayn*, 391.

224   "in spite of all other deductions he always came up with the decided feeling that England would give in and America would not intervene." Falkenhayn's interlocutor remarked, "You can't argue against this [sort of reasoning]."[134]

In a last attempt to bring Bethmann around, Falkenhayn pulled out all the stops. He claimed that USW was an integral part of his Verdun strategy and that without USW the campaign would fail and Germany would lose the resulting war of attrition. In fact, Falkenhayn had calculated USW into his original Verdun plan, but had never made that connection clear to other commanders or civilian leaders.[135] Bethmann, who had effectively asserted himself against the navy, was now speechless—as a civilian he could not counter the chief of staff's military appraisal of the land war, nor could he answer the argument from direct military necessity. The USW decision might yet have been reversed but for Admiral Holtzendorff's timely admission that USW would only be effective if the United States did not enter the war. Because Bethmann had previously shown that American entry meant losing the war, the Kaiser shrank from unlimited warfare—for the time being.[136]

Falkenhayn's actions in 1916 prefigure almost exactly the patterns of 1917 and 1918. The difference was that Falkenhayn had been forced (back) into the position of pursuing a purely military victory by Russia's unwillingness to negotiate, while Ludendorff and Hindenburg voluntarily embraced this position and refused to consider negotiations until the very end. Once a military commander found himself in this position, however, the default mechanisms took him down the path of extremes. The military solution required taking all-or-nothing risks, which, in the hopelessness of the strategic situation, were reckoned at the level of operations or, often, of mere tactics. Victory, even merely tactical victory (taking Fort Douaumont), began to be pursued for its own sake, even if it led in antistrategic directions; or, victory became redefined technically or mechanically as the mere possession of territory or the loss of fewer men than the enemy. One tried to overcome material and numerical inferiority by applying one's organizational virtues, which led to the seemingly self-contradictory combination of recklessness with detailed planning. One interpreted negative signs as positive ones, one relied on technical virtuosity and wonder weapons. One calculated, it is true, but according to wishful thinking; one doctored data to support one's wishes, one reckoned on psychology and morale and bluff. And, one stretched one's own troops to the limit, or beyond. The willingness to sacrifice one's own troops undercut whatever limits had existed for treating one's own civilians, for, after all, troops were more valuable and were making the greater sacrifices. Not surprisingly then, the enemy's civilians seemed even more appropriate for exploitation in the name of victory and of military necessity. Because no high officer was well versed in economics, corporate experts provided the details for exploitation. And when none of these steps worked, one tried them again, with more risk and more force.

With the exception of Verdun, which certainly qualifies as "total combat," Falken-

---

134. Janssen, *Der Kanzler*, 198, and Afflerbach, *Falkenhayn*, 392.

135. Herwig, *First World War*, 186, but cf. Kronprinz Wilhelm von Preussen, *Erinnerungen des Kronprinzen Wilhelm*, ed. Karl Rosner (Stuttgart, 1922), 157–58.

136. Afflerbach, *Falkenhayn*, 398–403.

hayn's plans did not reach the extremes to which they tended. They were checked by braking mechanisms that still operated among the civilian administrators and among those military administrators, such as the governors-general of occupied areas, whose jobs brought with them a civilian-like larger and longer-term viewpoint. These administrators factored in the larger world of international and domestic law, economics, domestic politics, neutral opinion, and even Allied opinion. But after August 1916, when Ludendorff and Hindenburg replaced Falkenhayn, these braking mechanisms worked less and less well, and the spiral that had commenced at the very beginning of the war spun out of control.

10

Civilians as Objects of Military Necessity

The military's treatment of civilians, which contains many parallels to colonial conflict, shows how far the spiral of force, driven and justified by "military necessity," actually went in the "nontotal" First World War.

Foundations of Policy toward Enemy Civilians

Germany entered the war with a newly updated manual (1914) for the rear areas, the *Kriegs-Etappen-Ordnung*, or KEO.[1] Because German military planners imagined that the coming war would be brief, the manual did not prepare its readers for a long occupation but for a short war of movement.[2] Nowhere did it give general guidelines for treating civilians, nor did it discuss the international law of occupation. Nevertheless, the KEO laid down four fundamental principles that one can discern in subsequent practice. First, "The preparedness of the field army comes unconditionally before the welfare of the rear zone."[3] Second, civilians were liable to collective punishment for sabotage in their district and to being held hostage to protect trains and villages from sabotage or enemy attack—in short, civilians did *not* automatically enjoy the protections afforded them by the Hague Convention on Land Warfare, which prohibited these practices.[4] Third, the rear zones,

1. Prussia, War Ministry, *Kriegs-Etappen-Ordnung* (KEO). The principles of the KEO applied to both the occupied zones and the front areas under the *Feldintendantur*. For the latter, see Germany, General Staff, *Heeresverpflegung* (Berlin, 1913), 279–311.
2. Freytag-Loringhoven, *Menschen und Dinge*, 136.
3. KEO, p. 52 (para. 103); Germany, General Staff, *Heeresverpflegung*, 290.
4. KEO, p. 68 (para. 137), p. 69 (para. 141). Cf. "The Hague Convention of 1907 Respecting the Laws and Customs of War on Land," para. 49, 50, and 52, in James Brown Scott, ed., *The Hague Conventions and Declarations of 1899 and 1907* (New York, 1915), 124–25, and commentaries by Meurer, *Die Haager Friedenskonferenz*

"especially in enemy territory," were expected to furnish "stores of provisions, all kinds of instruments, vehicles, [and] factory and construction materials." Rear echelon officers were to "use systematically the available factories, bakeries, butcher shops, mills, distilleries and breweries, refrigeration facilities, and threshing machines." Above all, they were to do so "beyond the current needs of the army," "foreseeing coming requirements and considering every possibility."[5] Finally, underscoring the desire to go beyond mere duty, the manual urged subordinates to behave independently. Corps, divisions, and the rear echelon inspectorate should communicate with each other directly; the army command was to intervene only if problems surfaced.[6] Like the field army, the rear was supposed to run according to "mission tactics" (*Auftragstaktik*) and the staff system.[7]

The bulk of the KEO was simply military-bureaucratic: it set up the administrative hierarchy and outlined how to keep track of supplies in a uniform way. The local commandants were enjoined to feed the poor and to respond quickly and fairly to civilian complaints.[8] The manual made clear that if the rear happened to be in Germany, the same principles would generally apply.[9] The problem lay in the dynamic assumptions incorporated in the KEO: the imperative predominance of the fighting army, the lack of absolute legal boundaries protecting the civilian population, the lack of limits to material exploitation, and the expectation that each local commander would go beyond what was necessary. In the absence of occupation policy coordinated from above, these assumptions filled the void. And there was no overall occupation policy, any more than there were uniform occupation institutions. Policy and institutions emerged gradually out of practices, supplemented by belated, sporadic interventions from the Reich Interior Office, the Foreign Office, the Chancellor's Office, various Prussian ministries, and even the Reichstag. Once again, the polycratic nature of Wilhelminian government created the vacuum within which military-cultural practices became policy.

There were four institutional forms of German occupation: the military governorships of Belgium and Poland; the rest of the east (especially the Baltic region) united under the eastern Supreme Command (Ober-Ost); the areas designated as the rear echelon in occupied France, Luxemburg, and westernmost Belgium (administered individually by the rear echelon administrators [*Etappeninspektionen*] of each of the seven armies manning the front lines); and the field administrations (*Feldintendanturen*) of the various armies directly on the front. The Feldintendantur position was established as a result of the lessons of 1866 and 1870. Headed by an *Armeeintendant* at the army level, it had special officers down to the division level. Its job was to supervise the collection and distribution of food and money for the fighting troops at and just behind the front.[10] The high com-

---

2:244–45, 289; Westlake, *International Law*, part 2: *War*, 102, 269; and the dissenting opinion of Lueder, "Das Landkriegsrecht im Besonderen," in *Handbuch des Völkerrechts*, ed. Holtzendorff, 4:475–76, 504–5.

5. KEO, pp. 57–58 (para. 114), 52–53 (para. 104); General Staff, *Heeresverpflegung*, 286–90.
6. KEO, p. 16 (para. 18, 19); Germany, General Staff, *Heeresverpflegung*, 285–86, 288.
7. KEO, p. 10 (para. 4), pp. 23–24 (para. 34).
8. Anlage 7: "Anweisung für den Etappen-Kommandanturen," KEO, 93–98.
9. KEO, p. 65 (para. 130); Germany, General Staff, *Heeresverpflegung*, 290.
10. Germany, General Staff, *Heeresverpflegung*, 287–89, 324.

228 mand (*Armeeoberkommando*) decided where the area of operations (front) ended and the rear (*Etappe*) began.

No central office coordinated or guided these institutions. Yet the form and extent of exploitation was remarkably similar in each, because the three main parameters determining occupation policy were the same everywhere: the military definition of the task (establishing its understanding of order and authority, and the "military necessity" involved in serving the goal of military victory); the instruments at its disposal (bureaucratic administration and force); and the problem of overcoming Germany's inferiority in materials, food, and manpower. When the military set about solving these problems it came up with broadly the same techniques wherever it was.

The military met surprisingly little resistance from German civilian government. There was apparently widespread agreement among civilians about the assumptions contained in the KEO, or as Maj. Albrecht von Thaer, chief of staff of the 9th Reserve Corps in northern France summed them up for his wife in early 1915, "Egoism for our troops is simply a duty."[11] Ludwig Köhler, the chief administrator for commerce and trade in occupied Belgium, wrote after the war that "naturally, the economic life of the occupied zone had to be made to serve German prosecution of the war to a much higher degree than was true for the homeland."[12] At the very beginning of September 1914 the Prussian finance minister was already stressing the bottom line: "It's better that the Belgians starve than that we do," he wrote to the chancellor. Bethmann tried to rein him in, arguing that Germany had "naturally assumed the duty of satisfying the most pressing needs of the population," but only, he added, "as far as this can be reconciled with our own needs."[13]

Indeed, the first instance of force used against enemy civilians for war purposes was orchestrated by the Reich Office of the Interior to apply to draft-age, male Russian-Polish agricultural workers in the German eastern provinces.[14] In the two years before the war, civilian planners had decided to follow recommendations from agrarian circles to ensure the foreign labor on which German agriculture depended. On 3 August 1914 the Interior Ministry of Mecklenburg-Schwerin ordered that foreign workers were to be disarmed, guarded by armed (if necessary, civilian) personnel, and kept away from alcohol and towns, and were to be arrested if they tried to leave their workplace. This typical order was confirmed and made uniform for other provinces by the Prussian war minister and the chancellor in separate regulations in subsequent days.[15] Although government leaders

11. Thaer to his wife, 6 Feb. 1915, in Thaer, *Generalstabsdienst*, 25.

12. Ludwig Köhler, *Die Staatsverwaltung der besetzten Gebiete*, vol.: *Belgien* (New Haven, 1927), 119.

13. Cited in Frank Wende, *Die belgische Frage in der deutschen Politik des Ersten Weltkrieges* (Hamburg, 1969), 24n42.

14. On forced laborers in Germany during the First World War: Ulrich Herbert, *Geschichte der Ausländerbeschäftigung in Deutschland 1880 bis 1980* (Berlin, 1986), 82–113; Lothar Elsner, "Ausländerbeschäftigung und Zwangsarbeitspolitik in Deutschland während des Ersten Weltkrieges," in *Auswanderer-Wanderarbeiter-Gastarbeiter*, ed. Klaus J. Bade (Ostfildern, 1984), 527–57; Elsner, "Der Übergang zur Zwangsarbeit für ausländische Arbeiter in der deutschen Landwirtschaft zu Beginn des 1. Weltkriegs," *Wissenschaftliche Zeitschift der Wilhelm-Pieck-Universität Rostock, Gesellschafts- und Sprachwissenschaftliche Reihe* 26:3 (1977), 291–98; Friedrich Zunkel, "Die ausländischen Arbeiter in der deutschen Kriegswirtschaftspolitik des 1. Weltkriegs," in *Entstehung und Wandel der modernen Gesellschaft*, ed. Gerhard A. Ritter (Berlin, 1970), 280–311.

15. Elsner, "Übergang," 295.

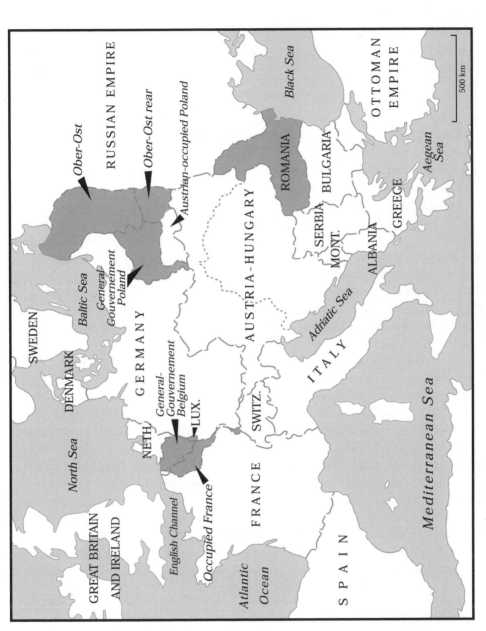

Areas occupied by Germany during World War I (shaded).

230 were clearly embarrassed by the orders to detain foreign laborers illegally, they did so and thus had clearly adopted the principle that military necessity trumped law even before the war began.[16]

Belgium

During the war, Entente propaganda painted Belgium as the chief victim of German occupation policies. Hugh Gibson, the American legation head in Brussels, said that Gen. Moritz von Bissing (the governor-general of Belgium from November 1914 to April 1917) "was the only German general who could strut sitting down."[17] But, for all Bissing's soldierly rigor, his administration, like that of his counterpart, Gen. Hans von Beseler in Poland, reflected a longer-term perspective and more economic realism than the other, more strictly military, types of occupation. Although neither Bissing nor Beseler ever received any instructions about the future of the territories they were governing, both aimed at either annexation or very close ties of dependency.[18] For Bissing this meant reviving industry, sparing as much of the infrastructure as possible, and creating the conditions for the acceptance of Belgium's future status, both externally among the Allies and internally among the population.[19] This latter consideration sensitized him to international law, which emerged as a major Allied concern.

Bissing's job was made easier by the Committee for the Relief of Belgium (CRB).[20] Both Belgium and Germany had been heavy importers of food before the war. General v. Moltke's scheme to deport Belgian workers and the harsh statement from the Prussian Finance Ministry cited previously reflected the view of military and civilian leaders that Germany was unable to share its scarce resources with occupied areas, and in fact would not do so. The CRB was founded by private persons from neutral states (chiefly Spain and the United States), led by Herbert Hoover, and funded by Belgium, France, Britain, and later mostly by the United States. As of mid-October 1914 the CRB covered two-thirds of Belgium's civilian food needs, with their own harvests covering the remainder. The food was imported through neutral nations and distributed by a vast network of CRB employees—all on the condition that no food fall into German hands. The existence of this state-within-a-state was a major infringement on German authority, but one that Germany gladly accepted, rather than deplete its own resources.[21] Without the CRB, Belgians probably would have faced mass starvation.[22]

Even with CRB aid, Belgium faced stringent military administration, far-reaching economic exploitation, forced labor, and deportation. We will never know how Britain

---

16. Zunkel, "Ausländischen Arbeiter," 287n27.

17. Herbert Hoover, *American Epic* (Chicago, 1959), 51.

18. Wild, *Briefe*, 121; Ernst von Wrisberg, *Heer und Heimat, 1914–1918* (Leipzig, 1921), 131.

19. Köhler, *Staatsverwaltung*, 104.

20. CRB: see George H. Nash, *The Life of Herbert Hoover*, 4 vols. (New York, 1988), vols. 2 and 3.

21. On the CRB see Hoover, *American Epic*; Köhler, *Staatsverwaltung*, 70–80; and Helen McPhail, *The Long Silence* (New York, 2000), 63–74.

22. As it was, the CRB barely covered subsistence needs and often fell below: Bissing to Hindenburg (no date given, but must be 24 Sept. 1916), in *UA* 3:1, 347.

and France might have conducted an occupation—they did not face the problem save for a tiny sliver of Alsace. And they had access to greater resources, thus removing one main temptation to full-scale exploitation. Presumably, they would have been equally interested in establishing clear authority and would have luxuriated in the bureaucracy and economic waste typical of military government.[23] But at least three factors seem to have made the German occupation harsher than contemporaries had expected. The first was Germany's chronic shortage of matériel and labor power. These were the civilian counterparts of the military disadvantages the Schlieffen Plan was designed to overcome, and military administrators applied equivalent techniques to solve them. The manpower shortage also meant that Germany's occupation forces were spread too thin. As in the colonies, where the same was true, terror and exemplary punishments replaced dense administration. The pattern began during the "Belgian atrocities," as we have seen, but it continued. Gen. August Keim (military governor of Limburg Province, a Pan-German, and former head of the Army League) was accused of liberal use of the death penalty, which he defended by reference to widespread spying.[24] Huge punitive fines were routinely levied against communities, and the military courts punished all sorts of offenses, many of them trivial. A German Social Democratic critic alleged that between October 1915 and September 1916, 103,902 people were judged guilty of war treason (*Kriegsverrat*) in Belgium.[25] The delict "war treason" held enemy civilians to the same standards of (relatively enthusiastic) behavior expected of Germans in wartime. And this brings us to the second and third factors: the military held a much more elaborate and rigid conception of order than civilians were used to, and Germans appeared to have been much more used to deferential behavior toward superiors than were the Belgians and French. The clash of cultures caused widespread misunderstanding, and the chasm between higher standards and too few policemen produced great anxiety among the Germans about their authority—an anxiety that encouraged more harshness.[26]

Economic exploitation reached proportions that no one would have predicted, although the dynamic was present from the beginning. In August 1914 the Foreign Office fought the General Staff over how much money Belgium could legally (according to the Hague Convention on Land Warfare) be expected to pay. Moltke said Belgium must "militarily, economically, and financially be so exploited that it largely covers the needs of our army concerning provisioning and certain items of war matériel and substitutes," meaning the fighting army, not the army of occupation.[27] The Foreign Office read international law—correctly—to mean that an occupier could demand payment only to cover occupation costs, not the costs of fighting the war. On 29 August 1914 the Kaiser ordered that the Supreme Command should determine the level of "contributions," which it did largely

---

23. David Mitrany, *The Effect of the War on Southeastern Europe*, Carnegie Endowment for International Peace (New Haven, 1936), 83–84, 138–39, 146–52, 163–65.

24. Coetzee, *German Army League*, 110.

25. Ernst, *Der grosse Krieg*, 118.

26. Wild to wife, 3 Dec. 1914, Mézières, *Briefe*, 45, and the citation from General Wandel's diary of 23 Feb. 1915, ibid., 45n1.

27. Brigitte Hatke, *Hugo Stinnes und die drei deutsch-belgischen Gesellschaften von 1916* (Stuttgart, 1990), 48.

232

Belgians read an official notice in Brussels. *Der Weltkrieg, illustrierte Kriegs-Chronik des Daheim* (Bielefeld: Velhagen & Klasing, 1915–), vol. 1, 235.

without regard either to law or the needs of the population.[28] Both "contributions" and requisitions gutted the economy, reducing Belgium's population to extreme poverty.

Bissing countered the antieconomic pressure from the Supreme Command by trying to jump-start Belgian industry, which had been made lame by extensive requisitions. But he failed, because neither German heavy industry nor the raw materials "centrals" [*Zentrale*] in Berlin (which oversaw the collection and distribution of essential raw materials for the war effort) wanted Belgium to recover. Heavy industry pursued its own interest, which was to take over Belgian competitors, for instance, by forced expropriation of non-Belgian-owned or-managed firms, or to ruin those it could not take over.[29] The third Supreme Command finished the job in February 1917 by closing all "nonessential" factories, a step it had tried, but failed to achieve, in Germany. One way or another, by war's end, of 260,000 businesses in Belgium, only 3,013 had survived.[30] By December 1917, 106 iron and steel factories had been dismantled and shipped to Germany, along with the entire interurban and streetcar systems.[31] Requisition and expropriation reached deep into the Belgian infrastructure. Mass Belgian unemployment then suggested one solution to

28. Wende, *Die belgische Frage*, 22–23.
29. Gerald Feldman, *Hugo Stinnes* (Munich, 1998), 374–511.
30. Hatke, *Hugo Stinnes*, 53–62; Gatzke, *Germany's Drive*, 87–92, 155.
31. Köhler, *Staatsverwaltung*, 130–32.

the German manpower problem. The resulting experiment created a scandal even larger than the "Belgian atrocities"—the Belgian deportations.

The Deportations of Belgian Workers

The forcible mass movement of populations has two forms: getting rid of the unwanted (criminals, putatively disloyal elements, or "useless mouths") and importing the needed (laborers). Wartime Germany engaged in both sorts. Deportation was a new departure, for Germany had only a slender previous history of such actions—once in 1886, when Bismarck forced thirty thousand Poles and Polish Jews from Posen into Congress Poland, and again in the colonies, as in the Witboi deportation to Togo.[32] And yet deportation was already an option for Moltke on 23 August 1914. Where did the idea come from?

Colonial rhetoric seems to have been the largest source for Germany, at least. Originally, liberals in the mid-nineteenth century debated deportation as a solution to social problems by removing criminals, the poor, and socialist revolutionaries. Those schemes never materialized. The broad stream of public and governmental opinion rejected deportation before 1914. But the idea lived on among social Darwinists, theorists of racial degeneration, and above all, supporters of the Pan-Germans and the right wing of the German Colonial Society.[33] Writing pseudonymously in 1912, Heinrich Class, the Pan-German leader, recommended evacuating French and Russian territory for German colonization in the event of a successful war. He coyly nodded to the moral disapproval he knew would greet his suggestion, saying forced evacuation was "only a tool to be used in the extreme case," but he immediately hastened to outline that case: a "defensive" war in which Germany was forced to attack its enemies, followed, in the interests of "ultimate security" against France and "a better border and also land for colonization" in Russia, by "evacuation" of the native inhabitants.[34] It is unclear whether Class's book inspired the naval officers whom the publicist Ernst Jäckh overheard in 1913 discussing "evacuation," "expropriation," and German colonization.[35] Class repeated his ideas openly after 28 August 1914 as war aims.[36] The ethnic cleansing variety of deportation is more clearly linked to civilian, rather than to military, circles, however. Already by early December 1914 Chancellor Bethmann Hollweg favored ethnic cleansing and German colonization of a strip of Poland bordering Prussia, and he appears to have arrived at this idea himself. He appointed Pan-German and procolonial members of the Prussian government to hone the details. Prussian high officialdom was divided about evacuation, and even most of the

32. Hans-Ulrich Wehler, "Polenpolitik im Deutschen Kaiserreich," in Wehler, *Krisenherde des Kaiserreichs 1871–1918*, 2nd ed. (Göttingen, 1979), 184–202.

33. Johannes H. Voigt, "Die Deportation," in *Ausweisung und Deportation*, ed. Andreas Gestrich (Stuttgart, 1995), 83–101.

34. Class, *'Wenn ich der Kaiser wär'* (Leipzig, 1912), 140–42, 152 (France); 170 (Russia).

35. Ernst Jäckh to Friedrich Naumann, Norway, Aug. 1913, in Jäckh's *Der goldene Pflug* (Stuttgart, 1954), 291, cited by Imanuel Geiss, *Der polnische Grenzstreifen, 1914–1918* (Hamburg, 1960), 42. See also Wernecke, *Der Wille zur Weltgeltung*, 302–4.

36. Gatzke, *Germany's Drive*, 26–27.

234 supporters, including the chancellor, rejected force and haste in favor of inducements to lure the unwanted over the border.[37] Ludendorff adopted the idea with his typical vehemence, but the Polish border scheme was the creation of civilians, not the military.[38]

There were other precedents for deportation. Every newspaper reader knew of the violent ethnic evacuations that had occurred during the Balkan Wars of 1912 and 1913, but references to these among German officers seem uncommon.[39] It is perhaps more surprising that the Russian precedent was so rarely cited in Germany. Unlike Germany, Russia had a long history of internal deportation, for punitive and demographic-colonization purposes. At the outbreak of war in 1914 its army received sweeping wartime powers very similar to those of the German army, including the explicit power to deport. Obsessed with spies whom they imagined were rife among Russia's unusually large foreign population, Russia's high command began the internal deportation of male enemy aliens living near the front even before fighting started. Driven by the army, together with conservative and right-wing newspapers, deportation swiftly expanded geographically to "exclusion zones" such as railways, major roads, defense factories, and the coastline, and demographically to include women and children aliens, and then Russian subjects of non–Great Russian nationality. Deportation became popular as an occasion for expropriation of property, especially of land. One million aliens and eight hundred thousand ethnic Russian subjects may have been deported, the highest number for any country during the war. Like all deportations under military control in this period, Russia's were poorly prepared for the journey and the resettlement.[40] Everyone suffered, many died. The deportation of ethnic Germans (Russian subjects) began on 7 September 1914, on the initiative of a corps commander, whose action was quickly backed by the local governor (of Suvalki province) and then by the chief of staff. As with other ethnic groups, the deportation swiftly widened its scope until whole provinces were "empty" of German speakers.[41]

Despite the enormous scale of the Russian operations, they seem to have been rarely discussed in German circles, and even after the war they were not commonly mentioned as exculpatory (along the tu quoque model). An exception was, again, a civilian, the president of East Prussia, Adolf Batocki, who in December 1914 cited the Russian precedents "in the last few years" as proof that "with the right preparation" governments could move

---

37. Geiss, *Der polnische Grenzstreifen*: Bethmann (71–72); other civilian supporters (49–60); Prussian division (129–32); lack of force (104).

38. Ibid., 128. Col. Thaer (a Silesian) thought he had authored the idea, but, because the plans were top secret, he could not know that the chancellor was already way ahead of him. Like Bethmann, Thaer wanted to compensate the inhabitants and have them leave voluntarily. Thaer, *Generalstabsdienst*, 43, 165, 205.

39. Geiss believes 1912–13 was an important precedent in Germany: Imanuel Geiss, "The Civilian Dimension of the War," in *Facing Armageddon*, ed. Hugh Cecil and Peter Liddle (London, 1996), 17.

40. Despite some prewar planning for this eventuality: Peter Holquist, "To Count, to Extract, to Exterminate," in *A State of Nations*, ed. Terry Martin and Ronald Suny (Oxford, 2001), 111–44, here 121–22; Dittmar Dahlmann, "Die Deportationen der deutschen Bevölkerungsgruppe in Russland und in der Sowjetunion 1915 und 1941," in *Ausweisung und Deportation*, ed. Andreas Gestrich (Stuttgart, 1995), 103–14, here 105.

41. This account is based on the excellent study by Eric Lohr, "Enemy Alien Politics within the Russian Empire during World War I," Ph.D. diss., Harvard University, 1999, revised ms. See his article, "The Russian Army and the Jews," *Russian Review* 60:3 (July 2001), 404–19.

masses of people "without harming them."[42] The phrase "in the last few years" suggests Batocki may not have been thinking of the current wartime deportations.

The modern history of deportation in Germany and Europe is still understudied, but the current state of research suggests that ideologically motivated deportation ideas had penetrated further into civilian than into German military circles, and that the Balkan or Russian precedents were not objects of imitation. Instead, Moltke's idea and the military pressure for Belgian deportations were immediate, short-term solutions to specific problems: fear of resistance and inability to feed Belgian workers before the CRB, and the manpower shortage in ammunition factories. The knowledge of deportations elsewhere made it easier to conceive of this tactic, but it appears to have been more a logical extension of the application of force to problems than part of an ideological worldview.

The process by which Germany came to deport tens of thousands of Belgian workers illustrates well the incremental, short-term nature of decision making, the lack of overt guiding principles, and the strength of covert assumptions.[43] The slide appears to have begun in early 1915 when some Rhenish industrialists called for Belgian workers to help alleviate the labor shortage.[44] In March 1915 the Prussian war minister asked Governor-General Bissing to arrange for volunteer laborers, which he did, but with little success. In the next year, thanks to German occupation policies, Belgian unemployment grew parallel with the labor shortage in Germany. By March 1916 a different motive moved the military: to free up reserves for the front, the war minister demanded four hundred thousand forced deportees to replace German factory workers. Bissing refused, citing the unfavorable effect that this clear breach of international law would have on foreign, especially neutral, public opinion, and the low quality of forced labor.[45] Bissing turned to the chancellor, who avoided the principled rejection Bissing sought and temporized, suggesting that other measures be tried first.[46] Lacking firm support from the chancellor, it became harder, even for a military man responsible only to the Kaiser, to hold out against military logic. Bissing now began a series of compromises that inadvertently undermined his principled opposition. In May he cut off public works assistance to localities to increase the number of unemployed. Then, building on his earlier orders (starting in November 1914) against those refusing to accept work, he shifted jurisdiction over such people from civil to military courts (15 May 1916) and legalized their deportation to Germany as individual miscreants. Bissing had thus expanded and militarized the penal model to force individuals to "volunteer," creating in the process both the mechanism and the excuse for later forcible mass deportation. For the moment, the 15 May ordinance remained merely a threat, however.

42. Adolf Tortilowicz v. Batocki-Friebe to Arnold Wahnschaffe, 20 Dec. 1914, cited in Geiss, *Der polnische Grenzstreifen*, 76.

43. Still the best account: Ritter, *Sword and Scepter*, 3:361–72; also, Köhler, *Staatsverwaltung*, 144–68; and Belgium, Ministry of Foreign Affairs, *Report Laid before the Belgian Parliament by the Minister of Foreign Affairs in Answer to the Reichstag Report on Belgian Deportations, 1916–1917* (Brussels, 1928).

44. Zunkel, "Ausländischen Arbeiter," 289.

45. Köhler, *Verwaltung*, 146–51.

46. Bethmann to Bissing, draft, 17 Apr. 1916, and Wahnschaffe's marginalium on Bissing to Bethmann, Brussels, 28 Apr. 1916, in *UA* 3:1, 336, 338; Ritter, *Sword and Scepter*, 3:361–62.

236   Meanwhile, the number of volunteers remained low and the pressure increased. In August 1916 Ludendorff and Hindenburg replaced Falkenhayn and immediately announced plans for the Hindenburg program to triple munitions production by spring and to increase Germany's troop levels. Forced labor would do both. Leaders of heavy industries, eager for cheap labor, became active lobbyists for it in September 1916. Carl Duisburg, head of Bayer Corporation, argued that industry could fulfill OHL's demand for the "impossible" (*Menschenunmögliche*) only if all limits, which he labeled "bureaucratism," were removed. For instance, he suggested that Bissing should lower food rations to create more "volunteers."[47] Walter Rathenau went further: "The solution to the Belgian worker problem can only be achieved by ignoring international prestige questions [i.e., international law], so that the seven hundred thousand workers in Belgium are made available to the home market, even if it means American aid [the CRB] will end."[48] The civilian "experts" thus agreed with OHL that force was the solution and that, as Hindenburg had told Bissing days earlier, "the necessity to use all labor power forces us to these sorts of measures and all social and international-legal considerations must be absolutely subordinate."[49]

On 4 August, before Ludendorff and Hindenburg had assumed supreme command, and responding to increasing pressure from the war ministry, Bissing had already taken the next step, telling the provincial and county administrators to begin deporting individuals under the order of 15 May.[50] Nonetheless, in September he held firm against the third OHL's insistent pressure. Bissing cited international law first, but apparently sensing that this argument was no longer strong enough, he listed practical objections: forced deportation would cause mass unrest and labor stoppages in Belgium, American aid would cease, neutrals would protest, and "since a means to force intransigent workers to work has not to date been used in a civilized state," the workers would become useless eaters.[51] The day after the 16 September meeting at which industrialists so enthusiastically supported the OHL, Bissing clashed personally with Ludendorff and thereupon offered the Kaiser his resignation, which Wilhelm rejected. Forced to stay in office, Bissing tried to be accommodating. When OHL suggested deporting only draft-age men, Bissing considered it, but demurred after one of his aides informed him that this, too, contravened international law.

The issue was supposed to be concluded at a 28 September conference in Berlin among the two military governors-general and representatives of the Foreign Office, the Reich Office of the Interior, the Supreme Command, and the War Ministry. This meeting formally met the conditions for a "strategic" decision-making session, insofar as military and civilian offices were present, but it did not function that way. The economic feasibility of deportation was never discussed, only the narrower issue of what circumstances

47. Protocol of the meeting (between leading industrialists and the war minister), 16 Sept. 1916, in *UA* 3:1, 385, 387.

48. Rathenau to Ludendorff, 16 Sept. 1916, *UA* 3:1, 383; Ritter, *Sword and Scepter*, 3:364–65.

49. OHL to the governors-general of Belgium and Warsaw, draft, II Nr. 34 648 op., 13 Sept. 1916, *UA* 3:1, 339.

50. Köhler, *Verwaltung*, 150–51; *UA* 3:1, 422; Zunkel, "Ausländischen Arbeiter," 298.

51. Bissing to Hindenburg, Ia Nr. 7793, Brussels, 15 Sept. 1916, *UA* 3:1, 341–44.

might make deportations legal.[52] Bissing's representatives rejected OHL's demand to use two hundred thousand forced laborers to build defensive positions (the "Siegfried line") behind the front in France. OHL's spokesman, Quartermaster General von Sauberzweig, made two arguments for mass deportation and forced labor: military necessity ("It is possible that the entire outcome of the war depends on this"),[53] and the duty of the occupying power to uphold "law and order" against idlers. The general government responded that all was quiet in Belgium. The representative of the War Ministry and the military men present agreed with Sauberzweig, and surprisingly, the Foreign Office raised no strong objection. The meeting ended inconclusively, but it led to a legal opinion by the Foreign Office that the military danger posed by masses of unemployed Belgians permitted deportation under international law.[54]

With the ground being cut out from under him, Bissing still maintained (4 October) that forced labor was "against my conscience."[55] Bissing had written to the chancellor, rehearsing the many practical (but not legal) reasons against deportation and forced labor. While he was awaiting the reply, the general government and representatives of OHL began outlining the logistics of deportation, just in case. On 7 October 1916 Bethmann followed the Foreign Office's legalistic reasoning.[56] He declared that international law did not forbid using civilian labor to build fortifications.[57] Deportations to Germany could be made to seem legal by declaring the (willfully) unemployed a threat to security and using Bissing's 15 May order to cover their mass deportation. Their forced labor was then legal because they were criminals, not simply civilian deportees.[58] Bethmann did underscore that deportees should perform no munitions work. ·

What seems to have happened is that civilians (in the Reich Office of the Interior, the Foreign Office, the general government, and the Chancellor's Office) had followed the long trend of German judicial thinking that held that military necessity—in this case, potential danger to occupation troops—or even the duty to uphold order in occupied territory superseded international law. International law had been Bissing's chief argument against the deportations. He used this argument less and less as September wore on. Without the shield of international law, both he and the civilian leaders who opposed deportation—and this included the chancellor and the foreign secretary—were exposed to the unanswerable claim of military necessity to win the war. Years later, Bethmann characterized the Belgian deportations as "a forced measure of military necessity" to the investigating parliamentary committee. "The military branch claimed that they were matters of necessity," Bethmann explained, "regulations resulting from a forced situation,

---

52. Ritter, *Sword and Scepter*, 3:366.

53. Köhler, *Verwaltung*, 151. Köhler was present at the meeting, but the protocols do not contain this citation: *UA* 3:1, 349–54.

54. Dr. Kriege's testimony, *UA* 3:1, 332, 409.

55. Bissing to Hindenburg, Brussels, 4 Oct. 1916, ibid., 356.

56. Bethmann to Bissing, 7 Oct. 1916, ibid., 366.

57. Bethmann may have been following a decision made earlier in discussions between the Reich Office of the Interior and General Moltke. Lewald's testimony, protocol of 28 Sept. 1916 meeting, in ibid., 352.

58. Bissing's civilian administration chief, v. Sandt, had already argued along these lines: Sandt to Bissing, 5 Sept. 1916, draft, and protocol of conference of 6 Oct. 1916, Brussels, in ibid., 395, 359.

238 essential for the purpose of carrying out the Hindenburg program, required in order to carry it out at all. So far as I know, it was not possible to carry out this program even then; but the argument of inexorable military necessity always confronted me."[59] The chancellor therefore tried only to mitigate the deportations, not to stop them. Deprived of support from the highest political office, Bissing finally gave in on 11 October.[60]

A week later (19 October) the decision-making process lurched to its next phase: preparation. Bissing apparently received the figure of twenty thousand deportees a week from industrialists and forwarded that to OHL. Rather than planning for this large number, representatives from the general government of Belgium and the relevant Berlin offices, meeting in Berlin, agreed on a typically fuzzy and self-contradictory policy. Although the aim was to increase "volunteers," the method was threatened or actual punishment. On the one hand, the deportations were justified as necessary for security under a penal order (15 May 1916); on the other, "the planned measures were to be stripped of the appearance of punishment" by calling the camps that housed the deportees "collection areas" rather than "concentration or prison camps."[61] In part, self-contradiction arose from the compromise necessary to paper over disagreements among policy makers. But it indicates, too, an incomplete decision-making process in which the government apparatus was willing to *act* according to "military necessity" but was reluctant to accept the consequences of this extremism, and thus was unwilling to think the process and its ramifications through to the end. Years later, Bissing's administrative assistant, Köhler, who was heavily involved in overseeing the deportations, concluded that the deportations "showed lack of psychological understanding, the absence of a steady leading hand, the incompleteness of decisions, and also the retreat before resistance that one should have taken into account from the outset."[62]

Deportations began a week after this last meeting, on 26 October—two days *before* the written guidelines for deportation were issued by the general government and three weeks *before* the War Office (Kriegsamt) issued its own instructions.[63] These guidelines clearly show that work, not punishment, was the intended object. But force had its own logic,[64] and, together with the military manner of doing things, the punitive or repressive character of deportation eclipsed everything else. The delicate balance the military was supposed

59. Germany, National Constituent Assembly, *Official German Documents Relating to the World War*, 412. "It was even for the Imperial Chancellor a matter of immense difficulty, if not of impossibility, to do away with a measure concerning which the military authorities said: 'If this measure is not carried out, we shall simply be unable to win the war'" (419).

60. Köhler, *Staatsverwaltung*, 151.

61. Ibid., 153; Erich Ludendorff, *Urkunden der Obersten Heeresleitung über ihre Tätigkeit 1916–18*, 2nd ed. (Berlin, 1921), 127–28.

62. Köhler, *Staatsverwaltung*, 166.

63. "Anweisung des General-Gouvernements in Belgien an die ihm untergeordneten deutschen Militär- und Zivilstellen über die Ausführung der Abschiebung arbeitsscheuer Belgier nach Deutschland," Sektion I c Nr. 7900, Brussels, 28 Oct. 1916; and "Die vom Kriegsministerium (Kriegsamt) aufgestellten Grundsätze über Heranziehung arbeitsscheuer Belgier zu Arbeiten nach Deutschland," Berlin, 15 Nov. 1916, UA 3:1, 239–45.

64. This is the theme of Ulrich Herbert's work on forced labor in the First World War: *Ausländerbeschäftigung*, 82–113, and Herbert, "Zwangsarbeit als Lernprozess," *Archiv für Sozialgeschichte* 24 (1984): 285–304.

to observe, and could not, was summed up in the governor-general's order that the transports were to be commanded by "an especially appropriate, energetic, but calm officer" who was to "to avoid all unnecessary harshness" and "to overlook small instances of disobedience but to intervene strenuously against large ones."[65] The transports were to be handled like troop transports. The War Office guidelines revealed the logic of force even more clearly. Camp commanders were told not to use outright force to get the Belgians to work; instead, "through stringent discipline and strict enlistment for necessary work in the camps, the prerequisites will be laid down such that the Belgians will greet every opportunity for well-paid work outside the camp as a desirable improvement of their condition." Once the Belgians were working, the guidelines foresaw pay equal to that of German workers (minus upkeep costs), and the deputy military commanders were ordered to make sure just complaints were swiftly and fairly settled. Nonetheless, the "volunteers" were to be kept in groups, so that they could easily be overseen and if necessary guarded by armed German workers. And their clothing was to carry a permanent label marking them as Belgian deportees.[66] Forced labor therefore automatically militarized the workplace and required uniform-like insignia to ensure different treatment for suspect laborers.

The actual treatment of the deportees fell below these standards. Belgian resistance was partly to blame because withholding unemployment lists meant that the Germans, who initially did not examine the deportees medically, filled their quotas with many sickly nonworkers. But the sheer organizational inability of the German military bore a greater share of the blame. Rear echelon troop strength had fallen by one-third in the autumn of 1916;[67] Germany lacked the personnel to carry out a successful, humane deportation of large numbers of unwilling people.[68] Knowing that they would have great trouble rounding up non-"volunteers" who knew they would be deported, the general government instructed district commanders to hold these people at the collection centers, "without [giving them] the opportunity of going home again."[69] They were thus unable to collect food, winter clothing, or blankets—nor, despite the governor-general's orders, did they receive them. Some deportees went sixty-three hours without food, and most were without blankets in the cold and drizzly fall and winter.[70] Typical of the organizational chaos was the fluctuating number of deportees demanded from week to week: OHL requested first eight thousand, then twenty thousand, then the next day revised that figure to twelve to thirteen

---

65. "Anweisung des General-Gouvernements," 239.

66. "Die vom Kriegsministerium (Kriegsamt) aufgestellten Grundsätze," 243–45. In response to military security concerns about enemy alien workers, Krupp managers in 1915 had suggested labeling Polish workers' clothing, but nothing came of it: Herbert, "Zwangsarbeit," 296, and Herbert, *Ausländerbeschäftigung*, 105.

67. Testimony of Lt. Col. Koch (Reichswehr), 16 Sept. 1925, in *UA* 3:1, 414, 416.

68. The same was true in the east, where the governor-general acceded to the same pressure as Bissing and in October 1916 deported five thousand Jewish forced laborers to Germany. Half of them were too frail to work and the deportation was called off before the planned thirty thousand had been rounded up. Ludendorff's successor at Ober-Ost commented on the failure of Germany's forced labor policy: "Our organs are simply inadequate to round up all the people forcibly." Herbert, *Ausländerbeschaftigung*, 92; Zunkel, "Ausländischen Arbeiter," 301–2.

69. Draft telegraphic instructions to the district chiefs, 6 Oct. 1916, *UA* 3:1, 373.

70. Munro, Sellery, and Krey, ed., *German War Practices*, part 1, 76.

240 thousand, and finally to two thousand after it became clear that Germany could not handle anything larger.[71]

Deportees arrived at ill-equipped former POW camps, where many waited weeks to be placed in factories. The camps displayed the typical range of humane to punitive treatment and competent to incompetent management that characterized military camps housing civilians, for example, in the Boer War. Some commandants recognized that the poor condition of many deportees required extra rations beyond the official 1,745 calories; others held scrupulously to the official order; and still others reduced rations to induce "volunteers." Some commandants were able to scrape up sufficient coal to heat barracks, others were not.[72] The food and coal shortages in Germany made the commandants' job much more difficult.

The combination of poor health, resistance, and poor coordination with industry meant that five weeks into the deportation, only 20 percent of the deportees were working.[73] Even Ludendorff quickly recognized that the experiment had been a disaster. Deportations halted in February 1917 even before the order came to do so.[74] In the interim almost sixty thousand men had been deported to Germany. All who refused the massive pressure to sign "voluntary" labor contracts were repatriated by mid-July 1917, despite General Ludendorff's attempt to have them diverted as forced laborers into occupied France.[75] There they would have joined over sixty thousand more men, women, and children, who had already been deported from Belgium to do military work behind the lines in the rear echelons (beyond Bissing's control). These persons were never released during the war.[76] The official Belgian report says that among deportees to Germany 3–4 percent died, 5.2 percent were maimed or permanently invalided, 6.5 percent had "scars from ill-treatment," 4.4 percent suffered frostbite, and 35.8 percent were ill when they returned from Germany.[77] German investigators reported a death rate of 1.8 percent by the end of March 1917 (annualized, that would be 4.46 percent), a figure they said was "high."[78] These statistics were the results of malnutrition, poor original health, overwork, ill-treatment, poor hygiene, no extra clothing, and bad housing. Malnutrition was partly the result of Germany's meager food ration in 1916–1917, which required supplements to reach the subsistence level.[79] Unlike French civilian prisoners, the Belgian deportees did not re-

71. Köhler, *Verwaltung*, 164.

72. Protocol of the Kriegsministerium Unterkunftsabteilung, Nr. 12 833/3. 17 MA, Berlin, 31 Mar. 1917, in *UA* 3:1, 374–80.

73. Ritter, *Sword and Scepter*, 3:370.

74. Ibid., 3:371.

75. Zunkel, "Ausländischen Arbeiter," 299n76.

76. Belgium, Ministry of Foreign Affairs, *Report Laid before*, 29–41.

77. "Observations Made on the State of Health of the Deportees on Their Return from Germany and from the German Front in Belgium and France," in Belgium, Ministry of Foreign Affairs, *Report Laid before*, 42–51, here 47. There is disagreement on the death toll: cf. Ritter, *Sword and Scepter*, 3:369, 567n45, and Gatzke, *Germany's Drive*, 157.

78. Protocol of the Kriegsministerium Unterkunftsabteilung, 375.

79. Bumm calculated that the average daily civilian ration in Germany was falling from 1,500 to 1,000 calories per day in the late fall and winter of 1916–17: Franz Bumm, *Deutschlands Gesundheitsverhältnisse unter dem Einfluss des Weltkrieges*, Carnegie Endowment for International Peace (Stuttgart, 1928), 72, cited in Chickering, *Imperial Germany*, 143.

ceive Red Cross or other extra food packages until the end of March.[80] Inmates (in any sort of institution) generally suffered a much higher malnutrition and death rate than did noninmates during the war. Nevertheless, the other conditions listed were caused by the same combination of logistical inattention, "lovelessness," and hostile disdain that reigned in the colonies. As the historian Gerhard Ritter observed, "The whole scheme had the appearance of regular slave transports and slave markets, which mitigation by some well-intentioned local commandants could not alter."[81]

Internationally, the Belgian deportations were equally disastrous. They produced an enormous international uproar that went beyond the Entente powers to include all the neutral states, the pope, and legions of private citizens.[82] No issue did more to turn American public opinion against Germany.[83] And the deportations coincided with Bethmann's peace initiative of December 1916, discrediting it as a cruel hoax.

Yet even after the war was over, neither former Foreign Secretary Arthur Zimmermann, who referred to the deportations as "a domestic measure," nor Bethmann seemed to understand their significance.[84] It may be understandable that Bethmann dismissed international opposition as mere Allied propaganda, for he could point to the (illegal) British blockade as a major factor forcing Germany to exploit all the resources at its disposal. But for our purposes, Bethmann's obtuseness is significant because it coexisted with his otherwise trenchant criticism of military "necessities" and how these blocked wiser political viewpoints.[85] Despite this insight, Bethmann seems to have regarded the Belgian deportations as an unimportant sideshow where the details of execution somehow went wrong and had to be mitigated, rather than as emblematic of a systematic pattern of extreme war conduct. Bethmann ended his postwar Reichstag testimony on the deportations by implicitly justifying them in the same tit-for-tat, tu quoque terms typical of everyone who accepted the argument from military necessity:

"The violation of international law was unquestionably to be found in the execution [of the deportations]; but this plea, I believe, will not be denied me: Are we forever to talk of nothing but our own sins, even those consisting in the violations of international law, we who stand face to face with an anomaly of international law like England's blockade through which (raising his voice) our people have been relegated to an existence of misery for generations?"
(Loud applause from the spectators.)
The Chairman: "That closes the matter."[86]

---

80. Protocol of the Kriegsministerium Unterkunftsabteilung, 376.

81. Ritter, *Sword and Scepter*, 3:369.

82. *UA* 3:1, 212–13, 246–78.

83. Germany, National Constituent Assembly, *Official German Documents*, 2:253–54; Prince Max v. Baden, *Erinnerungen und Dokumente* (Stuttgart, 1927), 78.

84. Germany, National Constituent Assembly, *Official German Documents*, 1:412.

85. Ibid., 1:419–20.

86. Ibid., 1:420.

242   Ludwig Köhler, Bissing's assistant, recognized that the problems in execution came from the nature of the policy itself as it arose out of "military necessity." "This compulsory reason for the entire action could not fail to have its effects on the manner of execution," he wrote in his contribution to the Carnegie Commission reports after the war. "The organs responsible for carrying out the forcible deportation thought they were only doing their duty when they placed the relentless fulfillment of the demands of the Supreme Command ahead of all other, including political, viewpoints." Having seen how extremism replicated itself throughout the system, Köhler nonetheless seems, like Bethmann, to have been unable to extricate himself from the chains of military-necessity thinking. He, too, relapsed into the tu quoque argument, citing the blockade and the Allied aerial bombardment of Karlsruhe: "Why should Germans be more punctilious [than the Entente] when it was a matter of life or death for the fatherland?"

And then Köhler recounted a final reason for the brutality involved in deportations: Belgian resistance and German fear of weakness. The Belgians had refused to produce lists of the unemployed; German officers responded by forced roundups of all available men, regardless of their skills or physical appropriateness. Köhler echoed the officer in charge of deportations at Mons, who claimed that resistance threatened "to stop the measure almost entirely and to prove the German administration powerless."[87] The necessity to demonstrate authority became greater as Germany's relative power declined, that is, as it came to rely more on foreign labor. This was a typical colonial situation of resistance and dependence, and it elicited a similar administrative response.

The Belgian deportations showed how military occupation policy developed as a seemingly logical response to the wartime situation, braked for a time by longer-term, postwar considerations and by sensitivity to the opinions of foreigners, on whom Germany was dependent for imports and (indirectly, via the CRB) food. That dependence increased Germany's otherwise comparatively weak attention to international law. But none of these brakes could stop indefinitely the inexorable argument from military necessity, which civilians such as the leaders of heavy industry could easily also claim when it coincided with their material interests. Military necessity was so indisputable that civilian leaders could not free themselves from it even after the war had been lost; they continued to argue according to its precepts (tit-for-tat, tu quoque, and the requirement to uphold authority based on force by applying more force).[88]

But the Entente propagandists were wrong if they thought Belgium was the paradigm case of military rule. The general government in fact shielded Belgium from the full force of a military-practical regime. General v. Einem's opinion of Bissing was widespread: "For the army he was not a good governor, because he was always too much concerned with sparing the Belgians; the army could only get things out of Belgium with difficulty."[89] It had a much easier time where it ruled directly: in the Baltic areas under Ober-Ost and in northern France.

---

87. Köhler, *Staatsverwaltung*, 163.
88. The Reichstag's majority opinion also absolved the government of wrongdoing: *UA* 3:1, 193–97.
89. Einem, *Armeeführer*, diary entry of 19 Apr. 1917, 304.

The Occupation under Ober-Ost

Although most Polish-speaking areas under German control were united under one governor-generalship, the rest of a vast occupied zone, reaching from the easternmost Polish counties to Courland on the Baltic Sea, Lithuania, and parts of White Russia (forty-two thousand square kilometers and three million people), was ruled directly by the eastern Supreme Command, Ober-Ost (see map 3).[90] A centralized military occupation hierarchy presided over four, later two, military districts that were subdivided along the Prussian model, down to individual villages and estates.[91] Next to this were an independent military railroad administration (formally similar to the independence of the railroad section of the General Staff) and the military police. The bureaucrats proliferated to between ten and eighteen thousand in number.[92] But they were never sufficient to permeate the large areas they were charged with administering, and so the colonial pattern of great expectations and inadequate means was repeated once more. The great expectations of the military recall the colonial, too: establishing order and security, living off the occupied zone (which made them independent of civilian oversight from Berlin), providing a surplus to the Reich, and demonstrating the superiority of the occupied administration to its Russian predecessor, which might "justify keeping the area forever."[93]

Although Ludendorff called a number of civilians from the Reich to help with administration, all officials were enjoined to stress the military nature of occupation at every turn.[94] The principles of occupation government, as Ludendorff set them down, were exactly those guiding the officer in combat: "to act quickly and energetically in unknown circumstances"; "to work not bureaucratically, but according to the requirements of the situation. Thank God there was no 'precedent,' that grave-digger of free power of decision."[95] Of course no "precedent" did not mean "free" decisions but rather ones determined by the habits of military culture. Friedrich von Payer, the leader of the Left Liberal Party, who became vice-chancellor in November 1917 and who had investigated the failures of German occupation administration in the east, summed up the main principle there as "nothing but the demand for a rigid, suffocating order."[96]

As is usual in systems aspiring to extreme "order," the result was disorder. The luxuriant bureaucracy produced a thicket of ordinances no orderly mind could penetrate. As one denizen of the lower bureaucracy claimed, "I have not spoken to a single one of our men in serious conversation who does not admit the convoluted counterproductiveness of our administrative measures . . . but each participates in the madness, because he feels

90. Aba Strazhas, *Deutsche Ostpolitik im Ersten Weltkrieg* (Wiesbaden, 1993), 13n5; Vejas Liulevicius, *War Land on the Eastern Front* (Cambridge, 2000), 21.

91. Liulevicius, *War Land,* 62–63.

92. Ibid., 56–57.

93. Ibid., 54–55.

94. Strazhas, *Deutsche Ostpolitik,* 33.

95. Ludendorff's memoirs as cited in Liulevicius, *War Land,* 59. Also, Eisenhart-Rothe, *Im Banne der Persönlichkeit,* 145–50.

96. Payer, *Von Bethmann Hollweg,* 201.

244 himself helplessly clamped into the paperwork machine."[97] The thin occupation put a premium on the *Auftragssystem*, the autonomy of each administrator to fulfill the principles of occupation in his own manner.[98] There was wide latitude for bizarre, brutal, or idiosyncratic behavior.[99] The overlapping jurisdictions of administration, railroad, and military police produced chaos of their own that Ober-Ost never resolved. And the statistics that were supposed to be an objective record of resources were often the amalgam of subjective impressions by local officials and absurd formalism, according to which, for example, all cows gave the same amount of milk and did so in winter as well as in summer.[100]

Military "order" was a solid tripod resting on identification and definition (of people and resources); hierarchy (the proper relationship of authority and subordination); and control (the exercise of authority or, failing that, of mere power).

Identification began with people. Every inhabitant over the age of ten was to receive a pass photo, which he or she was required to show on command. Photos were taken of five people at a time, each with numbers pinned to their chests. In 1917 1.8 million people were processed. This sort of objectification merely extended to civilians what soldiers had already undergone. It is typical of the military bureaucracy that it applied the same level of scrutiny to itself, reporting that the 1.8 million passes had cost 12,000 pens and 177 liters of ink.[101] Next, the occupiers attempted surveys of the entire resources of the area: factories, houses, buildings, livestock, down to household utensils.

Hierarchy rested on two simple principles: "No native could command or be set above any German,"[102] and, as the Order of Rule stated, "The interests of the army and the German Reich always supersede the interests of the occupied territory."[103] Military authorities demanded constant demonstrations of deference from the occupied, who, for example, were required to step off the sidewalk and deferentially tip their hats when they met a German officer.[104]

As control, "order" expressed itself in the prohibition of all unauthorized travel, even to the next village. All movement required passes, and thus the normal intercourse of life was either minutely regulated or stopped altogether.[105] Other behavior was equally subject to a flood of minute, self-contradictory prohibitions: "not working on Sundays and holidays, eating or selling meat or meat products, baking or eating cakes, brewing home-made beer, entering railroad cars reserved for Germans, hunting, feeding horses with oats, going to the market more than once per week, sending letters or packages other than by the official post, etc. etc."[106] Many prohibitions naturally produced many contraven-

97. Richard Dehmel, cited in Liulevicius, *War Land*, 177.

98. Liulevicius, *War Land*, 63.

99. Payer, *Von Bethmann Hollweg*, 234.

100. Alfred Vagts, "A Memoir of Military Occupation," *Military Affairs* 7:1 (spring 1943), 16–24, here 23; Liulevicius, *War Land*, 66–67.

101. Liulevicius, *War Land*, 101–3.

102. Ibid., 58.

103. Ibid., 66.

104. Strazhas, *Deutsche Ostpolitik*, 28–29.

105. Liulevicius, *War Land*, 89–100, 108.

106. Strazhas, *Deutsche Ostpolitik*, 28.

tions, and these were met with drastic punishment, from heavy collective fines to executions and, everywhere, beatings. A "memorandum on the most important abuses in Lithuania" that the presidium of the Lithuanian Landrat sent to the German chancellor on 20 October 1917 closed by saying, "There are many proven facts that show there are beatings at work, beatings at the police station, beatings during investigations, beatings when one has caught escaped prisoners, beatings during requisitions, beatings in prisons, beatings of children at schools, beatings because people fail to doff their hats, beatings because they come too late, etc."[107]

The *manner* of occupation combined the capricious control, brutality, and petty humiliation of the barracks, while the *content* of occupation was defined by the military necessity of victory. In the east, as in Belgium, exorbitant requisitions, expropriation, and forced labor were how the military tried to overcome Germany's material and manpower deficiencies.

Requisitions and expropriations of property were pushed way beyond the subsistence limit. A modern study estimates that in 1916 the Lithuanian population was left with 0.7 percent of the wheat and 1 percent of the rye harvest, no oats, 0.5 percent of the potatoes, 13 percent of the butter, 67 percent of the eggs (which were hard to transport), and virtually no meat.[108] In some areas, even seeds and seed potatoes were requisitioned.[109] Livestock disappeared into the military maw: 38 percent of the horses, 48 percent of cows, 30 percent of the sheep, and 44 percent of the pigs.[110] A postwar evaluation estimated that the German military occupation had removed 261 million marks worth of resources.[111] The occupiers "paid" for requisitions in worthless chits and met resistance with beatings, collective fines, exemplary punishments (such as being marched from village to village in chains), or worse.[112] There were few factories to shut down and confiscate (it was Poland that suffered more from the systematic stripping of metals and factory machines),[113] but forests were plentiful; by war's end 20 percent of these had disappeared into the German war effort.[114] In the absence of outside aid such as Belgium enjoyed from the CRB, the areas of eastern occupation, including the governor-generalship of Poland, suffered deaths from starvation and increases in mortality from diseases caused by malnutrition.[115] By 1916 the piecemeal efforts at expropriation had been systematized, so that when German troops took over most of Romania in the fall, an economic section of the General Staff moved in right behind the troops, setting up offices in the Ministry of Agriculture,

107. "Denkschrift, die wichtigsten Missstände in Litauen betreffend," 20 Oct. 1917, cited in Werner Basler, *Deutschlands Annexionspolitik in Polen und im Baltikum, 1914–1918* (East Berlin, 1962), 282.

108. Strazhas, *Deutsche Ostpolitik*, 47n203.

109. Ibid., 30.

110. Basler, *Deutschlands Annexionspolitik*, 280.

111. Liulevicius, *War Land*, 73.

112. Basler, *Deutschlands Annexionspolitik*, 279; Liulevicius, *War Land*, 67–68, 75; Strazhas, *Deutsche Ostpolitik*, 48.

113. Antony Polonsky, "The German Occupation of Poland during the First and Second World Wars," in *Armies of Occupation*, ed. Roy A. Prete and A. Hamish Ion (Waterloo, Ont., 1982), 127; Basler, *Deutschlands Annexionspolitik*, 108–11.

114. Basler, *Deutschlands Annexionspolitik*, 280.

115. Ibid., 380; Liulevicius, *War Land*, 68, 75.

NCO requisitioning a cow (probably in Poland), First World War. *Der Weltkrieg, illustrierte Kriegs-Chronik des Daheim* (Bielefeld: Velhagen & Klasing, 1915–), vol. 2, 127.

from where it presided over the plunder of that country with "rational ruthlessness," as a reporter for the Carnegie Commission noted.[116]

Of all the great economic hardships, the population hated forced labor the most. Impressing people for forced labor emerged as an ad hoc practice in the first months of the occupation (autumn 1915), and it was regularized and extended throughout 1916. An order of 6 May 1916 made all persons with ragged clothing liable to forced labor; on 26 June all adults, male and female, were declared subject to forced labor, and on 6 November 1916 all men between seventeen and sixty were ordered to report to work camps.[117] The military authorities therefore succeeded in "militarizing labor" in the occupied zones, where they had failed in Germany because the trade unions and the Reichstag refused to accept the original form of the Hindenburg program. The Reichstag protested forced labor and deportations in the east, too, but despite promises by Ober-Ost, the practices continued to the end of the war.[118] Richer people could commute their forced labor by payment. The poor were rounded up like cattle: "At night people in the countryside are taken prisoner and collected together. Even in the suburbs there are regular hunts."[119]

As in the other examples of forced labor we have seen, the ostensible economic goals were contradicted by bad treatment. Rations in the east were a half pound of bread and a

116. Mitrany, *Effect of War*, 141–50, here 141.
117. Strazhas, *Deutsche Ostpolitik*, 38, 39; Liulevicius, *War Land*, 73.
118. Strazhas, *Deutsche Ostpolitik*, 39–40; Basler, *Deutschlands Annexionspolitik*, 281.
119. "Memorandum on abuses," in Basler, *Deutschlands Annexionspolitik*, 281.

liter of soup a day.[120] This appears to have been at least 20 percent less than what German civilians were receiving in spring 1917, 35 percent less than the daily rations of the Belgian deportees, and a little less than Entente prisoners of war received at the worst periods of detention, in 1914 and again in 1918.[121] Unlike prisoners of war from the west, who received Red Cross packages, there were no such supplements for eastern forced laborers. More work needs to be done on comparative rationing, but it appears that these forced laborers were receiving perhaps half of what contemporaries believed necessary to sustain a heavy laborer.[122] Many died. Their suffering occurred as tons of food were being shipped from the occupied zone to Germany, or consumed by German troops. Pay, when it came, was a pittance, and housing and working conditions mirrored the wretchedness of the food allotments.

Most forced laborers in the east faced deportation to worksites inside the occupation zone. But at least thirty-four thousand were forcibly transported to Germany to work in agriculture.[123] An unknown number "volunteered," together with the five hundred to six hundred thousand or more Russian-Polish workers.[124] Even after their "voluntary" contracts expired, however, these civilians were compelled to continue working in Germany, making the label "volunteer" meaningless.[125] Prisoners of war and forced laborers were the single largest category of worker in agriculture during the war.[126]

There were other deportees from Ober-Ost whose plight developed directly from occupation practices, not from the need for labor. As the front moved eastward in the autumn of 1915, behind it German police and gendarmes imported from Prussia swept the land hunting for spies. Their suspicions were as latitudinarian as those of the troops in Belgium in 1914. They arrested so many "spies" that in January 1916 the military administration of Courland ordered the deportation of the entire population of a ten-kilometer strip along the coast and behind the lines.[127] These deportations mixed punitive and security motives.

The result of all this order and security was revolt. Thousands of suffering civilians, Russian prisoners of war, and forced laborers escaped into the woods and began partisan warfare. Even after Russian aid to the partisans stopped at the end of 1916, resistance con-

---

120. Ibid.

121. Civilians: Prussia, War Ministry and Supreme Command, *Die deutsche Kriegführung und das Völkerrecht* (Berlin, 1919), 41–42 (hereafter *Die deutsche Kriegführung*); deportees: Belgium, Ministry of Foreign Affairs, *Report Laid before*, 44; prisoners of war: Conrad Hoffman, *In the Prison Camps of Germany* (New York, 1920), 111; Robert Jackson, *The Prisoners, 1914–1918* (New York, 1989), 2.

122. Belgium, Ministry of Foreign Affairs, *Report Laid before*, 45.

123. Elsner, "Ausländerbeschäftigung," 539–40.

124. Herbert, *Ausländerbeschäftigung*, 91; 750,000: Carnegie Endowment for International Peace, Division of International Law, *Violations of the Laws and Customs of War*, pamphlet no. 32 (Oxford, 1919), 33. The Polish report on which this charge was based said the Poles were "induced by German agents to work under conditions depriving them of all their rights. They endured very harsh treatment in regard to work and food, and were frequently beaten."

125. Zunkel, "Ausländischen Arbeiter," 295; Basler, *Deutschlands Annexionspolitik*, 281.

126. Elsner, "Übergang," 291.

127. Strazhas, *Deutsche Ostpolitik*, 15.

248 tinued, and the partisans successfully wrested control of whole areas from German troops, especially at night. The occupiers appear not to have understood that they had created this state of affairs; they referred to the resisters as "robber bands," suggesting mere criminality rather than a political response to systematic ill-treatment.[128]

The extent of the brutality and exploitation in the east has invited comparison to the far worse occupation under National Socialism. World War I certainly provided a foundation for later developments.[129] The experience of administering an area as though it were a tabula rasa, the disdain in which the inhabitants were held, the aspiration to showcase superior culture as order and organization—these "pathologies of power" were swiftly combined after the war into the militarized, *völkisch* ideology that became National Socialism.[130] But one should be cautious in concluding that utopian ideology, which Ludendorff expressed and probably only consolidated after the war was already over, caused the immense extremity of the eastern occupation of World War I.[131] It developed instead out of the frames that the military applied to the problems it faced of establishing security and winning the war. The extent to which the military was unhampered by political interference (from civilian government, the Reichstag, foreign opinion, local resistance) is the extent to which it would travel up the spiral of force to the end of destructiveness and dysfunctionality. The best proof of this contention is that the same pattern had already occurred, not in the east, where traditional disdain for the non-German speakers was being recast into modern racism and where vast tracts of land excited the imagination with boundless possibilities, but in northern France, whose occupation shared with the east the one really important factor in determining the spiral of extremity: untrammeled military power.

Northern France

The occupation of northern France reached such a degree of completion in instrumentalizing the civilian population, expropriating wealth, and destroying the infrastructure that it merits without hyperbole the word "total." And yet no single hand or handbook guided the policies. With the exception of the destruction during the retreats of 1917 and 1918, which the third OHL ordered, all other actions occurred in the familiar sliding fashion at the initiative of the six separate armies whose purview stretched from the frontlines to the border.[132] Each army had its field administration directly at the front, and behind it an occupation zone run by the rear echelon inspector (a general) and his (reserve) troops. Civilians were gradually seconded from Germany to aid the soldiers, but the oc-

---

128. Ibid., 14, 50.

129. Herbert, *Ausländerbeschäftigung*, 83, 113.

130. This is Liulevicius's argument in *War Land*; citation, 176.

131. Ludendorff's later ideology: Eisenhart-Rothe, *Im Banne der Persönlichkeit*, 167–74; Siegfried Kaehler, "Vier quellenkritische Untersuchungen zum Kriegsende 1918," *Nachrichten der Akademie der Wissenschaften in Göttingen*, Philologisch-Historische Klasse 8 (1960), 423–81, here 451. Ideology as cause: Liulevicius, *War Land*, 7–9, 69.

132. Except for Longwy-Briey, which was slated for annexation from the beginning and which fell under a separate administration; see Gatzke, *Germany's Drive*, 85.

cupation remained firmly military and unremittingly short term, that is, the occupation aimed exclusively at contributing to the success of the fighting troops. No grander goal (of annexation, or demonstration of organizational superiority) clouded this practical aim. Beneath the military pyramid were usually a French mayor and his staff, though not all of these survived the war.[133] When the occupation began, about 2.25 million people lived in this heartland of French industry. There were 1.6 million surviving in a moonscape when it ended.[134]

The occupation authorities in northern France subjected their areas to the same identification and control techniques that suffocated the east, but in France there were few woods or swamps to escape to and from which to take up armed resistance.[135] Every person received an identity card specifying name, date of birth, profession, marital status, and state of health.[136] Each house had to post a list of occupants in the window.[137] But instrumentalizing civilians as forced laborers brought forth new inventions: external labels indicating work status. People who had been deported to Germany and returned or those who were liable to deportation to Germany wore a red label that subjected them to greater scrutiny. Gray and red meant you had signed a "voluntary" labor contract. A red label with the letters "Z.A.B." signified you were part of the civilian work brigades (*Zivilarbeiter-Bataillonen*), the lowest rung of the forced labor ladder.[138] This system unknowingly fulfilled a similar scheme of Trotha's, to affix to Herero prisoners tin IDs stamped "G.F." (*gefangener Herero*).

Because the French zone was smaller and had been much more routinized and charted by its own government than the east, it was possible to impose a much more complete degree of control there. A similar flood of minute prohibitions and exhortations inundated each zone. There was a permanent curfew, doors and windows were forbidden to be locked during the day, correspondence was forbidden except to prisoners of war interned in Germany. No travel was permitted without a pass (for which one had to pay), and by 1917 there was virtually no movement, as the economy ceased to function and the land disintegrated into isolated units.[139]

As it did everywhere, the quest for perfect security quickened the pervasive interest in demonstrating authority.[140] The *Grusserlass* (the requirement to step off the sidewalk and tip one's hat in deference to officers) had appeared in some districts in 1914. Interestingly,

---

133. For instance, the mayor of Lille was sacked in Feb. 1916: Rupprecht Kronprinz v. Bayern, *Mein Kriegstagebuch*, 1:432.

134. Georges Gromaire, *L'occupation allemande en France (1914–1918)* (Paris, 1925), 193, 199. No recent history has equaled or surpassed Gromaire's excellent account, which is based on official investigations and supplemented by many interviews he conducted in January 1919 and throughout 1921. Recent works: McPhail, *Long Silence*; Annette Becker, *Oubliés de la Grande Guerre* (Paris, 1998), 27–88; and Leonard V. Smith, Stéphane Audoin-Rouzeau, and Annette Becker, *France and the Great War, 1914–1918* (Cambridge, 2002), 45–53. On population: Hoover, *American Epic*, 388; McPhail, *Long Silence*, 36n3.

135. (Weak) resistance: Becker, *Oubliés*, 77–88.

136. Wilhelm Appens, *Charleville* (Dortmund, 1919), 34.

137. Gromaire, *L'occupation*, 76.

138. Ibid., 74, 220, 242.

139. Ibid., 75–79.

140. Many examples: ibid., 15, 16, 220, 342, 347.

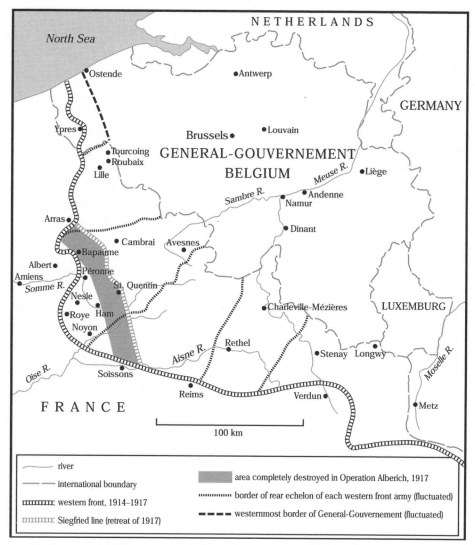

General-Gouvernement (German civil administration) in occupied Belgium, 1914–1917, and occupied zone in northern France, 1914–1918. Sources: Georges Gromaire, *L'occupation allemande en France (1914–1918)*, 44; Rupprecht Kronprinz von Bayern, *Mein Kriegstagebuch*, vol. 2, map 8; *UA* Reihe 3, vol. 1, "Karte der Zerstörungen beim Rückzug 1917"; Germany, Reichsarchiv, *Der Weltkrieg 1914 bis 1918*, vol. 6.

it was introduced at Charleville not because the Kaiser's headquarters were temporarily located there but at the initiative of the rear commander after the Kaiser had already moved on.[141] Even women and children seemed threatening. In February 1915 Crown Prince Rupprecht tried to stop women and children from wearing the tricolor by demonstrating France's defeat and humiliation. He ordered prisoners of war to be paraded through the streets of Lille. The resulting enthusiastic patriotic demonstration, mainly by women and children, was not what he had had in mind. "This nonsense must absolutely be ended," he wrote, "and the people shown that they cannot fool with us, in order to stop serious risings." As "atonement" for the demonstration, he fined Lille half a million francs.[142]

Requisitions were heavy from the beginning because the Schlieffen Plan had largely left logistics to chance, which meant living off the occupied land. A list from Avesnes in November 1914 shows how far requisitions reached into the household even at the start: "inkwells, a broom, 2 lavatory buckets, bells, 2 coffee pots, 8 coffee spoons, 8 sets of table silver and crockery, 3 forks, a coffee mill, 2 lamps."[143] France enjoyed one big advantage over the east, however. Beginning in March 1915, the CRB began feeding France too, though initially, because of transport problems, at a lower ration than for Belgium.[144] But there is little reason to believe that requisitions would have diminished much if the CRB had not existed. Crown Prince Rupprecht, commander of the 6th Army, was a politically astute and humane commander, who in 1916 ended up sharing precious rations with seventeen thousand French miners—who were necessary to the war effort—and their dependents. But in February 1915 he noted the principle of requisitioning in France: "The task of the economic section of our occupation administration lay mainly in the systematic removal of all raw materials needed by our industry and the seizure of food for the army. . . . It was regrettable that the population for a time suffered real shortages."[145] Rupprecht tried to ameliorate these shortages; he sent the French mayor of Lille to unoccupied France to try to overcome French opposition to paying Switzerland for extra food shipments. But these actions did not change the basic situation, which was that the German war effort and the good of the troops superseded elementary civilian needs.[146]

Requisitioning drifted into outright expropriation. By February 1916 (that is, *before* the radicalization normally attributed to the third OHL after August 1916) a team of two hundred economic experts visited over four thousand firms, compiling a detailed report that was the basis for the dismantling of whole factories and their shipment to Ger-

141. Appens, *Charleville*, 12.

142. Rupprecht Kronprinz v. Bayern, *Mein Kriegstagebuch*, diary entries of 4 Feb. and 5 Mar. 1915, 1:307, 309.

143. McPhail, *Long Silence*, 48.

144. Nash, *Life of Hoover*, 2:109.

145. Rupprecht Kronprinz v. Bayern, *Mein Kriegstagebuch*, diary entry, 9 Feb. 1915, 1:298, 321, 437; also, Wild, *Briefe*, letter to wife of 1 Jan. 1915, 50. Chronic malnutrition: Becker, *Oubliés*, 44.

146. When Bethmann, in arguing against unrestricted submarine warfare, said that the entry of the United States into the war would mean the end of food aid to Belgium, he still did not appear to think Germany would take up the slack: "The insecurity behind our front will increase if the Belgians must go hungry." *Betrachtungen* 2:267. In July 1916 the military occupation authorities almost cancelled CRB aid: Nash, *Life of Hoover*, 2:179–82.

252 many.[147] Agriculture was similarly surveyed, transformed into a command economy, and confiscated. Four-fifths of the grain harvest went to Germany, and the remaining one-fifth was used to pay the CRB.[148] Livestock disappeared eastward. The command economy led to wastage typical of military management. One member of the occupation remembered later how the military tried to reform agriculture in the Ardennes. Because Germany needed grain, the officers consolidated the small dairy farms, herding the cows into huge holding areas and planting pasturage with wheat. The cows, unused to such treatment, sickened and died. The wheat did not do much better because the climate was too wet, which is why the natives had turned to dairy farming in the first place. The Germans produced two hundredweights of grain per morgen (2.1 acres) of land, when the French had offered to deliver eight, if they could manage their own property. That offer was refused because, as a German observer ironically noted, "everything had to be militarized and run by officers. Fields were planted on command, harvested on command, and grain was threshed on command; but growth and sunshine can't be commanded—they haven't yet been drilled in the royal Prussian manner."[149] Despite the wastage, from July 1917 to the end of the war Belgium and France accounted for 20 percent of Germany's raw material needs.[150]

Like their fellow sufferers in the east, the French found forced labor the worst aspect of occupation. The work requirement was like requisitioning, expropriation, and deportation: present as a presumptive right of necessity from the beginning, it grew like Topsy, expanding in all directions, encompassing more categories of people, more kinds of work, and more geographical areas. It was driven by the independent initiatives of rear echelon administrators of lesser or greater rank and by the needs of troop commanders.[151] So, labor conscription began with healthy men, as in the order of the 1st Army's commander of the rear (29 October 1914) making any able-bodied man liable for work in the fields, and it spread from there. On 18 November 1914 the rear administration at Sissone ordered that unemployed men could be put in worker columns; on 25 March 1915, the rear commander at St. Quentin laid out times for obligatory work for men, but added that women and children could also be held to smaller tasks. By 20 July 1915 all men, women, and children were held to fourteen-hour days in the fields at Holnon (Aisne).[152] By 24 April 1916 one finds an order in Avesnes announcing that all persons, male or female, from twelve to sixty-four, were liable to forced labor.[153] In this piecemeal manner the entire French population was subject to forced labor long before the radicalization associated with the third OHL and before Ober-Ost had established its full regime in the east. By 1918 not only was

---

147. Gromaire, *L'occupation*, 110.

148. Ibid., 137.

149. Appens, *Charleville*, 35–36.

150. *Die deutsche Kriegführung*, 34.

151. Gromaire believes that orders came from above, but his documents suggest the reverse. Gromaire describes women's forced work as proceeding "with [the Germans'] slow and progressive movement" from local work, to work afar, deportation, and finally the general mobilization of women. Gromaire, *L'occupation*, ordered from above: 209; women: 247–70.

152. *Violation of the Laws*, 39.

153. For the orders: Gromaire, *L'occupation*, 208–212, 214, 215.

everyone theoretically liable for work, they were in fact working.[154] Their work ran from office cleaning to snow shoveling, agricultural labor, repairing guns, building the huge fortifications for the Siegfried line in 1917, and digging the labyrinth of trenches in 1918 (where in late September over half a million civilians labored).[155] That is, some of the work was directly war-related (especially that performed by the Z.A.B.), and therefore forbidden under international law. Payment was generally by chit, which was in the long run worthless and in the short run paid for by the municipalities as "contributions," not by the occupation authority. This was the same system in use in the east.[156]

Because of the CRB, French rations were better than those of forced laborers in the east, but the other conditions were identically bad.[157] Work columns rose at 4 A.M.; they might be sheltered in private homes, but they could land in barracks, tents, or abandoned buildings, often without straw or blankets; hygiene was miserable, medicine nonexistent; clothing and shoes simply wore out and were not replaced.[158] The Z.A.B. laborers were treated worse than people in the work columns. There were at least fifty thousand, maybe as many as one hundred thousand, in at least twenty-five brigades.[159] The Z.A.B. workers were interned in camps, guarded by police dogs, and subjected to rigorous discipline enforced by severe punishments. Another category of worker was men of conscription age who were treated like prisoners of war and subject to martial law. And finally the many evacuees (from the front or from destroyed or confiscated houses) were simply used for labor as the occasion seemed to require. All these various groups of workers seem to have been managed in the rotation system: they were worked until they became ill or exhausted, were rotated elsewhere to recover, and then brought back.[160] An unknown but probably significant number died.[161] As the war continued, France became crisscrossed with a network of labor camps, sixty-eight around Verdun (containing deported Belgians) and seventy-eight between Lille and St. Quentin.[162] When Herbert Hoover returned from an inspection tour of northern France, he said, "In every respect the land is like a vast concentration camp."[163]

One of the most remarkable proofs of the total disposability of the French population was the ubiquity and variety of deportation. Chronologically, the first deportations involved men of draft age, civilian hostages, and large numbers of "spies," who were transported by train to Germany with the same lack of preparation that Belgian deportees experienced.[164] Many of these people were returned to France after several months.

154. Ibid., 221; Becker, *Oubliés*, 57–61.

155. Germany, Reichsarchiv, *Der Weltkrieg 1914 bis 1918*, 12:63, 123–24; 14: Beilage 41.

156. Gromaire, *L'occupation*, 208. In one area in April 1916 wages were set at 2.25 francs a day, "of which 1.75 franc was deducted, leaving 50 centimes pay, of which only 25 centimes was paid in cash." *Violation of the Laws*, 37. See also Reinhold Zilch, *Okkupation und Währung im Ersten Weltkrieg* (Goldbach, 1994).

157. Smith et al., *France*, 48. undervalue the contribution of the CRB.

158. Gromaire, *L'occupation*, 232–34.

159. Ibid., 245.

160. Ibid., 214, 230; McPhail, *Long Silence*, 164, 177.

161. Gromaire, *L'occupation*, 435; McPhail, *Long Silence*, 172; Becker, *Oubliés*, 64.

162. McPhail, *Long Silence*, 178.

163. Ibid., 55.

164. Gromaire, *L'occupation*, 34–36, 73–74.

254   Deportation was also a common punishment for certain crimes or occupation infractions.[165] A third type of deportation struck people who lived just behind the front; when the war became stalemated, many of them were evacuated.[166] As evacuees, they became a disposable labor force whose work might return them to the areas from which they had originally been deported.

A fourth kind of deportation began in spring 1915 when the Swiss government offered to be a conduit for the "repatriation" of elderly, very young, or frail civilians to unoccupied France. Trains of five hundred persons each began leaving for Schaffhausen, while others went through Belgium. Most persons departed voluntarily in the sense that conditions and treatment were so poor that leaving their home, friends, and surroundings seemed better than staying.[167] But these "repatriated" largely coincided with the population that was unable to work, and it seems that some of them (especially at the beginning) were simply forced to leave and others belonged to groups (such as prostitutes) that some officers wanted deported.[168] Very large numbers of mostly women, children, old, and sick people were thus removed from the occupied zone by war's end, probably as many as half a million (almost 25 percent), which was the German figure.[169] The quartermaster general of the Field Army in 1915, Gen. Hugo von Freytag-Loringhoven, later recalled that he had wanted to deport even more people, but Switzerland limited the number of trains.[170]

The ubiquitous shuttling of forced laborers to and fro inside the occupied zone was another sort of deportation that characterized the occupation to its last days. But the limits of forced labor deportation had been tested in April 1916 in an experiment conducted by the quartermaster general of the 6th Army. He applied military logic to solving in his district Germany's two major problems simultaneously: lack of food and lack of labor, and in so doing, he also tested the proposition that all civilians had to work for their keep and that any civilian could be made to work successfully anywhere.

By spring 1916, feeding the urban population of Lille, Roubaix, and Tourcoing had become more and more difficult for the 6th Army's rear echelon. Most men were already detained or working, leaving a dependent population of women, children, the infirm, and the elderly. The quartermaster general aimed to solve the problem in a single stroke. He ordered each company of occupation troops to round up two hundred people, beginning with the unmarried or the childless, if possible from the working class, and forcibly deporting them to the countryside, where agricultural labor was needed and food was more plentiful. This military solution contained the usual contradiction. It had a humanitarian

---

165. Ibid., 228, 357.

166. Testimony of 1st Lt. Otto v. Stülpnagel, *UA* 3:4, 25.

167. Some people reportedly paid five hundred francs each to be "repatriated" to France: Smith et al., *France*, 50; Becker, *Oubliés*, 66–67.

168. Gromaire, *L'occupation*, 426–31; "forced": 427; Rupprecht Kronprinz v. Bayern, *Mein Kriegstagebuch*, 1:307; "prostitutes": Wild, *Briefe*, 56n1.

169. *Die deutsche Kriegführung*, 42. Hoover, in charge of postwar feeding of refugees, also speaks of five hundred thousand returnees from southern France; *American Epic*, vol. 1: *Relief of Belgium*, letter of 28 Dec. 1918, 399. Gromaire, *L'occupation*, 474, writes of a minimum of two hundred thousand, which is consistent with his usual underestimation of numbers.

170. Freytag-Loringhoven, *Menschen und Dinge*, 295.

side—better provisioning—and it targeted the most mobile or versatile sections of the remaining population. The deportees were supposed to receive advance notice and could take thirty kilograms of belongings with them. But its other face was involuntary labor, and its method was force. And above all, it was animated by the same wishful and antieconomical thinking characteristic of military problem solving.[171] In the end, therefore, force and unrealism carried the day.

Inevitably, the execution of the plan went awry. Some people were not notified and had fifteen minutes to pack. Some deportations occurred at 3:30 A.M.; people were snatched randomly to fulfill the quota.[172] These results were systematic, if unintentional, because compulsion was the bottom line. The covering order made this principle clear: "The execution of these orders shall be done energetically. A certain coarseness is inevitable, but one should avoid all useless hardship and brutality. Resulting trouble should be handled without pity."[173] This mixed message therefore ultimately decided for force. Furthermore, preparations for transport and billeting were as insufficient as they would be for the Belgian deportees. Between twenty-four and thirty thousand people, mostly women, arrived in the countryside to find few accommodations; they lived in ruins or abandoned buildings with little or no sanitation.[174] There was no medicine, but the women were vaccinated against typhus and checked for venereal disease, suggesting that the occupation authorities were diligent only in those matters that they thought might affect their own health.[175] The women were regimented like soldiers, given numbers, and formed into work groups; they were permitted to write only once a month, less than was true for prisoners of war.[176]

Not surprisingly, the city women of Lille, Roubaix, and Tourcoing were barely able to perform agricultural labor. On 9 August 1916 (after protests from Switzerland and the Vatican) the quartermaster general admitted defeat and ordered all women under thirty returned.[177] The one lasting success of the episode was that more women "volunteered" for local work, hoping to escape another deportation.

The deportations of Lille, Roubaix, and Tourcoing illustrate once again the path that military problem solving typically took when left to its own devices. The quartermaster general did not intend to create suffering; indeed, he probably intended to alleviate it. But a whole chain of assumptions and habits doomed the project to disaster: the insistence that food be obtained only in exchange for work (the same foundational assumption of the Hindenburg program to be applied to German civilians);[178] regarding people as in-

---

171. Becker imagines the Germans aimed specifically to humiliate French women, but there is no evidence of this: Becker, *Oubliés*, 73–74, and Smith et al., *France*, 49–50.

172. Gromaire, *L'occupation*, 280; Munro, Sellery, and Krey, eds., *German War Practices*, 1:82–83.

173. Gromaire, *L'occupation*, 280. Apparently, some officers and men refused to roust women from their beds and were imprisoned for it: Becker, *Oubliés*, 76.

174. Numbers: ibid., 277n1; Munro, Sellery, and Krey, eds., *German War Practices*, 1:86.

175. Conditions: Gromaire, *L'occupation*, 287–91.

176. Munro, Sellery, and Krey, eds., *German War Practices*, 1:86–87.

177. Rupprecht Kronprinz v. Bayern, *Mein Kriegstagebuch*, diary entry, 9 Aug. 1916, 1:515. Protests: *UA* 3:1, 360, 362, 363.

178. Hindenburg to Bethmann, II Nr. 34 647, 13 Sept. 1916: "The principle 'who does not work, will not eat' is in our current situation more than ever justified, *also vis-à-vis women*." Cited in Ludendorff, *Urkunden Obersten Heeresleitung*, 67, emphasis in original.

256 terchangeable material (*Menschenmaterial*); instrumentalizing civilians for the war effort; attempting to solve knotty problems in a single blow, which led to mixed motives and wishful thinking; force and violence as methods of execution; holding subordinates to the fulfillment of their duty "energetically" and "without pity"; haste, which precluded adequate logistical preparation; malignant neglect, the result of disdain for the nonsoldier (in this case the threefold condition of being the enemy, civilian, and female); and lack of realistic economic knowledge or judgment. These small cogs could produce major catastrophes.

Not all military men were so blinkered by military culture, however. The commander of the 6th Army, Crown Prince Rupprecht, was skeptical of the experiment from the moment the quartermaster general informed him of it: "The execution of this very harsh measure will not be without friction, and it will cause many abuses," he wrote in his diary. "Its success will be extremely small, since clerks and factory workers aren't appropriate for agricultural work."[179] But Rupprecht did not stop the project. His own responsibility lay with the fighting troops; mission tactics and regulations discouraged micromanaging one's subordinates. Rupprecht therefore allowed the quartermaster general to exercise authority, however misguided, in his own bailiwick. Apparently the chancellor learned of the results of the experiment only through American protests.[180]

The final kind of deportation was not a result of occupation but of combat. In preparation for the German offensives of 1918, masses of civilians were removed from their homes.[181] More, however, were removed during the two major retreats in the west. One was the intentional retreat in spring 1917 to the Siegfried line, which forced laborers had helped to build; the other was the unplanned, grudging withdrawal in summer and fall of 1918 prior to Germany's defeat. During both, German troops were ordered to destroy everything they could and forcibly to remove the remaining civilians farther into the still-occupied zones.[182] In both cases, civilians were deported almost without notice and could take little or nothing with them. Ostensibly, these harsh actions were done to save civilian lives, but the real goals seem mixed. Otherwise, it is hard to explain why only those capable of working were deported in 1917, leaving fourteen thousand dependants behind for the Entente to take care of.[183] As it was, 125,000 people became instantly homeless and propertyless and, falling into the category of the evacuated, became fodder for the involuntary work columns. The 1918 deportations were naturally even hastier and much less complete, as German soldiers abandoned their positions spontaneously and civilians strove to stay put. Opposition by the German political leadership also hampered the complete deportation that OHL evidently wanted.[184] Because the military goal during both retreats was complete destruction of the area, civilians were simply accounted as assets, whose disappearance (as potential laborers) was just part of the scorched earth policy. As

179. Rupprecht Kronprinz v. Bayern, *Mein Kriegstagebuch*, diary entry, 4 Apr. 1916, 1:443.
180. Munro, Sellery, and Krey, eds., *German War Practices*, 1:88.
181. Herwig, *First World War*, 397; Max von Gallwitz, *Erleben im Western* (Berlin, 1934), 309.
182. Kuhl's testimony, *UA* 3:1, 93.
183. Kuhl, *Weltkrieg*, 2:64; *Die deutsche Kriegführung*, 43.
184. Stülpnagel's testimony, *UA* 3:4, 25.

late as 29 September 1918, the day Ludendorff admitted the war was lost, he ordered the flooding of the mines of Carvin and Dourges and the removal of the French miners to other areas farther behind the lines.[185]

Even this very short account should have made clear that deportation was a normal event in occupied northern France. However, none of the six types of deportation aimed at "ethnic cleansing"; none was the expression of a grand ideological scheme to empty the area of its original population. But there were also very few hindrances to conceiving of deportation or putting it into practice. Indeed, in 1914 the French government briefly considered evacuating the entire population (rather than permit food shipments to the enemy zone), until Herbert Hoover convinced them of its impracticality.[186] Although Germany did not have a monopoly on deportation as a possible solution to various problems, the German military was quick to resort to *actual* deportation, which its officers invoked for all sorts of local reasons. The patchwork of local deportations in France became ever denser until it covered the entire zone, just as if it had been a centralized, coordinated policy. Repetitive practice demonstrated and justified the principle that civilians were entirely disposable; they could be shifted around at will, or simply made to disappear, in the sense used by Trotha in SWA. The ubiquity of deportation lowered the barriers even further to ideologically motivated deportation for "security" or colonization reasons, ideas that were already present in the far right wing in 1914 and that were now freer to enter the mainstream.[187]

If not everyone was a forced laborer (the occupation forces intentionally made it difficult to distinguish forced from "voluntary" labor), if not everyone was deported, still, everyone was working for the occupiers, and everyone without exception was liable to becoming a forced laborer or a deportee. Requisitions and expropriations had also reached the point of near totality. And perhaps more important, no principle or institution existed in Germany that was powerful enough to hinder the development toward totality in any of these areas. The same was true for the final demonstration of extremity: the willful destruction of northern France during the retreats of 1917 and 1918.

The Destruction of Northern France

Northern France was, of course, a battlefield for the entire war, and artillery fire churned a swath of ruin on either side of the trenches. But purposeful destruction is a different phenomenon. It was little discussed or prepared for in prewar official handbooks. The KEO said that during retreat the rear inspectorate was to order specifically

185. *UA* 3:1, 105. The next day Ludendorff amended his order to say that only the aboveground machinery should be destroyed, but it does not appear that he called off the deportation: *UA* 3:1, 105; Reichsarchiv, *Weltkrieg*, 14:656.

186. Nash, *Life of Hoover*, 2:107; McPhail, *Long Silence*, 68–69.

187. The right-wing *Deutsche Tageszeitung* had already asked on 15 Aug. 1914 if "evacuation of all inhabitants in the occupied zones" were not the best guarantee of security. Wieland, *Belgien 1914*, 22n139. Duke Johann Albrecht of Mecklenburg, president of the German Colonial Society, favored deporting all Walloons from Belgium: Ritter, *Sword and Scepter*, 3:26. And in excitable moments, the Kaiser would call for removing all the inhabitants from those areas in France and Belgium that Germany might annex: Ritter, *Sword and Scepter*, 3:34.

258   "which railroads, telegraph lines and other communications, depots, and storage facilities" were to be destroyed.[188] Wholesale destruction was evidently not foreseen.[189] There were several possible precedents in the First World War. Both the Belgians and the French had effectively hampered Germany's advance in 1914 by blowing up transport and communication networks, and France had flooded two of its coal mines.[190] Russia had been more thorough in East Prussia in 1914, and especially in 1915 by pursuing a scorched earth policy during its retreat from Warsaw.[191] But Gen. Hermann von Kuhl, the chief of staff of the army group that carried out the bulk of the devastation in 1917, did not recall these precedents when Reichstag investigators questioned him after the war. He explained that "war-historical studies concerning similar destruction were never done by the General Staff, so far as I can recall. It's a question that simply happens from case to case in wartime. It happened during the [German] retreat in Poland in 1914, when one destroyed as much as one could."[192] It was thus Germany's own experience that served as the model, an experience that, like the "Belgian atrocities," the early deportations, the grasp for the wonder weapon, gas, and other examples of extremity, occurred at the very beginning of the war out of what the actors understood as the logic of warfare.[193] Gen. Max Hoffmann wrote during the October 1914 retreat that the army had destroyed the (militarily important) railroads and bridges so thoroughly "that it will take the Russians weeks before they can advance. In addition, I've ordered all Russian coal mines to be flooded. One comes up with the finest ideas."[194] By no means were German assets exempt from this sort of thinking: the eastern commanders in 1914 also wanted to destroy the Upper Silesian mines, but the chief of staff of the 6th Army district (in which the mines were located), the deputy war minister, and civilian leaders got the order rescinded.[195] The category of militarily significant objects had therefore immediately expanded to include economic targets.

     One week after taking over the Supreme Command (28 August 1916), Ludendorff and Hindenburg surveyed the western front for the first time and concluded that Germany had to fortify its defensive lines and go on the defensive to save manpower. They ordered the preparation of the Siegfried line, located fifteen to forty-five kilometers to the rear of the front trenches. Although the decision to undertake a strategic retreat to the Siegfried line (code-named Alberich) was not taken until February 1917, on 2 October 1916 OHL ordered the army commanders to prepare plans for the complete destruction of areas that would be abandoned:

---

188. The General Staff recommended the total destruction of food stores during retreats: Germany, General Staff, *Heeresverpflegung*, 310.

189. KEO, p. 16 (para. 20).

190. Peter Graf Kielmansegg, *Deutschland und der Erste Weltkrieg* (Frankfurt, 1968), 62; Herwig, *First World War*, 97; *UA* 3:1, 63.

191. Reichsarchiv, *Weltkrieg*, 12:121; *UA* 3:1, 153.

192. *UA* 3:1, 81, 82.

193. Kuhl explained this logic in ibid., 82.

194. Hoffmann to his wife, 21 Oct. 1914, Max Hoffmann, *Aufzeichnungen des Generalmajors Max Hofmann* (Berlin, 1929), 1:59, cited in Geiss, *Der polnische Grenzstreifen*, 33n97.

195. Wrisberg, *Heer und Heimat*, 23.

It is necessary to make extensive preparations for the complete destruction of all rail lines, and further, all streets, bridges, canals, locks, localities, and all equipment and buildings that we cannot take with us but that could be of any use at all [*von irgendwelchem Nutzen*] to the enemy. The enemy must find a countryside completely sucked dry in which his own mobility is made as difficult as possible.[196]

The phrase "any use at all" was infinitely elastic and meant in practice total destruction of one-fourth of Germany's entire occupation zone in France.[197] Apparently the idea was to prevent an Allied attack for long enough to give the German troops, exhausted and decimated by the battle of the Somme, a chance to rest.[198]

Destruction, like combat and occupation, followed mission tactics, so the details were left to the army and army group commanders. They mounted significant opposition to this order. Army group commander Crown Prince Rupprecht protested that it was both militarily unnecessary, since Entente troops could shelter in ruins as well as in intact buildings, and impossible to carry out.[199] But he could not stop it. At most, he was able to limit the destruction to a strip fifteen kilometers in front of the Siegfried line and to save Noyon, Vesle, and Ham, three of the larger localities. "I would have liked to resign," he wrote, "but I was told it would do no good and would not have been approved anyway for political reasons, since it would have given the impression abroad of a rift between Bavaria and the Reich. So I had to limit myself to refusing to sign the order of execution."[200]

Unfortunately, the destruction turned out to be quite feasible. The operation was minutely planned. Nothing was spared, not the wells, which were made "unusable,"[201] not even the orchards, which were felled to prevent soldiers from taking shelter under them.[202] After the war, one German officer said that the area had been rendered "literally unrecognizable"; it had been turned into "a desolate, dead desert."[203] In all, 2.5 million kilograms of dynamite were used and the destruction was even filmed.[204] The commander of the 3rd Army found the film shocking: "We saw factories fly into the air, rows of houses fall over, bridges break in two—it was awful, an orgy of dynamite. That this is all militarily justified is unquestionable. But putting *this* on film—incomprehensible!"[205]

Efforts were made to ease the conditions of the 125,000 deportees, many of whom were removed overnight with no notice (because the operation was to be kept secret from the Allies). The extensive preparation, and probably the fundamental opposition of Rup-

196. Order of 2 Oct. 1916, in Kuhl, *Weltkrieg*, 2:62–63.
197. Rupprecht Kronprinz v. Bayern, *Mein Kriegstagebuch*, 3:128.
198. Kuhl's testimony, *UA* 3:1, 73.
199. Rupprecht Kronprinz v. Bayern, *Mein Kriegstagebuch*, diary entry of 17 Oct. 1916, 2:47.
200. Ibid., diary entry of 15 Mar. 1917, 2:116.
201. Kuhl, *Weltkrieg*, 2:63; or "poisoned"—there was a major argument about this after the war.
202. Ibid., 2:63.
203. Captain W. Meyer, in the *Münchner Post* 216 (1919), cited in Ernst, *Der grosse Krieg*, 100.
204. Kuhl, *Weltkrieg*, 2:63.
205. Einem, *Armeeführer*, 318, emphasis in original.

260 precht's army group, meant that this was the only deportation of the war that went smoothly and with a minimum of immediate hardship for the deportees.[206] But the fundamental hardship could not be ameliorated. When the Entente troops gingerly went forward into the moonscape, they were deeply shocked. Bethmann believed that peace with France was made immeasurably more difficult because of the hatred the military's action had engendered.[207] The destruction was counterproductive militarily, too; it was so total and so irrevocable that it hampered German troops during their advance through the same area in the March 1918 offensive.[208]

In the summer and fall of 1918 the pattern repeated itself: wholesale destruction of all property and forced removal of the population. OHL's general outlines for a planned retreat in 1918 had called for eleven days of thorough destruction.[209] But, as we shall see, army commanders found it impossible to get Ludendorff to agree to a planned retreat, so the German army fell back as the situation dictated. It had no time to destroy as thoroughly as it had in 1917. Nevertheless, General von Lüttwitz remarked that the destruction "went beyond the bounds of the necessary."[210] Only when Ludendorff had admitted that the war was lost did the order go out to cease burning down houses and villages.[211] But widespread devastation, including of houses, continued in many areas.[212]

The Allies used their increased leverage against these actions. In his note of 14 October 1918, President Woodrow Wilson required the "acts of inhumanity, spoliation, and desolation" to stop, or the Allies would refuse to sign the armistice.[213] At a cabinet meeting three days later, Ludendorff defended the army's actions as limited to what was militarily necessary, but the cabinet assured the U.S. president that the army would be ordered to avoid destruction of private property.[214] This intervention may have saved Belgium's coal mines, but those of northern France were destroyed; the Supreme Command admitted that 40 of the 111 mines were entirely destroyed, while the rest lost all aboveground facilities.[215]

Internal opposition also hindered even more extreme planned destruction. Crown Prince Rupprecht, who favored targeting only transportation and communication lines, energetically repeated the order to restrict destruction to these traditional military objects. German mine managers in one area refused to carry out orders to blow up the

206. *UA* 3:1, 75.

207. Rupprecht Kronprinz v. Bayern, *Mein Kriegstagebuch*, diary entry of 1 June 1917, 2:181.

208. General Kuhl's report, *UA* 4:3, 105, 142; Rupprecht Kronprinz v. Bayern, *Mein Kriegstagebuch*, diary entries of 17 Jan. and 20 Jan. 1918, 3:251–52, 263–64.

209. Gallwitz, *Erleben im Westen*, 353–54.

210. Cited in Klein, *Deutschland*, 3:445.

211. *UA* 3:1, 92; Erich Matthias and Rudolf Morsey, ed., *Die Regierung des Prinzen Max von Baden* (Düsseldorf, 1962), 121.

212. See War Minister Scheüch's explanation to the cabinet on 28 Oct. 1918, Matthias and Morsey, *Regierung*, 416.

213. President Wilson Note to German Government, 14 Oct. 1918, in U.S. Department of State, *Papers Relating to the Foreign Relations of the United States, 1918*, Supplement 1: *The World War*, 2 vols. (Washington, D.C., 1933), 1:358–59, here 359.

214. Prince Max v. Baden, *Erinnerungen*, 443, 457.

215. *Die deutsche Kriegführung*, 37–38.

aboveground facilities in late October, instead removing critical machine parts. Their ac-   261
tion was blessed by their chief quartermaster.[216]

Despite lack of time, Allied intervention, and some resistance, the 1918 destruction of
northern France was clearly excessive. Thorough devastation was the counterpart in situations of retreat to the absolute, no-holds-barred precepts governing attack and sweeping
advance. In the same way that they had decisively influenced the Schlieffen Plan, Germany's weakness and numerical inferiority in 1918 encouraged scorched earth. As General
v. Kuhl later explained, Germany had not even begun to prepare the Antwerp-Maas defensive line that would have permitted it to fend off Allied attacks, at least for a time. It
lacked the manpower to do so. "Considering this deficiency, it was all the more urgent to
hold up the opponent by other means."[217]

There were other reasons as well. The military regarded anything built or improved
during the occupation as German property, even though it had been "paid" for by French
municipal "contributions" and largely built by forced civilian labor. The Supreme Command and the War Ministry defended the destruction of these facilities, which otherwise
would have helped the enemy: "Can one really demand this of us? Can anyone deny that
the law of war permits this destruction for this reason?"[218]

Desire to wreck postwar economic competition was another reason that had been operating strongly during the previous phases of requisitions and expropriations.[219] Revenge and frustration over losing the war were also widespread motives. The bloodthirsty
"plans" to fight the Allied advance every step of the way reveal this undercurrent of emotion. Colonel Schwertfeger wrote in November 1918:

> It will be necessary for our enemies to pay for every step ahead with streams of
> blood. Large areas that so far have been unaffected by war will be wrecked com-
> pletely. If the enemy wants to push us out of the occupied parts of northern
> France, and if they want to force a retreat from Belgium, they will have to count
> on an extended period of bloody battles and the completely useless destruction of
> their own territory.[220]

The same motive seems to be behind the useless continuation of destruction that was
originally part of expropriation. One critical German observer in Charlesville noted that
"two days before the retreat even the lampposts were struck down and sawed apart. There
was not enough time to cart them off, so they at least had to be destroyed."[221] And, finally,
the breakdown of discipline, the result of the officers' loss of authority and of the troops'

---

216. *UA* 3:1, 115.
217. Ibid., 90.
218. *Die deutsche Kriegführung*, 29.
219. Gatzke, *Germany's Drive*, 91–92, 154, 160; Hatke, *Hugo Stinnes*, 53–54; Wende, *Die belgische Frage*, 193–95; McPhail, *Long Silence*, 34; Munro, Sellery, and Krey, eds., *German War Practices* 2:8.
220. Schwertfeger in the *Nationale Zeitung*, Nov. 1918, cited in Michael Geyer, "Insurrectionary Warfare," *Journal of Modern History* 73 (Sept. 2001), 459–527, here 495. Trotha had referred in July 1904 to the "streams of blood" necessary to force colonization: Trotha, diary, 1 July 1904, Trotha Papers, Nr. 315, p. 15.
221. Appens, *Charleville*, 27.

262 material deprivation for the past two years, meant widespread plunder. The same observer wrote that "the civilian population is not even left with the smallest appliance or even a chicken."[222]

The results of the devastation were staggering. There was nothing left but mud. In November 1918 half a million "repatriates" from southern France and three hundred thousand French deportees in Belgium trekked home. They found nothing. Herbert Hoover, in charge of their relief, wrote, "The destruction of twenty principal towns and literally hundreds of villages renders the return of these refugees a stupendous problem."[223] By one estimate, 850,000 buildings in France had been destroyed or seriously damaged;[224] combat accounted for much of this number, but the greater part resulted from gratuitous destruction understood by the Supreme Command as "military necessity."

222. Ibid., 36.

223. Hoover, letter of 28 Dec. 1918, *American Epic*, vol. 1: *Relief of Belgium*, 399.

224. For purposes of comparison, in the Lithuanian areas of occupation the number of buildings destroyed was about fifty-seven thousand: Basler, *Deutschlands Annexionspolitik*, 280. The German government said that the Russian army in East Prussia had destroyed twenty thousand buildings and eighty thousand dwellings: *UA* 3:1, 153.

11

The Armenian Genocide

In the spring of 1915 Germany's new Turkish ally began systematically murdering its Armenian population. The most radical reformers in the ruling Committee of Union and Progress (CUP) used the cover of war to "deport" the Armenians from their homes in Anatolia. Special armed units, Kurdish and other ethnic bands, and sometimes the regular army then slaughtered the defenseless refugees on their way to equally lethal concentration camps in the Syrian desert. The genocidal campaign continued through 1917 and picked up again in 1918, when Turkish troops entered the Caucasus. In the end, Anatolia's three thousand-year-old, 1.5–2 million-strong Armenian community was gone. That was the CUP's goal—to build a nation-state around a homogenous Turkic-Islamic population, stripped of its Christians (Armenians, Greeks, Nestorians, and some Syrians) and Jews. This genocidal project killed at least eight hundred thousand Armenians, most likely a million or more.[1]

---

1. Death estimates: Arnold J. Toynbee, *Armenian Atrocities* (London, 1915), 6, see also 92–105; Consul Rössler to Chancellor Bethmann Hollweg, Aleppo, 20 Dec. 1915, Nr. 116, Politisches Archiv, Auswärtiges Amt, Bonn, Türkei 183, vol. 40 (hereafter PA-AA). War's end, German estimates: Johannes Lepsius, *Der Todesgang des armenischen Volkes* (Potsdam, 1930), 297; Vahakn N. Dadrian, "The Naim-Andonian Documents on the World War I Destruction of the Ottoman Armenians," *International Journal of Middle East Studies* 18:3 (1986), 342. Turkish estimates: Norman Naimark, *Fires of Hatred* (Cambridge, Mass., 2001), 41; Gerard J. Libaridian, "The Ultimate Repression," in *Genocide and the Modern Age*, ed. Isidor Wallimann and Michael N. Dobrowski (New York, 1987), 206. German Admiral Souchon, who spent the war in Constantinople, confided to his diary on 15 Aug. 1915 that "three-quarters of the Armenians living in Turkey have been liquidated." BA-MA Freiburg, Nl. Souchon, no. 15, cited in Christoph Dinkel, "German Officers and the Armenian Genocide," *Armenian Review* 44, no. 1/173 (spring 1991): 77–133, here 115. See also Robert Melson, "Provocation or Nationalism," in *The History and Sociology of Genocide*, ed. Chalk and Jonassohn, 266–89, here 269–70; Robert Melson, *Revolution and Genocide* (Chicago, 1992), 145–47, 312–13nn18, 23; Marjorie Housepian, *The Smyrna Affair* (New York, 1966).

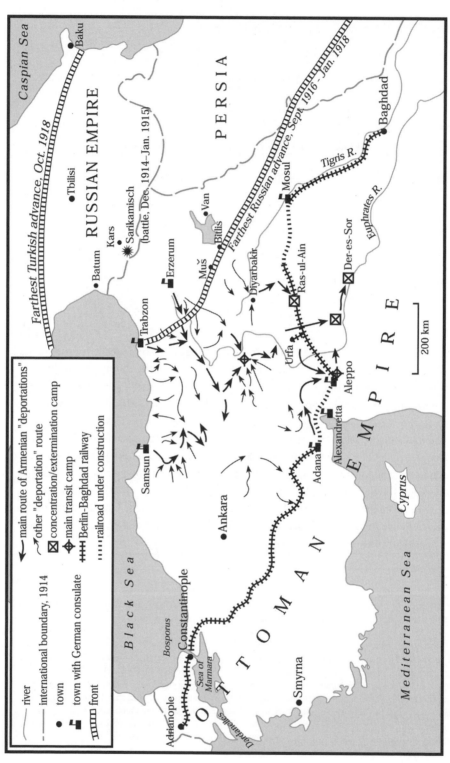

Routes of deportations of Armenians in Turkey, 1914–1918. Sources: Gerayer Koutcharian, *Der Siedlungsraum der Armenier unter dem Einfluss der historisch-politischen Ereignisse seit dem Berliner Kongress 1878* (Berlin, 1989), map 5; Jürgen Herrmkind, Helmut Kistler, and Herbert Raisch, eds., *Atlas zur Universalgeschichte* (Munich, 1979), map 83; Hermann Kinder and Werner Hilgemann, *The Anchor Atlas of World History*, vol. 2, (New York, 1968), 126.

United States and Allied commentators quickly suspected German involvement.[2] Powerful Germany seemed likely to be the dominant partner in the alliance, especially in wartime because of the German military mission. German officers and consuls were scattered across Anatolia where the killing occurred. And most of all, German official statements and (censored) newspaper accounts were at best pusillanimous; at worst they denied the killings or even blamed the Armenians.[3] The CUP assiduously spread rumors that German officials had ordered the killings, and these rumors filtered out to foreign observers, as they were intended to do.[4]

Like contemporaries, scholars today remain divided on Germany's role. Ulrich Trumpener, in a careful, archivally based study, concludes that Germany "neither instigated nor welcomed" the genocide. But he finds that both Austrian and German officials "were guilty of extremely poor judgment, a considerable degree of moral callousness, and an altogether excessive concern with what was or seemed to be politically expedient." They shrank from "drastic" measures to stop the Turks, though Trumpener doubts even those would have been successful.[5]

On the other side, Vahakn N. Dadrian argues most forcefully for Germany's complicity. His case could be summarized like this: two Germans (Colmar von der Goltz and Paul Rohrbach) contributed the ideology of ethnic consolidation through deportation; German officers suggested or ordered the deportations, and some participated in them; the Kaiser's pro-Turkish enthusiasm dictated that Germany's diplomats weakly and insincerely "protest" the killings after they came to light; and Germany continued to support the genocide, as evidenced by medals bestowed on some of the main perpetrators, their rescue from Allied hands after the war, and the Foreign Office's refusal to extradite them for war crimes.[6]

Germany's role in the Armenian genocide was, in fact, complicated and riddled with contradiction. Germany's foreign policy goals were incompatible with those of its ally,

---

2. Toynbee, *Armenian Atrocities*, 6.

3. Examples of this reasoning: Docs. 55, 110, 124, 139, 236, 531 in Arthur Beylerian, *Les grandes puissances* (Paris, 1983); James Bryce and Arnold Toynbee, ed., *The Treatment of the Armenians in the Ottoman Empire, 1914–16*, ed. Ara Sarafian (London, 2000), xxxii; Armen Hairapetian, " 'Race Problems' and the Armenian Genocide," *Armenian Review* 37 (spring 1984): 41–59; and Armen K. Hovannisian, "The United States Inquiry and the Armenian Question, 1917–1919," *Armenian Review* 37 (spring 1984): 146–63.

4. Austrian Consul Nadamlenzki to Ambassador Pallavicini, Adrianople, Nr. Z.100/P, 10 Nov. 1915, reprinted in Institut für Armenische Fragen, *The Armenian Genocide*, 3 vols. (Munich, 1987), 2:274; Pallavicini, Konfidenten-Bericht, Nr. 444, Constantinople, 2 Dec. 1915, cited in ibid., 294–96; Scheubner-Richter to Hohenlohe-Langenburg, Erzerum, Nr. 580, 5 Aug. 1915, PA-AA, Türkei 183, vol. 39; Rössler to Bethmann, Aleppo, Nr. 110, 30 Nov. 1915, ibid., vol. 40; Gunz to Embassy, Constantinople, 10 Aug. 1915, ibid., vol. 55; Ambassador Wolff-Metternich to Bethmann, Pera, Nr. 725, 18 Dec. 1915, ibid., vol. 40; Wolff-Metternich to Bethmann, Pera, 7 Dec. 1915 (citing a report of Gen. Friedrich Kress v. Kressenstein), in Johannes Lepsius, *Deutschland und Armenien, 1914–1918* (Potsdam, 1919), 201–2; Lepsius, *Todesgang*, x.

Lepsius's collection *Deutschland und Armenien* omits portions of some documents and occasionally sanitizes others. Nevertheless, it gives a generally accurate and detailed view of how the genocide unfolded. I have checked Lepsius's edition with the filmed version of the originals, available in U.S. National Archives Microfilm Rolls 139/463–64, 136/77, 136/81–82, and with the originals in the PA-AA, Türkei 183, vols. 36–40, 43–45, and 51.

5. Ulrich Trumpener, *Germany and the Ottoman Empire* (Princeton, 1968), 204–5, 269.

6. Vahakn N. Dadrian, *The History of the Armenian Genocide* (Providence, R.I., 1995), and Vahakn N. Dadrian, *German Responsibility in the Armenian Genocide* (Watertown, Mass., 1996).

266 and its institutions in Turkey, as at home, were internally fractious and uncoordinated. On the one hand, German policy regarding the genocide was largely the product of the same military-cultural assumptions that animated German wartime policies in Europe. These assumptions were most strongly articulated by some German officers in Turkey, but they also had penetrated the thinking of certain influential diplomats. On the other hand, other German foreign-political interests were clearly harmed by military "requirements." More than anything else, however, the stark result of unalloyed "military necessity" horrified most German observers who were on the spot, driving some to intervene against the killing. The resulting German policy was typically at cross purposes, ineffective, and (self-) destructive. But it is a brilliant illustration, if another is needed, of the logic and cost of "military necessity."

The German-Turkish Alliance and the Military Mission

The German-Turkish alliance was a shotgun marriage of two partners whose immediate aims coincided but whose long-term goals (insofar as Germany had any) were contradictory. Three men, War Minister Enver Pasha, Interior Minister Mehmet Talât Pasha, and the later commander of the 4th Army in Syria and Palestine, Cemal Pasha, were the most powerful core of a government of perhaps fifty shifting members. It was Enver who proposed the alliance to a reluctant Ambassador Hans von Wangenheim on 22 July 1914. The CUP hoped to use German support to create a modern, homogeneous state free of foreign tutelage and interference. Specifically, the CUP wanted to remove or renounce the reserve rights that foreign powers had gained over financial, judicial, and other internal matters (the "capitulations") and to revoke the Reform Agreement of February 1914 that Russia, seconded by Britain and France, had forced on Turkey. The agreement had established Armenian autonomy in areas of Anatolia, guaranteed by Russian intervention if necessary. Once freed of these limits to Turkish sovereignty, the CUP dreamed of expansion into Russia and into the Balkans, from which the Ottoman Empire had recently been expelled.[7]

The war doubtless came sooner than Enver expected; he and Talât had to maneuver hard to push their fellow governors to begin hostilities (November 1914). But Enver and his fellow radicals wanted war. Only war permitted them to abrogate the capitulations and the Reform Agreement. Cemal remembered, "Our only hope was through the world war to free ourselves from all conventions that were so many attacks on our independence and in future to be able to live as an independent and free people. . . . Similarly, it was our main goal . . . to dissolve the Armenian reforms that had been forced on us by Russia."[8] The "complete independence" from foreign intervention that Talât once summed up as Turkey's war aim meant freedom to "solve" the Armenian question; it is quite likely that

---

7. Trumpener, *Germany*, 19, 28. The correspondence surrounding the alliance, its terms, and renegotiation: Carl Mühlmann, *Deutschland und die Türkei, 1913–1914*, Politische Wissenschaft, vol. 7 (Berlin, 1929), 92–101.

8. Ahmed Djemal, *Erinnerungen eines Türkischen Staatsmannes* (Munich, 1922), 353–54. Cf. Wangenheim to Bethmann, Pera, 2 Feb. 1915, Doc. 15 of Lepsius, *Deutschland und Armenien*, 29.

Enver and Talât envisioned some radical solution as they pushed for war.[9] In a long, careful memo written in April 1916 Austrian Ambassador Janós Pallavicini summarized how CUP leaders had instrumentalized the war:

> The current leaders saw in the outbreak of the world war the favorable moment to reshape things undisturbed by other states and to be able to establish a national Turkish state by repressing all other nationalities. . . . The Young Turks hoped to find in us and Germany in this war support against external and therefore also against internal enemies. This is the main reason that Turkey let us pull it into war so easily in autumn 1914.
>
> Unfortunately, the Young Turk leaders, who felt themselves strong enough in this alliance to execute their program, took advantage of the situation to go against the non-Turkish nationalities in the sharpest way. Only during the war could Talât and Enver and their followers proceed against the Armenians as they have done and also so frighten the other nations [ethnic groups] that today they appear to have virtually achieved their Turkish national state.[10]

The Armenian genocide was therefore a central goal of Ottoman policy.

For the CUP, the alliance with Germany was a means toward long-term and above all bigger goals. The same was not true for Germany. It had hastily concluded the alliance for purely short-term military reasons as the outbreak of war neared. There was considerable difference of opinion about Turkey's military value. Many officers in the military mission and Ambassador Wangenheim judged Turkey weak and unreliable.[11] Kaiser Wilhelm, at first, and then Chief of Staff Moltke, Chancellor Bethmann Hollweg, and the Foreign Office overrode Wangenheim's misgivings. When war actually did break out, almost as the alliance was being signed, they pressed for Turkey's immediate entry into the war.[12]

Turkey was militarily useful. It closed the Straits, thus cutting off Russia from direct Allied support; it tied down Russian troops (and during the Gallipoli campaign, those of Britain and France, along with Australia, New Zealand, and other members of the British Empire); it threatened the Suez Canal; and it lent troops to the European theater.[13] The alliance also strengthened Germany's hand in the Balkans, bringing Bulgaria closer to the Central Powers and encouraging Romania to remain neutral (for a time).[14] But Turkey's disastrous campaign against Russia in December and January 1914–15 and its never-ending financial and munitions crises made it "a heavy moral, financial, and military bur-

9. Matthias Erzberger memo of his conversation with Enver and Talât of 10 Feb. 1916, Doc. 238, in Lepsius, *Deutschland und Armenien*, 237.

10. Pallavicini to Foreign Minister Burián, Constantinople, Nr. 28/P.A., 8 Apr. 1916, HHStA PA XII 210, reprinted in Institut, *Armenian Genocide*, 2:342–43.

11. Friedrich Kress von Kressenstein, *Mit den Türken zum Suezkanal* (Berlin, 1938), 15–16.

12. Trumpener, *Germany*, 15, 22; Jehuda L. Wallach, *Anatomie einer Militärhilfe* (Düsseldorf, 1976), 158–61, 166–67; Djemal, *Erinnerungen*, 136–42.

13. Mühlmann, *Deutschland*, 81–85.

14. Bethmann, *Betrachtungen*, 2:12.

268 den," as Ambassador Count Johann Heinrich von Bernstorff later recalled.[15] More than anything else, OHL knew that the war would be won or lost in Europe, not in Turkey. Neither Falkenhayn nor Ludendorff harbored illusions about the Turks' military capacities.[16] OHL was therefore not the driving force behind Germany's Turkish policy in the war, despite worries about how the Allied invasion of the Dardanelles in spring and summer 1915 might harm Germany's war effort.[17] The most pro-Turkish voices in the government belonged to diplomats, especially to Arthur Zimmermann, undersecretary of the Foreign Office.

Turkey loomed large for those who thought in global, world-policy terms. Turkey was the only land route whereby Germany could strike directly at the British, either by cutting Britain off from India at Suez, or by threatening India via Persia. Hitting Britain was the object of the jihad, or holy war, for which Kaiser Wilhelm pressed and which the caliphate officially declared on 14 November 1914.[18] (The jihad helped fuel the atmosphere of intolerance that aided the genocide.)[19] But even if such grandiose plans failed, Turkey was still key to Germany's world power status. If Britain could not be beaten, Germany could compensate for stalemate in Europe and restriction of overseas colonies by predominating in the Near East through a Turkish client state beholden to it financially, technically (the Berlin-Baghdad railway), and militarily. Foreign Secretary Jagow wrote in July 1915 that "supporting Turkey is now and in the future for us a question of the foremost importance."[20] For this reason the chancellor and the Foreign Office pressed hard during the summer and early fall of 1915 for Falkenhayn to open a third front against Serbia to link up with the Turks. Zimmermann was so desperate to do so that on 1 August 1915 he turned directly to Turkish Foreign Minister Halil Bey to have Enver lobby the reluctant German chief of staff.[21] The Foreign Office's efforts on Turkey's behalf could rely on vocal support from the growing group of anti-English expansionists such as Admiral v. Tirpitz, important sectors of the National Liberals, and the Pan-Germans.[22]

The more important that Turkey seemed to Germany's future, the weaker Germany's own position in the alliance seemed to be.[23] The alliance was not popular outside the rad-

15. Johann Heinrich Graf Bernstorff, *Erinnerungen und Briefe* (Zürich, 1936), 129. Bernstorff became ambassador in September 1917.

16. Afflerbach, *Falkenhayn*, 336–37; Janssen, *Der Kanzler*, 67; Rupprecht Kronprinz v. Bayern, *Mein Kriegstagebuch*, 2:104, 250; Wild, *Briefe*, 64.

17. Afflerbach, *Falkenhayn*, 44, 58–59, 262–63.

18. Humann to embassy, Therapia, 17 Aug. 1914, BA-MA Freiburg, RM 40, vol. 456, Archiv der Marine, Kriegsakten, Politisches, Bd. 1, Akten der Mittelmeerdivision.

19. Libaridian, "Ultimate Repression," 205; Pallavicini to Burián, Constantinople, Nr. 95/P.A., "streng vertraulich," 12 Nov. 1915, HHStA PA I 944, cited in Institut, *Armenian Genocide*, 2:278.

20. "Zusatz zum Schreiben des Herrn Reichskanzler," by Jagow, 24 July 1915, cited in Janssen, *Der Kanzler*, 283. Also Bethmann's similar view of 4 July 1915, cited 138; and Zimmermann's, 42–43.

21. Janssen, *Der Kanzler*, 278–79; Germany, Reichsarchiv, *Die Weltkrieg 1914 bis 1918*, 6:409–11.

22. Wernecke, *Der Wille zur Weltgeltung*, 289–93, 298; Tirpitz, *Politische Dokumente*, 59; Tirpitz, *Erinnerungen* (Leipzig, 1919), 479.

23. Both Ambassadors Wolff-Metternich and Bernstorff criticized this misapprehension by their superiors in the chancellery and Foreign Office: Wolff-Metternich to Bethmann, Pera, Nr. 711, 7 Dec. 1915, PA-AA, Türkei 183, vol. 40; Bernstorff, *Erinnerungen*, 128, 140–41.

ical core of the CUP. Zimmermann claimed that "our alliance rests on the six eyes of Talât, Enver, and Halil."[24] The CUP aim of independence also predisposed the Turks to chafe at German or Austrian criticism, which sensitized German diplomats to the dangers of falling into "England's role after the Congress of Berlin, or recently Russia's as a protector of the Armenians," as Wangenheim put it.[25] Unfortunately, four of the six eyes on which the alliance allegedly rested belonged to the two men, Talât and Enver, most responsible for the genocide. And the chancellor's and Foreign Office's campaign for a third front coincided with the height of the killing. Germany's civilian, more than its military, leadership was strongly tempted to underestimate Germany's own strength in the alliance and to reckon according to the imagined expediencies of realpolitik.

If OHL chose a backseat regarding Turkey, the German military mission there could not. Allied contemporaries and some scholars subsequently have attributed great policy-making power to the military mission.[26] But it was as ill-defined and fractured as most official Wilhelminian institutions; it was incapable of forming consistent policy. The treaty setting up the military mission was an entirely military product; neither the chancellor nor the Foreign Office was well-informed about it.[27] It was designed for peacetime and had to be hastily renegotiated when war broke out. Its terms were vague.[28] Its head from the beginning in December 1913 to the end of the war was Gen. Otto Liman von Sanders. He became the second or third highest ranking officer in the Turkish army, after War Minister Enver, and the only German officer with ex officio command power. According to the treaty, he was to participate in military decision making and to inspect units and fortifications. The other forty German officers, whose duties were left unspecified, were placed in staff and management positions; that is, they functioned like the general staff system at home, where junior officers drew up plans but the command power rested with the (in this case, Turkish) senior commanders. Their numbers grew slowly until October 1915; they had reached 290 by early 1916 and ultimately rose to almost 800, with 32,000 German troops.[29] The number of German officers at the height of the genocide in 1915 was thus relatively small.

Both the military mission treaty and Wilhelm's parting instructions to his officers underscored that officers were to confine their activities to the purely military, leaving politics and internal matters to their Turkish hosts.[30] When Turkey entered the war, the influence of German officers increased because military operations were being conducted; the disastrous campaign of 1914–15 and the attack on Suez were both German ideas, for ex-

24. Zimmermann in a conversation with Lepsius: Johann Lepsius, "Mein Besuch in Konstantinopel, Juli-August 1915," *Der Orient* 1:3 (1919): 21–33, here 30; Djemal, *Erinnerungen*, 116.

25. Wangenheim to Foreign Office, Pera, Nr. 228, 15 Apr. 1915, PA-AA, Türkei 183, vol. 36, also Doc. 26 in Lepsius, *Deutschland und Armenien*, 48–49.

26. Dadrian, *German Responsibility*, 109–16; Dinkel, "German Officers," 100, 102, 104.

27. Wallach, *Anatomie*, 128.

28. It is reprinted in Mühlmann, *Deutschland*, Anlage 2, 88–92.

29. Wallach, *Anatomie*, 179; Lepsius, *Deutschland und Armenien*, xxvii; 25,000 troops: Trumpener, *Germany*, 104; Groener told the cabinet there were 32,000 troops in Turkey, Prince Max v. Baden, *Erinnerungen*, 566.

30. Otto Liman von Sanders, *Fünf Jahre Türkei* (Berlin, 1919), 12.

270 ample.[31] But the war also decreased the German officers' power in several ways. With three exceptions, no German officer commanded troops. Moreover, whereas a peacetime advisor might be able to afford to use threatened resignation to get his way, there was no question of that in wartime.[32] For the military, as for the diplomats, Germany's perceived need for allies and *Menschenmaterial* elevated the status of even weak allies in their eyes. And once the threat to the Dardanelles had been beaten off, Enver and the CUP leaders became swollen with self-confidence and were even less likely to let a foreign power, even an ally, interfere with "internal" matters.[33]

But more than this, the military mission was incapable of policy making altogether. Policy, or at least coordination, would have rested with the chief, Liman. Alas, Liman was not even on speaking terms with Ambassador Wangenheim, who complained that Liman kept the Austrian military attaché better informed than he was.[34] The archives are filled with vociferous official complaints about the (admittedly) misanthropic, paranoid, and downright peculiar head of the military mission. Furthermore, Liman and Enver were on equally bad terms, so Liman lost whatever potential there was to influence Turkish policy at the top. Liman's relations with his subordinates were no better. Neither those who supported or condoned the genocide nor those who actively opposed it could stand him. Once Liman left Constantinople on 25 March 1915 to command the defense of the coast, he was geographically cut off as well.

But even a congenial chief would have had to struggle against the familiar fracturing of military authority. OHL received reports directly from Liman, the German military and naval attachés, the chief of the Mediterranean naval divisions and coast fortifications, the German chief of the Turkish General Staff (Gen. Friedrich Bronsart von Schellendorf), Field Marshal Gen. Colmar von der Goltz (after December 1914, personal advisor to the sultan and the war minister), and later from General Falkenhayn, after he assumed command of Turkish and German troops in the Near East.[35] All of these incumbents were free to act independently. In short, policy making, or at least decisions with policy consequences, could and did easily devolve downward. There was a good chance that the embassy would learn of military decisions belatedly, if at all, and no chance that the decisions would be coordinated.

There was one more immense hindrance to concerted military policy. Only two officers, neither one a member of the military mission proper, knew anything about Turkey. General v. d. Goltz had supervised Turkish military education from 1883 to 1895. OHL re-exiled him to Turkey in December 1914 after he had demonstrated unacceptable leniency toward Belgian civilians as first governor-general there. His new position was personal

31. Wallach, *Anatomie*, 167–68.

32. Felix Guse, *Die Kaukasusfront im Weltkrieg bis zum Frieden von Brest* (Leipzig, 1940), 113.

33. Self-confidence: Colmar von der Goltz, *Denkwürdigkeiten*, ed. Friedrich von der Goltz and Wolfgang Foerster (Berlin, 1929), 427.

34. Wangenheim to Bethmann, Pera, Nr. 1629, 16 Dec. 1914, PA-AA, Türkei 139, "Überlassung von preussischen offizieren und Finanzbeamten an die Pforte zu Reorganisationszwecken," (1914–1920), vol. 33. Vols. 33–49 are replete with complaints about Liman. See National Archives Microfilm Roll T 136/81.

35. On personal and institutional hindrances to policy making: Carl Mühlmann, *Das Deutsch-Türkische Waffenbündnis im Weltkriege* (Leipzig, 1940), 285–314, esp. 291–96; Kress, *Mit den Türken*, 22; Wallach, *Anatomie*, 174–82, 189, 191, 206.

advisor to the sultan and, after February 1915, to Enver, who apparently agreed with OHL that Goltz was "too old" and "soft."[36] Goltz remained the outsider he had always been, institutionally isolated until his death in 1916 during the quixotic expedition to Mesopotamia and Persia.[37]

The second officer was naval attaché Lt. Cdr. Hans von Humann. The son of an archeologist, he had grown up in Turkey and had become friends with Enver during Enver's time as military attaché in Berlin. Humann's continued close personal ties made him useful as an unofficial conduit to the war minister for the German embassy during the war. Humann was a rabid anti-Semite and enthusiastic expansionist, whose views placed him close to the Pan-Germans. While his official position as attaché carried neither command nor policy-making power, his personal connections and ideological convictions opened the possibility of influence beyond his station.[38]

None of the other officers had prior experience in Turkey, nor could they speak Turkish (or Armenian or Greek). They were completely dependent for information on their Turkish fellow officers. The Turkish interpretation of the treacherous Armenians and Greeks and of the requirements of "military necessity" became for many German officers simply facts that formed the basis of their own reckoning. Developing or retaining a critical distance from Turkish (mis)information would have required considerably more historical, linguistic, and political education than most officers possessed. The credulity of many German officers toward the prodigious Turkish propaganda campaign thus came from several sources: tendentious information, lack of a robust contrary perspective (from prior education or from public announcements of the German government), contractual loyalty to their comrades and allies, and the similarity between the story that Turkish officers told and their own military-cultural assumptions about a world of enemies and traitors, the instrumentalization of civilians for military purposes, and the necessity of using force to the end.

Thus the embassy was hobbled by Turkish sensitivity to foreign meddling and by its own sense of weakness, while the military mission concentrated on military operations. Neither was nearly as powerful as contemporaries thought.[39] And neither controlled the officers on the spot. If there was direct German involvement in the Armenian genocide, it came from those officers.

The Deportation Orders

The radical wing of the CUP had been making ideological and institutional preparations for the "final solution to the Armenian problem" since 1909.[40] The 1909 CUP party

36. Enver, cited in Trumpener, *Germany*, 89.

37. Uninfluential in the army: Goltz, *Denkwürdigkeiten*, 154–57, 159–60, 377, 380–81, 393, 401.

38. BA-MA Freiburg, RM 40, Nr. 456, "Besprechungen mit Enver Pascha, Sammlung Humann," 1–105; "Vertrauliche Mitteilungen," 106–411; Ernst Jäckh Papers, Yale University Library.

39. Trumpener, *Germany*, 68–69; Wallach, *Anatomie*, 158, 167; Mühlmann, *Deutsch-türkische Waffenbündnis*, 285–314; Joseph Pomiankowski, *Der Zusammenbruch des Ottomanischen Reiches* (Graz, 1969), 163; Liman, *Fünf Jahre Türkei*, 31, 34; Pallavicini to Foreign Office, Pera, tel. Nr. 588, 10 Oct. 1914, in Institut, *Armenian Genocide*, 2:170–71.

40. Critical German consuls recognized the genocide as a final solution and used that language to describe

272

Portrait of the German embassy staff in Constantinople, 1914 or 1915. Painting by W. V. Krauss; in Joseph Pomiankowski, *Der Zusammenbruch des Ottomanischen Reiches* (Vienna: Amathea-Verlag, 1928), Tafel 3.

statute had proclaimed homogeneity as its national goal. In August 1910, a secret CUP assembly first discussed deportation as a possible route to this aim.[41] Two years later, the party entrusted the minority problem to its chief ideologue, Ziya Gökalp, the author of Pan-Turanism (the consolidation and expansion of Turkey from an Anatolian core), for study. Two weeks after the Reform Agreements were signed in February 1914, Enver convened the first of a series of secret meetings to plan for removal of the "non-Turkish population centers that were exposed to negative foreign influence and were located at strate-

it: For example, Hoffmann to embassy, Alexandrette, 8 Nov. 1915, Nr. 944, PA-AA, Türkei 183, vol. 41; Scheubner-Richter to Bethmann, Munich, 4 Dec. 1916, in Lepsius, *Deutschland und Armenien*, Doc. Nr. 309, p. 307; Bernstorff to Foreign Office, Constantinople, 23 May 1918, tel. Nr. 782, PA-AA, Türkei 183, vol. 51; Bergfeld to Bethmann, Trabzon, 9 July 1915, Nr. 35, ibid., vol. 37; Rössler to Bethmann, Aleppo, 27 July 1915, Doc. 120, Lepsius, *Deutschland und Armenien*, 110; Scheubner-Richter to Foreign Office, "Denkschrift über die Armenier-Frage," Erzerum, 10 Aug. 1915, Nr. 582, PA-AA, Türkei 183, vol. 39.

41. Taner Akçam, *Armenien und der Völkermord* (Hamburg, 1996), 36–37. My discussion of the early preparations for genocide follows Akçam, whose account is based on the documents admitted as evidence in the Istanbul war crimes trials of 1919.

gic points," as a participant later reported.[42] The Greeks of Thrace and western Anatolia were the first target. The Special Organization (armed irregulars used for guerrilla and terrorist warfare), assisted by government and army officials, deported all Greek men of military age to labor brigades beginning in summer 1914 and lasting through 1916. A leader of the Special Organization claimed that 1.15 million people had been deported. The postwar Turkish parliament spoke of five hundred to five hundred and fifty thousand deaths as a result of these actions.[43]

Preparations for "solving the Armenian problem" followed the same pattern and seem part of the same campaign. On 2 August 1914, the CUP ordered the formation of more Special Organization units under the leadership of CUP party leader Dr. Bahaeddin Shakir, who became the chief technician of the Armenian genocide. He established his headquarters at Erzerum in the heart of Armenian Anatolia. Later in August, moderate civil bureaucrats and military men were removed from office in Anatolia. The Special Organization bands began extortion and murder campaigns against Armenians in late August and September, apparently trying to provoke armed resistance that would provide an alibi for government retaliation.[44]

The CUP therefore hardly needed Colmar v. d. Goltz or Paul Rohrbach to give them the idea for mass population removal.[45] Mass deportation, together with widespread massacres and ethnic evacuations, had already characterized the Balkan Wars of 1912–13 and been under discussion in CUP circles for several years. Goltz did believe Turkey should cut its European losses and concentrate its strength in Anatolia, but at least in the 1890s, when he first expounded these views, he advocated liberal constitutional and economic reforms to integrate non-Turkish populations into a progressive state.[46] For his part, Rohrbach adamantly rejected the Armenian genocide, as he had the similar "solution" in SWA, and agitated tirelessly in Berlin to get the government to take active steps against it.[47] Anyway, as Arnold Toynbee remarked in 1915 against the same charge of German ideological authorship, "The Turks do not need tempters."[48] But the CUP went from mere preparation to actual deportation in winter and spring 1915. What precipitated this shift? The means of violence provide a clue.

42. Testimony of Kushçubashi Eshref, a leader of the Special Organization (Teskilat-i Muhsusa), cited in Akçam, *Armenien*, 41.

43. Akçam, ibid., 42–43. Bloxham disputes the deaths: Donald Bloxham, "The Beginning of the Armenian Catastrophe," in *Der Völkermord an den Armeniern und die Shoah*, ed. Hans-Lukas Kieser and Dominik J. Schaller (Zurich, 2002), 101–28, here 106.

44. Akçam, *Armenien*, 52–53; Yves Ternon, *Les Arméniens* (Paris, 1977), 201–3. On the military background of the Special Organization see James J. Reid, "Militarism, Partisan War, and Destructive Inclinations in Ottoman Military History," *Armenian Review* 39, no. 3/155 (autumn 1986): 1–21; Donald Bloxham, "Power Politics, Prejudice, Protest, and Propaganda," in *Völkermord*, ed. Kieser and Schaller, 213–44, here 220–21.

45. Dadrian, *German Responsibility*, 20, 113–16.

46. Colmar von der Goltz, "Stärke und Schwäche des Türkischen Reichs," *Deutsche Rundschau* 93:1 (Dec. 1897): 46–70, esp. 65, 70. The *Denkwürdigkeiten* are not a reliable source for Goltz's own views; they contain strong völkisch additions by Goltz's apparently National Socialist son, Friedrich, who edited them with Wolfgang Foerster.

47. Rohrbach to Ernst Jäckh, 15 Aug. 1916, copy, BA Koblenz, Nl. Rohrbach, vol. 112; Trumpener, *Germany*, 227n63.

48. Toynbee, *Armenian Atrocities*, 108. Same point: Pomiankowski, *Zusammenbruch*, 161.

274   The killings were mostly orchestrated and carried out by the Special Organization. These ad hoc units had been engaged in dirty, guerilla warfare against the Italians in Tripoli in 1911 and against Turkey's Balkan enemies during the First Balkan War.[49] The military mission had reorganized the Special Organization before the First World War.[50] After August 1914 the CUP organized such units again and used them in two mutually supporting ways to pursue the goal of Pan-Turanism: by engaging in guerrilla raids across the Russian border and by provoking Armenians through extortion and killings.[51] The Special Organization units began as a mixed military-CUP institution. Nominally subordinate to the local army (in Anatolia, the 3rd Army), they were called into existence by the CUP but drew arms and intelligence from the military. Units destined for trans-Caucasus fighting sometimes had German officers.[52] Beginning in February 1915 the Special Organization began to be removed from army control and placed entirely under the command of the CUP zealot Dr. Shakir. Shakir had returned to Constantinople on 13 March 1915 from his provincial headquarters in Erzerum in order to take part in several meetings of the CUP Central Committee. The process of transferring command of the Special Organization to CUP control was complete by May 1915 when the first mass deportations from eastern Anatolia started.[53] Thereafter, orders for "deportation" generally came from Talât's Ministry of the Interior and went to the Special Organization, to provincial heads of government (*valis*), half of whom in Anatolia served double duty as part of the Special Organization anyway, and occasionally to regular military units.[54] Institutionally, then, the mechanism for genocide shifted from the military to the CUP and the government at about the time the killings became widespread and systematic.

This institutional history suggests that an original military impetus was transformed and systematized by the CUP for its own ideological purposes.[55] The army in question was the Turkish 3rd Army, fighting in eastern Anatolia, commanded by Mahmut Kâmil, whose chief of staff was the German Lt. Col. Felix Guse. Military defeat was the precipitator. Pressured by Chief of the (Turkish) General Staff Bronsart, who wanted Turkey to tie down Russian troops as soon as possible, and fired by his own reckless ambition, War Minister Enver had forced the 3rd Army into a premature winter campaign against the Russians in the Caucasus in mid-December 1914. Liman had warned that Turkey was un-

49. Erik J. Zürcher, *Turkey* (London, 1997), 110–11, 114.

50. Bloxham, "Power Politics," 220–21.

51. Ternon, *Arméniens*, 202–3; Dadrian, *German Responsibility*, 44–46.

52. Austrian Consul Kwiatkowski to Foreign Minister Berchtold, Trabzon, Nr. Z. 79/P, 8 Nov. 1914, reprinted in Institut, *Armenian Genocide*, 2:171.

53. Akçam, *Armenien*, 64–65.

54. Ibid., 65–67; Dadrian, *German Responsibility*, 41.

55. The Turkish General Staff documents support the conclusion that "at the highest levels, Enver Pasha and the military staff appear to have generated the basic idea of the forced evacuation of the Armenians in response to a military problem which threatened the security of the Turkish Third Army and therefore of the empire itself." Edward J. Erickson, *Ordered to Die* (Westport, Conn., 2001), 103. Another recent survey based on archival documentation (and which hews to the current, official Turkish line of denial) also concludes that an original military situation was taken over by the Interior Ministry: Mim Kemâl Öke, *The Armenian Question, 1914–1923* (Nicosia, 1988), 127–33.

prepared. Of ninety thousand soldiers who set out in December, only twelve thousand lived through the frigid retreat in January and February.[56] That retreat took the army through largely Armenian-populated territory. Reports from the 3rd Army began to repeat the widespread fear that local Armenians would side with the advancing Russians and perhaps rise up in anticipation of being freed from centuries of Turkish oppression. An American military historian, Edward Erickson, who was recently permitted partial access to the Turkish General Staff archives, reports that the documents give the impression of "a rising pattern of civil unrest, followed by an armed rebellion [in mid-March in Van]." They "also show an escalating response by the military culminating in the mass deportation of the Armenians."[57] Erickson's impressions are precisely what German staff officers would have received from their Turkish sources.

There are excellent reasons to doubt the smooth narrative moving from revolt at Van to deportation.[58] The number of Turkish-Armenian defectors fighting with Russia was militarily insignificant.[59] Civil unrest was mostly provoked by the Special Organization. The major conflicts in Van (c. 20 April–17 May 1915), and later Urfa and Mossa Degh, were all cases where Armenians fought to save themselves from deportation and massacre.[60] Turkish government officials gave three conflicting accounts of events at Van. Chronology and geography also argue against Van as the "cause." Enver's directive for "increased security precautions" against Armenians preceded the Van conflict. So did deportations and massacres at Adana, Zeitun, Marash, and Dörtyol. Furthermore, these occurred in western not eastern Anatolia, where the 3rd Army operated. Deportations therefore began in two separate regions. Nonetheless, the legend that a dangerous uprising at Van caused and justified the deportations was almost universally accepted by contemporary German observers (even by those who tried to stop the genocide).[61]

Did German staff officers initiate the deportations in eastern Anatolia? And if they did, what did they mean by deportation? We know that some German staff officers did indeed advise the Turkish army to deport Armenian civilians. But the timing of their advice is unclear. After the war, Lt. Col. Otto von Feldmann (who had been head of operations in the Ottoman General Staff) wrote:

> Even *German officers*—I myself among them—were forced to advise freeing the rear of the army from Armenians in certain areas at certain times. The *duty of self-preservation* of the Turkish army did not permit leaving strong forces to guard rear lines. Without that, however, no operation was possible, no reverse at the

---

56. Zürcher, *Turkey*, 119.

57. Erickson, *Ordered to Die*, 96.

58. For a contrary but carefully differentiated view, see Bloxham, "Beginning," and Bloxham, "Power Politics," 219.

59. Akçam, *Armenien*, 380n39.

60. Dadrian, *German Responsibility*, 31–34.

61. Three accounts: Trumpener, *Germany*, 222. Timing: Erickson, *Ordered to Die*, 98; Akçam, *Armenien*, 63. Credulity of genocide critics: Scheubner-Richter to embassy, 5 Aug. 1915, Doc. 129 in Lepsius, *Deutschland und Armenien*, 117.

front could be sustained, so long as Armenians lived in the rear. The experience right at the beginning of the war in the east had shown this lesson.[62]

Feldmann's reference was to the disastrous retreat in January–February 1915, though his statement does not date the advice. His account suggests that German officers recommended not universal deportation but specific deportations, which nonetheless encompassed the entire Armenian population of an area, not just draft-age males. Guse, the chief of staff of the 3rd Army, described military fears as anticipatory: "In the event of a Russian advance one had to reckon with the possibility of an Armenian uprising," he noted in his memoirs.[63] Both Guse and Feldmann could have been referring to the period February to April 1915. The other three documented examples we have of German officers advising deportation all occurred after the genocide was well underway. Bronsart ordered Armenian males working in forced labor brigades to be removed on 25 July 1915; and he advised Liman (who refused) to deport Greeks from the coast in August 1916.[64] In October 1915 Lieutenant Colonel Böttrich appended his signature to a decree from the Turkish War Ministry for the deportation of 848 Armenian railroad workers from the Berlin-Baghdad railway.[65] No other documents directly linking German officers to deportation have come to light.

It is possible, in my judgment likely, that Bronsart, Guse, and Feldmann (who all accepted the standard Turkish stories of Armenian perfidy) recommended clearing the rear echelon of the 3rd Army by deportation in late winter and early spring 1915. That advice inadvertently gave Enver and Talât the cover they wanted to pursue the CUP's ideologically driven "final solution," whose first steps they had already taken.[66] Feldmann and Guse explained the standard logic behind the German recommendations: the military necessity to save the weak Turkish army required removing all potential threats and, without hesitation, instrumentalizing civilians. This thinking was consistent with standard assumptions of military culture as we have seen them operate elsewhere. Enver cloaked the provisional law of 27 May 1915, which was the legal cover for the genocide, in the mantle of military necessity. It gave military commanders from the division level and higher the power "in the case of military necessity, or when spying or treason are suspected, to remove inhabitants individually or en masse from villages or cities and settle them in other

---

62. Feldmann, "Zum Talaatprozess," *Deutsche Allgemeine Zeitung* 301 (30 June 1921), 2, cited (in a different translation) by Dinkel, "German Officers," 96. Emphasis in original.

63. Guse, *Kaukasusfront*, 27; Dinkel, "German Officers," 101.

64. Dadrian, *German Responsibility*, 117; Dinkel, "German Officers," 88.

65. The order is Anlage 3 of Foreign Minister to Treutler, Berlin, Nr. 209, 13 Nov. 1915, PA-AA, Türkei 152, vol. 83. Number: Neurath to Foreign Office, Pera, tel. Nr. 2532, 2 Nov. 1915, PA-AA, Türkei 183, vol. 39.

66. A German missionary with good sources of information from inside Turkey wrote unhesitatingly that German officers had suggested deportations as the Turkish 3rd Army retreated in January–February 1915: Julius Richter, "Die deutschen evangelischen Missionskreise und das armenische Volk," *Allgemeine Missions-Zeitschrift* 46:2 (Feb. 1919): 33–45, here 36. The Austrian consul Kwiatkowski also heard from "usually reliable German sources" that German officers advised deportation, "but not in the manner in which these were then done." Kwiatkowski to Burián, Nr. 70/P, Vertraulich, Trabzon, 22 Oct. 1915, HHStA PA XII 463, in Institut, *Armenian Genocide*, 2:252.

areas."[67] Apparently Enver showed this order to General v. d. Goltz, who approved it, since it was entirely consistent with military practice, especially in occupied zones.[68] Goltz's later actions to stop deportations indicate it is unlikely he understood its larger significance. Enver's order was simultaneously approved by the Interior Ministry and by the cabinet three days later, and was passed by the Ottoman Assembly on 15 September 1915.[69]

Standard military thinking easily suggested deportation, but not genocide. German officers had no plausible reason to recommend such a staggering breach of commonly accepted norms.[70] Genocide was not necessary to pursue the war; in fact, it was counterproductive. It harmed the war effort by consuming resources that might have supported the army; it ruined the economy (of which Armenian craftsmen and traders were the linchpin); and it destroyed the security of the rear lines it was supposed to protect, especially regarding the 4th Army, whose supplies stopped flowing on roads choked with corpses and rank with typhus.[71] And most German officers, like Guse and Feldmann, had no ideological reason to favor genocide.

Two officers, Bronsart and Humann, did seem ideologically prepared to accept or even advocate genocide. Bronsart's views at the time are hard to reconstruct because his memoirs project his later National Socialist convictions backward.[72] Certainly, Bronsart seemed well informed about the decision for "deportation." In February 1919, in a letter defending German officers' conduct, he wrote that "the entire plans and orders for the repression of the uprising [in Van, which Bronsart consistently interpreted as the "cause"] were done by Turks in the Turkish War Ministry (not the General Staff) and in the Ministry of the Interior."[73] When German civilian officials of the Baghdad Railway asked him to prevent the deportation of Armenian employees, Bronsart remained passive, hiding behind technical excuses, apparently motivated by careerism, not conviction.[74] However, as we have seen, Bronsart twice ordered deportations for military reasons.

But Bronsart's wartime job was to oversee the Turkish war effort, not to create the long-term circumstances for a consolidated nation-state, even if he believed that the permanent disappearance of the Armenians would have benefited that goal. In his memoirs, Bronsart remarked that he had to remind Enver repeatedly that the war would be won in Europe, not Turkey, which suggests that Bronsart kept his own eyes on the narrow mili-

---

67. Karl Axenfeld, "Zur Steuer der Wahrheit über die Deportation des armenischen Volkes," *Allgemeine Missions-Zeitschrift* 46:3 (Mar. 1919): 57–64, here 58; Erickson, *Ordered to Die*, 102.

68. Dinkel, "German Officers," 81.

69. Öke, *Armenian Question*, 132–33. Öke believes Talât authored the order at Enver's repeated request.

70. For a different argument arriving at the same conclusion: Bloxham, "Power Politics," esp. 214–17, 222.

71. Kress, *Mit den Türken*, 130, 132; Guse, *Kaukasusfront*, 64–65, 96; Trumpener, *Germany*, 67.

72. Dinkel, "German Officers," 103. On Bronsart in the Böttrich affair: Hilmar Kaiser, "The Baghdad Railways and the Armenian Genocide, 1914–1916," in *Remembrance and Denial*, ed. Richard Hovannisian (Detroit, 1999), 67–122, here 82–83.

73. Bronsart to Karl Axenfeld, Damerow, 10 Feb. 1919, copy, PA-AA, Nl. Göppert, Nr. 5. Emphases in original omitted.

74. Kaiser, "Baghdad Railways," 82–83.

278 tary task at hand.[75] His marginalia critical of consular intervention also focused on alleged Turkish military needs.[76] Despite his racially based anti-Armenianism, Bronsart continued to maintain that the annihilation was an unintended consequence of Turkey's technical inability to carry out a humane deportation, an unfortunate byproduct of "*military necessity*," as he put it.[77] Unlike Trotha, Bronsart did not explicitly embrace genocide as a policy.

Lieutenant Commander v. Humann was an earlier and better informed pro-Turkish ideologue than Bronsart. Unlike the chief of staff, Humann called a spade a spade—and cheered the results. Already on 15 June 1915 he informed his naval superiors in Berlin that "because of their conspiracy with the Russians, the Armenians are being more or less annihilated. That is hard, but useful." He cited Talât's words as to why it was useful: "In order to be better allies for you, that is, without the weakness of an internal enemy."[78] This was a longer-term, geopolitical perspective, far beyond merely securing the rear lines. But Humann's job as naval officer would not have positioned him to urge such a sweeping and expensive policy or even to broach the narrower issue of deportation from behind the 3rd Army. It is more likely that Humann learned early on of the true scope and goal of the "deportation" program from his friend Enver and gave it his blessing.

Although the documentary evidence will only permit us to speculate about whether German officers' recommendations helped precipitate the shift in CUP policy from provocative killing to mass murder via deportation, it clearly shows that a few officers advised deportation even after they knew that deportation meant death. It is impossible to tell if they actively approved of the consequences (as did Humann) or were simply indifferent to them. "Military necessity" covered both positions. And Guse, Feldmann, Humann, and Bronsart all continued to cite military necessity to justify the genocide into the 1920s and beyond.[79] Even Liman, who several times intervened to protect Armenians and Greeks from deportation, testified at the 1921 trial of Talât's assassin that military necessity caused the deportations, which had turned deadly because of mismanagement, not intention.[80]

Few German officers actively participated in the genocide. Field Marshal v. d. Goltz came close on one occasion. After having responded to a governor's request for military

---

75. Bronsart v. Schellendorf, "Lebenserinnerungen," BA-MA Freiburg, Nl. Fragment Bronsart (MSg. 1/2039), p. 164.

76. Dinkel, "German Officers," 106.

77. Bronsart, "Ein Zeugnis für Talaat Pascha," *Deutsche Allgemeine Zeitung* (*DAZ*) 342 (24 July 1921). Racism and military necessity: Bronsart to Hanseatische Verlagsanstalt Hamburg, 23 Nov. 1939, BA-MA Freiburg, Nl. Bronsart. Emphasis in original.

78. Humann marginalium (dated 15 June 1915) to a telegram of the consular deputy in Mosul of 10 June 1915, BA-MA Freiburg, RM 40, Nr. 456, p. 93, cited in Dinkel, "German Officers," 113.

79. "x—" (probably Humann, editor of the *Deutsche Allgemeine Zeitung*), "Zum Talaat Prozess," *DAZ* 255 (3 June 1921), 2; "x—," Der Freispruch des Mörders," *DAZ* 256 (4 June 1921), 2; "Zum Talaat-Prozess—von einer deutschen Persönlichkeit die in der kritischen Zeit lange in dem umstrittenen ostanatolischen Gebiet an leitender Stelle tätig war," whom Dinkel identifies as Guse, *DAZ* 297 (28 June 1921), 2; Feldmann, "Zum Talaatprozess," *DAZ* 301 (30 June 1921), 2; Bronsart v. Schellendorf, "Ein Zeugnis für Talaat Pascha," *DAZ* 342 (24 July 1921). See Dinkel, "German Officers," 93–99.

80. "Ks" (author), "Die Ermordung Talaat Paschas," *DAZ* 254 (3 June 1921), 2.

help against Armenian and Syrian Christian rebels near Mosul, Goltz was informed by the German deputy consul there that the "rebels" were defending themselves against the governor's designs to kill them. Goltz immediately called back the detachment, because he "did not want German officers to intervene in this matter."[81]

The only well-documented case of active German participation concerns the shelling of Urfa, where Armenians fought against their deportation and murder from fortified positions in the Armenian church and surrounding quarter. In early October 1915, Turkish commander Fakri Pasha ordered his aide, Maj. Eberhard Wolfskeel von Reichenberg, to train his artillery on the Armenian quarter. Wolfskeel complied and Urfa soon fell; its surviving inhabitants were driven off into the maelstrom they had fought to escape. Wolfskeel described the action to his wife as a regular battle, although he referred to the Armenians as "bands." "But it is a battle again, and it is truly a joy to hear bullets whistling once more," he reported enthusiastically. The artillery job itself he found "quite interesting and pretty [hübsch]. Now the unimportant part begins, the removal of the civilian population and the courts-martial. Thank God, I don't have to concern myself much with these. They are internal Turkish matters and don't concern me, but one can't avoid seeing them and that is not pleasant."[82] Wolfskeel participated in the house-to-house searches that followed, attributing resistance to fanaticism or bad conscience, never to desperation or innocence. Insofar as the fighting differed from the usual, he explained it as "the horror of civil war."[83] Consul Rössler protested Wolfskeel's participation at Urfa (and Mossa Degh), but the major found it merely his soldierly duty.[84] Wolfskeel denied rumors the Armenians had slaughtered Muslims or rebelled.[85] He did not act from revenge or from ideology. Wolfskeel, instead, neatly compartmentalized responsibility—here, military duty, there, Turkish internal affairs. He soldiered along the road to genocide one dutiful step at a time.

German Diplomatic Intervention

It is unclear how much embassy personnel knew about the role German officers played in the decision for deportation or in actual deportations themselves. Wangenheim, who was ambassador until his sudden death in October 1915, was on good terms with Bronsart and Humann. His reports, as we shall see, for too long uncritically accepted the "military necessity" argument. But the flap over Lieutenant Colonel Böttrich's signature suggests that civilian leaders, at least in Berlin, were shocked at any direct German involvement in deportation. Böttrich, railroad section chief in the General Staff, had signed an order to deport Armenian railroad workers.[86] The Foreign Office collected the agitated correspondence on the case under the heading "Mistakes of Lt. Col. Böttrich"; Legation

81. Neurath to Bethmann, Pera, Nr. 669, copy, 12 Nov. 1915, PA-AA, Türkei 183, vol. 40.

82. Wolfskeel to his wife, Urfa, 12 and 16 Oct. 1915, BA-MA Freiburg, Nl. Wolfskeel, vol. 6, pp. 14, 16–17.

83. Wolfskeel to his wife, Urfa, 19 Oct. 1915, ibid., 20. Also, Bloxham, "Power Politics," 219.

84. Dadrian, *German Responsibility*, 58.

85. Rössler to Bethmann, Aleppo, Nr. 108, 16 Nov. 1915; Oppenheim's report, forwarded by Wolff-Metternich to Bethmann, Pera, Nr. 701, 29 Nov. 1915, PA-AA, Türkei 183, vol. 40.

86. Kaiser, "Baghdad Railways"; cf. Dadrian, *Armenian Genocide*, 261–62; Dadrian, *German Responsibility*, 19, 22–23, 131–33.

280   Secretary Constantin von Neurath wrote that the case "showed again [Böttrich's] complete lack of understanding of conditions here."[87] Foreign Secretary Jagow was incensed that Böttrich "not only did *not* protest the committee decision [to deport the Armenians] to the war minister, but he condescended to send it on with his signature."[88] Jagow apparently expected German officers to protest Turkish policy. He tried to get Falkenhayn to remove Böttrich, but Falkenhayn refused, citing "military interests."[89] He seemed not to understand or share Jagow's fears that a German signature on a deportation document would play into Allied propaganda about Germany's complicity. However, Falkenhayn did follow Jagow's request to ask Enver to postpone deportation until after the war, a successful ploy that saved many of the Armenian workers from death.[90] It is hard to believe that Berlin would have attached such importance to Böttrich's signature if the diplomats had known about the deeper involvement of officers like Bronsart, Guse, or Feldmann.

  The story of Germany's inconsistent and ineffective diplomatic intervention has been well told by Trumpener.[91] It remains to focus on the military reasoning that saturated and paralyzed German diplomacy.

  The first (willing) victim of the military chimera was Ambassador Wangenheim.[92] Wangenheim had energetically protested "atrocities" (*Ausschreitungen*) against Armenians in late December 1914. In late March 1915, when the first deportations from Zeitun had begun, he supported Consul Rössler's efforts to stop these, and he substantiated the accounts by the Armenian Patriarch of Constantinople of what had happened.[93] But as reports of violence mounted, Wangenheim began to close ranks with the Turkish government. On 15 April he still believed the Armenians were largely innocent of organized revolutionary activity, but he began to have doubts because German officers reported disloyalty of Armenian troops in the campaign against Russia. These doubts conveniently ran in the same direction as diplomatic reason, which warned against assuming the same role as Armenian protector that the Allies had recently played. Protection seemed especially unwise because of the "currently so unfavorable mood in governmental circles against the Armenians. . . . Otherwise we run the danger of risking more important interests that are closer to us for a perhaps vain cause," he wrote.[94] Safeguarding these interests meant accepting inevitable Allied charges holding Germany responsible for the "injus-

87. Neurath to Foreign Office, Pera, Nr. 2563, 8 Nov. 1915, PA-AA, Türkei 152, vol. 83.

88. Marginalium to report A 32601, ibid.

89. Falkenhayn to Treutler, General Headquarters, Nr. 930, 19 Nov. 1915, ibid.

90. Kaiser, "Baghdad Railways," 86.

91. Trumpener, *Germany*, ch. 7.

92. U.S. Ambassador Henry Morgenthau pilloried his colleague in several influential memoirs. Unfortunately, parts of the memoirs were manipulated for wartime propaganda purposes. Rather than risk error, it is better to rely on contemporary German documents whose authenticity is unquestionable and whose scope reaches far beyond the limited sources available to the U.S. embassy in Turkey. Henry Morgenthau, *Ambassador Morgenthau's Story* (New York, 1918); Morgenthau, *Secrets of the Bosphorus, 1913–1916* (London, 1918); Morgenthau, *The Tragedy of Armenia* (London, 1918).

93. Wangenheim to Bethmann, Pera, Nr. 342, 30 Dec. 1914; Wangenheim to Bethmann, Pera, Nr. 191, 26 Mar. 1915; Wangenheim to Bethmann, Pera, Nr. 195, 29 Mar. 1915, PA-AA, Türkei 183, vol. 36.

94. Inevitability was also Bronsart's reasoning in the Böttrich case: Kaiser, "Baghdad Railways," 83.

tice" done to the Armenians.[95] Wangenheim thus outlined German policy for the next two years or more: If the CUP was set on persecution, Germany could not stop it anyway and might lose the alliance trying. Germany would simply have to accept Allied blame.

A week after writing these thoughts, Wangenheim received the first word of Van. German military confirmation of the "uprising" gave Wangenheim the excuse he needed to drop the balance he had hitherto uncomfortably maintained between the conflicting Armenian and Turkish accounts and to come down hard on the Turkish side.[96]

On 31 May Wangenheim telegraphed Berlin of his meeting with War Minister Enver about Enver's deportation order of 27 May. Enver, Wangenheim reported, had told him that Turkey would counter the Armenian revolts by using the wartime emergency to deport "from the insurgent Armenian areas all not *entirely* trustworthy families to Mesopotamia." Although the measures "certainly mean great hardship for the Armenian population, in my opinion we might mitigate the form but not fundamentally hinder the measures. The Armenian subversion, fed by Russia, has assumed dimensions that threaten the substance of Turkey."[97] Wangenheim's recommendation was exactly what Enver had requested: "He [Enver] asked urgently [*dringend*] that we not hinder him in this." Wangenheim thus did three things: he accepted the Turkish argument of military necessity, he acquiesced to Enver's request to let the Turks proceed, and he hinted by underlining "entirely" that the deportations would be massive and entail "great hardship."

Wangenheim instructed the German consulates identically.[98] The consuls resisted Wangenheim's view. In desperate, shrill reports they marshaled fact after gory fact to argue against the Turkish claims Wangenheim had accepted. They railed against the "barbaric" measures; they argued that a "deportation of this magnitude is synonymous with massacre."[99] And they argued that the measures were not justified by military necessity. The rejection of military necessity became a trope, showing the broad recognition that it was the fundamental justification for "deportation." Major General Posseldt had dismissed the military necessity claim out of hand already in April. Not surprisingly, military men, including Consul Max Erwin von Scheubner-Richter, who was also an officer, felt more secure than did mere civilians in contradicting the military excuse.[100] In the end, it

95. Wangenheim to Bethmann, Pera, Nr. 228, 15 Apr. 1915, PA-AA, Türkei 183, vol. 36.

96. Wangenheim to Bethmann, Pera, Nr. 286, 8 May 1915, ibid. The consul at Mosul also confirmed the uprising at Van: Wangenheim to Foreign Office, tel. Nr. 1091, 10 May 1915, ibid.

97. Wangenheim to Bethmann, Pera, tel. Nr. 1268, 31 May 1915, PA-AA, Türkei 183, vol. 37. Emphasis in original.

98. The embassy compiled a brief history of its diplomatic actions in report Nr. 669, 12 Nov. 1915, PA-AA, Türkei 175a, vol. 36.

99. Büge to embassy, Adana, 18 May 1915; Scheubner-Richter to embassy, Erzerum, tel., 2 June 1915; Rössler to embassy, tel., Aleppo, 6 June 1915; and so forth; PA-AA, Türkei 183, vols. 36 and 37. Also in Lepsius, *Deutschland und Armenien*, Docs. 20, 27, 42, 47, 58, 66, 73, 76, 78, 79, 80, 100, and so on.

100. Memo of German embassy Dragoman Mordtmann, 26 Apr. 1915; Rössler to embassy, Aleppo, tel., 20 Apr. 1915; Scheubner-Richter to embassy, Erzerum, tel., 2 and 26 June 1915; Rössler to embassy, 27 July 1915; Stange to German military mission, Erzerum, 23 Aug. 1918; Scheubner-Richter to Hohenlohe-Langenburg, Erzerum, Nr. 580, 5 Aug. 1915; Kress v. Kressenstein to Hertling, Tiflis, Nr. 787, 3 Sept. 1918; PA-AA, Türkei 183, vols. 36, 37, 53, and in Lepsius, *Deutschland und Armenien*, Docs. 27, 31, 81, 98, 120, 149.

282 was the consuls who gave Wangenheim the arguments he subsequently used to criticize deportation.

The intense pressure to which the consuls and other German critics in the Turkish countryside subjected Wangenheim was compounded by neutral and Allied opinion. After repeated urging by Russia, the Allies publicized on 24 May an extraordinary statement condemning what they called "massacres" and averring they would "hold all the members of the Ottoman Government, as well as such agents as are implicated, personally responsible for such massacres."[101] As Wangenheim had feared, the Allies used the deportations to their advantage. The German records show growing sensitivity to charges of German complicity; the desire to counter such charges surely encouraged the shift from passivity to official protest.[102] But the killings also had taken on dimensions that Wangenheim doubtless had not foreseen when he passed along Enver's order.

On 17 June Wangenheim began to retreat from Enver's position, citing his consuls' and other reports of massacres and pointing out that the "banning of the Armenians was not only motivated by military considerations," but aimed, as Talât had admitted to him, "thoroughly to cleanse [*aufzuräumen*] [Turkey] of its native Christians without being disturbed by diplomatic intervention."[103] Once Wangenheim had taken the first step, Undersecretary of Foreign Affairs Zimmermann okayed the first formal protest (of the execution of Armenian political leaders).[104] Berlin had thus left Turkish policy to its ambassador,[105] who in turn had subordinated diplomacy to alleged military necessity. Finally on 4 July Wangenheim delivered his first official protest of the deportations, but he did so within the military parameters that remained effective for Germany until the end of the war: "We approve of the deportation of the Armenian population only insofar as it is done because of military considerations and to secure against revolts"; removals outside military zones or massacres were unacceptable.[106]

Accepting "military considerations" was a fatal limit to effective intervention. Talât, Enver, and German military supporters of the genocide maintained to the end that the "deportations" were militarily necessary and that deaths were accidental.[107] Civilians found it hard to argue on military turf. German Turkish policy in 1915 displayed the same self-hobbling that civilian leaders suffered concerning the Belgian deportations the next year: if one could not reject the mass deportation of civilians on principle, one was left to

101. Cited from *The Times* (London) in Institut, *Armenian Genocide*, 1:306; Sir G. Buchanan to Sir Edward Grey, Petrograd, 11 May 1915; Sir Edward Grey to Sir Francis Bertie, Nr. 1168, 11 May 1915, and Nr. 1185, 12 May 1915, in David Stevenson, ed., *British Documents on Foreign Affairs; The First World War, 1914–1918; The Allied and Neutral Powers: Diplomacy and War Aims, August 1914–July 1915*, pt. 2, ser. H, vol. 1, general editors Kenneth Bourne and D. C. Watt (Frederick, Md., 1989), Docs. 585, 586, 594.

102. Blair believes Germany's protests were cynically designed for public relations: Susan K. Blair, "Excuses for Inhumanity," *Armenian Review* 37, no. 4/148 (winter 1984): 14–30, here 20–22.

103. Wangenheim to Bethmann, Pera, Nr. 372, 17 June 1915, PA-AA, Türkei 183, vol. 37.

104. Zimmermann to Wangenheim, Berlin, tel., 18 June 1915, Lepsius, *Deutschland und Armenien*, Doc. 83.

105. Trumpener, *Germany*, 215.

106. Wangenheim to Bethmann, Pera, Nr. 433, 7 July 1915, PA-AA, Türkei 183, vol. 37.

107. For example, Talât: Wolff-Metternich to Bethmann, Pera, Nr. 725, 18 Dec. 1915; Enver to Hindenburg, Constantinople, tel., 3 Aug. 1918 in Bernstorff to Foreign Office, Constantinople, tel. Nr. 1255, 3 Aug. 1918, ibid., vols. 40, 53.

ex post facto, generally ineffective efforts at amelioration. The deportees were usually already dead. The Turkish government responded not at all to Wangenheim's protests, and by 16 July Wangenheim had given up and gone on sick leave.

If Wangenheim had set diplomatic policy inside military parameters, he had done so with Zimmermann's blessing. Wangenheim's temporary successor, Prince Ernst zu Hohenlohe-Langenburg, protested much more energetically, but he still felt compelled to keep to the limits Wangenheim had recognized, focusing on *how* the deportations were being handled, rather than rejecting them outright. Hohenlohe-Langenburg's exhortations had no effect on the Turks, other than having them block his appointment as permanent ambassador. Meanwhile in Berlin, protests by influential private persons, such as Johannes Lepsius, Paul Rohrbach, and numerous pastors, missionaries, and professors caused Bethmann and Jagow temporarily to dislodge Zimmermann from his sway over Turkish policy.[108] Bethmann and Jagow appointed Paul Wolff-Metternich to replace Wangenheim, and Wolff-Metternich went on a crusade of vociferous criticism as soon as he arrived in Constantinople in November 1915.

By 7 December, in the face of continuing failure, Wolff-Metternich saw the situation clearly and presented Berlin with an ultimatum. He argued, first, that Germany must cease private, diplomatic protest and go public. Second, in its public statement Germany must declare that there was an absolute legal and moral limit to what war or self-defense permitted. That limit was reached at the point where "an entire ethnic group, including old people, women, and children, suffered." Third, Germany had to recognize that it, not Turkey, was the stronger alliance partner. "Without our help the bloated frog will collapse. We do not need to be so anxious in dealing with the Turks." And finally, "To have success in the Armenian question we must make the Turkish government fear the consequences. If military reasons prevent us from taking a stronger position, then nothing remains but, while continuing unsuccessful protests that anger more than they help, to look on as our ally goes on massacring." Not surprisingly, Zimmermann's first response was that such a declaration had to be watered down before Germany dared print it.[109] In the end, "military reasons" prevented such a statement from being issued at all. On 22 December 1915 the Turkish government made its first official reply to Germany's protests. Citing "military reasons" and "legitimate defense," it strongly rejected interference in its domestic affairs. This sufficed to stop Berlin.[110] Wolff-Metternich was left to periodic "unsuccessful protests" and became more and more isolated and ineffective in Constantinople.

German policy reverted to the position Zimmermann had published on 6 October 1915. In that official statement the Kaiserreich recognized "the harsh but militarily understandable measure," regretted the "primitive" conditions in Turkey that caused hardship, but in the end claimed that "moral guilt for these events belongs to the Armenians themselves [for revolting] and their instigators in London, Petersburg, and Paris." It continued, "As regrettable as it is from a Christian and general human viewpoint that, along with the

108. Trumpener, *Germany*, 227–28.
109. Wolff-Metternich to Bethmann, Pera, Nr. 711, 7 Dec. 1915, PA-AA, Türkei 183, vol. 40, incompletely reproduced in Lepsius, *Deutschland und Armenien*, doc. 209.
110. Trumpener, *Germany*, 232–33; Lepsius, *Deutschland und Armenien*, Doc. 218.

284 guilty, hundreds of thousands of innocents should perish by this Turkish measure, the sons of Germany, whose sacrificial bloody fighting in the west, east, and south is considerably eased by the military aid of our Turkish allies, stand closer to the German government than the Armenians." For this reason it was impossible to break relations with Turkey.[111] The official press guidelines for 1917 were more succinct: "It is best to keep silent about the Armenian question."[112]

Although the killing continued in 1916 and 1917, Germany made only sporadic verbal protests. The pattern in 1915 clearly shows that vigorous leadership made a difference, at least inside the German bureaucracy. Berlin had allowed Wangenheim (and occasionally Bronsart) to dampen the activities of the consuls, who chafed at these restrictions.[113] Hohenlohe-Langenburg and Wolff-Metternich encouraged more consular intervention; following their example, embassy personnel became more active, and even Berlin seemed more daring. But once Bethmann and Jagow shrank from the alternative Wolff-Metternich had so clearly outlined, they sent a message that activity was unwelcome. The next German ambassador to Turkey, Richard von Kühlmann, told his Austrian colleague when he arrived in Constantinople that he would not repeat Wolff-Metternich's mistake and begin his tenure lecturing the Turks on Armenia.[114] Consuls continued to channel relief and to intervene humanitarily, but their job was a lonely one.

One hundred years ago diplomacy was not generally the domain of humanitarianism, although beginning steps in that direction had been taken. Austria's record of insight and intervention in the Armenian genocide was no better than Germany's, and I am unaware of Entente protests to their Russian partner concerning the ill-prepared, deadly mass deportations it visited on its own citizens.[115] The Armenian case was different, of course, because it was obvious by late May 1915 that the *object* of Turkish policy was mass extermination. The question remains: Could Germany have stopped the genocide if it had threatened to revoke the alliance? Unfortunately, this seems improbable, given the importance of the genocide to CUP national policy. However, 1918 gave both allies the chance to replay 1915. This time, Germany was much more energetic and even proactive in trying to prevent genocide, but it was equally ineffective.

The Bolshevik Revolution took Russia out of the war and permitted Germany and Turkey in 1918 to expand into the Caucasus, where perhaps one million Armenians, some

---

111. Undated draft in PA-AA, Türkei 183, vol. 43; published version in Yale, Jäckh Papers, Box 2; also Trumpener, *Germany*, 221–22.

112. Guidelines issued by the Oberzensurstelle des Kriegspresseamts at the beginning of 1917, cited in Institut, *Armenian Genocide*, 1:609–10.

113. Wangenheim to consuls, 31 May 1915, slightly amended in Wangenheim to Consul at Erzerum, 21 June 1915, in Anlage to Report Nr. 669 of 12 Nov. 1915, PA-AA, Türkei 175a, vol. 36; Austrian Consul Kwiatkowski to Count Czernin, Samsun, Nr. A. 21/P, 26 May 1917, HHStA PA XII 463, in Institut, *Armenian Genocide*, 2:378; Scheubner-Richter to Hohenlohe-Langenburg, Erzerum, Nr. 580, 5 Aug. 1915, PA-AA, Türkei 183, vol. 38; Paul Leverkuehn, *Posten auf ewiger Wache* (Essen, 1938), 45.

114. Pallavicini to Burián, Constantinople, Nr. 89/P.A., 21 Nov. 1916, HHStA PA XII 463, in Institut, *Armenian Genocide*, 2:365.

115. Trumpener, *Germany*, 268; Institut, *Armenian Genocide*, vol. 2. U.S. Secretary of State Robert Lansing accepted Turkish claims of military necessity, though he condemned the brutality of the deportations: Samantha Power, *"A Problem from Hell"* (New York, 2003), 13.

of them survivors of 1915, now lived. The Treaty of Brest-Litovsk ceded three predomi-
nately Armenian districts (Kars, Ardahan, and Batum) to Turkey. As Turkish troops
moved in, they resumed the genocide by massacre and starvation. To make matters worse,
the Turkish army advanced farther into Armenian-settled lands, beyond the Brest-Litovsk
borders, into Baku.[116]

Germany's greater activity in protesting Turkish actions had many causes. By 1918
German officials knew the CUP's actual goal and recognized its lies and subterfuges.
Brest-Litovsk made Germany more obviously liable for Turkish misdeeds.[117] German
public opinion was also forewarned and organized: the German-Armenian Society predicted new massacres, and the Reichstag, led by the Independent Socialists, held a vigorous debate about Germany's responsibility for the Armenians under the treaty. More important, OHL and the Foreign Office pulled roughly in the same direction because
German national interests now clashed with Turkey's. OHL opposed Turkey's advance
across the designated line, and it wanted stable, pro-German successor states to emerge,
not embittered, depopulated zones of chaos. Until his dismissal in July, Foreign Secretary
Kühlmann issued repeated, energetic instructions to Ambassador Bernstorff to pressure
the CUP leaders to stop massacres and atrocities, and withdraw to the original treaty borders. Kühlmann made threats of real substance: if the Turks misbehaved, Germany would
abrogate that section of the alliance committing it to guarantee Turkish territory against
Allied occupation.[118] Finally, Germany had a dedicated and perceptive officer on the spot
(who was serving as diplomatic representative to the Transcaucasian Republic), Gen.
Friedrich Kress von Kressenstein, who acted independently and creatively to thwart Turkish measures.

Nonetheless, Turkey did just about as it pleased until the armistice caused the collapse
of the CUP government. The CUP government's war aims were expansion and eradication
of "internal weakness"; only force could make it abandon these. Stopping Turkish policy
in the Caucasus would have required Germany to send troops to the new Armenian state.
OHL was pleased to encourage Austria to do so but declined for itself. So, Enver was free
to counter Hindenburg's plea in August 1918 for the return of refugees with a lecture on
the military necessity of keeping the rear lines free of Armenians.[119] The events of 1918 suggest that even a courageous policy in 1915 probably would not have saved the Armenians.

Resistance to the Chimera of Military Necessity

Military culture predisposed officers to see enemies everywhere and to demand complete security from perceived threats. Instrumentalizing civilians in the name of military
necessity was built into the priorities of fighting and winning that saturated officers' assumptions about their jobs and themselves. But the Armenian genocide shows that it was

---

116. See the account in Trumpener, *Germany*, 248–68, and the documents in Lepsius, *Deutschland und Armenien*, 367–454.
117. Kühlmann to Berckheim, Berlin, Nr. 1178, 3 June 1918, PA-AA, Türkei 183, vol. 51.
118. Kühlmann to Berckheim, Berlin, Nr. 1178, 3 June 1918, ibid.
119. Trumpener, *Germany*, 260–61.

286 possible for officers to hold all the conventional ideas and still act against the grain. The surviving evidence is not rich enough to allow firm conclusions, but the cases that follow suggest some of the parameters that permitted (or hindered) counteraction.

Liman is instructive because he not only believed in the propriety of deportation under certain circumstances, he actually ordered one. After receiving reliable evidence in July 1917 that the Greeks in the coastal town of Ayvalik were helping the enemy prepare a landing on Mytelene, Liman ordered them all deported. He insisted on careful preparations and humane handling of the deportees. When local Turkish authorities failed to do so and two hundred people died, Liman cancelled his order, repatriated the survivors, and admitted that such a large deportation had been unwise and unnecessary.[120] In November 1916 Liman forced the return of Armenians just deported from Smyrna, thereby thwarting an order from Talât. Liman happened to be near Smyrna when the deportation occurred. Unable to discover any military reason for it, he forced the local vali to rescind the order. Liman succeeded because he commanded troops and threatened to use them.[121] Many of the people Liman saved did not live long, however; as soon as he left the area, the Turkish authorities tried again.[122] The last Armenian survivors in Smyrna were murdered in 1922 under the Kemalist regime.[123]

Liman's actions show that it was possible to interpret military necessity narrowly. His distrust of others and resulting isolation predisposed him to be skeptical of standard explanations and more likely to go see for himself. But, above all, Liman alone, except for Goltz and Falkenhayn, had command power. That increased his independence and made his interventions (momentarily) effective.

Field Marshal v. d. Goltz also enjoyed high rank, the independence of command, and a certain distance and unflappability that comes with age and experience. In December 1915, Goltz learned by chance that Armenian deportees who had made it to Mosul were about to be redeported on orders of the supreme commander in Mesopotamia. Goltz intervened immediately, at first without effect. Persisting, he forced the authorities to postpone the decision, and when no formal resolution had been reached by mid-January 1916, he simply forbade the Armenians' departure. When Constantinople continued to insist, Goltz threatened to resign. Enver then acceded to Goltz's wish but pointed out that "his command authority did not entitle him to intervene in Turkish domestic affairs."[124] Goltz persisted in wanting to resign, which probably indicated his disgust at the deportations in general, not simply this one episode. But "he felt it his duty to remain at his post in view of the difficult military situation." He was also on record as protesting deportations of Greeks.[125] His success in the Mosul case rested entirely on his unequalled reputation and

120. Dinkel, "German Officers," 86–93.

121. Lepsius, *Deutschland und Armenien*, Docs. 306, 307; Kühlmann to Bethmann, Nr. 710, Pera, 17 Nov. 1916, PA-AA, Türkei 183, vol. 45, which contains the complete version of Liman's memorandum.

122. Austrian Consul Radimsky to Pallavicini, Smyrna, Nr. 90/P., 13 Dec. 1916, HHStA PA XII 463, in Institut, *Armenian Genocide*, 2:367–68.

123. Housepian, *Smyrna*.

124. Legationsrat Dieckhoff memo Nr. A. 49466, Berlin, 19 Nov. 1918, PA-AA, Türkei 183, vol. 53; also Lepsius, *Deutschland und Armenien*, Doc. 224.

125. Dadrian, *German Responsibility*, 127.

high status as advisor to the sultan and the war minister, and hence on the forcefulness of his threat. It was unheard of for a military man to resign in wartime, and in the end Goltz was too much a soldier to take that final step. His actions, like the others taken by military men, did not become publicly known and therefore had no larger political effect.

Unlike Liman and Goltz, Kress v. Kressenstein lacked command power when he intervened to help deportees, but he was experienced, thoughtful, and independent-minded.[126] As operations chief in the Turkish General Staff in September 1914, he arranged for his dour assessment of Turkish military strength to find its way to Moltke behind Liman's back.[127] Still, Kress depended on his Turkish comrades for information and accepted their negative views of Armenians; he never seems to have concluded that the genocide was due to policy rather than ineptitude.[128] But on a return trip to the Turkish 4th Army in late October 1915, he saw the full extent of the horror and was galvanized into action. He convinced his Turkish commander, Cemal, to inspect the transit camp at Aleppo, and then, using funds at his own disposition, he paid to clean the camp and erect a hospital and orphanage. Next, he and Cemal journeyed to Constantinople to complain in person that the deportations were destroying the rear echelon of the 4th Army. Kress also tried to fire up Germany's diplomatic protests.[129]

In November 1917 Kress intervened again, this time to prevent Cemal's scheme to deport the entire Jewish and Christian populations of Jerusalem (seventy thousand people). He convinced the German consul to pressure the embassy, while he went through military channels to Enver. Kress threatened to withdraw all German officers from the southern front if Enver did not relent.[130]

And then in 1918 Kress found himself in Tiflis (Tbilisi), where the Caucasus front was in danger of dissolving and taking the remaining Armenians with it. He worked tirelessly that summer to move Germany to force Turkey to withdraw its troops, permit the Armenians to take in the harvest, and let refugees return to eastern Anatolia. He proposed using German and Austrian troops to provide "safety" for Turkey's rear lines (thus disposing of that excuse for genocide); he wanted to divert precious stores of central European grain from Turkey to Armenia; he called for a German battalion to enter Baku to protect civilians there. Finding a reasonable Turkish leader in Gen. Halil Pasha, Kress worked to convince him that "the slogans like 'military necessity,' 'threat to rear lines' and whatever else . . . are devoid of *any justified basis*."[131] In short, Kress was daring and imaginative in thinking of diplomatic, military, political, and economic solutions. His arguments to the Foreign Office were equally interesting, for he dared to represent the plight of the Arme-

126. Kress joined the military mission as a major and swiftly became a lieutenant colonel. He was promoted to colonel in Feb. 1917 with the Turkish rank of major general and briefly commanded the Turkish 8th Army until Liman removed him in Nov. 1917 after the defeats in Gaza. Kress left the military mission and returned to the area in 1918 with the rank of general as diplomatic representative to the Transcaucasian Republic in Tiflis (Tbilisi). Wallach, *Anatomie*, 218–19, 220, 231–32.

127. Schulte, *Europäische Krise*, 258.

128. Kress, *Mit den Türken*, 127–29, 133.

129. Ibid., 132–37.

130. Ibid., 248–49.

131. Kress to Hertling, Tiflis, Nr. 787, 3 Sept. 1918, PA-AA, Türkei 183, vol. 53.

288 nians as a moral, not just a practical, issue. He wrote to the chancellor that "it is not my place to remind Your Excellency of the duties that Germany as a Christian nation has vis-à-vis the Christian Armenians, and of the impression it will make upon our public opinion and that of the entire Christian world, if we fail to save the Armenians from downfall." But having done so, he only then went on to adduce economic and geopolitical reasons to do the moral thing. Two weeks later he repeated these arguments, in the same order.[132] Kress was one of the few contemporaries to write (in 1938!) that the failure of the German government and of public opinion to disassociate themselves from Turkey during the war had made them "moral accomplices" to the killings.[133] Kress was an unusual man. He was also a disappointed man, because neither the Foreign Office nor OHL adopted his schemes in 1918. A German coconspirator of Kress's, Lieutenant Colonel Paraquin, Halil's chief of staff, was abruptly removed from his post for trying to protect the Armenians of Baku.[134]

The examples of Liman, Goltz, and Kress show that successful intervention required real power: command power, the use or withholding of troops, independent resources (Kress's funds), or threatening with one's very high status. Three other, lower-ranking German officers, whose documented opposition to the genocide has survived, illustrate the hurdles they faced.

Major General Posseldt commanded the fortress at Erzerum. He rejected the cover story of military necessity from the beginning, in April 1915, and, working together with Consul Scheubner-Richter, tried to prevent the arrests of Armenians. Posseldt was promptly replaced by a Turkish commander.[135]

Lt. Col. August Stange had commanded one of the Special Operation units involved in guerrilla activity in the Caucasus from December 1914 to August 1915. Ill and no longer silenced by his command duties, Stange wrote a thorough report about the genocide while waiting in Erzerum to return to the western front (where he died in a gas attack in 1918).[136] Stange's report named names and exposed the "deportations" for what they really were. He reasoned from the fact that "hundreds and thousands have simply been murdered" that "military reasons are only secondarily behind the evacuation." Instead, the Turks were fulfilling "a long-held plan fundamentally to weaken, if not to destroy, the Armenian people." Because of Stange's position in the Special Organization, he knew that the "destruction" of the Armenians "was decided on and well organized in Constantinople by the Young Turk Committee using the army and voluntary bands with members of the CUP present at the localities."[137] Stange sent his report to the military mission, where it rested in the files.

132. Kress to Hertling, Tiflis, 11 July, and tel. of 26 July 1918, ibid.

133. Kress, *Mit den Türken*, 138, cited by Wallach, *Anatomie*, 207.

134. Trumpener, *Germany*, 266.

135. Lepsius, *Deutschland und Armenien*, Doc. 31; Lepsius, *Untergang*, 36.

136. Stange's command over the Special Organization detachment ended on 15 Aug. 1915: BA-MA Freiburg, MSG. 2, Nr. 3739, preface to Stange's war diary.

137. Stange to Military Mission, Erzerum, 23 Aug. 1915, Lepsius, *Deutschland und Armenien*, Doc. 149; Dadrian, *German Responsibility*, 61–62.

Scheubner-Richter, temporary consul at Erzerum until August 1915 and then, like Stange, detached as officer to a guerrilla unit, is an interesting case for several reasons. Scheubner-Richter's political views were heavily influenced by Friedrich Naumann, who was one of the most vociferous defenders of wartime Turkey and belittlers of the Armenian genocide.[138] Scheubner-Richter's prewar attachment to Naumann and his early membership in the Nazi Party (and "martyr's death" during the Beer Hall Putsch) run directly counter to his stance toward the Armenians—again a warning against reasoning "logically" from ideology. For no consul was more vocal or active in the defense of the Armenians than Scheubner-Richter. He early recognized that the "deportations" were not justified by military necessity but aimed at extermination. He intervened with military and civilian Turkish authorities to stop deportations and personally organized food relief for deportees, actions that earned him a veiled threat to his safety from the local vali.[139] Wangenheim's instructions in late May 1915 that consuls limit intervention to friendly advice undercut Scheubner-Richter.[140] The consul felt embattled enough to defend his actions in a long report submitted as he left the consulate for the field. Two months later Zimmermann retrospectively approved of Scheubner-Richter's actions as consul.[141] As a field officer, Scheubner-Richter continued to help Armenians, but he explained to the chancellor in 1916 that being directly subordinate to a Turkish commander "naturally burdened me with greater caution [*Zurückhaltung*] regarding intervention in Armenian questions."[142] Scheubner-Richter's position as an officer was thus double-edged. On the one hand, it carried greater authority. For example, he reported that a moderate CUP general-inspector, Omer Nadji, who opposed the Armenian policy, "was happy to have in me, a German officer, support for his moderate position against other committee members."[143] On the other hand, Scheubner-Richter's status as an officer subordinated him to anti-Armenian pressure from Bronsart in the military mission and from Turkish commanders. Military prestige, and especially the military command system, were thus powerful tools that could work in either direction; a coherent military policy (as opposed to piecemeal interventions) would have given Germany much more leverage to affect Turkish policy.

Like Stange, when Scheubner-Richter was finally released from the fetters of direct military duty, he wrote a long report to the chancellor in which he denounced Turkish policy as "annihilation," not only of Armenians but of all non-Muslims and also Islamic non-Turkish peoples (Arabs) in the service of Pan-Turanism. Military necessity was the

138. Leverkuehn, *Posten*, 187; Trumpener, *Germany*, 252.

139. Scheubner-Richter to Hohenlohe-Langenburg, Erzerum, Nr. 580, 5 Aug. 1915, PA-AA, Türkei 183, vol. 39.

140. Dinkel writes that Bronsart "influenced" Wangenheim's instructions, which is possible, although Bronsart's dismissive marginalia about Scheubner-Richter's stance are appended to a report that arrived at the embassy on 1 June, ten to twelve days after Wangenheim's first instructions to Erzerum and Adana and a day after Wangenheim's general instruction to all consuls dictating that they not hinder Enver's "security measures." Dinkel, "German Officers," 107; Anlage to Embassy Report Nr. 669, 12 Nov. 1915, PA-AA, Türkei 175a, vol. 36.

141. Scheubner-Richter to Hohenlohe-Langenburg, Erzerum, Nr. 580, 5 Aug. 1915; Zimmermann to Wangenheim, Berlin, Nr. 782, 20 Oct. 1915, PA-AA, Türkei 183, vol. 39.

142. Scheubner-Richter to Bethmann, Munich, 4 Dec. 1916, ibid., vol. 45; also, with some changes, in Lepsius, *Deutschland und Armenien*, Doc. 309.

143. Scheubner-Richter to Bethmann, Munich, 4 Dec. 1916, PA-AA, Türkei 183, vol. 45.

290 excuse used to dupe Germany. He recommended strong public repudiation, because Germany's silence "is interpreted by many in Turkey and Persia as weakness."[144] Scheubner-Richter's report, like Stange's, was apparently laid *ad acta*.

Scheubner-Richter was not a professional officer; he had volunteered when the war broke out. And his position as consul encouraged the wider, extramilitary perspectives he brought to his job. It is telling that when he argued with the Turks he cited practical, mostly foreign-political reasons for rescinding the killing policy, but when explaining his actions to his own government, he said he proceeded from moral and legal conviction. "I assumed," he wrote, "that my government would be pleased to know its representative used every legal means at his disposal to intercede for humane and just treatment for suffering innocents."[145]

About a year later, Legation Secretary Hoesch explained the two principles that were the basis of governmental policy: "First, not to interfere in the business of a foreign state, especially of an ally, and, next, the consideration that a state fighting for its existence is justified in the interests of its internal security to take extraordinary measures that could be labeled as acts of self-defense."[146] The standards of existential military struggle that Germany applied to itself, its troops, civilians, and those in its occupied zones, it also applied to Turkey, where going to extremes took the form of genocide. As long as German leaders, civilian and military, acted from these premises, they could not take effective action—or permit other Germans to do so—to stop this process.

We now return to the last act of existential military struggle back in Europe. There, the process of going to extremes seemed almost as hard to stop as in Anatolia.

144. Scheubner-Richter to Bethmann, Munich, 4 Dec. 1915, PA-AA, Türkei 175a, vol. 36.

145. Scheubner-Richter to Hohenlohe-Langenburg, Erzerum, Nr. 580, 5 Aug. 1915, PA-AA, Türkei 183, vol. 39. After Germany's defeat, Scheubner-Richter embraced a German version of Pan-Turanism. He called for the "ruthless fight against everything foreign in Germany's national/racial body." Cited in Leverkuehn, *Posten*, 190.

146. Historical report by Legation Secretary Hoesch, in Wolff-Metternich to Bethmann, Therapia, Nr. 567, 12 Sept. 1916, PA-AA, Türkei 183, vol. 44.

12

Repetition and Self-Destruction

The acquiescence of Ludendorff and Hindenburg to strategic retreat and the defensive in 1917 shows that the third OHL was capable of departing from the set script of German military wisdom, even if the manner of the retreat—absolute destruction—was consistent with it. The combat of 1917 also demonstrated movement on the operative and tactical level, for example, the willingness to abandon territory under attack in order to defend more flexibly.[1] But apart from such mostly tactical lessons that the German army continued to learn, it was the retreat and consolidation of 1917 that were uniquely at variance with the default program. Otherwise, the third OHL continued to follow this program to the end: it pursued a purely military victory of force, rejecting negotiations out of hand. This all-or-nothing stance required taking extreme risks, which it attempted to counterbalance with a series of techniques: taut, detailed planning combined, inconsistently, with high reliance on the individual initiative of unit commanders (*Auftragstaktik*); operative and tactical excellence at the expense of strategy; and the use of wonder weapons. The cleft between reach and grasp, made worse by willful ignorance of economic realities, made poor treatment of soldiers inevitable and encouraged the instrumentalization of civilians for a conception of military necessity that steadily expanded to fill that cleft. The risks were apparently too great to allow realistic assessment of danger, making the risk takers unwilling to admit when the gamble had failed. The feedback loop did not function; instead, the unrealistic conviction of professional superiority, wishful thinking, belief in miracles or in *Kriegsglück* (the fortunes of war), and compulsory optimism created a working atmosphere in which admitting defeat became almost impossible.

1. Lossberg, *Meine Tätigkeit*, 250–51; Kuhl, *Weltkrieg*, 2:11; Einem, *Armeeführer*, 309; Germany, Reichsarchiv, *Die Weltkrieg 1914 bis 1918*, 12:29, 40–50 (hereafter Reichsarchiv, *Weltkrieg*).

292   The radicalization that characterized the German war effort after mid-1916 was achieved not because of something qualitatively different in military practices or because ideology now drove processes forward (though ideologization began to happen) but because the same military frames and procedures met with less resistance from civilian government and parliamentary leaders, and the inherent dynamic pushing toward extremity was allowed to develop further than it had ever done before. The great catastrophe was reached with small steps, which is why the actors thought they were defending an old order rather than ushering in a new one. The ideological justifications and reinterpretations came later, after the war was over. The accommodation the German military made to the changed circumstances of combat—for example, the use of small groups of storm troopers operating opportunistically or the checkerboard system of flexible defense—became part of a new military culture, especially among younger officers. But that is another story. Ours concerns the older officers in leadership positions, who continued to act largely within the confines of the military culture of the Bismarckian-Wilhelminian period. The extremes of World War I on the German side were its product.

It is not possible to present an adequately detailed account of the last two and one half years of the war. Instead, the following pages will highlight the recurring patterns in the third OHL's conduct of the war. The retreat and strategic defensive of 1916–17 occurred simultaneously with three major initiatives running in the opposite, offensive direction: the Hindenburg program (October 1916), the decision to begin unrestricted submarine warfare (winter 1916–17), and the decision in late fall 1917 to launch an all-out offensive in March 1918.

The Decisions for Retreat and the Defensive, 1916–1917

Most historians present Germany's defensive posture in 1917 as self-evident, given the lack of reserves, ammunition, transport (horses), and the general depletion of the army after Verdun and the Somme.[2] In similar situations in 1918, however, OHL was not so sensitive to the data of reality. Why was 1917 different? The main reason is probably that when Ludendorff and Hindenburg took over supreme command they had no knowledge of the western front. They canvassed and recanvassed the western commanders, whose much more modest views of military possibilities (caused by the repeated frustrations of 1914–16) provided the basis for OHL's assessment of the military situation. Unlike Falkenhayn, who made decisions almost by himself, Ludendorff and Hindenburg relied heavily on the advice of both field commanders and General Staff officers, even if they did not always follow it. In 1916 and 1917 they were more dependent than at any other time. Fortifying the Siegfried line was a relatively easy decision for Ludendorff, since his "gigantic" eastern offensives had always occurred with strong defensive lines to his rear.[3] It was more remarkable that Falkenhayn had prosecuted the war in the west for almost two years without them. Finally, the third OHL encouraged self-criticism, especially at the tactical

2. Reichsarchiv, *Weltkrieg*, 12:1; Klein, *Deutschland*, 2:584; Chickering, *Imperial Germany*, 173; Herwig, *First World War*, 246, 249.

3. Reichsarchiv, *Weltkrieg*, 12:61. "Gigantic": Eisenhart-Rothe, *Im Banne der Persönlichkeit*, 103.

and technical levels. Hindenburg produced a major document, "War Conduct and the General Staff," which he distributed to all General Staff officers at the end of November 1916.[4] In it he charged that the army "had learned more slowly than its enemies." Staff officers "must think *ahead* of our own experiences and continuously develop tactics and techniques." But Hindenburg's criticism even reached to strategy. The nature of war had changed: "The idea of destruction [*Vernichtungsgedanke*] now seeks its goal [through attrition]." Therefore, saving resources was paramount, making the defensive more appropriate than the offensive.

The hardest decision for Ludendorff was the retreat to the Siegfried line. It took him over four months of constant discussion from the time he ordered it fortified to the time he gave in to Crown Prince Rupprecht's arguments for retreat. Rupprecht had to insist that "many experienced troop commanders with very good judgment, who are not pessimists," favored it.[5] The commanders Rupprecht had in mind were doubtless subordinates close to the troops. For even well-prepared strategic retreat was so at odds with German military culture that the decision was opposed by the army commanders in Crown Prince Wilhelm's army group, by Gen. Max von Gallwitz, and by some army commanders under Rupprecht himself.[6] Even after he had been persuaded, Ludendorff called the retreat "highly regrettable" and continued to worry that it broadcast Germany's weakness and undermined troop morale.[7] Once convinced, however, Ludendorff made what German military language called an "entire decision," meaning he held firm against pressure from his staff officers and from Crown Prince Wilhelm to sweeten the pill by making limited attacks.[8]

Most remarkable of all, Ludendorff's decision brought with it a modified view of victory. Instead of the usual standard of the battle of annihilation, Ludendorff now (February 1917) claimed that "we will win [the campaign of 1917] if we hold on to our [occupied] territory throughout the great coming defensive battles."[9]

This was not a permanent insight, however, but a temporary expedient. OHL had given up on neither military victory nor the verities of military culture. Hindenburg said as much in his November statement to General Staff officers. Having acknowledged the need to cater to the war of attrition, Hindenburg nonetheless continued: "The offensive battle that seeks decision in movement and great battles with other armies, and which we know how to execute correctly, remains our military ideal of the future, on which Germany's future will continue to be built."[10] Both Hindenburg and Ludendorff believed that Germany would return to this type of warfare, if the war continued long enough. For them, 1917 was analogous to the "risk years" when Germany built its battle fleet; it was a

4. Reichsarchiv, *Weltkrieg*, 12:56–57. Emphasis in original.

5. Kuhl's testimony, *UA* 3:1, 71.

6. *UA* 3:1, 71–72; Gallwitz, *Erleben im Westen*, 163; Kuhl, *Weltkrieg*, 2:61; Rupprecht Kronprinz v. Bayern, *Mein Kriegstagebuch*, 3:126.

7. Reichsarchiv, *Weltkrieg*, 12:25, also 129, 145.

8. Ibid., 12:72–73; Kronprinz Wilhelm v. Preussen, *Deutschlands Heldenkampf*, 279.

9. *UA* 3:1, 69.

10. Reichsarchiv, *Weltkrieg*, 12:57.

294   moment of inactivity while Germany built up its offensive capability through the Hindenburg program. In the meantime, the offensive had shifted to another theater: the sea. The third OHL expected unrestricted submarine warfare to bring Germany its military victory, or to so weaken its opponents that Germany could once again wage offensive land warfare according to the Schlieffen model.[11] Unlike the rethinking that Falkenhayn had done in November 1914, for Ludendorff and Hindenburg none of the basic operating assumptions had been dislodged in 1917. We now turn to the expedients by which the third OHL hoped to return to the default program.

The Hindenburg Program

The Hindenburg program reprised Falkenhayn's idea of militarizing the civilian population, that is, making all civilians of both sexes from their late teens on liable to conscription for war work. Subjecting the nation to forced labor was supposed to solve Germany's fundamental raw materials and manpower problems by doubling munitions and tripling artillery and machine gun production, while simultaneously bringing three hundred thousand more workers into the factories. What is more, it was to do so by May 1917.[12] The Hindenburg program was thus a gigantic program of imperative wish fulfillment. The temptation simply to order an end to Germany's problems by force was so strong that the idea occurred three times: once under Falkenhayn, once as the Hindenburg program of October 1916, and again in June 1918.

One historian has suggested that the Hindenburg program was modeled after forced labor in the occupied zones.[13] Although the utter disposability of civilians for military purposes was a principle that saturated occupation policy, it is unlikely that it was imported from the occupied zones into Germany. Falkenhayn's plan (of June 1915) arose simultaneously with and independent of local calls for forced civilian labor in France and Belgium. Instrumentalizing civilians was a widespread underlying assumption of military necessity shared by most officers, and so it surfaced repeatedly in different contexts.[14] Nor was the proindustrialist bias of the Hindenburg program new; both plans relied on the self-interested "expertise" of the leaders of heavy industry to work out the economic details of which officers were ignorant.

The Hindenburg program went beyond Falkenhayn's in three ways, however. First, Falkenhayn had been open to the excellent economic and political arguments against his idea; Hindenburg and Ludendorff were not. Bethmann produced an impressive list of reasons why the Hindenburg program was doomed: all able-bodied men had been either drafted into the army or were working; drafting sixteen year olds would pull them out of factories; more women were already looking for work than were finding it; and creating a tier of forced or conscripted laborers would disturb the economy and foster political dis-

---

11. Gallwitz, *Erleben im Westen*, 163, 508–9; Kuhl's testimony, *UA* 3:1, 68; Reichsarchiv, *Weltkrieg*, 12:2–4, 62; Kielmansegg, *Deutschland*, 339.

12. Chickering, *Imperial Germany*, 76–81.

13. Liulevicius, *War Land*, 55, believes the eastern occupation was the model for the Hindenburg program.

14. For example, Einem, *Armeeführer*, diary entry, 18 Nov. 1916, 267.

content. Ludendorff never bothered to counter these arguments, he simply restated his opinion: "In my view there is lots of hidden manpower that has not yet been used, or used enough for the common [cause]."[15] Opinion was the only thing Ludendorff could offer, since the Hindenburg program was based not on fact but fantasy. In historian Gerald Feldman's words, the Supreme Command had "decided to dismiss all financial considerations and to embark upon a program whose practical feasibility . . . had never been seriously investigated. The deadline for the fulfillment of the program, May 1917, was based upon purely military calculations."[16] Military considerations were, of course, behind Falkenhayn's idea too, but under the third OHL they now became not merely predominant but exclusive. The bitter, peremptory tone of the program was new as well. Hindenburg told Bethmann that "the whole German people must live only in service to the fatherland. Achieving success makes quick action necessary. *Every day is of importance.* The necessary measures are to be taken *immediately.*"[17] If put into practice, the requirement that civilians had to work to receive food meant that some would surely have starved to death. The command tone of the battlefield, with all its ruthlessness and haste, now resounded in matters that were essentially political and economic.

The Hindenburg program was not implemented as OHL had drafted it. Ludendorff and Hindenburg insisted on plebiscitary approval by the Reichstag, which substantially modified the most outlandish and draconian features. The Reichstag acted as a brake on military extremism at home. But in the occupied zones, where the military faced fewer hindrances to its logic, parts of the program went ahead, as in the Belgian and Polish-Jewish deportations, with the results we have seen.

Unrestricted Submarine Warfare

The January 1917 decision to carry out unrestricted submarine warfare (USW) shows how mired the Supreme Command and the political system were in the assumptions and doctrines of military culture and the decision-making processes that followed from them. It is striking how closely USW repeated the formal patterns of the Schlieffen Plan and the decision to go to war in July 1914. And, as with the Hindenburg program, Falkenhayn had already blazed the trail.

Originally skeptical of USW, Falkenhayn had embraced it in the winter of 1915–16 as the last chance to win the war. Indeed, he felt the decision was simply inevitable for this reason; no one could fight that existential logic.[18] Ludendorff and Hindenburg arrived at the same conclusion: given the stalemate on land and with time running against Germany, only the submarine could win the war. As Hindenburg later put it, in an unconscious echo of Lothar v. Trotha in 1904, "[Doing] anything else would have appeared as

---

15. Bethmann to Hindenburg, 30 Sept. 1916, Ludendorff to war minister, 5 Oct. 1916, in Ludendorff, *Urkunden*, 72–73, 76.

16. Gerald D. Feldman, *Army, Industry, and Labor in Germany, 1914–1918* (Princeton, 1966), 154.

17. Hindenburg to Bethmann, II Nr. 34 647 op., 13 Sept. 1916, cited in Ludendorff, *Urkunden*, 67. Emphasis in original.

18. Falkenhayn to Wild, 5 Feb. 1917, Wild, *Briefe*, 223.

296 cruelty against our own blood."[19] OHL therefore issued what Bethmann called "an open threat" to civilian leaders in December 1916. USW, they claimed, was "the only means whereby we shall be enabled to bring the war to an end promptly. . . . Our military situation is such as not to permit negotiations of any kind to divert from their course military measures that have finally become recognized as correct, and thereby to cripple the energetic conduct of the war."[20] Again we see the standard argument: the need for haste, rejection of negotiation, and the requirement to use any means necessary for a purely military victory. USW, like the Schlieffen Plan, was thus not a sign of "exuberant confidence" but of desperation.[21] It risked the almost certain entry of the United States into the war in favor of a wonder weapon pitting German technical ability and daring against the superior sea power of Germany's strongest foe, Britain. Like all wonder weapons, it was experimental, which meant that opponents, such as the chancellor, had little data they could use to argue against it.[22] Expert testimony therefore weighed heavily. The navy had learned from its earlier policy defeats; Admiral v. Holtzendorff had honed his statistics and presented an essentially technical case with "mathematical precision."[23]

The errors in Holtzendorff's reasoning have been nicely dissected by Holger Herwig.[24] His findings can be consolidated into four categories of mistakes that illustrate the limits of the navy's technical thinking. First, the navy assumed a static, autistic world resembling the one it mentally inhabited, rather than an interactive, mutually dependent system in which learning and accommodation took place. Therefore, it failed to see that domestic economic damage could be made good with foreign credit, that modern economies were flexible, that one could substitute other starches for grain, that prices and wages would move up together, or that defensive techniques, such as the convoy, might be developed. The second error lay in uncritically accepting data favorable to the navy's case, for example, taking the poor U.S. grain crop of 1916 as typical, or optimistically undercounting the gross tonnage available to Britain. Third, the navy underestimated Britain. It ascribed less intelligence and less willpower to its foe than it assumed for Germany. Underestimating the enemy is one of the ubiquitous patterns in German military thinking of this period—indeed, many officers mentioned it self-critically at specific moments, but rarely managed to banish it from their reasoning.[25] It is evident again in the blithe attitude toward the entry of the United States into the war. Its undeniable economic resources

19. Hindenburg, *Aus meinem Leben*, 220.

20. Bethmann, testimony before the Reichstag, 31 Oct. 1919, Germany, National Constituent Assembly, *Official German Documents*, 1:344.

21. Prince Max v. Baden's characterization of the earnest impression the naval officers made on him as they argued for USW, *Erinnerungen*, 53.

22. Bethmann called it an "experiment," *Betrachtungen*, 2:132.

23. Prince Max v. Baden, *Erinnerungen*, 53.

24. Holger Herwig, "Total Rhetoric, Limited War," in *Great War, Total War*, ed. Chickering and Förster, 189–206, here 200–204.

25. Concerning Falkenhayn, see Janssen, *Der Kanzler*, 51, 51n3, 100, 184, 222; Thaer, letter of 24 Aug. 1916, *Generalstabsdienst*, 86; Hugo von Freytag-Loringhoven's observation of 14 Feb. 1915, in Rupprecht Kronprinz v. Bayern, *Meine Kriegstagebuch*, 1:300; Rupprecht's self-criticism, diary entries of 16 June 1917, 20 Aug. 1917, 20 Sept. 1917, yet his return to the same thinking on 31 Dec. 1917, 2:200, 247, 263, 305–7; Wild, *Briefe*, diary entries of 4 Nov. 1915, 11 Dec. 1915, 6 July 1916, and then his admission of 15 July 1916, 101, 120, 176, 177.

were discounted as irrelevant because USW was supposed to force the war to end early; militarily, the United States was dismissed out of hand, even by opponents of USW.[26] The final sort of error was the corollary to underestimating the enemy: overestimating oneself. In this case that meant "forgetting" a 1914 internal naval study that had estimated it would take 222 submarines to blockade Britain effectively. On 1 February 1917, when USW went into effect, Germany had 111 submarines, of which only 32 could be on duty at any given time, not all of them in British waters.[27] This was a staggering shortfall. The twinning of wishful thinking and risk, the hallmarks of the Schlieffen Plan, had now moved firmly into the realm of the unreal.

Holtzendorff's predictions for victory were as fantastic as the Hindenburg program. The navy promised to "bring England to its knees" in six months. But one can detect two backhanded acknowledgments that the whole house of cards was extremely fragile. One was a "window of opportunity" caveat: USW could only be successful if it were launched by 1 February 1917; otherwise the harvest would save England, while the time deadline for Germany elapsed. When USW failed, one could always argue, as Tirpitz and many officers did, that it simply had not been resorted to early enough.[28] The window of opportunity was the same argument Moltke had made for going to war in 1914 (before the Russian railroads were finished), and, as in 1914, it placed great pressure on the chancellor to acquiesce to the military experts.

There was a second indirect admission that the navy's plan was hollow. As in Falkenhayn's justification for Verdun, Holtzendorff explained that "bringing England to its knees" did *not* mean materially forcing it to quit but making the cost so great that England, unwilling to make the same heroic sacrifices as Germany, would negotiate on Germany's terms.[29] That is, it was at base a psychological argument.[30]

As in the decision to replace Falkenhayn with Ludendorff and Hindenburg, there was a strong plebiscitary element in USW. Admiral v. Tirpitz's propaganda machine had drummed up widespread support in the press and Reichstag for USW. USW functioned as a wartime analog to the navy's peacetime role as flagship of Weltpolitik. Holtzendorff included a panoply of civilian economic experts as scientific witnesses for his economic predictions. In October, the Reichstag went on record in favor of USW, thereby, in the words of one of its leaders, "renouncing entirely its own judgment in favor of the authority of the [Supreme Command]."[31] The Reichstag's action left the chancellor's opposition to USW without organized public support.

26. Rupprecht Kronprinz v. Bayern, *Meine Kriegstagebuch*, diary entry of 11 Feb. 1917; he changed his mind on 6 May 1917: 2:97, 161. Tirpitz, *Politische Dokumente*, 455–56. Ludendorff was still denying U.S. troops were militarily significant on 17 Oct. 1918, Prince Max v. Baden, *Erinnerungen*, 426; and Hindenburg denied in 1920 that they had been significant in causing the German defeat, *Aus meinem Leben*, 324.

27. Bernd Stegemann, *Die deutsche Marinepolitik, 1916–1918* (Berlin, 1970), 26–29; Herwig, "Total Rhetoric," 204–5.

28. Tirpitz, *Politische Dokumente*, 564, 588; Einem, *Armeeführer*, 413.

29. Stegemann, *Die deutsche Marinepolitik*, 57–64; and Herwig, "Total Rhetoric," 195–97.

30. Groener recognized its psychological basis and rejected USW on this account. Diary entry of 25 Sept. 1916, *Lebenserinnerungen*, 325–26. Also, Tirpitz, *Politische Dokumente*, 525–26.

31. Payer, *Von Bethmann Hollweg*, 195, 206–7.

298   There was, nevertheless, strong opposition to USW among both civilian and military leaders; they recognized that unleashing USW was probably the pivotal decision of the war. But they had been worn down by the juggernaut of interlocking arguments that mutually supported one another and reflected the most basic assumptions of military thinking. Bethmann tried a last tactic—his peace proposal of December 1916. When the Allies rejected it out of hand, he had no further fallback position. On 9 January 1917 the Kaiser adopted USW effective 1 February. And then one last repetition occurred, the analogue to the Halt-in-Belgrade scheme of late July 1914. President Wilson's offer of peace mediation, which Bethmann learned about on 28 January, moved the chancellor to plead for postponement of USW until Germany could sound out the proposal. But the U-boats were already at sea and the navy argued that it was technically impossible to contact them in time, just as it had been technically impossible to meddle with the Schlieffen Plan to suit diplomatic requirements.[32] Visiting Berlin in late January, Prince Max von Baden "found the politicians in a frame of mind that can only be described as stolid loyalty." Bethmann, he thought, could not bring himself "to be responsible for a rotten peace without having used the last chance of victory."[33]

     Among officers, widespread happiness at the decision was probably the most common response.[34] But there were also doubters (including many who simply believed the navy was the inferior service and could not possibly win the war by itself). Powerful forces, both personal-psychological and institutional, hindered thoughtful officers from resisting the logic of the wonder weapon once it had been adopted. The skeptics now had to accommodate themselves to it. Some did so by agnostic deference to their fellow experts. Gen. Max Hoffmann declared the matter "beyond my judgment"; Col. Albrecht v. Thaer thought that "if the navy feels certain it can do it, then one must not consider [the danger from the United States]."[35] Others, such as Crown Prince Rupprecht, let themselves be convinced against their better judgment. But such people were probably more inclined to let the navy's assertions be tested and then become disillusioned when the six-month deadline passed with England still on its feet. Still, it was hard not to hope; the psychological need to believe, the peer pressure to be upbeat, the emotional preparation necessary for the spring offensive, all these kept Rupprecht nursing his hopes into November 1917 that, even if they could not win the war by themselves, perhaps the U-boats might yet make a difference.[36] Tirpitz's figures had converted General v. Einem, but he too had doubts as the six-month period ended inconclusively. "I don't want to be a pessimist, but I cannot believe in a big victory now, unless God works a wonder. May he do so!"[37] But Einem only definitively gave up on the submarine wonder in June 1918.[38]

32. Bethmann's testimony before the Reichstag, 31 Oct. 1919, Germany, National Constituent Assembly, *Official German Documents*, 350.

33. Prince Max v. Baden, *Erinnerungen*, 54.

34. Lossberg, *Meine Tätigkeit*, 277.

35. Hoffmann, *Aufzeichnungen*, diary entry of 9 Jan. 1917, 153; Thaer, *Generalstabsdienst*, had adopted this position during the first debate: letter of 14 Mar. 1916, 61.

36. Rupprecht Kronprinz v. Bayern, *Mein Kriegstagebuch*, diary entries of 15 Feb. 1917, 2:9; 20 Aug. 1917, 2:248; 17 Nov. 1917, 2:289.

37. Einem, *Armeeführer*, letter of 4 July 1917, 324.

38. Ibid., diary entry, 30 June 1918, 413.

The March Offensive

The United States joined Germany's enemies in April 1917, and most historians agree with Bethmann that the war was definitively lost at that point. But it was lost more quickly and spectacularly because of the March offensive of 1918. The offensive squandered Germany's last reserves of troops and made it incapable of sustaining a longer defense that might have frustrated the Allies into negotiating before it was too exhausted to resist their terms. By 1918 Germany lacked both the manpower and mobility to convert a breakthrough into a strategic victory; the March offensive demanded the impossible.[39] The alternative most suitable to Germany's eroded position in 1917–18 would have been the strategic defensive and the simultaneous pursuit of negotiations. But OHL never seriously considered this alternative, and no institutions or civilian or military leaders were strong enough to stop the decision for self-destruction.

The March offensive and the three mini-offensives that followed it in April, May–June, and July 1918 repeated the old pattern once again: a rush to embrace an unrealistic risk; the attempt to master the risk by technical virtuosity (detailed, taut planning) or by contradictory measures or by sheer denial; the trust in a wonder weapon; and the omission of preparations for possible failure. This template had failed all its strategic tests so far, yet the third OHL tried it again. It had been successful, however, in achieving operative victories against Russia, where Ludendorff and Hindenburg had amassed most of their practical experience and their nimbus of fame. Russia's collapse in revolution encouraged the comforting illusion, widespread in the upper officer corps, that the old lessons were right after all.

Ludendorff had contemplated a 1918 offensive since April 1917; concrete planning had begun in October.[40] Those plans originally envisaged a limited attack designed to spoil Allied plans, but even before the Bolshevik Revolution, Ludendorff had approved the idea of his operations chief, Maj. Georg Wetzell, for an "annihilating blow" against the British.[41] Just three days after Lenin announced on 8 November 1917 that Russia would withdraw from the war, Ludendorff told the two royal army group commanders, Crown Prince Rupprecht and Crown Prince Wilhelm, that Germany would launch a major offensive that spring.[42] Russia's withdrawal evened the military strength of the Central and Entente powers, but it did not create the numerical superiority with which Moltke the elder had defeated France in 1870. The submarine campaign had failed to knock England out of the war,[43] but it had brought the United States into the war, which made the blockade for the first time truly strangling. Germany's reserves of munitions and manpower

39. Deist, "Der militärische Zusammenbruch des Kaiserreichs," 215; Deist, "Strategy and Unlimited Warfare," 278; Kuhl's testimony, *UA* 4:3, 56, 97, 144–45, 200; Delbrück's testimony, *UA* 4:3, 301–3; Groener, *Lebenserinnerungen*, 427. The recent historical revision of Dieter Storz is self-contradictory but ultimately concludes that the plan was impracticable: Storz, "'Aber was hätte anders geschehen sollen?'" in *Kriegsende 1918*, 62, 69.

40. Martin Kitchen, *The German Offensives of 1918* (Charleston, S.C., 2001), 21–26.

41. Herwig, *First World War*, 393–94; Meier-Welcker, "Deutsche Führung," 166.

42. Rupprecht Kronprinz v. Bayern, *Meine Kriegstagebuch*, entry of 11 Nov. 1917, 2:285.

43. Ludendorff had given up on USW by November 1917, Rupprecht Kronprinz v. Bayern, *Mein Kriegstagebuch*, 2:287.

300 now neared their absolute limit, and U.S. troops were expected to arrive in Europe in the summer. This dismal situation starkly repeated Germany's old military dilemma, which OHL and many commanders interpreted as the same kind of limited "window of opportunity" for offensive action as in July 1914 or January 1917.[44]

After the war had been lost, defenders of OHL's decision claimed that the defensive alternative had been carefully weighed.[45] It had not. Ludendorff was set on an offensive since at least 11 November; the planning sessions he held thereafter with his western commanders focused purely on tactical questions.[46] Whereas Ludendorff had found the decision for retreat in 1917 "uncommonly difficult," the decision to attack he characterized as "not hard, even if the task is huge."[47] Gen. Hermann von Kuhl, who was skeptical of the offensive's chances at the time, later explained that the decision itself "seemed almost self-evident. It lay, so to speak, in the air." He then recounted Germany's critical military situation, its increasingly despondent home front and weakening allies, and concluded that one simply could not wait until fresh American troops arrived on the scene. "The 'half-year danger zone' [for the Allies] could not be left unused," when Germany finally had more troops free to deploy in the west than ever before. And finally, Kuhl cited Germany's military culture, without calling it that, of course: "Attack is the strongest form of war; it alone leads to a decision. It gives the troops pep and raises their spirit. In peacetime we were raised to go on the offensive, it was our strength."[48] In Germany's hour of greatest need, it therefore reached for its strength. Most officers welcomed the offensive plan.[49]

Nonetheless, important military and civilian voices counseled against it. Doubts within the military concerning the March offensive (and USW) showed that military culture did not operate like indoctrination; it did not make it impossible to see danger or to appreciate the limits of reality. Instead, it provided strong reasons to overcome the resulting caution or to discount it as pessimism or as being incompatible with the proper performance of one's duty. The most severe skeptics were Crown Prince Rupprecht, his chief of staff, Kuhl, and Crown Prince Wilhelm's chief of staff, Count Friedrich von der Schulenburg.[50] None believed Germany had much chance of success. Yet none of them recommended the "pure defensive."[51] They preferred the active defensive of German counterattacks, which worked only if the Allies attacked first and thus wore themselves out. The plans they submitted to OHL in October 1917 were thus limited offensives, and easily became not a stark alternative to the grander offensive but a basis for one of the elements of it.[52] Once OHL had decided for the March offensive, the skeptics were called on to hone

44. Schwertfeger's report, *UA* 4:2, 90; Reichsarchiv, *Weltkrieg*, 14:686–87.

45. Hindenburg, *Aus meinem Leben*, 299; Kuhl, *Weltkrieg*, 2:289.

46. Rupprecht sent his recommendation for the March offensive to Ludendorff on 20 Nov. 1917; the big planning session of 19 Jan. 1918 was strictly tactical: Rupprecht Kronprinz v. Bayern, *Mein Kriegstagebuch*, 3:222–24, 2:319–20.

47. Reichsarchiv, *Weltkrieg*, 12:129; Meier-Welcker, "Deutsche Führung," 166, 181.

48. Kuhl, *Weltkrieg*, 2:288–90; identically: Kronprinz Wilhelm v. Preussen, *Deutschlands Heldenkampf*, 293.

49. Thaer, diary of 12 Feb. 1918, letter of 16 Aug. 1918, *Generalstabsdienst*, 164, 223; Lossberg, *Meine Tätigkeit*, 314; Storz, "'Aber was hätte,'" 56.

50. Reichsarchiv, *Weltkrieg*, 14:92–93.

51. Kuhl, *Weltkrieg*, 2:293.

52. Klein, *Deutschland*, 3:232, 236. See also Army Group Crown Prince Rupprecht to OHL, 20 Nov. 1917, Ia Nr. 4501, *geheim* (secret), in Rupprecht, *Mein Kriegstagebuch*, 3:222–38.

offensive alternatives among which OHL would choose. Their doubts then became veiled and merged with the position of another group of officers who favored the last-ditch effort, but who knew that the war was lost if it failed. To increase its chances of success, Rupprecht, Kuhl, Gallwitz, and Lossberg recommended flexibility: if the original attack stalled at an enemy strongpoint, it should immediately be shifted elsewhere in hopes of finding a weak spot for the breakthrough.[53] This view made incisive criticism of the ensuing campaign more difficult for at least two reasons. It increased uncertainty among commanders about the nature of the attack in their sector: Was it a probe, a diversion, or an attempt at a breakthrough?[54] That uncertainty encouraged attempts to achieve breakthrough where diversion was the operative goal. And it opened the door to Ludendorff's senseless repetition of attacks, which became hard to distinguish from flexibility. In fact, the skeptics were mostly inconsistent in their advice and criticism during the series of offensives after the first one, which was code-named Michael.

In late 1917 and early 1918, the drift of military culture toward a last, huge risk was again supported by a faulty political process. It is unclear whether a better process would have made any difference, however. After all, the fatal decision for USW was taken despite significant extramilitary input and many rounds of discussion involving the Reich's political leadership. The weak position of the navy as a new service had permitted that uniquely broad decision-making process, but the political leadership still could not outweigh the military during an existential-seeming war. The General Staff's competence for land warfare was so unchallenged, however, that no war council occurred in 1917–18 to discuss the merits of an offensive strategy versus a defensive strategy combined with negotiations.[55]

Instead, individuals tried to influence OHL directly. Government officials were severely hampered by the absence of leadership provided by the aged Georg von Hertling (chancellor from 25 October 1917 to 3 October 1918).[56] Meanwhile, Ludendorff rejected the arguments of influential public figures who feared a complete military victory was no longer possible, with the words: "Only action brings success. That has been proven by the success of our arms in other theaters. . . . Attack has always been the German method of combat."[57]

The plan displayed the strengths of the German military establishment but developed the characteristic weaknesses ever further. Ludendorff meticulously and creatively retrained the exhausted army in the techniques of breakthrough. He built on and extended Falkenhayn's innovation of the storm battalion. Substantial quantities of ammunition had been stockpiled. And the enormous buildup was successfully kept secret. When the attack came on 21 March it was wildly successful in the first days. General v. Kuhl described it to the Reichstag later as "*an astonishing organizational and tactical achieve-*

---

53. Gallwitz, *Erleben im Westen*, 294; Lossberg, *Meine Tätigkeit*, 314; Reichsarchiv, *Weltkrieg*, 59, 59n1, 67, 682–83.

54. See the disagreements in Reichsarchiv, *Weltkrieg*, 14:313–14, 314n1, 317.

55. Deist, "Der militärische Zusammenbruch," 213–14; Friederike Krüger and Michael Salewski, "Die Verantwortung der militärischen Führung deutscher Streitkräfte in den Jahren 1918 und 1945," in *Kriegsende 1918*, 386.

56. Prince Max v. Baden, *Erinnerungen*, 231, 235; Schwertfeger's report, *UA* 4:2, 179.

57. Ludendorff to Ernst Jäckh, 22 Feb. 1918, cited in Schwertfeger's report, *UA* 4:2, 93; Rüdiger Schütz, "Einführende Bemerkungen," in *Kriegsende 1918*, 41–44.

302 *ment.*"[58] But it was fatal strategically and harmful operationally, for Ludendorff had reduced planning and action to the most technical level, the tactical. Rupprecht noted in early April 1918 that OHL's orders suggested it was "living from hand to mouth, without recognizable operative intentions."[59]

The tendency in the Wilhelminian military to substitute operations for strategy had now plunged a notch further, to substitute tactics for operations. The operational was now as fraught with depressing limits as the strategic had been earlier, so Ludendorff and his advisors focused on the technical problem of breaking through the enemy's lines, but not on sustaining and developing that breakthrough into an operative, much less a strategic, victory. For by 1918 Germany lacked every objective measure for such an operative success: it had numerical parity but not superiority (and even with superiority, the Allies had never broken through the German lines); it lacked adequate reserves (one million men remained in the east); it had fewer heavy artillery and airplanes than the Allies; and above all, it lacked trucks, horses, and horse fodder for the transportation needed to pour troops and supplies through the hole.[60] Faced with these dismal figures but unwilling to give up on military victory, Ludendorff abandoned the operational. He blurted out to Rupprecht, "I forbid the word 'operation.' We are simply going to punch a hole [in the lines] and everything will happen from there. That is how we did it in Russia!"[61]

Like Schlieffen in a similar operative dilemma, Ludendorff now tried overcontrol and taut planning, intruding into tactical decisions normally reserved for lower command levels.[62] But, also like Schlieffen, he depended at the same time on the creative leadership of lower-ranking officers to exploit victory opportunistically, wherever it arose. He did not see the contradiction.

Virtually everybody at the time realized that Ludendorff was playing Germany's last card—this was the phrase they commonly used.[63] Yet Ludendorff constantly expanded the risk. He took Rupprecht's plan, which aimed at rolling up and defeating part of the British army, and extended it to target the entire British army. Then, in March, Ludendorff followed the advice of Gen. Oskar von Hutier of the 18th Army to transform a diversionary attack against the French into a second encirclement/annihilation. Ludendorff thus proposed to defeat *both* his enemies in a dual, simultaneous encirclement.[64] This grandiosity cancelled Ludendorff's earlier insight of 11 November 1917 that Germany had troops enough for only a single offensive.[65] And, of course, it split Germany's limited strength.

What Ludendorff failed to do was to prepare strong rear defenses to shield retreating troops and check Allied counterattacks. Several commanders and staff people suggested

---

58. Kuhl's report, *UA* 4:3, 128–29, emphasis in original.

59. Rupprecht Kronprinz v. Bayern, *Mein Kriegstagebuch*, diary entry of 5 Apr. 1918, 2:372.

60. Deist, "Der militärische Zusammenbruch," 215.

61. Rupprecht Kronprinz v. Bayern, *Mein Kriegstagebuch*, 2:372n.

62. Ibid., diary entries of 11 Feb. 1918, 28 Feb. 1918, 3:283, 287.

63. Prince Max v. Baden, *Erinnerungen*, diary entry of 19 Feb. 1918, 235; Thaer, *Generalstabsdienst*, diary entries of 31 Dec. 1917 and 12 Feb. 1918, 151, 164; Rupprecht Kronprinz v. Bayern, *Mein Kriegstagebuch*, diary entry of 19 Feb. 1918, 2:324; Lossberg, *Meine Tätigkeit*, 318; Kuhl, *Weltkrieg*, 2:292.

64. Reichsarchiv, *Weltkrieg*, 14:55, 91–92, 257.

65. Kuhl's report, *UA* 4:3, 102.

this obvious measure.[66] But no preparations were made. This omission reflected the ingrained bias against the defensive typical of the German military, ironically despite its enormous success in defense during the first three years of the war. It was also a consequence of the decision to launch an offensive, which diverted Germany's inadequate manpower resources entirely into hurried preparation for the coming attack—there was scarcely labor left to strengthen defenses.[67] And the lack of preparation for defeat reflected the wishful thinking and unreality at the base of the decision.[68] When Prince Max von Baden confronted Ludendorff on 19 February 1918 about Germany's slim, perhaps nonexistent, chances for success, Ludendorff could only reply, "You have to believe in victory."[69] Hindenburg had trouble explaining his and Ludendorff's thinking to his postwar readers:

> It is a reasonable question: What justified our hope for one or more sweeping [offensive] victories [in spring 1918], when our opponents had always failed [to achieve breakthroughs]? The answer is easy to give, but hard to explain. You can say it in a single word, 'trust.' Not trust in your lucky star or vague hopes, even less trust in numbers or external strengths. It was the trust a leader feels when he sends his troops into enemy fire, convinced that they will bear the utmost burden and make the seemingly impossible possible.[70]

Hindenburg's admission is extraordinary for its candor: even after the war he had not thought of anything more reasonable to say in his defense. Equally striking is his rejection of objective indicators such as numbers or troop or material strengths. Germany's abiding inferiority made bracketing them essential to acting according to the military culture's aggressive expectations of a proper commander. And so one was left with the Wilhelminian conundrum, "the necessity of the impossible."

The March offensive, launched on the 21st, pushed back the front forty miles before it bogged down on the 30th and was cancelled on 5 April. Just four days later, Ludendorff launched a second offensive in Flanders that foundered in two days. Having twice failed to defeat the main target, the British, Ludendorff planned the next offensive against the French, to be launched at the end of May. It and the offensive that followed it in July were ostensibly designed to lure British reinforcements away from Flanders, where Ludendorff intended to try again (at the end of July). But a larger design was in fact lacking. When the first assault against the French unexpectedly took Soissons, OHL immediately dumped its limited goal of diversion and went for a sweeping "decisive" victory. The result was the same as in March: an indefensible salient and the "wastage" and exhaustion of troops.[71] Einem described the first two offensives as "a wild slaughter"; the victories had been won "in a purely mechanical fashion" by repeating the same tactics. Ludendorff repeated them

---

66. Thaer, *Generalstabsdienst*, diary entry of 18 Apr. 1918, 183; Kuhl's report, *UA* 4:3, 97, 200.

67. Schwertfeger's report, *UA* 4:2, 259; Kuhl's testimony, *UA* 3:1, 90; Meier-Welcker, "Deutsche Führung," 182.

68. Michael Epkenhans, "Die Politik der militärischen Führung 1918," in *Kriegsende 1918*, 220.

69. Prince Max v. Baden, *Erinnerungen*, 236.

70. Hindenburg, *Aus meinem Leben*, 299.

71. Ibid., 333; Kuhl's report, *UA* 4:3, 167, 171–72; Kuhl, *Weltkrieg*, 2:359.

304 again on 15 July, but by then the French had finally caught on; they stopped the fourth and final offensive on 17 July and the next day began the Allied counteroffensives that ended the war.[72]

Admitting Defeat

Admitting defeat is probably the most difficult task any organization faces. It was doubly difficult for the German army because of its role as national symbol and its privileged place in the state, which rested on its guarantee to deliver military victory. Defeat would sweep away the old order and, along with it, its army. The political stakes strongly encouraged blindness to the catastrophic situation. But so did military culture, which affected behavior more thoroughly and systematically than abstract political worries. The self-destructive dynamic that characterized the end of the war can only be understood if one appreciates the organizational imperatives that kept officers from recognizing defeat, adapting to it (operationally or strategically), and thus halting the spiral of violence.

From the foregoing chapters, the chief military-cultural mechanisms guarding against (re)thinking will be abundantly clear. We must now ask, What experiences or subject positions allowed officers to escape these frames? and How did military culture tend to thwart their insights?

Critical realism could sprout where military culture was weakest. Thus, younger OHL staffers and those only recently called to the OHL were less saturated by the institutional habits of denial. Two other groups benefited from reality checks powerful enough—finally—to break through received wisdom. Extensive experience at the front helped Colonel v. Thaer and General v. Lossberg, for example, to arrive at critical views, while other, politically well-connected officers, such as Crown Princes Rupprecht and Wilhelm (and possibly Gen.-Maj. Paul von Bartenwerffer, head of the political section of OHL) had the advantage of extramilitary information and secret reports, which helped them put the military situation into its larger strategic perspective. These officers arrived at their dour conclusions independently over a period of months from April to early September 1918. They did not always conclude that the war was lost; the more palatable view held that Germany could no longer win a purely military victory and therefore had to adopt the defensive and open negotiations. In either case, they faced tremendous opposition from inside the military institution.

One source of friction was not peculiar to Germany. Denial of impending catastrophe is quite common, especially among organizations dealing with physical danger, and particularly when its warning signs become most apparent.[73] Such organizations typically place a high premium on physical courage and nurse feelings of invulnerability, both of which would be injured by sounding a premature alarm. Any army is liable to this.

In Germany's end phase, the first such alarm should have come with the stalemate of the "Michael" offensive. Several younger officers in the operations section at OHL, Maj.

---

72. Einem, *Armeeführer*, diary entry of 1 May 1918, 392, and letter of 19 July 1918, 418.
73. Turner, "Organizational and Interorganizational Development of Disasters," 390–91.

Baron Erich von der Bussche-Ippenburg and Capts. Bodo von Harbou and Geyer, did conclude that a Siegfrieden was now impossible and that Germany should give up its recent gains, return to the Siegfried line, and hold out on the defensive.[74] Their views were probably not widely known, however. Their section chief, Major Wetzell, did not share their opinion and would have been unlikely to pass it on. Two other factors would have discouraged them from pressing further. One was Ludendorff's intemperate criticism of his subordinates, behavior consistent with the ruthless forcefulness appropriate to officers, which led his staff to suppress negative information "because they are loath to report anything unpleasant."[75] The other was the disposability of staff officers, an institutional adaptation to the army's bifurcated organization. While the Military Cabinet overprotected commanders, the General Staff compensated by making staff officers particularly vulnerable to removal. The unintended result was that staff officers "oriented themselves more toward their superiors and Ludendorff than toward the enemy," Gen. Adolf Wild v. Hohenborn noted in late 1916. "Independence and willingness to act suffer from this. Everybody is afraid of being thrown out."[76] Wild's observation may have been truer at the front than at OHL, but clearly systemic hindrances discouraged younger officers from expressing unpopular views to superiors.

What happened when one persevered anyway is shown by the case of Col. Albrecht v. Thaer, chief of staff of the Wytschaete Korps in Flanders. Thaer had commanded seventy different divisions before being appointed in April 1918 as Ludendorff's chief of staff for provisioning. Thaer's extensive battlefield experience convinced him that Germany's troops were worn out and near collapse. On 1 May 1918 he summoned up his courage and reported his views to Hindenburg and Ludendorff. Hindenburg brushed him off with the Russian precedent. "There we did the same thing, attacking first here, then there, and all at once it succeeded. That's how it will go in the west, too. You see, thank God we have five more months until winter during which we can try a whole row of offensive attacks, attacking here and there, here and there." In Thaer's view, Hindenburg's answer was simply "irrelevant." Ludendorff's response was typically pungent. "What is all this belly-aching [*Geunke*]? What do you want me to do, conclude peace at any price?" Thaer replied that he "must leave all the consequences to OHL." "The result of my step with our great men: zero," Thaer concluded. "They are firmly convinced that they can wear the enemy down to peace; Hindenburg believes it, and Ludendorff certainly hopes so."[77]

OHL's adamant refusal to recognize the situation made critics inside the military question their own judgment. Thaer was no exception.[78] But he recovered his confidence

74. Wolfgang Foerster, *Der Feldherr Ludendorff im Unglück* (Wiesbaden, 1952), 31; Siegfried A. Kaehler, "Vier quellenkritische Untersuchungen zum Kriegsende 1918," *Nachrichten der Akademie der Wissenschaften in Göttingen* I. Philologisch-Historische Klasse, no. 8 (Göttingen, 1960), 428n2.

75. Thaer, *Generalstabsdienst*, diary entry of 26–27 Apr. 1918, 187.

76. Wild, *Briefe*, letter of 18–19 Dec. 1916, 208; also, Einem, *Armeeführer*, diary entry of 3 July 1916 and letter of 17 Nov. 1916, 238, 267; Rupprecht Kronprinz v. Bayern, *Mein Kriegstagebuch*, diary entry of 1 Nov. 1915, 1:402; 9 May 1916, 1:461; 20 May 1918, 2:396.

77. Thaer, *Generalstabsdienst*, 196–97.

78. See also Crown Prince Wilhelm's self-doubts about countering Ludendorff's after-offensives: Kronprinz Wilhelm v. Preussen, *Deutschlands Heldenkampf*, 333–34; Herwig, *First World War*, 393.

306 through self-criticism: "Unfortunately, I have caught myself up till now being too much of an optimist."[79] Still, Thaer made sure to keep his doubts from his fellow staff officers.[80] The atmosphere is clear from another officer's remark (at the end of July 1918): "Anyone who regarded the slogan 'forcing the enemy down' with skepticism was branded a weakling."[81] The stereotypical virtues of the officer undermined realism.

Higher-ranking officers were more secure than their younger colleagues, but they were also more securely fettered by Imperial military culture. The advice of the highest-ranking skeptics after the failure of the "Michael" offensive makes the problem clear. None advocated going on the defensive. Instead, they advocated a truly strategic offensive that concentrated Germany's forces in a single spot.[82] Even as each offensive failed, attack still seemed to them the best bet. Despite his skepticism about the prospects for success, for example, General v. Einem recommended the more ambitious of two proposed offensives for his army in July 1918.[83] And General v. Kuhl, who otherwise opposed Ludendorff's decisions in 1918, urged him to continue attacking on 15 July, after Einem had persuaded Ludendorff to halt this last offensive because of excessive losses. Kuhl wrote that if excessive losses were the reason, "then we cannot expect anything great; without losses nothing big can be gained."[84] Even after the successful French counterattack, Kuhl rejected the pure defensive, because "we must not relinquish the initiative to the enemy."[85]

In short, critical leaders within the military did not provide a clear alternative to Ludendorff's "buffalo" tactics.[86] The realism of the most realistic commanders and staff officers was severely checked by their standard assumptions about combat. The tactical perspective overwhelmed them. They remained convinced that, whether you aimed for a "real" military victory (of annihilation), a lesser victory of attrition, or even a negotiated peace, the *method* remained the same. The agreement on the general superiority of inherently risky offensive as against defensive tactics made it harder for critical commanders to separate themselves from the repetitious, willful use of those tactics in strategic and operative situations where they could no longer succeed.[87]

Ludendorff and Hindenburg were, of course, both subject to the same pressures stemming from military culture as were their subordinates. While popular opinion and professional hopes had elevated Hindenburg to symbolic ersatz-kaiser, Ludendorff had to incorporate the virtues of the fearless Schlieffen-genius, the guarantor of victory in actual war, not just in war planning. He was in some ways a prisoner of that role, which military

79. Thaer, *Generalstabsdienst*, 194–99, here 196, 195, 197, 198.

80. Ibid., diary entry of 29 Apr. 1918, 190.

81. Major Niemann's pamphlet, "Zur politischen Lage" (20 July 1918), cited in Schwertfeger's report, *UA* 4:2, 216; Niemann, *Kaiser und Revolution*, 28; Meier-Welcker, "Deutsche Führung," 179.

82. Gallwitz: On 3 June 1918, Gallwitz, *Erleben im Westen*, 323, 327. Rupprecht and Kuhl: Reichsarchiv, *Weltkrieg*, 14:320–21; Meier-Welcker, "Deutsche Führung," 170, 171–36; Rupprecht Kronprinz v. Bayern, *Mein Kriegstagebuch*, diary entries of 8 Apr. 1918, 2:374, 12 Apr. 1918, 2:388, 3 Oct. 1918, 2:455.

83. Einem, *Armeeführer*, diary entry of 17 June 1918, 408.

84. Foerster, *Ludendorff*, 17.

85. Reichsarchiv, *Weltkrieg*, 14:534.

86. That includes Hoffmann, who in principle favored a single concentrated blow but who nevertheless in June believed Germany should try yet another attack against the French. Hoffmann, *Aufzeichnungen*, diary entry of 4 June 1918, 197, 198. "Buffalo strategy" was Foch's term: Herwig, *First World War*, 233.

87. For example, Kuhl, *Weltkrieg*, 2:351–52; Lossberg, *Meine Tätigkeit*, 346.

culture had created and political culture supported. Like the keystone of an arch, Ludendorff was supposed to hold the edifice together. He dared not weaken. Confronted with the views of military skeptics, he seemed to fear, as Col. Herman Ritter Mertz von Quirnheim noted in his diary, "that people would accuse him of losing his nerve."[88]

The genius motif encouraged contemporaries (and some historians) to locate the main obstacle to realistic military policy in Ludendorff's personality and mental health.[89] There is no question that the de facto head of an imperative chain of command exercises great personal influence on decisions and staff. Ludendorff did become anxious, inconsistent, and refractory during Germany's long defeat in 1918. But it is helpful to see how much system there was to Ludendorff's behavior.

Ludendorff reacted to defeat much as Falkenhayn had done in 1916. Ludendorff too clutched at a failed plan and attacked repetitively, as Falkenhayn had done at Verdun. Ludendorff too became lost in details: he micromanaged the March offensive and during briefings ducked the unpleasant larger issues by changing the subject to minutiae.[90] He too began reckoning victories mechanically, claiming success "so long as we inflict more losses on the enemy than we suffer ourselves."[91] He too vastly overestimated enemy losses.[92] And he too lied. Two months after he had calculated that Germany lacked the necessary manpower reserves, he nonetheless told the new foreign secretary, Paul von Hintze, that Germany could indeed win a final, military victory, implying that negotiations were unnecessary.[93] Unlike Falkenhayn, however, Ludendorff kept on lying to the civilian leadership, which made it impossible for them to prepare for the impending defeat.[94]

In the end Ludendorff (and Hindenburg) behaved according to the expectations that military culture and the war-transformed political culture held of them. This is surely one reason why even officers who should have known better did not blame them for the defeat or for their reluctance to admit it. For all his postwar criticism of Ludendorff, for example, in the end Col. Bernhard Schwertfeger, appointed by the Reichstag to analyze Germany's defeat, exonerated OHL before the parliamentarians: "Courage and confidence are career requirements for soldiers, and no one should expect from the commanders after such incredible battlefield achievements that they would dwell on the reverse side of the medal. Considering that was the job of politics."[95]

Or, take General v. Kuhl's lengthy report to the postwar Reichstag. Even though he disagreed with almost every action Ludendorff took in 1918, Kuhl defended the quartermaster general's step-by-step descent into the abyss because each decision was eminently

---

88. Diary entry of 26 July 1918, cited in Foerster, *Ludendorff*, 28.

89. Foerster, *Ludendorff*, provides the results of the Reichsarchiv's research into the question of Ludendorff's mental health. Blaming Ludendorff: Kitchen, *German Offensives*, 233–34.

90. Lossberg, *Meine Tätigkeit*, 326, 345; Foerster, *Ludendorff*, 35, 44–45, 56; Storz, " 'Aber was hätte,' " 95.

91. June 1918, cited in Storz, " 'Aber was hätte,' " 90.

92. Reicharchiv, *Weltkrieg*, 14:314–15.

93. Discussion of 9 July 1918, Schwertfeger's report, *UA* 4:2, 209.

94. The most infamous example was the crown council of 14 August: Germany, Foreign Office and Ministry of the Interior, ed., *Amtliche Urkunden zur Vorgeschichte des Waffenstillstandes 1918*, 2nd ed. (Frankfurt, 1988; orig., 1924), 3–6 (hereafter *Amtliche Urkunden*); Schwertfeger's report, *UA* 4:2, 224–32, quotations, 224, 229–30.

95. Schwertfeger's report, *UA* 4:2, 180.

308   reasonable according to conventional military wisdom.[96] Thus, the March offensive was defensible because Germany was "checkmated" and the visible risks "could not hold the commander back from seeking a decision of force so long as there was any chance of victory. He had no choice. It was conceivable that the fortunes of war" would have granted victory. Kuhl found the idea for the offensive "a great 'attack plan,' a 'convincing and rousing idea.'" When it failed, it was understandable that "the strong will of OHL did not want to let go of the goal. Often in war standing firm has led to surprising victory in the last second." Negotiations were in any case unimaginable: "In this war it was a matter of victory or defeat." The continued offensives in May and June were logical: "One had to act. Even most critics of the OHL agree with this." Remaining on the defensive would have meant losing the war: "Arriving at this timid conclusion was not necessary before the last attempt at a favorable decision had been made." And so forth.[97] Kuhl and other public defenders of OHL chose the arguments they found most convincing, those that were most firmly anchored in Imperial military culture.[98]

Meanwhile, as OHL stalled, the skeptics among high-ranking commanders and younger General Staff officers grew. Those of April and May were joined by others in June.[99] The successful French counterattack on 17 July hastened the process. Now Generals v. Gallwitz and v. Lossberg thought defense and negotiation were the only paths open.[100] They and the crown princes pressed in July, August, and September to conduct a prepared strategic retreat to establish deep lines of defense from which Germany could frustrate the Allies while initiating peace negotiations. Ludendorff resisted this advice until the Allied breakthrough at Arras-Cambrai on 2 September forced him to order a retreat—though it was too late to do so in the way the critics desired. (Even then, some OHL staffers opposed this heresy.)[101]

It was not until early September that the General Staff prepared itself organizationally for admitting defeat. At the urging of Ludendorff's advisor, Col. Max Bauer, and with Ludendorff's acquiescence, two younger officers, Maj. Joachim von Stülpnagel and Col. Wilhelm Heye, joined the staff on 11–12 September in order to bring a fresh viewpoint. Around the 25th, together with younger staffers and the older General v. Bartenwerffer, they began to prepare Ludendorff to face the facts. Finally, on 29 September 1918 Ludendorff and Hindenburg admitted to their staff and to civilian leaders that Germany had lost the war; without an immediate armistice, they claimed, the army would suffer com-

---

96. Cf. Niemann, *Kaiser und Heer*, 360–61, who called Ludendorff's decisions in 1918 "not always 'the best,'" but "reasonable," and then cited Moltke the elder as having said that "it is enough if the commander always orders the 'reasonable'; then he will always have the prospect of reaching his goal, although not the certainty, since 'even the best man can fail because of the irresistible power of circumstance.'"

97. Kuhl's report, *UA* 4:3, quotations in order: 189, 144, 136–37, 138–39, 165, 183.

98. For further examples, see Reichsarchiv, *Weltkrieg*, 14:691; Freytag-Loringhoven, *Menschen und Dinge*, 329–30; Niemann, *Kaiser und Heer*, 141; Kronprinz Wilhelm v. Preussen, *Erinnerungen*, 186–87; Foerster, *Ludendorff*, 58, 68, 129.

99. Meier-Welcker, "Deutsche Führung," 173n50.

100. Lossberg, *Meine Tätigkeit*, 346–47; Gallwitz, *Erleben im Westen*, 340–41. Foerster distrusts Lossberg's account, but most historians accept it. Foerster, *Ludendorff*, 22–25.

101. Kuhl diary, 3 Sept. 1918, cited in Foerster, *Ludendorff*, 55.

plete military collapse. Ludendorff's admission ended what one close observer described as the "terrible inner battle in which one saw the catastrophe, on the one hand, but on the other could not and did not want to understand it."[102]

OHL's inability to admit defeat, its choice to conduct the war by relentless offensives and then by a bitter fighting retreat without relinquishing territory drifted toward totality by driving up the casualty rate and exhausting an ever higher percentage of "human material." In the five months after the March offensive began, Germany suffered one million casualties (dead, wounded, missing, captured). From mid-July to the armistice, another 420,000 were killed or wounded and 340,000 were missing or captured.[103]

In the course of this organizational denial, a line was crossed separating mere "wastage" from national suicide. Maj. Alfred Niemann was one of the first to recognize that line, on 20 July 1918, two days after the French counterattacks threw German troops onto the defensive, permanently. "The slogan 'holding out for a victorious end' is just a slogan, a euphemistic expression for voluntary 'honorable death,' which is only understandable to German idealism."[104] As a policy, "honorable death" developed in the summer and fall of 1918, unclearly and piecemeal by extending dicta or assumptions that had been operating the entire time. It ended as one of the versions of Endkampf (final battle) envisioned by high-ranking officers that risked or even embraced the destruction of Germany in a final battle against the Allies.[105] In the Endkampf the full destructive force inherent in the military's operative maxims turned on itself in a pyre of self-destruction.

Endkampf

Because of its obvious military-cultural logic, Endkampf was visible in outline long before it became an actual plan. Crown Prince Wilhelm had expressed the logic in July 1917 when he proposed offering the Allies a negotiated settlement on the basis of the status quo (a "peace of understanding"). If they rejected it, then one would rally the German people and "strain the last nerve to block the [Allies'] plan [to destroy Germany]."[106] The practical foundation for Endkampf began the next year, in April 1918, with the defensive plans of the younger staff skeptics and realistic commanders.[107] They advocated a flexible defense in depth that would have created a broad swath of destruction across the rest of occupied France and Belgium in order to slow or stop the Allied advance.[108] By late July, when the offensive was no longer possible, Rupprecht and other commanders now also

---

102. Maj. Gen. Hermann Mertz v. Quirnheim, note of 29 Sept. 1922, cited in Schwertfeger's report, *UA* 4:2, 428.

103. Deist, "Der militärische Zusammenbruch," 228–29. In the end, 3% of the German population and 15% of its soldiers were killed in the war: Afflerbach, " 'Bis zum letzten Mann und letzten Groschen?' " in *Die Wehrpflicht*, 89.

104. Major Niemann, memo, 20 July 1918, cited in Schwertfeger's report, *UA* 4:2, 216.

105. The best account is Geyer, "Insurrectionary Warfare," 459–527. Also Krüger and Salewski, "Die Verantwortung."

106. Kronprinz Wilhelm v. Preussen, *Erinnerungen*, 165.

107. Geyer, "Insurrectionary Warfare," 496.

108. Ibid., 495–97; Kaehler, "Vier quellenkritische Untersuchungen," 428n2.

310 called for such a defense from which "we can exercise resistance successfully for a long time. Our last hope is to hold out long enough until the enemy concludes that the sacrifices in blood and material are out of proportion to the results, especially since every one of our retreats means the complete destruction of the land between the lines." This plan assumed the severe destruction that Germany had used during its "Alberich" retreat of 1917. But Rupprecht's goal was limited: after the first major repulse of an Allied attack he wanted to enter negotiations to end the war, even if that should mean "great sacrifices" on Germany's part.[109] The means were thus more absolute than the end.

Three weeks later, at the crown council on 14 August, Ludendorff and Hindenburg also adopted a bloody, destructive defense. Their plan differed from Rupprecht's in two ways. OHL still claimed it could win the war by using more violent techniques. And it ordered a slow fighting retreat, clinging to every inch of territory, instead of Rupprecht's plan for a large strategic retreat, with systematically scorched earth and then limited counterattacks. Ludendorff's type of retreat became the reality; it caused huge casualties and much destruction, but it was not as systematic or thorough as 1917 had been.

These were the practical foundations of Endkampf. But the temptation to resort to increased force had obviously spread far beyond the military. OHL's shocking announcement on 29 September immediately elicited all sorts of versions of the Endkampf idea, many of them from civilians. The spectrum reached from Foreign Secretary Hintze's scheme to threaten (but not really carry out) all-out resistance in order to fool the allies into offering better peace terms to industrialist Walter Rathenau's romantic call for a German popular insurrection to win the war.[110]

The most realistic Endkampf conception took shape under Prince Max von Baden's new government, which had succeeded Chancellor Hertling's on 3 October and inaugurated constitutional reforms designed to make Germany acceptable as a negotiating partner with the Allies and to legitimate a disappointing peace at home. Prince Max's plan was not a bluff; he and the cabinet were willing to break off armistice negotiations and continue the war for some months, if necessary by drafting the very last man capable of holding a gun, thereby shutting down industry in Germany—but only if the broad populace supported such a move, and only if it stood a real chance of military success, defined as getting better peace terms. The cabinet discussed Endkampf at great length on 9 October and 17 October, and again on the 19th and the 28th. At no time could military spokesmen persuade the cabinet that Endkampf was either militarily or politically viable. Reluctantly, Prince Max and the cabinet abandoned the scheme and voted to sign the armistice.[111]

The military's version of Endkampf differed from the cabinet's conception in two ways. First, the goal was not limited to better peace terms, because much more was at stake for the army as an institution than for Germany as a nation. Except perhaps for France (which Britain and the United States would restrain), the Allies did not intend to "destroy" Germany, that is, erase it as a sovereign entity. The officers and Wilhelminian

---

109. Rupprecht Kronprinz v. Bayern, *Mein Kriegstagebuch*, diary entry of 27 July 1918, 2:428–29.

110. Schwertfeger's report, *UA* 4:2, 251; Geyer, "Insurrectionary Warfare," 482–85; Prince Max v. Baden, *Erinnerungen*, 309, 466; Rupprecht Kronprinz v. Bayern, *Mein Kriegstagebuch*, entry of 17 Oct. 1918, 2:463.

111. Matthias and Morsey, *Die Regierung*, 116–23, 205–15, 217, 226–53, 283, 398–411.

leaders who hyperbolically claimed that the Allies were out to destroy Germany were elid-ing the Kaiserreich's outmoded institutions, preeminently the army and the Kaiser's Kom-mandogewalt, with Germany, tout court.[112] These were the institutions the Allies were bent on destroying, and with them the military's status, independence, and ethos. There-fore, for officers, Endkampf was not about amelioration of the peace terms for the nation but about salvation for the military.

Consequently, Endkampf for them was not the first act of a reform government or the insurrectionary harbinger of a revolutionary age but the continuation to the death of the old habits, scripts, and assumptions of Wilhelminian military culture. These now made their final, dramatic appearance: the principled rejection of negotiation, claiming it would appear an admission of weakness or of failure to achieve military victory; the con-comitant inability to admit defeat; the narrow understanding of defeat as destruction of troops (not as the inability to prosecute the war economically or politically); the desper-ate belief that the fortunes of war (*Kriegsglück*) might turn; the personal identification with military honor; and the narrowly professional concern to save the army's and navy's reputations for the future.

Endkampf's radical quality came from taking the old ways of doing business to their logical extremes. These continuities are visible, for example, in the most concrete mea-sure for Endkampf, which came from War Minister Heinrich Scheüch. On 9 October he offered a two hundred thousand man one-time levy, and on 17 October he raised this fig-ure to over six hundred thousand. These men were to be scraped up from industry, schools, hospitals, and the premature call-up of draftees born in 1900.[113] The levy was ex-traordinary in one sense, because it committed absolutely all the reserves and required entirely shutting down the non-war-related economy. But in another sense it was simply another—albeit final—solution to Germany's chronic reserve problem, raising and train-ing men in the usual way for the front.[114] Indeed, Scheüch's predecessor, War Minister Hermann von Stein, had already made the two-hundred-thousand-man offer in June 1918, contingent on OHL's promise that the additional troops would permit Germany to win the war.[115] The drafting of every last man, at the cost of closing factories and shutting down civilian life, had already been proposed twice by the OHL, once in the Hindenburg program in 1916 and again in June 1918.[116] The police measures to enforce the six-hun-dred-thousand-man levy, that is the elimination of freedom of movement by a pass sys-tem, had been in force in the occupied territories almost from the beginning of the war. Even the recognition that Endkampf needed popular approval was a typically Wilhelmin-

---

112. The elision of military capacity with sovereignty was widespread during the war and became a major political trope during the Weimar Republic.

113. Matthias and Morsey, *Die Regierung*, 122, 226, 240, 242n58; *Amtliche Urkunden*, 90–91, 133–35, 145–46, 150.

114. Reserves: Groeber and Foreign Secretary Wilhelm Solf in smaller cabinet session of 16 Oct. 1918, *Amtliche Urkunden*, 121; Erich von Gündell, *Aus seinen Tagebüchern*, ed. Walther Obkircher (Hamburg, 1939), diary entry of 18 Oct. 1918, 292. Training: Groener in cabinet meeting of 5 Nov. 1918, *Amtliche Urkunden*, 249.

115. Ludendorff, *Urkunden*, 115; Prince Max v. Baden, *Erinnerungen*, 439–45. Solf remarked at the 17 Oct. cabinet meeting that the measure was not new: *Amtliche Urkunden*, 150.

116. OHL to Chancellor, II Nr. 877, geh. op., 18 June 1918, in Ludendorff, *Urkunden*, 108.

312   ian half-measure; instead of democracy or plebiscites, proponents wanted a carefully or-chestrated patriotic announcement from the Kaiser, the chancellor, and the Reichstag.[117]

For the military, Endkampf thus meant simply the continuation of the war and its ad hoc measures. It was the culmination of a series of small, unremarkable steps. Neverthe-less, Endkampf risked complete destruction. Was the military serious, or just bluffing? How far was it prepared to take (self-)destruction?

As early as 10 October, some cabinet members thought Endkampf was a bluff, a way for the military to claim they had tried to continue the war but had been blocked, and thus to shift the blame for losing the war from the army to the new government.[118] Histo-rians are still divided, though most modern accounts tend to doubt OHL's sincerity.[119] There are good reasons for skepticism. Endkampf seems hard to reconcile with Luden-dorff's call for an immediate armistice. Ludendorff rejected Scheüch's first offer of troops to make Endkampf possible.[120] Ludendorff could risk big talk because after mid-October he could count more and more on being stopped by the cabinet's scrupulousness. And most important, the mere bluff of the Endkampf that never happened was enough to launch the hugely successful "stab-in-the-back" myth that saved the army's reputation and poisoned the democratic Weimar Republic.[121]

However, many factors indicate that Ludendorff was serious about the Endkampf. The possibility of fighting on if the Allies refused to treat with Germany or offered a bad armistice or peace terms was present in OHL's plans from the beginning.[122] Hintze had had to argue with Ludendorff against the idea on 29 September, when Ludendorff made his armistice announcement.[123] Ludendorff had instructed Major v. d. Bussche to outline the Endkampf possibility to Reichstag leaders, which he did on 2 October.[124] Ludendorff also discussed Endkampf privately with Gen. Ernst von Eisenhart-Rothe, and with Colonels v. Thaer and v. Haeften on various days from 29 September to 1 October. He told Thaer, "If we win some rest by the armistice, or if the enemy is too impertinent in its demands, or if some other possibility appears to improve our situation by bitter fighting, then, believe me, we will fight to the utmost."[125]

In the first half of October, Endkampf for Ludendorff was probably more a consola-tion than a plan. He had called for an immediate armistice because he feared an imminent

---

117. Matthias and Morsey, *Die Regierung*, cabinet meeting of 28 Oct. 1918, 402, 406, 407; Payer, *Von Beth-mann Hollweg*, 142.

118. Solf and Roedern in cabinet meeting of 10 Oct. 1918, Matthias and Morsey, *Die Regierung*, 127.

119. Serious: Foerster, *Ludendorff*, 88, 97, 129; Reichsarchiv, *Weltkrieg*, 14:631–32; Goerlitz, *Kleine Geschichte*, 210–11, 212, 214; Geyer, "Insurrectionary Warfare," 494. (Probably) bluffing: Kaehler, "Vier quellenkritische Un-tersuchungen," 432; Klein, *Deutschland*, 3:440, 470, 473; Erdmann, *Der Erste Weltkrieg*, 138; Kitchen, *Silent Dicta-torship*, 265; Chickering, *Imperial Germany*, 189–90.

120. Prince Max v. Baden, *Erinnerungen*, 449n1.

121. Ludendorff claimed that "only the revolution" had hindered Endkampf: Kuhl's report, *UA* 4:3, 215; Wild, *Briefe*, letter of 5 Nov. 1918, 249.

122. Klein, *Deutschland*, 3:432.

123. Foerster, *Ludendorff*, 90–91.

124. *Amtliche Urkunden*, 66–68.

125. Quote: Thaer diary, 30 Sept. 1918, *Generalstabsdienst*, 236; Eisenhart-Rothe, *Im Banne der Persönlichkeit*, 122–25; Prince Max v. Baden, *Erinnerungen*, diary entry of 2 Oct. 1918, 340.

Allied breakthrough and the consequent destruction of the German army. He held to this view until around 14 October. On the 10th, the new foreign Secretary, Wilhelm Solf, reported that Ludendorff still believed the army could not hold out for three months. Ludendorff therefore pressed the reluctant cabinet to accede to President Wilson's demand to evacuate the occupied territories, which it did in the German reply of 12 October.[126] A quick evacuation would have made Endkampf impossible. But Ludendorff and Hindenburg thought Wilson would permit a slow retreat during which the army and its equipment could be safely brought back to the German border where it would stand ready to take up the fight again, if peace or armistice terms were unacceptable.[127]

Two factors in mid-October moved Ludendorff to back off his admission of 29 September. The most important, as Ludendorff told the cabinet on 17 October, was that the Allies had not mounted the breakthrough he had feared, from which he concluded that they were war-weary themselves and incapable of doing so. The "crisis" on the western front was over, he claimed, and if Germany held out for another four weeks, it would be "out of the woods."[128] The second factor was Wilson's note of 14 October, his second. It said the Allies would determine the timing of evacuation (which would doubtless be quick); it demanded an end to the "illegal and inhumane practices" of the destructive retreat in Belgium and France; it required Germany to stop its only offensive weapon, the submarine; and it repeated Wilson's determination "to destroy every arbitrary power anywhere."[129] For Ludendorff, these demands were "nothing more or less than putting down one's arms and unconditional capitulation."[130] He advised the cabinet on 17 October to continue to seek an armistice, but to counter these demands with a strong note, while preparing the public to continue the war.[131] A week later he and Hindenburg rejected Wilson's third note, and with it the possibility of an armistice, demanding a fight to the end. The chancellor and cabinet refused; the Kaiser supported them and accepted Ludendorff's, but not Hindenburg's, resignation on 26 October.

This chronology suggests that Ludendorff's insight of 29 September was a momentary doubt, not a genuine recognition of facts.[132] It was so at odds with his usual thinking that he was unable to hold on to it for more than two weeks. The widespread suspicion among the officer corps that it had been due to an attack of nerves was their way of expressing the same judgment.[133] In embracing Endkampf, its proponents reverted to the logic of military culture. Its unreality did not hinder proponents from making the sugges-

---

126. *Amtliche Urkunden*, 92, 97; Gündell, *Tagebüchern*, 289–90.

127. Report of Berckheim to Foreign Office, General Headquarters, 11 Oct. 1918, *Amtliche Urkunden*, 96.

128. *Amtliche Urkunden*, 138, 139, 148, 150; Matthias and Morsey, *Die Regierung*, 251.

129. Wilson Note of 14 Oct. 1918, U.S. State Department, *Papers Relating to the Foreign Relations*, Supplement 1, vol. 1: 359.

130. Admiral Levetzow's summary of Ludendorff's views in a memo on the cabinet meeting of 17 Oct. 1918, at which Levetzow was present, cited in Foerster, *Ludendorff*, 111.

131. *Amtliche Urkunden*, 150.

132. Even Hindenburg had once (March 1915) doubted whether Germany could defeat its enemies militarily, though he quickly recovered his adamantine optimism: Janssen, *Der Kanzler*, 90–91, 90n23.

133. Ferguson claims (incredibly) that Germany's defeat was due to Ludendorff's nervous admission: Niall Ferguson, *The Pity of War* (New York, 1998), 310–14.

314   tion seriously, since it proposed a continuation of usual war conduct, not a break with it. Furthermore, it was no more unreal than unrestricted submarine warfare or the March offensive(s). And nobody had ever promised it would succeed (which is why the chancellor and cabinet rejected it).

Endkampf reprised the old thinking and assumptions. It built on what Schwertfeger later called the myth of the impregnability of the western front, that is, the fact that it had held so far meant it could hold indefinitely.[134] Behind that myth was the much larger one, that Germany had not really been defeated. Michael Geyer, and before him Fritz Klein and Joachim Petzold, have argued that the military leadership did indeed admit Germany's defeat and that historians should be wary of seeming to give credence to the stab-in-the-back legend by imagining that they did not.[135] Yet even the admission of 29 September was only partial. Although Ludendorff said from one side of his mouth that Germany was "militarily finished," apparently it was not entirely defeated. The armistice, he told his staff, was designed to save the army from "final defeat."[136] For "defeat" still meant military destruction on the battlefield, which officers (and civilians) imagined à la Schlieffen as the result of breakthrough, encirclement, and annihilation.[137] That is why Ludendorff's successor, Gen. Wilhelm Groener, was still repeating to the cabinet on 5 November (six days before the armistice) that OHL's "first duty is and will remain to avoid a decisive defeat of the army."[138] It was in this Schlieffen sense that Germany was undefeated, and this operative sense was what had always counted for the old officer corps, not the strategic (political and economic) sense.

If Ludendorff had truly accepted Germany's strategic defeat, it is hard to see how he could have imagined that the Allies would permit Germany to keep its huge eastern gains (except for Romania); to withdraw at leisure in the west, keeping its army at full fighting strength; and to appear at the peace conference as an equal negotiating partner. Yet that is what he and apparently most officers believed.[139] As it was, the lack of a "decisive defeat" was enough to allow the old illusions to surge back. The arguments for Endkampf were replete with the old errors: underestimating the enemy, overestimating oneself, projecting one's methods onto the enemy, and so forth. For example, Ludendorff denied to the end the importance of Allied matériel and manpower superiority. He allowed that the Allies had more tanks and trucks, but told the cabinet (9 October) that he hoped to have six hundred tanks by spring 1919 and he "did not believe that other forms of superiority were dangerous."[140] Asked on the 17th about American reinforcements, Ludendorff discounted them, even though he knew that the six-hundred-thousand-man call-up would face 1.1

134. Schwertfeger's report, *UA* 4:2, 276–80. This is the same use of history as positive feedback that Hindenburg and Ludendorff adduced to silence critics such as Thaer about the March offensive.

135. Geyer, "Insurrectionary Warfare," 462–64; Klein, *Deutschland*, 3:431–32.

136. Thaer, *Generalstabsdienst*, 233, 234.

137. Niemann, *Kaiser und Revolution*, 122; Kronprinz Wilhelm v. Preussen, *Erinnerungen*, 229; "Auffassung der Lage," Political Section of OHL, 6 Oct. 1918, in Reichsarchiv, *Weltkrieg*, 14:661; Matthias and Morsey, *Die Regierung*, 211 and 246 (Haussmann), 340 (Friedberg), 373 (Scheüch), 402 (Gallwitz).

138. Matthias and Morsey, *Die Regierung*, 530.

139. Berckheim to Foreign Office, General Headquarters, 11 Oct. 1918, *Amtliche Urkunden*, 96.

140. Matthias and Morsey, *Die Regierung*, 121–22.

million fresh American troops.[141] So convinced was OHL that the Schlieffen break-through was the only way to fight that it misinterpreted the Allies' "bite-and-hold" tactics as proof that they were unable to prosecute a winning campaign.[142] In their last instructions to the German armistice commission on 23 October, Ludendorff and Hindenburg even indulged once more the fond dream of splitting the Allies and defeating them individually. They thought France and Britain would insist on such harsh armistice terms that Wilson would refuse further American military aid. OHL accounted Germany's chances against Britain and France alone as "not at all hopeless, especially if Belgium also breaks down and the war is limited to the German-French border."[143] Five days later, General v. Gallwitz was still repeating to the cabinet the old hope to which the officer corps had been clinging since at least April 1918: one last concerted effort would cause the war-weary Allies to sue for peace.[144] Endkampf understood cognitively was thus merely another repetition of the standard assumptions, methods, and problem-solving techniques, and it was by no means limited to Ludendorff.

However, Endkampf exceeded the usual by realizing the full extent of destruction and objectification of civilians that military practices contained as potentials. We have already seen that military necessity "required" the total destruction and evacuation of a wide strip of northern France during "Alberich" in 1917. Endkampf now elevated these means to the end. Total destruction would not simply hinder the Allied military advance, it would make it unthinkable, because Belgium and France would not be liberated but annihilated. "Through the fault of the Entente the occupied areas will be given over to devastation [*Verwüstung*]," declared the political section of OHL on 6 October 1918.[145]

This sort of destruction had already begun in August. Ludendorff interrupted it with his order of 30 September that suspended destruction of housing while armistice negotiations proceeded. But once Ludendorff felt the "crisis" on the western front had passed, he returned to total devastation. The general explained to the cabinet on 17 October what conduct of the war in preparation for Endkampf entailed. First, "The general-government of Belgium must become part of the rear echelon," which would strip it of the protections it had hitherto enjoyed and place it directly under military control. Next, Ludendorff proposed expelling the Committee for the Relief of Belgium, which would be told:

> Do not send any more food. That will have a good effect in Belgium. In Tournai the population did not want to leave [be deported], because they thought that peace was now going to come. That idea cannot be allowed to crop up: one has to say to Belgium, peace is a long way off and the horror [*das Furchtbare*] of war can

141. Prince Max v. Baden, *Erinnerungen*, 437.

142. Geyer, "Insurrectionary Warfare," 468.

143. "Anweisung für die Waffenstillstandskommission," 23 Oct. 1918, *Amtliche Urkunden*, 191.

144. Matthias and Morsey, *Die Regierung*, 402. War Minister Scheüch had also indulged this illusion two days earlier, 368, 373.

145. "Auffassung der Lage," Political Section of OHL, 6 Oct. 1918, Reichsarchiv, *Weltkrieg*, 14:661, also cited in Geyer, "Insurrectionary Warfare," 474. See, too, Bernhard Schwertfeger's article in early Nov. 1918 saying the same thing (Geyer, "Insurrectionary Warfare," 495), and Rupprecht's statement of 27 July, cited earlier.

316   also happen in Belgium, compared to which 1914 will be mere child's play. One knows that even when commanders try hard, they cannot prevent all four million people [of the German army] from engaging in acts of violence.

After complaining that not destroying houses was already militarily "irresponsible," Ludendorff explained that the CRB had to end because Germany was already breaking the contract: "Troops are quartering themselves and taking the cow from the field and food from the house. They have no choice."[146]

Ludendorff in October 1918 was in the same position as General v. Trotha had been in October 1904. The practice of unlimited violence was already occurring; he proposed to make it explicit policy.[147] Endkampf embraced the horror of war against "peace foolishness" (*Friedensduselei*)[148] and widened that horror in extent (making Belgium a battle zone) and degree (plunging the Belgian population into starvation, fighting a war in its midst, and visiting uncontrolled acts of individual terror against it). Endkampf used the civilian population as hostages to achieve its goals.[149] The tactic of 1870 had become widespread practice during the war and now was elevated to a wonder weapon against defeat.[150]

Destruction of occupied territory was one thing, but the destruction of Germany was another. Whether one should risk national destruction by fighting inside Germany seems to have depended on how one defined the goal of Endkampf. If one aimed to force better peace terms, then clearly one stopped Endkampf at the border. This was the position of the chancellor, the cabinet, the Foreign Office, and many officers (for example, Colonel Heye and Generals Bruno v. Mudra and Max v. Gallwitz).[151] Ludendorff and Hindenburg always gave the cabinet the impression that fighting would not reach Germany, but it is hard to gauge what they really thought.[152] Prince Max suspected that Ludendorff believed fighting would eventually occur on Germany's borders or inside them.[153] OHL's last instructions to the armistice commission (23 October) suggest that, while they preferred "resuming the war in Belgium and before Metz," they thought it possible that Germany

146. Matthias and Morsey, *Die Regierung*, 240–41; cf. Geyer, "Insurrectionary Warfare," 497.

147. In the 23 Oct. 1918 statement, in which Ludendorff sketched some of the features of an "intensified" continuation of the war, he specifically mentions two things, both of which meant returning to older practices: dropping the post–30 Sept. limits on destruction of civilian infrastructure and reactivating unrestricted submarine warfare (which the government had agreed to halt on 21 Oct.). Reichsarchiv, *Weltkrieg*, 14:671.

148. Ludendorff, in Prince Max v. Baden, *Erinnerungen*, 444.

149. Geyer, "Insurrectionary Warfare," 495.

150. Recall Ludendorff's proposal in 1917 to use the forty thousand inhabitants of St. Quentin (France) to prevent Allied shelling of that part of the Siegfried line. Colonel v. Haeften had to talk Ludendorff out of "terror attacks on London" on 8 Oct. 1918. Klein, *Deutschland*, 3:467.

151. Matthias and Morsey, *Die Regierung*, 217, 243–46, 339, 405–7; Kaehler, "Vier quellenkritische Untersuchungen," 435; telephone conversation between Haniel and Foreign Office representative to the OHL Kurt Baron v. Lersner, 25 Oct. 1918, in *Amtliche Urkunden*, 199; Gallwitz, *Erleben im Westen*, 423; Böhm, *Adjutant*, 38; Matthias and Morsey, *Die Regierung*, 403.

152. Matthias and Morsey, *Die Regierung*, 118, 205, 244.

153. Prince Max v. Baden, *Erinnerungen*, 395. Groener in July or August favored fighting even behind the Rhine, but by November he had changed his mind; *Lebenserinnerungen*, 436, 446–47.

might fight on the border "under very undesirable circumstances (war in one's own land, heavy loss of iron and steel production, endangerment of the entire war industry of western Germany, a difficult transportation situation)."[154] But there is nothing to indicate that they rejected this possibility.[155] After the war, Rupprecht's chief of staff, Kuhl, admitted that German troops would have had to retreat to the border and then to the Rhine fortifications, destroying everything on the left bank of the Rhine. But typically, a few pages later, Kuhl seems to retract the admission.[156]

It seems likely that the widespread flirtation with the Endkampf idea among officers was not any more realistic about actual costs than had been true of "planning" for some time. But that does not mean they were unprepared to risk it. For much of the motivation for Endkampf was not about planning and policy but about honor and humiliation. Vice-chancellor Friedrich von Payer described the arguments that Ludendorff, General Hoffmann, Colonel Heye, and Admirals Ernst Ritter von Mann (secretary of the Naval Office) and Reinhard Scheer (chief of the Admiralty) made at the 17 October cabinet meeting: "There were lots of hopes and fears, surmises and reckonings, that were half-reasonably, half-emotionally expressed, but then taken back or otherwise contradicted; they gave no satisfactory basis for an objective judgment."[157] On the 25th Ludendorff and Hindenburg made a last attempt to convince the government to adopt the Endkampf. Accompanied by Admiral Scheer and War Minister Scheüch, they met with Payer because Prince Max was in bed with influenza. Again Payer noted the unusual use of emotional words such as "dishonorable" and "disgrace." When he repeatedly pressed them about whether continued fighting would bring better armistice or peace terms, he received "no direct answer."[158]

Payer had discovered that army and naval officers could not politically or militarily defend their emotionally motivated plan. They wanted to fight the Endkampf to preserve what they called "honor." Partly, honor signified the personal identification of each officer with his corporate status-group, or *Stand*. Understood this way, it had a reactionary political valence. But honor was also the term used to sum up all those professional characteristics and expectations of the proper officer that the military culture had worked out over decades of trial and error. Defeat and armistice were so thoroughly incompatible with these expectations that it is hardly surprising to see honor reemerge as the emotional weapon to reassert one last time the worth of the whole enterprise. Honor was always a guide in bad times, and no times were worse than these. Honor was therefore a shorthand formula standing for the entire way of thinking that had just failed, so it was not, as Payer sharply observed, an actual argument; it substituted for one.

In difficult situations military honor drifted toward self-destruction. We have seen this in the exemplary case of Captain Klein in SWA. The same maxim reappeared often during the World War, now not only for individuals but for a larger "we." Falkenhayn, for

---

154. *Amtliche Urkunden*, 192.

155. Geyer, "Insurrectionary Warfare," 499.

156. Kuhl, *Weltkrieg*, 2:506, 511. Gallwitz foresaw war inside Germany if it agreed to evacuate the occupied zones; *Erleben im Westen*, 410.

157. Payer, *Von Bethmann Hollweg*, 133.

158. Ibid., 141–44.

318 example, had told an American journalist in January 1915, "If we shall go under in this war . . . then we shall do so with honor, by relinquishing not a foot of territory and fighting to the last man."[159] Einem's reaction to the launching of USW in January 1917 was almost identical: "We will defend ourselves [including against America] and then go down with honor."[160] When Wild heard that Austria had capitulated, his first response was, "Then we had better go down with honor!"[161] The self-destruction of the Endkampf was therefore well prepared, if unintentionally. It began with accepting death for one's person, then as appropriate for one's corps, and it had expanded to include the entire army. Ludendorff's fighting retreat since July 1918 had already shown his disdain for the unnecessary German casualties. On 31 October Ludendorff wrote that he was prepared in the Endkampf "to risk actual defeat," meaning a Schlieffen-type annihilation of the German army on the battlefield.[162] Cabinet members thought this was no empty threat, and it seems likely that many high-ranking officers preferred "actual defeat" to capitulation.[163] Equating the army with the nation, a widespread position, suggested the next step: national suicide. But few officers appear to have been ready to take that step in autumn 1918. Ludendorff gave it voice, however: "A people that accepts humiliation and conditions that destroy its existence without having done its utmost is ruined. If it is forced to do the same after making a last, extreme exertion, then it will live."[164]

Although not all officers supported the Endkampf (Crown Prince Rupprecht rejected it out of hand as useless and harmful because Germany had, in fact, been defeated),[165] it appears that some version of it enjoyed wide support among high-ranking officers.[166] Even after Ludendorff had been dismissed on 26 October, the two generals whom the cabinet had called for advice, Generals v. Gallwitz and v. Mudra, defended the Endkampf. More straightforward than Ludendorff, they admitted that Germany's chances were slim if Austria signed the armistice (which it did on 3 November). But significantly, after they had left the meeting and conferred together, they informed the cabinet that they had been too pessimistic.[167] Their retraction says a great deal about the pressure officers felt to go against their reason in the direction of risk and destruction.

The cabinet and Reichstag stopped the Endkampf, though it lived on in powerful myths and interwar planning.[168] The navy, however, launched its version of the Endkampf. The navy's last battle, of course, was considerably less radical than the army's, because the glorious deaths would have been confined to the sailors, not spread to civilians

159. Afflerbach, *Falkenhayn*, 263.

160. Diary entry of 3 Feb. 1917, cited in Wild, *Briefe*, 247n6.

161. Wild, *Briefe*, letter of 5 Nov. 1918, 249.

162. Ludendorff note of 31 Oct. 1918, Schwertfeger's report, *UA* 4:2, 365.

163. Conrad Haussmann on 17 Oct., Matthias and Morsey, *Die Regierung*, 246; Kaehler, "Vier quellenkritische Untersuchungen," 436.

164. Ludendorff note of 31 Oct. 1918, cited in Schwertfeger's report, *UA* 4:2, 367.

165. Rupprecht Kronprinz v. Bayern, *Mein Kriegstagebuch*, diary entries of 17 and 30 Oct. 1918, 2:463, 469.

166. Kaehler, "Vier quellenkritische Untersuchungen," 436.

167. Payer, *Von Bethmann Hollweg*, 145.

168. Geyer, "Insurrectionary Warfare."

and possibly to Germany. Nonetheless, the navy's action shows how acceptable self-destruction had become among the German military.

The navy and the army had been arguing with a single voice since 1916 when Falkenhayn embraced unrestricted submarine warfare. Both services clung to the old logic of ultimate risk/ultimate force. The navy was as loath to admit the defeat of USW as the army was to admit its own defeat on land. As late as the cabinet meeting of 17 October, Admiral Scheer repeated the claim that sooner or later USW would "be politically effective."[169] The navy had also steadily produced ever more radical plans that were the reverse image of its actual strength. In July 1918 the admiralty twice proposed increasing USW by extending the blockade to the coast of the United States. The navy was prepared to risk a cascade of war declarations by the neutral states that mostly steamed these waters, even though only three U-boats were available to enforce the blockade![170] The Kaiser, guided by reasonable arguments from the Foreign Office and two years of failed submarine policy, rejected this idea. He and the chancellor also rejected (28 July 1918) the proposal to attack the British fleet in the English Channel.[171] This hopeless enterprise returned to the "single battle of annihilation" that, like the Schlieffen Plan for the army, had been the basic doctrine of Tirpitz's battle fleet and the founding assumption behind naval officer training and socialization.[172] In October 1918 naval leaders dusted off this plan to show that the battle fleet (as opposed to submarines) had, in fact, been useful to the war effort and deserved future appropriations.[173] They did not aim to send the German navy to a glorious doom, but they were prepared to risk it. Captain Michaelis summed up the navy's thinking: "I know it is a pure risk, but if there is no alternative, then a risk is justified. If it succeeds, then I'm convinced everything has been won; if it fails, nothing more is lost than is the case anyway without it."[174] No one at OHL could have put the pure risk theory better, or have demonstrated more succinctly the blindness caused by identifying the interests of one's own service with those of the nation. The naval command went ahead and ordered the last battle without the approval of either the Kaiser or the chancellor. Only the sailors' revolt, which ushered in the revolution, stopped it. The suicidal aspect of the plan, however, was carried out in spite of everything, when the skeleton crews sank the German fleet after it had surrendered at Scapa Flow.[175]

The Endkampf had to be stopped by external intervention, from the cabinet, the Reichstag, and popular revolt. Inside the military the pressure to repeat violence through to annihilation seemed almost irresistible. In this process the end, which had once been victory, had now become death. The means had become the end.

---

169. Prince Max v. Baden, *Erinnerungen*, 439–40.

170. Schwertfeger's report, *UA* 4:2, 347, 349–52.

171. Ibid., 212.

172. Gross, "Eine Frage der Ehre?" 353–54, 358–59; Holger Herwig, *"Luxury Fleet"* (London, 1980).

173. Gross, "Eine Frage der Ehre?"

174. Michaelis to Levetzow, Berlin, 5 Oct. 1918, cited in Gross, "Eine Frage der Ehre?" 355n32. See also Prince Max v. Baden, *Erinnerungen*, 574–75.

175. Gross, "Eine Frage der Ehre?" 365; Andreas Krause, *Scapa Flow* (Berlin, 1999).

Allied Comparisons

No comparative study of war conduct (*Kriegführung*) exists for the First World War.[176] It is only possible here to offer some observations about how Germany might fit into such a comparison with its fellow belligerents. The broadly shared military culture of Western armies plus the length and difficulty of the war produced many basic similarities in conduct. All the officer corps seemed to learn slowly: they remained fixated on numbers and for a long time on clinging to territory; they indulged in staggering human "wastage"; and they continued to champion the same sorts of soldierly virtues as they had before 1914.[177] Tim Travers found that, in addition to these similarities, the British and French armies shared a number of characteristics, among them a personalized system of advancement, devotion to the cult of the offensive, discouragement of criticism and innovation at higher command levels, and stifling hierarchy.[178] Like most historians, Travers is struck by the greater adaptability and tactical effectiveness of the German army, which means he underestimates how much the doctrinal hegemony of the offensive and hierarchical drag also marked it. In Germany criticism and innovation were generally limited to the tactical level and occurred where the patterns of military culture permitted, but not generally and not strategically.

All of the belligerent armies (and governments) interpreted international law in ways most favorable to their own armed strengths and the new technologies that they successfully developed. Thus, Britain engaged in an illegal naval blockade and France accepted "terror" as a legitimate goal in exercising its relative air superiority over Germany.[179] But Britain continued to show more spontaneous interest in and respect for international law than Germany, which is why Allied propaganda could so successfully use allegations of war crimes for popular mobilization.[180] Britain rejected the French argument about air terror, for example, and it managed the blockade against neutral shipping as gently as possible.[181] Nonetheless, an estimated seven hundred thousand German civilians died directly or indirectly as a result of the Allied blockade. In Germany, sensitivity to international law centered institutionally in the Foreign Office as an effect of concern about foreign public opinion. But the Foreign Office had so thoroughly accepted the dictum of military necessity that it was a weak and uncertain bulwark against military pressure. Occasionally a minister or secretary would raise international law objections to a proposed

---

176. The prosecution of the war has been more fully studied regarding economic mobilization, technological development, and more recently the experience of trench warfare.

177. David French, "The Strategy of Unlimited Warfare?" in *Great War, Total War*, ed. Chickering and Förster, 281–95; David Stevenson, "French Strategy on the Western Front, 1914–1918," in *Great War, Total War*, 297–326.

178. Tim Travers, *The Killing Ground* (London, 1993), 253–57. Travers also lists lack of heavy artillery and poor coordination of artillery and infantry; the latter was true of the German army until far into the war.

179. Christian Geinitz, "The First Air War against Noncombatants," in *Great War, Total War*, 207–25, here 213.

180. Horne and Kramer, "German 'Atrocities,'" 10, 32.

181. Geinitz, "First Air War," 214; Paul C. Vincent, *The Politics of Hunger* (Athens, Ohio, 1985), 35, 38–39, 44.

policy, but they did so unreliably and with less success as time went on.[182] The weakness of institutions meant that the strongest opposition to military contravention of international law tended to come from individuals, like the much maligned Governor-General Bissing, who acted from conscience.

It is still uncertain how Germany's treatment of prisoners of war compares with that of other belligerents.[183] On the one hand, POWs interned by Germany had a good overall survival rate that compared favorably with that of POWs captured by France and Britain.[184] On the other, the Reichstag committee that investigated Allied charges produced a vigorously critical minority report.[185] The Geneva Convention had found greater sympathy in German military circles than had other international agreements. Nevertheless, no prewar planning for prisoners occurred (nor did it among the Allies), and no central coordinating office was ever established, so the same variation from camp commander to camp commander occurred here as in occupation policy and in the various military districts in Germany. Provisioning was terrible at both the beginning and the end of the war and may have been worse than what poor planning and the blockade accounted for. In terms of prewar planning, the pattern of provisioning shortfalls, lack of coordination, and the use of some POW laborers under harsh conditions, the German pattern seems like the Russian, but with a much lower mortality rate.[186] Discipline in the German camps was harsh and had the same punitive quality that characterized the treatment of occupied civilians, and prisoners of war were instrumentalized in the same way for labor.[187] There were persistent reports that Russian and Romanian prisoners of war were treated worse, not only in the east where the infrastructure hampered provisioning, but in the west, where they were used as laborers.[188] It is unclear how this situation compares with severe violations of the Geneva Convention by Italy, Bulgaria, and others.[189] Britain (which had many fewer prisoners to worry about) and France both appear to have treated German prisoners fairly well.[190]

Concerning treatment of enemy civilians under occupation, the western Allies had little chance to demonstrate how they would have behaved.[191] Germany's ally Austria built

---

182. Stenzel, _Kriegführung_, 51–52. Arnold Wahnschaffe welcomed potential Russian violations of law so he could justify deportation as reprisal: Geiss, _Der polnische Grenzstreifen_, 77–78; but Minister of the Interior Friedrich Wilhelm v. Loebell opposed the recruitment of Polish soldiers because it violated international law, 117–18.

183. As this manuscript was finished, Uta Hinz's study of POWs had not yet appeared.

184. Rachamimov, _POWs_, 107, citing Prussian War Ministry statistics.

185. _UA_ 3:3.1 and 3.2, minority report: 3:3.1, 24–27. Robert Jackson's research in _The Prisoners_ confirms the minority report, while Bruno Thoss wrote recently that German treatment was "comparatively decent"; "Militärische Entscheidung und politisch-gesellschaftlicher Umbruch," in _Kriegsende 1918_, 17–37, here 32.

186. Rachamimov, _POWs_, 48–56, 93–96, 108–14.

187. Stenzel, _Kriegführung_, 49; minority report, _UA_ 3:3.1, 24–25.

188. Jackson, _Prisoners_, 42, 48; Hoffman, _In the Prison Camps of Germany_, 119–20; Strazhas, _Deutsche Ostpolitik_, 24–25.

189. István Deák, _Beyond Nationalism_ (Oxford, 1990), 203; _Violations of the Laws_, 56; Mitrany, _Effect of the War_, 150–51.

190. Jackson, _Prisoners_, 138–40.

191. Horne and Kramer believe that "differences in past experience and mentality" would have caused the Allies to react differently: _German Atrocities_, 424.

322   civilian expertise into its occupation administrations and pursued occupation more systematically and professionally than did Germany. Austria handled its occupied Poles with more sensitivity and success than Germany did, though the occupation was still oppressive. The Austrian occupation of Serbia was much harsher, particularly in its political repression and massive economic exploitation. Nevertheless, the most recent study concludes that the principles of the bureaucratic *Rechtsstaat*, visible in the army's autonomous interest in international law, limited the violence there.[192] The Austrian occupation did not reach the same extremes as Germany's occupation of northern France.[193] Russia's scorched earth retreats and mass deportations (of its own population!) are indeed comparable to those of Germany and were perhaps signs of Russia's own impending experiment with extremes in the Soviet Union.

The predominance of the military over the political that had distinguished Germany from other countries before the war increased after 1914 and produced the main systematic differences between Germany's conduct of the war and that of other countries. Nowhere else did the General Staff run the war. Typically, other militaries enjoyed their greatest reach of power at the beginning of the conflict. As things soured, the political branch made a resurgence. Germany went the opposite way, leaving the field free for its military peculiarities to luxuriate even further. Stalemate in the west seduced all the armies into focusing narrowly on tactics, for example, but none inflated tactics to the level of operations or even strategy, as occurred in Germany.[194] British Field Marshal Douglas Haig represented the opposite tendency; he underestimated the operative success of the tactics the Allies had devised in summer and fall of 1918. Both the British and French armies displayed a livelier sense of their limitations: they could conceive of losing a battle, they did not underestimate their enemy.[195] They were also more economical or realistic about their resources, apparently on their own, not simply because of political intervention. Although it took until spring 1918, the Allies also achieved much better coordination among their armies; that is, they were less solipsistic.[196] Their armies and navies also appear to have worked together better. Finally, one misses among the Allies the same repetitive move or urge to self-destruction. The potential may have existed, however, visible in the repeated failed offensives both Britain and France undertook for three years. But by fall 1917 the French army mutinies had led to political intervention that stopped this repetition; British politics finally hindered it without being prodded by mutiny. We cannot know how France or Britain would have reacted to impending defeat. Would their desperation have produced an equivalent to Endkampf? Perhaps, given the potential of modern militaries at that time to go to the limit of force. But an Allied Endkampf would likely

---

192. Jonathan Gumz, "'Streams of Violence in the Land of Milk and Honey'" (Ph.D. diss., University of Chicago, 2003), introduction accessed 4 July 2003 at cas.uchicago.edu/workshops/meurhist/paper.pdf, pp. 6, 14, 16–20. Aviel Roshwald disagrees: *Ethnic Nationalism and the Fall of Empires* (New York, 2001), 125–26.

193. Basler, *Deutschlands Annexionspolitik*, 112–13n106; Hugo Kerchnawe et al., *Die Militärverwaltung in den von österreich-ungarischen Truppen besetzten Gebieten* (New Haven, 1928), 19–21, 53–268, esp. 57–58 on administrative principles.

194. Strachan, "From Cabinet War," 31.

195. Burchhardt, *Friedenswirtschaft*, 248; David Stevenson, "French Strategy," 324.

196. Thoss, "Militärische Entscheidung," 28–29.

have been more firmly anchored in a popular uprising, such as the one that occurred in France in 1870. It would have been a *levée en masse* instead of a General Staff scheme to continue the old destructive tactics to the point of self-annihilation.

There were four kinds of constraints that operated against the tendencies within the German military to run to extremes. First, Germany reacted to international pressure, which was usually expressed in the language of international law. It altered military policy according to such objections when it recognized that the war effort might be more harmed by international reaction than it was helped by the policy. Submarine warfare in 1914–16 and the Belgian deportations are two examples. It is typical that both cases were reactive; the policies were launched despite foreknowledge of heavy objection to them, and then they were annulled.

A second constraint came from political considerations funneled mostly through civilian government or the Reichstag. These were most successful against the junior service, the navy, and before the third OHL, after which civilian self-confidence collapsed. Even before August 1916, however, civilians readily acquiesced to the disabilities produced by the military's high status in Germany and they never dared to contradict "military necessity."

The weakness of civilian constraints also weakened critics within the military itself, the third type of restriction. Governor-General Bissing, abandoned by Bethmann Hollweg, is a good example of this. Of course the imperative command system common to all militaries was probably the greatest overt hindrance to successful internal criticism. But the more subtle disincentives located in the expectations of military culture were equally strong, both in promoting "institutional blindness" (*Betriebsblindheit*) and in discouraging "pessimism." OHL's secretive information policy relieved even army commanders of responsibility to judge policy according to the entire situation, of which they were kept ignorant.

And finally, there were circumstantial constraints: lack of time (to destroy northern France more thoroughly in 1918), lack of resources (to build more submarines to produce a truly unlimited submarine warfare), failing troop morale and civilian support (for the Endkampf), and so forth.[197] The weakness of the first three constraints strongly suggests that, had the fourth not operated, the German military might have reached far greater extremes in World War I.

197. Herwig, "Total Rhetoric," 206.

Conclusions and Implications

Imperial Germany and its military culture exemplify Hannah Arendt's insight that "the danger of violence, even if it moves consciously within a nonextremist framework of short-term goals, will always be that the means overwhelm the end."[1] In the Kaiserreich, that is exactly what happened. The institutional locus of violence as means (to political ends) in the state is the military. By examining how that institution operated, I have tried to demonstrate how and why the means might come to displace the end or, to put it another way, how and why the institution designed to wield controlled violence exceeded the reasonable, effective, or goal-oriented limits to its use.

A study of institutional extremes is therefore a study of limits and their transgression. Most explanations for the kind of massive state-sanctioned violence we have been examining have concentrated on the transgressive aspect. They ask what impels organizations, groups, or leaders to use excessive violence, and they often find the answers in ideology (like racism or imperialism, which we will discuss below). In ideologically driven systems, extremes are contained as ends or goals in the motivating ideas themselves, and thus the means stay subordinate to the ends, giving the extreme results a seeming Weberian rationality. The Imperial German case shows that militaries, because violence is their business, do not need external ideologies or motivations to encourage excess; their task and the doctrines, habits, and basic assumptions (the military culture) they develop to handle it may be sufficient in themselves. Even a defined (and therefore limited) goal—of crushing a revolt, for example—can be enough to trigger a procedural dynamic ending in genocide. In such cases, the rationality of extreme actions develops from the means, not from the original end or goal.

---

1. Arendt, *On Violence*, 80.

If we allow that military institutions, at least in the late nineteenth and early twentieth centuries, contained the transgressive within them, then our attention turns away from the drive to excess and instead toward the limits and why they failed. There were limits to excess internal to the military, based on humanitarian, practical, political, legal, and other considerations. But the military culture arising from the "strong" organization made it very hard for even critically minded, high-ranking officers to buck the scripts and deeply ingrained expectations that constituted "military necessity." Therefore, the main effective limits to excess lay outside the military, in government, politics, law, and public opinion. These could reinstate the superiority of the (limited) ends to the means. In Imperial Germany, these forces were too weak—or unwilling—to do this. That is what distinguished Germany from other European states and what sustained and intensified its particular military culture.

Germany's military culture developed inside a threefold vacuum. First, the constitution shielded it from civilian oversight and external criticism. Second, the constitution and the political system provided little coordination among agencies, which led to ministerial particularism and reinforced the military's solipsism. Finally, after Bismarck's fall, the government barely provided a coherent policy (foreign or otherwise) that might have guided or countered the drift of military activity.

The First World War is a splendid example. Having entered the war without war aims, Germany's leadership did not dare expose domestic political disharmony by setting goals with which the left or center-right inevitably would have disagreed. On the one hand, silence left the field open to those with unattainable visions of immense annexation, which could hardly act as a limit to action.[2] On the other hand, the government provided no counter guidelines. The oft-repeated phrase about attaining or maintaining world power status was actually a negative goal; it meant the destruction of Britain and its circle of allies. The most positive formulation of that goal was the claim that Germany was fighting for its existence. Contemporaries lamented the fact that, in Prince Max v. Baden's words, "Our claim to power has until now [1918] been justified only as securing our existence or interests."[3] No ethical, moral, or universal grounds could be found to express the "national power-idea."[4] Why? Because the "national power-idea" was an empty substitute for policy.

In the absence of a positive national war policy, practices and actionism took over. The experts in war (the army and especially the General Staff) did their job according to the assumptions, scripts, and expectations of military culture. Strategy dissolved into operations and finally, in 1918, into mere tactics. The military's default programs expanded to fill the policy vacuum. And they were remarkably effective at the levels of tactics and operations for which they had been honed. Years of careful training meant that despite

---

2. The Pan-Germans among the annexationists were ideologues, but most of the enthusiasts were opportunists who joined the bandwagon after the war began, such as Matthias Erzberger or Hugo Stinnes.

3. Prince Max v. Baden's memorandum on "Ethical Imperialism," in his *Erinnerungen*, 253.

4. Ethical: Prince Max v. Baden, *Erinnerungen*, 254. Moral: Niemann, *Kaiser und Revolution*, 57; Niemann, *Kaiser und Heer*, 108–9. Universal: Ludwig Dehio, cited in Erdmann, *Der Erste Weltkrieg*, 91. "National power-idea": Volkmann report, "Die Annexionsfragen des Weltkrieges," *UA* 4:12 pt. 1, 23.

326 the lack of overall coordination there was system to the practices of the officer corps; officers produced the same sort of ordering and exploitation of human and material resources wherever they were. And, lacking braking mechanisms from without or within the military, they repeated the script of violence, ratcheting it higher and higher, moving closer and closer to an extreme end that they did not "intend."

This processual understanding of Wilhelminian Germany will remind some readers of Hans Mommsen's structural explanation for the Third Reich. Rather than privileging ideology as a causal factor, Mommsen concluded that the radicalization of Nazi (genocidal) policy and its irrationality were the result of several qualities of its government.[5] Three of these—fragmentation (or polycratic administration), postponed decisions (or policy unclarity), and lack of feedback—are much like what one sees in the Kaiserreich. But there are important differences. Mommsen characterizes the "Führer myth" and leadership rivalries as "atavistic principle(s)" at odds with "a great modern industrialized state." And he finds that decision making had reverted to the "personal level," that is, it had become simply idiosyncratic.[6] The processes I have described as issuing from military culture are organizational, meaning that they are not personal or idiosyncratic; furthermore, they are products of bureaucratic functioning. If one regards bureaucracy as a modern phenomenon (which one need not do), then they are "modern." More important, in the Third Reich radicalization (and not chaos) resulted from this kind of government because the "line of least resistance" through which policies developed was indeed set by Nazi ideology as interpreted by Hitler: "The utopian dream of exterminating the Jews could become reality only in the half-light of unclear orders and ideological fanaticism. Then, despite all opposing interests, the process developed its own internal dynamic."[7] In the Kaiserreich, the coordinating, magnetic pull of ideology was missing. The smaller logic of practices and basic assumptions provided the motor and the direction of radicalization.

The Kaiserreich was much less an outlaw state than the Third Reich. The extremes it reached both in the colonies and in European warfare were strongly supported by international norms and assumptions that eroded limits to extremism. It is important to repeat: Germany was at the end of a spectrum it shared with the rest of the Western world. The two most important shared norms concerned national sovereignty and war. The international system that had emerged from Napoleonic Europe placed the independent state at the center of law and right. The more sacrosanct national sovereignty, the larger its demands for sacrifice from its own soldiers and civilians, and the weaker the limits of international law on its actions against others. As to war, no Western government rejected it as a legitimate tool of politics, and all considered the ability to wage war a defining characteristic of a sovereign state. The late-nineteenth-century Western world thus placed

5. Hans Mommsen, "National Socialism," in *From Weimar to Auschwitz*, trans. Philip O'Connor (Princeton, 1991), 141–62, esp. 157–61. I disagree with Mommsen's interpretation of the Third Reich; I think ideology was central to its genocidal policies.

6. Ibid., 161.

7. Least resistance: ibid., 158. Utopian dream: Hans Mommsen, "The Realization of the Unthinkable," in *From Weimar*, 224–53, here 251.

military might at the heart of state self-definition, though nowhere was the emphasis so central as in Germany. By the beginning of the twentieth century, however, international opinion among the self-proclaimed "civilized nations" (i.e., those organized as states) increasingly believed that war should be limited to self-defense, thus potentially placing a limit on states' untrammeled use of violence for political ends. Nonetheless, once World War I broke out, the Allies' reluctance to consider a negotiated peace encouraged the German military interpretation of (all) war as existential and fed the vicious circle of expanding violence to which the German military tended anyway.

The military's default program of escalating violence was positively reinforced from inside Germany, as well. Military culture, for all its autism, was enmeshed in a dialectical relationship with government and political culture. The incapacities of Wilhelminian government (to rein in, correct, or guide the military) intensified military culture, making it seem stronger and more reliable than mere "politics." That encouraged civilian leaders to rely more and more on the military and to submit to its perceptions of and solutions to problems, which increased the pressure on the army to succeed, which in turn encouraged more extremes in the institution and its culture. Political culture reacted with similar intensifying circularity.

Here Arendt's distinction between power and violence is especially important. Power is the strength and legitimacy that comes from (political) agreement, or as she puts it, from "the human ability to act in concert."[8] The incomplete political system of Imperial Germany lacked power in this sense. Its foreign policy was equally isolated and weak. Again, as Arendt writes, "Loss of power becomes a temptation to substitute violence for power."[9] As the Wilhelminian leaders succumbed to this temptation, the wielders of violence, the military, became more and more important. The military became a kind of charismatic institution in the sense that its continued status and privileged place in government and society depended on its success.[10] This is the reason, in abstract terms, why the victory of annihilation, the tendency to "final" solutions, was so predominant in prewar German military culture.

The interaction between military culture, government, and political culture seems to have produced increasing congruence between military culture, foreign policy, certain ideological trends, and some social groups—despite the absence of formal coordination. The military's default program, for example, was consistent with Germany's foreign policy, Weltpolitik, which rested on the risk (or bluff) of pure force. Yet military and foreign policy had never been synchronized, and the main contours of German military culture had developed for twenty years under Bismarck's "satiated" foreign policy. Nevertheless, it is certainly true that once Weltpolitik was inaugurated in 1897, nothing in Germany's

8. Arendt, *On Violence*, 44.

9. Ibid., 54.

10. Weber used the term "charisma" to define a type of legitimate authority of individual leaders that could not be institutionalized and still retain its essential character. Nonetheless, the term is apt for describing the Wilhelminian military because of the way charismatic authority is sustained—by success recognized by the "followers." See Max Weber, *On Charisma and Institution Building*, trans. S. N. Eisenstadt (Chicago, 1968), 3–77, esp. 20–22, 51.

328 foreign policy ran counter to its military-cultural habits. The military default program, which amounted to the reduction of politics to the exercise of force, was also consistent with ideologies such as social Darwinism and imperialism, which were fashionable among the educated, organized, and politically indispensable middle strata. Support for the military way of doing things also came from the "double militarism" that had saturated much of prewar civilian life.[11] During the First World War, that process deepened as military service became a kind of ersatz political participation and lent the military a deep national legitimation it would ordinarily not have possessed.[12] The war also seemed to confirm the military's indispensability and its paranoid view of existential struggle; in a world of total victory or total defeat, there could be no negotiation, only fighting on until death and destruction enveloped everything.

Germany's military culture was thus multiply supported from outside itself. Inside, it was even harder to break out of its thought and behavior patterns. Culture, after all, operates precisely to smooth operations, that is, to minimize resistance. "Strong" organizations, those characterized by rigid discipline and imperative command, are hardest to counter, and these were surely the main hindrances to independent criticism from within the officer corps. The military also made it easy to focus on one's narrow, technical task and to compartmentalize. Finally, the scripts and procedures of military culture were effective on the tactical and operative levels. It was hard to argue against (partial) success, easy to imagine that just a bit more effort, a bit more luck, would convert the tactical into the operative and the operative into strategic victory.

This study of military culture in practice raises questions about the possible relation of the army's institutional extremism to other causal explanations, such as technology, ideology, racism, and imperialism. This is the place to draw together the implications of what we have seen for these important subjects.

Technology

Already in the 1860s and 1870s Europeans were projecting onto Prussia/Germany their nightmare vision of a new kind of warfare, war as machine. The Prussian General Staff seemed to epitomize a conduct of war that followed the "logic of technology, science and planning" and its excesses.[13] Moltke's use of modern management techniques would seem to confirm their intuition. But there is no simple causal relation between technology and extremism. Above all, the organizational-cultural mechanisms we have studied do not appear to have been "caused" by changes in industry and technology.

Technology seems most obviously to have been an enabler. Industry and technology created the power gap between Europeans and non-Europeans, thus making possible the second wave of imperialism in the nineteenth century. They greatly magnified firepower, leading to the deadly trench stalemate of World War I and the unimaginable casualty rates

11. Förster, *Der doppelte Militarismus*; Rohkrämer, *Militarismus*.

12. Michael Geyer, "The Place of the Second World War in German Memory and History," *New German Critique*, no. 71 (spring–summer 1997): 5–40, here 28–29.

13. Pick, *War Machine*, 165; excess: 154.

of the fruitless attempts at breakthrough. Increased firepower put armies under pressure to become or stay technically up to date. But if technology had been a prime mover, then one would expect the armaments race to have begun in 1871, not after 1906, and one would expect greater technological acceptance and innovation among militaries.[14] Armies did learn from technology, but they did so relatively slowly and unevenly.[15]

For the German army, trapped in its manpower dilemma, technology's multiplier effect was indeed important: it made the army stronger than its numbers. New weapons (gas, submarines, tanks, planes) might make the difference in a stand-off. But that possibility simply encouraged the already existing propensity of the German military elite to focus on techniques in order to escape the bad news of Germany's relatively weak strategic situation. Technological innovation was another factor contributing to the positive feedback loop inside military culture.

Arden Bucholz has made the strongest argument for the causal effect of technology on the German military. He has shown how the centrality of the railroad to mobilization and deployment caused the railroad section of the General Staff to swell in importance, and how it encouraged the expectation that exact, timetable-like advance planning could overcome chance and friction in war. However, in other areas, such as transport, weapons, and communications, the German army was no better at assimilating technical advances than other armies, and was sometimes worse.[16] Preexisting institutional predilections thus seem to determine which aspects of technology will be adopted and developed. Once adopted, these new technologies are integrated into the existing military culture and work in the same, often unintended, ways characteristic of military culture.

Ideology

Ideology is fundamentally different from the hidden basic assumptions of military culture, and even from the explicit doctrines or norms and values of any culture or organization. Ideology is bigger, more systematic, and more all-encompassing. Ideology, in Roger Chickering's helpful words, is "a highly structured belief system," a "political cosmology" that tries "to bring conceptual order to a world in which questions of power are being debated."[17] The Third Reich was highly ideological and so was its Final Solution. There is something logical and even comforting in expecting that ideology will always be at the base of genocide or other forms of horrible extremity. In that case, human action would follow a plan and thus lend itself to analysis according to goal rationality. Irrationality is thus displaced into the ideas themselves, exonerating, so to speak, the mechanisms (organization, bureaucracy, legalism, group pressure, and so on) to which we are all subject as cultural creatures.

14. David G. Herrmann, *The Arming of Europe and the Making of the First World War* (Princeton, 1996), 7–36.
15. Storz, *Kriegsbild.*
16. Bucholz, *Moltke, Schlieffen*, 179–85, 241.
17. Chickering, *We Men*, 75.

But the ideological explanation is often too simple. It ignores the common, even usual, contradiction between norms or overt values and behavior. It overlooks the role that ideologies very often play in culture as ex post facto justifications for action.[18] In the events treated in this book, ideology is much more visible as a rationalization than a cause. It appears because actors found it necessary to explain why they had caused tremendous destruction or loss of life. Falkenhayn is a good example. His social Darwinism played no role in planning for Verdun, but he used social Darwinist verbiage in an "attempt to obscure with argumentation a disaster that was growing daily," as his biographer writes.[19] Ludendorff is another. He practiced "total war," in the sense of operations without limit, for four years without enunciating its principles or reifying it. Only after the defeat did he do so.[20]

Racism is a subcategory of ideology and is often used as a similar explanatory black box. Yet it, too, often appeared as a result of imperial experiences, rather than being their cause. Hannah Arendt recognized this chronology in her useful distinction between eighteenth- and nineteenth-century race-thinking and late-nineteenth- and twentieth-century racism:

> Race-thinking was a source of convenient arguments for varying political conflicts; . . . it never created new conflicts or produced new categories of political thinking. Racism sprang from experiences and political constellations which were still unknown. . . . Imperialism would have necessitated the invention of racism as the only possible "explanation" and excuse for its deeds, even if no race-thinking had ever existed.[21]

The memoirs of soldiers in SWA and China are replete with examples of the transformation of vague race-thinking into racism.

Yet there are undeniable racists in our story: Lothar v. Trotha, who became a racist during his time of service in German East Africa in the 1890s, and Hans v. Humann (and possibly Friedrich Bronsart v. Schellendorf). However, Trotha did not enact the race war idea from the moment he landed in SWA. He pursued the usual illusions of envelopment and military annihilation; only when these had turned nightmarish did he adduce the "race war" to explain the results to Berlin. Trotha's racist convictions made it easier for him to resort to and name a "final solution," but they did not cause it. Racism is not necessary to produce such final solutions. We have seen many examples of people performing the same actions and pursuing the same ends without benefit of racism or other ideological motives. And we have examples of racists who explicitly rejected "final solutions." Paul Rohrbach is the most stunning example, for nobody justified violent imperialism

---

18. Kluckhohn, "Concept of Culture," 71.

19. Afflerbach, *Falkenhayn*, 455.

20. Speier, "Ludendorff," 318. Even then, he clung to the hollow Wilhelminian claims that it was "defensive."

21. Arendt, *The Origins of Totalitarianism* (New York, 1951), 183. Robert Miles makes a similar distinction between "racialization" and "racism": Miles, *Racism* (London, 1989), 75–77.

and even the genocide of "useless" natives (such as the Nama, he thought) in more straightforward language than Rohrbach.[22] But he heatedly opposed the mass annihilation of both the Herero and later the Armenians, the first apparently for practical reasons but the latter for moral-ethical ones that were absent from his thinking in 1907. Like Rohrbach, there were many soldiers whose race-thinking or even conventional racism (toward Africans, Chinese, or Armenians) is evident but who acted against the grain of mass slaughter or complicit cynicism. Obviously, the relation between race-thinking—and even racism—and action is extremely complicated. Furthermore, the ubiquity of racialist thinking in Europe and the West before 1914 makes it hard to see how racism could tell us why Europeans went to extremes in some situations and not in others.

One of the most interesting cautions against using racism too freely as an explanation is the German wartime treatment of Europeans. We have forgotten how thoroughly civilians in the occupied zones were instrumentalized in the name of war: photographed, numbered, listed, labeled, expropriated, reduced to involuntary laborers, deported, beaten, starved, and executed. This treatment was not meted out only to eastern Europeans, where it may seem to us in retrospect as a kind of preparation for the Third Reich; it was equally the lot of Belgians and French. And wherever the limits to military rule were weakest, there the process quickly reached what we think of as colonial extremes. Indeed, contemporaries used the colonial analogy themselves. Wild von Hohenborn, for example, advocated creating a postwar Belgium "like a kind of independent colony" along the English dominion model. Friedrich von Schwerin, commissioned in 1915 by Bethmann to redraw the map of eastern Europe, advocated creating a colony out of the border strip to be annexed from Poland; while farther east, the Lithuanian Social Democrats protested that area's treatment by asserting that Lithuania "was not Central Africa."[23]

Actions that seem racist can develop out of ordinary organizational dynamics. The practices of occupation in Europe are one example; the conviction of German qualitative military superiority is another. German military culture coped with Germany's numerical manpower inferiority by assuming that superior organization and discipline would compensate for smaller numbers. The postulate of qualitative superiority became necessary to the system, and it operated like racism, producing the same peculiar mix of arrogance and anxiety and the same cognitive blinders.

Distinguishing actual racism from military-cultural effects that functioned in the same way is also difficult because the ideologies of racism and social Darwinism shared significant aspects of content and form with the practices of imperialism and war. Through their shared logical structures, they mutually supported one another. A scholar of racism has called this phenomenon "ideological articulation," but it can be equally true of practices.[24] Racist and social Darwinist ideologies, on the one hand, and imperial and modern warfare practices, on the other, reinforced each other, and ultimately they co-

22. Rohrbach, *Deutsche Kolonialwirtschaft*, 1:352.

23. Wild to his wife, 13 Apr. 1915, *Briefe*, 92; Geiss, *Der polnische Grenzstreifen*, 85; Strazhas, *Deutsche Ostpolitik*, 60.

24. Miles, *Racism*, 87; also Finnemore, "Constructing Norms," 173–74.

alesced in National Socialism. But before the 1920s they were separate phenomena, and their uneven mutual articulation is important in understanding the earlier period.

Imperialism

Imperialism did more than provide the European powers with the venue for their wars from 1871 to 1914. The colonial situation itself was identical to war; it unleashed the same dynamic of extremism and directly predicted the fate of the occupied populations of Europe in the First World War.

Imperialism *was* war. As Governor Götzen of German East Africa explained in the context of the Maji-Maji Revolt, "Colonial policy has always been conquest, and nowhere in the world will the taking of land by a foreign people occur without fighting."[25] "Colonization is a question of power [*Machtfrage*]" was the pithier formulation repeated by countless soldiers in the colonies.[26] The point was power instead of law: "Here only power counts, which substitutes for law," as a missionary told Bismarck in 1889.[27] General v. Hartmann had also postulated that in the absence of the limits of law that occurred in the existential struggle of war, violence could develop untrammeled. Hannah Arendt thought this development was the most destructive feature of modern imperialism:

> Violence has always been the *ultima ratio* in political action and power has always been the visible expression of rule and government. But neither had ever before been the conscious aim of the body politic or the ultimate goal of any definite policy. For power left to itself can achieve nothing but more power, and violence administered for power's (and not for law's) sake turns into a destructive principle that will not stop until there is nothing left to violate.[28]

The "economy of violence" in the colonies then began to unfold.[29] The original violence begat resistance that refuted the self-expectation of European superiority and exposed the weaknesses of the colonizers in imposing their will. The fear of appearing weak demanded a greater outlay of violence, a crushing demonstration of power that, in the absence of legitimacy, promised (temporary) success. No limits of morality or international law—in the fighting words of the times, no "moralizing self-deception or hesitant sentimentality," no "sweet old wives' views"—could be permitted to dull the edge of violence.[30] The spiral was free to run its course; a "final solution" was at hand.

Europe embarked on imperialism in the comforting illusion that the "civilized world" was insulated from the results. Military men (and too many military historians)

25. Götzen, "Denkschrift über die Ursachen des Aufstandes in Deutsch-Ostafrika, 1905," Dar es Salaam, 26 Dec. 1915, BA-MA Freiburg, RM 5, Nr. 6036, 133.

26. Max Schwabe, "Einige Lehren," 461; Kurd Schwabe, *Krieg in Südwestafrika*, 18; Major Heydebreck, "Betrachtungen," 462 (Heydebreck opposed Trotha's Vernichtungspolitik).

27. Missionary Brinker cited by Rohrbach, *Deutsche Kolonialwirtschaft*, 1:230.

28. Arendt, *Origins*, 137.

29. Trutz v. Trotha's phrase, in " 'The Fellows Can Just Starve,' " 422; Trotha, *Koloniale Herrschaft*, 37–44.

30. Rohrbach, *Deutsche Kolonialwirtschaft*, 1:285–86; Dove, "Deutsch-Südwest Afrika," 195.

continued to believe the myth that imperial warfare had nothing whatever in common with wars fought in Europe. The point, at least for this study, is not that Europeans learned beastliness from their imperial encounters but that they could try out abroad the techniques, assumptions, doctrines, and scripts they carried with them, in an atmosphere relatively unlimited by law and conducive to the application of more force when the first allotment failed to achieve the goal. The Germans at least learned nothing from colonial warfare that did not confirm their prejudices about the correct way to fight wars.[31] Imperialism strengthened the military template.

The Legacy of Germany's Military Culture

One of the most striking qualities of the imperial German military establishment was the combination of operative and tactical effectiveness with apparent irrationality: the inflated and exclusivist definition of victory (in the Clausewitzian sense of complete annihilation of the enemy forces); the rigid adherence to the tactic of offensive envelopment; the rejection of realistic planning for provisioning and maintenance; the inability to estimate the enemy's strengths (a product of the necessity to assume professional superiority); the tendency to repetitive actionism at the cost of disproportionate destruction and even self-annihilation; the inability to admit defeat or to learn from it; and the overreliance on officers' moral qualities of daring, foolhardiness, and optimistic self-sacrifice. Other explanatory frameworks, such as professionalism, doctrinalism, or the peculiar sociology of the officer corps, cannot account for this odd mixture. Military culture does a much better job because, while it takes these factors into consideration, it emphasizes the operation of hidden, prerational assumptions, the products of the organization's history, which actually motivate action and which are likely to produce seeming irrationality. Actual behavior, habitual practices, and powerful, motivating expectations are the results of (military) culture.

It is in the realm of behavior that I believe military culture left its greatest unintentional legacy to National Socialism, a legacy of a different order from that of the prewar extremist ideologies. Military culture bequeathed practices, habits of action, and ways of behaving that were far more robust than flat and lifeless ideas such as anti-Semitism or social Darwinism, whose believers might or might not ever translate them into deeds. The part of National Socialist ideology that came from the practices of military culture transcended the conventional split between norms and actions by elevating the actions themselves to norms. The "cult of violence" that epitomized National Socialism was simply the reification of practices and behavior (that is, action templates) that had become severed from the old Imperial military culture.[32] In the Third Reich they were easily harnessed for the ideological ends of even greater mass destruction and death.

31. Also, Trotha, "'The Fellows Can Just Starve,'" 433; Glenn Anthony May, "Was the Philippine-American War a 'Total War?'" in *Anticipating Total War,* ed. Boemeke et al., 437–59, here 457.

32. On the structural relation between World War I and National Socialism: Hans Mommsen, "Militär und zivile Militärisierung in Deutschland 1914 bis 1938," in *Militär und Gesellschaft,* ed. Frevert, 265–76, esp. 276.

Bibliography

UNPUBLISHED SOURCES

Bundesarchiv (Berlin-Lichterfelde)

R 1001 (Reichskolonialamt)

Nrs. 286–288: Militärische Expeditionen der Schutztruppe: Feb. 1895–Dec. 1897

Nrs. 721–725: Unruhen und Aufstände in verschiedenen Teilen Deutsch-Ostafrikas im Jahre 1905 und ihre militärische Unterdrückung, Bde. 1–4, 4 Aug. 1905–19 July 1912

Nr. 771: Bekämpfung von Hungersnöten in Deutsch-Ostafrika, Jan. 1899–Sept. 1917

Nr. 774: Bericht des Obersten v. Trotha über politische Verhältnisse, Missionen, kulturelle Entwicklung, Organisationen und Stationen in Deutsch-Ostafrika

Nr. 784: Sammlung der Gouvernementsbefehle des Kaiserlichen Gouvernements (DOA), Bd. 3, 30 July 1895–23 Jan. 1905

Nr. B 786/2: Runderlasse des Kaiserlichen Gouvernements, Bd. 4, Dec. 1895–March 1897

Nr. 1496: Informationsreise des Staatssekretärs Dr. Solf, Enthält: Denkschrift über SWA im Vergleich mit Britisch-Südafrika, June 1912–Aug. 1912

Nr. 2089: Differenzen zwischen Generalleutnant v. Trotha und Gouverneur Leutwein über das Verhältnis von militärischen und politischen Massnahmen zur Beendigung des Krieges

Nrs. 2090–2091: Deportation der Kriegsgefangenen aus SWA in andere Kolonien

Nrs. 2111–2119: Aufstand der Hereros 1904–1909

Nr. 2120: Schriftliches Material aus Swakopmund

Nr. 2121: Denkschrift des Reichskanzlers für den Reichstag, Mar. 1904

Nrs. 2133–2134: Aufstand im Namalande im Jahre 1904, Bd. 1, Aug. 1904–1 Jan. 1905

Nrs. 2140–2141: Aufstand im Namaland und seine Bekämpfung, 8 Feb. 1907–June 1914

Nrs. 4704–4705: Bericht über die einheimische Bevölkerung SWA und ihre Behandlung durch die Deutschen (Englisches Blaubuch), Bd. 1 und 2, Jan. and Dec. 1918

Nrs. 6466–6467: Deutsch-Ostafrika Allgemeine Jahresberichte, Bde. 1–2, Jan. 1894–Jan. 1989

R 151 F (Kaiserliches Gouvernement in Deutsch-Südwestafrika, 1884–1915)

Film FC 4704: Feldzug gegen die Hereros und Khauas-Hottentotten, 1895–1896 [D.IV.c.1., Nr. 436, orig. microfilm 250]

Film FC 4705: Expedition gegen die Afrikaner-Hottentotten, 1897 [D.IV.d, Nr. 438] und gegen die Zwartbooi Hottentotten, 1898 [D.IV.f., Nr. 440, orig. microfilm 251]

Film FC 4706: Expedition gegen die Afrikaner-Hottentotten, 1897 [D.IV.d, Nr. 438], und gegen die Zwartbooi Hottentotten, 1898 [D.IV.f., Nr. 440, orig. microfilm 251]

Film FC 4711: Feldzug gegen die Herero, 1904–1906

Film FC 4712: Feldzug gegen die Herero, 1904–1906

Film FC 4713: Feldzug gegen die Herero, 1904–1906

336   Film FC 4714: Feldzug gegen die Herero, 1904–1906, Kriegsgefangene [D.IV.l.3, Nr. 454–456, orig. microfilm 260]

Film FC 4715: Feldzug gegen die Herero, 1904–1906, Kriegsgefangene [D.IV.l.3, Nr. 454–456, orig. microfilm 261]

Film FC 4720: Feldzug gegen die Hottentotten, 1904–1907

Film FC 4721: Feldzug gegen die Hottentotten, 1904–1907

Film FC 4722: Feldzug gegen die Hottentotten, 1904–1907, Kriegsgefangene [D.IV.m.3, Nr. 465–66. orig. microfilm 268]

Film FC 4723: Feldzug gegen die Hottentotten, 1904–1907, Kriegsgefangene [D.IV.m.3, Nr. 465–66. orig. microfilm 269]

61 Ko 1 (Deutsche Kolonialgesellschaft)

Film 39521: Deutsche Kolonialgesellschaft, Herero Aufstand

Film 39522: Deutsche Kolonialgesellschaft, Herero Aufstand

R 43 (Alte Reichskanzlei)

Film 13209/13210: Türkei

Bundesarchiv (Koblenz)

N 1408 (Nachlass Paul Rohrbach [1869–1956])

Bd. 25: Lebenserinnerungen, Bd. 1, Ausführliche Erstfassung, nur für die Familien, nicht zur Veröffentlichung bestimmt, Teile I–VI. S. 1–196

Bd. 67: Briefe an die Frau aus SWA, Sept. 1903–Apr. 1905

Bd. 68: Briefe an die Frau aus SWA, May–Dec. 1905

Bd. 69: Briefe an die Frau aus SWA, Jan. 1906–Mar. 1907

Bd. 112: Briefe u.a. von Ernst Jäckh, 1916

Bd. 123: Briefe u.a. von Ernst Jäckh, 1920

Kl. Erw. 16 (Carl Peters)

Briefe an Seine Excellenz betr. Fragwürdigkeit des preussischen Systems bei der Ausbildung der ostafrikanischen Schutztruppe, Kilimandschar Station, 27 Oct. 1891

Kl. Erw. 275 (Friedrich v. Lindequist)

"SWA Erlebnisse," ms.

Nl. 1030 (Nachlass Viktor Franke [1866–1936])

Bd. 3: Tagebuch, 5 Sept. 1903–18 Dec. 1904

Bd. 21: Der Aufstand in Deutsch-Südwestafrika und die nachfolgenden Jahre, 1903–1906

Bundesarchiv-Militärarchiv (Freiburg i. Br.)

RM 2 (Kaiserliche Marine-Kabinett)

Nr. 186: Expedition nach SWA, 1904

RM 3 (Reichsmarineamt)

Nr. 4745: Allerhöchste Befehle und Berichterstattung an Seine Majestät über China, 1900

Nr. 6822: Kriegszustand und Oberbefehl: Anweisung für die Kommandeur des Ostasiatischen Expeditionskorps

RM 5 (Admiralstab der Marine)

Nr. 6035: Aufstand in Deutsch-Ostafrika, Bd. 1, Aug. 1905–Nov. 1905

Nr. 6036: Aufstand in Deutsch-Ostafrika, Bd. 2, Nov. 1905–1908

RM 40 (Reichs-Marine, Dienst- und Kommandostellen der Kaiserlichen Marine im Mittelmeer und im Osmanischen Reich)

Nr. 456: Archiv der Marine, Kriegsakten, Politisches, Bd. 1, Akten der Mittelmeerdivision, Aug. 1914–Feb. 1916

RM 121 (Landstreitkräfte der Kaiserlichen Marine)

Nr. 396: Tagebuch des Boxeraufstands vom 30. Mai bis Ende 1900 (Bd. 1)

Nr. 397: Tagebuch des Boxeraufstands vom 1. Januar bis Anfang Juli 1901 (Bd. 2)

Nr. 398: Befehle an den Oberbefehlshaber Graf Waldersee und Gen. Lt. von Lessel

Nr. 399: Nachrichten vom Oberbefehlshaber Graf Waldersee und Gen. Lt. von Lessel, Oct. 1900–Aug. 1901

Nr. 400: Kriegstagebuch des Kommandos des Expeditionskorps nach China, Befehlshaber: Generalmajor von Hoepfner, 25 June 1900–26 Nov. 1900

Nr. 422: Militärische Operationen, Bd. 1, 20 Jan. 1904–10 Mar. 1904

Nr. 423: Militärische Operationen, Bd. 2, 13 Mar. 1904–25 Sept. 1904

Nr. 424: Kriegstagebuch des Kommandos des Marine-Expeditionskorps, 1 Feb. 1904–7 Apr. 1904

Nr. 427: Kriegstagebuch des Korvetten Kapitäns Gudewill, 18 Jan. 1904–29 Feb. 1904

Nr. 429: Kriegstagebuch: Landungskorps SMS Habicht, 24 Feb. 1904–Feb. 1905

Nr. 430: Kriegstagebuch: 1. Feldkompanie, Marine-Inf.-Bataillon, 17 Jan.–4 June 1904

Nr. 431: Kriegstagebuch: 2. Feldkompanie, Marine-Inf.-Bataillon, 14 Jan.–9 July 1904

Nr. 432: Kriegstagebuch: 4. Feldkompanie, Marine-Inf.-Bataillon, 17 Jan.–18 June 1904

Nr. 434: Kriegstagebuch: 3. Kompanie, Marine-Inf.-Bataillon, Bd. 1, 10 Feb.–21 Nov. 1904

Nr. 435: Kriegstagebuch: 3. Kompanie, Marine-Inf.-Bataillon, Bd. 2, 23 Nov. 1904–5 Mar. 1905

Nr. 438: Kriegstagebuch: SMS Thetis (Ältester Offizier der Ost-Afrikanischen Station), Berichte und Meldungen über Aufstand, 29 Sept. 1905–13 Mar. 1906

Nr. 439: Anlage zum Kriegstagebuch SMS Thetis (Ältester Offizier der OA Station), Bd. 1, 20 Oct. 1905–15 Dec. 1906

Nr. 440: Anlage, Bd. 2, 16 Dec. 1906–5 Mar. 1907

Nr. 441: Ältester Offizier der Ost-Afrikanischen Station: Geheim! Akten: Anlagen zum Kriegstagebuch, Fol. I, Aug.–Oct. 1905

Nr. 442: Aufstand in Deutsch-Ostafrika. Kriegstagebuch, 26 Sept. 1905–29 Mar. 1906

Nr. 443: Berichte und Meldungen über Aufstand, Sept. 1905–Dec. 1905 ["Der Älteste Offizier der Ostafrikanischen Station. Geheim! Akten betr. Aufstand in Deutsch-Ostafrika, August-Sept. 1905"]

Nr. 448: Kriegstagebuch: Detachements, Samange, Kilwa, Mohorro, Lindi, Mikinda + Beilagen

338

Nr. 449: Berichte und Meldung des Hauptmanns v. Schlichting, Mtindji, Nov.–Dec. 1905

Nr. 450: Berichte und Meldung des Lt. Frhr. v. Stengel, Kilwa, Oct.–Dec. 1905

Nr. 451: Kriegstagebuch des Lt. v. Milczewski, Muansa, Oct. 1905–Feb. 1906

Nr. 452: Kriegstagebuch Oblt. z. See Paasche, Aug. 1905–Feb. 1906

Nr. 453: Kriegstagebuch Stabsarzt Dr. zur Verth, Mohorro, Nov. 1905–Jan. 1906

Nr. 454: Kriegstagebuch Seesoldatendetachment Kibata, Mtinzi, Sept. 1905–Feb. 1906

Nr. 455: Kriegstagebuch Matrosendetachement Wachtel, Oct. 1905–Feb. 1906

Nr. 456: Kriegstagebuch Detachement Mikindana, Aug. 1905–Feb. 1906

Nr. 457: Kriegstagebuch Detachement Kissidju, Oct.–Nov. 1905

Nr. 458: Kriegstagebuch Detachement Engelbrecht, Oct. 1905–Mar. 1906

Nr. 459: Kriegstagebuch Seesold, Detachement Lindi, Sept. 1905–Feb. 1906

RW 51 (Kaiserliche Schutztruppen und sonstige deutsche Landstreitkräfte in Übersee)

Bd. 2: Dokumentenzentrale, Schutztruppe Südwestafrika

Bd. 12: Bestimmungen für das Militärgerichtsverfahren, etc. während des Kriegszustandes in Deutsch-Südwest-Afrika, 1904

Bd. 18: Überblick über die bei der Entsendung von Verstärkungen für die Schutztruppe in SWA gesammelten Erfahrungen und die in den Kommissionsberatungen zu erörternden Fragen, 1 Nov. 1908

Bd. 19: Ergebnis der Arbeiten der durch AKO vom 14.11.1908 berufenen Kommission zur Beratung aufgrund der bei der Entsendung von Verstärkungen für die Schutztruppen in SWA gesammelten Erfahrungen, 1908

N 38 (Nachlass Arnold Lequis [1861–1949])

Bd. 4: Privatkorrespondenz

Bd. 16: Urschrift: Erfahrungsbericht aus SWA, 15 May 1904–14 Dec. 1904

Bd. 17: Durchschrift und Abschrift des Erfahrungsberichts

Bd. 18: Erinnerungen an SWA, 1904–1905

Bd. 29: Kämpfe während des Boxer-Aufstandes, 13 June 1900–16 Oct. 1900

Bd. 30: Kriegstagebuch des Kompanie-Führers Lequis im Boxeraufstand, 17 July 1900–11 June 1901

Bd. 31: Anlage zu Kriegstagebuch

Bde. 35–38: Etappenkommandeur Süd: Tätigkeit während des Herero- und Witboi-Feldzugs (3 May 1904–22 Jan. 1908)

Bd. 57: Schriften: u.a., "Militarismus und Weltpolitik"

Bd. 59: Kommission zur Bewertung der bei der Entsendung von Verstärkungen für die Schutztruppen in SWA gesammelten Erfahrungen. Bericht des Gen.-Majors und Quartiermeisters v. Gündell an Kaiser Wilhelm II: Abschrift, 28 Mar. 1909

N 103 (Nachlass Paul v. Lettow-Vorbeck [1870–1964])

Bd. 1: Korrespondenz

Bd. 25: Einsatz beim Boxeraufstand in China, 1901

Bd. 32: Persönliche Tagebücher, Handschriften, 24 Sept. 1900–5 Jan. 1901: Lageskizzen von Kämpfen in China

Bd. 34: Persönliche Tagebücher, Handschriften, 9 Aug. 1904–4 Oct. 1905: Kämpfe in Afrika

Bd. 35: Persönliche Tagebücher, Handschriften, 18 Oct. 1904–30 Apr. 1906

Bd. 43: Tagebuchartige Aufzeichnungen: Erinnerungen an den Einsatz während des Boxeraufstandes, 1900–1901

Bd. 44: Persönliches Tagebuch: Einsatz während des Boxeraufstands, 19 Oct. 1900–15 Apr. 1901

Bd. 70: Tagebuchaufzeichnungen, in SWA, 1905

Bd. 73: Kampfhandlungen während des Hottentottenaufstandes: Konzept-Kriegstagebuch, 17 May–18 Oct. 1904; Skizze Waterberg, 5 Aug. 1904

Bd. 74: Kriegstagebuch, 27 Aug. 1904–25 Sept. 1905

Bd. 75: Verlauf des Aufstandes in SWA: Denkschrift des Grossen Generalstabs, 16 Jan. 1904–3 Apr. 1905, u.a.

Bd. 77: Aufstand, erzählende Niederschrift von Lettow-Vorbeck, 1910

Bd. 84: Räumung der Malagarossi-Stellung: Antrag des Korvetten-Kapitäns Zimmer auf Einleitung eines Kriegsgerichtsverfahrens wegen der ihm zu last gelegten Massnahmen: Beweisunterlagen hierzu, 5 Sept. 1916–30 June 1917

Bd. 113: SWA: Hereroaufstand: Bilderfolge zusammengestellt von General-Leutnant v. Trotha, 1904–1906

N 138 (Nachlass Eberhard Graf. v. Wolfskeel [1875–1954])

Bd. 6: Privatkorrespondenz mit seiner Frau, 1 Oct. 1915–28 Feb. 1916 (Urffa)

N 156 (Wilhelm Souchon)

Bd. 2: Privatdienstliche Korrespondenz, u.a. mit Bronsart v. Schellendorf

N 187 (Nachlass Martin Chales de Beaulieu [1857–1945])

Bd. 3: Erinnerungen aus meinem Leben (Ausarbeitung des Gen. d. Inf. a.D. Martin Chales de Beaulieu), Nov. 1940

N. 247 (Nachlass Hans v. Seeckt)

Nr. 42: Aufzeichnungen aus Konstantinopel und der Türkei, von der Hand Seeckts, 1917–1918

Nr. 50: Niederschrift: die Gründe des Zusammenbruches der Türkei Herbst 1918

Nr. 88: (Privat-) Dienstlicher Schriftwechsel 1919–1920

Nr. 175: Schriftwechsel

Nr. 178: Korrespondenz, 1914–1918

N 559 (Nachlass Berchtold v. Deimling)

Nr. 7: Nordfeldzug: Kriegstagebuch des Regimentsstabes des 2. Feldregiments für SWA, 1904 und Südfeldzug

Nr. 8: Telegramme des Südfeldzuges, 11 June 1906–29 Jan. 1907

MSg. 1 (Militärbiographische Sammlung)

Nr. 2038: Aufzeichnungen, Korrespondenz und Presseausschnitte aus der Tätigkeit von Oberleutnant Eberhard v. d. Hagen bei der Schutztruppe in SWA 1905–1911.

Nr. 2039: Fritz Bronsart von Schellendorf, Autobiographie

340 *MSg. 2 (Militärgeschichtliche Sammlung)*

Nr. 3039: Einsatz des Hauptmanns Frhr. v. Welck in SWA, Schriftwechsel, Zeitungsausschnitte, 1904–1909.

Nr. 3739: Kriegstagebuch Oberstlt. August Stange, 7 Dec. 1914–10 Mar. 1915.

Nr. 5196: Tagebuch des Leutnants Franz Westermayer über den Boxeraufstand in China.

Nr. 5646: Expeditions-Korps in China: Kriegstagebuch und Bericht von Arthur Langlet, 1900–1901

Politisches Archiv des Auswärtigen Amtes (Bonn)

Türkei 152: betr. Eisenbahnen in der Türkei

Bd. 83: 1. Oct. 1915–30 Nov. 1915

Türkei 175: betr. Katholiken in der Türkei

Bd. 3: 1 Apr.–14 Dec. 1915

Türkei 183 (Armenien)

Bde. 36–55: 1914–1919

Nachlass Paul Weitz

Bd. 1: Briefe verschiedener Mitglieder des Auswärtigen Amtes, 1902–1917
Bd. 3: Briefe v. *Frankfurter Zeitung,* 1903–1920
Bd. 6: Briefe v. Richard v. Kühlmann, 1915–1916
Bd. 13: Verschiedenes
Bd. 14: Aufzeichnung mit 3 Anlagen

Nachlass Dr. Otto Göppert (20 May 1872—3 July 1943)

VI. Sonderaufgaben, 1907–1935
Nr. 5: Türkei- und Armenienfrage (1918–1919)
VII.
Nr. 1: Notizbücher (11 Stück), 1896–1921
Nr. 3: Persönliche Briefe (Curtius, Bülow, Köpke)

Politisches Archiv des Auswärtigen Amtes (Used in microfilm form from the United States National Archives)

Türkei No. 139: Überlassung von preussischen Offizieren und Finanzbeamten an die Pforte zu Re-organisationszwecken, Bde. 33–49, 1914–1920 [Microfilm Roll T 136/77]
Türkei No. 142: Militär- und Marine-Angelegenheiten, Bde. 39–56 (1 July 1914–31 Jan. 1916) [Microfilm Rolls T 136/81–82]
Türkei No. 183: Armenia, Bde. 35–56, 11 Mar. 1914–Jan. 1920 [Microfilm Rolls T 139/463–464]

Archiv der Vereinigten Evangelischen Mission (Wuppertal) (Now called Archiv- und Museumsstiftung Wuppertal)

RMG 1.606c: Philipp Diehl [previous Nr. B/c II 35,3]

RMG 1.609e: Wilhelm Eich, Bd. 5, Korr. 1906 [previous Nr. B/c II 36]

RMG 1.615: Eduard Dannert [previous Nr. B/c II 43]

RMG 1.644: August Kuhlmann (1871–1945), Bd. 1 (1892–1907) [previous Nr. B/c II 72]

RMG 1.660a: Heinrich Vedder (1876–1972), Bd. 1 (1894–1906) [previous Nr. B/c II 87]

RMG 2.499a: Franzfontein [previous Nr. C/h 8 a]

RMG 2.597: Die Witboois: ihre Geschichte und ihr Schicksal in Kamerun, 1894; 1904–1913 [previous Nr. C/i 17]

RMG 2.602: Herero-Aufstand, dazu Briefe aus Deutschland [previous Nr. C/i 22 (1903–1909)]

RMG 2.660: Deutsche Kolonialbehörden in SWA: u.a. Fürsorge für die Herero, 1901–1907 [previous Nr. C/o 5]

RMG 2.697e: Afrikareisen von Inspektor J. Spiecker (1902–1903; 1905–1906), Bd. 5, 1906 [previous Nr. C/s 5, 5]

Archive of the von Trotha Family (Private Papers)

Lothar von Trotha Nachlass

Nr. B69: Tagebuch Lothar v. Trotha, May 1904–Dec. 1905 (typescripts)

Nr. 314: Lose Blätter (copies of original typewritten letters, speeches, plus other handwritten notes)

Nr. 315: Tagebuch Lothar v. Trotha, May 1904–Dec. 1905 ("Zusammengestellt von Frau Lucy von Trotha, Bonn am Rhein 1930, Mit Anhängen")

Yale University Library

Ernst Jäckh Papers

PUBLISHED SOURCES

Newspapers and Journals

Berliner Lokalanzeiger, 1904

Berliner Neueste Nachrichten, 1 Feb.–30 Mar. 1909

Berliner Zeitung, 1904

Deutsche Allgemeine Zeitung, 1921

Deutsch-Südwestafrikanische Zeitung, 1904–1905

Kölnische Zeitung, 1915

Militär-Wochenblatt, 1900–1914

Der Reichsbote, Jan.–June 1904

Vierteljahrshefte für Truppenführung und Heereskunde, 1904–1914

Official Document Collections and Reports

Andonian, Aram, ed. *Documents officiels concernant les massacres arméniens*. Paris, 1920.

Belgium. Ministry of Foreign Affairs. *Report Laid before the Belgian Parliament by the Minister of Foreign Affairs in Answer to the Reichstag Report on Belgian Deportations, 1916–1917*. Brussels, 1928.

Belgium. Official Commission of the Belgian Government. *Reports on the Violation of the Rights of Nations and of the Laws and Customs of War in Belgium*. 2 vols. London, 1915–16.

Beylerian, Arthur. *Les grandes puissances, l'empire ottoman et les arméniens dans les archives françaises (1914–1918)*. Paris, 1983.

342   Bland, J.O.P. *Germany's Violations of the Laws of War, 1914–1915: Compiled under the Auspices of the French Ministry of Foreign Affairs.* New York, 1915.

Bryce, James, and Arnold Toynbee, eds. *The Treatment of the Armenians in the Ottoman Empire, 1914–16: Documents Presented to Viscount Grey of Fallodon by Viscount Bryce; Uncensored Edition.* Ed. Ara Sarafian. London, 2000.

Carnegie Endowment for International Peace, Division of International Law. *Violations of the Laws and Customs of War: Reports of the Majority and Dissenting Reports of American and Japanese Members of the Commission of Responsibilities, Conference of Paris, 1919.* Pamphlet no. 32. Oxford, 1919.

Eiswaldt's Handbuch für Einjährig-Freiwillige, Reserve-Offizieraspiranten und Offiziere des Beurlaubtenstandes des Trains. 10th ed. Berlin, 1915.

Elsner von Gronow, Kurt, and Georg Sohl, eds. *Militärstrafrecht für Herr und Marine des Deutschen Reichs: Handbuch für Kommando- und Gerichtsstellen, für Offiziere und Juristen.* Berlin, 1906.

Fitzner, Rudolf. *Deutsches Kolonial-Handbuch: Nach amtlichen Quellen bearbeitet.* Vol. 1, 2nd ed. Berlin, 1901.

France. Foreign Office. *Les Violations des lois de la guerre par l'Allemagne.* Paris, 1915.

Germany. Admiralty [Admiralstab der Marine]. *Die Kaiserliche Marine während der Wirren in China 1900–1901.* Berlin, 1903.

Germany. Foreign Office [Auswärtiges Amt]. *Die völkerrechtswidrige Führung des belgischen Volkskriegs.* Berlin, 1915.

Germany. Foreign Office and Ministry of the Interior [Auswärtiges Amt and Reichsministerium des Innern], eds. *Amtliche Urkunden zur Vorgeschichte des Waffenstillstandes 1918. Auf Grund der Akten der Reichskanzlei, des Auswärtigen Amtes und des Reichsarchivs.* Berlin, 1924.

Germany. General Staff [Grosser Generalstab]. *Heeresverpflegung.* Berlin, 1913.

——. "Aus dem Südafrikanischen Kriege 1899 bis 1902." In *Kriegsgeschichtliche Einzelschriften*, Hefte 32–35. Berlin, 1903–5.

——. *Die Kämpfe der deutschen Truppen in Südwestafrika; Auf Grund amtlichen Materials.* Vol. 1: *Der Feldzug gegen die Herero* (1906). Vol. 2: *Der Hottentottenkrieg* (1907). Berlin, 1906–7.

——. *Kriegsbrauch im Landkriege.* Vol. 31 of *Kriegsgeschichtliche Einzelschriften.* Berlin, 1902.

——, ed. *Moltke's militärische Korrespondenz: Aus den Dienstschriften des Krieges 1870/71.* Berlin, 1896.

Germany. National Constituent Assembly. *Official German Documents Relating to the World War.* 2 vols. Translated by Division of International Law, Carnegie Endowment for International Peace. New York, 1923.

Germany. Parliament. *Stenographische Berichte über die öffentlichen Verhandlungen des 15. Untersuchungsausschusses der Verfassungsgebenden Nationalversammlung nebst Beilagen.* 2 vols. Berlin, 1920.

——. *Stenographische Berichte über die Verhandlungen des Reichstages.* Berlin, 1904–1907. (*Sten. Ber.*)

——. *Das Werk des Untersuchungsausschusses der Verfassungsgebenden Deutschen Nationalversammlung und des Deutschen Reichstages 1919–1928, Verhandlungen, Gutachten, Urkunden.* Ed. Eugen Fischer, Berthold Widmann, Walter Bloch, Walter Schücking, Johannes Bell, Georg Gradnauer, Rudolf Breitscheid, and Albrecht Philipp. Berlin, 1921–1930. Reihe 1, vol. 5 (*Deutschland auf den Haager Friedenskonferenzen*); Reihe 3, vols. 1–4 (*Das Völkerrecht im Weltkrieg*); Reihe 4, vols. 2–3, 6 (*Die Ursachen des deutschen Zusammenbruchs im Jahre 1918*). (*UA*)

Germany. Reichsarchiv. *Der Weltkrieg 1914 bis 1918.* 14 vols. Berlin, 1925–1944.

——. *Kriegsrüstung und Kriegswirtschaft.* Vol. 1: *Die militärische, wirtschaftliche und finanzielle Rüstung Deutschlands von der Reichsgründung bis zum Ausbruch des Weltkriegs.* Berlin, 1930.

Great Britain. *Report of the Committee on Alleged German Outrages Appointed by His Britannic Majesty's Government and Presided over by the Right Hon. Viscount Bryce.* Cd. 7894. London, 1915.

Great Britain. Parliament. *Evidence and Documents Laid before the Committee on Alleged German Outrages.* Cd 7895. London, 1915.

——. *Papers Relating to German Atrocities and Breaches of the Rules of War in Africa.* Presented to both Houses of Parliament by Command of His Majesty, July 1916. London, 1916.

——. *Report of His Majesty's Commissioners Appointed to Inquire into the Military Preparations and Other Matters Connected with the War in South Africa.* Cd. 1789. London, 1903.

——. *Report on the Concentration Camps in South Africa by the Committee of Ladies Appointed by the Secretary of State for War; Containing Reports on the Camps in Natal, the Orange River Colony, and the Transvaal.* Cd. 893. London, 1902.

——. *The Treatment of the Armenians in the Ottoman Empire: Documents Presented to Viscount Grey of Fallodon, Secretary of State for Foreign Affairs.* London, 1916.

Institut für Armenische Fragen. *The Armenian Genocide.* 3 vols. Munich, 1987.

Kommando der Schutztruppen im Reichs-Kolonialamt. *Sanitäts-Bericht über die Kaiserliche Schutztruppe für Südwestafrika während des Herero- und Hottentottenaufstandes für die Zeit vom 1. Januar 1904 bis 31. März 1907.* Berlin, 1909.

Lepsius, Johannes. *Bericht über die Lage des armenischen Volkes in der Türkei.* Potsdam, 1916.

——. *Deutschland und Armenien, 1914–1918. Sammlung Diplomatischer Aktenstücke.* Potsdam, 1919.

——. *Der Todesgang des armenischen Volkes: Bericht über das Schicksal des armenischen Volkes in der Türkei während des Weltkrieges.* Potsdam, 1930.

Lepsius, Johannes, Albrecht Mendelssohn-Bartholdy, and Friedrich Thimme, eds. *Die Grosse Politik der Europäischen Kabinette 1871–1914; Sammlung der Diplomatischen Akten des Auswärtigen Amtes; Im Auftrage des Auswärtigen Amtes. Rings um die Erste Haager Friedenskonferenz.* Vol. 15. Berlin, 1924.

Michaelis, Herbert, and Ernst Schraepler, eds. *Ursachen und Folgen; Vom deutschen Zusammenbruch 1918 und 1945 bis zur staatlichen Neuordnungen Deutschland in der Gegenwart; Eine Urkunden- und Dokumentensammlung zur Kriegsgeschichte.* Berlin, 1959.

Munro, Dana C., George C. Sellery, and August C. Krey, eds. *German Treatment of Conquered Territory, Being Part II of "German War Practices."* Washington, D.C., 1918.

Munro, Dana C., George C. Sellery, and August C. Krey, eds. *German War Practices, Part 1: Treatment of Civilians.* Washington, D.C., 1917.

Ohandjanian, Artem. *Dokumente über Armenien im Österreichischen Staatsarchiv.* 2 vols. Vienna, 1988.

Prussia. War Ministry [Kriegsministerium]. *D.V.E. Nr. 53. Grundzüge der Höheren Truppenführung.* Berlin, 1910.

——. *Exerzir-Reglement für die Infanterie.* Berlin, 1888. [Often spelled "Exerzier"]

——. *Exerzir-Reglement für die Infanterie.* 2nd ed. Berlin, 1889.

——. *Felddienst-Ordnung.* Berlin, 1900.

——. *Felddienst-Ordnung.* Berlin, 1908.

——. *Kriegs-Etappen-Ordnung* (12 March 1914) (D.V.E. Nr. 90). Berlin, 1914. (KEO)

Prussia. War Ministry and Supreme Command [Kriegsministerium and Oberste Heeresleitung]. *Die deutsche Kriegführung und das Völkerrecht; Beiträge zur Schuldfrage.* Berlin, 1919.

344   Scott, James Brown, ed. *The Hague Conventions and Declarations of 1899 and 1907, Accompanied by Tables of Signatures, Ratification and Adhesions of the Various Powers, and Texts of Reservations.* New York, 1915.

——. *The Proceedings of the Hague Peace Conferences; Translation of the Official Texts; The Conference of 1899.* New York, 1920.

Stevenson, David, ed. *British Documents on Foreign Affairs; The First World War, 1914–1918; The Allied and Neutral Powers: Diplomacy and War Aims, August 1914–July 1915.* Pt. 2, ser. H, vol. 1. General editors Kenneth Bourne and D. C. Watt. Frederick, Md., 1989.

Toynbee, Arnold J. *Armenian Atrocities: The Murder of a Nation; with a Speech Delivered by Lord Bryce in the House of Lords.* London, 1915.

Union of South Africa. *Report on the Natives of South West Africa and Their Treatment by Germany.* London, 1918.

U.S. Department of State. *Papers Relating to the Foreign Relations of the United States, 1918.* Supplement 1: *The World War.* 2 vols. Washington, D.C., 1933.

Zimmermann, Alfred, ed. *Die deutsche Kolonial-Gesetzgebung; Sammlung der auf die deutschen Schutzgebiete bezüglichen Gesetze, Verordnungen, Erlasse und internationalen Vereinbarungen, mit Anmerkungen und Sachregister. Auf Grund amtlicher Quellen und zum dienstlichen Gebrauch herausgegeben.* Bd. II. Berlin, 1898.

Memoirs and Diaries

Alverdes, Hermann. *Mein Tagebuch aus Südwest: Erinnerungen aus dem Feldzuge gegen die Hottentotten.* Oldenburg, 1906.

Auer von Herrenkirchen, Hellmuth. *Meine Erlebnisse während des Feldzuges gegen die Hereros und Witbois nach meinem Tagebuch.* Berlin, 1907.

Baden, Prince Max von. *Erinnerungen und Dokumente.* Stuttgart, 1927.

Bauer, Max. *Der grosse Krieg in Feld und Heimat; Erinnerungen und Betrachtungen.* Tübingen, 1921.

Bayer, Maximilian. *Mit dem Hauptquartier in Südwestafrika.* Berlin, 1909.

Bayern, Rupprecht Kronprinz von. *Mein Kriegstagebuch.* 3 vols. Ed. Eugen von Frauenholz. Munich, 1929.

Belwe, Max. *Gegen die Herero 1904–05; Tagebuchaufzeichnungen.* Berlin, 1906.

Bernstorff, Johann Heinrich Graf. *Erinnerungen und Briefe.* Zürich, 1936.

Bethmann Hollweg, Theobald von. *Betrachtungen zum Weltkriege,* Vol. 2: *Während des Krieges.* Berlin, 1922.

Binder-Krieglstein, E. Baron. *Die Kämpfe des Deutschen Expeditionskorps in China und ihre militärischen Lehren.* Berlin, 1902.

Böhm, Gustav. *Adjutant im preussischen Kriegsministerium Juni 1918 bis Oktober 1919; Aufzeichnungen des Hauptmanns Gustav Böhm.* Ed. Heinz Hürten and Georg Meyer. Stuttgart, 1977.

Bülow, Bernhard von. *Denkwürdigkeiten.* 4 vols. Berlin, 1920.

Deimling, Berthold Karl Adolf von. *Aus der alten in die neue Zeit; Lebenserinnerungen.* Berlin, 1930.

——. *Südwestafrika: Land und Leute; Unsere Kämpfe; Wert der Kolonie.* Vortrag, gehalten in einer Anzahl deutscher Städte. Berlin, 1906.

Djemal, Ahmed. *Erinnerungen eines Türkischen Staatsmannes.* Munich, 1922.

Einem, Karl von. *Ein Armeeführer erlebt den Weltkrieg; Persönliche Aufzeichnungen.* Ed. Junius Alter. Leipzig, 1938.

Eisenhart-Rothe, Ernst. *Im Banne der Persönlichkeit: Aus den Lebenserinnerungen des Generals der Infanterie a.D.* Berlin, 1931.

Ernst, Carl. *Der grosse Krieg in Belgien; Beobachtungen seinen ehemaligen hannoverschen Landsleuten gewidmet.* Gembloux, Belgium, 1930.

Estorff, Ludwig von. "Kriegserlebnisse in Südwestafrika; Vortrag gehalten in der Militärischen Gesellschaft zu Berlin am 8. Februar 1911." *Beiheft zum Militär-Wochenblatt*, Heft 3 (1911): 79–101.

———. *Wanderungen und Kämpfe in Südwestafrika, Ostafrika und Südakrifa 1894–1910.* Wiesbaden, 1968.

Falkenhayn, Erich von. *Die Oberste Heeresleitung 1914–1916 in ihren wichtigsten Entschliessungen.* Berlin, 1920.

Freytag-Loringhoven, Hugo Frhr. von. *Heerführung im Weltkriege; Vergleichende Studien.* Berlin, 1920.

———. *Menschen und Dinge, wie ich sie in meinem Leben sah.* Berlin, 1923.

Friedrich III. *Das Tagebuch des Kronprinzen; Aussprüche, Briefe und andere Kundgebungen 1831–1886.* Berlin, 1886.

Gallwitz, Max von. *Erleben im Westen.* Berlin, 1934.

———. *Meine Führertätigkeit im Weltkriege 1914–1916: Belgien—Osten—Balkan.* Berlin, 1929.

Giehrl, Rudolf. *China-Fahrt; Erlebnisse und Eindrücke von der Expedition 1900–1901.* Munich, 1903.

Goltz, Colmar von der. *Denkwürdigkeiten.* Ed. Friedrich von der Goltz and Wolfgang Foerster. Berlin, 1929.

Götzen, Gustav Adolf Graf von. *Deutsch-Ostafrika im Aufstand, 1905–06.* Berlin, 1909.

Groener, Wilhelm. *Lebenserinnerungen; Jugend, Generalstab, Weltkrieg.* Ed. Friedrich Frhr. Hiller von Gaertringen. Göttingen, 1957.

Gündell, Erich von. *Aus seinen Tagebüchern: Deutsche Expedition nach China 1900–1901, 2. Haager Friedenskonferenz 1907; Weltkrieg 1914–1918 und Zwischenzeiten.* Ed. Walter Obkircher. Hamburg, 1939.

Guse, Felix. *Die Kaukasusfront im Weltkrieg bis zum Frieden von Brest.* Leipzig, 1940.

Hindenburg, Paul von. *Aus meinem Leben.* Leipzig, 1920.

Hoffmann, Max. *Die Aufzeichnungen des Generalmajors Max Hoffmann.* 2 vols. Ed. Karl-Friedrich Nowak. Berlin, 1929.

Hürten, Hans, and Georg Meyer. *Adjutant im preussischen Kriegsministerium Juni 1918–Oktober 1919; Aufzeichnungen des Hauptmanns Gustav Böhm.* Stuttgart, 1977.

Jäckh, Ernst. *Der goldene Pflug, Lebensernte eines Weltbürgers.* Stuttgart, 1954.

Kress von Kressenstein, Friedrich. *Mit den Türken zum Suezkanal.* Berlin, 1938.

Kühlmann, Richard von. *Erinnerungen.* Heidelberg, 1948.

Lettow-Vorbeck, Paul von. *Meine Erinnerungen aus Ostafrika.* Leipzig, 1920.

———. *Mein Leben.* Biberach an der Riss, 1957.

Leutwein, Paul. "Meine Erlebnisse im Kampf gegen die Hereros." In *Mit der Schutztruppe durch Deutsch-Afrika*, ed. "Simplex Africanus." Berlin, 1909.

———. *Afrikanerschicksal; Gouverneur Leutwein und seine Zeit.* Stuttgart, 1929.

Leutwein, Theodor. "Der Aufstand in Deutsch-Südwestafrika." *Deutsche Revue* (1907).

———. *Elf Jahre Gouverneur in Deutsch-Südwestafrika.* Berlin, 1906.

Liman von Sanders, Otto. *Fünf Jahre Türkei.* Berlin, 1919.

Lossberg, Fritz von. *Meine Tätigkeit im Weltkriege 1914–1918.* Berlin, 1939.

Ludendorff, Erich. *Kriegführung und Politik.* Berlin, 1922.

346 ——. *My War Memories 1914–1918.* 2 vols. London, 1922.

——. *The Nation at War.* Trans. A. S. Rappoport. London, n.d.

——. *Der totale Krieg.* Munich, 1935.

——. *Urkunden der Obersten Heeresleitung über ihre Tätigkeit 1916–18.* 2nd ed. Berlin, 1921.

Moltke, Helmuth von. *Erinnerungen, Briefe, Dokumente 1877–1916.* Ed. Eliza v. Moltke. Stuttgart, 1922.

——. *Gesammelte Schriften und Denkwürdigkeiten.* 5 vols. Berlin, 1892–93.

Payer, Friedrich von. *Von Bethmann Hollweg bis Ebert: Erinnerungen und Bilder.* Frankfurt, 1923.

Preussen, Kronprinz Wilhelm von. *Erinnerungen des Kronprinzen Wilhelm; Aus den Aufzeichnungen, Dokumenten, Tagebüchern und Gesprächen.* Ed. Karl Rosner. Stuttgart, 1922.

——. *Meine Erinnerungen aus Deutschlands Heldenkampf.* Berlin, 1923.

Rohrbach, Paul. *Aus Südwestafrikas schweren Tagen: Blätter von Arbeit und Abschied.* Berlin, 1909.

Rust, Conrad. *Krieg und Frieden im Hererolande; Aufzeichungen aus dem Kriegsjahre 1904.* Leipzig, 1905.

Salzmann, Erich von. *Im Kampfe gegen die Herero.* 2nd ed. Berlin, 1905.

Scheibert, Justus. *Der Krieg in China 1900–1901 nebst Beschreibung des Landes, seiner Sitten und Gebräuche.* Berlin, 1909.

Schmidt, Max [Div.-Pfarrer]. *Aus unserem Kriegsleben in Südwestafrika. Erlebnisse und Erfahrungen.* Berlin, 1907.

Schumann (Mission Superintendent). "Die Schreckenstage auf der Missionsstation Jakobi." *Missionsberichte der Gesellschaft zur Beförderung der Evangelischen Missionen unter den Heiden zu Berlin für das Jahr 1906,* February 1906, 62–76.

Schwabe, Kurd. *Der Krieg in Deutsch-Südwestafrika, 1904–1906.* Berlin, 1907.

——. *Mit Schwert und Pflug in Deutsch-Südwestafrika.* Berlin, 1904.

Seeckt, Hans von. *Aus meinem Leben 1866–1917; Unter Verwendung des schriftlichen Nachlasses im Auftrage von Frau Dorothee von Seeckts.* Ed. Friedrich von Rabenau. Leipzig, 1938.

Sonnenberg, Else. *Wie es am Waterberg zuging; Ein Beitrag zur Geschichte des Hereroaufstandes.* Berlin, 1905.

Stülpnagel, C.. *Heisse Tage; Meine Erlebnisse im Kampf gegen die Hereros.* Berlin, 1905.

Stürghk, Josef Graf. *Im deutschen Grossen Hauptquartier.* Leipzig, 1921.

Stürmer, Harry. *Zwei Kriegsjahre in Konstantinopel; Skizzen deutsch-jungtürkischer Moral und Politik.* Lausanne, 1917.

Thaer, Albrecht von. *Generalstabsdienst an der Front und in der OHL.* Abhandlungen der Akademie der Wissenschaften in Göttingen, philologisch-historische Klasse, Dritte Folge, Nr. 40. Ed. Siegfried Kaehler. Göttingen, 1958.

Tirpitz, Alfred von. *Erinnerungen.* Leipzig, 1919.

——. *Politische Dokumente: Deutsche Ohnmachtspolitik im Weltkriege.* Hamburg, 1926.

Treutler, Karl Georg von. *Die graue Exzellenz; Zwischen Staatsräson und Vasallentreue; Aus den Papieren des kaiserlichen Gesandten Karl Georg von Treutler.* Ed. Karl-Heinz Janssen. Frankfurt, 1971.

Trotha, Lothar von. *Meine Bereisung von Deutsch-Ostafrika; Vortrag des Oberst von Trotha gehalten in der Sitzung der Gesellschaft für Erdkunde am 12. Juni 1897.* Berlin, 1897.

Valentini, Rudolf von. *Kaiser und Kabinettschef; Nach eigenen Aufzeichnungen und dem Briefwechsel des Wirklichen Geheimen Rats Rudolf von Valentini Dargestellt von Bernhard Schwertfeger.* Ed. Bernhard Schwertfeger. Oldenburg, 1931.

Wandt, Heinrich. *Etappe Gent.* Vienna, 1926.

Wegner, Armin. *Die Verbrechen der Stunde, die Verbrechen der Ewigkeit*. Hamburg, 1982.

Westarp, Kuno von. *Konservative Politik im letzten Jahrzehnt des Kaiserreiches*. 2 vols. Berlin, 1935.

Wild von Hohenborn, Adolf. *Briefe und Tagebuchaufzeichnungen des preussischen Generals als Kriegsminister und Truppenführer im Ersten Weltkrieg*. Ed. Helmut Reichold and Gerhard Granier. Boppard am Rhein, 1986.

Wrisberg, Ernst von. *Heer und Heimat, 1914–1918*. Leipzig, 1921.

SECONDARY SOURCES

Adas, Michael. *Machines as the Measure of Men: Science, Technology, and Ideologies of Western Dominance*. Ithaca, N.Y., 1989.

Afflerbach, Holger. " 'Bis zum letzten Mann und letzten Groschen?' Die Wehrpflicht im Deutschen Reich und ihre Auswirkungen auf das militärische Führungsdenken im Ersten Weltkrieg." In *Die Wehrpflicht: Entstehung, Erscheinungsformen und Politisch-Militärische Wirkung*, Beiträge zur Militärgeschichte, vol. 43. Ed. Roland G. Foerster, 71–90. Munich, 1994.

——. *Falkenhayn: Politisches Denken und Handeln im Kaiserreich*. Munich, 1994.

Ahmad, Feroz. *The Young Turks: The Committee of Union and Progress in Turkish Politics, 1908–1914*. Oxford, 1969.

Akçam, Taner. *Armenien und der Völkermord; Die Istanbuler Prozesse und die türkische Nationalbewegung*. Hamburg, 1996.

Albertini, Luigi. *The Origins of the War of 1914*. Edited and translated by Isabella Massey. 3 vols. Oxford, 1952–57.

Amery, L. S., ed. *The Times History of the War in South Africa*. 7 vols. London, 1900–1909.

Anderson, Eugene Newton. *The Social and Political Conflict in Prussia, 1858–1864*. Lincoln, Neb., 1954.

Andreopoulos, George J. *Genocide: Conceptual and Historical Dimensions*. Philadelphia, 1994.

Angress, Werner T. "Das deutsche Militär und die Juden im Ersten Weltkrieg." *Militärgeschichtliche Mitteilungen*, no. 1 (1976): 77–88.

Anonymous. "Aus den Denkwürdigkeiten und militärischen Werken des General-Feldmarschalls Grafen v. Moltke." *Vierteljahrshefte für Truppenführung und Heereskunde* 7 (1910): 337–61.

——. "Das türkisch-russische Grenzgebiet in Armenien." *Vierteljahrshefte für Truppenführung und Heereskunde* 10, no. 3 (1913): 512–22.

——. "Der Train in den Verhandlungen der Kommission für den Reichshaushaltsetat." *Militär-Wochenblatt* 98, no. 72 (1913): cols. 1643–45.

——. "Informal Social Organization in the Army." *American Journal of Sociology* 51, no. 5 (March 1946): 365–70.

——. "Kriegsgefangenentransporte." *Vierteljahrshefte für Truppenführung und Heereskunde* 9, no. 3 (1912): 505–27.

——. "Patrouillenritte in Südwestafrika (August bis Oktober 1904)." *Vierteljahrshefte für Truppenführung und Heereskunde* 2, no. 3 (1905): 452–95.

——. "Was sagen wir zum Herero-Aufstand?" *Barmer Missionsblatt* (Barmen) (March 1904), 19.

Anonymous ["M"]. "Etwas über Verpflegung." *Militär-Wochenblatt* 97, no. 132 (1912): 3032–34.

Appens, Wilhelm. *Charleville: Dunkle Punkte aus dem Etappenleben*. Dortmund, 1919.

Arendt, Hannah. *Eichmann in Jerusalem: A Report on the Banality of Evil*. New York, 1962.

——. *On Violence*. New York, 1970.

——. *The Origins of Totalitarianism*. New York, 1951.

348 Argyris, Chris, and Donald A. Schön. *Organizational Learning 2: Theory, Method, Practice.* New York, 1996.

Armeson, Robert B. *Total Warfare and Compulsory Labor: A Study of the Military-Industrial Complex in Germany during World War I.* The Hague, 1964.

Avant, Deborah D. *Political Institutions and Military Change: Lessons from Peripheral Wars.* Ithaca, N.Y., 1994.

Axenfeld, Karl. "Zur Steuer der Wahrheit über die Deportation des armenischen Volkes." *Allgemeine Missions-Zeitschrift* 46, no. 3 (March 1919): 57–64.

———. "Der ostafrikanische Aufstand." *Missionsbericht der Gesellschaft zur Beförderung der evangelischen Missionen unter den Heiden zu Berlin* (April 1906), 215–17.

Baba, Marietta L. "Organizational Culture." In *Encyclopedia of Cultural Anthropology*, vol. 3, ed. David Levinson and Melvin Ember, 891–95. New York, 1996.

Baedeker, Diedrich. "Kolonialstatistik und Bemerkungen." *Jahrbuch über die Deutschen Kolonien* 4 (1911): 218–37.

Bahrdt, Hans Paul. *Die Gesellschaft und ihre Soldaten; Zur Soziologie des Militärs.* Munich, 1987.

Bailes, Howard. "Military Aspects of the War." In *The South African War; The Anglo-Boer War 1899–1902*, ed. Peter Warwick and S. B. Spies, 65–102. London, 1980.

Balck, Major. "Die Entwicklung der taktischen Anschauungen in der englischen Armee nach dem Burenkrieg." *Vierteljahrshefte für Truppenführung und Heereskunde* 3, no. 3 (1906): 449–89.

Bald, Detlef. "Afrikanischer Kampf gegen koloniale Herrschaft; Der Maji-Maji-Aufstand in Ostafrika." *Militärgeschichtliche Mitteilungen* 19 (1976): 23–50.

———. *Der deutsche Generalstab 1859–1939; Reform und Restauration in Ausbildung und Bildung.* Sozialwissenschaftliches Institut der Bundeswehr, Heft 7. Munich, 1977.

Barnett, Correlli. *Britain and Her Army, 1509–1970: A Military, Political, and Social Survey.* New York, 1970.

Basler, Werner. *Deutschlands Annexionspolitik in Polen und im Baltikum 1914–1918.* East Berlin, 1962.

Bauer, Yehuda. *Rethinking the Holocaust.* New Haven, 2001.

Bauman, Zygmunt. *Modernity and the Holocaust.* Ithaca, N.Y., 1989.

Becker, Annette. *Oubliés de la Grande Guerre. Humanitaire et culture de guerre 1914–1918. Populations occupées, déportés civils, prisonniers de guerre.* Paris, 1998.

Belfield, Eversley. *The Boer War.* London, 1975.

Bentheim, Ferdinand von. *Leitfaden zum Unterricht in den Kriegswissenschaften. Für Lehrer und zum Selbstunterricht.* Berlin, 1840.

Berger, Thomas U. "Norms, Identity, and National Security in Germany and Japan." In *The Culture of National Security: Norms and Identity in World Politics*, ed. Peter J. Katzenstein, 317–56. New York, 1996.

Berghahn, Volker R. *Germany and the Approach of War in 1914.* 2nd ed. New York, 1993.

———. *Militarism: The History of an International Debate, 1861–1979.* Leamington Spa, U.K., 1981.

———. "War Preparations and National Identity in Imperial Germany." In *Anticipating Total War: The German and American Experiences, 1871–1914*, ed. Manfred F. Boemeke, Roger Chickering, and Stig Förster, 307–26. Cambridge, 1999.

———, ed. *Militarismus.* Cologne, 1975.

Bernard, Viola W., Perry Ottenberg, and Fritz Redl. "Dehumanization." In *Sanctions for Evil: Sources of Social Destructiveness*, ed. Nevitt Sanford and Craig Comstock, 102–24. San Francisco, 1971.

Bernhardi, Friedrich von. "Clausewitz über Angriff und Verteidigung; Versuch einer Widerlegung." *Beiheft zum Militär-Wochenblatt*, no. 12 (1911): 399–412.

——. *Deutschland und der nächste Krieg.* Stuttgart, 1912.

Best, Geoffrey. "How Right Is Might? Some Aspects of the International Debate about How to Fight Wars and How to Win Them, 1870–1918." In *War Economy and the Military Mind,* ed. Geoffrey Best and Andrew Wheatcroft, 120–35. London, 1976.

——. *Humanity in Warfare: The Modern History of the International Law of Armed Conflicts.* London, 1980.

Blair, Susan K. "Excuses for Inhumanity: The Official German Response to the 1915 Armenian Genocide." *Armenian Review* 37, no. 4/148 (winter 1984): 14–30.

Blell, Hauptmann Wolfgang. "Das Völkerrecht im Landkriege." *Militär-Wochenblatt* 86, no. 70–71 (1901): 1841–47, 1870–75.

Bley, Helmut. *South-West Africa under German Rule, 1894–1914.* Evanston, Ill., 1971.

Bloxham, Donald. "The Beginning of the Armenian Catastrophe: Comparative and Contextual Considerations." In *Der Völkermord an den Armeniern und die Shoah,* ed. Hans-Lukas Kieser and Dominik J. Schaller, 101–28. Zurich, 2002.

——. "Power Politics, Prejudice, Protest, and Propaganda: A Reassessment of the German Role in the Armenian Genocide of World War I." In *Der Völkermord an den Armeniern und die Shoah,* ed. Hans-Lukas Kieser and Dominik J. Schaller, 213–44. Zürich, 2002.

Boemeke, Manfred F., Roger Chickering, and Stig Förster, ed. *Anticipating Total War: The German and American Experiences, 1871–1914.* Washington, D.C., 1999.

Boguslawski, Albrecht v. *Der kleine Krieg und seine Bedeutung für die Gegenwart; Nach zwei Vorträgen, gehalten in der Militärischen Gesellschaft.* Berlin, 1881.

——. "Guerrilla War—A Prussian View." In *The Guerrilla Reader: A Historical Anthology,* ed. Walter Laqueur, 106–9. New York, 1977.

Bond, Brian, ed. *Victorian Military Campaigns.* London, 1967.

Bonn, M. J. "Die wissenschaftliche Begründung der Trotha'schen Eingeborenenpolitik." *Frankfurter Zeitung,* no. 45 (14 September 1909).

Bredow, Wilfried von. "Erkundungsziel Militärwelt; Vorüberlegungen zu einer ethnomethodologischen Erweiterung der Militärsoziologie." In *Militär als Lebenswelt; Streitkräfte im Wandel der Gesellschaft,* ed. Wolfgang R. Vogt, 171–79. Opladen, 1988.

Breit, Gotthard. *Das Staats- und Gesellschaftsbild deutscher Generale beider Weltkriege im Spiegel ihrer Memoiren.* Boppard am Rhein, 1973.

Bridgman, Jon. *The Revolt of the Herero.* Berkeley, 1981.

——, ed. *German Africa: A Select Annotated Bibliography.* Stanford, 1965.

Brunsson, Nils. "The Irrationality of Action and Action Rationality: Decisions, Ideologies, and Organizational Actions." *Journal of Management Studies* 19, no. 1 (1982): 29–44.

Bucholz, Arden. *Moltke, Schlieffen, and Prussian War Planning.* New York, 1991.

——. *Moltke and the German Wars, 1864–1871.* New York, 2001.

Bumm, Franz. *Deutschlands Gesundheitsverhältnisse unter dem Einfluss des Weltkrieges.* Carnegie Endowment for International Peace. Berlin, 1928.

Burchardt, Lothar. *Friedenswirtschaft und Kriegsvorsorge: Deutschlands wirschaftliche Rüstungsbestrebungen vor 1914.* Boppard am Rhein, 1968.

Büttner, Kurt, and Heinrich Loth, eds. *Philosophie der Eroberer und koloniale Wirklichkeit; Ostafrika 1884–1918.* Berlin, 1981.

Callwell, Charles Edward. *Small Wars: Their Principles and Practices.* 3rd ed.; orig. 1906. London, 1976.

Cecil, Hugh, and Peter Liddle, eds. *Facing Armageddon: The First World War Experienced.* London, 1996.

350   Chalk, Frank, and Kurt Jonassohn. "The Conceptual Framework." In *The History and Sociology of Genocide: Analyses and Case Studies*, ed. Frank Chalk and Kurt Jonassohn, 3–43. New Haven, 1990.

———. "The History and Sociology of Genocidal Killings." In *Genocide: A Critical Bibliographic Review*, ed. Israel W. Charny, 39–59. London, 1988.

———, eds. *The History and Sociology of Genocide: Analyses and Case Studies*. New Haven, 1990.

Charny, Israel W. "Toward a Generic Definition of Genocide." In *Genocide: Conceptual and Historical Dimensions*, ed. George J. Andreopoulos, 65–94. Philadelphia, 1992.

———, ed. *Genocide: A Critical Bibliographical Review*. London, 1988.

———, ed. *Toward the Understanding and Prevention of Genocide*. Boulder, Colo., 1984.

Chickering, Roger. "Der 'Deutsche Wehrverein' und die Reform der Deutschen Armee 1912–1914." *Militärgeschichtliche Mitteilungen* 25 (1979): 7–35.

———. *Imperial Germany and the Great War, 1914–1918*. Cambridge, 1998.

———. *We Men Who Feel Most German: A Cultural Study of the Pan-German League, 1886–1914*. Boston, 1984.

———. "World War I and the Theory of Total War: Reflections on the British and German Cases, 1914–1915." In *Great War, Total War: Combat and Mobilization on the Western Front, 1914–1918*, ed. Roger Chickering and Stig Förster, 35–53. Cambridge, 2000.

Chickering, Roger, and Stig Förster, eds. *Great War, Total War: Combat and Mobilization on the Western Front, 1914–1918*. Cambridge, 2000.

Class, Heinrich. *Wenn ich der Kaiser wär—Politische Wahrheiten und Notwendigkeiten*. Leipzig, 1912.

Clayton, Anthony. *France, Soldiers, and Africa*. London, 1988.

Coetzee, Marilyn Shevin. *The German Army League: Popular Nationalism in Wilhelmine Germany*. Oxford, 1990.

Cohen, Paul A. *History in Three Keys: The Boxers as Event, Experience, and Myth*. New York, 1997.

Conrad, Joseph. *Heart of Darkness*. London, 1902.

Craig, Gordon. *The Politics of the Prussian Army, 1640–1945*. Oxford, 1955.

Crothers, George Dunlap. *The German Elections of 1907*. New York, 1941.

Dabringhaus, Sabine. "Anticipating Total War? The United States and Germany, 1871–1914." Paper presented at the conference "Anticipating Total War? The United States and Germany, 1871–1914," Augsburg, 27–29 July 1994.

———. "An Army on Vacation? The German War in China, 1900–1901." In *Anticipating Total War: The German and American Experiences, 1871–1914*, ed. Manfred F. Boemeke, Roger Chickering, and Stig Förster, 459–76. Cambridge, 1999.

Dadrian, Vahakn N. "Genocide as a Problem of National and International Law: The World War I Armenian Case and Its Contemporary Legal Ramifications." *Yale Journal of International Law* 14, no. 2 (summer 1989): 221–334.

———. *German Responsibility in the Armenian Genocide: A Review of the Historical Evidence of German Complicity*. Watertown, Mass., 1996.

———. *The History of the Armenian Genocide: Ethnic Conflict from the Balkans to Anatolia to the Caucasus*. Providence, R.I., 1995.

———. "The Naim-Andonian Documents on the World War I Destruction of the Ottoman Armenians: The Anatomy of Genocide." *International Journal of Middle East Studies* 18, no. 3 (1986): 311–60.

———. "A Textual Analysis of the Key Indictment of the Turkish Military Tribunal Investigating the Armenian Genocide." *Armenian Review* 44, no. 1/173 (spring 1991): 1–36.

——. "A Typology of Genocide." *International Review of Modern Sociology* 5 (fall 1975): 201–12.

351

Dahlmann, Dittmar. "Die Deportationen der deutschen Bevölkerungsgruppe in Russland und in der Sowjetunion 1915 und 1941; Ein Vergleich." In *Ausweisung und Deportation: Formen der Zwangsmigration in der Geschichte*, ed. Andreas Gestrich, 103–14. Stuttgart, 1995.

Dahn, Felix. "Der deutsch-französische Krieg und das Völkerrecht." In *Bausteine; Gesammelte kleine Schriften* (Berlin, 1884), 122–224.

——. *Das Kriegsrecht; Kurze, volksthümliche Darstellung für Jedermann zumal für den deutschen Soldaten*. Würzburg, 1870.

Deák, István. *Beyond Nationalism: A Social and Political History of the Habsburg Officer Corps, 1848–1918*. Oxford, 1990.

Dedering Tilman. "The German-Herero War of 1904: Revisionism of Genocide or Imaginary Historiography." *Journal of Southern African Studies* 19, no. 1 (March 1993): 80–88.

Dehio, Ludwig. "Um den deutschen Militarismus." *Historische Zeitschrift* 180 (1955): 43–64.

Deist, Wilhelm. "Armee in Staat und Gesellschaft, 1890–1914." In his *Militär, Staat, und Gesellschaft*, 19–42. Munich, 1991.

——. "The German Army, the Authoritarian Nation-State, and Total War." In *State, Society, and Mobilization in Europe during the First World War*, ed. John Horne, 160–72. Cambridge, 1997.

——. "Der militärische Zusammenbruch des Kaiserreichs; Zur Realität der 'Dolchstosslegende.'" In his *Militär, Staat, und Gesellschaft*, 211–33. Munich, 1991.

——. *Militär und Innenpolitik im Weltkrieg, 1914–1918*. 2 vols. Quellen zur Geschichte des Parlamentarismus und der Politischen Parteien. Düsseldorf, 1970.

——. "Remarks on the Precondition to Waging War in Prussia-Germany, 1866–1871." In *On the Road to Total War: The American Civil War and the German Wars of Unification, 1861–1871*, ed. Stig Förster and Jörg Nagler, 311–25. New York, 1997.

——. "The Road to Ideological War: Germany, 1918–1945." In *The Making of Strategy: Rulers, States, and War*, ed. Williamson Murray, MacGregor Knox, and Alvin Bernstein, 358–65. Cambridge, 1984.

——. "Strategy and Unlimited Warfare in Germany: Moltke, Falkenhayn, and Ludendorff." In *Great War, Total War: Combat and Mobilization on the Western Front, 1914–1918*, ed. Roger Chickering and Stig Förster, 265–79. Cambridge, 2000.

——. "Voraussetzungen innenpolitischen Handelns des Militärs im Ersten Weltkrieg." In his *Militär, Staat, und Gesellschaft; Studien zur preussisch-deutschen Militärgeschichte*, 103–52. Munich, 1991.

——. "Zur Institution des Militärbefehlshabers und Obermilitärbefehlshabers im Ersten Weltkrieg." *Jahrbuch der Geschichte Mittel- und Osteuropas* 13–14 (1965): 222–40.

Demeter, Karl. *Das deutsche Offizierkorps in Gesellschaft und Staat, 1650–1945*. 2nd ed. Frankfurt, 1962.

Dessauer, Lothar. *Der Militärbefehlshaber und seine Verordnungsgewalt in der Praxis der Weltkrieges*. Berlin, 1918.

de Vries, Johannes Lucas. *Namibia—Mission und Politik (1880–1918). Der Einfluss der deutschen Kolonialismus auf die Missionsarbeit der Rheinischen Missionsgesellschaft im früheren Deutsch-Südwestafrika*. Neukirchen-Vluyn, 1980.

Dinkel, Christoph. "German Officers and the Armenian Genocide." *Armenian Review* 44, no. 1/173 (spring 1991).

Dobrowski, Michael N., and Isidor Wallimann, eds. *Genocide in Our Time: An Annotated Bibliography with Analytical Introductions*. Ann Arbor, 1994.

352 Dove, Karl. *Deutsch-Südwestafrika.* 2nd ed. Berlin, 1913.

Dower, John W. *War without Mercy: Race and Power in the Pacific.* New York, 1986.

Drechsler, Horst. *Aufstände in Südwestafrika; Der Kampf der Herero und Nama 1904 bis 1907 gegen die deutsche Kolonialherrschaft.* Berlin, 1984.

——. *"Let Us Die Fighting": The Struggle of the Herero and the Nama against German Imperialism, 1884–1915.* Trans. Bernd Zollner; orig. 1966. London, 1980.

——. *Südwestafrika unter deutscher Kolonialherrschaft.* Berlin, 1966.

du Preez, Peter. *Genocide: The Psychology of Mass Murder.* London, 1994.

Dülffer, Jost. *Regeln gegen den Krieg? Die Haager Friedenskonferenzen 1899 und 1907 in der Internationalen Politik.* Berlin, 1981.

Duppler, Jörg, and Gerhard P. Gross, eds. *Kriegsende 1918: Ereignis, Wirkung, Nachwirkung.* Munich, 1999.

Dupuy, Colonel Trevor Nevitt. *A Genius for War: The German Army and the General Staff, 1807–1945.* Englewood Cliffs, N.J., 1977.

Duster, Troy. "Conditions for Guilt-Free Massacre." In *Sanctions for Evil: Sources of Social Destructiveness,* ed. Nevitt Sanford and Craig Comstock, 25–36. San Francisco, 1971.

Eley, Geoff. *Reshaping the German Right: Radical Nationalism and Political Change after Bismarck.* New Haven, 1983.

Elsner, Lothar. "Ausländerbeschäftigung und Zwangsarbeitspolitik in Deutschland während des Ersten Weltkrieges." In *Auswanderer-Wanderarbeiter-Gastarbeiter; Bevölkerung, Arbeitsmarkt und Wanderung in Deutschland seit der Mitte des 19. Jahrhunderts,* ed. Klaus J. Bade, 527–57. Ostfildern, 1984.

——. "Der Übergang zur Zwangsarbeit für ausländische Arbeiter in der deutschen Landwirtschaft zu Beginn des 1. Weltkriegs." *Wissenschaftliche Zeitschift der Wilhelm-Pieck-Universität Rostock, Gesellschafts- und Sprachwissenschaftliche* Reihe 26, no. 3 (1977): 291–98.

Endres, Franz. "Militarismus als Geistesverfassung des Nichtmilitärs." In *Militarismus,* ed. Volker R. Berghahn, 99–101. Cologne, 1979.

Epkenhans, Michael. "Neuere Forschungen zur Geschichte des Ersten Weltkrieges." *Archiv für Sozialgeschichte* 38 (1998): 458–87.

——. "Die Politik der militärischen Führung 1918: 'Kontinuität der Illusionen und das Dilemma der Wahrheit'." In *Kriegsende 1918: Ereignis, Wirkung, Nachwirkung,* ed. Jörg Duppler and Gerhard P. Gross, 217–33. Munich, 1999.

Epstein, Klaus. "Erzberger and the German Colonial Scandals, 1905–1910." *English Historical Review* 74 (1959): 637–63.

Erdmann, Karl-Dietrich. *Der Erste Weltkrieg.* 5th ed. Munich, 1985.

Erickson, Edward J. *Ordered to Die: A History of the Ottoman Army in the First World War.* Westport, Conn., 2001.

Esherick, Joseph W. *The Origins of the Boxer Uprising.* Berkeley, 1987.

Evans, R.J.W., and Hartmut Pogge von Strandmann, eds. *The Coming of the First World War.* Oxford, 1989.

Farrar, Lancelot L. *Arrogance and Anxiety: The Ambivalence of German Power, 1848–1914.* Iowa City, 1981.

——. *The Short-War Illusion: German Policy, Strategy, and Domestic Affairs, August–December 1914.* Santa Barbara, 1973.

Featherstone, Donald. *Colonial Small Wars, 1837–1901.* Newton Abbot, U.K., 1973.

Fein, Helen. "Genocide, Terror, Life Integrity, and War Crimes: The Case for Discrimination." In

Genocide: Conceptual and Historical Dimensions, ed. George J. Andreopoulous, 95–107. Philadelphia, 1992.

———. *Imperial Crime and Punishment: The Massacre at Jallianwala Bagh and British Judgment, 1919–1920.* Honolulu, 1977.

Felber, Roland, and Horst Rostek. *Der "Hunnenkrieg" Kaiser Wilhelms II. Imperialistische Intervention in China 1900–01.* Illustrierte Historische Hefte Nr. 45. Berlin, 1987.

Feld, Maury. *The Structure of Violence: Armed Forces and Social Systems.* Beverly Hills, Calif., 1977.

Feldman, Gerald. *Army, Industry, and Labor in Germany, 1914–1918.* Princeton, 1966.

———. *Hugo Stinnes; Biographie eines Industriellen, 1870–1921.* Munich, 1998.

———. "Hugo Stinnes and the Prospect of War before 1914." In *Anticipating Total War: The German and American Experiences, 1871–1914,* ed. Manfred F. Boemeke, Roger Chickering, and Stig Förster, 77–95. Cambridge, 1999.

———. "War Aims, State Intervention, and Business Leadership in Germany: The Case of Hugo Stinnes." In *Great War, Total War: Combat and Mobilization on the Western Front, 1914–1918,* ed. Roger Chickering and Stig Förster. Cambridge, 2000.

Ferguson, Niall. *The Pity of War: Explaining World War I.* New York, 1998.

Finnemore, Martha. "Constructing Norms of Humanitarian Intervention." In *The Culture of National Security: Norms and Identity in World Politics,* ed. Peter J. Katzenstein, 153–85. New York, 1996.

Fischer, Fritz. *Germany's Aims in the First World War.* New York, 1967.

———. *Weltmacht oder Niedergang; Deutschland im Ersten Weltkrieg.* Frankfurt, 1965.

———. *World Power or Decline: The Controversy over Germany's Aims in the First World War.* New York, 1974.

Foerster, Wolfgang. *Der Feldherr Ludendorff im Unglück: Eine Studie über seine seelische Haltung in der Endphase des ersten Weltkrieges.* Wiesbaden, 1952.

Foley, Robert T. "Schlieffen's Last Kriegsspiel." *War Studies Journal* 3 (1998): 117–33; 4: 97–115.

———. "The Origins of the Schlieffen Plan." *War in History* 10, no. 2 (April 2003): 222–32.

Förster, Stig. "Der deutsche Generalstab und die Illusion des kurzen Krieges, 1871–1914: Metakritik eines Mythos." In *Lange und kurze Wege in den Ersten Weltkrieg,* ed. Johannes Burkhardt et al., 115–58. Munich, 1996.

———. *Der doppelte Militarismus; Die deutsche Heeresrüstungspolitik zwischen Status-Quo-Sicherung und Aggression, 1890–1913.* Stuttgart, 1985.

———. "Der Sinn des Krieges; Die Deutsche Offizierselite zwischen Religion und Sozialdarwinsimus, 1870–1914." In *"Gott mit Uns"; Nation, Religion und Gewalt im 19. und frühen 20. Jahrhundert.* Ed. Gerd Krumeich, 193–211. Göttingen, 2000.

———. "Dreams and Nightmares: German Military Leadership and the Images of Future Warfare, 1871–1914." In *Anticipating Total War: The German and American Experiences, 1871–1914,* ed. Manfred F. Boemeke, Roger Chickering, and Stig Förster, 343–76. Cambridge, 1999.

———. "Militär und staatsbürgerliche Partizipation; Die allgemeine Wehrpflicht im Deutschen Kaiserreich 1871–1914." In *Die Wehrpflicht: Entstehung, Erscheinungsformen und Politisch-militärische Wirkung,* Beiträge zur Militärgeschichte, vol. 43, ed. Roland G. Foerster, 55–70. Munich, 1994.

———. "Optionen der Kriegführung im Zeitalter des 'Volkskrieges'—Zu Helmuth von Moltkes militärisch-politischen Überlegungen nach den Erfahrungen der Einigungskriege." In *Militärische Verantwortung in Staat und Gesellschaft; 175 Jahre Generalstabsausbildung in Deutschland,* ed. Detlev Bald, 83–108. Koblenz, 1986.

354 ——. "The Prussian Triangle of Leadership in the Face of the People's War: A Reassessment of the Conflict between Bismarck and Moltke, 1870–71." In *On the Road to Total War: The American Civil War and the German Wars of Unification, 1861–1871*, ed. Stig Förster. New York, 1997.

Förster, Stig, and Jörg Nagler, eds. *On the Road to Total War: The American Civil War and the German Wars of Unification, 1861–1871*. New York, 1997.

Fourniau, C. "Colonial Wars before 1914: The Case of France in Indochina." In *Imperialism and War: Essays on Colonial Wars in Asia and Africa*, ed. J. A. de Moor and H. L. Wesseling, 72–86. Leiden, 1989.

François, Hermann von. *Der Hottentotten-Aufstand; Studie über die Vorgänge im Namalande vom Januar 1904 bis zum Januar 1905 und die Aussichten der Niederwerfung des Aufstandes.* Berlin, 1905.

François, Curt v. *Kriegführung in Süd-Afrika.* Berlin, 1900.

François, Major-General v. "Der Herero-Aufstand." *Militär-Wochenblatt* 89:1–2 (1904), Hefte 18, 19, 21, 33, 34, 40, 49, 61, 69, and 76.

François, Major v. *Lehren aus dem Südafrikanischen Kriege für das Deutsche Heer.* Berlin, 1900.

French, David. "The Strategy of Unlimited Warfare? Kitchener, Robertson, and Haig." In *Great War, Total War: Combat and Mobilization on the Western Front, 1914–1918*, ed. Roger Chickering and Stig Förster, 281–95. Cambridge, 2000.

Frey, Marc. "Bullying the Neutrals: The Case of the Netherlands." In *Great War, Total War: Combat and Mobilization on the Western Front, 1914–1918*, ed. Roger Chickering and Stig Förster, 227–44. Cambridge, 2000.

Frevert, Ute. *Die kasernierte Nation: Militärdienst und Zivilgesellschaft in Deutschland.* Munich, 2001.

——. "Der Militär als 'Schule der Männlichkeit': Erwartungen, Angebote, Erfahrungen im 19. Jahrhundert." In *Militär und Gesellschaft im 19. und 20. Jahrhundert*, 145–73. Stuttgart, 1997.

——, ed. *Militär und Gesellschaft im 19. und 20. Jahrhundert.* Stuttgart, 1997.

Freytag-Loringhoven, Hugo v. "Die Exerzier-Reglements für die Infanterie von 1812, 1847, 1888, und 1906; Ein Jahrhundert taktischer Entwicklung; Vortrag gehalten in der Militärischen Gesellschaft zu Berlin am 14. November 1906." Berlin, 1906.

Friedrichsmeyer, Sara, Sara Lennox, and Susanne Zantop, eds. *The Imperialist Imagination: German Colonialism and Its Legacy.* Ann Arbor, 1998.

Gasman, Daniel. *The Scientific Origins of National Socialism: Social Darwinism in Ernst Haeckel and the German Monist League.* London, 1971.

Gatzke, Hans W. *Germany's Drive to the West.* Baltimore, 1966.

Geinitz, Christian. "The First Air War against Noncombatants: Strategic Bombing of German Cities in World War I." In *Great War, Total War: Combat and Mobilization on the Western Front, 1914–1918*, ed. Roger Chickering and Stig Förster, 207–25. Cambridge, 2000.

Geiss, Imanuel. "The Civilian Dimension of the War." In *Facing Armageddon: The First World War Experienced*, ed. Hugh Cecil and Peter Liddle, 16–24. London, 1996.

——. *July 1914: The Outbreak of the First World War: Selected Documents.* New York, 1968.

——. *Der polnische Grenzstreifen, 1914–1918.* Hamburg, 1960.

Genocide: Crime against Humanity. Special issue of the *Armenian Review* 37, no. 1 (1984).

George, Alexander. "The Causal Nexus between Cognitive Beliefs and Decision-Making Behavior: The 'Operational Code' Belief System." In *Psychological Models in International Politics*, ed. Laurence S. Falkowski, 95–124. Boulder, Colo., 1979.

——. "The 'Operational Code': A Neglected Approach to the Study of Political Leaders and Decision-Making." *International Studies Quarterly* 13 (June 1969): 190–222.

Gestrich, Andreas, ed. *Ausweisung und Deportation: Formen der Zwangsmigration in der Geschichte.* Stuttgart, 1995.

Gewald, Jan-Bart. *Herero Heroes: A Socio-Political History of the Herero of Namibia, 1890–1923.* Oxford, 1999.

——. *Towards Redemption: A Socio-Political History of the Herero of Namibia between 1890 and 1923.* Leiden, 1996.

Geyer, Michael. "German Strategy in the Age of Machine Warfare, 1914–45." In *Makers of Modern Strategy: From Machiavelli to the Nuclear Age,* ed. Peter Paret, 527–97. Princeton, 1986.

——. "Die Geschichte des deutschen Militärs von 1860 bis 1945; Ein Bericht über die Forschungslage (1945–1975)." In *Die moderne deutsche Geschichte in der internationalen Forschung 1945–1975,* ed. Hans-Ulrich Wehler, 256–86. Göttingen, 1978.

——. "Insurrectionary Warfare: The German Debate about a *Levée en Masse* in October 1918." *Journal of Modern History* 73 (September 2001): 459–527.

——. "Militarismus." In *Geschichtliche Grundbegriffe; Historisches Lexikon zur politische-sozialen Sprache in Deutschland,* vol. 4, ed. Otto Brunner, Werner Conze, and Reinhart Koselleck, 1–48. Stuttgart, 1978.

——. "The Past as Future: The German Officer Corps as Profession." In *German Professions, 1800–1950,* ed. Geoffrey Cocks and Konrad H. Jarausch, 183–212. Oxford, 1990.

——. "The Place of the Second World War in German Memory and History." *New German Critique,* no. 71 (spring–summer 1997): 5–40.

Goerlitz, Walter. *Kleine Geschichte des deutschen Generalstabes.* Berlin, 1967.

Goltz, Colmar von der. "Stärke und Schwäche des Türkischen Reichs." *Deutsche Rundschau* 93, no. 1 (December 1897): 46–70.

Goodenough, Ward H. "Culture." In *Encyclopedia of Cultural Anthropology,* vol. 1, ed. David Levinson and Melvin Ember, 291–99. New York, 1996.

Gromaire, Georges. *L'occupation allemande en France, 1914–1918.* Paris, 1925.

Gross, Gerhard P. "Eine Frage der Ehre? Die Marineführung und der letzte Flottenvorstoss 1918." In *Kriegsende 1918: Ereignis, Wirkung, Nachwirkung,* ed. Jörg Duppler and Gerhard P. Gross, 349–65. Munich, 1999.

Gründer, Horst. *Geschichte der deutschen Kolonien.* 3rd ed. Paderborn, 1995.

Gumz, Jonathan. "Streams of Violence in the Land of Milk and Honey": Habsburg Serbia in the Era of Total War, 1915–1918." Ph.D. diss., University of Chicago, 2003. Accessed 4 July 2003 at cas.uchicago.edu/workshops/meurhist/paper.pdf.

Guse, Felix. "Der Armenieraufstand 1915 und seine Folgen." *Wissen und Wehr* 10 (1925): 609–21.

Haeften, v. [Hauptmann]. "Eine deutsche Kolonialarmee." *Vierteljahrshefte für Truppenführung und Heereskunde* 2, no. 4 (1905): 609–31.

Hagenlücke, Heinz. *Deutsche Vaterlandspartei; Die nationale Rechte am Ende des Kaiserreichs.* Düsseldorf, 1997.

Hairapetian, Armen. "'Race Problems' and the Armenian Genocide: The State Department File." *Armenian Review* 37 (spring 1984): 41–59.

Harff, Barbara. "The Etiology of Genocides." In *Genocide and the Modern Age: Etiology and Case Studies of Mass Death,* ed. Isidor Wallimann and Michael Dobrowski. New York, 1987.

Harff, Barbara, and Ted Robert Gurr. "Toward Empirical Theory of Genocides and Politicides:

356   Identification and Measurement of Cases since 1945." *International Studies Quarterly* 32 (1988): 359–71.

Hartmann, Julius von. "Militärische Nothwendigkeit und Humanität; ein kritischer Versuch." *Deutsche Rundschau* 13–14 (1877–78): vol. 13: 111–28 and 450–71; vol. 14: 71–91.

Hatke, Brigitte. *Hugo Stinnes und die drei deutsch-belgischen Gesellschaften von 1916.* Stuttgart, 1990.

Heinemann, Ulrich. *Die verdrängte Niederlage; Politische Öffentlichkeit und Kriegsschuldfrage in der Weimarer Republik.* Göttingen, 1983.

Herbert, Aubrey. "Talat Pasha." *Blackwood's Magazine* 208, no. 1290 (April 1923): 425–40.

Herbert, Ulrich. *Geschichte der Ausländerbeschäftigung in Deutchland 1880 bis 1980; Saisonarbeiter, Zwangsarbeiter, Gastarbeiter.* Berlin, 1986.

——. "Zwangsarbeit als Lernprozess; Zur Beschäftigung ausländischer Arbeiter in der westdeutschen Industrie im Ersten Weltkrieg." *Archiv für Sozialgeschichte* 24 (1984): 285–304.

Herrmann, David G. *The Arming of Europe and the Making of the First World War.* Princeton, 1996.

Herwig, Holger. *The First World War: Germany and Austria-Hungary, 1914–1918.* London, 1997.

——. *"Luxury Fleet": The Imperial German Navy, 1888–1918.* London, 1980.

——. "Total Rhetoric, Limited War: Germany's U-Boat Campaign, 1917–1918." In *Great War, Total War: Combat and Mobilization on the Western Front, 1914–1918,* ed. Roger Chickering and Stig Förster, 189–206. Cambridge, 2000.

Hiller von Gaertringen, Friedrich Frhr. " 'Dolchstoss-Diskussion' und 'Dolchstoss-Legende' im Wandel von vier Jahrzehnten." In *Geschichte und Gegenwartsbewusstsein. Festschrift für Hans Rothfels zum 70. Geburtstag,* 122–60. Göttingen, 1963.

Hirschfeld, Gerhard, Gerd Krumeich, Dieter Langewiesche, and Hans-Peter Ullmann, eds. *Kriegserfahrungen; Studien zur Sozial- und Mentalitätsgeschichte des Ersten Weltkrieges.* Stuttgart, 1997.

Hobhouse, Emily. *The Brunt of War and Where It Fell.* London, 1902.

——. *War without Glamour.* London, 1924.

Hobson, John A. *Imperialism: A Study.* 2nd ed., 1902. Ann Arbor, 1967.

Hoffman, Conrad. *In the Prison Camps of Germany: A Narrative of the "Y" Service among Prisoners of War.* New York, 1920.

Hofmann, Hanns Hubert, ed. *Das deutsche Offizierkorps, 1860–1960.* Boppard am Rhein, 1980.

Holmes, Terence M. "The Reluctant March on Paris: A Reply to Terence Zuber's 'The Schlieffen Plan Reconsidered'." *War in History* 8, no. 2 (April 2001): 208–32.

——. "The Real Thing: A Reply to Terence Zuber's 'Terence Holmes Reinvents the Schlieffen Plan'." *War in History* 9, no. 1 (January 2002): 111–20.

Holquist, Peter. "To Count, to Extract, to Exterminate: Population Statistics and Populaton Politics in Late Imperial and Soviet Russia." In *A State of Nations: Empire and Nation-Making in the Age of Lenin and Stalin,* ed. Terry Martin and Ronald Suny, 111–44. Oxford, 2001.

Hoover, Herbert. *An American Epic,* vol. 1: *Introduction: The Relief of Belgium and Northern France, 1914–1930.* Chicago, 1959.

Horne, John. "Introduction: Mobilizing for 'Total War,' 1914–1918." In *State, Society, and Mobilization in Europe during the First World War,* ed. John Horne, 1–18. Cambridge, 1997.

Horne, John, and Alan Kramer. *German Atrocities, 1914: A History of Denial.* New Haven, 2001.

——. "German 'Atrocities' and Franco-German Opinion, 1914: The Evidence of German Soldiers' Diaries." *Journal of Modern History* 66, no. 1 (March 1994): 1–33.

——. "War beween Soldiers and Enemy Civilians, 1914–1915." In *Great War, Total War: Combat and Mobilization on the Western Front, 1914–1918,* ed. Roger Chickering and Stig Förster, 153–68. Cambridge, 2000.

Horowitz, Irving Louis. *Taking Lives: Genocide and State Power*. New Brunswick, N.J., 1980.

Housepian, Marjorie. *The Smyrna Affair*. New York, 1966.

Hovannisian, Armen K. "The United States Inquiry and the Armenian Question, 1917–1919." *Armenian Review* 37 (spring 1984): 146–63.

Hovannisian, Richard G. "The Armenians in Turkey." In *The History and Sociology of Genocide*, ed. Frank Chalk and Kurt Jonassohn, 249–66. New Haven, 1990.

Howard, Michael. "Colonial Wars and European Wars." In *Imperialism and War: Essays on Colonial Wars in Asia and Africa*, ed. J. A. de Moor and H. L. Wesseling, 218–23. Leiden, 1989.

———. *The Franco-Prussian War: The German Invasion of France, 1870–1871*. New York, 1961.

Hughes, Daniel J. "Schlichting, Schlieffen, and the Prussian Theory of War in 1914." *Journal of Military History* 59 (April 1995): 257–78.

Hull, Isabel V. *The Entourage of Kaiser Wilhelm II, 1888–1918*. Cambridge, 1982.

———. "Military Culture, Wilhelm II, and the End of the Monarchy in the First World War." In *The Kaiser*, ed. Wilhelm Deist and Annika Mombauer, 235–58. Cambridge, 2003.

Huntington, Samuel P. *The Soldier and the State: The Theory and Politics of Civil-Military Relations*. Cambridge, 1957.

Iliffe, John. *A Modern History of Tanganyika*. Cambridge, 1979.

———. *Tanganyika under German Rule, 1905–1912*. Cambridge, 1969.

Immanuel. "Der offensive Geist in unserer neuen Felddienst-Ordnung." *Militär-Wochenblatt* 93, no. 71 (1908): cols. 1664–67.

International Council on Archives. *Quellen zur Geschichte Afrikas südlich der Sahara in den Archiven der Bundesrepublik Deutschland*. Zug, 1970.

Irle, J. *Was soll aus den Herero werden?* Gütersloh, 1906.

Jackson, Robert. *The Prisoners, 1914–1918*. New York, 1989.

Jahr, Christoph. "Zivilisten als Kriegsgefangene; Die Internierung von 'Feindstaaten-Ausländern' in Deutschland während des Ersten Weltkrieges am Beispiel des 'Engländerlagers' in Ruhleben." In *In der Hand des Feindes; Kriegsgefangenschaft von der Antike bis zum Zweiten Weltkrieg*, ed. Rüdiger Overmans, 297–322. Cologne, 1999.

Janis, I. L. "Groupthink among Policy Makers." In *Sanctions for Evil: Sources of Social Destructiveness*, ed. N. Sanford and C. Comstock. San Francisco, 1971.

Janowitz, Morris. "The Ineffective Soldier: A Review Article." *Administrative Science Quarterly* 5, no. 2 (September 1960): 296–303.

———. *Military Conflict: Essays in the Institutional Analysis of War and Peace*. Beverly Hills, Calif., 1975.

———. *The Professional Soldier: A Social and Political Portrait*. New York, 1971.

Janssen, Karl-Heinz. *Der Kanzler und der General; Die Führungskrise um Bethmann Hollweg und Falkenhayn, 1914–1916*. Göttingen, 1967.

Jochmann, Werner. "Die Ausbreitung des Antisemitismus." In *Deutsches Judentum in Krieg und Revolution, 1916–1923*, ed. Werner E. Mosse, 409–510. Tübingen, 1971.

Jonassohn, Kurt, and Frank Chalk. "A Typology of Genocide and Some Implications for the Human Rights Agenda," In *Genocide and the Modern Age: Etiology and Case Studies of Mass Death*, ed. Isidor Wallimann and Michael N. Dobrowski, 3–20. New York, 1987.

Kaehler, Siegfried A. "Vier quellenkritische Untersuchungen zum Kriegsende 1918." *Nachrichten der Akademie der Wissenschaften in Göttingen I*. Philologisch-Historische Klasse, No. 8, 423–81. Göttingen, 1960.

Kaiser, Hilmar. "The Baghdad Railways and the Armenian Genocide, 1915–1916: A Case Study in

358   German Resistance and Complicity." In *Remembrance and Denial: The Case of the Armenian Genocide*, ed. Richard Hovannisian, 67–122. Detroit, 1999.

Kalshoven, Frits. *Belligerent Reprisals*. Leyden, 1971.

Kaminski, Andrzej J. *Konzenstrationslager 1896 bis Heute; Geschichte, Funktion, Typologie*. Orig. 1982. Munich, 1990.

Kanya-Forster, A. S. *The Conquest of the Western Sudan: A Study of French Military Imperialism*. Cambridge, 1969.

———. "The French Marines and the Conquest of the Western Sudan, 1880–1899." In *Imperialism and War: Essays on Colonial Wars in Asia and Africa*, ed. J. A. de Moor and H. L. Wesseling, 121–45. Leiden, 1989.

Katzenstein, Peter J., ed. *The Culture of National Security: Norms and Identity in World Politics*. New York, 1996.

Kehr, Eckart. "Zur Genesis des Königlich Preussischen Reserveoffiziers." In *Primat der Innenpolitik*, ed. Hans-Ulrich Wehler, 53–63. Berlin, 1965.

Keiger, John F. V. "Poincaré, Clemenceau, and the Quest for Total Victory." In *Great War, Total War: Combat and Mobilization on the Western Front, 1914–1918*, ed. Roger Chickering and Stig Förster, 247–63. Cambridge, 2000.

Kelman, Herbert C. "Violence without Moral Restraint: Reflections on the Dehumanization of Victims and Victimizers." *Journal of Social Issues* 29, no. 4 (1973): 25–61.

Kerchnawe, Hugo, et al. *Die Militärverwaltung in den von österreich-ungarischen Truppen besetzten Gebieten*. Carnegie Endowment for International Peace. New Haven, 1928.

Ketchum, J. Davidson. *Ruhleben: A Prison Camp Society*. Toronto, 1965.

Kielmansegg, Peter Graf. *Deutschland und der Erste Weltkrieg*. Frankfurt am Main, 1968.

Kier, Elizabeth. "Culture and French Military Doctrine before World War II." In *The Culture of National Security: Norms and Identity in World Politics*, ed. Peter J. Katzenstein, 186–215. New York, 1996.

———. *Imagining War: French and British Military Doctrine between the Wars*. Princeton, 1997.

Killingray, David. "Colonial Warfare in West Africa, 1870–1914." In *Imperialism and War: Essays on Colonial Wars in Asia and Africa*, ed. J. A. de Moor and H. L. Wesseling, 146–67. Leiden, 1989.

Killingray, David, and David Omissi, eds. *Guardians of Empire: The Armed Forces of the Colonial Powers c. 1700–1964*. Manchester, 2000.

Kilmann, Ralph H., Mary J. Saxton, and Roy Serpa, eds. *Gaining Control of Corporate Culture*. San Francisco, 1985.

Kitchen, Martin. *The German Offensives of 1918*. Charleston, S.C., 2001.

———. *The German Officer Corps, 1890–1914*. Oxford, 1973.

———. *The Silent Dictatorship: The Politics of the German High Command under Hindenburg and Ludendorff, 1916–1918*. New York, 1976.

Klein, Fritz, ed. *Deutschland im Ersten Weltkrieg*. 3 vols. Berlin, 1968–69.

Klein, Paul, and Ekkehard Lippert, eds. *Militär und Gesellschaft; Bibliographie zur Militärsoziologie*. Munich, 1979.

Kluckhohn, Clyde. "The Concept of Culture." In *Culture and Behavior*, ed. Richard Kluckhohn, 19–73. New York, 1962.

Koch, H. W. "Social Darwinism as a Factor in the 'New Imperialism.'" In *The Origins of the First World War*, ed. H. W. Koch, 319–42. London, 1984.

———, ed. *The Origins of the First World War: Great Power Rivalry and German War Aims*. 2nd ed. London, 1984.

Köhler, Ludwig. *Die Staatsverwaltung der besetzten Gebiete*. Vol.: *Belgien*. Carnegie Foundation for International Peace. New Haven, 1927.

Kramer, Alan. "'Greueltaten.' Zum Problem der deutschen Kriegsverbrechen in Belgien und Frankreich 1914." In *"Keiner fühlt sich hier mehr als Mensch . . .": Erlebnis und Wirkung des Ersten Weltkriegs*, ed. Gerhard Hirschfeld and Gerd Krumeich, 83–112. Essen, 1993.

Krause, Andreas. *Scapa Flow; Die Selbstversenkung der Wilhelminischen Flotte*. Berlin, 1999.

Krüger, Friederike, and Michael Salewski. "Die Verantwortung der militärischen Führung deutscher Streitkräfte in den Jahren 1918 und 1945." In *Kriegsende 1918: Ereignis, Wirkung, Nachwirkung*, ed. Jörg Duppler and Gerhard P. Gross, 377–98. Munich, 1999.

Krüger, Gesine. *Kriegsbewältigung und Geschichtsbewusstsein; Realität, Deutung und Verarbeitung des deutschen Kolonialkriegs in Namibia 1904 bis 1907*. Göttingen, 1999.

Kuhl, Hermann von. *Der Weltkrieg 1914–1918; Dem deutschen Volke dargestellt*. 2 vols. Berlin, 1929.

Kuhn, Ph. (Stabsarzt). "Die Gesundheitsverhältnisse in unseren Kolonien." *Jahrbuch über die deutschen Kolonien* 1 (1908): 42–61; 2 (1909): 79–96.

Kundhardt von Schmidt, General-Major. "Betrachtungen über die Verluste der deutschen Heere im Kriege gegen Frankreich 1870–71." *Militär-Wochenblatt* 95, no. 43 (1910): 1040–45.

Kutz, Martin. *Realitätsflucht und Aggression im deutschen Militär*. Baden-Baden, 1990.

Langdon, John W. *July 1914: The Long Debate, 1918–1990*. New York, 1991.

Langewiesche, Dieter. "Die Rolle des Militärs in den Europäischen Revolutionen von 1848/49." In *Ungarn-Deutschland*, ed. W. Bachofer and H. Fischer, 273–88. Munich, 1983.

Laqueur, Walter. *Guerrilla: A Historical and Critical Study*. London, 1977.

Lasson, Adolf. *Princip und Zukunft des Völkerrechts*. Berlin, 1871.

Lau, Brigitte. "Uncertain Certainties: The Herero-German War of 1904." *Mibagus* 2 (April 1989): 4–5, 8.

Legro, Jeffrey W. *Cooperation under Fire: Anglo-German Restraint during World War II*. Ithaca, N.Y., 1995.

———. "Military Culture and Inadvertent Escalation in World War II." *International Security* 18, no. 4 (spring 1994): 108–42.

LeJuge, Lt. Col. "Eine amerikanische Stimme über 'German Militarism.'" *Militär-Wochenblatt* 99, no. 167–68 (1914): 3604–8.

Lemkin, Raphael. *Axis Rule in Occupied Europe: Laws of Occupation, Analysis of Government, Proposals for Redress*. Washington, D.C., 1944.

Lerman, Katherine. *The Chancellor as Courtier: Bernhard von Bülow and the Governance of Germany, 1900–1909*. Cambridge, 1990.

Leutwein, Theodor. "Die Kämpfe der Kaiserlichen Schutztruppe in Deutsch-Südwestafrika in den Jahren 1894–1896, sowie die sich hieraus für uns ergebenden Lehren." Vortrag, gehalten in der Militärischen Gesellschaft zu Berlin am 19. Februar 1898. *Beiheft zum Militär-Wochenblatt*, no. 1 (1899): 1–30.

———. "Die Rassengegensätze als eine der Ursachen des südwestafrikanischen Aufstandes." *Deutsche Revue*, October 1911.

Leverkuehn, Paul. *Posten auf ewiger Wache; Aus dem abenteuerreichen Leben des Max von Scheubner-Richter*. Essen, 1938.

Levitt, Barbara, and James G. March. "Organizational Learning." *Annual Review of Sociology* 14 (1988): 319–40.

Lewis, Bernard. *The Emergence of Modern Turkey*. Oxford, 1961.

Libaridian, Gerard J. "The Ultimate Repression: The Genocide of the Armenians, 1915–1917." In

360   *Genocide and the Modern Age: Etiology and Case Studies of Mass Death*, ed. Isidor Wallimann and Michael N. Dobrowski, 203–36. New York, 1987.

Lindeiner gen. von Wildau, Major. "Gefangenenfürsorge." *Militär-Wochenblatt* 98, no. 126 (1913): 2855–58.

Lindqvist, Sven. *'Exterminate All the Brutes': One Man's Odyssey into the Heart of Darkness and the Origins of European Genocide*. Trans. Joan Tate. New York, 1996.

Liulevicius, Vejas Gabriel. *War Land on the Eastern Front: Culture, National Identity, and German Occupation in World War I*. Cambridge, 2000.

Lohr, Eric. "Enemy Alien Politics within the Russian Empire during World War I." Ph.D. diss., Harvard University, 1999, revised ms.

——. "The Russian Army and the Jews: Mass Deportation, Hostages, and Violence during World War I." *Russian Review* 60, no. 3 (July 2001): 404–19.

Looff, Max. *Tufani; Sturm über Deutsch-Ostafrika*. 3rd ed. Berlin, 1941.

Lueder, C. "Krieg und Kriegsrecht im Allgemeinen." In *Handbuch des Völkerrechts*, ed. Franz von Holtzendorff, 169–367. Hamburg, 1889.

——. "Das Landkriegsrecht im Besonderen." In *Handbuch des Völkerrechts*, vol. 4, ed. Franz von Holtendorff, 369–544. Hamburg, 1899.

Lupfer, Timothy. *The Dynamics of Doctrine: The Changes in German Tactical Doctrine during the First World War*. Fort Leavenworth, Kans., 1981.

MacIntyre, Alasdair. "Rationality and the Explanation of Action." In *Against the Self-Images of the Age: Essays on Ideology and Philosophy*, by Alasdair MacIntyre, 244–59. New York, 1971.

Maercker, Major. "Die militärische Lage in Süd-Westafrika." *Jahrbuch über die deutschen Kolonien* 1 (1908): 39–41.

——. *Unsere Kriegführung in Deutsch-Südwestafrika. Vortrag*. Berlin, 1907.

Maltzahn, Capt. Frhr. v. "Der Abschluss des Burenkrieges." *Vierteljahrshefte für Truppenführung und Heereskunde* 6, no. 3 (1909): 435–67.

Mann, Heinrich. *Man of Straw*. New York, 1984.

March, James G. "Decision Making Perspectives: Decision in Organizations and Theories of Choice." In *Perspective on Organization Design and Behavior*, ed. Andrew H. Van de Ven and William F. Joyce, 205–44. New York, 1981.

March, James G., and Roger Weissinger-Baylon, eds. *Ambiguity and Command: Organization Perspective on Military Decision Making*. Marchfield, Mass., 1986.

Markusen, Eric. "Genocide and Warfare." In *Genocide, War, and Human Survival*, ed. Charles B Strozier and Michael Flynn, 75–86. Totowa, N.J., 1996.

Matthias, Erich, and Rudolf Morsey, eds. *Die Regierung des Prinzen Max von Baden*. Vol. 2 of Quellen zur Geschichte des Parlamentarismus und der politischen Parteien, Erste Reihe. Düsseldorf, 1962.

Maurice, J. F., and M. H. Grant, eds. *History of the War in South Africa, 1899–1902*. 8 vols. London, 1906–10.

May, Glenn Anthony. "Was the Philippine-American War a 'Total War?'" In *Anticipating Total War: The German and American Experiences, 1871–1914*, ed. Manfred F. Boemeke, Roger Chickering, and Stig Förster, 437–59. Cambridge, 1999.

McPhail, Helen. *The Long Silence: Civilian Life under the German Occupation of Northern France, 1914–1918*. New York, 2000.

Meier-Welcker, Hans. "Die deutsche Führung an der Westfront im Frühsommer 1918; Zum Problem der militärischen Lagebeurteilung." *Die Welt als Geschichte* 21 (1961): 164–84.

——. *Seeckt*. Frankfurt, 1967.

Melson, Robert F. "Provocation or Nationalism: A Critical Inquiry into the Armenian Genocide of 1915." In *The History and Sociology of Genocide: Analyses and Case Studies*, ed. Frank Chalk and Kurt Jonassohn, 266–89. New Haven, 1990.

——. *Revolution and Genocide: On the Origins of the Armenian Genocide and the Holocaust*. Chicago, 1992.

Merker, Hauptmann. "Über die Aufstandbewegung in Deutsch-Ostafrika." *Militär-Wochenblatt* 91 (1906): cols. 1021–30, 1085–92, 1119–26, 1530–38.

Messerschmidt, Manfred. "Die Armee in Staat und Gesellschaft—Die Bismarckzeit." In *Das kaiserliche Deutschland; Politik und Gesellschaft 1870–1918*, ed. Michael Stürmer, 89–118. Düsseldorf, 1970.

——. *Militär und Politik in der Bismarckzeit und im wilhelminischen Deutschland*. Darmstadt, 1975.

——. "The Military Elites in Germany since 1870: Comparisons and Contrasts with the French Officer Corps." In *The Military, Politics, and Society in France and Germany in the Twentieth Century*, ed. Klaus-Jürgen Müller. Oxford, 1995.

——. "The Prussian Army from Reform to War." In *On the Road to Total War: The American Civil War and The German Wars of Unification, 1861–1871*, ed. Stig Förster and Jörg Nagler, 263–82. New York, 1997.

——. "Völkerrecht und 'Kriegsnotwendigkeit' in der deutschen militärischen Tradition." In *Was damals Recht war . . . NS-Militär- und Strafjustiz im Vernichtungskrieg*, by Manfred Messerschmidt, 191–230. Essen, 1996.

Meurer, Christian. *Die Haager Friedenskonferenz; Vol. 2: Das Kriegsrecht der Haager Konferenz*. 2 vols. Munich, 1907.

Meyer, Hans, ed. *Das Deutsche Kolonialreich; Eine Länderkunde der deutschen Schutzgebiete, Vol. 1: Ostafrika & Kamerun*. Leipzig, 1909.

Miles, Robert. *Racism*. New York, 1989.

Militärgeschichtliches Forschungsamt. *Operatives Denken und Handeln in deutschen Streitkräften im 19. und 20. Jahrhundert*. Vol. 9 of Vorträge zur Militärgeschichte. Bonn, 1988.

Mitrany, David. *The Effect of the War on Southeastern Europe*. Carnegie Endowment for International Peace. New Haven, 1936.

Mombauer, Annika. *Helmuth von Moltke and the Origins of the First World War*. Cambridge, 2001.

——. "Wilhelm, Waldersee, and the Boxer Rebellion." In *The Kaiser*, ed. Wilhelm Deist and Annika Mombauer, 91–118. Cambridge, 2003.

Mommsen, Hans. "National Socialism: Continuity and Change." In *From Weimar to Auschwitz*, trans. Philip O'Connor, 141–62. Princeton, 1991.

——. "The Realization of the Unthinkable: The 'Final Solution of the Jewish Question' in the Third Reich." In *From Weimar to Auschwitz*, trans. Philip O'Connor, 224–53. Princeton, 1991.

——. "Militär und Zivile Militärisierung in Deutschland 1914 bis 1938." In *Militär und Gesellschaft im 19. und 20. Jahrhundert*, ed. Ute Frevert, 265–76. Stuttgart, 1997.

Moor, J. A. de, and H. L. Wesseling, eds. *Imperialism and War: Essays on Colonial Wars in Asia and Africa*. Leiden, 1989.

Morgenthau, Henry. *Ambassador Morgenthau's Story*. New York, 1918.

——. *Secrets of the Bosphorus, 1913–1916*. London, 1918.

——. *The Tragedy of Armenia*. London, 1918.

Mosse, George L. *Fallen Soldiers: Reshaping the Memory of the World Wars*. Oxford, 1989.

Mossolow, Nicolai. *Waterberg: Beitrag zur Geschichte der Missionsstation Otjozomdjupa, des Kambazembi-Stammes und des Hererolandes*. Windhuk, [1976].

362 Mühlmann, Carl. *Deutschland und die Türkei, 1913–1914; Die Berufung der deutschen Militärmission nach der Türkei 1913, das deutsch-türkische Bündnis 1914 und der Eintritt der Türkei in den Weltkrieg.* Politische Wissenschaft, vol. 7. Berlin, 1929.

——. *Das Deutsch-Türkische Waffenbündnis im Weltkriege.* Leipzig, 1940.

Müller, Georg Alexander von. *Regierte der Kaiser? Kriegstagebücher, Aufzeichnungen, und Briefe des Chefs des Marine-Kabinetts, 1914–1918.* Ed. Walter Görlitz. Göttingen, 1959.

Müller, Klaus-Jürgen. *The Military and Politics and Society in France and Germany in the Twentieth Century.* Oxford, 1995.

Müller, Rolf-Dieter. "Total War as the Result of New Weapons? The Use of Chemical Agents in World War I." In *Great War, Total War: Combat and Mobilization on the Western Front, 1914–1918,* ed. Roger Chickering and Stig Förster, 95–111. Cambridge, 2000.

Naimark, Norman. *Fires of Hatred: Ethnic Cleansing in Twentieth-Century Europe.* Cambridge, Mass., 2001.

Nash, George H. *The Life of Herbert Hoover.* 4 vols. New York, 1988.

Niemann, Alfred. *Kaiser und Heer; Das Wesen der Kommandogewalt und ihre Ausübung durch Kaiser Wilhelm II.* Berlin, 1929.

——. *Kaiser und Revolution; Die entscheidenden Ereignisse im Grossen Hauptquartier.* Berlin, 1922.

——. *Revolution von oben, Umsturz von unten; Entwicklung und Verlauf der Staatsumwälzung in Deutschland 1914–1918.* Berlin, 1927.

Nigmann, Ernst. *Geschichte der Kaiserlichen Schutztruppe für Deutsch-Ostafrika.* Berlin, 1911.

——. *Die Wahehe; Ihre Geschichte, Kult-, Rechts-, Kriegs- und Jagdgebräuche.* Berlin, 1908.

Noske, Gustav. *Kolonialpolitik und Sozialdemokratie.* Stuttgart, 1914.

Nuhn, Walter. *Flammen über Deutschost; Der Maji-Maji-Aufstand in Deutsch-Ostafrika 1905–1906, die erste gemeinsame Erhebung schwarzafrikanischer Völker gegen weisse Kolonialherrschaft.* Wilhelmshaven, 1991.

Öke, Mim Kemâl. *The Armenian Question, 1914–1923.* Nicosia, Cyprus, 1988.

Opton, Edward M., Jr. "It Never Happened and Besides They Deserved It." In *Sanctions for Evil: Sources of Social Destructiveness,* ed. Nevitt Sanford and Craig Comstock, 49–70. San Francisco, 1971.

Ott, J. Steven. *The Organizational Culture Perspective.* Chicago, 1989.

Otto, Helmut. *Schlieffen und der Generalstab; Der preussisch-deutsche Generalstab unter Leitung des Generals von Schlieffen, 1891–1905.* East Berlin, 1966.

Pakenham, Thomas. *The Boer War.* London, 1979.

Palmer, Alison. *Colonial Genocide.* Adelaide, 2000.

Pettigrew, Andrew M. "On Studying Organizational Cultures." *Administrative Science Quarterly* 24, no. 4 (1979): 570–81.

Petzold, Joachim. *Die Dolchstosslegende; Eine Geschichtsfälschung im Dienst des deutschen Imperialismus und Militarismus.* Berlin, 1963.

Pick, Daniel. *War Machine: The Rationalization of Slaughter in the Modern Age.* New Haven, 1993.

Poewe, Karla. *The Namibian Herero: A History of Their Psychosocial Disintegration and Survival.* Lewiston, N.Y., 1985.

Polonsky, Antony. "The German Occupation of Poland during the First and Second World Wars: A Comparison." In *Armies of Occupation,* ed. Roy A. Prete and A. Hamish Ion, 97–142. Waterloo, Ont., 1982.

Pomiankowski, Joseph. *Der Zusammenbruch des Ottomanischen Reiches.* Graz, 1969.

Pool, Gerhardus. *Samuel Maherero.* Windhuk, 1991.

Porch, Douglas. "Bugeaud, Galliéni, Lyautey: The Development of French Colonial Warfare." In 363
    Makers of Modern Strategy: From Machiavelli to the Nuclear Age, ed. Peter Paret, 376–407.
    Princeton, 1986.

Posen, Barry R. *The Sources of Military Doctrine: France, Britain, and Germany between the World
    Wars.* Ithaca, N.Y., 1984.

Power, Samantha. *"A Problem from Hell": America and the Age of Genocide.* New York, 2003.

Prager, Oberlt. "Ein französisches Reglement für die Kriegführung in Afrika." *Vierteljahrshefte für
    Truppenführung und Heereskunde* 6, no. 3 (1909): 475–92.

Prein, Philipp. "Guns and Top Hats: African Resistance in German South West Africa, 1907–1915."
    Journal of Southern African Studies 20, no. 1 (1994): 99–121.

Prete, Roy A., and A. Hamish Ion, eds. *Armies of Occupation.* Waterloo, Ontario, 1982.

Rachamimov, Alon. *POWs and the Great War: Captivity on the Eastern Front.* Oxford, 2002.

Reid, James J. "Militarism, Partisan War, and Destructive Inclinations in Ottoman Military History:
    1854–1918." *Armenian Review* 39, no. 3/155 (autumn 1986): 1–21.

Renner, Major. "Wechselwirkung zwischen Heereszucht und Verpflegung im Kriege." *Viertel-
    jahrshefte für Truppenführung und Heereskunde,* 6, no. 3 (1909): 413–20.

Richter, Julius. "Die deutschen evangelischen Missionskreise und das armenische Volk." *Allgemeine
    Missions-Zeitschrift* 46, no. 2 (February 1919): 33–45.

Riezler, Kurt. *Die Erforderlichkeit des Unmöglichen; Prolegomena zu einer Theorie der Politik und zu
    anderen Theorien.* Munich, 1913.

Ritter, Gerhard. *Der Schlieffenplan; Kritik eines Mythos.* Munich, 1956.

——. *The Sword and the Scepter: The Problem of Militarism in Germany.* 3 vols. Trans. Heinz Nor-
    den. Coral Gables, Fla., 1969–73.

Roghmann, Klaus, and Rolf Ziegler. "Militärsoziologie." In *Handbuch der empirischen Sozial-
    forschung,* ed. René König, vol. 2:514–66. Stuttgart, 1977.

Rohrkrämer, Thomas. *Der Militarismus der "kleinen Leute"; Die Kriegervereine im Deutschen Kaiser-
    reich, 1871–1914.* Beiträge zur Militärgeschichte. Munich, 1990.

Rohrbach, Paul. *Deutsche Kolonialwirtschaft.* 2 vols. Vol. 1: *Südwest-Afrika.* Berlin, 1907.

Ropp, Theodore. *War in the Modern World.* Durham, N.C., 1959.

Roshwald, Aviel. *Ethnic Nationalism and the Fall of Empires: Central Europe, Russia, and the Middle
    East, 1914–1923.* New York, 2001.

Rossi, Ino. "The Development of Theories of Culture." In *People in Culture: A Survey of Cultural
    Anthropology,* ed. Ino Rossi, 31–78. New York, 1980.

Rothenberg, Gunther. "Moltke, Schlieffen, and the Doctrine of Strategic Envelopment." In *Makers of
    Modern Strategy: From Machiavelli to the Nuclear Age,* ed. Peter Paret, 296–325. Princeton, 1986.

Sackmann, Sonja A. "Culture and Subcultures: An Analysis of Organizational Knowledge." *Admin-
    istrative Science Quarterly* 37, no. 1 (1991): 140–61.

——. "Uncovering Culture in Organizations." *Journal of Applied Behavioral Science* 27, no. 3 (1991):
    295–317.

Sander, L. *Zur Lage in Südwestafrika.* Vortrag am 8. Feb. 1904 in Abteilung Berlin der Deutschen
    Kolonial Gesellschaft. Berlin, 1904.

Sanford, Nevitt, and Craig Comstock, eds. *Sanctions for Evil: Sources of Social Destructiveness.* San
    Francisco, 1971.

Sapienza, Alice M. "Believing Is Seeing: How Organizational Culture Influences the Decisions Top
    Managers Make." In *Gaining Control of the Corporate Culture,* ed. Ralph H. Kilmann, Mary J.
    Saxton, and Roy Serpa, 66–83. San Francisco, 1985.

364 Schein, Edgar. H. *Organizational Culture and Leadership.* San Francisco, 1985.

——. "How Culture Forms, Develops, and Changes." In *Gaining Control of Corporate Culture,* ed. Ralph H. Kilmann, Mary J. Saxton, and Roy Serpa, 17–43. San Francisco, 1985.

Schlieffen, Alfred von. "Der Krieg in der Gegenwart." *Deutsche Revue* 34, no. 1 (January–March 1909): 13–24.

Schmid, Michael. *Der "Eiserne Kanzler" und die Generäle: Deutsche Rüstungspolitik in der Ära Bismarck, 1871–1890.* Paderborn, 2003.

Schmidt-Bückeburg, Rudolf. *Das Militärkabinett der preussischen Könige und deutschen Kaiser; Seine geschichtliche Entwicklung und staatsrechtliche Stellung, 1787–1918.* Berlin, 1933.

Schmidt-Richberg, Wiegand. *Die Generalstäbe in Deutschland 1871–1945; Aufgaben in der Armee und Stellung im Staate.* Beiträge zur Militär- und Kriegsgeschichte, vol. 3. Ed. Militärgeschichtliches Forschungsamt, 11–120. Stuttgart, 1962.

Schulte, Bernd F. *Die deutsche Armee, 1900–1914: Zwischen Beharren und Verändern.* Düsseldorf, 1977.

——. *Europäische Krise und Erster Weltkrieg; Beiträge zur Militärpolitik des Kaiserreichs, 1871–1914.* Frankfurt am Main, 1983.

Schütz, Rüdiger. "Einführende Bemerkungen." In *Kriegsende 1918: Ereignis, Wirkung, Nachwirkung,* ed. Jörg Duppler and Gerhard P. Gross, 41–47. Munich, 1999.

Schwabe, Max [Hauptmann]. "Einige Lehren aus dem Kriege in Südwestafrika." *Vierteljahrshefte für Truppenführung und Heereskunde* 1, no. 3 (1904): 461–79.

Seeberg, Karl-Martin. *Der Maji-Maji-Krieg gegen die deutsche Kolonialherrschaft.* Berlin, 1989.

Seifert, Ruth. *Individualisierungsprozesse, Gechlechterverhältnisse und die soziale Konstruktion des Soldaten; Eine theoretische und empirische Studie zur soldatischen Subjektivität und zu ihrer Wechselwirkung mit der Gesellschaft.* Sozialwissenschaftliches Institut der Bundeswehr, Heft 61. Munich, 1993.

——. "Krieg und Vergewaltigung; Ansätze zu einer Analyse." In *Massenvergewaltigung; Der Krieg gegen die Frauen,* ed. Alexandra Stiglmayer, 87–112. Freiburg, 1993.

——. "Militär und Ordnung der Geschlechter; Vier Thesen zur Konstruktion von Männlichkeit." In *Ordnung zwischen Gewaltproduktion und Friedensstiftung,* ed. Klaus Dieter Wolf, 213–29. Baden-Baden, 1993.

Semmel, Bernard. *Imperialism and Social Reform: English Social-Imperial Thought, 1895–1914.* Cambridge, Mass., 1960.

Senghaas, Dieter. *Rüstung und Militarismus.* Frankfurt, 1972.

Shaw, Stanford J., and Ezel Kural Shaw. *History of the Ottoman Empire and Modern Turkey,* vol. 2: *Reform, Revolution, and Republic: The Rise of Modern Turkey, 1808–1975.* Cambridge, 1977.

Showalter, Dennis. "From Deterrence to Doomsday Machine: The German War of War, 1890–1914." *Journal of Military History* 64 (July 2000): 679–710.

——. "German Grand Strategy: A Contradiction in Terms?" *Militärgeschichtliche Mitteilungen* 48, no. 2 (1990): 65–102.

——. "Mass Warfare and the Impact of Technology." In *Great War, Total War: Combat and Mobilization on the Western Front, 1914–1918,* ed. Roger Chickering and Stig Förster, 73–93. Cambridge, 2000.

Siemann, Wolfram. *Gesellschaft im Aufbruch; Deutschland 1849–1871.* Frankfurt, 1990.

Smelser, Neil J. "Some Determinants of Destructive Behavior." In *Sanctions for Evil: Sources of Social Destructiveness,* ed. Nevitt Sanford and Craig Comstock, 15–24. San Francisco, 1971.

Smith, Helmut Walser. "The Talk of Genocide, the Rhetoric of Miscegenation: Notes on Debates in the German Reichstag concerning Southwest Africa, 1904–1914." In *The Imperialist Imagina-*

tion: German Colonialism and Its Legacy, ed. Sara Friedrichsmeyer, Sara Lennox, and Susanne Zantop, 107–23. Ann Arbor, 1998.

Smith, Leonard V., Stéphane Audoin-Rouzeau, and Annette Becker. *France and the Great War, 1914–1918*. Cambridge, 2002.

Smith, Roger. "Human Destructiveness and Politics: The Twentieth Century as an Age of Genocide." In *Genocide and the Modern Age: Etiology and Case Studies of Mass Death*, ed. Isidor Wallimann and Michael Dobkowski. Westport, Conn., 1987.

Snook, Scott A. *Friendly Fire: The Accidental Shootdown of U.S. Black Hawks over Northern Iraq.* Princeton, 2000.

Snyder, Jack. "Civil-Military Relations and the Cult of the Offensive, 1914 and 1984." *International Security* 9, no. 1 (summer 1984): 108–46.

——. *The Ideology of the Offensive: Military Decision Making and the Disasters of 1914.* Ithaca, N.Y., 1984.

Sösemann, Bernd. "Die sogenannte 'Hunnenrede' Wilhelms II; Textkritische und interpretatorische Bemerkungen zur Ansprache des Kaisers vom 27 Juli 1900 in Bremerhaven." *Historische Zeitschrift* 222, no. 2 (1976): 342–58.

——. "'Die Erforderlichkeit des Möglichen': Kritische Bemerkungen zu der Edition Kurt Riezler, Tagebücher, Aufsätze, Dokumente." *Blätter für Deutsche Landesgeschichte* 110 (1974): 261–75.

Speier, Hans. "Ludendorff: The German Concept of Total War." In *Makers of Modern Strategy: Military Thought from Machiavelli to Hitler*, ed. Edward Mead Earle, 306–21. Princeton, 1943.

Sperber, Jonathan. *The Kaiser's Voters: Electors and Elections in Imperial Germany.* Cambridge, 1997.

Spies, S. Burridge. *Methods of Barbarism? Roberts and Kitchener and Civilians in the Boer Republics, January 1900–May 1902.* Cape Town, 1977.

——. "Women and the War." In *The South African War: The Anglo-Boer War 1899–1902*, ed. Peter Warwick and S. B. Spies, 161–85. London, 1980.

Spraul, Gunter. "Der 'Völkermord' an den Herero; Untersuchungen zu einer neuen Kontinuitätsthese." *Geschichte in Wissenschaft und Unterricht* 39, no. 12 (1988): 713–39.

Stadelmann, Rudolf. *Moltke und der Staat.* Krefeld, 1950.

Stargardt, Nicholas. *The German Idea of Militarism; Radical and Socialist Critics, 1866–1914.* Cambridge, 1994.

Staub, Ervin. *The Roots of Evil: The Origins of Genocide and Other Group Violence.* Cambridge, 1989.

Stavenhagen, Hptm. v. "Aus der Geschichte des Militär-Versorgungswesens." *Militär-Wochenblatt* 95, nos. 24, 25, 26 (1910).

Stegemann, Bernd. *Die deutsche Marinepolitik, 1916–1918.* Berlin, 1970.

Stenzel, Ernst. *Die Kriegführung des deutschen Imperialismus und das Völkerrecht; Zur Planung und Vorbereitung des deutschen Imperialismus auf die barbarische Kriegführung im ersten und zweiten Weltkrieg, dargestellt an den vorherrschenden Ansichten zu den Gesetzen und Gebräuchen des Landkrieges, 1900–1945.* Berlin, 1973.

Stevenson, David. *The First World War and International Politics.* Oxford, 1988.

——. "French Strategy on the Western Front, 1914–1918." In *Great War, Total War: Combat and Mobilization on the Western Front, 1914–1918*, ed. Roger Chickering and Stig Förster, 297–326. Cambridge, 2000.

Stone, Jay, and Erwin Schmidl. *The Boer War and Military Reforms.* Lanham, Md., 1988.

Stoneman, Mark R. "The Bavarian Army and French Civilians in the War of 1870–1871: A Cultural Interpretation." *War in History* 8, no. 3 (July 2001): 271–93.

Storz, Dieter. "'Aber was hätte anders geschehen sollen?' Die deutschen Offensiven an der West-

366   front 1918." In *Kriegsende 1918: Ereignis, Wirkung, Nachwirkung*, ed. Jörg Duppler and Gerhard P. Gross, 51–95. Munich, 1999.

———. *Kriegsbild und Rüstung vor 1914: Europäische Landstreitkräfte vor dem Ersten Weltkrieg*. Herford, Germany, 1992.

Strachan, Hew. "From Cabinet War to Total War: The Perspective of Military Doctrine, 1861–1918." In *Great War, Total War: Combat and Mobilization on the Western Front, 1914–1918*, ed. Roger Chickering and Stig Förster, 19–31. Cambridge, 2000.

———. *The First World War*. Vol. 1. Oxford, 2001.

Strazhas, Aba. *Deutsche Ostpolitik im Ersten Weltkrieg; Der Fall Ober-Ost, 1915–1917*. Wiesbaden, 1993.

Strozier, Charles B., and Michael Flynn. *Genocide, War, and Human Survival*. Lanham, Md., 1996.

Sudholt, Gert. *Die deutsche Eingeborenenpolitik in Südwestafrika; Von den Anfängen bis 1904*. Hildesheim, 1975.

Ternon, Yves. *Les Arméniens: Histoire d'un génocide*. Paris, 1977.

Thoss, Bruno. "Militärische Entscheidung und politisch-gesellschaftlicher Umbruch; Das Jahr 1918 in der neueren Weltkriegsforschung." In *Kriegsende 1918: Ereignis, Wirkung, Nachwirkung*, ed. Jörg Duppler and Gerhard P. Gross, 17–37. Munich, 1999.

———. "Nationale Rechte, militärische Führung und Diktaturfrage in Deutschland 1913–1923." *Militärgeschichtliche Mitteilungen* 42 (1987): 27–76.

Travers, Tim. *The Killing Ground: The British Army, the Western Front, and the Emergence of Modern Warfare, 1900–1918*. London, 1993.

Trotha, Trutz von. "'The Fellows Can Just Starve': On Wars of "Pacification" in the African Colonies of Imperial Germany and the Concept of "Total War." In *Anticipating Total War: The German and American Experiences, 1871–1914*, ed. Manfred F. Boemeke, Roger Chickering, and Stig Förster, 415–35. Cambridge, 1999.

———. *Koloniale Herrschaft; Zur Soziologischen Theorie der Staatsentstehung am Beispiel des "Schutzgebietes Togo."* Tübingen, 1994.

Trumpener, Ulrich. *Germany and the Ottoman Empire, 1914–1918*. Princeton, 1968.

Turner, Barry A. "The Organizational and Interorganizational Development of Disasters." *Administrative Science Quarterly* 21, no. 3 (1976): 378–97.

Vagts, Alfred. *A History of Militarism, Civilian and Military*. Rev. ed. London, 1959.

———. "A Memoir of Military Occupation." *Military Affairs* 7, no. 1 (spring 1943): 16–24.

van Crefeld, Martin. *Command in War*. Cambridge, Mass., 1985.

———. *Supplying War: Logistics from Wallerstein to Patton*. Cambridge, 1977.

van Evera, Stephen. "The Cult of the Offensive and the Origins of the First World War." *International Security* 9, no. 1 (summer 1984): 58–107.

Vassilian, Hamo B. *Armenian Genocide: A Comprehensive Bibliography and Library Resource Guide*. Glendale, Calif., 1992.

Vaughan, Diane. *The Challenger Launch Decision: Risky Technology, Culture, and Deviance at NASA*. Chicago, 1996.

Vincent, C. Paul. *The Politics of Hunger: The Allied Blockade of Germany, 1915–1919*. Athens, Ohio, 1985.

Vogt, Wolfgang R., ed. *Militär als Gegenkultur; Streitkräfte im Wandel der Gesellschaft (I)*. Opladen, 1986.

Voigt, Johannes H. "Die Deportation—Ein Thema der deutschen Rechtswissenschaft und Politik im 19. und frühen 20. Jahrhundert." In *Ausweisung und Deportation; Formen der Zwangsmigration in der Geschichte*, ed. Andreas Gestrich, 83–101. Stuttgart, 1995.

Wallach, Jehuda L. *Anatomie einer Militärhilfe; Die preussisch-deutschen Militärmissionen in der Türkei, 1835–1919.* Düsseldorf, 1976.

———. *Das Dogma der Vernichtungsschlacht; Die Lehren von Clausewitz und Schlieffen und ihre Wirkungen in zwei Weltkriegen.* Frankfurt, 1967.

Wallimann, Isidor, and Michael N. Dobrowski, eds. *Genocide and the Modern Age.* New York, 1987.

Walter, Dierk. *Preussische Heeresreformen 1807–1870: Militärische Innovationen und der Mythen der 'Roonschen Reform'.* Paderborn, 2003.

Warwick, Peter. "Black People and the War." In *The South African War: The Anglo-Boer War, 1899–1902,* ed. Peter Warwick and S. B. Spies, 186–209. London, 1980.

Warwick, Peter, and S. B. Spies, eds. *The South African War: The Anglo-Boer War, 1899–1902.* London, 1980.

Weber, Max. *On Charisma and Institution Building: Selected Papers.* Trans. S. N. Eisenstadt. Chicago, 1968.

Wehler, Hans-Ulrich. *The German Empire, 1870–1918.* Leamington Spa, U.K., 1985.

———. "Polenpolitik im Deutschen Kaiserreich." In *Krisenherde des Kaiserreichs 1871–1918; Studien zur deutschen Sozial- und Verfassungsgeschichte,* 2nd ed., ed. Hans-Ulrich Wehler, 184–202. Göttingen, 1979.

Wende, Frank. *Die belgische Frage in der deutschen Politik des Ersten Weltkrieges.* Hamburg, 1969.

Wernecke, Klaus. *Der Wille zur Weltgeltung; Aussenpolitik und Öffentlichkeit im Kaiserreich am Vorabend des Ersten Weltkrieges.* Düsseldorf, 1970.

Westlake, John. *International Law,* part 2: *War.* Cambridge, 1907.

Wieland, Lothar. *Belgien, 1914: Die Frage des belgischen 'Franktireurkrieges' und die deutsche öffentliche Meinung von 1914 bis 1936.* Frankfurt, 1984.

Willeke, Hptm. "Die Ausbildung der kaiserlichen Schutztruppe für Südwest Afrika." *Militär-Wochenblatt* 97, no. 69 (1912): 1586–89.

Willems, Emilio. *Der preussisch-deutsche Militarismus; Ein Kulturkomplex im sozialen Wandel.* Cologne, 1984.

Winzen, Peter. *Bülows Weltmachtkonzept; Untersuchungen zur Frühphase seiner Aussenpolitik, 1897–1901.* Boppard am Rhein, 1977.

Young, George. *Nationalism and War in the Near East (by a Diplomatist).* Carnegie Endowment for International Peace. Oxford, 1915.

Zantop, Susanne. *Colonial Fantasies: Conquest, Family, and Nation in Precolonial Germany, 1770–1870.* Durham, N.C., 1997.

Zechlin, Egmont. "Friedensbestrebungen und Revolutionierungsversuche im Ersten Weltkrieg." *Aus Politik und Zeitgeschichte; Beilage zur Wochenzeitung Das Parlament,* B20/1961, B24/1961, B25/1961, B20/1963, B22/1963 (1961–63).

———. *Krieg und Kriegsrisiko; Zur deutschen Politik im Ersten Weltkrieg; Aufsätze.* Düsseldorf, 1979.

Zeller, Joachim. " 'Wie Vieh wurden hunderte zu Tode getrieben und wie Vieh begraben'; Fotodokumente aus dem deutschen Konzentrationslager in Swakopmund/Namibia 1904–1908." *Zeitschrift für Geschichtswissenschaft* 49, no. 3 (2001): 226–43.

Zilch, Reinhold. *Okkupation und Währung im Ersten Weltkrieg; Die deutsche Besatzungspolitik in Belgien und Russisch-Polen 1914–1918.* Goldbach, 1994.

Zimmerer, Jürgen. *Deutsche Herrschaft über Afrikaner; Staatlicher Machtanspruch und Wirklichkeit im kolonialen Namibia.* Hamburg, 2001.

———. "Kriegsgefangene im Kolonialkrieg: Der Krieg gegen die Herero und Nama in Deutsch Südwestafrika, 1904–1907." In *In der Hand des Feindes; Kriegsgefangenschaft von der Antike bis zum Zweiten Weltkrieg*, ed. Rüdiger Overmans, 277–94. Cologne, 1999.

Zirkel, Kirsten. "Military Power in German Colonial Policy: The Schutztruppen and Their Leaders in East and South-West Africa, 1888–1918." In *Guardians of Empire: The Armed Forces of the Colonial Powers, 1700–1964*, ed. David Killingray and David Omissi, 91–113. New York, 1999.

Zmarzlik, Hans-Günter. "Social Darwinism in Germany: An Example of the Socio-Political Abuse of Scientific Knowledge." In *The Human Creature*, ed. Günther Altner, 346–77. Garden City, N.Y., 1974.

Zorn, Albert. *Das Kriegsrecht zu Lande in seiner neuesten Gestaltung*. Berlin, 1906.

Zorn, Philipp. *Die beiden Haager Friedenskonferenzen von 1899 und 1907*. In *Handbuch des Völkerrechts*. Vol. 5, pt. 1. Ed. Fritz Stier-Somlo. Stuttgart, 1915.

Zuber, Terence. *Inventing the Schlieffen Plan: German War Planning, 1871–1914*. Oxford, 2002.

——. "The Schlieffen Plan Reconsidered." *War in History* 6, no. 3 (1999): 262–305.

——. "Terence Holmes Reinvents the Schlieffen Plan." *War in History* 8, no. 4 (2001): 468–76.

——"Terence Holmes Reinvents the Schlieffen Plan—Again." *War in History* 10, no. 1 (2003): 92–101.

Zunkel, Friedrich. "Die ausländischen Arbeiter in der deutschen Kriegswirtschaftspolitik des 1. Weltkriegs." In *Entstehung und Wandel der modernen Gesellschaft; Festschrift für Hans Rosenberg zum 65. Geburtstag*, ed. Gerhard A. Ritter, 280–311. Berlin, 1970.

Zürcher, Erik J. *Turkey: A Modern History*. London, 1997.

Zwehl, Hans von. *Falkenhayn*. Berlin, 1926.

Index

References to illustrations are in bold type.